Human Rights

Human Rights

Politics and Practice

THIRD EDITION

Edited by

Michael Goodhart

OXFORD
UNIVERSITY PRESS

Great Clarendon Street, Oxford OX2 6DP,
United Kingdom

Oxford University Press is a department of the University of Oxford.
It furthers the University's objective of excellence in research, scholarship,
and education by publishing worldwide. Oxford is a registered trade mark of
Oxford University Press in the UK and in certain other countries

First edition 2009
Second edition 2013
Impression: 5

Published in the United States of America by Oxford University Press
198 Madison Avenue, New York, NY 10016, United States of America

British Library Cataloguing in Publication Data
Data available

Library of Congress Control Number: 2015953376

ISBN 978–0–19–870876–6

Printed by CPI Group (UK) Ltd, Croydon CR0 4YY

For people everywhere engaged in struggles for their rights.

New to this edition

- A new chapter on religion and human rights addresses key controversies in this contested area.
- A new chapter on sexual orientation and gender identity reflects the growing prominence of this topic and demonstrates its centrality to human rights theory and practice.
- 'Challenging assumptions' boxes ask students to become aware of and question their own attitudes and assumptions about the topics being explored.
- 'Critical thinking' features invite students to reflect on critical questions throughout each chapter.
- 'Alternative points of view' boxes highlight differing perspectives on key issues and direct students to readings that take positions on controversial terms and concepts to encourage them to weigh up the evidence for themselves.
- 'Deconstructing' features unpack controversial terms and concepts for students.

Preface to the Third Edition

Once again, I have the privilege to present a new edition of *Human Rights: Politics and Practice*. Once again, the book has been fully revised, reorganized, and updated. I am particularly delighted that we have been able to add two timely and important new chapters—on religion and human rights, and on sexual orientation, gender identity, and human rights—without making substantive cuts to the text. We have also introduced some enhanced pedagogical features that we hope will make the book a more useful tool for students and instructors.

It is tempting to try to situate this new edition amidst the ongoing tumult, promise, and peril evident in global politics. I shall resist this temptation, for it seems plain to me that even the most casual observer must quickly realize that we can't make sense of our world without understanding the politics and the practice of human rights. It is my hope that this book will help students to understand not simply the facts about human rights, but also the deeper legal, historical, philosophical, and conceptual issues that make them so problematic and so indispensable politically.

I want to again thank the editorial staff of Oxford University Press for their support and hard work. In addition, I am grateful to Caitlin Corrigan for her assistance in the preparation of this edition. Thanks are also due to the anonymous reviewers who have shared their experiences with teaching this text and their insights into the subject matter to help make the book better. Last, and most importantly, I am deeply grateful to the wonderful and obliging authors for their ongoing commitment to this project and to human rights education and scholarship more broadly.

Michael Goodhart
Pittsburgh, USA, February 2016

Brief Contents

Detailed Contents

PART II   Human Rights in Practice   145

Notes on Contributors

Brooke Ackerly is Associate Professor of Political Science at Vanderbilt University. Her interests include democratic theory, feminist methodologies, human rights, social and environmental justice. She integrates into her theoretical work empirical research on activism. Her publications include *Political Theory and Feminist Social Criticism* (2000, Cambridge), *Universal Human Rights in a World of Difference* (2008, Cambridge), and *Doing Feminist Research* with Jacqui True (2010, Palgrave Macmillan). She is currently working on the intersection of global economic, environmental, and gender justice. She teaches courses on feminist theory, feminist research methods, human rights, contemporary political thought, and gender and the history of political thought. Winner of the Graduate Teaching Award and the Margaret Cuninggim Mentoring Prize, she is also the founder of the Global Feminisms Collaborative, a group of scholars and activists developing ways to collaborate on applied research for social justice. She advises academics and donors on evaluation, methodology, and the ethics of research. She has been a member of the editorial board for *Politics and Gender* (Journal of the APSA, Women and Politics Section) and is currently a member of the editorial boards of the *Journal of Politics* and *Politics, Gender and Identities*.

John Barry is Professor of Green Political Economy at the School of Politics, International Studies and Philosophy, Queens University Belfast. His areas of research include green political economy and green economics; governance for sustainable development; the greening of citizenship and civic republicanism; green politics in Ireland, North and South; the politics, ethics, and economics of peak oil and climate change; the link between academic knowledge, political activism, and policy making; post-conflict politics and political economy in Northern Ireland and theories and practices of reconciliation in Northern Ireland. His latest book is *The Politics of Actually Existing Unsustainability: Human Flourishing in a Climate-Changed, Carbon-Constrained World* (2012, Oxford University Press). He is a former co-leader of the Green Party in Northern Ireland and is a Green Party councillor on Ards and North Down Council.

Andrea M. Bertone has nineteen years of international development and research experience in anti-human trafficking, gender equality, girls' education, gender-based violence, and female economic empowerment. She has managed large, complex development projects and conducted research in Afghanistan, Thailand, Nigeria, Guinea, Tanzania, Ghana, South Africa, Kenya, Myanmar, and Zambia. From 2003 to 2010, Dr Bertone managed a US State Department-funded project called http://HumanTrafficking.org, the pre-eminent web resource on human trafficking at the time. She has authored several peer-reviewed articles on human trafficking. Currently, Dr Bertone is the Director of the Gender Department of a large international development organization, FHI 360. She serves as Adjunct Professor at George Washington University where she teaches graduate-level courses on human trafficking, gender and development, and gender advising. Dr Bertone earned her doctorate in Government and Politics from the University of Maryland, College Park.

Cynthia Burack is Professor of Women's, Gender and Sexuality Studies at The Ohio State University. She is the author or editor of six books, the most recent of which are *Tough Love: Sexuality, Compassion, and the Christian Right* (2014, SUNY Press), *Right-Wing Populism and the Media* (2014, Routledge, co-edited with Claire Snyder-Hall), and *Sin, Sex, and Democracy: Antigay Rhetoric and the Christian Right* (2008, SUNY Press). With Jyl J. Josephson, she co-edits the SUNY Press series, *Queer Politics and Cultures*, in which *Tough Love* and *Sin, Sex, and Democracy* were published. Burack's current research focuses on US government interventions and advocacy on behalf of sexual orientation and gender identity (SOGI) human rights abroad.

Sonia Cardenas is Professor of Political Science and Dean of Academic Affairs at Trinity College in Hartford, Connecticut. Working at the intersection of international relations and human rights, her research explores the relationship between international norms and state practices around the world. She has published over fifteen journal articles and book chapters, in addition to numerous opinion pieces and reviews. She is also the author of *Conflict and Compliance: State Responses to International Human Rights Pressure* (2007), *Human Rights in Latin America: A Politics of Terror and Hope* (2010), and *Chains of Justice: The Global Rise of National Human Rights Institutions* (2014), all from the University of Pennsylvania Press. Cardenas has been active in advancing the interdisciplinary study of human rights.

David Chandler is Professor of International Relations and Director of the Centre for the Study of Democracy, Department of Politics and International Relations, University of Westminster, London. He is the editor of the journal *Resilience: International Policies, Practices and Discourses*, and his recent books include: *Resilience: the Governance of Complexity* (2014, Routledge), *Freedom vs Necessity in International Relations* (2013, Zed Books), and *International Statebuilding: The Rise of Post-Liberal Governance* (2010, Routledge).

Christian Davenport is Professor of Political Science & Faculty Associate in the Center for Political Studies, University of Michigan, Ann Arbor, as well as Director of the Radical Information Project (RIP) and Stop Our States (SOS). Primary research interests include political confl ict (e.g. human rights violations, genocide/politicide, torture, political surveillance/covert repressive action, civil war, and social movements), measurement, and racism. Professor Davenport is the author of *State Repression and the Promise of Democratic Peace* (2007, Comparative Politics, Cambridge: Cambridge University Press) and *Media Bias and State Repression* (to appear, Contentious Politics, Cambridge: Cambridge University Press).

Tim Dunne is the Executive Dean, Faculty of Humanities and Social Sciences, and Professor of International Relations at The University of Queensland. Previously he served as Research Director at the Asia Pacific Centre for the Responsibility to Protect at the same university.

Roja Fazaeli is Assistant Professor in Islamic Civilizations at the Department of Near and Middle Eastern Studies, Trinity College Dublin. She received her PhD from the Irish Centre for Human Rights at the National University of Ireland. Roja has published widely on Islamic feminisms, female religious authorities, women's rights in Iran, and human rights and religion. She has a number of book contributions and has published articles in the *International Journal of Middle East Studies*, *Muslim World Journal of Human Rights*, and the *Journal of Religions and Human Rights*. Her book on Iranian Women's Rights and Activisms will soon be published. Previous to joining Trinity, Roja worked for Amnesty International Irish Section and a number of other non-governmental organizations. She previously served on the executive boards of the Irish Refugee Council, UN Women Ireland, the Association for the Study of Persianate Societies, and the board of directors of Amnesty International Irish Section. She is currently on the editorial board of the journal *Religion and Human Rights*, is the Scholars at Risk representative in Trinity College Dublin, and serves as a member of Immigrant Council of Ireland's Research and Policy Steering Group.

Sakiko Fukuda-Parr is Professor of International Affairs at the New School. She is a development economist who has published widely on a broad range of development policy-related issues including poverty, gender, technology, capacity development, and agriculture. She is best known for her work as director and lead author of the UNDP Human Development Reports 1995–2004. She started her career at the World Bank working on agricultural projects and moved to UNDP where she worked on aid coordination in Africa. Her current research projects include: the role of economic policy in realizing the Right to Food and the political economy of the MDGs. She is a member of the UN's Committee on Development Policy, the Lancet-Norway Commission on Global Governance for Health, and serves on the Boards of the International Association of Feminist Economics, Centre for Economic and Social Rights, and the Knowledge Ecology International. She is a co-convenor of Metrics for Human Rights, and of a research initiative: The Power of Numbers: Critical Review of MDG Targets for Human Development and Human Rights.

Ronald D. Gelleny is Associate Professor of Political Science and Fellow in the Ray C. Bliss Institute of Applied Politics. Ron specializes in the areas of comparative and international politics. His research focuses on political economy, human rights, and cross-national political behaviour. His research has been published in the *Canadian Journal of Political Science, European Union Politics, International Studies Quarterly, Journal of Peace Research*, and *Political Research Quarterly*.

Marlies Glasius is Professor in International Relations at the Department of Politics, University of Amsterdam. She also holds the IKV Special Chair in Citizen Involvement in Conflict and Post-Conflict Situations, Free University, Amsterdam. She was previously the managing editor of the *Global Civil Society Yearbook*, coordinator of the Study Group on European Security, and a Lecturer in Global Politics at the LSE. She holds a PhD *cum laude* from the Netherlands School of Human Rights Research. Marlies Glasius's research interests include the theory and practice of global civil society, international criminal justice, human security, and authoritarian rule. Current projects include an investigation of discursive diffusion among recent social movements; and the changing nature of authoritarian rule in its adaptation to globalization. She is the author of *The International Criminal Court: A Global Civil Society Achievement* (2006) and co-editor with Mary Kaldor of *A Human Security Doctrine for Europe: Project, Principles, Practicalities* (2005) and with David Lewis and Hakan Seckinelgin of *Exploring Civil Society: Political and Cultural Contexts* (2004), all with Routledge, and the annual *Global Civil Society Yearbook*. Recent articles have appeared in *Development and Change, International Journal of Transitional Justice, Human Rights Quarterly*, and *International Studies Review*.

Michael Goodhart is Associate Professor of Political Science, and he holds secondary appointments in Philosophy and in Gender, Sexuality, and Women's Studies. He is the Interim Director of the Global Studies Center at the University of Pittsburgh and a University Honors College Faculty Fellow. His current research focuses on problems of global injustice; he is also interested in challenges to the theory and practice of democracy and human rights in the context of globalization and in related questions concerning democratic governance and accountability at the international and transnational levels. Dr Goodhart is author of *Democracy as Human Rights: Freedom and Equality in the Age of Globalization* (2005, Routledge) and contributing co-editor of *Human Rights in the 21st Century: Continuity and Change since 9/11* (2011, Palgrave); he is also author of numerous articles and book chapters. He is an affiliate of the Human Rights Institute at the University of Connecticut, a member of the Center for Ethics and Policy at Carnegie Mellon University, and sits on several editorial boards. In 2008–9 he was an Alexander von Humboldt Foundation Research Fellow and Guest Professor in the Hertie School of Governance, Berlin.

Marianne Hanson is Associate Professor of International Relations at the University of Queensland. Her publications are in the fields of international security, weapons control, and human rights.

Paul Havemann is adjunct Professor of Law at James Cook University and Senior Research Fellow at the Institute of Commonwealth Studies, School of Advanced Studies, University of London; he has previously taught in Canada, Australia, New Zealand, and the UK. His published work addresses law and order for Indigenous peoples in Canada and the 'indigenization' of social control; Indigenous peoples' coerced placelessness in Australia; Indigenous peoples and the Internet, genetic modification and risk in New Zealand; and contractualism, modernity and the demise of social citizenship. He has studied traditional hunting and conservation in the Torres Strait; the exclusion of Indigenous peoples from international climate change governance; and, a human rights-based approach to climate change mitigation, adaptation, and governance. Currently he is researching how neoliberal ideology promotes the commodification of nature to the detriment of Indigenous peoples and of humankind. He is editor of *Indigenous Peoples Rights in Australia, Canada and New Zealand* (1999, Oxford: Oxford University Press).

Christine (Cricket) Keating is Associate Professor of Women's, Gender, and Sexuality Studies at Ohio State University and a member of the popular education collective Escuela Popular Norteña. Her research focuses on feminist political theory, decolonial theory, and comparative political thought. She is the author of *Decolonizing Democracy: Transforming the Social Contract in India*.

Larissa C. S. K. Kersten is a PhD candidate in the Department of Government at the University of Essex. Some of her research focuses on the measurement of economic and social rights. She holds an LLB in Law and Human Rights from the University of Essex, and studied economics and international relations in Germany, France, and Korea (MSc Economics, University of Muenster).

Alan J. Kuperman is Associate Professor at the LBJ School of Public Affairs, University of Texas at Austin. He is editor of *Constitutions and Conflict Management in Africa: Preventing Civil War through Institutional Design* (2015, Philadelphia, PA: University of Pennsylvania Press), co-editor of *Gambling on Humanitarian Intervention: Moral Hazard, Rebellion and Civil War* (with Timothy Crawford; 2006, New York: Routledge), and author of *The Limits of Humanitarian Intervention: Genocide in Rwanda* (2001, Washington, DC: Brookings). In 2013–14, he was Jennings Randolph Senior Fellow at the US Institute of Peace, in Washington, DC.

Todd Landman is Professor in the Department of Government and Executive Dean of the Faculty of Social Sciences at the University of Essex. He has numerous publications on comparative methods and human rights, and he has carried out a variety of international consultancy appointments relating to the measurement of human rights.

Anthony J. Langlois is Associate Professor in the School of History and International Relations at Flinders University, Adelaide, Australia. He was educated at the University of Tasmania and the Australian National University. Langlois is the author of *The Politics of Justice and Human Rights: Southeast Asia and Universalist Theory* (2001, Cambridge University Press) and co-editor of *Global Democracy and its Difficulties* (2009, Routledge) and *Australian Foreign Policy: Controversies and Debates* (2014, Oxford University Press). He has published in many leading scholarly journals, including *Millennium*, *European Journal of International Relations*, *Review of International Studies*, *Political Studies*, *Human Rights Quarterly*, *Human Rights Review*, *Journal of Human Rights*, *International Journal of Human Rights*, *Critical Review of International Social and Political Philosophy*, and *Australian Journal of Political Science*. His areas of academic endeavour include human rights, international relations, international political theory, global sexuality politics and ethics.

Doutje Lettinga has a doctorate in Sociology from the VU University Amsterdam and a double Master's in History and Political Science from the University of Amsterdam. She has worked as a researcher and project manager for various organizations and institutions including Human Rights Watch and the EU Fundamental Rights Agency. She currently works for Strategic Studies, an initiative of Amnesty International Netherlands, where she works on the nexus of research and policy advice. Doutje Lettinga's research projects include work on social justice and human rights activism, the human rights diplomacy of rising powers, human trafficking policies in the EU, the politics of the Islamic veil in Europe, rights to protection from violence against migrant women, surveillance and human rights, and the effects of counter-terrorism mechanisms on minorities.

Gil Loescher is Visiting Professor at the Refugee Studies Centre, University of Oxford, and Professor Emeritus at the University of Notre Dame. He is the author, co-author, and co-editor of numerous publications on refugee policy including *UNHCR: The Politics and Practice of Refugee Protection*, 3rd edn (2016, Abingdon, UK: Routledge), *The Oxford Handbook on Refugee and Forced Migration Studies* (2014, Oxford: Oxford University Press), *Refugees in International Relations* (2011, Oxford: Oxford University Press), *Protracted Refugee Situations: Political, Security and Human Rights Implications* (2008, Tokyo: UN University Press), *The UNHCR and World Politics: A Perilous Path* (2001, Oxford: Oxford University Press), *Beyond Charity: International Cooperation and the Global Refugee Crisis* (1993, New York: Oxford University Press), *Refugees and International Relations* (1989, Oxford: Clarendon Press), and *Calculated Kindness: Refugees and America's Half-Open Door* (1986, New York: Simon & Schuster).

Vanessa Pupavac is Associate Professor in the School of Politics and International Relations at the University of Nottingham. She has previously worked for the United Nations and has published extensively on human rights and humanitarianism, including *Language Rights: From Free Speech to Linguistic Governance* (2012).

Joanna R. Quinn is Associate Professor of Political Science and Director of the Centre for Transitional Justice and Post-Conflict Reconstruction at The University of Western Ontario. Since 1998, Dr Quinn has been engaged in research that considers the role of acknowledgement in overcoming the causes of conflict, which has the potential to effect real and lasting change. She has written widely on the role of acknowledgment in truth commissions and in customary law in Uganda, Haiti, Canada, Fiji, and Solomon Islands.

David L. Richards is Associate Professor of Human Rights and Political Science at the University of Connecticut. His current book, *Violence Against Women and the Law* (2015, Paradigm), is co-authored with Jillienne Haglund and uses original data on 196 countries to examine what gender violence laws exist in these countries, how these laws come to be enacted, and with what outcomes they are associated. His most current work can be found at http://www.davidlrichards.com.

William F. Schulz, President of the Unitarian Universalist Service Committee, Adjunct Professor of Public Administration at the Wagner School of Public Service at New York University, and Affiliated Professor at Meadville Lombard Theological School in Chicago, served as Executive Director of Amnesty International USA from 1994 to 2006. He is the author of *What Torture Taught Me and OtherReflections on Justice and Theology* (2013, Boston, MA: Skinner House Books), *In Our Own Best Interest: How Defending Human Rights Benefits Us All* (2001, Boston, MA: Beacon), and *Tainted Legacy: 9/11 and the Ruin of Human Rights* (2003, New York: Nation Books). He is also a contributing editor of *The Phenomenon of Torture: Readings and Commentary* (2007, Philadelphia, PA: University of Pennsylvania Press) and *The Future of Human Rights: US Policy for a New Era* (2008, Philadelphia, PA: University of Pennsylvania Press).

Damien Short is Reader in Human Rights at the School of Advanced Study, University of London. Much of his research has focused on the rights of Indigenous peoples, settler colonialism, reconciliation projects, cultural genocide, and extractive industries, along with sociological and anthropological approaches to human rights. In his more recent work he has investigated the institutional history of 'ecocide' within the United Nations and its relationship to the Genocide Convention. A new monograph, *The Genocide Ecocide Nexus,* will be published by Zed Books in 2016. Damien is the Editor in Chief of the *International Journal of Human Rights*.

Rhona K. M. Smith is Professor of International Human Rights in the School of Law at Northumbria University, Newcastle, UK. She has authored various books on international human rights including *Textbook on International Human Rights,* 7th edn (2016, Oxford University Press) and *Text and Materials on International Human Rights,* 3rd edn (2012, London: Routledge-Cavendish). She has also worked with the Nordic human rights centres and institutes, most recently on human rights capacity-building projects in China and Southeast Asia.

Scott Straus is Professor of Political Science and International Studies at UW-Madison. He is the author of *Making and Unmaking Nations: War, Leadership, and Genocide in Modern Africa* (2015, Cornell University Press) and *Fundamentals of Genocide and Mass Atrocity Prevention,* forthcoming from the United States Holocaust Memorial Museum. He also co-edited with Steve Stern *The Human Rights Paradox: Universality and its Discontents* (2014, University of Wisconsin Press).

Kerri Woods is Lecturer in Political Theory at the University of Leeds. Dr Woods has published on human rights theory and environmental rights, and is author of *Human Rights* (2014, Palgrave Macmillan) and *Human Rights and Environmental Sustainability* (2015, Edward Elgar).

Guided Tour of the Textbook Features

This text is enriched with a range of learning tools to help you navigate the text material and reinforce your knowledge and understanding of human rights. This guided tour shows you how to get the most out of your textbook package.

Introduction: Human
Rights in Politics
and Practice

Michael Goodhart

Chapter Contents

- Why Human Rights?   2
- The Politics of Human Rights   5
- The Practice of Human Rights   5
- Human Rights as an Object of Enquiry   6
- About this Book   7

Reader's Guide

This introduction aims to provide the historical and conceptual background necessary for informed critical engagement with the ideas and arguments presented throughout this book. It begins by considering why human rights have emerged as a particularly powerful and important moral and political discourse since the middle of the twentieth century, stressing their modernity, their invention, and their revolutionary character. It examines the work that human rights do as moral and political value claims with powerful social, political, and economic implications. Next, it shows why this political character means that human rights play out in complex and divergent ways in practice. This makes human rights difficult to study, as they are inherently multifaceted and necessarily interdisciplinary. This introduction concludes with a brief overview of the aims, structure, and objectives of the book.

Reader's Guide

Reader's Guides at the beginning of every chapter set the scene for upcoming themes and issues and indicate the scope of coverage within the chapter.

Reader's Guide

This introduction aims to provide the historical and conceptual background necessary for informed critical engagement with the ideas and arguments presented throughout this book. It begins by considering why human rights have emerged as a particularly powerful and important moral and political discourse since the middle of the twentieth century, stressing their modernity, their invention, and

---

**BOX 1.3 FROM THE UNIVERSAL DECLARATIO
OF HUMAN RIGHTS (1948)**

Now, Therefore The General Assembly proclaims this Universal Declaration of Human Rights as a common standard of achievement for all peoples and all nations, to th

Boxes

A range of boxes interspersed throughout the chapters provide further insight into specific topics and issues, including through the use of case studies.

**BOX 5.1 CHALLENGING ASSUMPTIONS:
VIOLENCE AND HUMAN NATURE**

Many popular accounts of human rights abuse, especially those involving massacres and genocide, assume that violence of a certain magnitude necessarily reflects evil in the world.

Challenging Assumptions

Challenging Assumptions boxes throughout the text invite you to become aware of and question your own attitudes and assumptions about the topics being explored.

**BOX 3.4 ALTERNATIVE POINTS OF VIEW: THE
R2P DEBATE**

Some argue (Evans, 2013) that the inability to take strong action in Syria has not damaged the norm of R2P irreversibly. By contrast, others 'only see a doomed fate for R2P as an

Alternative Points of View

Alternative Points of View boxes highlight differing perspectives on key issues, and encourage you to weigh up the evidence and come to your own conclusions.

Critical Thinking Question:

If states have the responsibility to protect vulnerable populations in conflict situations abroad, do they also have responsibility for providing such populations with adequate and housing? If not, what is the salient difference in the two

Critical Thinking Questions

Critical Thinking Questions throughout the text challenge you to critically reflect on the chapter material.

BOX 1.5 DECONSTRUCTING THE LIBERALISM OF HUMAN RIGHTS

Many people who are enthusiastic about the value of human rights, and who recognize their historical connections with liberalism, nonetheless question whether liberalism is an adequate or desirable basis for a global and universal human rights movement. Various possible forms of critique include the following:

* Many theorists argue that the key concepts liberals use to ground human rights (agency, choice, freedom, etc.) are not

its development out of imperi political orders. Liberalism's cla of equal rights is undermined i continued investment in a glob inegalitarian and unequal.

* Critical theorists often go bey value claims and focus on phile unexpected consequences, so

Deconstructing Features

Deconstructing features unpack controversial terms and concepts to further develop your understanding of key ideas.

KEY POINTS

The foundation for rights is a puzzling philosophical questio

The early natural law foundation for rights became vulnerab during the Enlightenment because of the decline of Christia

Key Points

Key Points follow each main section of text in every chapter and summarize key themes and issues to reinforce your learning.

? QUESTIONS

Individual Study Questions

1. What is the process followed for a state wishing to be bound to the provision
2. What are the benefits of listing human rights in treaties?
3. What is the effect of a reservation on a state's legal obligations under a treaty? that seek to defeat the object and purpose of the treaty?

Questions

Individual study questions at the end of each chapter test your understanding, while group discussion questions spark debate and additional reflection.

FURTHER READING

Alfredsson, G. and **Eide, A.** (eds) (1999). *The Universal Declaration of H Achievement*. The Hague: Martinus Nijhoff.

This text comprises a series of chapters in which experts analyse the impact of each in the Universal Declaration.

Hathaway, O. (2002). Do treaties make a difference? Human rights treaties and

Further Reading

Annotated further reading guides at the end of every chapter recommend key readings on important issues, helping you to navigate the key academic literature in the field.

WEB LINKS

http://www.ohchr.org The website of the United Nations Office of the Higl (OHCHR) provides access to all UN human rights treaties as well as the texts c body) reports. It is easy to navigate around and contains copious links to additiona

http://www.bayefsky.com Professor Bayefsky's website focuses on the work of United Nations. It has a particularly useful thematic search facility.

Web Links

A list of helpful web links is provided at the end of each chapter, directing you towards useful reports, organizations, data, and other information to take your learning further.

Glossary

Abrogation of rights The failure to honour rights.
Accession or accretion The acquisition of territory that has emerged from the action of the forces of nature.

the behavioural sciences, which we the natural sciences.
Bilateral treaty A treaty conclude parties only.

Glossary Terms

Key terms are highlighted throughout the text and are defined in a glossary at the end of the book.

Guided Tour of the Online Resource Centre

www.oxfordtextbooks.co.uk/orc/goodhart3e

The Online Resource Centre that accompanies this book provides students and instructors with ready-to-use teaching and learning materials designed to maximize the learning experience.

FOR STUDENTS:

A **flashcard glossary** allows you to test your understanding of key terminology.

Links to key human rights documents direct you to important documents and human rights declarations discussed in the text.

Web links help you to take your learning further and conduct independent research on the topics covered in the text.

FOR REGISTERED LECTURERS:

Which are the most common sources of International Human Rights law?

○ Treaties
○ Reservations
○ Customary international laws
○ Declarations

2 out of 2
Treaties can be broadly compared to legislative acts. They specify the legal obligation of the state, a
Customary international laws also represent a source of international human rights law, whereas rese
'sources' themselves but legal ways in which a state can avoid responsibility for treaties' terms.
Page reference: 62-65.

A **test bank** with a variety of multiple-choice, true-or-false, fill-in-the-blank, and essay questions provides you with a range of testing options.

Monitoring and enforcing international
human rights law: international systems

• **Primary (UN charter) bodies**
  – The Human Rights Council (HRC) is the principal

Fully adaptable PowerPoint slides complement each chapter and can form the basis of lecturer presentations or in-class handouts.

Introduction: Human Rights in Politics and Practice

Michael Goodhart

Chapter Contents

Reader's Guide

This introduction aims to provide the historical and conceptual background necessary for informed critical engagement with the ideas and arguments presented throughout this book. It begins by considering why human rights have emerged as a particularly powerful and important moral and political discourse since the middle of the twentieth century, stressing their modernity, their invention, and their revolutionary character. It examines the work that human rights do in politics, explaining them as value claims with powerful social, political, and economic implications. Next, it shows why this political character means that human rights play out in complex and divergent ways in practice. This makes human rights difficult to study, as they are inherently multifaceted and necessarily interdisciplinary. This introduction concludes with a brief overview of the aims, structure, and objectives of the book.

Consider the following political events: an authoritarian government silences a critical independent media; rural villagers and the urban poor endure sickness caused by the lack of clean water; criminal networks traffic women and girls for sex; transnational corporations shift manufacturing jobs to low-wage countries with lax labour standards; gay men and women organize to win the right to marry and found families; refugees fleeing tribal or religious violence are denied asylum in nearby wealthy countries; suspected terrorists are captured and detained without trial or review; workers and their allies build a campaign to demand a living wage; reformers organize resistance to a repressive military regime; internationally orchestrated air strikes help to topple a regime that has threatened to massacre its own people; activists successfully work to eliminate school fees and make education available for all. What do such disparate events have in common? It would be difficult to talk about any of them without invoking human rights.

The decades since the **Universal Declaration of Human Rights** (UDHR) was approved by the United Nations General Assembly in 1948 have witnessed what one writer aptly calls 'the rise and rise of human rights'.[1] Human rights have become so pervasive that it is hard to imagine making sense of, or even talking about, the political world without them.

Why Human Rights?

The advancement of human rights to the forefront of global politics has been as remarkable as it has been improbable. The UDHR, an abstract and non-binding collection of noble words and sentiments, has engendered a vast and growing body of international law that is challenging the ideal of sovereignty and transforming relations among states. This transformation includes the creation and development of a diverse array of international institutions concerned with human rights monitoring, compliance, and, increasingly, enforcement. Human rights have inspired domestic and transnational social movements that have toppled repressive regimes and won protection for oppressed and marginalized people; these movements have emerged as powerful political actors in their own right. While the idea of human rights has provoked sometimes sharp controversy, it has nonetheless become the dominant normative or moral discourse of global politics and a major standard of international legitimacy. Why?

Although this text focuses on the post-Second World War era of human rights, understanding the contemporary state of human rights politics and practice requires some sense of their logic and appeal. It would be impossible to summarize the history of human rights here; instead, in the following sections I shall focus on several essential features of human rights that help to explain their emergence and their success, as well as some of the controversies surrounding them. The point of doing so is to provide the historical and conceptual background necessary for informed critical engagement with the ideas and arguments presented throughout this book. Three related features of human rights deserve special emphasis in this respect:

- human rights are distinctively modern;
- human rights are a political invention;
- human rights are inherently revolutionary.

The Modernity of Human Rights

To say that human rights are distinctively modern is not to deny the long history of the values that animate them. Human rights are closely tied historically to notions of justice and human dignity that are as old as human society. To stress the modernity of human rights is rather to stress two important contrasts, one with the corporate conception of rights that dominated medieval Europe and many other pre-modern societies, the other with notions of justice and dignity based in religious cosmology.

Medieval conceptions of rights were anchored in social status. Rights pertained to classes or categories of persons rather than to individuals, and they were strongly supportive of hierarchical notions of social organization. The rights one possessed depended upon and varied with one's status or social position. Rights and duties defined the social roles that constituted society; they were in this sense conservative (norm-preserving) and stabilizing (order-preserving) features of society. Rights were often also anchored in cosmological conceptions or religious views that interpreted the existing social order as divinely orchestrated (or at least sanctioned). That is, the organization of society, including the rights and duties of different groups of people, was seen as reflecting a divine will or plan.

In Western Europe, where the idea of human rights first emerged in its modern form, this way of viewing society and social organization underwent a profound and sustained transformation beginning as early as the twelfth and thirteenth centuries. The transformation entailed economic development, artistic and literary renaissance, religious reformation, and intellectual flowering. Together, these trends fostered *humanism* (a concern with the achievements and potential of human beings), *rationalism* (an emphasis on reason and science rather than on belief or superstition), and *individualism* (a differentiation of persons from the social groups or classes to which they belong).

My point is not that these are necessary elements of any account of human rights, but rather that these elements shaped the emergence of the particular form of human rights that appeared in early modern Europe. In describing human rights as rights that belong to everyone, they make a powerful statement about human capabilities and potential. They simultaneously assert a far-reaching normative and political programme for protecting and respecting people's ability to exercise those capabilities and realize that potential. In relying on reason in their justification, human rights embody a political logic that transcends—and thus threatens—traditional values and beliefs. Finally, in ascribing rights to everyone, the modern conception of rights challenges conventional understandings of social and political order.

Human Rights as a Political Invention

This radicalism indicates that human rights were less the product of evolution than of invention (see Minogue, 1979). The idea of rights in Europe can be traced back to its origins and meanings in Roman law (Tuck, 1979), but in seventeenth-century England it became a radical and disruptive notion. This development would have horrified one of the key figures responsible for this change, the political philosopher Thomas Hobbes (1588–1679). Hobbes was a devoted monarchist who tried to develop a justification for royal absolutism that would be more persuasive than the divine right of kings, which was increasingly under challenge from theologians and rebellious Parliamentarians. Hobbes's key innovation was to suggest that, in a hypothetical 'state of nature' before the creation of society, all individuals should be considered free and equal. Hobbes believed that this natural freedom and equality would result in chaos and war, to which an all-powerful ruler was the logical and best solution (see Hobbes, 1968 [1651]).

Although Hobbes used freedom and equality to justify absolute authority, others quickly saw the potential to put them to other, very different purposes. The most famous and important of them was the philosopher and Whig revolutionary John Locke (1632–1704). Locke saw that Hobbes's arguments about natural freedom and equality had the potential to justify political revolution by making authority depend on the consent of the governed (Locke, 1960). Locke understood this freedom and equality in terms of natural or human rights enshrined in natural law. Government was established, in Locke's view, to provide means to interpret, judge, and execute this natural law—in other words, to protect rights. When government lacked consent or failed to respect and protect rights, Locke argued, it made itself illegitimate, and the people had the right to replace it.

The Revolutionary Character of Human Rights

Their revolutionary character is the third feature essential for understanding the politics and practice of human rights and the success and controversy they have generated. By the close of the eighteenth century, rights had become a moral standard for assessing the legitimacy of governmental authority and the battle cry of revolutionaries in the United States, France, Haiti, and elsewhere. This revolutionary character is inherent in the logic of human rights themselves. As Carole Pateman (1988, pp. 39–40) has argued, the simple premise of natural freedom and equality undermines justifications for natural authority and subjection: 'the doctrine of natural individual freedom and equality was revolutionary precisely because it swept away, in one fell swoop, all the grounds through which the subordination of some individuals, groups or categories of people to others had been justified'.

This is what Kenneth Minogue (1979, p. 11) meant in describing human rights as the leading edge of the axe of rationalism, which toppled monarchies and cleared the ground for democracy. The great revolutions of the eighteenth and nineteenth centuries marched under the banner of human rights precisely because of the power of this argument against monarchy and aristocracy. Yet these human rights revolutions were at best partial and incomplete. Women, labourers, slaves, and 'natives' in areas subjected to European rule were denied the 'universal' rights that the revolutions themselves proclaimed (see Pateman,

1988; Mills, 1997; Goodhart, 2005). Social, economic, and cultural rights were mostly ignored and often brutally suppressed.

This was as the early proponents of 'the rights of man' had always intended. Their cause was narrowly political and concerned with empowering a small class of landowning gentry chafing under a hereditary monarchy and aristocracy. The logic of consent and natural rights justified their revolution, but in the end it justified much more besides. The logic of human rights extended much further than Locke or his contemporaries could have imagined or endorsed, and over time the axe of rationalism came more to resemble a double-edged sword, as those excluded from enjoyment of their rights used the logic of universality to challenge their subjection and the hypocrisy that supported it. It is this revolutionary potential and emancipatory logic that make human rights particularly appealing to people struggling against domination and oppression and that explain a large part of their 'rise and rise'.

Appeal and Criticisms

Yet the universal aspiration of human rights is itself double-sided. The failure of human rights in practice to live up to their universal promise has been the source of much of the criticism lodged against them, and this criticism has often been justified. It was perfectly obvious for a long time that who qualified as 'human' in most conceptions of human rights was a fairly narrow group of wealthy European males. This criticism has been amplified by the invocation of human rights in justifying all sorts of domination—from colonialism and imperialism to patriarchy, preventive war, and the global **neoliberal** economic order. Human rights have often been used by elites of various stripes to institutionalize and protect their power and privilege.

Criticism of human rights for failing to live up to their universal promise has often been conflated with another prominent criticism: that their origin in a particular Western cultural and philosophical context makes them an intrinsically Western concept, one at odds with cultural and philosophical traditions elsewhere. This criticism is more suspect. It comes mainly from economic and political elites whose status is threatened by human rights and from Western intellectuals interested in discrediting human rights; the latter presumably aim to head off the misuses of human rights as tools of domination referred to in the

previous paragraph. Whatever the intentions of this latter set of critics, their position winds up supporting autocrats and plutocrats whose abuse of power and privilege the critics would no doubt also condemn. It does so by endorsing the idea that cultures are monolithic and homogeneous and by undermining what is best understood as the global and inclusive nature of human rights claims. This makes it difficult for critics of the status quo in any given society to challenge the hegemonic interpretation of 'culture' invoked by elites; it also makes it difficult for advocates of democracy and social justice to invoke human rights in their fight against domination, oppression, and exploitation.

As a practical matter, people everywhere—not just or even primarily in the West—invoke human rights in their struggles against sexism, racism, poverty, political exclusion, foreign intervention, and so on. Often, in doing so, they link human rights claims to elements of their own cultural, religious, and philosophical traditions—typically elements ignored or repressed by elites. Activists find the logic and power of human rights an invaluable tool for mobilizing and organizing people and for challenging power; this is the case even though these same activists are often among the most eloquent and persuasive critics of partial and prejudicial applications and implementations of human rights.

With respect to the philosophical point regarding the incompatibility of human rights with Indigenous cultural and philosophical traditions, the critics are correct—yet the implications of this fact are quite the opposite of what they imagine. The incompatibility of human rights with traditional cultures and philosophies explains their appeal to those suffering from injustice—as much in the West as elsewhere. It is precisely the point of human rights claims that they disrupt tradition, upend convention, and undercut hierarchy. Human rights provide a critical resource for activists in their struggles against domination and oppression *because* they supply a different way of thinking about justice, dignity, and respect. To take just one example: it is not as if Western civilization—whatever that means—has historically embraced equality of the sexes; the struggle for women's rights has been a struggle against cultural and philosophical tradition in the West, as it is everywhere.

These arguments reveal the inherently political character of human rights and highlight why attention to context and to power dynamics is essential for understanding the controversy surrounding human rights wherever they are invoked. This controversy is a reaction to the radical, revolutionary work that human rights do in the world—work that explains why human rights, despite their theoretical baggage and chequered past, remain so appealing and so indispensable in practice.

The Politics of Human Rights

To assert a human right is to make a fundamentally political claim, in two senses. First, it is to make a demand on society, to insist that things be arranged—economically, politically, culturally—so that everyone enjoys equal respect and dignity. This explains why human rights resonate with ancient and global notions of justice and human dignity. Yet human rights are not simply equivalent with human dignity or justice; they represent a certain kind of dignity or justice, one incompatible with domination, oppression, or exploitation. As the images of the axe and the double-edged sword suggest, human rights imply the levelling or cutting down of traditional forms of status and hierarchy. Another way of saying this is that human rights are normative claims. They express a certain set of political convictions and aspirations concerning the freedom and equality of all people. This makes the concept or ideology of human rights incompatible with any system of values that regards some persons as naturally or divinely subordinate to others. This point is vital: when opponents of human rights argue that they clash with traditional values or cultures, they are perfectly correct.

To deny or downplay this clash is to miss what is happening politically when human rights are invoked: power is being challenged, domination contested, authority questioned. The issue is not whether human rights are compatible with existing beliefs and practices around the world; in many instances they are not. The issue is rather whether one endorses the values expressed through human rights or the values underlying beliefs and practices that might conflict with human rights. This points to the second way in which human rights are inherently political claims: the very act of claiming them helps to constitute people as political subjects (Zivi, 2012).

Human rights can also be asserted, as I alluded to earlier, as rhetorical or ideological cover for political choices motivated by other considerations. Examples of such behaviour are familiar: European powers justified colonial enterprises as 'civilizing missions'; American politicians cite human rights abuses in launching 'preemptive' military attacks and monitoring the private communications of citizens. The rejection of human rights often works in a similar way, as when authoritarian rulers decry human rights as cultural imperialism to secure their grip on power. The important point here is that it is impossible to understand the advantage to be gained from trumpeting or denouncing human rights without understanding what various actors are doing *politically* when they claim or reject them—namely, taking sides.

The Practice of Human Rights

Human rights are inherently political; to embrace or contest them is to take sides on questions of power. I began this introduction by arguing that human rights have in effect become the coin of the realm in global politics, the dominant normative discourse, and a benchmark for legitimate authority. If traditional politics—laws, governments, policies—are the face of that coin, its flip side is the long record of human rights practice that has developed over the past four centuries and accelerated dramatically in recent decades. One can no more understand human rights purely as an abstract moral or political idea than one can understand football by reading the rulebook without watching a match.

This practice is evident in the history of social movements, legal challenges, political argumentation, and public discourse. It represents the real world of human rights, the empirical record of their use by all kinds of people in varied contexts over time. Regardless of what one might think of the philosophical arguments in favour of human rights, there exists this legacy of their actual use and effects in the world that must be reckoned with. Just as it is perfectly possible to be an atheist and still recognize that religion exists and has a real and significant impact on social life, one need not find the moral or philosophical arguments for human rights conclusive or even persuasive to acknowledge that human rights practice is a significant political phenomenon in our world.

How widely or narrowly one reads this history of human rights is itself probably determined in large part by where one's ideological sympathies lie (for a very broad reading, see Ishay (2004); for a very narrow one, see Moyn (2010)). Was the democratic political revolution that began with seventeenth-century opposition to monarchy and aristocracy a human rights movement? What about the struggles for labourers and for abolition of slavery? Women's rights? Resistance to colonial rule? One way to answer these questions is by studying the rhetoric and beliefs of the participants. Another is to argue that what the actors said or thought is less important than the thrust and logic of their arguments. Still another is to focus on outcomes, assessing how these movements contributed to the realization of human rights as we understand them today. In making such studies, the history of misuses of human rights cannot be ignored.

Ultimately there is no single or correct way to define the history of human rights practice. How one defines it is never merely an objective decision about 'the facts' because the stories we tell reflect our political values and have practical consequences. This is, at least in part, what makes human rights so challenging, so important, and so rewarding to study.

Human Rights as an Object of Enquiry

Human rights are an amazingly rich and complex object of enquiry. Their study involves normative, empirical, and critical approaches and has historical, legal, sociological, anthropological, comparative, and international dimensions.

One complexity in the study of human rights is that they simultaneously demand normative and empirical analysis. Normatively-oriented scholars primarily concern themselves with philosophical and policy questions, while empirically-oriented scholars focus mainly on trying to understand how human rights work in the world. Both are crucially important, and they are much more closely entwined than many scholars seem to realize.

In fact, one of the chief difficulties in the study of human rights is that the normative and the empirical, which are deeply entangled in practice, are usually treated as separate questions. Consider human rights' status as a global standard of legitimacy. Political theorists might be concerned with the appropriateness of this standard and with what exactly it entails. These normative questions are distinct from, but closely related to, empirical questions about how human rights came to function as a global standard in the first place and how effectively global human rights mechanisms

work. These questions can be answered in part by tracing the history of the laws and institutions that have evolved over time and of the social actors and movements that advocated their development. Trying to understand either the empirical or the normative dimensions of these processes in isolation seems guaranteed to result in partial or distorted understandings. In order to grasp this history and its significance properly, we need to inquire not only about what various actors have done but also about what they thought they were doing; why, politically, they wanted to do it; the resulting norms to which their actions contributed; the identities they helped to create or strengthen; and the effectiveness of their efforts in varied contexts.

Despite these difficulties, some generalizations can be made. **Empirical** studies of human rights, both **qualitative** and **quantitative**, aim to help us understand the reality of human rights politics and practice. These studies might focus on laws, movements, or institutions, or on levels of achievement or violation of human rights standards, trying to uncover the factors that contribute to them. Alternatively, they might seek to trace how the discourse of human rights works to socialize political actors through a combination of pressure and persuasion. Or, they might study the politics of human rights within a particular country or region, trying to explain why certain policies or practices have emerged. They might also focus on how states and other international actors use human rights politically—as a tool of foreign policy, a condition of aid, and so on.

Normative studies of human rights aim to understand the philosophical bases of human rights. They focus on the justifications given for human rights and on the values that human rights claims embody. Normative studies might track the intellectual development of human rights arguments, clarify concepts (such as freedom), or try to justify a particular way of understanding human rights or the obligations they entail. They might also critique (analyse and endorse or criticize) past or present practice on moral grounds (see Table 0.1).

Legal and policy approaches draw on the normative and the empirical. One can study the law from an empirical point of view, emphasizing its content, development, and enforcement, or from a normative perspective, emphasizing its moral character and its interpretation. Similarly, one can try to understand the effects of existing policy or predict the effects of a new policy by relying on empirical analysis, and one

Table 0.1 Human rights as an object of enquiry

	Empirical	Normative
Scope of analysis	*What is*; the practice of human rights in the world	*What ought to be*; moral, philosophical, or conceptual questions about human rights
Objects of analysis	*Real-world phenomena*, e.g. treaties and conventions, institutions, violations, enforcement, social movements, historical records, interviews, opinion surveys, statistical measures	*Concepts*, e.g. democracy, freedom, obligation, rights *Arguments*, e.g. freedom requires X; one should do Y if Z applies
Aims of analysis	*Description* or observation of what is actually going on *Explanation* of what accounts for the patterns and relationships in our observations or predicts what is likely to occur	*Clarification* of key concepts and definitions *Justification* or moral arguments that support human rights *Moral critique* or critical evaluation of existing laws, policies, and practices using normative standards

can argue for or recommend new policies because of the values they embody or promote.

About this Book

This book attempts to provide a comprehensive introduction to the theory and practice of human rights from the perspective of politics and cognate disciplines. It has three principal aims:

- To introduce students to human rights, both as they are studied by scholars and as they are used in the world.

- To provide detailed treatment of some key issues in contemporary human rights in ways that simultaneously illuminate those issues and illustrate the approaches that various disciplines employ in studying them.

- To stimulate critical thinking about how human rights work and how they might play a role in shaping our future.

The book is divided into two parts that reflect these complementary objectives. Part I comprises eight chapters showcasing the 'state of the art' of the study of human rights in various fields and disciplines. These chapters both introduce the main approaches to the study of human rights as a political phenomenon and survey the

key findings they have yielded. These chapters also highlight the primary challenges and controversies involved in the study of human rights.

Part II encompasses fifteen thematic chapters written to investigate important topics in contemporary human rights politics and practice. Through the use of varied and extensive case studies, these chapters provide fresh insights into important issues while also providing students with clear examples of how scholars undertake research on human rights. The chapters were all purpose-written for this text by an impressive group of international scholars of human rights. The topics covered represent only some of the important themes and issues in the contemporary study and practice of human rights.

The chapters reflect a variety of perspectives on human rights; there has been no attempt to impose a standard definition of human rights, and no ideological litmus test for authors to pass regarding their views on human rights. The chapters also contain significant overlap, with numerous themes, cases, treaties, and institutions being mentioned in several chapters. This diversity and overlap are intentional and serve an important pedagogical purpose, illustrating that there is no one way to understand human rights or to study them. Students can benefit from comparing the views of different authors on refugees, the International Criminal Court, the Responsibility to Protect, environmental crisis, feminist activism, and many others that appear in several chapters.

In the end, human rights are important not because of the conclusions we reach about them but because of the work that they do in the world.

As you explore this book, you will begin to appreciate how indispensable human rights have become in global politics and to form your own opinions about their value, their limitations, and their potential.

 NOTE

1. Kirsten Sellars (2002). *The Rise and Rise of Human Rights.* Stroud, UK: Sutton Publishing.

Visit the **Online Resource Centre** that accompanies this book for updates and a range of other resources:
www.oxfordtextbooks.co.uk/orc/goodhart3e/

PART I
Human Rights and Politics

1

Normative and Theoretical Foundations of Human Rights

Anthony J. Langlois

Chapter Contents

Reader's Guide

Human rights have come to provide a powerful basis for an ethical critique of international politics and policy. This chapter examines the theoretical basis for the **normative** ideas advanced by those who offer critiques using the language of human rights. It recognizes that the idea of human rights has a philosophical and a political history, a history that emerges out of political liberalism, and one that resonates still in many of the contemporary controversies surrounding the development and use of human rights. The rhetoric of human rights declares the idea to be universal; in this chapter we look at the various ways in which this claim may be interpreted, including the views of cultural relativists and others who deny the universality of human rights. The chapter concludes by emphasizing the way in which the human rights agenda is deeply political: it privileges a certain set of normative commitments that its proponents hope will become, in time, the ethical constitution of the international system.

Introduction

Understanding the history of the human rights idea is essential to understanding the debates and problems that arise when we try to theorize human rights. Despite the rhetoric of human rights—that they are universal, inalienable, inherent, and so on—the contemporary usage of rights is a very recent affair, emergent out of the history of the West. Neither Socrates nor Jesus, neither Confucius nor Buddha, would have claimed—in the face of injustices they experienced—that their universal human rights were being abused. Today, however, the language of human rights has become globally recognized as a response to injustice. The way in which we think about this transition, the emergence and spread of the idea of rights, is important for the way in which we seek to justify and theorize human rights.

The Emergence of Rights Language

Rights language did not appear out of a vacuum, but developed gradually through Western political history, reaching its first golden age in the European Enlightenment. Prior to the Enlightenment, social, moral, and political values were spoken of in relation to the right—that is, in relation to an objective moral order that stood over and above all people. This order was conceptualized as the natural law, which, after the rise of Christianity, became associated with the Church. Under the natural law, people had duties to one another and to God; rights were derived from the duties we owed one another under God. The practice of claiming modern secular rights, rights that have as their focus the subjective freedoms and liberties of individuals, rather than *objective right* (the divinely sanctioned moral order of the day) is associated with the long development of the idea of individual liberty, culminating in the Enlightenment.

The rights claimed in the Enlightenment made sense to the people of that period because they had been preceded by the development of specific conceptions of society, individuality, freedom, liberty, government, and religion. These conceptions laid the groundwork for human rights—or, as they were called at the time, the rights of man. As these subversive ideas gained critical influence, they began to appear in the political documents known as rights declarations.

These documents, the most important of which were drafted in the final decades of the 1700s, are the early rhetorical and legal masterpieces of rights politics (Fields, 2003, p. 22). They were created under the influence of both a long chain of political events and the intellectual ferment of the Enlightenment. The former included crucial historical events such as the illegal and confused but fabulously daring trial of King Charles I of England, in 1649 (Kamenka, 1978). With this trial, the English monarch's rights were made a function of the rights of the people. These same rights were to be discussed and promoted by a host of Enlightenment *philosophes* over the ensuing 130 years. Despite their differences with one another, these thinkers demanded individual freedom from absolutist control.

The Revolutionary Uses of Human Rights

It was this demand for freedom that led American colonists to revolt against their British masters, a revolt that led to the creation of the first grand document of the 'age of rights': the US Declaration of Independence of 1776 (see Box 1.1). While not the first American rights document (there had been a Bill of Rights in 1774 in the First Continental Congress; and the state of Virginia also declared a Bill of Rights on 12 June 1776), the Declaration of Independence penned by Thomas Jefferson (1743–1826) gave poetic and radical voice to the claim that all men (*sic*) should be free to live independently and with equality (Lauren, 1998, p. 17). Jefferson argued that people are entitled to a bill of rights to guard their freedoms against all governments. Americans subsequently gained these entitlements through the US Constitution (1789) and its first ten amendments, which constitute the Bill of Rights (1791).

In France, too, revolution against a despotic monarch and regime led to the creation of that other grand rights document: The Declaration of the Rights of Man and of the Citizen (1789; see Box 1.1). The French were inspired by the Americans—indeed, key French citizens had fought in the American Revolutionary War—and they sought to secure rights, not just for their countrymen, but for everyone: '*all men* are born free and equal in rights' (Article 1, emphasis added).

These Declarations encapsulate what we now call liberal democracy. They do not merely set out an

BOX 1.1 REVOLUTIONARY STATEMENTS OF HUMAN RIGHTS

From the United States Declaration of Independence (1776)

We hold these truths to be self-evident, that all men are created equal, that they are endowed by their Creator with certain unalienable Rights, that among these are Life, Liberty and the pursuit of Happiness … That to secure these rights, Governments are instituted among Men, deriving their just powers from the consent of the governed … That whenever any Form of Government becomes destructive of these ends, it is the Right of the People to alter or to abolish it, and to institute new Government, laying its foundation on such principles and organizing its powers in such form, as to them shall seem most likely to effect their Safety and Happiness.

From the French Declaration of the Rights of Man and of the Citizen (1789)

The representatives of the French people, organized as a National Assembly, believing that the ignorance, neglect, or contempt of the rights of man are the sole cause of public calamities and of the corruption of governments, have determined to set forth in a solemn declaration the natural, unalienable, and sacred rights of man, in order that this declaration, being constantly before all the members of the Social body, shall remind them continually of their rights and duties; in order that the acts of the legislative power, as well as those of the executive power, may be compared at any moment with the objects and purposes of all political institutions and may thus be more respected, and, lastly, in order that the grievances of the citizens, based hereafter upon simple and incontestable principles, shall tend to the maintenance of the constitution and redound to the happiness of all. Therefore the National Assembly recognizes and proclaims, in the presence and under the auspices of the Supreme Being, the following rights of man and of the citizen:

Article 1: Men are born and remain free and equal in rights. Social distinctions may be founded only upon the general good.

Article 2: The aim of all political association is the preservation of the natural and imprescriptible rights of man. These rights are liberty, property, security, and resistance to oppression.

---

action plan for short-term political goals; rather, they articulate a philosophical account of what it means to have legitimate government (Kamenka, 1978). Central to this is an egalitarian philosophy of what it means to be human.

Philosophical Questions

The political consequences of these rights declarations continue to escalate today. But ever since these rights were first advanced they have been dogged by philosophical questioning. Natural and imprescriptible rights had their critics; and even those who wished to embrace such rights had questions.

Philosophical Foundations

The difficulty concerned the underlying philosophy from which the notion of rights was derived. The rights described in the Declarations are moral ideas known as **natural rights**, derived from the natural law, which in Christian civilization had to do with the moral character given by God to his creation. This is very clear, for example, when one reads the work of John Locke (1632–1704), who laid the foundation for much of the subsequent enthusiasm about rights. However,

the period in which the early rights theorizing occurred was also the period in which Christian theism gradually lost its hold on the allegiance of the *philosophes*. The reason of man came to replace the word of God as the highest authority, fracturing the logic of natural law and duty that lay behind the Christian natural rights framework (Waldron, 1987). New theories were developed—by Hugo Grotius (1583–1645) and Thomas Hobbes (1588–1679), for example—that sought to derive rights, not from the natural law (ordained by God), but from our basic humanity. These theories were for a time quelled by powerful restatements of natural law theories (such as Samuel Pufendorf's (1632–94)). Nonetheless they added force to the general cultural shift under way during this period. This shift would over time highlight the moral autonomy of the individual, undermine the derivative natural law–duty–rights structure of political morality, and focus the popular imagination on the idea of basic, inalienable rights. These rights would come to be understood as natural rights that could be derived from our natural humanity, rather than from God's natural law (Haakonssen, 1991, p. 61). Over time, the natural rights idea became more and more politically efficacious; it also became more philosophically tenuous. If natural rights were no longer justified by direct appeal to God via the natural law, how were they to be justified? Nature by itself evinced a bewildering array of values, with no consensus about which were the correct ones. It seemed that the fate of natural rights was to be a political idea that came too late to be awarded philosophical respectability (Waldron, 1987, p. 13).

Early Critics of Rights

By the time of the Rights Declarations, key philosophers were forcefully attacking the idea of natural rights. These attacks came from across the philosophical spectrum—from conservatives, liberals (particularly utilitarians), and socialists (see Box 1.2).

Conservatives are most famously represented by Edmund Burke (1729–97), author of *Reflections on the Revolution in France* (Burke, 1971); here, the French Declaration of the Rights of Man and of the Citizen is denounced in strong terms. Burke's denunciation concerned the basis on which people were thought to have rights. He did not reject rights as such, but rejected the idea that rights were natural, that they existed as an 'Archimedean point' outside society by which government could be judged. Such abstractions were wrongheaded, he argued. Rather, man had rights because of the organic traditions and institutions of his society. Rights were the rights of *Englishmen* or *Frenchmen*, not of *man*. Different political communities may construct different rights, he argued. The attempt to impose one list of abstract rights on all men would issue in the breakdown of social bonds, the eruption of chaos, and eventually tyranny—expectations that for Burke were vindicated by subsequent events in France.

Liberals, in the form of utilitarians, also attacked natural rights. Jeremy Bentham (1748–1832) declared in 'Anarchical Fallacies' (Bentham, 1843): '*Natural rights* is simple nonsense: natural and imprescriptible

---

BOX 1.2 THE PHILOSOPHERS ON THE RIGHTS OF MAN

Bentham (1748–1832)

How stands the truth of things? That there are no such things as natural rights—no such things as rights anterior to the establishment of government—no such things as natural rights opposed to, in contradistinction to, legal: that the expression is merely figurative; that when used, in the moment you attempt to give it a literal meaning it leads to error, and to that sort of error that leads to mischief—to the extremity of mischief. ('Anarchical Fallacies', see Bentham (1843))

Burke (1729–97)

As to the share of power, authority, and direction which each individual ought to have in the management of the state, that I must deny to be amongst the direct original right of man in civil society; for I have in my contemplation the civil social man, and no other. It is a thing to be settled by convention. (*Reflections on the Revolution in France*, see Burke (1971))

Marx (1818–83)

Thus none of the so-called rights of man goes beyond egoistic man, man as he is in civil society, namely an individual withdrawn behind his private interests and whims and separated from the community. Far from the rights of man conceiving of man as a species-being ... The only bond that holds them together is natural necessity, need and private interest, the conservation of

their property and egoistic person. ('On "the Jewish Question"', see Marx (1987))

Hobbes (1588–1679)

The Right of Nature ... is the Liberty each man hath, to use his own power, as he will himselfe, for the preservation of his own nature; that is to say, of his own Life; and consequently, of doing any thing, which in his own Judgement, and Reason, hee shall conceive to be the aptest means thereunto. (*Leviathan*, see Hobbes (1968))

Locke (1632–1704)

Men being ... by nature all free, equal, and independent, no one can be put out of his estate and subjected to the political power of another without his consent. (*The Second Treatise of Government*, see Locke (1952))

Kant (1724–1804)

So act that the maxim of your will can at the same time be a universal law ... Treat all humans as ends in themselves rather than as mere means ... Conduct yourself as a member of a kingdom of ends. (*Groundwork for the Metaphysics of Morals*, see Kant (2002))

(Edmundson, 2004)

rights, rhetorical nonsense—nonsense upon stilts.' Natural rights were 'unreal metaphysical phenomena', unreal rights that stemmed from an unreal law, the natural law, which itself was dismissed due to the absence of a divine lawgiver. If one wanted to advance liberal democracy, one should speak of the reform of actual rights and laws—positive rights and laws—not fanciful ones.

Radicals criticized the rights of man for being the rights of bourgeois man. Rights to liberty, property, and personal security gave the entrepreneur a relatively free hand in his capitalist occupations. The economic well-being of the masses would remain of little concern. Karl Marx's (1818–83) passion was the emancipation of the **proletariat** or wage workers, to be achieved via revolution with the backing of rigorous science. In practice, rights were part of the general capitalist system of domination that stood in the way of the achievement of equality and well-being for all human persons.

The great irony of the rights revolution, then, is that, just when the language of natural rights became extraordinarily efficacious in dealing with social and political issues, the main currents of political and philosophical thought became ambivalent about the idea (Langlois, 2001, Chapter 3).

KEY POINTS

The foundation for rights is a puzzling philosophical question.

The early natural law foundation for rights became vulnerable during the Enlightenment because of the decline of Christian theism.

At the same time the idea of rights became more politically effective.

Conservatives, liberals, and radicals all criticized the idea of natural rights.

Critical Thinking Question:

Which criticisms of natural rights do you find important? Why?

Modern Human Rights

This was all changed by the Second World War (1939–45). The horror of total war and, in particular, the atrocities of the Jewish Holocaust 'outraged

the conscience of mankind'—to cite the language of the UN's **Universal Declaration of Human Rights** (UDHR; see Box 1.3). In moral shock, the response of the collective Western social imagination was to return to the natural law. Members of the Nazi leadership were charged and tried at the **Nuremberg Tribunal** (1945–9), under the auspices of the natural law, with **crimes against humanity**. This charge was not extant in any formal international document or law, but was one that, so it would be held, was patently clear and known to any reasonable person *because* it was a part of the natural law. The point here—one to which we shall return—is that positive law, be it domestic or international, is held to account by a higher moral standard. Natural law, then, was invoked as the legal basis for the indictments against the Nazis and as the moral foundation for liberal democracy and human rights.

Human rights standards were placed centrally in the United Nations Charter (1945), and in 1948 the UN promulgated its Universal Declaration. The UDHR has a preamble and thirty articles, the first of which declares that 'all human beings are born free and equal in dignity and rights'. A quick perusal of the Declaration is sufficient for the reader to recognize all the main elements of liberal political theory: the emphasis on freedom and liberty, dignity, and equality; the importance of the rule of law, freedom from slavery and torture, and the presumption of innocence; the ownership of private property, freedom of religion

BOX 1.3 FROM THE UNIVERSAL DECLARATION OF HUMAN RIGHTS (1948)

Now, Therefore The General Assembly proclaims this Universal Declaration of Human Rights as a common standard of achievement for all peoples and all nations, to the end that every individual and every organ of society, keeping this Declaration constantly in mind, shall strive by teaching and education to promote respect for these rights and freedoms and by progressive measures, national and international, to secure their universal and effective recognition and observance, both among the peoples of Member States themselves and among the peoples of territories under their jurisdiction.

Article 1: All human beings are born free and equal in dignity and rights. They are endowed with reason and conscience and should act towards one another in a spirit of brotherhood.

and expression, and the right to take part in the government of one's country (liberty rights); and, more controversially, rights to adequate standards of living, education, and cultural participation (welfare rights).

This modern account of human rights contains philosophical tensions. The whole underlying *structure* of the human rights idea is linked to ideas of natural law and natural right that, as we have seen, are philosophically problematic. The *content* of the new human rights represented a very specific philosophical account of human society: that of liberal political thought. Thus, the new universal human rights were highly *particularistic*: they emerged out of Western philosophy and politics, and they embodied a distinct ideological position. The sense in which these ideas are universal has neither to do with their history (which is one thread in the larger history of the West) nor with any form of global **empirical** reality (modern human rights are not found indigenously occurring in all human societies). Instead, the universality of these rights derived from their proponents' belief that human sociability *should* be articulated (at least in part) by the use of rights language, and that these particular rights *should* be the moral norms by which human behaviour is judged and evaluated.

The Moral Basis of Human Rights

We see, then, that for proponents, human rights are viewed as a set of moral demands, demands that should be institutionalized in our corporate political life—within states and internationally. How is it that these moral demands are justified? The UDHR powerfully articulates the moral urgency that energized the world after the Second World War. Crucially, however, the UN document makes no attempt at explanation, justification, or philosophical defence. This was a deliberate strategy. The Human Rights Commission, the body given the responsibility to draft the UDHR, was well aware of the differences that would have to be managed. Its strategy was to focus on norms or rules, leaving aside questions of justification (Morsink, 2000).

Much has been written in the years since the UDHR's promulgation about how to reconcile the specificity of the political and moral claims made in the name of human rights with the multiplicity of human ethical, religious, philosophical, cultural, and social traditions. The dilemma is this: the UDHR engages a universalist rhetoric to present a particular

position, that of the liberal rights tradition. This position is *normatively* universal, to be sure; but it is not shared universally by all human persons, and the traditions and communities in which they live.

Much of the subsequent controversy associated with arguments about universalism and relativism has been complicated by the failure of rights proponents either to be clear about or to properly understand the liberal nature of the political project in which they are involved. In the same way that believers in natural law and rights often claimed that these ideas were self-evident, so too, for many believers in human rights, the liberal values that they articulate are held to be universal, values of the common human sense. But, in fact, they are not common or universal, despite the desire of many that they be so. And it is this that makes the philosophical justification of human rights so important: the proponents of human rights need to have good reasons with which to defend human rights, and by which to attempt to persuade others to support human rights.

One might argue that the difficult task of philosophical justification has been superseded by the creation of the international human rights regime. It may be observed that we have had almost seventy years of the development and implementation of human rights law, both domestically within states and internationally; that human rights have 'worldwide acceptance' and 'global legitimacy'; that, by signing on to the UN Charter, the UDHR, and subsequent human rights instruments, states have ceded some measure of their sovereignty and may legitimately and legally be held accountable for their behaviour in relation to human rights standards. It may be argued: given that the political philosophers were unable to persuade the world of the veracity of rights before the Second World War, perhaps the defence of human rights is rightly given to the international lawyers and diplomats who have made such progress in expanding the remit of human rights in the decades since. We have human rights now, and they are protected because of the laws and institutions these people established and maintained.

The technical description of this approach is 'the argument from **legal positivism**' (Langlois, 2004). The main fault in the argument is that it risks equating or *reducing* human rights to legal rights. The potential danger in this approach is clear: it would mean that human rights *only* exist where there are actual laws or agreements or institutions that say they exist.

Take these away, and you no longer have human rights. Clearly this is a perilous doctrine, one that runs against the thrust of the human rights movement. The historical development of human rights has depended on the conviction that rights exist as *moral demands* that need to be translated into legal and institutional contexts in order to be effectively protected and policed. These moral demands stand behind any laws, agreements, or institutions, and are the impetus for the creation of such. The ability to claim or argue for rights is often most important to us when we *do not* in fact have a well-functioning legal and institutional context by which to claim them—what Jack Donnelly (1989) terms the 'possession paradox' (see Box 1.4). This ability is dependent upon people being able to understand and identify with certain moral requirements—one of the goals of philosophical justification.

The Philosophical Justification of Modern Human Rights

We have seen that the idea of human rights emerged out of the political history of the West and, in particular, out of liberal political theory. There are many varieties of liberalism, but they are all fundamentally linked by their regard for the individual human subject. In Immanuel Kant's (1724–1804) phrase, individuals are always to be regarded as ends, not means. All individuals are to be considered of equal moral worth

BOX 1.4 THE POSSESSION PARADOX

'Having' a right is … of most value precisely when one does not 'have' the object of the right—that is, when one is denied direct, objective enjoyment of the right. I call this 'the possession paradox' of rights: 'having' and 'not having' a right at the same time, the 'having' being particularly important precisely when one *does not* 'have' it. This possession paradox is characteristic of all rights … We must distinguish between *possession* of a right, the *respect* it receives and the ease or frequency of *enforcement* … It is the ability to claim the right if necessary—the special force this gives to the demand and the special social practices it brings into play—that makes having rights so valuable and that distinguishes having a right from simply enjoying the benefit of being the (right-less) beneficiary of someone else's obligation.

(Donnelly, 1989, pp. 11–12)

and standing. But exactly how this is understood varies between different proponents of liberalism.

The basic dignity of the human person has often been argued to ground rights, and in the Western tradition, a principal historical source for this idea of human dignity was the Christian idea that man was made in the image of God—in the *imago dei*. More commonly today, however, liberal approaches stress human characteristics rather than divine ones. So, for example, the human capacity for rationally purposive agency is determined to be the distinguishing characteristic of human beings; this in turn becomes the basis for a fuller doctrine of human rights (see Gewirth, 1996). Or, similarly, autonomy and choice are taken to be fundamental ingredients in any valuable life, and rights are derived from the conditions— the liberties and freedoms—that are needed in order to sustain such a life (see Raz, 1986).

Another way of deriving rights is through the idea of political equality: the idea that each individual has equal moral worth and should be accorded this by equal respect in a political community's political processes (see Dworkin, 1977). This political equality is sometimes linked to our equal basic needs: the most obvious ones having to do with security and subsistence (see Shue, 1980). Alternatively, it can be linked to our capabilities, which are future-oriented: directed to the requirements for a life of full dignity (see Sen, 1999a; Nussbaum, 2000b). Pragmatic approaches, on the other hand, are reluctant to be too specific about a particular foundation for human rights, focusing instead on areas of consensus among diverse people, and using this agreement as the basis for legitimating rights (see Rawls, 1971, 1993, 1999).

The Universalism of Human Rights

The UDHR's claim to have *universal* application is commonly challenged in one of two related ways (Freeman, 2002, Chapter 6). The first is the argument from **cultural relativism**, a conceptual rejection of rights which states that norms are only appropriate for the cultures out of which they emerge, and that therefore the norms of human rights emergent out of the West only apply in the West. Related to this is the argument from **imperialism**, which—often using cultural relativism as a supporting argument—states that, far from being about the protection of all people everywhere, human rights is a political tool which has been used to promote and defend Western interests. The argument from imperialism suggests that the 'truths' of human rights are disguised forms of power, part of a complex system of global political manipulation.

Cultural Relativism

The cultural relativist often criticizes the human rights doctrine for failing to respect different cultural, religious, and philosophical traditions, and therefore, ultimately, for failing to respect or recognize peoples' identities. **Tolerance** and respect are the key values here; the irony is supposed to be that liberals, in the form of human rights proponents, are being *illiberal* by expecting everyone else to become liberals (see Box 1.5 for further discussion of liberalism and human rights). However, this is an inconsistent use of the cultural relativist argument, precisely because it is not relative *enough*.

A consistent relativist is refuted by her own doctrine: by claiming that all truths are relative, she proclaims the relativism of her own truths, and the incoherence of her position. A consistent relativist cannot prioritize any values at all. A relativist has no basis on which to hold that tolerance or respect are *universal* values which can be used to discredit the supposed interference of specific liberal values (note the double irony that tolerance and respect, along with an appreciation

of pluralism, are liberal values anyway: the so-called relativist may simply be a confused liberal). All that a consistent cultural relativist can do in politics is to note that people have different values: the relativist has no basis for ordering or prioritizing these values, and is thus reduced to political quietism and irrelevance.

A quite common source of this inconsistency is a failure to differentiate between the theoretical claims of cultural relativism, and the empirical fact of cultural relativity. The former undermines any attempt to establish a basis for universal human rights; the latter simply recognizes that people (as individuals and groups) are different from one another. What one does with this recognition will depend entirely on one's broader philosophical approach.

Human Rights Imperialism

A similar confusion is played out by those who charge human rights universalists with being imperialistic. Ironically, the anti-imperialism of the human rights challengers must also appeal to a universal principle—a universal principle of anti-imperialism. This principle must either be a principle of freedom, a principle of tolerance, or a principle of equality. It would suggest that people should be free to believe what they like or belong to whichever culture they like; or, people

---

BOX 1.5 DECONSTRUCTING THE LIBERALISM OF HUMAN RIGHTS

Many people who are enthusiastic about the value of human rights, and who recognize their historical connections with liberalism, nonetheless question whether liberalism is an adequate or desirable basis for a global and universal human rights movement. Various possible forms of critique include the following:

- Many theorists argue that the key concepts liberals use to ground human rights (agency, choice, freedom, etc.) are not sufficient to capture what is intended by the use of the term *human* in human rights. Liberalism's philosophical focus is argued to be too narrow.

- Communitarian thinkers across a range of traditions argue that liberalism's attempts to abstract the human person from their community or tradition undermines key features of what it means to be human and to pursue specific visions of the good life.

- Radical philosophers argue that liberalism is compromised by its own constitutive inequalities, those engendered by

its development out of imperial and racially discriminatory political orders. Liberalism's claim to promote a just world of equal rights is undermined by both its historical and continued investment in a global world order that is deeply inegalitarian and unequal.

- Critical theorists often go beyond liberalism's face value claims and focus on philosophical ambiguities, unexpected consequences, social outcomes, and the tensions within and between human rights claims and practices. These explorations often challenge naïve beliefs in human rights claims.

- Queer thinkers examine the ways in which gender and sexuality upset conventional liberal categories of identity and politics; queer thinkers show how unstable many of liberalism's claims are and delight in upsetting the power relationships normalized by these claims.

References: Benhabib, 2011; Holder and Reidy, 2013; Douzinas and Gearty, 2014; Lutz-Bachmann and Nascimento, 2014; Picq and Thiel, 2015 should tolerate the differences of others and respect their right to be different; or, people should regard other people's capacity to belong to a culture and to have beliefs as equal to their own such capacity. In any of these cases, the argument of the cultural imperialists seems to reduce to an argument along these lines: 'we *do not* agree with you imposing your will on us, because we *do* agree with you that we have certain rights to liberty of action and belief'. The anti-imperialist's argument, like that of the confused relativist's, seems to be a form of nascent liberalism.

There is a crucial question which must be addressed to political leaders who engage in the human rights challenging rhetoric of anti-imperialism: are the cultural beliefs and practices which they defend using the rhetoric of anti-imperialism consistent with the principles that are logically required to frame that anti-imperialism? In all too many of the political disputes over human rights in international politics, those taking the anti-imperialist line against human rights fail to apply the principles which support their anti-imperialism *within* the jurisdictions over which they have authority. Strongman authoritarian leaders argue against human rights on the basis of universal principles that give state leaders freedom, autonomy, and equal respect in the community of sovereign states, and then impose policies which deprive their citizens of that same freedom, tolerance, and equality within the domestic polity. Or, similarly, religious leaders demand freedom of belief, tolerance, and equal treatment for their religious values and practices—and then proceed to deny freedom, tolerance, and equal treatment to members of their communities who may have minority or dissenting opinions. The anti-imperialist rhetoric is useful for drawing our attention to the universal principles we use to frame our responses to injustice; however, rather than succeeding as a critique of the liberalism which grounds human rights, this rhetoric's failures and inconsistencies serve to further support human rights themselves as safeguards against imperialism.

Human rights have become institutionalized globally. The political leaders, officials, and organizational bodies of the movement have become powerful in their own right; that power can easily be misused and employed as a tool of domination. While the anti-imperialist and cultural relativist arguments are often invoked to challenge such domination, the above discussion suggests that the challenge comes more consistently from within human rights norms themselves—norms which privilege equality and freedom and warn against domination

and arbitrary power. The theory of human rights stands as an important corrective to any abuse in the implementation or practice of human rights.

KEY POINTS

The Second World War was the catalyst for the modern redeployment of the idea of the rights of man, now called human rights.

The United Nation's Universal Declaration of Human Rights was promulgated in 1948.

While the rights in the new Declaration emerge out of the liberal political tradition, no philosophical justification is formally given for the rights declared because of the variability of human belief systems. Individuals and groups are left to expound their own justifications for the rights in the Declaration.

Moral justifications for human rights have been presented on the following grounds: human dignity, our ability to reason, the autonomy of individuals, the equality of all persons, our common needs, the capabilities of the human person, and the consensus of diverse parties on key beliefs.

Cultural relativists criticize human rights for illegitimately privileging one set of values over others; rights defenders respond that it is the relativists whose views are inconsistent and that there are very good reasons for privileging rights values.

Human rights are criticized for being the exercise of an imperialist politics; however, those who make this argument are shown to be inconsistent and not genuinely concerned with protecting the victims of authoritarian rule.

Critical Thinking Question:

Which justification for human rights do you find attractive? How would you defend it against those who claim that it wrongly privileges one set of values over others?

Types of Human Rights: Liberty and Welfare Rights

Human rights today have three core texts, The Universal Declaration of Human Rights, the International Covenant on Civil and Political Rights (ICCPR), and the International Covenant on Economic, Social and Cultural Rights (ICESCR). These texts collectively make up the International Bill of Human Rights. The two covenants are human rights treaties which operationalize the Universal Declaration of Human

Rights—they adumbrate what are often seen to be the two different forms of rights within the UDHR, articulating them more fully, and in a manner that responded to the necessities of international politics and the emerging machinery of human rights in the United Nations. For our purposes, what is interesting about the two covenants is the way in which they have come to represent a series of debates regarding the political and normative nature of human rights.

Civil and political rights are often seen to be the core rights at the heart of the tradition of political rights talk and practice, especially as it emerged in Europe and the United States of America in the eighteenth century. Rights such as freedom of speech, freedom from slavery, freedom of religion, and equality before the law are paradigmatic examples. By contrast, many of the rights set out in the International Covenant on Economic, Social and Cultural Rights are seen to fall into a different class: it has often been argued that whereas the rights of the ICCPR are the core and basic rights of the liberal tradition ('liberty rights'), those of the ICESCR are aspirations and goals that we collectively share regarding the good human life well lived ('welfare rights'). These rights include, among others, just and favourable conditions of work, an adequate standard of living, education, healthcare, and participation in cultural life.

Embedded within this debate are historical, ideological, political, normative, and philosophical differences regarding what political ideas can legitimately be promoted by the use of 'rights language'. Here we will examine one of the key fault lines in this debate, which has often been thought to usefully connect all of these differences.

The Negative/Positive Distinction

The classic fault line in the theorization of types of human rights is that described by the negative/positive distinction, a distinction that refers to the normative and philosophical character of the rights in question. On this schema, civil and political rights are considered to be 'negative rights' and economic, social, and cultural rights are considered to be 'positive rights' (see also Box 1.6). What do these terms mean?

The idea behind negative rights is that they only require governments to *refrain* from doing things. In order for a person to have the right to freedom of association, so the argument might go, a government merely needs

BOX 1.6 CHALLENGING ASSUMPTIONS: NEGATIVE AND POSITIVE RIGHTS

Negative rights are commonly thought of as rights of non-interference; positive rights as activity-based. On this basis, for me to have free speech I just need to be let alone to do my speaking; but to have my right to education, someone will need to do a lot of work to build the school and train the teachers. However, if we think closely about free speech and education as rights—not just as activities we undertake—then both need theoretical and material supports which erase this allegedly clear negative/positive distinction. Free speech as a guaranteed right requires positive support from the state in the same way that education does: an institutional system which sets out the right and has the material means to protect it when it is infringed. Creating and insuring the social and institutional space for people to speak freely, it turns out, involves the same sorts of active investment as does the provision of education as a right.

to refrain from obstructing them. By contrast, a positive right requires a government to do a considerable amount: a right to healthcare provision requires (at the least) a government to have some mechanism to connect you with a doctor when you are ill.

Another key element of the distinction is that negative rights are said to be immediately implementable, whereas positive rights require progressive realization. So, for example, if you are in a society where there is no freedom of speech, this can be changed in an instant by a government simply repealing all the measures it had in place to limit that freedom, thus allowing people to say, write, and print what they like as they please. However, access to a reasonable standard of living is not a right that a government can procure for its citizens simply by government decree; in impoverished societies this right might only be met after years of sustained development, even under the best of possible circumstances.

A further argument would be that positive rights are not justiciable in the manner of negative rights; that is, one cannot settle who has responsibility for the satisfaction of a given right in the same manner. Let us take the case of civil and political rights: if I am deprived of my freedom of religion, tortured, or am not treated equally before the law, it is a relatively straightforward matter for a court to determine who is to blame, and who is responsible to do something about it. The abuse of my rights has a justiciable remedy. If I live in an underdeveloped society with little access to food, healthcare, work, or education, the question of who is responsible for this situation and who should remedy it are much more difficult indeed; many have argued that the matter is so complex that it cannot be thought justiciable.

The Indivisibility of Rights

Further investigation reveals, however, that this now classic distinction goes both too far and not far enough in the manner in which it distinguishes between the different types of rights and the circumstances under which they might be attained. Let us briefly see why, before going on to suggest a better approach.

If we go back to our earlier examples we can see on second glance that we need a more sophisticated analysis. Freedom of association may be experienced by a person when a government simply refrains from activity. However, in order for you to enjoy your freedom as a right, there needs to be an institutional structure in place for you to utilize should an arm of government (or some other agent) seek to infringe your right. If a policeman were to detain you wrongly, you need courts, lawyers, statutes, and other state apparatus to exist and to be at your disposal in order to claim your right. It turns out that there is much the state must do in order to ensure your negative rights. Similarly with freedom of speech: a government can grant you freedom of speech as a right if it is the case that all such rights granting and protecting mechanisms are already in place. If they are not in place, they will take time to be established and become operational. 'Negative' rights need positive government action in order to be granted, protected, and to be justiciable. 'Positive' rights to healthcare or education and so on operate in a similar way: in societies where these rights are institutionalized, they are similarly justiciable. In societies where levels of development mitigate against institutionalization, it may well be the case that the right to freedom of the press and the right to healthcare both face the same structural difficulties.

Recognizing this, scholars have moved on to develop more sophisticated typologies of rights, which allow for differentiation between rights that need more or less activity in order to be met, and that have varying normative character (Koch, 2009). Henry Shue (1980) wrote of the obligation to avoid depriving, to protect from deprivation, and to aid the deprived. Asbojorn Eide (1989) formulated obligations to respect, protect, facilitate, and fulfil. Others created similar scales.

Collectively they reinforce Eide's key point: that 'each and every human right—economic, social, cultural, civil and political—may require various measures from (passive) non-interference to (active) insurance of the satisfaction of individual needs all depending on the concrete circumstances'. (Quoted in Koch, 2009, p. 15.)

Such a conclusion suggests that while not all human rights are the same, there is a strong sense in which they are 'indivisible, interdependent and inter-related', to use the rhetoric of the Vienna Declaration and Programme of Action, 1993. The Declaration goes on to say that 'The international community must treat human rights globally in a fair and equal manner, on the same footing and with the same emphasis …'. It is evidently the case that this latter set of injunctions is not followed; one of the reasons for hope and evidences of progress in human rights protection over recent decades, however, has been the reclaimed understanding that the various types of human rights—civil, political, economic, social, cultural—are not easily divorced from one another, and that the practical and institutional realization of any one set of these rights has follow-on effects for the broader political objective articulated by the Vienna Declaration.

KEY POINTS

The Universal Declaration and other UN Human Rights instrumentalities contain both liberty rights and welfare rights.

The difference between these two types of rights has often been mapped out using the classic negative/positive distinction.

Negative rights are said to require only passive non-interference to be realized, whereas positive rights need to be actively pursued by state or intergovernmental agents.

Closer inspection reveals this to be a false dichotomy, with both liberty and welfare rights needing complex combinations of respect, protection, facilitation, and fulfilment by a range of different actors.

This analysis reinforces a repeated theme in the history of modern human rights, that they should be understood as indivisible, interdependent, and interrelated.

Critical Thinking Question:

Why is it important to recognize that both liberty and welfare rights require institutions and state action to be realized?

Group Rights

Many of the rights that have been developed within the contemporary human rights project have a collective or group dimension. The two UN Covenants discussed in the previous section ascribe certain rights to all 'peoples'—most famously the right to self-determination. As well as the liberty and welfare rights already discussed, which are conventionally understood as individual rights, the evolution of modern human rights has seen the development of 'solidarity rights'. These group or collectively oriented rights are 'to goods such as development, peace, a healthy environment, communication, humanitarian assistance, and a share in the common heritage of mankind' (P. Jones, 2008b).

Human rights theorists have been significantly divided over how to understand such rights. Some theorists have argued that while we can talk of groups having rights under certain conditions, these rights cannot be understood as human rights. Human rights understood as the rights of individuals remain the only 'real rights', because of the role they play in protecting individuals from the interests, intentions, and 'rights' of hostile groups. Others will point to the solidarity rights listed above and argue that many of the goods that we discuss under the rubric of human rights are experienced collectively—that, indeed, many of the abuses of human rights we fight against have collective as well as individual dimensions. This line of argument is often extended to include a broader debate about culture, and has particular resonance for those working with human

rights in post-colonial and other non-Western contexts. Another related complication involves how we think about minority rights (see Box 1.7). Thus, the discussion of group rights provides a clear entrée into discussions of cultural difference and its significance for understanding human rights.

A most useful way of understanding the terms of the debate is provided by the analysis of Peter Jones (P. Jones, 1999a, 1999b, 2008a, 2008b). Jones identifies two different conceptions of group rights that are used in the discussion: the *collective conception* and the *corporate conception* of group rights. He argues that the distinction 'is crucial to the issue of whether group rights are in sympathy with, and perhaps form part of, the morality of human rights, or whether they belong to a quite different and potentially conflicting morality'. (P. Jones, 1999b, p. 107.)

The Collective Conception of Group Rights

To best understand what it means to have a group right on the collective conception, let us first go back one step and ask what it means to have a right in the first place. Jones answers this with the aid of an 'interest theory of rights' (drawn from Raz, 1986). In this theory, we have a right to something if we have an interest in that something—not any kind of interest though; it has to be an interest of 'sufficient moment'. This sufficiently important interest provides a justification for us to impose a duty on another person. Using this interest theory of rights, we can see how it might be that we can talk sensibly of group rights: people who

---

BOX 1.7 MINORITY RIGHTS

Minority rights are similar to group rights, in that they apply to a subset of group-differentiated people: the rights of women or the rights of native language speakers for example. Two features of minority rights make them appropriate for positioning within the family of human rights. First, they are rights which apply to individuals who have a minority status of some form; this is a feature they share with the collective conception of group rights. Second, minority rights may be thought of as human rights because they are what James W. Nickel terms 'URAMs': universal rights applied to minorities. On close examination, minority rights turn out to be the application of universal rights to the specific needs or vulnerabilities of minority populations. As Nickel argues, even strongly differentiated minority rights can

be instances of universal rights applied to minorities. An example he uses here is the right of women to prenatal care. This appears to be a right men can't share, one that does not apply to all persons, and therefore one that is not a *human* right, properly understood. However, the right to prenatal care can be understood as an instance of the universal human right to basic medical care, in its specific application to pregnant women. It is a sub-specification of a universal human right. Nickel concludes that minority rights can be understood as human rights in cases where they can be shown to derive from such a broader universal right.

Reference: Nickel, 2007, Chapter 10

belong to a group might have a shared interest which as an individual is not very strong, but when shared with others is of sufficient moment to be considered a right and thus to ground duties which other persons or groups may be obliged to discharge.

Jones uses a couple of examples to illustrate how this works: one involves the interests of people living in the vicinity of a polluting factory, and one involves people who belong to a cultural minority group. The individuals alone in these examples may not have a sufficiently strong interest to oblige others to change their behaviour—whether that is to stop polluting or to extend consideration to certain aspects of their cultural identity (language use, for example). However, the combined interests of people who come together to form a group may well provide the strength of justification necessary.

For our purposes, the crucial points are these: the group comes into play through the aggregation of the shared interests of its separate members; the group's moral standing is derived from that of its members and their interests and does not exist separately; and, finally, the group's import is that it provides a right that may not exist without the sharing of interests that it facilitates. On this conception, we can indeed speak of group rights, but these rights depend on and advert to the interests of the individuals who collectively form the group.

The Corporate Conception of Group Rights

In the corporate conception, the idea of 'groupness' is different from what we have just discussed. Rather than the group being made up of a collection of individuals with shared interests, the group itself is thought of as an individual: it is 'conceived as a single, integral entity' (P. Jones, 1999b, p. 86). Any given right that the group might have is to be thought of as *its right*, not as the right of its members thought of as individuals.

Can a group, thought of in these terms, have rights? Jones argues that when we ask this question, we are asking a question similar to the one we ask when we ask whether animals or future generations can be thought of as having rights. The answer lies in the way in which we attribute moral standing to these entities. Here, the key question is whether a group as an entity can have moral standing in a way that is not simply a function of the moral standing of its members. For it to do so, a group must be understood as an entity that has an identity of moral significance that is morally prior to the interests and rights it may then be said to possess.

For example, a nation, on this account, would be conceptualized as an entity that has an identity, a way of life, a self-understanding, a character, that should be respected and granted political recognition for its own sake—including rights such as self-determination. By contrast, the collective conception of group rights would see nationhood as having value only in that it recognizes and serves the interests and well-being of the individuals who are its citizens (see Box 1.8).

Group Rights as Human Rights

The key contrast can be briefly summarized: on the collective conception, group rights are a function of the interests of the group members' individual interests, and thus the rights of the group will always be a function of the rights of its members. Because of this, we can conclude that some group rights can be understood within the discourse of human rights. By contrast, group rights understood on the corporate conception cannot be thought of as human rights. They belong to a separate moral subject, the community, or group, whose rights exist in some sense independently of the rights of its members.

BOX 1.8 THE ASIAN VALUES DEBATE

The so-called Asian values debate is a vivid illustration of the political nature of human rights, providing us with a range of controversies to examine, which engage with the different forms of human rights discussed in this chapter: liberty rights, welfare rights, and group rights. In the 1990s in particular, a variety of Asian political elites used a mixture of arguments about economic development, self-determination, culture, philosophy, and religion to contest the political priorities set by 'Western' discourses of human rights (Langlois, 2001).

The 'Asia' advanced here by many of the anti-democratic ruling elites of the region, however, was itself a political vision, and one as contested within Asia as it was elsewhere (similar debates have been held in other regions, most notably Africa). The elites' use of economic rights (especially around the discourse of development) to limit liberty rights and their invocation of cultural and religious traditions and identities of the corporate conception have received rigorous criticism. In turn, however, many of these critical voices are themselves not happy with the dominant global discourse of human rights, and also draw on intellectual and social resources based in different cultural traditions and embodying different political priorities to the dominant human rights discourse (Langlois, 2001).

The danger with the corporate conception of group rights is that the proponents of a group right may argue that it is a matter in relation to which it is only the group that has moral standing, not individuals or minorities within the group. This would authorize rejecting, ignoring, or silencing competing claims from individuals—thus opening a space for group rights to threaten human rights. By contrast, the collective conception protects against such conflict by requiring the group's rights to respect those of the individual; it does not allow for the group to be able, in Jones's evocative phrase, to write the individual out of the moral calculation (P. Jones, 1999b, p. 93). It is only with a conceptual scheme that guarantees this protection of an individual's human rights that we can endorse group rights as human rights; thus, we can conclude that for group rights to be understood as a part of the morality of human rights they must be construed with the use of the collective conception of group rights.

KEY POINTS

The effective implementation of human rights norms has a significant collective dimension, but group or solidarity rights have always been controversial.

Group rights can be understood under two conceptions: the collective and the corporate conception.

The collective conception allows for a form of group rights that also preserve the integrity of people's individual rights.

The corporate conception of group rights conflicts with the broader morality of human rights because it provides no basis to protect individuals and subgroups against the potential coercive power of the group.

Critical Thinking Question:

Why is it that the discussion of group rights demonstrates the importance of the individual in the overall morality of human rights?

Human Rights as a Political Project

The rhetoric of human rights can sometimes obscure the many ways in which the human rights movement is a *political* movement. The talk of universalism, of common standards for human kind, and of inalienable and self-evident rights can give the impression that all the big questions about human rights are settled. As even a cursory investigation of the history of the human rights idea shows, however, the greater part of what we appeal to when we appeal to human rights is controversial and contested. There are four levels at which the political nature of human rights is important.

The first level has to do with the normative tradition out of which human rights historically emerge. The normative under-girdings of human rights are from liberal political theory and, before that, from the natural law tradition. In our contemporary world, the language of human rights is being spoken by people who work in a great variety of other traditions, and the confluence of these traditions with that of the liberal one produces contestation, dispute, and disagreement. The claim that the liberal approach should continue to be the arbiter or referee in the continued development of human rights as they go global is deeply controversial. Similarly, any change to the existing human rights corpus brought on by adopting values from other traditions is also deeply controversial. There are no fixed answers about how to resolve these conflicts.

A second level at which human rights are political concerns rights declarations—quintessentially the UDHR, but also its precursors, and the subsequent human rights instruments created through the UN and regionally. Human rights declarations are usually the product of a committee appointed by a political authority. What goes into a declaration and what is left out is determined by those involved in the drafting. They do not have clear and pristine access to human reason or religious revelation; the rights that they declare are heavily contingent on the historical and political framework in which they work. However good or bad a particular rights declaration may be, it is always a political outcome, a compromise, or a diplomatic resolution of competing interests. Rights declarations, then, must also be recognized as political instruments.

The implementation of a rights regime is the third level at which rights are political. The decision to describe certain states of being as human rights abuses, the decision to use state power to change circumstances or to detain or free individuals in the name of human rights—these are all profoundly political decisions, and they are decisions that of necessity are engaged with in a local context. The diversity of human communities may well mean that behaviour that in one place is considered a rights abuse is routinely accepted somewhere else. There is no settled means for universal resolution of these differences.

The fourth level at which human rights are political is the most familiar: rights emerged within the Western tradition as a way of preserving the freedoms and liberties of individuals and groups against the powers of the state. The political project of human rights is a strategy for fighting against existing power structures in the hope of creating a social environment that is more nearly just. Local context is everything in this equation, and where that local context is inhospitable to the principles embedded in received human rights norms, the struggle can be interminable and disheartening.

What is common across these four areas is the way in which the normative agenda pursued by human rights practitioners is both displayed and questioned, challenged and interrogated (Langlois, 2001; Baxi, 2006). Whether one is explaining a normative tradition, declaring a right, applying some aspect of a rights regime, or defending the rights of the abused against powerful interests, one is asserting a set of political beliefs about the value of human beings and the way in which they should be treated. Defending those convictions is an essential part of the human rights project

> ## KEY POINTS
>
> Human rights are political in the following four senses:
>
> - Human rights are political because they embody a set of norms that emerged out of the tradition of political liberalism, with which not all identify.
>
> - Specific human rights regimes are created by groups of people who have their own political agendas and constituencies, and who must make decisions about what to include and exclude that cannot satisfy everyone.
>
> - The implementation of any established human rights regime is subject to interpretation, political context, and local circumstances.
>
> - The pursuit of human rights translates into local engagement, and quite often bitter confrontation, with prevailing unjust power structures.
>
> ## Critical Thinking Question:
>
> Which political aspects of human rights do you think make human rights a radical or revolutionary political doctrine?

and is ultimately what we are doing when we engage in debates about the normative and theoretical justification of human rights.

Conclusion

The language of human rights is fundamentally a normative or ethical language, one that emerged out of the political liberalism of the Enlightenment, and one that leads to a very distinctive form of political engagement. In our modern period, the Universal Declaration of Human Rights is the defining text of the human rights movement; but behind the rights that are declared in that document are layers of history and philosophy.

These in turn are present in many of the debates in contemporary global politics over the meaning, usefulness, and effective implementation of human rights. This chapter has shown that understanding the history and philosophy of human rights is essential to being able to navigate the complex political debates surrounding the desirability and normative content of human rights reform in the international system.

? QUESTIONS

Individual Study Questions

1. Why do the rights of international human rights law need philosophical or moral foundations?

2. Explain why having a right is most important when we lack the object of that right.

3. What are the common elements of the various liberal justifications for rights?

4. What lessons can we learn from the Asian values debate?

5. Why and in what senses are human rights political?

Group Discussion Questions

1. Why is the history of the human rights idea important today?

2. What are the strengths and limitations of Jacques Maritain's position on the justification of rights?

3. Why is the negative/positive distinction an inadequate way of thinking about the differences between liberty and welfare rights?

FURTHER READING

Baxi, U. (2006). *The Future of Human Rights*. Oxford: Oxford University Press.

The author connects the sometimes complacent arguments about human rights theory with the lives of those suffering human rights abuse and considers the new challenges facing human rights today.

Beitz, C. (2009). *The Idea of Human Rights*. New York: Oxford University Press.

This book questions how we should best understand the contemporary practice of human rights in international politics.

Brysk, A. (2013). *Speaking Rights to Power: Constructing Political Will*. Oxford: Oxford University Press.

An examination of how it is that talk of human rights can transform the world. The author examines many cases where proponents of human rights have made them matter in the battle against powerful interests.

Griffin, J. (2008). *On Human Rights*. Cambridge: Cambridge University Press.

A state-of-the-art attempt to provide a substantive theory of human rights.

Ignatieff, M. (2001). *Human Rights as Politics and Idolatry*. Princeton, NJ: Princeton University Press.

In two highly accessible essays, Ignatieff sets out all the major issues to do with human rights in contemporary international politics; his views are then interrogated by a number of eminent commentators.

Langlois, A. J. (2001). *The Politics of Justice and Human Rights*. Cambridge: Cambridge University Press.

This book considers the questions of universalism and pluralism through an examination of the so-called Asian values debate of the 1990s.

Mahoney, J. (2007). *The Challenge of Human Rights*. Oxford: Blackwell Publishing.

This book traces the rise of human rights as a resource for ethical reasoning in politics.

Reus-Smit, C. (2013). *Individual Rights and the Making of the International System*. Cambridge: Cambridge University Press.

An account of the evolution of the contemporary system of states, in which the role played by individual rights in shaping that system is examined anew.

Zivi, K. (2012). *Making Rights Claims: A Practice of Democratic Citizenship*. Oxford: Oxford University Press.

An examination, both theoretically and practically, of what happens when people make the bold claim that they have rights, particularly when those rights are not yet enjoyed.

WEB LINKS

http://plato.stanford.edu/entries/rights-human/   The human rights entry in the online Stanford Encyclopedia of Philosophy, which provides valuable discussion and useful links to related topics.

http://philpapers.org/browse/human-rights/   This is the link to the Human Rights category at the website PhilPapers: 'a comprehensive directory of online philosophical articles and books by academic philosophers'.

http://europa.eu/pol/rights/index_en.htm   The European Union Human Rights website provides a discussion of the role of human rights in the EU, including legislation and other activities.

http://www.hurisearch.org/   A search engine specifically for human rights, with coverage of over 5,000 human rights websites.

Visit the **Online Resource Centre** that accompanies this book for updates and a range of other resources: **www.oxfordtextbooks.co.uk/orc/goodhart3e/**

2

Feminist and Activist Approaches to Human Rights

Brooke Ackerly

Chapter Contents

Reader's Guide

Human rights are an ethical tool for political criticism in domestic and transnational struggles for justice. This chapter emphasizes the theoretical and political history of human rights that emerges out of the struggles that have been waged by feminists and other non-elites. First, I discuss the bases for the moral legitimacy of human rights and consider challenges to those arguments. Second, I outline three aspects of feminist approaches to human rights: their criticism of some aspects of human rights theory and practice, their rights claims, and their conceptual contributions to a theory of human rights. According to feminists, human rights are indivisible, interrelated, and intersectional. That feminist theory of rights comes from the struggles of women's human rights activists around the world and in their communities.

Introduction

Despite the tremendous diversity among people and sociocultural contexts, human rights possess a kind of universality. That universality is grounded in the struggle for those rights. These struggles too are very different, as people must confront myriad forms of oppression. What they have in common is their reliance on the broad moral resonance of universal human rights. This moral resonance is grounded in the confidence or hope that those who hear a cry out for 'human rights' will recognize in it a legitimate political claim and will take action to help those making that claim to secure their rights. This *hope* that 'human rights' have universal moral legitimacy is not the same as the recognition of human rights, however. Their universal moral resonance must not be confused with universal political efficacy; the former is no guarantee that any particular rights claims will be effective. Regardless of the effectiveness of particular struggles for human rights, these struggles convey the meaning of human rights.

The universality and legitimacy of human rights have long been questioned, with feminists among their most powerful and incisive critics. Much of this criticism addresses problems that trace back to the grounding of the modern conception of human rights in the **Western** intellectual tradition of the **Enlightenment** (see Chapter 1). This is the same intellectual tradition that justified colonization in the name of bringing 'civilization' to colonized peoples. It is the same intellectual tradition that privileges individual rights over those of the community and has been uncomfortable with group claims to self-determination. Despite this history, the concept of human rights has been used globally by people struggling against injustice, people making political claims about justice, even claims that challenge the political power of Western countries and of their own governments.

This chapter takes the perspective that the material bases of struggles for human rights, that is, the actual cultural, economic, and political contexts of daily life, have helped to shape human rights norms themselves. Women's quite specific experiences of exclusion, domination, and oppression were crucial to the feminist theoretical **critique** of human rights and to the movements that have worked to redefine women's rights as human rights. The methodological assumption of this chapter is that if we want to understand human rights, we have to pay attention to the political struggles that use 'human rights' in their struggles. When we do this, we see the role of these movements in shaping and reshaping what human rights mean.

Today, scholars generally recognize that substantive claims made by those engaged in struggle have brought about important transformations in the theory of human rights (Bob, 2009; Mertus, 2009; Ackerly and Cruz, 2010; Zivi, 2012). Women in particular have been concerned with how human rights function and malfunction in practice, leading them to develop substantive criticisms of human rights as theorized in the Enlightenment tradition and institutionalized

in the **Universal Declaration of Human Rights** (UDHR). The **conceptual** developments propelled by these insights have been realized in international instruments regarding women's rights, such as the **Convention for the Elimination of All Forms of Discrimination Against Women** (CEDAW, 1979). Feminists' substantive criticisms have transformed the way we think about human rights generally, not just for women's issues. Feminist contributions to human rights theory are apparent in subsequent conventions, such as the Convention on the Rights of Persons with Disabilities (CRPD, 2006), particularly where these mention the political, economic, and social institutions and practices necessary for rights enjoyment (see Box 2.1). Additionally, international institutions such as the **World Bank**, the International Labor Organization (ILO), and the UN Security Council have sought to implement this transformed view.

Of course, even though the theory of human rights has been transformed, many of the real-world issues that prompted those changes remain politically contentious in many parts of the world. A robust human rights theory is not enough to ensure that everyone is secure in their enjoyment of rights. This chapter will discuss the theoretical and substantive insights gained from feminist approaches to human rights, including the diverse bases for asserting the moral universality of human rights. It will also highlight the ways in which feminists and other activists for marginalized groups have used human rights in their struggles and how these struggles have in turn shaped the theory of human rights.

Universal Human Rights and Cultural Relativism

There is no universal agreement about the foundations of human rights. Theorists have proposed many different foundations, typically grounding them in some pre-existing intellectual or cultural tradition (see Chapter 1). Some of these proposals with rich theoretical legacies include: individual moral standing of the person,[1] individual autonomy,[2] reciprocity,[3] human agency,[4] human dignity,[5] equal creation by a divinity,[6] membership in the human family,[7] membership in political society,[8] well-being,[9] and human functioning.[10] Some theorists seek foundations for human rights in the common ground among competing, or at least very different, traditions and an engagement across

---

BOX 2.1 SAMPLE EVIDENCE OF 'RIGHTS ENJOYMENT' LANGUAGE IN SELECTED INTERNATIONAL CONVENTIONS AND DECLARATIONS

UDHR article 22

Everyone, as a member of society, has the right to social security and *is entitled to realization*, through national effort and international co-operation and in accordance with the organization and resources of each State, *of the economic, social and cultural rights indispensable for his dignity and the free development of his personality*.

UDHR article 26

(2) Education shall be directed to the full development of the human personality and to the strengthening of respect for human rights and fundamental freedoms. It shall promote understanding, tolerance and friendship among all nations, racial or religious groups, and shall further the activities of the United Nations for the maintenance of peace.

CEDAW article 1

For the purposes of the present Convention, the term 'discrimination against women' shall mean any distinction, exclusion or restriction made on the basis of sex which has the effect or purpose of impairing or nullifying the *recognition, enjoyment or exercise* by women, irrespective of their marital status, on a basis of equality of men and women, of human rights and fundamental freedoms in the political, economic, social, cultural, civil or any other field.

CEDAW article 3

States Parties shall take in all fields, in particular *in the political, social, economic and cultural fields*, all appropriate measures, including legislation, to ensure the full development and advancement of women, for the purpose of guaranteeing them the *exercise and enjoyment of human rights and fundamental freedoms* on a basis of equality with men.

CRC article 3

... States Parties undertake to ensure the child such protection and care as is necessary for his or her well-being, taking into account the rights and duties of his or her parents, legal guardians, or other individuals legally responsible for him or her, and, to this end, shall take all appropriate legislative and administrative measures.

... States Parties shall ensure that the institutions, services and facilities responsible for the care or protection of children shall conform with the standards established by competent authorities, particularly in the areas of safety, health, in the number and suitability of their staff, as well as competent supervision.

CRPD article 1

The purpose of the present Convention is to *promote, protect and ensure the full and equal enjoyment* of all human rights and fundamental freedoms by all persons with disabilities, and to promote respect for their inherent dignity ... Persons with disabilities include those who have long-term physical, mental, intellectual or sensory impairments which *in interaction with various barriers* may hinder their full and effective participation in society on an equal basis with others.

---

them.[11] Still others have attempted to anchor them in their historical and functional evolution.[12]

During the 1980s and 1990s, while activists were using human rights to mobilize and develop networks, some political leaders were arguing that human rights were 'Western values' and inconsistent with their local values, and feminist, post-colonial, and post-structuralist theorists joined in questioning the universality of human rights. Meanwhile, scholars debated the merits of **cultural relativism**.

Cultural relativists raise both theoretical and historical objections to the universality of human rights. In this section we consider both, along with some of the responses that defenders of universal human rights

have offered. In the next section, we shall see how feminist approaches to human rights specifically address the historical and theoretical challenges explored here.

Theoretical Dimensions of Cultural Relativism

Cultural relativism is the view that ethics develop within a particular social context; because social contexts are distinct from one another, relativists argue, there cannot be a moral or ethical framework that applies in all contexts (Rorty, 1993). Instead, cultural relativists hold that ethics and moral values are specific to a particular social or cultural milieu.

To cultural relativists, human rights' emergence from the Western Enlightenment tradition demonstrates their inappropriateness for societies with their own diverse cultural, religious, and philosophical traditions. Critics often cite several ways in which modern, Western theories of human rights clash with non-Western cultures. Human rights are said to construct an ideal of the autonomous individual, while many cultures value the group or community above the individual. Human rights are said to be legalistic, while many cultures prefer (seemingly) consensual modes of resolving differences to adversarial ones; human rights are supposedly rationalistic, while many cultures rely on traditional beliefs and practices that conflict with Western conceptions of reason and of the related concepts of rationality and autonomy. Finally, human rights presume a modern, bureaucratic state concerned with the private liberties of citizens, while many cultures understand the relationship between society and its members differently. These differences, cultural relativists allege, make Western notions of human rights inappropriate in cultures with differing traditions.

One frequently noted problem with cultural relativist critiques of human rights is that they are self-defeating.[13] The claim that truths and values are relative to particular cultures seems itself to be a universal claim, forcing the relativist to concede either that there are some universal moral principles or that even relativist claims must be viewed as non-generalizable. While there might be just one universal moral principle, it is hard to imagine an account that generates just this particular universal principle (the principle of relativism) and no others. Often, the basis of the relativist critique is that 'imposing' Western notions of human rights in non-Western contexts exhibits a kind of intolerance. While correct as far as it goes, this critique too is self-defeating, insofar as it establishes toleration as a universal value (see Chapter 1).

A deeper objection to the relativist position is that it wrongly accepts a very narrow, Western view of human rights as a distinctively Western concept. However much the existing scholarship on human rights, most of which originates in the **global North**, seems to reinforce this view, the theoretical underpinnings of human rights are in fact vast—much broader than what the literature reflects—drawing on a broad range of theoretical perspectives and intellectual histories (An-Na'im, 1992b, 2002; Sobrino, 2001; Sachedina, 2009; John D'Arcy May, 2012). Perhaps

more importantly, the relativist premise that cultural transformation is problematic because of the incompatibility between human rights and certain cultural traditions has been challenged on the ground by activists who argue that dominant practices within their own cultural traditions should be transformed to eliminate the oppression of women and minorities (Narayan, 1997; Rao, 2003b). In fact, in relativist criticisms of human rights there is a rhetorical appeal to anti-Westernism that has been used to silence rights claimants who wish to transform oppressive structures within their own societies (Kim Dae, 1994; Zakaria, 1994; Narayan, 1998; Rothschild, Long, and Fried, 2005). These rights claimants are often demonized as foreign agents, pawns of the West, and so on.

Finally, the cultural relativist criticism of human rights relies on a sociological account of culture for which there is little **empirical** evidence. The relativist view assumes that 'cultures' must be profoundly different from one another. At the same time, it also assumes that cultures contain no diversity of norms internally. The advocates of cultural relativism themselves contradict this point; the counter-evidence is provided in their view that legal and social institutions are needed to maintain local norms. If these norms need maintenance, it must be because they are more dynamic or contested than the cultural relativist account suggests. The work of activists provides further evidence that such contestation exists.

Historical Dimensions of Cultural Relativism

The origins of this anti-Westernism in connection with human rights trace back to the condescending way that Europeans used human rights historically to justify colonialism, imperialism, slavery, and the exclusion of women, religious and ethnic minorities, and other marginalized people from the category of 'human'. Indeed, the development and confidence in Europe of the belief in European moral superiority and the universal relevance of European moral values coincides uncomfortably with the colonizing imperialism of the eighteenth and nineteenth centuries that denied most of the world (and all women) these rights. Relativist critics—including leaders of authoritarian regimes in Singapore and South Korea—argued not only that the rational, autonomous, rights-bearing individual was a Western historical construct, but also that this construct was used to justify European domination in the name of 'civilizing' non-European peoples. This historical abuse of human rights discourse can hardly be denied; more important is the question of whether this history of misuse should invalidate the entire concept of human rights. We shall return to this question, in connection with feminist approaches.

Another historical argument made by relativists is that small and non-Western states were excluded from participating in the development of the contemporary international human rights framework. This argument turns out to be largely inaccurate. While it is true that the foundations of the contemporary human rights regime were worked out before decolonization, small states and non-Western states were in fact involved in developing the theoretical and political framework reflected in the UDHR (Waltz, 2001, 2002) (see Box 2.2). The contributions of participants from smaller and non-Western states went to the core commitment to inclusion and universality of human rights. In particular, women from these countries pushed for gender-inclusive language: Hansa Mehta of India and Minerva Bernardino from the Dominican Republic argued successfully for the Universal

---

BOX 2.2 CHALLENGING ASSUMPTIONS: DIVERSITY AND THE DRAFTING OF THE UDHR

The presence of non-Western and small states in these discussions did not always promote more inclusive outcomes. Many Arab delegations declined to endorse the UDHR by abstaining, citing conflicts between the Declaration's views on women and their own religious and cultural views. Though communist and Arab delegations favoured minority rights and a provision explicitly condemning cultural genocide, the United States, fearful of the implications for its own system of oppressing its African American minority, was staunchly opposed (see Chapter 8), as were most other countries of the Americas. On the question of minority rights, a proposed article protecting groups from cultural attack was not included (Morsink, 1999).

Think about the political environment of the drafting of the UDHR. How does US opposition to minority rights protections affect your broader understanding of the US role in international human rights politics? Do you think the smaller countries in Latin American went along with the United States because they had significant minority populations and shared its concerns, or do you think the political power of the United States played a part?

Declaration to be a 'Universal Declaration of Human Rights' and not a 'Declaration of the Rights of Man' and for it to state specifically in the Preamble that the document applied to 'men and women' (Parisi, 2002; Arat, 2008).

Some of these same theoretical and historical criticisms resonate today in debates concerning the universalizing discourse of **neoliberal** economic globalization (Parisi, 2010b). Critics, including feminists and activists from the global South, worry that this discourse is being used to undermine traditional cultural practices, institutions, and knowledge as a tool for reconfiguring non-Western societies and economies in ways that make them more open to corporate exploitation and more vulnerable to control by international financial institutions (IFIs). For example, the International Monetary Fund (IMF), whose structural adjustment programmes promise prosperity, have instead worsened inequality and increased poverty in many parts of the world. Likewise the World Bank, while purportedly working to alleviate poverty, has increased **gender** and economic inequality through its funding priorities, which include support for export-led industries and industrial-scale agriculture. These sectors bring women and subsistence farmers into the formal economy as labourers who need to work for wages, which are often insufficient to enable workers to live above the poverty line. Critics are concerned not just with the discursive aspects of neoliberalism, but also wrestle with various legal and technological aspects of exploitation, which may have global causes and which are often locally varied (Shiva, 1991, 2005).

Importantly, human rights often figure as a tool for combating neoliberal economic policies by criticizing their impact on people's lives. This fact, along with the use of human rights by domestic activists working to transform gender relations and combat various forms of marginalization, show that while the theoretical and historical problems with human rights are real and serious, the cultural relativist critique does not capture the complexity of human rights or their varied sources of strength and legitimacy.

Universal human rights have been gaining traction globally for addressing the issues raised by culturally, politically, and economically marginalized groups. Part of their legitimacy can be found in the varied moral foundations actually underlying human rights. The consultative process led by the

United Nations Educational, Scientific and Cultural Organization (UNESCO), which was to inform the drafting of the UDHR, drew on the religious, cultural, and intellectual backgrounds of member states. These included Jewish, Greek, and Roman histories of ideas, Buddhism, Hinduism, Confucianism, Christianity, and Islam. Again, while this process preceded the decolonization of the latter part of the twentieth century, the traditions that informed the process were multiple and diverse—though disproportionately informed by elites' perspectives on each tradition. There are two reasons for this elite bias: elites have been the authors of history (in both senses), and elites dominate in the representation of states and selection of experts in the UN system (see Box 2.3). As we will see, by the 1990s political tides were turning; UN conferences, under pressure, developed lobbying and caucusing tools that enabled non-elite voices to influence the political negotiations of member states. Still, elites dominated the formation of the UN and the drafting of the Universal Declaration itself.

For those people who have struggled for their rights, debates about the foundations of human rights are academic unless they lead to a recognition of them as human beings and of their rights as legitimate. Human rights have become a common framework for thinking about many questions of justice ranging from Indigenous rights to disability rights; their development as an appropriate moral basis for assessing the legitimacy of political claims and their codification in international law and institutions has developed in parallel with activist critiques of an engagement with human rights. In the next section we consider how that process has unfolded, paying particular attention to feminist critiques as an example of the kind of theoretical and practically anchored analysis that has transformed human rights.

BOX 2.3 CHALLENGING ASSUMPTIONS: WHO WON THE COLD WAR?

Consider the ways in which human rights theory and practice privilege elite perspectives on ideas and politics. These are the ideas of the winners in intellectual, economic, and political conflict, the ideas of those whose ideas and actions are recorded by history. Who were the winners and losers of the Cold War (see Chapter 3)? Who are the authorities of religious interpretation (see Chapter 10)?

KEY POINTS

Cultural relativism is the view that ethics or moral values are specific to the cultures in which they arise.

The theoretical critique based on cultural relativism views human rights as Western constructs that are inappropriate for other cultures. This view involves a contradiction and ignores the demands for human rights by activists in those cultures.

The historical critique based on cultural relativism views human rights as a tool of Western imperialism. While correct, this historical baggage has not affected the popularity or legitimacy of the global human rights discourse for addressing oppression in the global South or in transnational politics.

The cultural relativism debate, as well as the evolution of the contemporary human rights regime, was elite-driven, though recently the system has become more open to activist influence.

There are many possible foundations defended as the source of moral and political legitimacy for human rights, all of which draw on pre-existing (elite-defined) traditions.

Critical Thinking Questions:

Is 'feminism' a Western idea? What experiences and struggles would you need to learn about in order to answer this question?

Can we celebrate our cultural traditions and also want to change them to be more respectful of human rights?

Feminist and Activist Approaches to Human Rights

Feminist activists have been at the forefront of the practical and theoretical analysis of human rights. There are many different feminist theoretical perspectives, drawing on a wide variety of justifications or foundations for human rights. Moreover, feminists disagree among themselves about many of the substantive and strategic issues related to human rights. Therefore, feminist contributions to human rights must be understood as reflecting a range of the variety of *feminisms*. Despite this diversity, there are some common and recurring themes in feminist approaches to human rights, themes that are also prominent in many other activists' approaches.

Rights as Entitlements

Even if those in a struggle for their human rights do not share a common foundation, they may share a common conception of rights (Sobrino Sj, 2001). Today a broad range of groups use rights language to press their claims. What are they asking for?

Western theorists have commonly conceived of human rights as entitlements (Donnelly, 1982). An **entitlement** can be thought of as a benefit secured by law or contract, something that one is due (in common speech we say that someone is *entitled* to something or simply that she has a right to it). Feminists and many human rights activists have focused instead on the *enjoyment* of human rights (see Box 2.1). Those who have human rights have the personal and social capacity to enjoy them, meaning that they are in a position actually to benefit from the substance of the right (which corresponds to the meaningful thing promised in the legal or contractual guarantee). If one does not enjoy one's rights, one doesn't really have them at all in an important sense. Having rights is like having ice cream: you can have ice cream in the freezer, but unless you are actually *eating* the ice cream you are not really *enjoying* it. Similarly, one can have rights as entitlements in a legal or even a moral sense, but unless you are benefiting from the substance of those rights, you are not enjoying them. One of the key insights of feminist and other activist work on human rights is that if individuals or groups face cultural, economic, or other obstacles to the enjoyment of their rights, then in a very important sense they don't really have those rights at all, even if the law says they do.

The UDHR includes many rights that can be interpreted as entitlements: the right not to be tortured (Article 5); the right to assemble and associate (Article 20); the right to vote (Article 21); the right to free expression (Article 19); and the right to work (Article 23). Where the import of the entitlement is unclear, the article clarifies that the measure of one having the right is in whether he can exercise or enjoy the right.

From this perspective, the UDHR makes a good start at spelling out what rights people have (what rights they ought to have, or are owed morally). However, in many different contexts people are not able to enjoy these rights. For example, a woman who endures domestic violence does not *enjoy* the right not to be tortured. (As we shall see, part of the problem here is theoretical, and part of it is contextual.) Indigenous people who worry that they will be picked up for questioning if they travel in groups, even if they have never personally been picked up, do not *enjoy* the rights to assemble and associate. Many different cultural, political, or economic barriers can impede the enjoyment of rights. These barriers represent exercises of power; the denial of rights enjoyment to some people usually serves to advance or protect the power or privilege of others. People struggling for their rights are often struggling to have their *enjoyment* of rights recognized and protected by governments, social or cultural institutions, or legal systems. In these struggles they draw on theoretical and practical reasoning in demanding the substance of their rights (see Box 2.4). They also challenge power.

BOX 2.4 COMPARING CONVENTIONS

In the CEDAW, activists lobbied for and governments recognized the need for all social, political, and economic institutions in a society 'to ensure the full development and advancement of women, for the purpose of guaranteeing them the *exercise and enjoyment of human rights and fundamental freedoms* on a basis of equality with men' (CEDAW 3). This language in the convention articulated a recognition that legal institutions alone were not sufficient for the enjoyment of rights. A decade later, the Convention on the Rights of the Child (CRC 1989) used similar language and expanded its application. For example, in the article on protecting children from abuse, appropriate measures are explicitly social and educational:

Article 19, 1. States Parties shall take all appropriate legislative, administrative, social and educational measures to protect the child from all forms of physical or mental violence, injury or abuse, neglect or negligent treatment, maltreatment or exploitation, including sexual abuse, while in the care of parent(s), legal guardian(s) or any other person who has the care of the child.

The Convention on the Rights of Persons with Disabilities (CRPD) illustrates a further advance on the articulation of the importance of addressing not just legal, but also social and cultural obstacles to rights enjoyment. For example, Article 4(1) enumerates a list of nine obligations. The second of these—'To take all appropriate measures, including legislation, to modify or abolish existing laws, regulations, customs and practices that constitute discrimination against persons with disabilities'—articulates a state responsibility to challenge certain customs and practices.

The Feminist Critique of Traditional Human Rights Theory

Feminist scholarship and activism work to make visible the complex ways in which human rights theory and various cultural and institutional practices connected to human rights can serve as invisible barriers to women's enjoyment of their rights. To see this, we shall focus on three aspects of the normative theory underlying human rights as understood and implemented in the West, with a strong focus on individualism and on the protection of civil and political rights.

First, the unarticulated notion that a human rights victim was typically a man rendered some *kinds* of violations that women experienced politically invisible. Consider the ways in which the assumed rights victim was male and why this might be a problem. For example, the prototypical torture victim is imagined to be a political prisoner in a government cell being 'interrogated'—beaten, abused, water-boarded (see Chapter 15). The agent of torture is a state official, a military man, or someone acting on behalf of the government. Around the world women and men are tortured in this way. Yet consider also that around the world women (much more often than men) experience similar levels of violence at the hands of intimate partners (see Box 2.5). Before feminist criticism, the **normative** theory of human rights through which the Universal Declaration is interpreted and implemented in the West didn't invite us to think about domestic violence as torture. Theorists call this problem '**androcentrism**' in human rights law (Charlesworth, 1995; Arati Rao, 1995). Androcentrism constitutes a significant obstacle to women's enjoyment of their rights. Further, as the analysis in the following section

will show, in criticizing androcentrism and other dimensions of privilege in the early framing and application of human rights theory, feminists developed analytical frameworks that helped them to broaden the very meaning of human rights by clarifying the interdependence of political and social rights. This helped to advance human rights enjoyment not just for women but for anyone struggling for enjoyment of their rights.

The second aspect of human rights theory and practice on which feminist criticism and activism have focused is the conceptual division between the public, political sphere and the private sphere of domestic or personal relations, sometimes referred to as the **public/private dichotomy**. This division has made the *places* where women's rights are frequently violated politically invisible. Domestic, private violence is not visible as torture, not only because its victims are most often women abused by intimate partners or family members, but also because the violence itself generally takes place in private spaces—in the home (see Box 2.6). Yet feminists argue that domestic violence is a human rights issue because civil laws have proven incapable of curtailing the levels of violence women experience within the home, contributing to the high probability that women will experience such violence in their lifetimes (Bunch, 1990).

This analysis is not limited to domestic violence. When families favour boys and men over girls and women in their decisions about relative investments in the health and education of household members, they create significant obstacles to girls' and women's enjoyment of their rights. Where gender is a predictor of health and educational outcomes, feminist analysis shows that these differences are not natural, but rather

---

BOX 2.5 WOMEN'S HUMAN RIGHTS ACTIVISM: WOMEN'S COURAGE IN KANPUR, INDIA

In March of 1981, a group of women activists organized a two-day march against dowry and rape in Kanpur, India. After some discussion, the activists formed Sakhi Kendra, a group where problems could be discussed fearlessly and where collective social action could be encouraged. Sakhi Kendra provides housing, legal services, and medical assistance to survivors of dowry abuse, rape, forced prostitution, domestic violence, and other forms of violence against women. Over half of the women in Uttar Pradesh, where Kanpur is located, have reported physical assault by an intimate partner. Many women are killed and others driven to suicide in increasing incidents of

domestic violence. In the face of institutional and intimate-partner violence, Sakhi Kendra publishes women's rights newsletters in Hindi, runs micro-funding and employment workshops, and offers training to emerging women's groups in vulnerable and poor areas. In conjunction with its gender sensitivity training for girls, boys, couples, media, and the police, the group also coordinates festivals and street dramas to raise public awareness of gender issues, dowry, and violence against women. Sakhi Kendra provides its services to women throughout Kanpur, regardless of caste, creed, or social standing.
Excerpted from (Murray, 2008, p. 121).

BOX 2.6 WOMEN'S HUMAN RIGHTS ACTIVISM: WOMEN'S COURAGE IN DURBAN, SOUTH AFRICA

Founded in 1992, the Wings of Love Care Centre of South Africa is dedicated to supporting women in domestic violence situations. As in many cities, in Durban, where crime and unemployment rates are high, domestic violence cases often go overlooked by law enforcement agencies. Among several programmes to combat the results of domestic violence, the Centre runs a shelter for women who run away from their abusers, and provides psychological and legal counselling,

education sessions on victim empowerment, child abuse, and parenting skills for women in the region. To change the attitude of indifference among law enforcement officers and raise awareness for domestic violence issues, the Centre provides sensitivity training to police officers and to others in community organizations.

Excerpted from Murray (2008, p. 115).

the result of formal laws, policies, and resource allocations controlled by the state as well as of less formal but equally systemic cultural norms and beliefs.

A third problem for women posed by the traditional theory of human rights concerns its assumption about the nature of social norms violations. The Universal Declaration expects that the *way* that social mechanisms violate rights is through discrimination. This means that some of the social mechanisms that determine the contexts of women's rights violations go unexamined. For example, Article 2 of the UDHR states, 'Everyone is entitled to all the rights and freedoms set forth in this Declaration, without distinction of any kind, such as race, colour, sex, language, religion, political or other opinion, national or social origin, property, birth or other status.' The phrase 'without distinction' signals that the Declaration follows an anti-discrimination paradigm. That is, it argues that if people are the same, they should be treated the same.

This lens for thinking about justice dates back to Aristotle's Nicomachean Ethics (Book V). Discrimination means some people who are alike in the relevant sense have nonetheless been treated differently. However, there are two problems with the seemingly straightforward anti-discrimination approach to injustice. The first is that in cases where discrimination is a problem, the assumption that people are alike in the relevant sense usually doesn't hold. When women's right of expression isn't respected, it is often because social norms do not support the idea that women should be heard (MacKinnon, 1993, 1987). So the problem is not that equals are denied their rights; it is that women are not considered equals in the relevant sense to begin with. Social norms teach us that different people have different relative worth and that different expectations apply to them. Anti-discrimination arguments require that people already agree that the people being discriminated against are equal in a relevant sense—that

the problem is one of unequal treatment of equals. In many cases involving women's human rights, there is no agreement that women are men's equals in the first place.

The second problem with the anti-discrimination framework is that it treats equality for women as a question of sameness rather than of equity. Formal legal equality does not ensure equal enjoyment of rights. That is, the injustices women experience are not only about levelling the legal playing field between men and women, but also about realizing that social norms create unequal forces, not just unequal ground. For example, equal suffrage does not ensure that women will be able to get their interests represented by the political leaders vying for their vote in places where social norms discount the political views of women. Equal legal opportunity for education does not mean that girls and boys will be equally encouraged to take up those opportunities or be enabled to do so by fair shares of food or school monies at home. Equal access to healthcare will not decrease maternal mortality without addressing the specific local dimensions of its causes.

For some feminist scholars, the problems of androcentrism, the public/private dichotomy, and the anti-discrimination paradigm make the universality of human rights and their usefulness for feminist movements suspect (Peterson and Parisi, 1998). Others point out that these criticisms are not really directed at human rights themselves but are better understood as criticisms of how rights have been conceived and used. This view helps to explain why women's movements continue to use rights despite their problems (Peters and Wolper, 1995; Parisi, 2010b, p. 217). They have used a framework of human rights developed through critique and practical experience to assert the need for special attention to context and to the specific obstacles that block women's enjoyment of their human rights. This framework, and the movements that use it, have proven effective in making women's struggles for rights and justice visible and in forging links with others engaged in similar struggles.

Making a Rights Claim

Making rights claims is an important aspect of any struggle for rights. Any human rights claim involves two more specific claims or arguments: (1) that the claimant is the kind of being who gets to make a claim—that is, a *human*; and (2) that the substance of the claim is one that should be recognized as a *right*. Either of these elements can be the basis of a struggle for rights, or both together.

The claim to be part of humanity might seem trivial, but it is actually a crucial consideration. To see this, consider the treatment of those whose rights have been most famously violated. In slavery, segregation, apartheid, and genocide, the oppressed and murdered are treated not only in death but also in life as less than human. They are compared in the media and political discourse to vermin. They are forced to live in conditions suitable only for vermin. Images of their inhumane treatment are renewed and normalized through popular culture, social norms, and historic reminders. In different contexts, women, *dalits*, ethnic minorities, Indigenous people, and people with disabilities have had to struggle to establish that they are the kinds of beings entitled to have and enjoy rights.

That the substantive benefit being claimed should count as a right—rather than simply a wish or complaint—is equally important. The same groups who struggle for recognition must often also struggle to show that the treatment they suffer and the obstacles they face in different contexts are indeed rights violations, no matter how familiar or socially accepted they are. Feminists have used the slogan 'women's rights are human rights' to emphasize this point: rights to choose a marriage partner, to choose the age of marriage, to inherit property, and to reproductive choice are not rights claims typically made by men. Women have had to argue that the substantive benefits at stake are *human* rights.

Consider again the case of domestic violence; because it systematically undermines women's security and liberty, feminists have argued that it should be understood as torture. The systematic dimension of this problem is essential: formal institutions, interacting with social norms and practices, allow for violence and abuse to persist throughout society. In such circumstances, being a woman significantly increases the likelihood of experiencing a rights violation. Recognition of this pattern of rights violations led women to understand this as a human rights issue and to assert their political claim under the banner of women's rights as human rights. In appealing to human rights discourse and to international human rights institutions, women made a conscious, strategic choice to enhance the visibility and legitimacy of their cause (E. Friedman, 1995). The strategic considerations and trade-offs are evident, as in the case of women active in Indigenous rights movements. They must balance their worries about the threat that individualistic conceptions of property rights pose to their communities against the benefits of using the discourse of human rights to press their demands for communal self-determination. Likewise, they must balance their communities' demands for self-determination against community practices that leave them economically vulnerable, often without the property rights that are a source of security in the global economy.

Not all such claims are uncontested. Recognition of rights related to reproduction, sexuality, and self-determination have often triggered fierce resistance. The assertion that these substantive benefits are universal human rights is not a claim about how widely recognized these rights are; rather, it is an acknowledgement that people fighting against injustice employ the human rights framework in all kinds of contexts all over the world. They use it to demand that the concept and the practice of human rights be expanded to incorporate recognition of them as human beings, to ensure protection of certain substantive benefits as legitimate rights, and to effectuate the removal of obstacles to the enjoyment of those rights or benefits. They often do so even when no treaty or international institution has recognized the legitimacy of these claims. As these demands are acknowledged, the theory and practice of human rights are transformed.

Feminist Conceptual Contributions to Human Rights

The transformative theory of human rights developed by feminists is informed by the concrete experiences of women and other marginalized groups. This theory has been articulated through particular struggles, but it has a particular theoretical architecture that stresses the indivisibility and interrelatedness of human rights and emphasizes how political, economic, and social structures are crucial to securing the enjoyment of human rights—and thus crucial targets of analysis and critique.

Indivisibility captures the idea that no right is secure unless all rights are secure. If the political right to associate is not protected, then people will not be able to strike to change their working conditions. Indivisibility suggests certain analytic and political strategies: for example, working for homeless women's rights requires attention to the histories of childhood sexual abuse that often lead to women's homelessness. One innovation in CEDAW is that specific articles spell out the achievements in health, education, and other areas necessary for women to be able to enjoy all their rights. Women cannot enjoy their right to work if they are not healthy enough to work; they cannot be healthy enough to work if they are surviving domestic violence. Rights are indivisible.

Feminist theories of human rights also emphasize that the rights of all people are interrelated (or interdependent). No person's rights are secure unless all people's rights are secure. If, for example, cultural norms constrain the freedom of association of lesbians (see Chapter 11), and if this violation of rights is tolerated by society, then the rights of other marginal or vulnerable groups, such as labour organizers, Indigenous peoples, and opposition political parties, can more easily be constrained. Once society accepts that there are some valid reasons for denying some people's rights, it embarks on a slippery slope.

The third element in feminist human rights theory follows from the first and second. Feminist approaches rely on structural analysis of human rights violations; this means that understanding how individual and social action is conditioned by the formal and informal structures of cultural, political, and economic life is crucial to identifying and eliminating the obstacles to rights enjoyment. These structures might be local or global, and might be beyond the control of particular governments or communities. It follows that a focus on individuals and the rights violations they endure is insufficient without attention to the structures that enable and condone those violations. Structural analysis is difficult because the structures themselves can be immensely complex, sometimes transnational or global, and often deeply rooted in tradition or ideology. Feminist human rights theory has to analyse the structures to understand why women suffer the human rights violations that they do; feminist human

rights activism has to take account of these structures in formulating rights claims.

Feminists and women activists have used concepts such as patriarchy, globalization, neoliberalism, militarization, global cycles of vulnerability, race, ethnicity, colonial legacy, contemporary imperialism, nationalism, self-determination, and gender-based violence to explain and critique particular structural configurations that affect women's lives and impinge on their rights. Some of these concepts are grounded in particular political struggles, like those against gender-based violence (Bunch, 1990) or self-determination (Parisi and Corntassel, 2007). Others serve as lenses to bring specific structural dynamics like global capital into focus for critique (Chowdhry, 2004: cited by Parisi, 2010a, p. 2203). While some of these substantive interests may seem peculiar to the particular concerns of women's rights activists, analyses of structural power have been used to articulate the rights concerns raised by feminists about the way marginalization works on various segments of humanity (see Box 2.7).

One tool that feminists have developed to assist in this kind of analysis is the concept of intersectionality (see Box 2.8). Intersectionality is the recognition that oppression works through multiple mechanisms; feminists argue (and show) that to understand the rights violations suffered by particular women, we need to understand how these different mechanisms intersect to produce specific forms of oppression. For instance, to comprehend the oppression experienced by, say, elite urban Indian lesbian heads of household, or Indigenous women who have lost their land and whose communities are engaged in struggles for self-determination, requires intersectional analysis. In each case, women experience multiple forms of oppression simultaneously, and the intersection of oppressions defines the concrete ways in which their rights are threatened.

In the face of this resistance to gender analysis, the human rights approach offered a strategically interesting possibility. Human rights and gender analysis share a critique of power. The growing legitimacy of human rights discourse for talking about a broad range of issues, particularly health issues, made it an attractive alternative, in part because this legitimacy made some aspects of gender and development seem less conceptually daunting. At the Fourth World Conference on Women in Beijing, activists and policy makers sought to integrate concerns about development, peace, and equality for women, and human rights provided a framework for doing so.

BOX 2.7 UNITED NATIONS FOURTH WORLD CONFERENCE ON WOMEN

In 1995, policy makers and activists from around the world met in Beijing for the United Nations Fourth World Conference on Women and for a parallel meeting of non-governmental organizations (NGOs) at the NGO Forum in Huairou. The meetings brought together political leaders to negotiate a highly contentious Platform for Action. The history leading up to this conference and the use of the Platform for Action afterwards illustrate an interesting dilemma for feminist approaches to human rights.

Throughout the 1970s and 1980s, the field of development was receptive to feminist influence. In the United Nations and in the **donor** agencies of many countries, androcentric models of development that focused on jobs for male heads of households and on infrastructural projects as drivers of

economic development were being criticized. Many people working on these projects, along with their academic allies, argued that development would not affect women for the better without programming that was attentive to the power dynamics of gender. These arguments led to a push for 'gender and development'. While some programmes targeting women's economic needs were conceived, they were typically underfunded relative to overall national aid budgets. In practice, the shift to 'gender' analysis was interpreted to require 'gender' experts (Snyder, 2006), and projects focusing on women were relegated to special women's bureaus. For these reasons, the move towards gender and development did not yield the desired scale and range of impact on development planning.

Despite an extensive preparatory meeting process, over a quarter of the text of the Platform for Action, including text related to health, remained disputed at the beginning of the conference (Doran et al., 1995). However, at the conclusion of the meeting, many feminists celebrated the Beijing Platform for Action for bringing human rights from the periphery to the centre of development thinking (Bunch and Fried, 1996; Antrobus, 2005).

The Platform for Action did so at a cost, however. There were twelve issue areas, ranging from poverty through issues concerning the girl child. These issue areas overlapped considerably, as one would expect. For example, poverty, education, health, and the girl child are obviously related. As we saw in the preceding section, a feminist human rights lens facilitates

seeing these connections. Yet instead of promoting integrated approaches to these related issues, the Platform for Action invited organizations and donors to focus on particular issue areas. So, while the Platform for Action marked a conceptual advance by incorporating the human rights lens into development thinking, it simultaneously set up obstacles to a structural analysis of power by encouraging institutional mechanisms to focus on limited dimensions of these complex problems.

The Beijing Platform for Action integrated development and human rights frameworks (at least conceptually). It also ushered in an era of 'gender mainstreaming' by calling on governments, international governance organizations, and others to use gender analysis in designing and assessing their work

BOX 2.8 DECONSTRUCTING INTERSECTIONALITY

For those who have studied feminism or sociology, the term 'intersectionality' is familiar. Often it is assumed to be shorthand for considerations of race, class, and gender. But its meaning is not broadly shared. For some, intersectionality focuses on identity politics, recognizing that identity categories intersect such that a professional African American straight woman may participate in a different identity politics from a college-age lesbian of Hispanic origin. Others think about intersectionality as an analytical lens. In this view, the forces of racism, homophobia, immigration status, and class intersect and impact each person differently. In the analytical view, we can see the impact of these forces in patterns of injustice without knowing how any particular person chooses to

identify or attributing any particular identity-based politics to any individual.

Some associate intersectionality with the political criticism of anti-racism and anti-sexism activism in the United States (Kimberle Crenshaw, 1991). Post-colonial scholars recognize the role of intersectional arguments in the anti-colonial political movements (Rao, 2003b).

A prominent critic of the identity-based view is K. Anthony Appiah. Scholars who might help you think through these differences include K. Crenshaw (1991); McCall (2005); A.-M. Hancock (2007, 2011); Jordan-Zachery (2007); Bowleg (2008); Weldon (2008); Duong (2012); and Verloo (2013).

(True and Parisi, 2010). **Gender mainstreaming** entails an attempt to institutionalize accountability for design programming and allocating resources in ways that promote human rights for all. It can be thought of as an institutional design implication of the feminist conceptual analysis of human rights.

Gender mainstreaming has been interpreted in widely varied ways. True and Parisi attribute the multiple interpretations of gender mainstreaming to the multiple theoretical lenses at work in the Beijing Platform for Action. Although the Platform for Action was the touchstone document for gender mainstreaming, it did not provide definitive guidance. This feminist approach can provide a conceptual architecture for thinking about rights in ways that lead to rights enjoyment not just for women, but for everyone.

Indivisibility, interrelatedness, and intersectionality are distinctive of feminist theories of human rights. These theories reveal human rights to be dynamic, growing out of diverse experiences and contexts rather than from a particular Western, Enlightenment tradition, as many have argued (Donnelly, 1985; Charvet and Kaczynska-Nay, 2008). Feminist human rights theory and practices are informed by a global history of struggle against complex modes of oppression, and they are constantly evolving in relation to these struggles. Feminist approaches to human rights are grounded in its struggles for justice against oppression.

KEY POINTS

Conceiving rights as entitlements, legal or contractual guarantees, ignores the question of whether people actually enjoy the substance of those rights.

Feminists argue that the Western, Enlightenment model of human rights is androcentric, relies on a false public/private dichotomy, and conceives of rights violations narrowly in terms of discrimination.

Making a rights claim involves asserting that one is the kind of being entitled to make rights claims and that the substance of the claim should be recognized as a right.

Feminist theories of rights emphasize the indivisibility of human rights, the interrelatedness of all rights and rights-bearers, and the intersectional nature of oppression, which suggests a structural analysis of obstacles to the enjoyment of rights.

Critical Thinking Questions:

What 'new terrain' for human rights do you see emerging, and could feminism contribute to our understanding of these issues?

Is sexual assault on college campuses a human rights issue?

What critical concerns do women's rights and labour rights activists have in common?

Conclusion

Because the source of political legitimacy of universal human rights is its moral legitimacy across boundaries of political authority, feminists have been critically attentive to the possibility that the moral resource of human rights is not 'universal'. The disagreements among feminists around the use of human rights and their universality reflect the political character of human rights. That political character enables them to be deployed for thinking about a wide range of injustices.

As we have seen, from their earliest criticisms of human rights as androcentric and blind to human rights violations that take place in private, feminist contributions to universal human rights have included a practice of deconstructing and revealing power dynamics, even those hidden within human rights discourse and practice itself. Even within feminist human rights theory and practice there is always an attention to the possibility that human rights may be used in ways that are not empowering to women (Peterson and Parisi, 1998).

Yet, this possibility has not inhibited activists—women and other marginalized people—from using the political legitimacy of human rights to press their claims. Feminists have used human rights to press for the full range of rights, including reproductive rights, sexuality rights, labour rights, property rights, and Indigenous rights. Through their political struggles, women have deployed and developed human rights theory and practice. Each achievement opens up new terrain for contestation. Feminist human rights activists use these opportunities to further develop human rights theory and practices, ever broadening it to be more inclusive of all people's rights violations.

QUESTIONS

Individual Study Questions

1. What are three criticisms of cultural relativism?

2. Name three challenges that the first formulations of universal human rights were not adequate for making visible the human rights violations women experience.

3. What are the three features of a feminist theory of human rights?

4. Why should we define human rights based on struggles?

5. Why do women's rights advocates want rights enjoyment and not merely entitlements?

Group Study Questions

1. If cultural relativism is so wrong, why do you think it is a common argument against rights?

2. Compare the cultural relativist and the feminist criticisms of human rights.

3. Are human rights 'meaningful' if people always have to struggle for them?

4. Why are reproductive rights human rights and not women's rights?

5. Why is intersectionality important to feminist approaches to human rights?

FURTHER READING

Arat, Z. (2008). Women's rights as human rights. *UN Chronicle*, 45 / 2–3, 9–13.

This essay provides a brief sketch of women's exclusion from rights discourse and subsequent inclusion in the UN rights instruments.

Bunch, C. (1990). Women's rights as human rights: Toward a re-vision of human rights. *Human Rights Quarterly*, 12 /November, 486–98.

This essay offers a clear account of the ways violations of women's human rights were invisible under the human rights framework, and was an important text for women's human rights advocates to build common ground across a range of rights concerns.

Doran, P., Wanhua, Y., Wagner, L., and **Wise, S.** (1995). Summary of the Fourth World Conference on Women. *A Daily Report on the Fourth World Conference on Women*, 14, 12.

This article summarizes the key contributions of the Fourth World Conference on Women.

Friedman, E. (1995). Women's human rights: The emergence of a movement. *Women's Rights, Human Rights: International Feminist Perspectives* (ed. J. Peters and A. Wolper). London: Routledge.

This article summarizes women's human rights activism and movement-building leading up to the United Nations Conference on Human Rights in Vienna.

Ishay, M. (2004). *The History of Human Rights: From Ancient Times to the Globalization Era*. Berkeley, CA: University of California Press.

This book provides a detailed history of the concept of human rights, focusing on its roots in Western political thought.

Murray, A. F. (2008). *From Outrage to Courage: Women Taking Action for Health and Justice*. Monroe, ME: Common Courage Press.

This book juxtaposes analysis of the state of women's rights violations in the area of health with examples of women's activism for their rights.

Parisi, L. and **Corntassel, J.** (2007). In pursuit of self-determination: Indigenous women's challenges to 'traditional' diplomatic spaces. *Canadian Foreign Policy*, **13**/3, 81–98.

This essay shows how Indigenous women have worked to be visible in traditional political spaces.

Parisi, L. (2010). Feminist perspectives on human rights. *The International Studies Compendium Project* (ed. R. A. Denmark). Oxford: Blackwell.

This article provides a survey of the feminist academic literature on human rights.

Rothschild, C., Long, S., and **Fried, S. T.** (eds) (2005). *Written Out: How Sexuality is Used to Attack Women's Organizing*. New York: International Gay and Lesbian Human Rights Commission & The Center for Women's Global Leadership.

This collaboratively written text provides illustrations of how anti-lesbian cultural presuppositions are used to intimidate feminist activism.

Spivak, G. C. (2005). Use and abuse of human rights. *Boundary 2*, **32** / 1, 131–89.

This provocative article takes a cross-cultural approach to the question of human rights and the ways in which humans wrong one another, arguing that there is an important role for the humanities in developing meaning and understanding necessary for addressing injustice.

WEB LINKS

http://www.globalfundforwomen.org/   The Global Fund for Women is a grant-making organization that supports women's rights activism.

http://www.awid.org/   Association for Women's Rights and Development (AWID) is an association of women's rights activists, policy makers, funding organizations, and academics interested in promoting women's rights.

http://www.femnet.or.ke/   The African Women's Development and Communication Network (FEMNET) is a network of women's rights activist organizations in Africa.

http://www.iisd.ca/vol14/enb1421e.txt   This text provides a summary of the Beijing Platform for Action drafting process.

NOTES

1. L. E. Goodman (1998).
2. Nagel (1979); Benhabib (2004, p. 133); Talbott (2005).
3. Benhabib (2004, p. 130).
4. Ignatieff (2001). Cf. Gould, who grounds norms in human agency and interaction (Gould, 2004, 1988).
5. Donnelly (1989, pp. 17, 28–37); Nino (1991); L. E. Goodman (1998); Muzaffar (2002). Note that Rorty argues that the universality of human dignity does not rest on their being any 'distinctively human attribute' (Rorty, 1993, p. 116).
6. Locke (1988 [1688]); Sachedina (2009).
7. Sobrino Sj (2001, p. 153).
8. Cohen (2004); Benhabib (2004, Chapter 4).
9. Bruton (1997); Yasuaki (1999).

10. Nussbaum (1997b, 2000a, 2000b); Sen (2004, 1999a); Gould (2004).

11. Maritain (1949); An-Na'im (1992a); Taylor (1999); Regan (2010).

12. Donnelly (1989); An-Na'im (1992b); Ishay (2004).

13. This section draws on Langlois (2009, pp. 19–20).

 Visit the Online Resource Centre that accompanies this book for updates and a range of other resources: www.oxfordtextbooks.co.uk/orc/goodhart3e/

3

Human Rights in International Relations

Tim Dunne and Marianne Hanson

Chapter Contents

Reader's Guide

Human rights have become firmly enmeshed in both the practice and study of international relations. Dominant theories of international relations explain the role of such rights in significantly different ways, and it is evident that their major claims carry persuasive arguments, indicating an uneasy juxtaposition of state sovereignty with ideas of a universal moral order. While the Cold War prevented the immediate focus on human rights that the United Nations system warranted, the growth of various international human rights regimes and the rise of international **non-governmental organizations** (NGOs) and human rights activists enabled a closer insertion of human rights into state diplomatic practices, a development that revealed the existence of human rights contestation itself as part of the Cold War. The ending of the Cold War heralded a 'springtime' for human rights and liberalism, but the advent of the 'war on terror' showed that the cascade of human rights norms might also be open to reversion, as particular states reinterpreted or rejected previously espoused principles. More recently, attempts to protect the vulnerable in internal conflicts in places like Darfur, Libya, and Syria reveal the complications of trying to uphold human rights as conflicting views on what ought to be done, and how, confront the international community. These developments raise important questions about state practice and human rights. But overall, and even though some norm reversion has occurred, it remains the case that states are bound up with human rights challenges and that they engage, to varying degrees, with evidence of human rights protection and promotion. Although much recent attention has rightly been focused on changes to the internalization of norms (such as reinterpretations of the **Convention Against Torture** or the restrictions of civil liberties in domestic arenas), we continue to see the reiteration of a view that human rights are important and an accompanying evolution—even if it is imperfect—of concepts and practices on protecting them at the international level. This is visible in formulations such as the responsibility to protect, with its potential for intervention to protect human rights and its recognition that the prevention of human rights abuses is vitally important.

Introduction

The prevalence of human rights in contemporary debates about world politics presents something of a puzzle to many academicians working in international relations (IR). In a geopolitical world that is dominated by states' claims to exclusive authority in their domain, human rights are a polite fiction. At least, such is the claim by political realists, who have been the dominant voice in IR since the emergence of the discipline.

As we show in the first section of this chapter, realists do not have it all their own way. Liberal thinking in IR argues that it is rational for states to pursue policies congruent with human rights principles. Constructivists are also critical of realism, although for different reasons. According to them, states pursue human rights goals for reasons to do with their identity and status. The fact that there is a lively debate among the main theories of IR as to what human rights are and why actors promote them reveals an important philosophical issue about the difference between 'reality' and our theories that interpret and explain it.

The second section of this chapter focuses on key controversies over human rights as understood in the discipline of IR. The first of these concerns the mismatch between the importance attached to human rights at the declaratory level and the prevalence of human rights abuses in reality. What explanation can be given for this double standard? One set of answers relates to the weak monitoring and enforcement mechanisms in the international human rights regime. Another takes us back to the question of state **sovereignty**, particularly the unrelenting tendency on the part of elites to support narrow national interests over universal values of justice and fairness. These controversies are discussed in accordance with the development of human rights norms in modern international society.

The third section follows organically from the narrative about the human rights story in international relations. If we are to take seriously the claim that there is a global human rights culture, then we are entitled to ask what duties that imposes on states and other actors to protect the rights of others when they are being systematically denied. The discussion will focus on two dimensions of international responsibility. The first is the duty of protection of their citizens that is incumbent on all states in light of their obligations under the various human rights covenants. In this discussion, protection applies to the 'internal' dimension of the norm of sovereignty as responsibility. The second dimension of international responsibility relates to the duty that falls on states to act as humanitarian rescuers in instances where a state is collapsing or a regime is committing gross violations of human rights.

Theoretical Issues and Context

It is commonplace in the mainstream study of IR to claim that the subject matter is 'the world of sovereign, independent states' and that these states are rational actors who seek to maximize their power or security. Both assumptions follow from what IR scholars call the assumption of *anarchy*. By this term, what is being signified is not a permanent state of war but rather the absence of an 'international state' that has the power and the authority to impose a just peace.

A good illustration of the problem of anarchy can be gleaned from Hobbes's description of how order emerges from a state of nature. In his famous book *Leviathan*, written in 1651, just as the states system was beginning to take hold in Europe, Hobbes argued that a state was a necessary condition for a durable domestic political order. The state was justified in terms of a bargain between the government, whose duty it was to provide security, and the people, who consented to obey the will of the sovereign. However, no such regulating authority was present at the international level. The Hobbesian world view is a continual reminder of the limits to cooperation—and the ever-present possibility of conflict—in a decentralized system where there is no 'global Leviathan' to watch over sovereign states. If we accept this as a starting point, the landscape of world politics immediately seems inhospitable to human rights. The **realist** world is one where rules are regularly broken, and agreements last only as long as they benefit the contracting parties. As Hobbes put the problem with characteristic clarity, treaties that are not imposed by force 'are but words'.

Today's realists continue to believe that, for the most part, the diplomacy of human rights is just talk. They understand that human rights are part of the vocabulary of modern international society: after all, no state leader openly challenges the principles underpinning the human rights regime. The realist contention is that, when push comes to shove, human rights are very low on the list of national policy goals. This explains the prevalence of *double standards* in international diplomacy, whereby political leaders pay lip service to protecting human rights while at the same time allowing these principles to be undermined by the pursuit of other goals. In other words, in the final analysis, unless the promotion of human rights is in the *national interest* why would it be rational for states to pursue such goals?

The condition of international anarchy and the pursuit of the national interest are two significant reasons why realists are sceptical about human rights. A third reason is an ethical objection to the assumption of a universal morality that is in many ways the bedrock of the existing human rights regime. As the great realists of the early part of the twentieth century argued (Carr, 1946; Morgenthau, 1948), exhortations to obey the universal moral law can be simply techniques to hide the pursuit of narrow selfish interests. All great powers in history have articulated universal claims: we should not be surprised if such measures benefited the dominant power. Such a convenient linkage between universal morality and the national interest was evident in the justifications for colonial possessions made by the European imperial powers in the nineteenth century, just as the promotion of democracy consolidated US hegemony in the modern era. Likewise, those living outside the 'greater West' today often complain that human rights are a tool wielded by the powerful to secure various goals such as favourable terms of trade or even a change of regime.

Liberalism is historically the main challenger to realism in the study of international relations. At the level of ideas, liberalism develops out of a Western tradition of thinking in which the individual has rights that public authorities must respect. While there are varieties of liberal thinking, the central idea is that individual persons have basic rights to free speech, fair treatment in terms of judicial process, and political equality enshrined in a political constitution. While Hobbes and Machiavelli are invoked by realists to justify the promotion of national self-interest, liberals look to Locke and Kant as their lodestars. Kant's pamphlet, 'Perpetual Peace' (Kant, 1991) builds a theory of international liberalism in which all individuals have equal moral worth, and in which an abuse of rights in one part of the world is 'felt everywhere'.

It is easy to dismiss liberalism as being utopian. The history of statecraft from the mid-seventeenth century onwards is more readily understood in terms of conflict and aggression. But, as liberals point out, moral universalism has continued to insert itself into the practice of international politics. From the birth of the **Enlightenment** onwards, states have made significant advances in terms of meeting universal principles central to liberalism. Many states have, over time, enshrined the rights of citizens in legal constitutions, ended the trade in slaves and then the institution of slavery, agreed to protect the condition of workers, and advanced international **humanitarian law** to protect wounded or captured soldiers and to criminalize the targeting of civilians. Many of these advances that took place between the mid-nineteenth and the early twentieth centuries became codified in the internationalization of human rights in the UN system after 1945 (see Chapters 1 and 2).

As will become apparent in the following section, the implementation of human rights standards in the twentieth century has been chequered. Liberals recognize that the division of global humanity into separate sovereign states presents particular problems when it comes to embedding universal moral principles. Two kinds of responses are triggered by this dilemma. The first is the attempt to expand the liberal 'zone' so that there are fewer authoritarian states in the world; the second is to strengthen international institutions in the expectation that they can alter the incentives of member states in ways that enhance respect for human rights and human dignity.

Constructivism offers a way of thinking about the relationship between norms and interests. Unlike realists and liberals, constructivists argue that there is no necessary tension between the interests of sovereign states and the moral principles associated with the promotion and protection of human rights.

The important theoretical point here concerns the constitutive nature of international political reality, specifically how states create—and are created by—shared norms and values.

The development of human rights needs to be understood according to this dynamic. As is often the case in social life, the international realm is made up of many contending sets of expectations and rules as to how actors ought to behave. While the historically dominant realist logic suggests one form of international conduct, constructivists and liberals argue that this inter-state order has been transformed by the emergence of universal values. The protection of human rights therefore becomes 'integral to the moral purpose of the modern state, to the dominant rationale that licences the organization of power and authority into territorially defined sovereign units' (Reus-Smit, 2001, p. 520). Constructivists argue that if states reject universal values outright, they will have to pay a price: this could take the form of condemnation, exclusion, or possibly coercive measures aimed at enforcing the new standard of legitimate statehood. (Realist, liberal, and constructivist views of human rights are summarized in Table 3.1.)

KEY POINTS

While they do not deny the existence of human rights, proponents of the various theories of IR examined here (realism, liberalism, and constructivism) view the role and promotion of human rights in world politics in different ways.

The clash between the division of the world into separate sovereign states and claims for universal moral principles is felt most keenly by realist scholars, for whom national interest will always trump calls for inserting human rights into foreign policy formulation.

Liberals view human rights as having an increasingly important role, and point to the spread of liberal democracy as well as the establishment of a global human rights regime as evidence of this; constructivists, for their part, note that respect for human rights can have an important effect on the forming of state identities, noting that some states seek to practise a foreign policy that is both pragmatic and principled.

Critical Thinking Question:

Why do we need to situate knowledge about human rights inside different theories of world politics?

Key Controversies

Human Rights in the Cold War—Organized Hypocrisy?

Liberal histories of human rights regard the 1948 **Universal Declaration of Human Rights** (UDHR) as a founding document that had been brought into being because of the horrendous destructive capacity of modern states. Eleanor Roosevelt, one of its main advocates, said that it had 'set up a common standard of achievement for all people and all nations' (cited in Risse and Sikkink, 1999, p. 1). Defenders of human rights believe the UDHR signalled a normative shift away from the absolute sovereignty presumed by states and towards the idea that all individuals should have rights by virtue of their common humanity.

The persistence of two sets of rival **normative** claims—one based on the rights of sovereign states and the other on the rights of individuals as members of a natural universal community—is traced back through many centuries by IR scholars. Theologians in the Columbian period debated the rights of the aborigines in the Americas (see Chapter 19); peacemakers at Westphalia in 1648 included minority rights in the final treaties; and the period of British hegemony in the nineteenth century witnessed the emergence of an anti-slavery norm—albeit coexisting with the practice of colonialism, which was anything but human rights-friendly.

The contemporary struggle between the universal and particular is brought into sharp relief by the doctrine of human rights. After the euphoria of the UN General Assembly's proclamation of the UDHR, human rights advocates had to wait a further three decades before such principles began significantly to constrain the behaviour of states. In the intervening period, the liberal call for states to live up to respecting universal rights was muted by two realist factors: first, the priority accorded to national security by the leading protagonists (and their allies) during the **Cold War**; and second, the fact that states did not allow multilateral monitoring of their human rights practices. This last point was illustrated by the first session of the UN **Commission on Human Rights** (in early 1947), which noted that it had 'no power to take any action in regard to any complaints concerning human rights' (Donnelly, 2003, p. 73). In other words, from the outset, human rights were overshadowed by systemic factors to

Table 3.1 Dimensions of human rights (HR) according to main IR theories

	Sectors		
IR theories	Moral basis of human rights	Status of institutions	Human rights in foreign policy
Realism	The logic of self-help in an anarchic system means HR are a luxury that states cannot afford. Claims to universal values mask the play of national interest.	Institutions are powerless—HR are left to the will of states. State leaders pay lip service to human rights standards.	HR can be a useful tool if they enhance the relative power of a state; the moment they work against the state's vital security interests, they must be abandoned. Using force to uphold HR values is almost always reckless and self-interested.
Liberalism	HR are an extension of natural and inalienable rights. States have a duty to protect rights—if they fail to do this their sovereign status is in question.	HR regimes (the informal rules) and institutions (e.g. the Human Rights Commission) are vital for monitoring compliance. If institutions are weak, states will 'cheat'. Legalization within the EU has meant that obligations are legally binding.	The promotion of HR is inextricably linked to the promotion of democracy and good governance. Unless HR values are embedded in state-based institutions, they will not be durable.
Constructivism	The basis of HR is the overlapping consensus that exists among actors and institutions in international and world society. It is not a 'natural' virtue but an inter-subjectively generated commitment.	Institutions matter, but the 'norm cascade' enables the researcher to track the process of socialization. Transnational social movements assist with the compliance problem by cajoling and shaming.	The realist claim about the primacy of the national interest is problematized by constructivists. Interests, they argue, are a product of the identity and values of a state or region. Therefore, we should expect rights-protecting states at home to promote HR abroad.

do with great power rivalry and the preference by members of international society to view human rights as standards and not as enforceable commitments. With the exception of the limited group of states who were signatories to the European Convention on Human Rights, the general picture from 1945 to 1973 was one in which there was a yawning gap between standards and delivery.

Several factors converged in the mid-1970s which together signalled a step-change in the human rights regime and which challenged realist assumptions about the nature of international relations. These can be grouped into the following themes (to be examined in turn): the growing legalization of human rights norms; the emergence of human rights INGOs (international non-governmental organizations); and

the increased priority accorded to human rights in the foreign policies of key Western states.

Development of Legal Norms

In 1976, the two international human rights covenants came into force. These instruments are significant because they help to transform international standards into domestic law; in so doing, they open up the possibility that non-governmental organizations and social movements will scrutinize and censure the behaviour of governments (described in Box 3.1). The pressure to comply with human rights norms on the part of domestic actors was supplemented by the growing importance of the UN Commission on Human Rights. While the work of the Commission—replaced in 2006 by the UN Human Rights Council—was largely that

BOX 3.1 THE 'NORM CASCADE'

Constructivists are interested in how beliefs about human rights are translated into global norms. This issue leads directly to the relationship between domestic political practices and international standards of right conduct. Drawing on sociological theory, constructivists have developed a model of norm socialization that is referred to as a 'norm cascade'. The cascade has five phases. *Phase one* is the repression of opposition groups and the effective blocking of the influence of transnational networks. *Phase two* is where advocacy groups begin to scrutinize the activity of governments that violate the basic rights of their citizens. The reaction of the target state is one of denial, i.e. a refusal to accept that the international human rights

standards invoked by INGOs are legitimate. *Phase three* is where forces of resistance are mobilized in the target state, aided and supported by the global human rights movement; the government is inclined to make a tactical concession hoping that the problem will go away. *Phase four* is where governments make an effort to improve their human rights practices, recording and regarding external standards as something they ought to aspire to; however, non-compliance continues despite recognition of the validity of the International Bill of Rights. Finally, *phase five* occurs when the institutions of the state see themselves as being guardians of human rights; conformity to the norm becomes automatic, making its operation difficult to discern.

of information gathering and sharing, its role raised the status of human rights in the UN system. The appointment of a UN High Commissioner for Human Rights in 1993 took the profile to an even higher level, illustrating the growth of legal and institutional norms emphasized by liberal and constructivist schools of IR theory.

Emergence of Human Rights INGOs

The 1970s also saw the emergence of INGOs committed to deepening state compliance with human rights law. Dismissed by Soviet diplomats in 1969 as 'weeds in the field' (Foot, 2000, p. 38), INGO activity was beginning to have a significant impact on state–society relations in all corners of the globe. Such activity also challenged the realist emphasis on states as the only important actors in IR. **Amnesty International** (AI) is a telling example of this shift. Its mission is to campaign for internationally recognized human rights (http://www.amnesty.org). Originally set up around a clutch of activists in 1961, it had over 150,000 members in more than 100 countries by 1977; in 2015, the membership is more than 2 million, with subscribers in over 150 states.

INGOs like Amnesty perform two vital functions. They act as information networks with a capacity to communicate evidence of human rights violations to their membership and the global media. If INGOs are believed to be authoritative and independent, as Amnesty is, then this information is taken seriously both by UN bodies entrusted with monitoring human rights and by other actors in global civil society. In 1977, Amnesty won the Nobel Peace Prize, and seven years later it was highly influential in the

drafting of the 1984 Convention Against Torture. The second key function that human rights INGOs play in world politics is one of monitoring governments' records in complying with the treaties they have signed. Significant in this respect is the annual Amnesty International Report, which documents non-compliance in countries throughout the world—a practice that other leading INGOs, such as **Human Rights Watch**, have emulated. When systematic non-compliance has been exposed, human rights INGOs are skilful at using print and digital media to embarrass those public bodies whose word is not as good as their bond, a technique known as **naming and shaming**. The growth of human rights networks and the intersubjective relationship between values and state practice are noted by constructivists, who describe a process of 'norm cascade' to show how ideas can take hold and grow in importance (see Box 3.1).

Insertion of Human Rights into Diplomacy

Of the three dynamics for change that became evident in the 1970s, probably the most significant was the intrusion of human rights into the diplomacy of Western states. The inclusion of these ideas into diplomacy and foreign policy showed that some states were beginning to define their identity and goals by reference to particular norms. In the USA, Congress was increasingly minded to pass legislation linking aid and trade to human rights. And when Jimmy Carter became President, the cause of human rights found a passionate advocate—in sharp contrast to the more realist-minded Nixon–Kissinger era, when they were thought to complicate the achievement of more important goals in the economic and security domains. In Western Europe, Norway and the Netherlands were becoming more activist in promoting human rights in their own foreign policies. Within the European Community (EC), and after 1993 the European Union (EU), respect for human rights had long been a condition for membership. Individuals in many European states could also bring human rights complaints against their governments through the Council of Europe's **European Court of Human Rights** (ECHR), indicating a much higher level of regional institutionalization than was the case in the UN system (which in some instances allows for individual complaint but in which the views of the treaty bodies are not binding).

The signing of the **Helsinki Accords** in 1975 illustrates each type of agency at work. This agreement was the culmination of three years of negotiation among thirty-five states involved in the *Conference on Security and Cooperation in Europe* (CSCE). The Soviet-led Eastern bloc was intent on normalizing relations with the rest of Europe and having the Cold War division of Europe recognized as permanent in an international treaty. The West Europeans were pushing hard for shared commitments to fundamental human rights: while this was resisted by the communist states, they eventually yielded in order to realize their gains in other issue areas. The Accords set out ten 'guiding principles for relations among European states', including 'respect for human rights and fundamental freedoms, including the freedom of thought, conscience, religion or belief' (Conference on Security and Cooperation in Europe, Final Act, 1975). While the communist elites chose to emphasize other articles in the final declaration that underscored the principle of non-intervention in their internal affairs, activists inside their societies began a period of intense mobilization that did untold

damage to the stability of communist rule. 'Less than a year after the Helsinki Final Act', Daniel Thomas argues (Thomas, 1999, p. 214), 'the combination of domestic mobilization and transnational networking had rendered the international normative environment inhospitable to the political status quo in Eastern Europe—precisely the opposite of what the Warsaw Pact elites intended when they called for a European security conference.' The novel feature of repeat meetings and robust and critical 'follow-up' among Helsinki states, a process not found in the UN human rights system at the time, was also instrumental in the reinforcement of these human rights norms (Hanson, 1994; see Box 3.2).

The CSCE process reminds us that the Cold War, while it was preoccupied with traditional realist security concerns (including nuclear arms and territorial aims in a divided Europe), was also, at its heart, a debate about human rights. From the Western viewpoint, the ideological divisions between East and West were not restricted to territorial contests and competing economic systems, but were also inherently about the relationship between governments and the rights they afforded their citizens. And even if Western outrage about the plight of dissidents and others in the Soviet bloc was not paramount in diplomatic discussions, neither had it been totally subsumed or forgotten in the need to avoid nuclear confrontation. Writing in 1986, R. J. Vincent reminded us that 'the history of East–West relations' was 'in an important sense the history of a dispute about human rights' (Vincent, 1986, p. 61).

Human Rights After the Cold War: Progress or Decline?

By the mid- to late 1990s, the international human rights norm had diffused widely. One key driver here

BOX 3.2 GORBACHEV'S ADHERENCE TO THE HELSINKI PROCESS

Mikhail Gorbachev, leader of the Soviet Union from 1985 until its demise in 1991, cited the Helsinki Final Act as a major influence on his decision to promote human rights in the Soviet Union in the late 1980s (Gorbachev, 1989). Unlike his predecessors, Gorbachev decided that the human rights provisions contained in the Helsinki Final Act and subsequent CSCE documents would be taken seriously by his government.

Demands were also mounting from the many human rights NGOs operating inside the Soviet bloc and outside it. Importantly, Gorbachev also cited the Helsinki Final Act's agreement that borders in Europe could be changed, but by peaceful means only, in 1989, thus allowing the peaceful revolutions in Eastern Europe and the Soviet Union that ultimately brought about the end of the Cold War.

was the rapid increase in the number of liberal democratic states. With the fall of communism, and countries transitioning to democracy in Latin America and Asia, it is now the case that a larger proportion of the world's population live in what could broadly be described as liberal democratic states. Around twenty states were democracies in 1945; by 2011 this figure had risen to well over a hundred (117 according to the INGO Freedom House). The organization's 2015 Report, however, warned of a decline in the numbers of free states in recent years: the 'Arab Spring' which started in late 2010, and ongoing conflict between Russia and its near neighbours demonstrated that it is not always straightforward for states to make a smooth transition from authoritarian systems to truly democratic ones, a point which is explored later in this chapter. Democracies are naturally hospitable to protecting individual rights; on occasions when citizens' rights are being curtailed by excessive presidential/executive authority, liberal states contain important countervailing legal mechanisms to protect individuals. (See Box 3.3 for more on liberal democracy and human rights.)

A second key driver was the growing acquiescence of non-liberal states in the human rights regime. The 1993 **Vienna World Conference on Human Rights** was an important signifier of the status of the standard, as was the signing of the International Covenant on Civil and Political Rights (ICCPR) by China in 1998. These tipping points illustrate the progressive socialization of states into a framework where their internal behaviour is subject to the scrutiny of other states as well as to international public opinion, a development incongruent with the realist emphasis on non-interference in the domestic affairs of states. Constructivist thinkers in IR talk about this process of socialization in terms of a 'norm cascade' (see Box 3.1).

Simply glancing at the website of a leading pro-democracy INGO such as Freedom House reveals

how much democratic socialization has taken place since 1990. Empirical data, however, is not in itself an explanation for how and why a norm of 'democratic entitlement' (Franck, 2000) emerged. Was it a triumph of political ideology (Fukuyama, 1992), a triumph of marketization, or a triumph of United States hegemony (Ikenberry, 2001)? In complex ways, all of these accounts overlap; what matters at this juncture is to point out that the landscape of international relations looked much more hospitable to human rights in the 1990s than it had ever done before. The decision by the North Atlantic Treaty Organization (NATO) in March 1999 to use force against the Federal Republic of Yugoslavia in an attempt to end human rights abuses against Kosovo Albanians prompted world leaders such as UK Prime Minister Tony Blair to declare that there was a 'new doctrine' of internationalism in which power and principle were at last converging.

After 9/11: The Challenge to the Convention Against Torture

The previous narrative about an expanding zone of peace in which the rights of ordinary citizens are upheld appeared, when viewed in the shadow of the 9/11 decade, to be something of an anachronism. Whereas the challenge to human rights during the Cold War originated from societies built on a collectivist ideology, the resistance to the human rights regime post-9/11 was displayed by leading liberal states such as the United States and the United Kingdom.

The most graphic representation of the retreat of human rights was the haunting images of naked prisoners, first aired on CBS news in April 2004. The official reaction of the Bush Administration to the Abu Ghraib scandal was that these incidents were committed by 'a few bad apples'. Such complacency was unfounded given that the USA had, since 9/11, systematically sought to reinterpret key articles of the International Bill of Rights, specifically in relation to the treatment of prisoners. The Secretary of Defense called for stronger interrogation techniques to be used against so-called high-value detainees. Far from refraining from cruel and degrading treatment, the Administration raised the bar for what counts as torture to the extent that it was equated with the infliction of lasting pain commensurate with 'serious physical injury such as death or organ failure' (Bybee, 2005; see Chapter 15).

The threat posed by al-Qaeda-inspired suicide bombers prompted voices inside the liberal

---

BOX 3.3 CHALLENGING ASSUMPTIONS: LIBERAL DEMOCRACY AND HUMAN RIGHTS

Is it inevitable that the number of liberal democracies will continue to increase despite the relative decline in Western power in the twenty-first century?

Can we claim that liberal democracies will always be the champions of human rights?

establishment to question whether certain human rights commitments were now in tension with national security. In relation to the Torture Convention, both Michael Ignatieff (2004) and Alan Dershowitz (2004) argued that the threat of apocalyptic terrorism was such that certain exceptions to the convention ought to be permissible (see Chapter 15). The former argued that human rights infringements ought to be seen as a lesser evil, while the latter believed that **torture warrants** should be considered as a way of regulating the practice. Needless to say, the response from the broadly international legal establishment was one of horror (Greenberg and Datel, 2005).

While liberal intellectuals slugged it out, governments around the world were quickly curtailing the rights of terror suspects—often so widely defined as to include political opposition movements. This general retreat from certain core human rights commitments after 9/11 reminded us that compliance with human rights norms is contingent and potentially reversible. Such retreats should not surprise us, but what is also clear is that the case for human rights is hard to dispel altogether; one of Barack Obama's first acts on gaining the US Presidency was to announce his intention to close the prison at Guantanamo Bay and to refrain from violating the Convention Against Torture. This was symbolically important; even though US Congressional politics has meant that Guantanamo is still operating, the statement indicated a clear break with the previous policy of reinterpreting human rights norms. The preceding discussion has endorsed Vincent's observation that 'there is an inescapable tension between human rights and foreign policy' (Vincent, 1986, p. 129). What is also evident is that this tension has not gone away, despite the best hopes of liberal internationalists after the fall of communism.

KEY POINTS

Although developed as part of the 1945 UN system, the international human rights regime was marginalized by the Cold War. Yet human rights concerns had always been part of this confrontation, and came to be incorporated into East–West diplomacy from the mid-1970s, thanks largely to the mobilization of transnational human rights NGOs.

The end of the Cold War and the subsequent spread of 'zones of peace and liberal democracy' created new hopes that human rights would gain ever greater importance in international relations. Paradoxically, however, this same period also saw some of the worst abuses of human rights, in states such as Somalia, Rwanda, Bosnia, and East Timor. These represented a serious challenge to states and international organizations that were still coming to grips with how to respond to such tragedies effectively.

The onset of the 'war on terror' focused attention on the human rights practices of the USA, Britain, and other states that had previously been seen as human rights champions. However, this 'roll-back' was always challenged by others and more recent policies indicate a resilience of the idea of human rights, regardless of calls for their reinterpretation.

Critical Thinking Questions:

How should we evaluate the policies and practices of Western states in relation to human rights? A sceptic could argue that, for much of the Cold War, the West turned a blind eye to extreme violations taking place in many conflicts in newly decolonized countries; or even worse, Western states perpetrated atrocities in situations where they were directly involved in geopolitical struggles (such as Indochina).

Similarly, how should we evaluate the claim that considerable progress in human rights occurred after the end of the Cold War, and yet the UN Security Council chose to look away when Rwanda was spiralling into genocide (in 1994)?

Findings: Human Rights and State Practice

In this section we illustrate the impact that human rights claims have had on state sovereignty in two key respects: first is the process by which human rights standards have become intertwined with the everyday practice of sovereign states at a domestic, or internal, level; second is the development of the idea of international responsibility, such that human rights are seen as the concern of all states, and have become integrated into the external policies of sovereign states and international institutions. A useful way to capture this historic shift is the idea of 'sovereignty as responsibility', articulated by Deng et al. (1996).

Internalization—Protecting Human Rights at Home

Internalization stresses the state's obligations to protect. There has been a tendency in the IR literature to focus on the narrow question of the promotion of human rights in foreign policy—often narrowing this still further to the question of forcible human rights protection. The danger here is that the spotlight falls on those states in the world which have the military capacity to respond to humanitarian emergencies, and that it also—even if unintentionally—diverts attention from the primary responsibility that states ought to fulfil, namely that of protecting their own populations. Instead of a focus which centres on foreign intervention, sovereign responsibility places the burden of upholding human rights first and foremost on the state. Remember that, for the most part, the protection of human rights begins at 'home'. It is noteworthy that former UN Secretary General Kofi Annan recognized the primacy of **national human rights institutions**. These institutions will, 'in the long run', ensure that 'human rights are protected', he argued. Importantly, the responsibility placed on the state also requires the state to engage in the *prevention* of human rights crimes, including their incitement, and calls on states to utilize the appropriate and necessary means to fulfil this responsibility.

The 'norm cascade' featured in Box 3.1 provides an analytical device for examining how far a particular state has progressed in terms of developing a comprehensive human rights policy. In broader terms, the first requirement for states to be able to claim that they take human rights seriously is 'to surrender a degree of sovereignty' and permit some degree of international scrutiny (Sikkink, 1993, p. 142). Such an injunction requires a detailed analysis of treaty ratification, or the mechanisms by which human rights standards are embedded in domestic law.

The question of ratification leads inexorably to the discussion of variations in domestic legal orders. Paradoxically, authoritarian states find the process of ratification easier given that the head of state retains supreme power to enact domestic laws. Democracies find the process of ratification is longer and more complex. The adoption of a treaty in the United States, for example, requires a two-thirds vote in the Senate, rendering the process vulnerable to partisan politics. We should not, however, automatically think that making a legal commitment is necessarily going to orient the behaviour of actors towards better protection of human rights. We have to be wary of methodological flaws in the study of compliance to human rights treaties (Simmons, 2009): false positives can result when, for example, liberal democratic states comply with a treaty because they are guided by the values and institutions that built the liberal political order in the first place;

false negatives can result when human rights norms are violated but for reasons that are independent of the norm (e.g. in the context of a protracted civil war).

Whether compliance to international human rights treaties is a good measure of the power of human rights is an important question. For this to be the case, international measures for protecting rights have to inform the policies of political parties, be advocated for in civil society, and be heard in law courts. Even in cases where there are strong regional or global treaties—such as the European Convention on Human Rights or the Rome Statute of the International Criminal Court—the principle of complementarity is asserted such that domestic courts have primary jurisdiction to prosecute alleged crimes against humanity.

Externalization—Promoting Human Rights in Foreign Policy

While internal human rights promotion remains highly important, we cannot get away from the fact that in IR, questions still abound within the international community over how to respond, who should act, and when, if violations are carried out with impunity elsewhere. There is now a general agreement that states have a responsibility to prevent and halt the worst abuses of human rights, especially episodes of genocide and other mass atrocities, if the leaders of the state in which these are being carried out are unwilling or unable to protect their populations. The international community, acting through the Security Council of the United Nations, has a responsibility to take timely and decisive action, including military force as a last resort, should national authorities 'manifestly fail' to protect their populations.

This incorporation of internationalist values and responsibilities into a country's (or conceivably a region's) foreign policy represents an important dimension of a comprehensive human rights policy. For it to be said that a state actor has an external human rights policy, two aspects need to be present. First, the pursuit of human rights values and policies must be given strategic importance such that many different ministries mainstream human rights into their activity. Second, there must be explicit policy instruments to promote, monitor, and evaluate compliance with international human rights norms by domestic state institutions, as well as scrutiny of the performance of other states, and, if needed, a response—in accordance with the UN's provisions—to uphold these values elsewhere.

The Responsibility to Protect: Combining Internalization and Externalization

This thinking of sovereignty as responsibility was crucial in the evolution of the doctrine of the **Responsibility to Protect** (or R2P), which brings together these internal and external dimensions. Especially after 1989, key Western states recognized that the liberal values that defeated communism were *universal* values. Having a comprehensive human rights policy meant insisting on the legitimate appraisal of the internal conduct of all states (Vincent, 1986, p. 152). For states to be in conformity with the norms of sovereignty as responsibility, they had not only to protect human rights inside their own borders, but also actively to support basic rights externally (Reus-Smit, 2001).

This duty to protect was being championed by norm entrepreneurs inside several key states as well as by the then UN Secretary General Kofi Annan, driven in part by the horrific abuses witnessed in Somalia, Rwanda, the Balkan wars, and in East Timor. By the end of the century, however, inconsistency in its application—or worse, inaction in the face of genocide in the case of Rwanda—triggered an important debate about the circumstances in which it is right to engage in armed intervention in the affairs of other sovereign states without their consent.

The Canadian government was particularly supportive of a new initiative to stop 'future Kosovos' (where there was international action but no UN mandate) or 'future Rwandas' (international action that came too late to prevent the genocide). It set up the International Commission on Intervention and State Sovereignty (ICISS) to update and defend the case for humanitarian intervention in a world that was not always receptive to the idea and which was rapidly coming to be dominated by the emphasis on the war on terrorism. This state-sponsored commission's task was to find a way to bridge the international community's responsibility to act when faced with clear violations of humanitarian norms, while still respecting the perennial issue of the sovereign rights of states. The new orientation which evolved from these discussions utilized the term 'the Responsibility to Protect'. One of the co-chairs of the ICISS, former Australian foreign minister Gareth Evans, put the shift from the 1990s to the early twenty-first century into context:

The international community has too often in the past stood paralysed between the competing imperatives of intervention to protect human rights catastrophically at risk, and that of non-intervention in the internal affairs of sovereign states. Throughout the 1990s there was fundamental disagreement between those—mainly in the global North—arguing for a 'right to humanitarian intervention', and those, mainly in the global South, who feared that any recognition of such a 'right' would mean a revival of old imperialist habits ... It was necessary to cut through that deadlock, and 'R2P' did so, by using language that clearly changed the emphasis from 'right' to 'responsibility', by approaching the issue from the perspective of the victims rather than any potential intervener.

(G. Evans, 2008)

The extensive deliberations of the ICISS firmly placed the responsibility to uphold human rights and protect citizens primarily on the state itself. All countries had a responsibility to protect their citizens from **genocide, war crimes, ethnic cleansing**, and **crimes against humanity**, it argued. But where a state manifestly failed to do this, the international community would now share a collective responsibility to respond. Thus, only in the event that a state would not or could not protect its people would outside intervention be considered; a respect for sovereignty was therefore coupled with a clearly articulated *responsibility* of the international community to respond appropriately in the event that a state failed to live up to its duties.

This formulation did much to strengthen the view that the responsibility to protect human rights lies first and foremost with individual governments, continuing the elaboration of the notion of responsible sovereignty, where sovereignty was no longer seen as a protection against intervention but rather as a notion and practice that carries with it undeniable obligations to citizens, to whom a sovereign government is accountable. The implication here is far-reaching: sovereignty as an entitlement is conditional on the promotion and protection of the rights of citizens. Further, accountability is due not only to a state's domestic population, but also to an international community (Thakur, 2002; Etzioni, 2006). Similar notions of sovereignty were elaborated in the United Nations (2004) publication 'A more secure world', the commissioned report of the High-level Panel on Threats, Challenges and Change, and these various reports have now come to influence academic thinking on human rights to a substantial degree. (There is likewise a resonance here with the conceptual and operational elements of the **International Criminal Court**, which also places responsibility primarily on the relevant state to prosecute its citizens who have violated international norms. Again, where a state fails or is unable to do this, the responsibility to do so falls on external bodies.)

In September 2005, representatives from 193 states met in New York for a World Summit on global security and development issues. R2P was placed on the agenda by the then Secretary General Kofi Annan. Months of drafting and negotiation preceded the meeting, including a call for a major redrafting by neoconservative US Ambassador to the UN John Bolton. The key R2P paragraphs survived, although it was a close call (Bellamy, 2010, p. 23). It is worth reiterating the text of the key paragraphs, which made it into the final World Summit document and which were unanimously adopted by the UN General Assembly:

138. Each individual State has the responsibility to protect its populations from genocide, war crimes, ethnic cleansing and crimes against humanity. This responsibility entails the prevention of such crimes, including their incitement, through appropriate and necessary means. We accept that responsibility and will act in accordance with it. The international community should, as appropriate, encourage and help States to exercise this responsibility and support the United Nations in establishing an early warning capability.

139. The international community, through the United Nations, also has the responsibility to use appropriate diplomatic, humanitarian and other peaceful means, in accordance with Chapters VI and VIII of the Charter, to help to protect populations from genocide, war crimes, ethnic cleansing and crimes against humanity. In this context, we are prepared to take collective action, in a timely and decisive manner, through the Security Council, in accordance with the Charter, including Chapter VII, on a case-by-case basis and in cooperation with relevant regional organizations as appropriate, should peaceful means be inadequate and national authorities are manifestly failing to protect their populations from genocide, war crimes, ethnic cleansing and crimes against humanity.

(UN General Assembly, 2005)

Human Rights and State Practice

The doctrine of R2P was put to the test in early 2011. A week after an uprising in Libya began, the government led by Muammar Gaddafi ordered a violent crackdown on the opposition movement. The League of Arab States (Arab League) suspended Libya from the organization on 22 February 2011, the first indication of the critical role that regional organizations were to play in the response to the crisis. On the same day, the UN Security Council issued a statement calling for the Libyan government 'to meet its responsibility to protect its population' (United Nations Security Council, 2011). This was an unusually quick response from the Security Council—only a week into the crisis.

Gaddafi's loyal forces continued to pound opposition strongholds in Eastern Libya. The Arab League—and the EU—called for the UN to authorize a **no-fly zone** to limit the extent of the terror perpetrated by government forces. On 17 March, the UN Security Council agreed to Resolution 1973 which mandated a no-fly zone (a rare measure for the Security Council to use). Resolution 1973 marked the first time the Security Council had authorized a no-fly zone with the explicit purpose of protecting civilians, and against the wishes of the host state. It illustrated how far R2P had travelled.

Yet both supporters and critics of the NATO-led action tended to overstate the extent to which the Libya case had set a precedent that would be likely to be repeated in other situations of grave human rights violations. Sceptics will point to the fact that a third of Security Council members abstained on Resolution 1973, highlighting the controversial nature of this decision. The main reason why these members abstained was not simply that they were acting as 'spoilers' seeking to halt Western state intervention; they had genuine concerns that the mission had a low chance of success and that there was too much indeterminacy in the resolution. Who was going to implement it? With how much force? For how long? None of these operational issues was addressed in the text of the resolution—and all of them became points of controversy during the period of NATO's enforcement action during the spring and summer of 2011. Additionally, the BRICS states (Brazil, Russia, India, China, and South Africa) on the UN Security Council argued that the Security Council's civilian protection mandate had been exceeded by the US, UK, and France, who appeared to favour a goal of regime change. These claims blemished the R2P doctrine somewhat, even as the Libya case was heralded as a triumph for the notion that human rights violations warranted an R2P response.

R2P supporters have a different view of the decision-making over Libya. On the vote itself, they would point to the fact that the text did not provoke a veto from a permanent member—a markedly different outcome to the diplomatic opposition that was mounted against Britain and the United States in 1999 when they sought to persuade the Security Council to authorize an intervention to protect Kosovo Albanians. Supporters also see Resolution 1973 as further evidence of a deeper normative consensus around the need to use force, as a last resort, in response to atrocities actually being committed and threatening to escalate further. But rather than viewing Libya as a precedent that is likely to be invoked at any point soon, there are good reasons for thinking of this case as a 'perfect storm' producing decisive action. Military force was necessary to prevent further atrocities, which Gaddafi was publicly threatening; Gaddafi had few friends in the region or allies in the Security Council to prevent action being taken against him; and the geo-strategic terrain was favourable to NATO. The situation in Libya put R2P front and centre in diplomacy and security, but the factors that aligned to authorize and implement the no-fly zone may not coincide in other cases. The dissatisfaction that the Libya case produced among some states has made it hard to command support for a muscular response to the ongoing crisis in Syria. The Responsibility to Protect doctrine has been invoked by the UN Security Council to provide humanitarian corridors and to condemn Syria for its grievous failure to protect its populations, but there has been no authorizing of forceful action in a 'timely and decisive' manner, as anticipated in the World Summit document. As Syria has proved, Libya was the exception rather than the 'rule' (see Box 3.4). When governments and insurgency groups decide to pursue their political goals through violent struggle, the options available to outsiders to constrain or end the harm are limited—and the risks of intervening and making matters worse are grave. Debates about coercive intervention by third party states remain a point of friction in the United Nations system.

Yet it is important to realize that the R2P framework requires not just intervention; it is also, at its core, an attempt to embed a greater sense of responsibility on the part of governments to protect their own populations and to assist other governments and peoples who are deemed to be 'at risk' of experiencing mass atrocity crimes (Bellamy, 2014). It is also the case that the norm against atrocities remains strong, that

> ### BOX 3.4 ALTERNATIVE POINTS OF VIEW: THE R2P DEBATE
>
> Some argue (Evans, 2013) that the inability to take strong action in Syria has not damaged the norm of R2P irreversibly. By contrast, others 'only see a doomed fate for R2P as an international norm' (Yaziji, 2013). Much depends here on whether the absence of consistent action on the part of the UN Security Council is condoned on the basis that different cases require different foreign policy instruments—or whether inconsistent action is viewed as the result of double standards.

all states have internalized the prospect of external scrutiny in the event of mass atrocities being committed (or at risk of being committed). Moreover, the language of R2P continues to be used widely and is not in itself disputed: Security Council discussions and various General Assembly debates since 2009 suggest that the doctrine has become embedded in human rights discourse, even if differences remain about Resolution 1973. That those differences centre on process—and not on principle—would indicate that the doctrine remains an incontestable milestone in efforts to protect human rights.

Human Rights and IR: The Expansion of the Discipline and the Application of Rights

The position of human rights in the study of international relations has been receiving attention in other areas also, reinforcing an analysis that the externalization of human rights norms is a growing trend. As the R2P doctrine shows, there is an increasing focus on *conflict prevention* as a key tool. Early warning mechanisms and conflict prevention are not only relatively new areas of study in the disciplines of IR and peace and conflict resolution, but have also been adopted as essential elements in the practice of human rights protection and humanitarian projects. Examples include the ongoing work of the Organization for Security and Co-operation in Europe (OSCE), the EU, and the African Union, clearly signalling a shift away from merely reactive responses towards global and regional proactive initiatives to protect populations.

The area of development studies in IR is also replete with the intrusion of human rights into its agenda (see

Chapter 12). While a rights-based approach might have been implicit in early formulations of development practice, the argument now is that it should be explicitly and firmly embedded in discourses of poverty reduction and on the operations of institutions such as the **World Bank** and the **International Monetary Fund** (Nelson and Dorsey, 2003; Gready and Ensor, 2005; Uvin, 2007).

KEY POINTS

Two elements of human rights protection in the practice of states need to be present in any claims that norm cascades are successfully occurring: first is the internalization of human rights norms, where the rights of citizens are enshrined in domestic legal and social practices; the second, an externalization of these norms, can be seen as a commitment to international human rights regimes and an acceptance of a responsibility to protect human rights where abuses are evident in other states.

The formulation of R2P takes forward the idea of responsible sovereignty and incorporates both internal and external obligations incumbent upon individual states and the broader international community.

State practice has also recognized the need to engage in early warning and conflict prevention, and this is a growing area of study in IR as well as in peace and conflict research and development studies.

Critical Thinking Question:

If states have the responsibility to protect vulnerable populations in conflict situations abroad, do they also have responsibility for providing such populations with adequate food and housing? If not, what is the salient difference in the two kinds of protection?

Conclusion

Do these new areas of discussion move us significantly forward in being able to uphold human rights in the practice of international politics? There are at least two criticisms that can be placed at the door of these innovations in thinking about human rights in international relations. The first is that they might foster expectations of protection that are unrealizable in reality—for every Libya there is a Syria, opening up the question of double standards on the part of intervening states (and their institutions like NATO). The second and related factor is that most humanitarian atrocities are not preventable (or resolvable) by the application of military power; and even in rare cases where the use of force has contributed to a positive outcome, there is no escaping the moral dilemma in which some innocent lives are lost in order to protect others. Wars of peace, as Kipling described them, are still wars.

Human rights and IR coexist at a complicated and uneasy level, reminding us of the complex nature of the relationship between state sovereignty, power, and norms. International human rights regimes are slowly evolving to make important symbolic, if not always substantive, progress. At the same time, the Human Security Report of 2013 reminds us that the number of conflicts worldwide, as well as the number of people killed in such conflicts, has decreased over time. Given that violent conflict is often the crucible in which human rights violations occur, it would seem important that this downward trend continues. All this would indicate that a continued emphasis on early warning, peacekeeping, and conflict prevention might be a key element in avoiding human rights abuses in the future.

But the gradual weaving of human rights threads into the fabric of international politics is not cause for complacency. The study of the nexus between human rights and IR is both productive and at the same time troublesome. It is productive in the sense that the normative choice about where to begin—with a world of individuals or a world of states—ineluctably makes the researcher consider the impact of the actors on the other side of the ledger. It is troublesome in that it requires human rights advocates to be aware of the complexities of the world political system, the as-yet limited abilities of this system to uphold rights in a consistent and effective manner, and the plain but uncomfortable truth that there are often competing justice claims on the part of different actors.

? QUESTIONS

Individual Study Questions

1. Why has the study of international relations not focused on human rights until relatively recently?

2. In what way might realists, who argue that human rights have no place in foreign policy, share views with those who claim that universal human rights are 'a Western imposition'?

3. How might we best explain the emergence of a universal human rights regime?

4. What role did human rights activists play in ending the Cold War?

Group Discussion Questions

1. Has the universal human rights regime been irredeemably damaged by the practices of certain Western states in the 'war against terror'?

2. Is R2P anything more than a slick acronym for an unworkable idea?

3. Are human rights issues 'here to stay' in international relations?

FURTHER READING

Bellamy, A. (2014). *Responsibility to Protect: A Defence.* Oxford: Oxford University Press.

This book considers the difficulties involved in upholding human rights, but defends the role and evolution of the R2P principle.

Donnelly, J. (2013). *Universal Human Rights in Theory and Practice* (3rd edn). Ithaca, NY: Cornell University Press.

A very useful overview of the theory and practice of human rights.

Dunne, T. and **Gifkins, J.** (2011). Libya and the State of Intervention. *Australian Journal of International Affairs,* **65**/5, 515–29.

This article examines the controversy surrounding R2P action in Libya.

Dunne, T. and **Wheeler, N. J.** (eds) (1999). *Human Rights in Global Politics.* Cambridge: Cambridge University Press.

A wide-ranging collection of writings on human rights and international relations.

Forsythe, D. P. (ed.) (2000). *Human Rights and Comparative Foreign Policy.* Tokyo: United Nations University Press.

Forsythe examines the role of human rights in the practice of various foreign policy approaches.

Forsythe, D. P. (2012). *Human Rights in International Relations* (3rd edn). Cambridge: Cambridge University Press.

A comprehensive examination of the place of human rights in international politics.

Freeman, M. (2011). *Human Rights: An Interdisciplinary Approach* (2nd edn). Cambridge: Polity Press.

A useful account of the various approaches to human rights.

Glanville, L. (2014). *Sovereignty and the Responsibility to Protect.* Chicago: Chicago University Press.

An excellent analysis of the idea of responsibility, especially as it pertains to the R2P doctrine.

Vincent, R. J. (1986). *Human Rights and International Relations.* Cambridge: Cambridge University Press.

A classic account of human rights, linking them to the theoretical approach of 'international society'.

Weiss, T. G. (2012). *Humanitarian Intervention* (2nd edn). Cambridge: Polity Press.

This book charts the evolution of ideas about humanitarian intervention.

Wheeler, N. J. (2001). *Saving Strangers: Humanitarian Intervention in International Society.* Oxford: Oxford University Press. An early analysis of the conceptual and practical challenges of interventions, especially those of the 1990s.

WEB LINKS

http://www.amnesty.org/   Amnesty International. Amnesty International is best known for its practices of campaigning and its international solidarity with the victims of human rights abuses. It works by mobilizing public pressure and lobbying directly to influence governments, companies, and international organizations worldwide. Established in 1961, by 2015 it had more than 2 million members in 150 countries.

http://www.hrw.org   Human Rights Watch. Human Rights Watch arose directly out of the Helsinki process and the Helsinki Watch human rights monitoring groups. Formed in 1978, it is the largest human rights organization based in the United States.

http://www.crisisgroup.org/home/index.cfm   The International Crisis Group (ICG). The ICG was formed in 1995 as a response to the human rights tragedies of Somalia, Rwanda, and Bosnia to provide early warning of conflicts, field-based analysis, and policy prescriptions to governments and other NGOs involved in conflict analysis, prevention, and resolution. Unlike many other similar NGOs, its senior management team comprises former government members and prominent statesmen and stateswomen.

http://www.osce.org/odihr/   The Office for Democratic Institutions and Human Rights (ODIHR) (Organization for Security and Co-operation in Europe (OSCE)). ODIHR is the subsidiary body within the OSCE (the successor to the Helsinki process) that seeks to protect human rights and fundamental freedoms in the member states of the OSCE, whose geographical scope extends from Vancouver to Vladivostock. Based in Warsaw, ODIHR is committed to the protection of minorities, upholding the rule of law, and the transition to democracy in the region.

http://www.cidh.org/DefaultE.htm   The Inter-American Commission on Human Rights (IACHR). The IACHR is an autonomous organ of the Organization of American States (OAS). It was established in 1959, following the American Declaration on the Rights and Duties of Man adopted in Colombia in 1948. In 1969, the IACHR adopted the American Convention on Human Rights. Although of relatively limited effectiveness during the early decades of its existence, the IACHR is reputed to have strengthened its capacities substantially since the late 1990s, as demonstrated, for instance, in its robust prosecution of former Peruvian leader Alberto Fujimori in 2008.

http://www.achpr.org/   The African Commission on Human and Peoples' Rights (ACHPR). The ACHPR was established under the authority of the African Charter of Human and Peoples' Rights, itself entering into force in 1986 under the aegis of the African Union.

http://www.globalr2p.org   Global Centre for the Responsibility to Protect. The most active site for R2P material, including a regular 'monitor' and key statements cajoling UN member states to take action in relation to actual or potential atrocities.

http://www.r2pasiapacific.org   The Asia-Pacific Centre for the Responsibility to Protect. The most active R2P research centre, focusing primarily but not exclusively on the Asia Pacific. Includes a great deal of academic material that is open access, including briefings and reports.

Visit the Online Resource Centre that accompanies this book for updates and a range of other resources: www.oxfordtextbooks.co.uk/orc/goodhart3e/

4

Human Rights in International Law

Rhona K. M. Smith

Chapter Contents

Reader's Guide

This chapter introduces the international legal context of human rights. It complements the preceding chapters by outlining the practical (rather than theoretical) framework for human rights. In summary, this chapter will consider where to find human rights (in law) and how to ensure those rights and freedoms are respected by states. From an initial focus on the principal instruments (treaties), the institutional framework will be considered, explaining the mechanisms for monitoring and enforcing human rights. Neither politics nor law can be considered in isolation: political will is needed to secure the drafting and adoption of international instruments; political will is also a factor in monitoring and enforcing international human rights. However, without law, international human rights would undoubtedly be a less tangible, measurable, and enforceable concept than is the case today.

Introduction

International human rights are now an integral part of public international law. Indeed, there is a strong argument for human rights being regarded as a distinct branch of international law, as respect for human rights is not primarily a characteristic of inter-state obligations, but rather a reflection of the state's undertakings in respect of its population. Acceptance of human rights is a manifestation of a state's acknowledgement of the pre-eminence of the rule of law. This chapter introduces the international legal context of human rights.

All states profess to respect certain international human rights, many of which are explored in detail elsewhere in this book. These rights are normally tabulated in a legally binding format as a **treaty** and are thus easily ascertainable. While their existence (in tangible legal form) is beyond question, their content remains hotly disputed. Every state claims to promote respect for key human rights and fundamental freedoms within its territory, but not all states accept all the tabulated rights and freedoms. Given that there are hundreds of instruments of varying legal force that purport to enumerate human rights, this is not entirely surprising. From a legal perspective, the most enforceable human rights are expressed in treaties, primarily **multilateral treaties** (i.e. international treaties with several states participating). Nevertheless, there are many examples of human rights that predate such multilateral treaties—these too can be enforceable against states. Moreover, many of these rights are now contained in treaties.

This chapter starts by exploring the origins of human rights law, considering the implications inherent in creating international human rights law. The seismic shift this reflects (and caused) in the conceptualization of international law will be highlighted. Tragic events around the world have frequently proved to be the prompt for articulating international human rights. Such a manifestation of political will is a crucial factor in ensuring the success of human rights: without consensus, no treaty can become 'law', be embedded into normal state practice, or be internationally monitored or enforced.

Following this overview of the evolution of international human rights law, the emphasis will move

BOX 4.1 FINDING INTERNATIONAL HUMAN RIGHTS LAW ONLINE

In the twenty-first century, engaging fully with international human rights law demands the use of online sources. All primary sources are freely available online in several languages. Once familiarity with the principal websites is achieved, it is possible to research any aspect of basic human rights. Space constraints restrict this guide to the official UN portal:
http://www.ohchr.org

The main website is that of the UN Office of the High Commissioner for Human Rights. Information can be found through a variety of routes—*quick links* on the right hand side of the home page take you directly to many relevant sites.

From the home page, note the following links from the top banner.

Your human rights

This links to *International law*, which in turn has a link to *The core international human rights instruments*, a hyperlinked list of the full text of all the principal UN human rights treaties, instruments, codes, and guidelines. A quick link to *Human rights instruments* is also available at the right-hand side of the home page. It links to the same page. This is the main primary source that you will require.

Countries

This links through *Human rights in the world* to a map and an alphabetical list of member states. For each country, you can obtain information on contracting status (ratifications, reservations, and derogations) as well as recent Special Procedures reports and concluding observations of treaty monitoring bodies.

Human rights bodies

This links to a portal for all the UN Charter and treaty monitoring bodies. It also has a link to the material on treaty body reform and the treaty body strengthening process. Each treaty monitoring body has its own page from which you can access the relevant treaty, reporting guidelines, committee information, the reports of each state to the committee, the concluding observations of the committee thereon (through *Sessions*), and general comments and recommendations of the committee.

Publications and resources

This links to *Publications* that give access to a variety of useful electronic publications on human rights, including *Fact sheets* and *Special issue* papers.

to elaborating the principal sources of international human rights law. The various forms of expressing human rights will be considered before identifying the core international human rights instruments. As will be apparent, even when a state accepts a particular human rights treaty, it can still avoid full legal responsibility by a variety of legal means. These are important as they impact, sometimes considerably, on the extent of a state's obligations.

While articulating lists of human rights has some merit in itself, ensuring that the rhetoric of the law is transformed into a practical reality is a major issue. Accordingly, attention will then move to the institutional framework, identifying the mechanisms for monitoring and enforcing human rights. Once more, political will is a factor in monitoring and enforcing international human rights. Are human rights enforceable in law? Most importantly, can an individual actually claim that a state has infringed his or her human rights? (See Box 4.1 for a guide to finding international human rights law online.)

Historical Evolution of International Human Rights Law

This section will outline the evolution of human rights, particularly charting the reincarnation of philosophical ideals as international laws (treaties). The next section will then consider the sources of contemporary international human rights law. There is evidence of laws and policies that ensured respect for some rights of individuals many centuries ago. Most religious texts promulgate certain rights and freedoms of followers, assuming they adhere to the codes for life enshrined in the tenets of the faith. **Enlightenment** philosophers also contributed to the development of human rights theories (see Chapter 1), although there are many examples of non-Christian philosophical contributions that help rebalance the alleged Eurocentricity of human rights' origins. Human rights have a long history, much of which is rarely discussed today (Burgers, 1992). What is beyond doubt is that the majority of legally binding instruments (treaties) that form the body of modern human rights law emerged during the twentieth century—although these were not the first treaties on international human rights. Early examples of 'human rights' instruments focused on the abolition of slavery, humanitarian law, and minority protection guarantees.

Following this brief review of early examples of human rights agreements, contemporary international human rights instruments will be discussed.

Abolition of Slavery

Slavery is now universally condemned, all states having outlawed it. Its prohibition is an obligation owed by all states to the entire international community (on such obligations, see Barcelona Traction Case (*Belgium v. Spain* (1970), ICJ Reps 32)). Some two hundred years ago, the UK and the USA claimed to begin the end of the slave trade by enacting national legislation prohibiting trade in people. Over the next sixty years, a series of **bilateral treaties** (legally binding agreements between two countries) was concluded between the UK and other states by which the two states involved agreed to prevent their subjects from engaging in the slave trade (see Martinez, 2008). In 1815, the international Congress of Vienna deemed the slave trade repugnant. Under the auspices of the **League of Nations**, a Slavery Commission was established and a 1926 Slavery Convention adopted (League of Nations, 1926). This was followed in 1956 by the Supplementary Convention on the Abolition of Slavery, the Slave Trade, and Institutions and Practices similar to Slavery. Despite this, modern incarnations of slavery remain, with human trafficking and forced labour being the most obvious examples. Human trafficking in particular appears to be a growth industry which various modern treaties and transnational initiatives seek to suppress in the twenty-first century (see Chapter 16).

Humanitarian Law and the Laws of War

Humanitarian law—agreements on the conduct of hostilities—also emerged comparatively early in the history of international human rights law. These agreements have as their goal the 'civilization' of conflict by ensuring that only enemy agents could be targeted, and that civilians are thus protected. Agreements also related to the types of killing to be deployed (humane deaths). Today, this body of law is still in existence. The Hague 1907 laws of war and the **Geneva Conventions and Protocols** of 1949 and 1977, respectively, are the most famous examples; more recent agreements include a ban on landmines and the Convention on Cluster Munitions, which was opened for signature in December 2008.

Individual legal responsibility arises for those who fail to respect the rights of combatants under these treaties. This was evidenced in the Tokyo Tribunal and the **Nuremberg Tribunal** following the Second World War. Those defeated leaders found responsible for mass violations of human rights were tried and sentenced (usually to death). Following a spate of special courts and ad hoc tribunals focusing on criminal justice, the **International Criminal Court** (ICC) was established by a treaty—the Rome Statute on the International Criminal Court—in 1998. The ICC has competence to investigate and consider war crimes and violations of humanitarian law when the national courts are unable or unwilling to do so. Violations of other human rights, in contrast, cannot be prosecuted in the court (as we will see).

Although closely related, humanitarian law and international human rights have evolved as discrete areas of law and policy. Human rights apply generally: the state is required to respect the declared and accepted human rights of all. Humanitarian laws, in contrast, are essentially minimum rights that must be respected during proclaimed emergencies or conflicts (see Chapter 21). Violations of international humanitarian law may result in individual prosecutions, whereas violations of general human rights will not, as liability rests with the state. Contemporary prosecutions include: Radovan Karadzic before the International Criminal Tribunal for the Former Yugoslavia; Charles Taylor's conviction by the Special Court for Sierra Leone; and Kaing Guek (Duch) Eav's conviction by the Extraordinary Chambers of the Courts of Cambodia.

Minority and Labour Rights

There are also historic minority protection regimes—for example, the 1878 Treaty of Berlin accorded special status in law to specified religious groups. Prior to this, 'aliens' (foreigners) were only accorded minimum rights and freedoms, based on the idea that an injury to an individual was tantamount to an injury to the individual's state of nationality. **Reparations**, or remedies for loss or damage suffered, could be sought. In the early twentieth century, there was a focus on ensuring the peaceful coexistence of peoples within states in the wake of the First World War—hence the minority guarantee treaty regimes instigated by the League of Nations and the creation of the **International Labour Organization** (ILO). The former sought to ensure respect for religious or linguistic minorities who found themselves in a 'foreign' state due to the redrawing of Europe's boundaries and/or the redistribution of the overseas territories of the defeated countries. The latter sought to regulate labour, assisting with rebuilding the economies of countries decimated by war, and ensuring fair working conditions for all.

In the aftermath of the collapse of the League of Nations and the Second World War, the international community had to rethink its approach to the maintenance of peace, law, and order. Although the ILO survived intact from this tumultuous period between the two World Wars, its minority protection system was discontinued; the newly established United Nations elected to focus on universal human rights, thereby obviating (it was hoped) the need for special minority guarantees. Despite the change in focus, minority groups (whether ethnic, religious, linguistic, or other) are all too often in a weaker position than majority groups in any given state. Still, with the emphasis on equality in international human rights, remedies may be available for such individuals, eliminating oppression and discrimination.

Contemporary human rights law has early antecedents, traces of which survive to the present day. The following section will examine the mechanisms for establishing binding obligations on states to protect human rights; thereafter the parameters of modern human rights law will be outlined.

KEY POINTS

There are early examples of international agreements on human rights issues.

Efforts to abolish all forms of slavery today focus on proscribing those practices analogous to slavery.

International humanitarian law and the laws of war have early origins. The formal laws were negotiated between the warring states and governed hostilities. Today, these laws are found in the Hague and Geneva conventions and associated instruments, and apply to most conflicts.

Critical Thinking Questions:

Do the origins of human rights outlined above indicate a global North or Western bias, as some commentators suggest? What evidence is there of human rights in early Buddhist, Confucian, Hindu, or Islamic writings and teachings? Are human rights really just a 'moral code' for the functioning of society?

Sources of International Human Rights Law

As with any area of law, it is necessary to establish what the building blocks are, to know 'where to find the law'. International law is a little different from national law in this respect—there is no single legislature passing laws that must be obeyed. Rather, there are various organizations from which treaties emanate and various other agreements made by states of their own volition. On top of this, there is a mass of additional materials that outlines and informs international law. In this section we will consider the key sources of international human rights law.

Treaties

Treaties are probably the closest thing to recognizable (in the national sense) law in international law. They are, for the purposes of human rights, written down and agreed by states. In this way, treaties are most obviously 'international legislation'. States have to 'agree' to treaties. They indicate their agreement through signature (generally a political act) followed by ratification (the legal act). For students, the most comprehensive guide to treaty law is the partial codification (collation of existing laws and practices) and partial progressive development (evolution of new law) of the pre-existing law found in the Vienna Convention on the Law of Treaties 1969. This treaty contains detailed (technical) guidance on the creation, dissolution, meaning, and enforcement of treaties. Not all states agree to its terms, but many do, and parts of the treaty represent customary international law (as we shall discuss).

Treaties contain statements of law. They can be broadly compared to legislative acts. The treaty specifies the legal obligation of the state, an obligation that can be enforced. Not all obligations are negative, requiring states simply to refrain from doing something; some are positive, with states obliged actively to do something to respect the right in question—passing homicide and assault laws to help ensure respect for the right to life is an obvious example. The state would not be directly at fault if an individual killed another individual, but nevertheless attracts responsibility if there is no national homicide law that can be invoked. For example, in *Ng* v. *Canada* (UN Doc. CCPR/C/49/D/469/1991—Human Rights Committee), the USA requested the extradition of Ng to stand trial for various counts of capital murder and other crimes in

BOX 4.2 CHALLENGING ASSUMPTIONS: BORDERS AND HUMAN RIGHTS

Many states rebut responsibility for violations which occur outside their territory. Should Canada have been found responsible in *Ng* v. *Canada*? Should a state be responsible for the actions of members of its military forces acting in their private capacity overseas (torture, food deprivation, physical and sexual assaults)? Should foreigners be able to claim asylum on the basis that the standard of medical care in their home state is much lower than in the state where they are claiming asylum?

California. Although the Canadian Supreme Court considered extradition not to infringe Canada's obligations, the *UN Human Rights Committee* (which monitors implementation of the **International Covenant on Civil and Political Rights** (ICCPR)) concluded that the resultant execution by gas asphyxiation, the penalty if convicted, was cruel and inhuman treatment in violation of Article 7. Clearly, Canada was not directly responsible for this, but its decision to extradite had a foreseeable consequence (an infringement of human rights). Such positive obligations have significant consequences for states when contemplating extradition, deportation, or asylum (see Box 4.2). Undertakings not to torture an individual or not to impose the death penalty are often required in advance.

Obviously treaties can have far-ranging consequences for states. They are legal obligations that should not be undertaken lightly. States can elect, through treaties, to alter aspects of their territorial **sovereignty** (e.g. Advisory Opinion on *Nationality Decrees Issued in Tunis and Morocco* (1922), PCIJ Series B, No. 4). This is noteworthy as many states claim that international human rights law impinges on their internationally protected (e.g. under the UN Charter) and virtually sacrosanct national sovereignty. There are, however, many reasons not related to law or sovereignty that states agree to treaties. Irrespective of the reason, states agreeing to international human rights law have agreed to any limitation on their sovereignty flowing therefrom.

How does a State Signify Acceptance of a Treaty's Terms?

Just as with contracts under national law, states must agree to be bound by a treaty (see Figure 4.1). Treaties are concluded in writing: thus a state has to indicate its consent to be bound by the signature of the Head of State or appropriately authorized representative. At

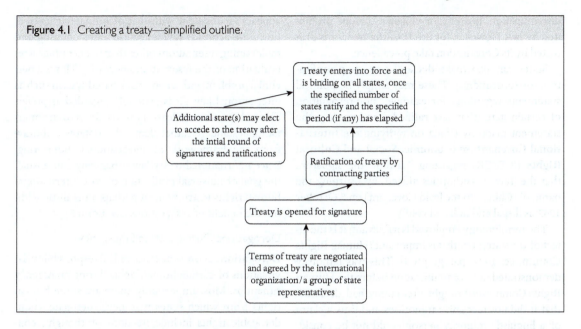

Figure 4.1 Creating a treaty—simplified outline.

this stage, the state is a signatory to the treaty. Most human rights treaties can have a large number of state parties. Article 18 of the Vienna Convention on the Law of Treaties stipulates that states should act in accordance with the terms of a treaty during the period between signature and ratification. That is not, however, the end of the matter. Generally, a state confirms its consent by **ratification** or acceptance of the treaty. This usually follows state-specific national procedures. The instrument of ratification should be deposited with the specified body, usually the UN Secretary General's office, for communication to other **contracting states**. Treaties usually specify a minimum number of ratifications necessary for the treaty to enter into force.

As commentators like Bayefsky (2001) note, some states may ratify a treaty as a political act, to enhance their reputation or placate critics, without having any intention of complying fully. The use of reservations (as we shall see) aids this. Hathaway (2007, p. 592) identifies the potential for domestic legal enforcement of the terms of the treaty and the positive collateral political consequences of the decision to ratify as key incentives for states to commit to international human rights treaties.

Reservations and Declarations after Ratification

Even if a state does elect to ratify a human rights treaty, there are a number of legal ways in which a state can avoid responsibility for its terms. States may enter reservations and declarations either on ratification or at any time thereafter. These are statements of intent entered by the state and communicated to

other parties to the treaty. In effect, they provide a mechanism for a state to opt out of the provision in question, either partly or in whole. A simple **reservation** may exclude liability for a specific article of the treaty. More controversial are those that seek to pervade the entire treaty—for example, Saudi Arabia's statement on ratification of the Convention on the Elimination of all Forms of Discrimination Against Women (CEDAW) that, in the event of a conflict between the Convention and Islamic law, the Kingdom would not be obliged to follow the Convention. Although objected to by a number of European states, the Saudi reservation remains in force.

International law treats reservations that are incompatible with the object and purpose of the treaty as void (ineffective). This view is derived from the opinions of the **International Court of Justice (ICJ or World Court)** in the Genocide Case (1951, ICJ Reps 15) and of the Human Rights Committee (1994). While the argument that states should not be able to opt out of fundamental human rights has merit, for states the process can be more complicated. Thus the USA's reservation transmitted on ratification of the ICCPR: 'That article 20 does not authorize or require legislation or other action by the United States that would restrict the right of free speech and association protected by the Constitution and laws of the United States.' This reservation is potentially problematic as Article 20 provides that any propaganda for war shall be prohibited by law and any advocacy of national, racial, or religious hatred that constitutes incitement to discrimination, hostility, or violence shall be prohibited by law. However, for the USA the freedoms protected by its Constitution take precedence.

States can also make **declarations** upon ratification, or subsequently. These may simply be political statements regarding, for example, non-recognition of certain states that have ratified the treaty (e.g. the statement made by China on ratifying the **International Covenant on Economic, Social and Cultural Rights** (ICESCR) regarding Taiwan: 'the signature that the Taiwan authorities affixed, by usurping the name of 'China', to the [said Covenant] on 5 October 1967, is illegal and null and void').

The terminology employed is irrelevant; it is the effect of the statement that is important (Human Rights Committee, 1994, paragraph 3). This was famously demonstrated in a communication before the Human Rights Committee brought after France had 'declared' that it did not recognize minorities and thus a claim of a linguistic minority person could not be considered by the Committee (*Guedson* v. *France*, UN Doc. CCPR/C/39/D/219/1986).

Reservations constitute a significant problem for proponents of universal human rights. While states will sign and ratify treaties, the efficacy of their actions can be undermined by reservations entered to negate key provisions. Although the concept of reservations appears inconsistent with that of human rights treaties, little action is taken against states entering and maintaining reservations other than to encourage a re-evaluation of the reservation's necessity. This is a perennial problem with a consensus-based system such as international law—it is generally regarded as preferable to have states at least try to conform to the international standard rather than to have states withdraw from the framework of international monitoring. Since international treaty law is basically consensual, the goal of universal ratification of core international human rights instruments is perhaps unrealistic without the benefit of reservations (see Box 4.3).

Derogations During a State Emergency

Derogations allow states to avoid all responsibility for violations of certain human rights during emergency situations. Most importantly, there are some human rights from which states may never derogate—non-derogable rights include freedom of thought, conscience, and religion, and the prohibition on torture (see, for example, Article 4(2), ICCPR). Each treaty stipulates whether derogation is possible and, if so, from which provision(s). Some treaties do not permit derogations (e.g. ICESCR, due to the nature of those rights—we will go on to discuss the African Charter on Human and Peoples' Rights).

BOX 4.3 ALTERNATIVE POINTS OF VIEW ON UNIVERSAL RATIFICATION OF THE CORE HUMAN RIGHTS TREATIES

For a great many states ratification has become an end in itself, a means to easy accolades for empty gestures. The problem has arisen in part because of a deliberate emphasis on ratification.

The primary goal of the UN community has been to achieve universal ratification of the human rights treaties. The underlying belief is that once universal ratification is realized, the implementation techniques can be strengthened. Once committed to participation, states will find it difficult to pull out and will find themselves ensnared in an ever-expanding network of international supervision and accountability.

In the meantime, ratification by human rights adversaries is purchased at a price, namely, diminished obligations, lax supervision, and few adverse consequences from non-compliance. The cost of membership has been deliberately minimized.

(Bayefsky, 1996)

The emphasis upon promoting universal ratification is an essential one in order to strengthen and consolidate the universalist foundations of the United Nations human rights regime. Despite the fears of some critics, the quest for universal ratification need not have any negative consequences for the treaty regime as a whole.

(Alston, 1997, paragraph 23)

There is clear evidence … that states with strong domestic institutions and poor human rights records are less likely to join human rights treaties than states with weaker domestic institutions that have similar records. That is true even though democracies as a whole—which realize more domestic collateral benefits from membership than non-democracies, because the constituencies favouring human rights treaties tend to be stronger—are more likely to join human rights treaties. Moreover, consistent with the prediction that collateral incentives are at work, newer regimes, which stand to gain larger collateral benefits from treaty membership, have a higher likelihood of joining human rights treaties. Also consistent with the approach, states in regions with higher levels of human rights treaty commitment are themselves consistently more likely to join those treaties.

(Hathaway, 2007, p. 613)

Measures justifying derogation must be of a temporary and exceptional nature. Generally, the emergency must pose a genuine threat to the existence or stability of the state and the state must have legally proclaimed a state of emergency. The UK has a notable history of entering lengthy derogations, claiming justification on the basis of the perceived threat from terrorists in Ireland and Northern Ireland in the latter part of last century.

The power to derogate should be limited to extreme situations. It is not a way for states to avoid human rights obligations. Moreover, even in emergency situations, human rights remain crucially important and international humanitarian law still applies. In times of war and other emergencies, human rights are more likely to be threatened and respect for them should therefore be regarded as more, not less, important.

Towards an International, Interdependent, and Indivisible System of Human Rights

Having outlined the process of becoming bound by a treaty, it is now appropriate to identify the legal obligations assumed by the states under the key international human rights treaties and to consider why there are so many treaties and other instruments.

At present, there are nine core international human rights instruments, concluded under the auspices of the United Nations (see Box 4.4). The most widely accepted treaty is the Convention on the Rights of the Child. Every UN member state, save the USA, South Sudan, and Somalia, has ratified it (on the USA and non-ratification, see also Chapter 17). Most UN states have agreed to be legally bound by several of these core treaties. They thus agree to respect the stipulated rights of individuals, protect those rights in law, and take all necessary measures to fulfil their treaty obligations.

Even in the era of the United Nations, drafting international human rights instruments proved initially to be a tortuous process. While agreement on punishing **genocide** was relatively easily reached as details emerged of the Holocaust in Europe during the Second World War, agreement on universal human rights proved more problematic. The former Commission

---

BOX 4.4 PRINCIPAL INTERNATIONAL HUMAN RIGHTS INSTRUMENTS (UN)

UN Nine Core Human Rights Treaties (note several have additional optional protocols containing further rights and/or individual communication or investigation regimes)

1. International Convention on the Elimination of All Forms of Racial Discrimination 1965.

2. International Covenant on Civil and Political Rights 1966.

3. International Covenant on Economic, Social and Cultural Rights 1966.

4. Convention on the Elimination of All Forms of Discrimination against Women 1979.

5. Convention against Torture and Other Cruel, Inhuman, or Degrading Treatment or Punishment 1984.

6. Convention on the Rights of the Child 1989.

7. International Convention on the Protection of the Rights of All Migrant Workers and Members of Their Families 1990.

8. Convention on the Rights of Persons with Disabilities 2006.

9. International Convention for the Protection of All Persons from Enforced Disappearances 2006.

Other Key United Nations Instruments

Convention Relating to the Status of Refugees 1951 (and 1967 protocol).

Standard Minimum Rules for the Treatment of Prisoners (ECOSOC) 1957.

Code of Conduct for Law Enforcement Officials 1979 (General Assembly (GA) Resolution 34/169).

Declaration on the Right to Development (GA Resolution 41/128).

Declaration on the Rights of Indigenous Peoples 2007 (GA Resolution 61/295).

The International Labour Organization's Eight Fundamental Treaties

Convention No. 29 on forced labour 1930.

Convention No. 87 on freedom of association and protection of the right to organize 1948.

Convention No. 98 on the right to organize and collective bargaining 1949.

Convention No. 100 on the issue of equal remuneration 1951.

Convention No. 105 on the abolition of forced labour 1957.

Convention No. 111 on discrimination (employment and occupation) 1958.

Convention No. 138 on minimum age 1973.

Convention No. 182 on worst forms of child labour 1999.

BOX 4.5 CHALLENGING ASSUMPTIONS: HIERARCHIES OF RIGHTS?

Are some rights more important than others? During the **Cold War**, a devastating polarization of attitudes towards human rights emerged. Communist states and many newly independent and developing states considered that rights pertaining to existence, such as rights to adequate food, shelter, education, and work were pre-eminent, while many older (Western) democracies emphasized civil and political rights such as free speech, the right to fair trials, etc. The two treaties are characterized by different obligations. The ICESCR requires states to realize the rights progressively, to the maximum of their available resources (Article 2(1)), while the ICCPR demands instant respect for its rights and provision of national remedies for violations (Article 2).

Critics argue that it is incompatible with the notion of universal human rights to have rights which are achieved progressively. Others argue that these rights (food, education, social security, work) should not necessarily be viewed as state functions. However, the millennium development goals (and the post-2015 agenda) emphasize the necessity of continually enhancing provision of basic economic and social rights (including food and healthcare). Without such basic needs, life itself is threatened. Other critics argue that economic and social rights are more expensive for states to realize—consider, however, the cost of establishing a full independent judicial system, or of training police in detention regulations and building appropriate detention facilities for use pre- and post-trial. It is clear that many rights and freedoms have explicit or implicit cost implications for states.

---

on Human Rights made great progress in drafting the Universal Declaration of Human Rights (UDHR) 1948, an aspirational tabulation of the fundamental rights and freedoms of all. Although the United Nations had only 56 member states in 1948, there were 193 member states in 2015, all of whom profess adherence to the UDHR. It is truly a universal declaration today.

The initial plan was for the 'blueprint' set out in the Declaration to be translated into treaty obligations binding on states. Unfortunately, international politics intervened and consensus could not be reached (see Box 4.5). As a result of the tension, the decision was taken to pursue two separate instruments: one focusing on economic, social, and cultural rights, the other on civil and political rights.

However, irrespective of the designation accorded to any given right, human rights are, above all, interdependent, indivisible, and universal. One cannot exercise rights of political participation without benefiting from the economic, social, and cultural right to education, to facilitate an informed choice. Similarly, the civil right to life is devoid of meaning if there is no food or clean water. The two Covenants combine to entrench the breadth of rights and freedoms espoused in the UDHR. Arguably, most of the other treaties and instruments simply elaborate their application.

Other Sources: Customary International Law and 'Soft' Law

Customary international law is the term applied to the body of rules and regulations that represent accepted state practice. Customary international law is usually agreed by most or all states, their agreement being signified by compliance rather than written agreement. Some aspects of human rights arguably reflect customary international law. The prohibition on torture and, more especially, the prohibition on slavery are examples. All states accept that slavery is contrary to international law. They are bound to prohibit slavery irrespective of whether or not they have ratified the anti-slavery treaties. More difficult is torture—although all states ostensibly prohibit it, state practice sadly seems to condone varying degrees of torture and related practices (see Chapter 15). It is thus more problematic to consider its prohibition as accepted custom. Other issues arise with definitions—there is no customary law definition of 'torture' and the treaty definition (e.g. Article 1, **Convention Against Torture and Other Cruel, Inhuman, or Degrading Treatment or Punishment**) cannot be imputed to obligations of non-contracting states. There continues to be debate over the existence and legal enforceability of customary international law. Given that so few disputes reach the ICJ, which could provide a definitive answer, a satisfactory resolution is not imminent. Moreover, with most states now party to some of the main international human rights treaties, there is less need to rely on customary international law to prove a legal obligation enforceable against the state.

In addition to the foregoing, human rights may also be found in **soft law**. Soft law is the term used to contrast with 'hard' (treaty / customary) law that produces legally binding obligations. Soft law includes a variety of different instruments concluded under the auspices of international organizations. These instruments are not technically legally binding but do enshrine principles agreed by states. Breaching soft law is not necessarily without consequences, but these are typically political rather than legal. As Shelton (2000) notes, non-binding measures are an increasing feature on the international stage. Examples include the Declaration on the Right to Development and the Standard Rules for the Treatment of Prisoners. Frequently, 'soft law' instruments precede 'hard' law—thus the Universal Declaration was subsequently legally expressed in the twin covenants, and the Declaration of the Elimination of Discrimination against Women (1967) was followed by the Convention on the Elimination of All Forms of Discrimination against Women (CEDAW) in 1979.

Soft law informs the obligations of states but does not define them. Forsythe (2006, p. 13) notes the importance of the full range of human rights 'soft law' in helping to realize non-governmental organizations' (NGO) and foreign policy objectives.

KEY POINTS

Treaties are the most common source of international human rights law. They are concluded in writing and states must accept their terms.

States can avoid certain treaty obligations through reservations, declarations, and derogations. However, reservations should not negate the object and purpose of the treaty. Derogations should only be used when absolutely necessary.

Customary international law is a source of international human rights: rights and freedoms regarded as so widely accepted that every state is bound by them.

'Soft law' constitutes another important source of international human rights insofar as it reflects the practice and opinion of states. It can be influential but is not legally enforceable.

Human rights are interdependent and indivisible. Most human rights are co-dependent on other human rights. Human rights thus form a cohesive web of rights and freedoms.

Critical Thinking Questions:

Does the existence of reservations and derogations undermine the universality of human rights, or is it simply a practicality to ensure states will agree to accept legal obligations? Would any state currently claiming to be under threat from terrorism be justified in seeking to derogate from treaty provisions? If so, which rights/freedoms and why?

Monitoring and Enforcing International Human Rights Law

A system of human rights law, as previously outlined, will clearly be of benefit in delineating the parameters of human rights protection and enshrining the entitlements of individuals (and occasionally groups). However, any benefit of having human rights is seriously eroded if those rights cannot be enforced. This section will thus examine the existing mechanisms for monitoring and enforcing human rights. The international system will be outlined first in this section, followed by regional and national systems. Inevitably, less recourse is available for the aggrieved individual at international level than at national level.

The International (United Nations) System for Monitoring and Enforcing Human Rights

In this section, the UN organs and bodies will be considered first, then the treaty monitoring bodies that oversee the implementation of the nine core human rights treaties. Other UN systems for monitoring human rights will then be outlined. Finally, a brief review of a major growth area of international activity—criminal and **transitional justice**—will complete this section.

The United Nations is clearly the most important source of human rights law. Most of the major treaties are adopted under the auspices of the United Nations or by organizations linked to the United Nations (such as UN Economic, Scientific and Cultural Organization (UNESCO), the World Health Organization (WHO), or the ILO). More pertinently, the United Nations system has developed a system of monitoring compliance with human rights (see Figure 4.2). Every single member state of the United Nations is monitored by these systems, as will be explained. However, as Tomuschat (2003, p. 7) notes, 'international protection of human rights is a chapter of legal history that has begun at a relatively late stage in the history of humankind'. Moreover, it is a system that exemplifies consensual diplomacy, with all that that entails. States will only actively participate when they feel it benefits them (politically, economically, or diplomatically). If a state feels victimized by the system, it is free to withdraw. There is thus a political balance to be achieved between effective monitoring and not alienating any state from the process. Inclusivity is important.

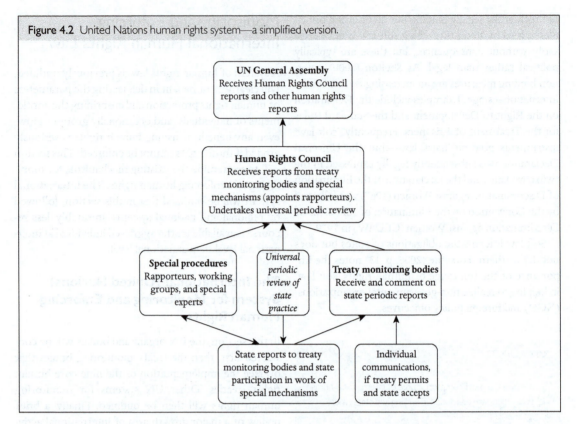

Figure 4.2 United Nations human rights system—a simplified version.

Primary (Charter) Bodies

The UN Charter and associated legislation includes machinery for monitoring compliance with international human rights law. The principal body with responsibility for monitoring compliance with human rights is the **Human Rights Council** (HRC), which was established in 2006 (see, for example, Oberleitner, 2007; Ramcharan, 2011; Freedman, 2013) following the dissolution of the much-derided Commission on Human Rights, a functional commission of the Economic and Social Council (see Article 61, UN Charter). The main criticisms against the Commission included that it was biased and secretive (e.g. Franck, 1984; Boekle, 1995; Annan, 2002, 2005).

The Human Rights Council is a subsidiary body of the United Nations General Assembly, to which it reports. It comprises forty-seven elected states and is 'responsible for promoting universal respect for the protection of all human rights and fundamental freedoms for all, without any distinction of any kind and in a fair and equal manner' (GA Resn 60/251 at 2; see United Nations General Assembly, 2006). It is imbued with power to undertake a universal periodic review

of the fulfilment by each state of its human rights obligations and commitments. This review was heralded as complementing the work of the treaty monitoring bodies (as we shall see) and not 'overly burdensome' to those involved (Human Rights Council Resolution 5/1 at 3(f) + (h)). Universal periodic review addresses international human rights law and, perhaps more controversially, international humanitarian law. However, not many states elect to comment on humanitarian issues when reviewing other states. As for the information to be consulted: states submit reports; the United Nations Office of the High Commissioner for Human Rights (OHCHR) compiles relevant reports of treaty bodies and special procedures; additional credible and reliable information provided by 'other relevant stakeholders' summarized by the OHCHR may also be used. A dialogue follows, with other states commenting, clarifying, and questioning the state report. The dialogue, including recommendations made to the state and any responses thereto, forms the basis of the final report which the Council adopts.

The HRC also has competence to receive complaints addressing 'consistent patterns of gross and reliably attested violations' of human rights and freedoms. This procedure draws heavily on its predecessor (the former Commission's 1253/1503 procedure). Human Rights Council Resolution 5/1 of 2007 provides information on the new process, which has three sequential stages: an initial admissibility review by a working group of independent experts; consideration of situations by a working group drawn from Council members; and review and/or action by the HRC. No information on the nature of the complaints or the discussions of the Council will be made public (unless the state consents).

The work of the Council is supported by a range of special procedures (*rapporteurs*)—private individuals, serving in their individual capacity to monitor compliance with human rights in different states through official visits, conceptualize potential developments in human rights, consider claims of violations of rights and freedoms, and articulate and address concerns. These special procedures may be appointed to consider a specific state (e.g. Somalia; Myanmar) or a theme (e.g. extreme poverty and human rights; rights of Indigenous peoples; freedom of religion or belief; or rights of older persons). Their appointments, terms, and conduct are governed by various instruments including a code of conduct (HRC Res 5/1 on institutional building and 5/2 on code of conduct).

The ILO and UNESCO both have distinct systems for ensuring the protection of rights protected by treaties concluded under their auspices. UNESCO also operates a system for considering communications concerning rights within its jurisdiction—primarily, the rights to education and to participate freely in cultural life as well as rights related to freedom of expression and information. Decision 104, EX/3.3 by UNESCO (1978) examines the procedures that should be followed in the examination of cases and questions that might be submitted to UNESCO concerning the exercise of human rights in the spheres of its competence. These proceedings are generally confidential.

Article 24 of the Constitution of the International Labour Organization allows for complaints by industrial associations of employers/workers who are claiming that any of the members has failed to secure effective observance of any convention. This is part of the ILO system for monitoring compliance with its human (workers') rights.

Undoubtedly, there are few remedies available to the individual under the primary international mechanisms. This is perhaps inevitable in an organization focused on the obligations that states owe each other. The confidential nature of the various systems is consonant with respect for national sovereignty and a reluctance to risk alienating states. All states are encouraged to participate, with a 'light touch' enforcement style being the inevitable consequence.

Secondary (Treaty) Bodies

In addition to the foregoing, each of the principal treaties includes a mechanism for monitoring compliance with human rights. This is a secondary system as it is based on the principal treaties and thus only applies to those states that have ratified the treaty in question. All the treaty bodies are centred and serviced in Geneva, home of the OHCHR. The composition of each committee, its powers, and functions are specified in the salient treaty (e.g. for Committee on the Rights of the Child, see the Convention on the Rights of the Child, Articles 43–5). Egan (2011) provides a detailed analysis of these bodies.

Each treaty receives and considers self-evaluative state reports at intervals specified in the relevant treaty or by the Committee. Concluding Observations issued in response to the state reports and deliberations thereon detail good practice and assess state compliance with their obligations. Non-compliance triggers no sanction. All reports are public and available online. Many committees are competent to receive complaints of violations of human rights from one state against another. However, for obvious diplomatic reasons (not least the fear of retribution) these procedures are not utilized. Some committees may undertake visits to states (e.g. Committee against Torture visits detention facilities). The core treaties can each now consider individual complaints. However, states must agree expressly, either contemporaneously with ratification or subsequently, to accept this competence and allow the relevant committee to hear individual complaints. Indeed, some of these procedures are contained in separate instruments (usually protocols) explicitly to emphasize a distinction from the scope of normal treaty obligations. In a conscious attempt to render the complaint system acceptable to states, non-legalistic terms are deployed. Thus communications are transmitted to a committee that considers the material submitted to it and issues an opinion thereon. Considering the number of assenting states, and especially in comparison to the regional systems (as we shall see), there are very few complaints by individuals. Yet surely no one can argue that this reflects predominant good state practice and contented individuals enjoying the full range of rights and freedoms to which their state has acquiesced!

The international system is often regarded as 'toothless': there is a plethora of international bodies that monitor compliance by states with accepted international human rights, but no real mechanisms for forcing states to honour their treaty obligations fully within their territory. Attempts are being made to streamline the system of reporting, rendering it less onerous on states (e.g. a core report with all the general information supported by treaty-specific information where required, rather than repeating information to different committees). Countering common state complaints should render the monitoring system more efficient. Alston (1997), Annan (2005), and Hathaway (2007), among others, suggest that, with universal ratification of many instruments approaching, improving the effectiveness of treaty obligations is the next hurdle to securing human rights. Political will has been expressed; the rhetoric must now become a reality.

Criminal Justice Mechanisms

Despite the idealistic and uniform statements on securing international peace and security that characterized the formative years of the United Nations, civil wars and international conflicts remain all too common, and they entail the violation of human rights. Although international human rights law imposes obligations on states, it is usually individuals who actually infringe rights and freedoms. This is most apparent when war crimes or crimes against humanity are committed. Can these individuals be held to account for their actions?

Following the tragedies of Rwanda and Yugoslavia in the 1990s, demands for ascribing criminal responsibility strengthened. Ad hoc international tribunals were established by resolutions of the United Nations Security Council to try those involved in the atrocities. Similar, self-funded tribunals and courts were created (e.g. Sierra Leone, Cambodia, and Indonesia) with varying degrees of involvement of the United Nations. Ultimately, the international community established a permanent International Criminal Court (see Box 4.6), with jurisdiction to prosecute individuals allegedly involved in violations of international criminal law (see Cassesse, 2003). The relevant treaty (Rome Statute of the International Criminal Court) only applies to

BOX 4.6 DECONSTRUCTING WORLD COURTS AND JURISDICTION

The International Court of Justice is often referred to as the World Court. It has jurisdiction over all international disputes referred to it by states. Individuals cannot bring complaints to the court. The ICJ can also issue advisory opinions on matters of international law.

The International Criminal Court has jurisdiction only over international criminal law violations which take place in states which have ratified the Rome Statute, and which have occurred after the Statute has entered into force for that state. Individuals allegedly responsible for atrocities are prosecuted in this court and, if convicted, can serve custodial sentences.

Many commentators (e.g. Nowak, Buergenthal) posit the creation of a new world human rights court which could hear complaints brought by individuals and groups against states concerning any human rights treaties that the relevant state has ratified. This would work with the treaty bodies. However, this option is not popular with states.

those states that accept its jurisdiction. The Rome Statute details all crimes within the jurisdiction of the court—Chapters 20 (Genocide) and 15 (Torture) in this book address two examples. Cases can be referred to the ICC by the Security Council of the United Nations (e.g. Sudan), by states themselves when they are unable (or unwilling) to prosecute (e.g. Uganda, Central African Republic), or by the Office of the Prosecutor as a result of investigations (e.g. Kenya). The ICC is effectively a last resort for bringing to justice individuals who commit specified heinous crimes. The first trials are only just concluding, so it is too early to assess its effectiveness. Still, the Court's very existence represents a significant achievement and addition to international humanitarian and human rights laws.

The emphasis in the international courts and tribunals is on prosecuting those higher up the chain of command. Slobodan Milošević (former President of Yugoslavia) was on trial for genocide and other war crimes at the ad hoc International Criminal Tribunal for the former Yugoslavia when he died in 2006 (*Prosecutor* v. *Milošević*, Case IT-02-54, incomplete). Previously, in Arusha, Tanzania the former Prime Minister of Rwanda, Jean Kambanda, was the first senior official convicted on counts of genocide (*Prosecutor* v. *Kambanda*, 4 September 1998, Case ICTR

97-23-S, upheld *Kambanda* v. *Prosecutor*, 19 October 2000, Case ICTR 97-23-A). This century, the ICC issued an arrest warrant for the then President of Sudan, Omar al Bashir, in connection with events in Darfur. There are also charges against William Samoei Ruto, suspended Minister for Higher Education, Science and Technology, and others in connection with the post-election violence in Kenya (2007–8).

Regional Human Rights Systems for Monitoring and Enforcement

Alongside the UN human rights system are a number of regional human rights systems. These are international systems, created by treaties and agreed by states. Even the rights and freedoms contained in the regional treaties bear striking similarities to those articulated in the UDHR and subsequent instruments. According to their proponents, there are many advantages to regional human rights arrangements. 'Peer pressure' is more likely to prompt a state to comply with human rights obligations within a smaller regional setting (though some regional systems have over fifty members, making that an increasingly moot point). Furthermore, the regional systems can enshrine a system of rights and freedoms that reflects regional characteristics. Nevertheless, similar rights appear in each instrument, although the African system uniquely includes collective 'peoples' rights' as well. Africa, the Americas, and Europe have adopted numerous treaties on human rights; the following brief discussion merely highlights the key arrangements of the principal regional systems.

The Organization of American States (OAS) is one of the oldest regional organizations. Its American Convention on Human Rights was, however, only adopted in 1969. This establishes a court to adjudicate disputes and allows the pre-existing American Commission on Human Rights to consider human rights infringements. The Commission can also be seized of complaints brought by individuals against states that have not ratified the Convention (e.g. *Mary & Carry Dann* v. *United States of America* (2002), Report 75/02).

The **Council of Europe** was established in 1949, after the OAS, and adopted its Convention for the Protection of Human Rights and Fundamental Freedoms in 1950. The treaty is restricted to a narrow band of civil and political rights, although the Council later adopted a Social Charter listing social and economic rights. Today, a **European Court of Human Rights** sits permanently, with competence to consider individual complaints brought by individuals against member states concerning any of the rights and freedoms in the European Convention (not Charter) and associated Protocols. It has heard two inter-state complaints (*Ireland* v. *UK* (1979), Series A, No. 25 and *Cyprus* v. *Turkey* [2001], ECHR 331) and over 100,000 individual complaints. The European Court officially supervises national conformity with human rights (another organ oversees observance of the Court's judgments). While national courts and governments retain primary responsibility for enforcing human rights, the jurisprudence of the Court is widely complied with by governments and is influential worldwide.

The African Charter on Human and Peoples' Rights (1981), more than any of the other regional systems, claims to reflect a distinctive regional set of values, giving an African 'spin' to pre-existing human rights. The Charter initially established a Commission to monitor compliance and had competence to receive individual and group complaints. These powers are being extended to a new Court created under the auspices of the African Union (which succeeded the Organization of African Unity).

In the countries of the League of Arab States, a revised Arab Charter on Human Rights entered into force in 2008 with a Committee receiving reports on progress made towards realizing human rights.

In South East Asia, the Association of South East Asian Nations (ASEAN) has adopted a human rights declaration but no formal monitoring mechanism.

National Human Rights Systems for Monitoring and Enforcing Human Rights

States, as signatories of international human rights treaties, have primary responsibility for ensuring those rights and freedoms within their territory. The obligation to protect human rights thus falls clearly on the state, but enforcement of human rights at the regional and international level remains open to criticism. States are all too often reluctant to accept the jurisdiction of international and regional bodies to receive complaints from individuals. However, some succour may be gleaned from national laws. It is ideal if individuals enjoy successful recourse to national law when human rights are infringed as the state can or should be able to remedy the raised problem swiftly.

National courts can also be used in the prosecution of violations of certain serious human rights.

National Courts: Universal Jurisdiction and Rights of Action

In terms of the core human rights treaties, states undertake to ensure that the human rights specified in the treaty are secured and guaranteed for all citizens within their jurisdiction. Most states have written constitutions, many of which enshrine human rights. An early example is the French Constitution of 1791, which included the 1789 Declaration of the Rights of Man and of the Citizen as its preamble. More recent examples are the Canadian Charter of Rights and the South African Constitution. There is usually a court empowered to review the compatibility of national law and policies with human rights. States may adopt a monist or dualist approach to treaties whereby treaties are, respectively, automatically part of national law or treated as external to national law. Creating a system whereby individuals can seek redress for violations of international and regional human rights at the national level is imperative to the success of international human rights law when the international systems appear impotent and some regional systems overburdened. There have been some successes with individuals and groups taking action in North American and European states against multinational enterprises headquartered there which are claimed to have violated rights in Asian and African states.

Additionally, violations of some human rights (e.g. torture, slavery, and genocide) are universal crimes and subject to **universal jurisdiction**—that is to say, the perpetrators can be tried anywhere in the world, irrespective of their nationality, that of the victim, or the state in which the violation occurred. Faryadi Zardad, an Afghan warlord, was convicted in the UK of conspiring to torture and kidnap in Afghanistan under the Taliban regime (first instance unreported, on appeal *R v. Zardad* [2007], All ER (D) 90). The USA has also expressed willingness to consider torture under national law (see *Filartiga v. Pena-Irala* 1980F. 2d 876 (2d cir) and Chapter 15). There should be no hiding place for those perpetrating atrocities.

National Human Rights Institutions

Given the lack of mechanisms available at the UN level and the costs and difficulties involved in engaging with the regional systems, it should be no surprise that the system of international human rights is predicated on the concept of national human rights institutions. The *Paris Principles* (see United Nations General Assembly, 1993; OHCHR, 1993) guide the international community as to what the powers, functions, and composition of a national human rights institution should be. National institutions are discussed in more detail in Chapter 5.

The systems that exist for protecting and promoting international human rights law are clearly fallible. However, in little over fifty years, a dramatic new web of mechanisms for monitoring and enforcing rights has created a paradigm shift in how individuals are viewed on the international stage.

KEY POINTS

No set of laws (international, regional, or national) can be developed and enforced without the will of the states concerned.

The United Nations has created a comprehensive system of bodies with responsibility for monitoring compliance with international human rights law. Their effectiveness depends on state cooperation in various 'constructive dialogue' processes.

The Human Rights Council has significant powers to review all state activities under its universal periodic review process. Treaty monitoring bodies have evolved over the years to become more proactive proponents of human rights, though they are dependent on the enabling treaty for their powers.

Criminal justice poses a new challenge for the international community. The International Criminal Court is one mechanism that seeks to ensure that those who seriously violate human rights can be held to account.

Regional systems operate alongside, not instead of, international human rights systems. These can be more successful at ensuring compliance with human rights having courts and/or commissions with competence to receive individual complaints against states.

Critical Thinking Questions:

Is the international system 'toothless' when it comes to protecting the rights of individuals against the actions of the states in which they find themselves? What alternative or additional enforcement mechanisms could work in the international arena? Are your suggestions likely to be acceptable to states, or is there a mechanism for imposing them on states?

Conclusion

As this chapter has demonstrated, states generally indicate their acceptance of international human rights law by agreeing to treaties. However, there are a number of ways in which states can avoid the full impact of such legal obligations: reservations, derogations, and declarations. Politically, states find adopting human rights a positive experience; legally, there are many ways they can avoid full legal responsibility for the rights and freedoms accepted. The existing mechanisms for monitoring human rights adopt a 'light' touch, encouraging states to comply with treaties through a constructive dialogue rather than forcing them through any court process. In contrast, individuals committing war crimes can be prosecuted anywhere. The 'common standard of achievement for all peoples and all nations' proclaimed sixty years ago in the Universal Declaration of Human Rights is not yet a reality. Nevertheless, without law, international human rights would be a less tangible, measurable, and enforceable concept than it is today.

? QUESTIONS

Individual Study Questions

1. What is the process followed for a state wishing to be bound to the provisions of a treaty?
2. What are the benefits of listing human rights in treaties?
3. What is the effect of a reservation on a state's legal obligations under a treaty? Can you find examples of reservations that seek to defeat the object and purpose of the treaty?
4. What is meant by interdependent and indivisible rights? Can you give some examples of this interdependence?
5. Why are the principal UN human rights treaties monitored through committees rather than courts? What benefits does such a system bring?
6. Research your state's ratification record, regional, and national human rights arrangements. What treaties have been ratified? Are there significant reservations or declarations? Can you directly action infringements of international human rights in national courts?

Group Discussion Questions

1. To what extent should the enforceability of treaties be prioritized over securing a high number of ratifications? (This is a debate that Alston and Bayefsky instigated in the 1990s.)
2. Should human rights be aspirational standards of achievement for states to strive for, or should they be clearly articulated and enforceable against each and every state under national and/or international law?
3. Examine news reports over a set period of time. Identify human rights stories. Are the human rights issues correctly identified and appropriately explored?

≈ FURTHER READING

Alfredsson, G. and **Eide, A.** (eds) (1999). *The Universal Declaration of Human Rights: A Common Standard of Achievement*. The Hague: Martinus Nijhoff.

This text comprises a series of chapters in which experts analyse the impact of each of the rights and freedoms contained in the Universal Declaration.

Hathaway, O. (2002). Do treaties make a difference? Human rights treaties and the problem of compliance. *Yale Law Journal*, **111**, 1932–2042.

Qualitative analysis of the relationship between human rights treaties and state practice.

Lijnzaad, L. (1995). *Reservations to UN-Human Rights Treaties: Ratify and Ruin?* The Hague: Martinus Nijhoff.

Expert monograph on the concept of reservations and their impact on international human rights law.

Shelton, D. (2006). *Remedies in International Human Rights Law* (2nd edn). Oxford: Oxford University Press.

The principal book reviewing remedies available for infringements of human rights.

Shelton, D. (2014). *Advanced Introduction to International Human Rights Law*. Cheltenham: Edward Elgar.

This is a very good introduction to international human rights law and the international regime.

Smith, R. (2011). *Textbook on International Human Rights* (5th edn). Oxford: Oxford University Press.

A basic introduction to international human rights law.

Steiner, H., Alston, P., and **Goodman, R.** (2007). *International Human Rights in Context: Law, Politics, Morals* (3rd edn). Oxford: Oxford University Press.

Comprehensive reader, with interpretation, on international human rights, focused primarily on legal and related philosophical issues.

Symonides, J. (ed.) (2003). *Human Rights: International Protection, Monitoring, Enforcement*. Aldershot: Ashgate and Burlington, VT: UNESCO.

Expert essays on the problems and processes of monitoring international human rights law.

 ## WEB LINKS

http://www.ohchr.org   The website of the United Nations Office of the High Commissioner for Human Rights (OHCHR) provides access to all UN human rights treaties as well as the texts of all Committee (treaty monitoring body) reports. It is easy to navigate around and contains copious links to additional materials.

http://www.bayefsky.com   Professor Bayefsky's website focuses on the work of the treaty monitoring bodies of the United Nations. It has a particularly useful thematic search facility.

http://www.icc-cpi.int   The website of the International Criminal Court provides access to the documentation surrounding the current warrants, and pre-trial and trial proceedings.

http://www.echr.coe.int   The website of the European Court of Human Rights includes a search engine facilitating access to the jurisprudence of the Court. This website is included as the European Court has produced the greatest volume of regional jurisprudence.

 Visit the Online Resource Centre that accompanies this book for updates and a range of other resources: www.oxfordtextbooks.co.uk/orc/goodhart3e/

5

Human Rights in Comparative Politics

Sonia Cardenas

Chapter Contents

Reader's Guide

Comparative politics—the study of political life within countries—has contributed significantly to our understanding of human rights. On the one hand, this subfield of political science has advanced our knowledge of why states sometimes violate internationally recognized human rights, whether by arbitrarily killing people or practising torture or by not assuring that they attend school, drink clean water, and have access to adequate healthcare. Both domestic incentives and exclusionary ideologies, we know, increase the likelihood of rights violations. On the other hand, comparative politics has attempted to explain human rights protection, showing how domestic structures (both societal groups and state institutions) can influence reform efforts. This chapter begins by considering alternative logics of comparison, including the merits of comparing a small versus a large number of cases and human rights within or across regions. The leading domestic-level explanations for why human rights are violated and protected are then reviewed, followed by a discussion of how domestic–international linkages can be indispensable for explaining otherwise perplexing human rights outcomes. The chapter concludes with an overview of the various ways in which, in the context of globalization, comparative politics shapes human rights practices.

Introduction

Human rights and domestic politics go hand in hand. Despite the importance of international relations (Chapter 3), domestic politics is vitally important to understanding contemporary human rights. Most human rights abuses occur within the borders of a single country, even if their effects spill over into neighbouring states and elicit global pressure. Human rights norms, moreover, are fundamentally about how states should treat those under their authority. When rights are violated, the domestic context helps to reveal the sources of abuse, the strength of resistance, and the prospects for change. Could we understand the killing fields of Cambodia, apartheid in South Africa, feminicide in Latin America, past civil rights struggles in the United States, the persistence of torture and child soldiers, or the proliferation of human rights treaties without examining domestic politics? Put simply, domestic factors (political, economic, and social) are inextricably linked to human rights practices.

Comparative politics—the systematic study of domestic political life, or politics within countries—is an essential tool for grappling with human rights complexities. Its focus is on how domestic interests, identities, and institutions shape political outcomes. Both the state and society are important domestic actors influencing human rights practice. Methodologically, comparativists highlight similarities and differences between countries and over time, seeking to isolate significant causes and offer compelling explanations. They compare, not only countries as wholes, but the many discrete and varied political phenomena within countries to achieve a better understanding of the rich diversity of political life in the world. These methods and explanations are the hallmark of comparative human rights research.

Indeed, human rights practices lend themselves particularly well to comparative research because they vary so widely. For example, it is not altogether self-evident why states violate (and protect) human rights to such differing degrees. Why do human rights violations occur, and what are the sources of human rights reform? This chapter is structured around these central questions. The chapter also discusses how comparative politics and international relations are closely interconnected. To put these issues in context, we open with an overview of alternative strategies for comparing human rights practices in an increasingly interdependent world.

The Logic of Comparison

Comparing human rights practices is an essential tool for understanding the sources of abuse and reform. Comparisons allow us to isolate similarities and differences meaningfully, in an attempt to understand underlying causal mechanisms. Take the example of truth commissions (see Chapter 22). If the goal is to understand the conditions under which truth commissions are effective, studying only one commission may be of limited value. Guatemala, for example, had a very well-known truth commission in the 1990s, but focusing on this alone could be misleading: the findings could be unique to Guatemala, given the country's long and bloody civil war and its large rural Indigenous population. A more useful approach would be to compare Guatemala's commission with its counterparts elsewhere (Hayner, 2002). In general, drawing broader conclusions about human rights practices requires comparing cases across space or over time.

Scholars have applied various logics of comparison to understand human rights outcomes better, and these strategies are available to any student of human rights. Three sets of approaches, in particular, depict the state of comparative human rights research: single case studies; multiple cases using **quantitative methods**; and a small number of cases, compared within a region or cross-regionally. Each approach has its strengths and weaknesses.

First, one can examine human rights in a single case, with an eye to determining changes over time. The advantage of focusing on only one case such as South Africa is that, given limited time and resources for conducting research, it affords greater depth and detail of coverage. The disadvantage is that evaluating human rights in a single episode can be of limited generalizability—that is, hard to extend to other cases.

Second, human rights practices can be compared across multiple cases, relying on either a large or small number of cases. A very large number of cases can be examined using statistical methods; this quantitative approach requires careful measurement of human rights conditions and other factors (see Chapter 8). The advantage of this approach is that numerous factors can be considered simultaneously and the findings can be relatively reliable. Large-scale comparisons are routinely used in studies seeking to explain why states engage in repression. A typical study might examine more than a hundred countries around the world over a ten-year period or longer, measuring different types of repression (e.g. torture and arbitrary killings) and a range of potentially relevant variables. The difficulty is that the analysis may not be as rich in historical or other detail. And while large-scale quantitative studies can tell us how different factors are related to one another—i.e. correlated in a statistically significant manner—these studies are not always capable of tracing causal mechanisms. For example, establishing that democracy and human rights protection are correlated is not the same as showing *why* democracy enhances human rights. Yet the logic underlying this claim may have important policy implications for those deciding whether force should be used to promote democracy abroad.

Third, fewer cases may be compared without having to rely on statistical methods. Such comparisons can either be restricted to a single region of the world or span more than one region. Even comparing two cases can be very productive, as long as the comparison is structured carefully so that the same questions are addressed across the different cases. A study (Hertel, 2006) comparing why transnational human rights campaigns vary in their effectiveness illustrates this. That study compared transnational campaigns surrounding economic and social rights in Bangladesh and Mexico: while the two countries were very similar in many ways, the campaigns succeeded to varying

degrees, revealing how domestic politics mediates transnational influence.

As for comparing human rights practices within a single region—Africa, Asia, Europe, or Latin America—there may be compelling reasons for doing so. The evidence suggests that countries within a single region are more likely to have similar human rights practices, including treaty ratification and levels of abuse (see Table 5.1). Comparative politics itself, moreover, has until recently been organized largely in terms of 'area studies', on the assumption that regions are somewhat unique. Likewise, elaborate regional systems of human rights protection—comprising **treaties** and other institutions—exist in Europe, the Americas, and Africa, reinforcing the view that regions are unique: rights protections are fairly similar within a region but rather different across regions.

Cross-regional human rights comparisons are nonetheless on the rise, as the previous example of Bangladesh and Mexico indicates. The area studies approach has come under critical scrutiny, as observers question the value of treating regions as unique entities in the context of globalization. The tendency today is to treat regions less as natural, discrete, and unchanging blocs—cultural stereotypes—and more as historically constructed, diverse, and dynamic entities. Cross-regional comparisons provide an emerging and potentially productive tool for understanding human rights practices around the world.

Table 5.1 Human rights practices by region, post-2000.

Human rights practice	Africa	Asia	Europe and North America	Latin America and the Caribbean
Disappearances	Low	Low	Low	Low
Extra-judicial killings	Medium	Medium	Low	Medium
Political imprisonment	Medium	Medium	Low	Low
Torture	High	Medium	Medium	Medium
Freedom of association	Medium	Medium	High	High
Freedom of movement and speech	Medium	Medium	Medium	Medium
Electoral self-determination	Medium	Medium	High	High
Religious freedom	Medium	Low	Medium	Medium
Workers' rights	Medium	Medium	Medium	Medium
Women's economic and social rights	Medium	Medium	High	Medium

Note: Adapted from CIRI Human Rights Data Project (http://www.humanrightsdata.com/).

The Sources of Human Rights Violations

Understanding why human rights violations occur is essential. Only by comprehending the root causes of abuse can effective human rights policies be devised to prevent future violence. It is no surprise that scholars have invested a great deal of energy in explaining the vexing question of why human rights abuses occur. What moves people to commit atrocities against others, even their neighbours, and why do states fail to protect people's basic economic and social rights? The conventional wisdom often points to evil or apathetic individuals as the source of human rights violations (see Box 5.1). A comparative perspective tells us, however, that most human rights violations are fundamentally political—i.e. acts of violence or exclusion, most often by the state, against those it considers a threat.

Human rights violations can take different forms and occur to varying degrees. Of all human rights abuses, **physical integrity violations** have perhaps attracted the most attention. More commonly known as repression, coercion, or state terror, physical integrity violations entail the use or threat of violence by the

government or its agents. These violations can include torture, extra-judicial killings, political imprisonment, and **disappearances**. Additionally, economic, social, and cultural rights, which span a broad range of subjects, can also be violated. Yet despite their basic significance, as we shall discuss, violations of economic and social rights have often been ignored in the human rights field (see Hertel and Minkler, 2007).

Incentives and Ideologies

Most accounts in comparative politics begin with the premise that human rights violations are choices made by rational decision makers. Accordingly, these decision makers calculate the costs and benefits of alternative courses of action and 'choose' to violate human rights. Proceeding from this assumption, scholars have attempted to understand which factors are most likely to be important. Under what conditions, that is, will decision makers think it is beneficial to violate human rights, or too costly not to do so? Here there is some disagreement.

One promising framework looks to both the incentives decision makers face and the role of ideologies. Incentives can take many forms; Table 5.2 identifies some of the most prominent (see Carey and Poe, 2004). While the evidence is mixed, some conditions do seem to increase substantially the likelihood of human rights abuse; these include past repression, low levels of democracy, weak economic development, and war, as well as the existence of domestic political threats and dissent. The effects of past abuse, in particular, are straightforward but crucial. For example, once a state

Table 5.2 Sources of human rights abuse: hypotheses and evidence

Source	Hypothesis	Evidence
Past repression	Repression in the recent past makes future abuse more likely	Strong
Democracy	Lower levels of democracy result in higher levels of rights abuse	Strong
Economic development	Human rights violations are greater in poorer countries	Strong
International and civil war	Human rights abuses are more likely in the context of war	Strong
Threats and dissent	Human rights abuses are greater when states face armed threats and social dissent	Strong
Population size	Countries with large populations have higher levels of human rights abuse	Strong
Military regimes	Countries with military regimes tend to violate human rights more frequently	Strong
Economic growth	Rapid economic growth leads to greater human rights violations	Mixed
Population growth	Human rights violations are greater in countries with high population growth	Mixed
British cultural influence	Human rights abuses are greater in countries that were *not* British colonies	Mixed
Leftist regime	Countries with a leftist political regime are more abusive	Mixed
International trade	Countries with low levels of international trade engage in greater human rights violations	Mixed
Ethnic or cultural diversity	Ethnically divided countries are more likely to abuse human rights	Mixed

engages in torture it can be difficult to break the cycle. Torture, after all, depends on an institutional apparatus that may be costly to dismantle. Rules and regulations often lay the foundations for torture, defining the permissible limits of state action; organizational structures arrange state agents into specialized units (e.g. death squads), while prisons and clandestine detention facilities allocate physical 'spaces' for torture to occur. In short, reversing a policy of human rights violations requires far more than sheer political will.

Beyond the structural incentives that shape decision makers' calculations about violating human rights, **exclusionary ideologies** define the conditions under which it is *acceptable* to target or exclude certain categories of people. Indeed, ideologies and identities can be powerful **non-materialist** sources of human rights abuse (Cardenas, 2007). Whereas international law stipulates that human rights be applied universally to all people, national ideologies and identities often exclude or marginalize groups of people from human rights protection.

Among the most powerful exclusionary ideologies is **national security doctrine**, which legitimates the state's use of extra-legal measures to contain social instability and guarantee national security. This ideology was very influential during the **Cold War**, especially in Latin America, and it has seen something of a resurgence in the context of the 'war on terror'

after 9/11. National security doctrine and similar ideologies provide a rationale for why it is acceptable and even necessary to respond to societal challenges with human rights abuse. Opponents are labelled 'enemies', 'subversives', and 'terrorists', regardless of the more complex political reality. Without understanding the role of such ideologies, it is not self-evident why states would so often respond to armed threats with violence. States tend to be far more powerful than extremist groups, capable of marshalling substantial bureaucratic resources (including law enforcement agencies and legal systems) to contain perceived threats. Violence is rarely *necessary*, but it is quite often deemed appropriate.

Exclusionary ideologies can also deny some people human rights protections on the basis of their identity. Those whose identity is perceived as somehow threatening to mainstream identities can become the targets of systemic discrimination. Such ideologies often underlie the marginalization of people on the basis of gender, sexual preference, race, religion, or ethnicity. For instance, in many parts of the world, gay, lesbian, bisexual, and transgendered persons are targets of violence (see Chapter 11). Even in cases where the state does not actively persecute people on the basis of their identity, it often fails to investigate cases of abuse and punish perpetrators. In Mexico, for example, *feminicide*—the systematic and targeted killing of poor women—continues unabated, with little intervention from state authorities. Similar stories can be told of the persecution of ethnic and religious minorities around the world.

Exclusionary ideologies are most influential when they are institutionalized. For instance, when exclusionary ideologies become embedded in national laws, they help structure the routines and procedures followed by state agencies. Remarkably, most states take the trouble to justify human rights abuses in terms of national laws, including resorting to 'emergency' (i.e. exceptional) rule or legislation to legitimize actions that are illegal internationally. Exclusionary ideologies also become part of professional training, part and parcel of how ordinary people can be transformed into torturers (Chapter 15). When agents of the state are indoctrinated about the threats that certain groups pose to national well-being and survival, and then given the tools to coerce, they are primed to commit unfathomable atrocities in the name of national security. In other cases, exclusionary ideologies can be transmitted by the media, as they were by powerful elites who used Rwanda's airwaves in the days preceding the 1994 **genocide** to fan the flames of Hutu animosity toward the Tutsi population. Exclusionary ideologies may not be as readily measured or tested as other factors, but they are no less fundamental, underlying virtually all human rights abuses.

To summarize, human rights are violated because decision makers calculate that there are benefits to doing so (or costs to not doing so). Perceived threats are especially significant and often underlie human rights violations. Yet what constitutes a threat can only be understood in the context of institutionalized ideas and ideologies. These non-material factors structure values, options, and identities, defining who is fully and equally human and which behaviours are appropriate. When ideologies and incentives converge, so that state actors view a group or situation as fundamentally threatening, human rights violations are likely to ensue.

The 'Invisibility' of Economic and Social Rights

Despite their differences, all human rights are to some extent interdependent, meaning that the protection of any one set requires to some extent the fulfilment of the others. This is because people have intersecting identities: those who are poor are also more likely to

belong to other marginalized groups, such as women, Indigenous people, undocumented workers, or those whose sexual identity does not conform to the mainstream. Thus, the targets of civil and political rights abuses are also more likely to be living on the economic margins of society and to be suffering social rights violations. Poverty, moreover, underlies the abuse of civil and political rights, just as it constitutes a violation of economic and social rights. In practice, rights are commonly abused in tandem, even if this is not a matter of intentional state policy.

The question still remains of why economic and social rights are so often disregarded despite international laws to the contrary. One possibility concerns the fact that these violations do not entail direct, intentional bodily harm, which tends to generate strong sympathy from onlookers (Keck and Sikkink, 1998). Neither can these abuses be readily traced to the state and its agents, making social mobilization less likely. Indeed, in the case of economic and social rights, *who* exactly is responsible for hunger, poverty, substandard education, or poor employment conditions is relatively uncertain; torture, in contrast, often leaves clear physical marks and can be traced more readily to a state hierarchy. Given these differences, it may be unsurprising that international actors have emphasized the *progressive realization* of economic and social rights, with the assumption being that these rights are costly to implement and can only improve gradually over the long term. That these were the rights supported by the Eastern bloc during the Cold War, most closely associated with communism and socialism, has only exacerbated their invisibility among some Western powers, including the United States.

Yet economic and social rights are central to domestic governance. Few people would dispute that economic policy making is important or that education, healthcare, employment, and housing are essential political topics. Both in developing countries and in advanced industrialized economies, poverty and income inequality mean that millions of people have their basic needs unmet—needs to sustain a simple life of dignity that most of us take for granted, including access to shelter and food; healthcare and education; a fair wage, earned under safe working conditions; and running water.

Despite the fact that these are internationally recognized human rights, governments often remain reluctant to support them. After all, once something is acknowledged to be a right within a domestic system, the failure to protect that right can lead to concrete social demands—in the courts or on the streets. In some cases, developing countries, which are often among these rights' strongest advocates, face especially daunting challenges in protecting economic and social rights; that is, even when the political will exists, the capacity to deliver basic rights may be missing. For post-colonial states, whose economic systems were heavily skewed by their incorporation into the world economy, placing them in a highly dependent position, their ability to develop at a pace that protects economic and social rights is often severely constrained. The politics of post-colonial states is also often such that ruling elites have an interest in maintaining the status quo and their own positions of power, whereas talk of economic and social rights may risk an unpalatable redistribution of resources.

In any country, awareness of economic and social rights can lead to vocal demands and grievances, as groups mobilize and deploy the powerful transnational discourse of human rights. This can be true of Indigenous peoples seeking to reclaim land from multinational corporations, sweatshop workers demanding a safer environment and higher wages, or healthcare advocates in rural villages wanting ready access to anti-retroviral drugs to combat HIV/AIDS. As these examples suggest, in a globalizing world, the demand for economic and social rights can clash with the interests of both states and 'markets'. For these reasons, governments often emphasize the difficulties in protecting these rights, or they reject them altogether, essentially rendering them invisible.

Can Human Rights Abuses be Prevented?

The sources of human rights abuse are no doubt complex, reflecting a combination of factors. Non-democracy, armed conflict, poverty, and exclusionary ideologies are especially significant. Together, these factors push state leaders to abuse human rights. If human rights abuses reflect to some extent political choices, and the evidence strongly suggests they do, then political reform is at least possible; and the policy implications of this analysis are quite substantial.

This analysis flies in the face of many popular explanations, which trace human rights abuses to static views of human nature and group conflict. Indeed, conventional accounts often assume that human rights atrocities occur because people (or at least some

people) are essentially evil or because some groups are simply too different, unlikely to live peacefully alongside one another, or to provide generously for each other. This **essentialist** perspective is deeply sceptical about the human capacity to overcome natural propensities or deeply ingrained patterns of interaction. In contrast, insights from comparative politics suggest that human rights violations can be combated with concrete strategies.

Preventing human rights abuses requires a comprehensive policy of promoting democratic forms of governance, demilitarization, and development, while challenging exclusionary ideologies. Unfortunately, there is no short cut to a world without human rights violations. Long before international human rights norms began to take hold in the twentieth century, sovereign states coerced and marginalized those within their borders, privileging some groups over others, as a way of retaining and extending their control. These dynamics will not disappear in contemporary politics just because certain practices are now internationally outlawed and labelled a human rights violation. Since human rights abuses remain fundamentally political acts, they can be prevented only by targeting their root causes. The alternative of simply promoting compliance with international norms or the virtues of human rights is, sadly, insufficient. At the same time, it is incumbent on activists to frame economic and social grievances—including the core problem of poverty—in terms of human rights. Showing how violations of one set of rights undermine other rights and how all rights abuses can be potentially destabilizing are other useful strategies. In general, arguments linking different human rights to one another are likely to have the most traction in a globalizing world.

Despite extensive research into the sources of human rights violations, students of human rights still have their work cut out for them. One crucial question concerns the role of international trade and globalization (see Hafner-Burton, 2009). Ongoing debates in this area have enormous policy consequences, since economic leverage remains a key foreign policy tool in the human rights arena (Chapters 12 and 13). Should countries continue trading with egregious rights violators such as China? In other words, is economic engagement ultimately better for human rights because it creates openness to new ideas as much as new markets? And how exactly do global trade and financial flows affect the protection of particular economic and social rights in local communities? If labour or subsistence rights, for example, are to be protected in a country, it is important to understand more precisely why they are violated. Indeed, preventing human rights abuses of all kinds requires grappling first with their underlying sources.

KEY POINTS

Physical integrity violations, also known as state repression, are among the most notorious human rights abuses. They are the product of both rational incentives and exclusionary ideologies.

Among the most significant incentives that state leaders face to violate human rights are past repression, low levels of democracy, poverty, war, and social threats or dissent. The role of other factors (including economic growth, trade, or ethnic and cultural diversity) is far more uncertain.

Exclusionary ideologies define the conditions under which it is deemed appropriate and even necessary to violate human rights norms. National security doctrines, which are used to justify suspending rights to maintain national stability, are one important type of exclusionary ideology; broader ideologies of discrimination like racism or sexism are others.

Although all human rights are interdependent, violations of economic and social rights have remained relatively invisible, as states resist the apparently high costs of protecting society's most marginalized groups.

Preventing human rights abuses requires targeting the roots of abuse—weak democracy, militarization, poor development, and exclusionary ideologies—not just promoting human rights standards.

Critical Thinking Questions:

Are human rights violations inevitable? What role, if any, does dehumanization play? When non-state actors commit human rights abuses, how should we understand the role of the state?

Internalizing Human Rights

If violations are one side of human rights practice, protection is the other. Comparative politics is crucial for understanding both dimensions, including the processes by which a system of abuses is reformed. Even if international actors exert pressure on non-compliant states to initiate human rights reform, the domestic context can be essential. Societal groups and state institutions must embrace international norms

if human rights protection is to take root. Where social support for human rights protection is absent, human rights reform is difficult to imagine, let alone realize. Where human rights norms are weakly embedded in state institutions—including the political regime, legal system, and governmental human rights agencies—human rights reforms are likely to remain superficial and weak. Just as preventing violations requires targeting the root sources of abuse, it also necessitates that human rights norms be incorporated into domestic structures. The **Vienna World Conference on Human Rights (Vienna Conference)**—a path-breaking global conference in 1993 that charted the course of post-Cold War human rights policy—recognized this. In its final document, the Conference highlighted the role of domestic legal systems, human rights education, national human rights institutions, **non-governmental organizations** (NGOs), and the media.

The 'Spiral Model'

In most cases, human rights change entails a long-term process, usually imperfect and contradictory, wherein state–society relations gradually evolve to accommodate human rights norms. This depiction is consistent with what some scholars have called the **spiral model of human rights change** (Risse, Ropp, and Sikkink, 1999). According to this model, human rights change tends to occur in stages, as states confront pressures both from 'above' (internationally) and 'below' (domestically). In response to these pressures, states initially deny abuses, then they begin making small concessions, move to more concrete if still sometimes cosmetic reforms, and eventually—in some cases—alter their behaviour so that it is consistent with internationally recognized human rights norms.

Whether or not human rights reform occurs is of course highly contingent. It depends on numerous factors, including whether human rights pressure is applied consistently, and how domestic conditions evolve. For example, some states may begin making nominal human rights reforms, including releasing political prisoners and undertaking legal reform, but fall short of full compliance. As long as armed conflict persists, or civil society remains weak and divided, human rights progress will be limited and incomplete.

The spiral model is most helpful in suggesting that human rights change occurs incrementally. Even government responses that seem purely cosmetic can lead over time to consequential reforms. The model also emphasizes the dual importance of state and non-state actors, domestically and internationally, who in the to-and-fro of communicating with each other contribute to human rights change. Even if critics sometimes question the model's more general applicability, it can be applied innovatively to a small number of cases to help elucidate complex human rights outcomes (see Shor, 2008).

Overall, the spiral model and broader comparative research emphasize the role of both societal groups and state institutions in shaping human rights protection. While social pressure is necessary, especially against highly repressive regimes, reform is most fully successful only when a state has 'internalized' human rights. For a state that has internalized human rights norms, national commitments stem from a sense of obligation rather than from external pressures or incentives. In short, human rights reforms succeed best when they reflect domestic commitments.

Societal Groups

From the Mothers of the Plaza de Mayo in Argentina, who marched weekly in the central government square to protest against the disappearance of their children, to national **Helsinki committees** formed secretly in East European countries during the Cold War to oppose Soviet rule, to student activists who defiantly blocked Chinese tanks in Tiananmen Square, the world has vivid images of human rights groups confronting repressive regimes. And yet it remains difficult to understand why and how people bravely mobilize on behalf of human rights, often at great risk to their lives; nor is it self-evident why such groups can ever be effective against highly repressive regimes. Comparative politics provides valuable insights into the origins and successes of domestic human rights movements.

Human rights groups and movements (see Chapter 9) can organize and mobilize for various reasons, reflecting both their own strength and the opportunities that the broader political environment provides them. Part of the reason why some groups mobilize relates to the power of individual leaders who inspire and energize others, such as Martin Luther King Jr, who was integral to the civil rights struggle in the United States, or Václav Havel, who bravely championed the cause of human rights in the former Czechoslovakia. Some groups also have long-standing experience and extensive resources, including moral authority, to take a firm stand against an oppressive regime: thus religious organizations or lawyers' unions, for example, have played powerful roles in many parts of the world.

Furthermore, when oppressive states make concessions, even if they are symbolic or hypocritical, such gestures create a political opportunity for human rights groups to mobilize. For instance, if a state begins to 'talk the talk' of human rights—such as introducing human rights laws, releasing political prisoners, or ratifying a treaty—domestic groups may gain some breathing room to mobilize. As states set a new standard for themselves, domestic groups can in turn demand consistency in practice. This partly explains why human rights groups can mobilize even at the height of repression, as they take advantage of even minute political openings to stake their claims. Over time, moreover, domestic pressures can intensify, as local human rights groups enter into broader alliances with other groups in civil society. As pressure mounts, a government may become unwittingly entrapped in a process of increasing concessions. If these dynamics are sustained over time, they can even contribute to the government's downfall.

Human rights groups tend to vary in terms of their identity, falling into several (sometimes overlapping) categories. Some form broad advocacy groups, committed to human rights protections generally or the promotion of specific rights (e.g. housing, employment, health). Others focus on the rights of certain groups of people, such as women, children, migrant workers, prisoners, or other vulnerable populations. Still others are primarily professional organizations, including lawyers and health workers, committed to using their specialized skills and expertise to improve human rights conditions. Finally, religious groups often promote social justice and human rights concerns closely overlapping with their broader convictions.

Despite their diversity, domestic human rights groups rely on a wide range of mutually reinforcing strategies. They directly assist human rights victims, from providing them with legal or medical assistance to assuring that they receive other essential social services. They also lobby governments directly, pressuring them to protect human rights, whether by halting abuses, securing economic justice in the face of global markets, implementing legal reform, or holding perpetrators accountable for their wrongdoings. In all of these efforts, domestic human rights groups rely extensively on **naming and shaming**. This entails first collecting information about abuses; such documentation can be critical for exposing the truth and mobilizing support on behalf of human rights. Activists then disseminate evidence of violations, drawing attention to the gap between human rights standards and state behaviour. The goal is to embarrass, or shame, governments into complying. Very often, moreover, domestic groups engage in socialization, targeted at both civil society and state actors, as they aim to spread awareness of internationally recognized human rights norms. Socialization efforts can range from distributing pamphlets outlining basic human rights, to training state officials about their obligations under international law.

Given these numerous strategies, local human rights groups can wield far-reaching influence. At a minimum, they can help place human rights issues on a state's agenda. Even if states continue committing violations, pressure from NGOs can be significant in eliciting concessions. Internationally, the information generated by domestic groups can be crucial in mobilizing transnational alliances. Once formed, the success of transnational networks depends in turn on domestic groups, who may be perceived as having greater legitimacy than foreign actors. Finally, when human rights groups join forces with broader currents in civil society, they can play a key role in democratization. Time and again, human rights demands have played a defining role in the fall of oppressive regimes around the world. While pressure from domestic activists is rarely sufficient for bringing about significant human rights change, it is almost always necessary.

State Institutions

If human rights standards are to be protected, they have to be incorporated into state institutions. The state, after all, is the basic guarantor of human rights. It is obligated both to desist from violating human rights and, in a positive sense, to ensure that non-state actors within its borders do not violate them. When violations do occur, the state is further obligated to ensure that victims have due recourse to legal protection, that violations are investigated, and abusers are punished. These are the touchstones of respect for human rights.

Four kinds of state institution are particularly important for assuring the protection of human rights

domestically: democratic structures of governance, domestic laws and rules, national and local courts, and governmental human rights institutions or agencies. In cases where human rights standards are weakly embedded in any of these institutions, human rights protection is likely to suffer. Consequently, human rights reform often requires the strengthening of these state institutions.

Democratic Governance

Human rights standards are most likely to be protected under democratic forms of governance (Chapter 14). Just as non-democratic regimes tend to engage in higher levels of repression, democratic governance facilitates human rights protection. This is true procedurally and substantively. In democracies, individuals whose rights have been violated typically have access to the state, where they can file complaints, demand investigation, and expect accountability. More fundamentally, representative democracies tend to embrace human rights standards, including notions of human freedom and equality (Goodhart, 2005). Democratic governments are therefore far less inclined than their autocratic counterparts to violate human rights, at least civil and political rights.

Democracy in and of itself, however, does not assure full respect for human rights (see, for example, Box 5.2). The *extent* of human rights protection depends on the quality of democratic governance. For example, in weak democracies human rights protections are more likely to be compromised. This explains why human rights violations can persist even under democratization.

BOX 5.2 ALTERNATIVE POINTS OF VIEW: HUMAN RIGHTS IN ANTI-TERRORISM

There are alternative schools of thought about the place of human rights in combating terrorism. Some view human rights abuses—including by democracies—as an unfortunate necessity in countering terrorist threats. Others assert the primacy of protecting human rights even when national security itself is at stake. How exactly can a commitment to democratic governance and human rights be reconciled with the need to confront terrorist threats? *Human Rights in the 'War on Terror'*, edited by Richard Ashby Wilson, explores this complex debate from the perspective of both scholars and practitioners.

Domestic Laws and Rules

Human rights protection also reflects domestic laws and rules, which define human rights standards and regulate relevant state–society interactions. In many countries, for example, international treaty obligations are not legally binding unless national implementing legislation is passed. Where domestic laws and rules do not conform to international human rights standards, a process of **harmonization** is required, in which domestic standards are aligned with international ones. Domestic laws and rules can be enshrined in the constitution and in bills of rights, as well as in special regulations, guidelines, and procedures.

Beyond constitutions and bills of rights, a wide range of rules can specify human rights standards, define the state's precise duties, and describe the procedures to be followed when rights are violated. Administrative state agencies, moreover, have their own internal rules of relevance for human rights. For example, the rules of conduct for police officials define humane treatment and detail the consequences of non-compliance. Unless human rights standards are incorporated into domestic laws and rules, they are unlikely to have day-to-day impact.

Court Systems

National and local courts are essential for guaranteeing human rights protection. Courts vary in the extent to which they provide victims with access, refer to international standards, and abide by the **rule of law** (i.e. apply legal standards fairly across cases, rather than arbitrarily in response to political calculations). Where human rights victims have no effective recourse to courts or the rule of law is weak, violators are not held accountable for their crimes and a climate of **impunity** reigns. Weak legal systems often reflect a broader problem of political corruption, as public officials do the bidding of powerful actors rather than protect the rights of individual citizens. Court systems enhance the predictability of justice, and they are a basic prerequisite for any rights-protective society.

As international human rights law (Chapter 4) evolves, moreover, the stock of national courts actually rises. While this may seem counter-intuitive, complaints and cases cannot generally be taken before international or regional bodies until all domestic remedies have been exhausted. The **International Criminal Court** (ICC) differs somewhat. It can initiate proceedings only when domestic courts fail to prosecute or where domestic proceedings are not credible. Likewise, notions of universal jurisdiction mean that, in principle, egregious human rights cases can be tried in any national court: thus, European countries have at various times attempted to try notorious dictators like Chile's Augusto Pinochet or Chad's Hissène Habré. Domestic courts increasingly complement international legal bodies.

National Human Rights Institutions

National human rights institutions (NHRIs) are relatively new governmental bodies, designed to promote and protect human rights domestically (Cardenas, 2014). Most of these institutions have been created since the 1990s, often with active support from the United Nations. Present in over a hundred countries, NHRIs are supposed to be both independent of the executive and representative of society. These are among the key criteria identified in the 1993 Paris Principles, a defining document that stipulates the internationally recognized duties of NHRIs (see Chapter 4). National institutions that do not meet these criteria are not accredited, or recognized, internationally.

These state agencies are charged with a broad range of tasks. On the protective side, they collect petitions from individuals who allege that their human rights have been violated, investigate complaints, and make recommendations to state bodies, though their decisions are not usually legally binding. They often produce an annual report, providing statistics about complaints. In a sense, they are the domestic version of international governmental human rights bodies such as the UN **Human Rights Council**. On the promotional side, NHRIs—often in cooperation with NGOs—promote human rights education. They may help to insert human rights into school curricula (e.g. holding essay and poster contests), engage in professional training (e.g. of law enforcement officers and health professionals), or launch public education campaigns (e.g. disseminating the **Universal Declaration of Human Rights** or running radio advertisements). Despite the scepticism of some observers, and the real limitations of many of these institutions, NHRIs can potentially serve as useful intermediaries between the state and society.

Just as understanding the sources of abuse is essential to devising effective human rights policies, sustainable human rights reforms require the commitment of both societal groups and state institutions. This suggests that domestic human rights groups should be empowered, and states must be supported in building effective democratic institutions, laws and rules, court systems, and governmental human rights bodies. Where existing institutions are weak, states should be challenged to incorporate human rights standards into their domestic structures. Human rights reforms can succeed only when they enjoy domestic support: societal groups promote human rights norms, assist victims, and keep governments in check; state institutions define standards and regulate human rights practices. Both sets of actors are necessary for a strong system of human rights protection to thrive.

KEY POINTS

Human rights reform requires embedding international human rights norms in domestic structures. Both societal groups and state institutions must support human rights standards.

The process by which human rights change occurs is gradual and contingent. Responding to domestic and international pressures, states build on their prior commitments: moving from denial of abuse to cosmetic changes, to increasingly substantial changes in some cases.

Domestic human rights groups mobilize according to their resources and the opportunities provided to them by the political environment. Human rights groups follow numerous strategies, from naming and shaming to assisting victims and lobbying governments.

State institutions are essential for guaranteeing the protection of human rights. Democratic structures of governance, laws and rules (including national constitutions), court systems, and governmental human rights institutions are especially significant.

Critical Thinking Question:

Consider recent police violence and social protests in the United States relating to racial discrimination. Would adopting a human rights framework lead to change, and why?

Domestic–International Linkages

As important as comparative politics is for understanding human rights issues, it would be a mistake to overlook the significance of international factors, especially in light of increasing global interdependence (Chapter 13). In particular, domestic–international linkages often shed light on otherwise puzzling human rights outcomes. These dynamics are evident in the South African case, where societal pressure and state institutions joined with a broad spectrum of international pressures to achieve meaningful human rights change (see Box 5.3). On the one hand, domestic politics can mediate the effects of international human rights treaties and pressures. On the other hand, international actors often shape human rights practices in ways that cannot be reduced to domestic politics.

One recurring puzzle is why international human rights pressure varies in its effectiveness, both cross-nationally and over time. Why was human rights pressure so successful in Eastern Europe, South Africa, and the Southern Cone of Latin America? And why has it proven relatively ineffective when applied against countries as different as China and Cuba? Some studies (e.g. Cardenas, 2007) show that for states to alter their human rights practices dramatically in response to human rights pressure certain domestic conditions have to be met: the incentives to violate human rights have to be very low while support for human rights has to be relatively strong. This does not mean that all human rights violations will disappear, only that conditions will improve in apparent response to international pressure.

A related puzzle concerns the reasons why states commit to human rights treaties (see Simmons, 2009). Treaties, in principle, can challenge traditional notions of state sovereignty and constrain the state's room to manoeuvre. There is widespread agreement that domestic interests and institutions help to explain why states join human rights treaties. For instance, among democracies, newer democracies are more likely than long-standing ones to accept human rights treaties. This counter-intuitive outcome can be traced to the domestic interests of leaders in newer democracies, who face higher uncertainty and therefore use treaties as a way of binding a country to long-term human rights compliance (Moravscik, 2000). Among dictatorships, scholars have also emphasized the importance of 'open' dictatorships, which permit multiple political parties. Such dictatorships provide greater access to political interest groups, who can demand treaty ratification.

BOX 5.3 HUMAN RIGHTS FROM THE INSIDE OUT: THE SOUTH AFRICAN CASE

South Africa was subject to human rights pressure longer than any other country in the twentieth century. For decades, an abhorrent system of apartheid stripped the black majority of its most basic human rights. And then, in the early 1990s, apartheid ended and the country democratized: Nelson Mandela was released in 1990 after decades in prison; apartheid was formally dismantled under President F. W. de Klerk, beginning in 1991; and universal-suffrage elections were held in 1994. What explains the timing of these dramatic changes?

Above all, domestic groups such as the African National Congress engaged in active resistance, without which change would have been highly unlikely. By persisting in their armed struggle against the apartheid regime, societal groups made it clear that the state could no longer provide national security. Unlike in other countries where the state was able to crush the opposition, the minority white government in South Africa proved incapable of containing the armed threat. The strength and resilience of domestic groups was therefore crucial.

International actors played a valuable and complementary role. In particular, they provided domestic groups with arms to oppose the state and funding to strengthen their capacities, as well as entering into transnational networks of solidarity that empowered domestic groups in their ongoing struggle. Concurrently, long-standing sanctions and boycotts targeted military and cultural relations (including sports), and made it more costly for the state to continue its abuses. The apartheid regime responded with numerous concessions, even while it continued to violate human rights. In the longer term, however, human rights change became an increasingly legitimate alternative. Once the incentives to repress were gone, with the state no longer capable of controlling the armed insurrection and the economy on the verge of collapse, the time was ripe for change. The fall of apartheid in the early 1990s was the result of both domestic *and* international factors.

Democratization alone, however, was insufficient to assure a high level of human rights protection. When Mandela became president in 1994, he immediately set out to embed human rights norms domestically. For example, in 1994 he signed the Human Rights Commission Act, which created the South African Human Rights Commission—a national human rights institution envisioned in both the country's constitution and bill of rights. In practice, the institution has promoted human rights extensively, especially economic and social rights like housing, both in South African society and within state agencies. But it has also not been sufficiently critical of and independent from the state. If human rights protection is to be fully internalized in post-apartheid South Africa, state institutions must commit more completely to implementing human rights standards. They must also target the root marginalization of those experiencing human rights abuses in South Africa, including refugees, migrants, and asylum seekers, as well as those living with HIV/AIDS, women, and prisoners.

This explains why open dictatorships are more likely to ratify the Convention against Torture, for example, even though they practise torture extensively (Vreeland, 2008).

Other human rights practices can also be difficult to explain when international factors are overlooked. Two types of international influence are especially important in shaping human rights outcomes. First, international actors contribute to state repression when they send contradictory messages: publicly promoting human rights, while privately accepting ongoing violations; or applying human rights pressure but continuing to sell military equipment, for instance (Sikkink, 2004). A classic example of this is US Secretary of State Henry Kissinger's suggestion to the Argentine junta in 1976 that they finish their dirty work as soon as possible, famously giving them a 'green light' to eliminate opponents.

International factors also help to clarify why states sometimes fail to live up to their human rights commitments, despite their good intentions. For instance, states (often developing countries) can lack the capacity to implement their treaty obligations. In the human rights arena, even foregoing torture may entail enacting new laws, training members of the coercive apparatus, and strengthening legal accountability. In such situations, international actors—governments, international organizations, or multinational corporations—can be part of the problem if they fail to do their part in building domestic capacities, or, worse still, if their activities undermine domestic actors. Domestic–international linkages therefore shed light on why violations sometimes persist even when states face human rights pressures, and why human rights reform can be relatively weak despite states' best intentions.

KEY POINTS

In an increasingly interdependent world, understanding human rights practices requires examining international factors alongside domestic ones.

Domestic factors help to explain otherwise puzzling human rights outcomes, including the conditions under which international human rights pressure matters and why states commit to human rights treaties.

Domestic interests and institutions account for why states ratify human rights treaties. For example, emerging democracies and 'open' dictatorships (i.e. those permitting multiple political parties) are most likely to accept a human rights treaty.

International actors can contribute to human rights violations, accounting for why abuses sometimes persist. They can also affect states' capacities to implement human rights obligations.

Critical Thinking Question:

Given what you have learned about the role of domestic and international factors in promoting human rights reform, when should ratifying human rights treaties lead to change? Should force be used in extreme cases?

Conclusion

Human rights practices cannot be understood without some appreciation for the insights provided by the study of comparative politics. By drawing attention to the role of domestic factors, including state–society relations, comparative politics sheds valuable light on why human rights violations occur and the conditions under which reform is possible. A systematic understanding of violations and reform, in turn, is a prerequisite for devising effective human rights policies and improving human lives.

Comparative politics highlights the roles of a wide range of factors that can influence human rights outcomes. For example, comparative politics traces physical integrity violations (or state repression) to several structural conditions: weak democratic institutions, poverty, war, armed threats, and exclusionary ideologies. These factors push states to abuse human rights, even when confronted with countervailing human rights pressures. Comparative studies also suggest that human rights reform is possible only when human rights norms enjoy domestic support, both from societal groups and state institutions. While it is tempting to focus on the role of either the state or society, comparative politics emphasizes that both actors are crucial for generating human rights change.

Insights from comparative politics, however, do not produce easy answers; rather, they confirm that human rights practices are highly complex and contested. In particular, the role of international factors cannot be overlooked. In a globalizing world, domestic–international linkages are crucial determinants of human rights practice. Domestic politics, for example, help to explain why similar types of regime commit differently to human rights treaties or why states respond in widely divergent ways, even to similar international human rights pressures. Likewise, international actors can sometimes spark or prolong human rights violations; but on the positive side, they can empower societal groups while building the state's institutional capacity to implement human rights. Methodologically, comparative politics reminds students of the value of comparing human rights practices, whether relying on a few or many cases or focusing on a single region or multiple regions.

The twentieth century saw the 'internationalization' of human rights, as new global standards and institutions were created to regulate state action. Despite enormous progress, today human rights abuses persist and reforms are often limited. Comparative politics suggests that a deeper understanding of the domestic dynamics underlying human rights practices is needed. If human rights are fundamental standards for the way the state should treat society, greater attention must be paid to the domestic roots of abuse and the role of societal groups and state institutions in producing sustainable change. The twenty-first century raises the challenge of how to internalize human rights standards, translating principled norms into concrete state practice.

? QUESTIONS

Individual Study Questions

1. What is comparative politics, and why is it considered important for understanding human rights practices?

2. What are some of the major strategies for comparing human rights practices?

3. What are different types of human rights violations, and why are they deemed to occur? How do exclusionary ideologies contribute to human rights abuse?

4. Why do economic and social rights remain relatively 'invisible'?

5. Can human rights violations be prevented, and if so, how?

6. Why do domestic human rights groups mobilize, and what are some of the more effective strategies they employ?

7. Are state institutions essential for understanding human rights reform? Why or why not?

8. How do you think domestic and international politics interact to shape human rights outcomes?

Group Discussion Questions

1. Which explanations for human rights abuse do you find most compelling, and why? Which surprise you most? Which do you find unconvincing?

2. Drawing on the contributions of comparative politics, what advice would you give human rights organizations targeting an abusive regime?

3. What lessons, if any, does the South African case provide for contemporary human rights campaigns?

4. In your view, what are the potential strengths and weaknesses of national (governmental) human rights institutions?

5. How well do comparative political insights help us understand human rights violations in the United States?

≋ FURTHER READING

Brysk, A., and **Shafir, G.** (eds) (2007) *National Insecurity and Human Rights: Democracies Debate Counterterrorism.* Berkeley, CA: University of California Press.

An exploration of how democracies respond to perceived terrorist threats, this volume examines the relationship between national security and human rights protection.

Cardenas, S. (2007). *Conflict and Compliance: State Responses to International Human Rights Pressure.* Philadelphia, PA: University of Pennsylvania Press.

This book examines how and why states around the world respond to international human rights pressure, emphasizing the domestic sources of abuse.

Carey, C. and **Poe, S.** (eds) (2004). *Understanding Human Rights Violations: New Systematic Studies.* Aldershot: Ashgate.

This important volume surveys the research on human rights violations, especially physical integrity violations, and the findings from statistical studies.

Davenport, C. (2007). *State Repression and the Domestic Democratic Peace.* Cambridge: Cambridge University Press.

This book uses quantitative methods to reveal which aspects of democracy lead to state repression and which favour human rights protection.

Hertel, S. and **Minkler, L.** (eds) (2007). *Economic Rights: Conceptual, Measurement, and Policy Issues*. Cambridge: Cambridge University Press.

This volume offers a thorough examination of economic rights from a human rights perspective.

Landman, T. (2002). Comparative politics and human rights. *Human Rights Quarterly*, **24**/4, 890–923.

This article provides a valuable overview of how comparative politics contributes to the study of human rights.

Landman, T. (2005). *Protecting Human Rights: A Comparative Study*. Washington, DC: Georgetown University Press.

Drawing on a broad range of social science perspectives, this accessible book offers a framework for studying human rights problems comparatively.

Risse, T., Ropp, S., and **Sikkink, K.** (eds) (1999). *The Power of Human Rights: International Norms and Domestic Change*. Cambridge: Cambridge University Press.

This path-breaking book introduced the 'spiral model', discussing how international and domestic factors interact to produce human rights change.

WEB LINKS

http://www.escr-net.org/caselaw/   The Caselaw Database on Economic, Social, and Cultural Rights examines legal strategies used around the world for claiming economic, social, and cultural rights.

http://www.hrcr.org/   Human and Constitutional Rights is a searchable database of bills of rights and human rights in national constitutions.

http://hdr.undp.org/en/reports   Human Development Reports detail the state of 'human development' around the world, attentive to both human rights and economic development.

http://www.cidcm.umd.edu/mar/   The Minorities at Risk Project provides comparative data on politically active ethnic groups around the world.

http://nhri.ohchr.org/   This is a comprehensive website devoted to national human rights institutions around the world.

http://www.statewatch.org/   Statewatch is a non-governmental organization that monitors the state and civil liberties in European democracies.

http://www1.umn.edu/humanrts/research/   Part of the University of Minnesota Human Rights Library, this invaluable site provides hundreds of resources for researching country conditions.

 Visit the Online Resource Centre that accompanies this book for updates and a range of other resources: www.oxfordtextbooks.co.uk/orc/goodhart3e/

6

Sociological and Anthropological Approaches

Damien Short

Chapter Contents

Reader's Guide

Anthropologists and sociologists have typically been either positivists or relativists. Consequently they have been slow to develop an analysis of justice and rights, and have therefore lagged behind other disciplines in examining the most significant institutional revolution of the twentieth century—the growth of universal human rights. This chapter will discuss how sociology and anthropology eventually broke free from the shackles of a disciplinary focus on cultural relativism and legal positivism, and finally engaged with the concept of universal human rights. We will examine the key contributions to this endeavour from sociologists and anthropologists. We will see how sociology expanded its analysis of citizenship rights to that of human rights, developing a broad, yet nuanced, social constructionist interpretation, and how anthropology turned its ethnographic methodology towards an examination of the 'social life of rights', thereby side-stepping the long-standing debate of 'universalism versus relativism'. The concluding sections identify 'social constructionism' as a common bond between the disciplines, and emphasize the importance of sociological and anthropological perspectives to the study of human rights.

Introduction

Until relatively recently, the discipline of sociology has largely confined its examination of rights to the realm of citizenship (Morris, 2006, p. 1). The concept of citizenship, however, is closely linked with the modern nation state, a political form that has been infected with the problems of imperialism, globalization, migrant workers, refugees, and Indigenous peoples (Turner and Rojek, 2001, p. 109). In a seminal essay for the journal *Sociology*, Bryan Turner (1993) suggested that globalization has created problems that are not wholly internal to nation states, and that consequently we should extend sociological inquiry to the concept of *human* rights. While few sociologists have attempted, like Turner (1993), to develop a foundational social theory of human rights, there is now a growing body of research, stimulated by recent anthropological contributions in particular, which analyses the 'social life of rights' (Wilson, 1997, 2001, 2006). Moving beyond legal positivism and investigating 'beneath the surface', such studies have shown that 'rights' are not simply givens, or necessarily beneficial to the rights-holders; rather, they are the products of social and political creation and manipulation and should be viewed accordingly. In addition, unlike philosophical debates, which attempt to foreclose the ontological status of rights, recent social research has analysed rights as socially constructed phenomena and attempted to explore their meaning and use. In 1997, Richard Wilson suggested a distinct need for more detailed studies of human rights according to 'the actions and intentions of social actors, within wider historical constraints of institutionalized power' (Wilson, 1997, pp. 3–4). Since then there has been a growth in such work from both sociologists and anthropologists. In the next section we will trace the development of sociological approaches to the study of human rights, from an initial position of non-engagement, due to an emphasis on positivistic social science, to an eventual **social constructionist** engagement. We will then turn to anthropological approaches and trace their development from the now infamous American Anthropological Association's (AAA) relativistic 'Statement on Human Rights' through to the years of explicit engagement with human rights and what has been identified as the 'emancipatory cultural politics' turn and the now dominant **ethnographic** strand of anthropological engagement.

Sociology of Human Rights

Despite the ubiquity of human rights after the Second World War, sociology has had remarkably little to say about this 'age of rights' (Bobbio, 1999). Bryan Turner (1993) was perhaps the first sociologist to confront this disciplinary problem. 'It was prescient of Turner to identify this gap, at a time when few other sociologists had recognised the area of rights as central to social structures, processes and identities, and his writing on the topic is a necessary starting point for all others wishing to focus on these issues' (Morris, 2006).

Classical Sociology

Turner (1993, p. 492) began by suggesting that sociology as a discipline has no obvious foundation for a contemporary theory of rights, the blame for which he lay firmly at the door of classical social theory and its scepticism towards normative analysis of legal institutions. Consequently, he argued that **classical sociology**, as outlined by the 'founding fathers'—Marx, Durkheim, and Weber—failed to provide an ontological grounding for a theory of rights. For example, Emile Durkheim's desire to distinguish sociology from philosophy, and his injunction to treat 'social facts' as 'things', precluded normative considerations and treated moral and legal norms merely as external restrictions on the behaviour of individuals. Durkheimian sociology suffered from a severely limited positivistic focus that failed to offer adequate causal explanations for issues such as social inequality and injustice (see Turner, 1993).

Similar problems arise if we consider Weber's emphasis on 'value-free' social science and his rejection of any normative foundation for law. In his classic text, *Economy and Society*, Weber (1978) focused on certain social developments that he showed 'relativized' the law. The axioms of natural law are discredited by the conflict between formal and substantive law, the relativization of legal norms as a consequence, juridical rationalism, the decline of religious tradition, and the spread of legal rationalism. Weber (1978, p. 875) emphasized the increasing 'rationality' of law and the decline of its 'metaphysical dignity'. Thus, Weber rejected the possibility of a universalistic normative foundation for law and hence for rights (Turner, 1993, p. 494).

Turning to Karl Marx, the basis of his views on rights were documented in the essay 'On "The Jewish

Question"' (Marx, 1987), his reply to his friend Bruno Bauer's views on Jewish emancipation. The essay reflected his great interest in the revolutionary activity so prevalent in Europe at that time and, in particular, the French Revolution and the ensuing Declaration of the Rights of Man and of the Citizen, and its various updated versions. Marx considered the rights to liberty, property, security, and equality as little more than individualistic rights that serve only to divorce the individual from society.

The essence of the charge was that the primary rights in the declaration are *individualistic* in nature, and only serve to secure the property interests of the rapacious individual. Such talk of rights blinds us to the gross inequalities inherent in the world between the workers and the owners of the means of production. Thus, the implication in Marx's work is that rights *only* have a place in a society with a capitalist industry and economy, with 'a private individual pursuing material gain in a context where all his relations with others are mediated by the market and commodity exchange'. For Marx, within political society people were seen as cooperative, while in the economic roles they were competitive, individualistic, and egoistic; the theory of rights merely expressed the division and alienation of human beings (Turner, 1993, p. 492). In short, in Marx's account of capitalist civil society, law is an instrument of class domination and human rights are no more than a tool to obscure fundamental social and economic inequalities.

Thus, the legacy of this sceptical heritage was an absence of a normative basis for the study of rights, which left sociologists with no means of responding to a relativist position on rights and values (Turner, 1993). Consequently, the only substantive disciplinary engagement with 'rights' came through the concept of **citizenship**—the bundle of rights granted by the nation state to the individual citizen, and which was perceived by sceptical sociologists as less problematic since it did not appear to raise problems about universal ontology (Turner, 1993, p. 496). Thus, a sociology of citizenship functioned as a somewhat inadequate substitute for a sociology of rights.

From Citizenship to Human Rights

The concept of citizenship is closely linked with the modern nation state, but this political form has been infected with numerous problems, such as imperialism, globalization, migrant workers, refugees, and Indigenous peoples, which has raised questions about the nation state as the framework for an adequate analysis of citizenship and rights (see Turner, 1993; Turner and Rojek, 2001). As globalization has created problems (or at least, greater awareness of problems) that are not wholly internal to nation states, so the concept of citizenship rights must be extended to that of human rights. The major problem with sociology's reluctance to engage with human rights is that human rights have now become a powerful institution and play a significant role in political mediation of social conflict (Turner and Rojek, 2001, p. 119).

Turner has argued that the concept of human rights can be understood sociologically by the need to protect vulnerable human beings with social institutions, which in turn can pose threats to those human beings (Turner, 1993, p. 502). The social and legal institutionalization of human rights is the predominant modern attempt to resolve this dilemma that is inherent in modern societies. Yet Turner's analysis goes further than mere explanation. He argues that, without some universal moral grounds, it is impossible to talk about justice: 'There has to be some foundation of a universalistic character in order for such discussions about justice to take place. Otherwise we are left with a mere talking shop of difference' (Turner and Rojek, 2001, p. 112). He persuasively deploys sociological theory to explore the moral basis of a universalist doctrine of human rights and proposes that a shared experience of 'human frailty' and the 'vulnerability of the human body' provides a common ground: 'Human frailty is a universal experience of human existence' (Turner, 1993, p. 505; Turner and Rojek, 2001, p. 110). Additionally he argues that we need universal human rights due to the 'precariousness' of 'social institutions', which 'stand in a fateful relationship to human purposes, because they contradict their origins'.

The institutions that are designed to protect human beings—the state, the law, and the church in particular, are often precisely those institutions which threaten human life by the fact that they enjoy a monopoly of power.

(Turner, 1993, pp. 501–2)

Finally, Turner (1993, p. 506 [my emphasis]) invokes the notion of **collective sympathy**: 'Ultimately my argument has to assume that sympathy is also a consequence of, or a supplement to, human frailty. Human beings will want their rights to be recognised *because they see in the plight of others their own (possible) misery.*'

Social Constructionism

A few years after Turner's initial contribution, Malcolm Waters (1996) took issue with Turner's **foundationalist** approach, and advocated a social constructionist interpretation of universal human rights. He writes:

I want to argue that an adequate sociological theory of human rights must ... take a social constructionist point of view, that human rights is an institution that is specific to cultural and historical context just like any other and that its very universality is itself a human construction.

(Waters, 1996, p. 593)

Waters approaches human rights through a social constructionist lens, which emphasizes the socially created nature of social life, and accordingly views the construction of universal human rights as the product of the balance of power between political interests at a particular point in history. The rise of human rights cannot be explained simply through notions of human vulnerability, institutional threats, and collective sympathy, but rather by the assertion of powerful class interests. The original design of the **Universal Declaration of Human Rights** (UDHR) and the subsequent expansion and enforcement of the human rights principles can be explained by reference to four sets of interests (see Box 6.1).

Yet, Turner (1997, p. 566) pointed out that 'it is perfectly consistent to argue ... that human rights can have a foundationalist ontology in the notion that human beings are frail and accept the argument that human rights will be constructed in a contingent and variable way according to the specific characteristics of the societies in which they are developed and as a particular outcome of political struggles over

---

BOX 6.1 INTERESTS RESPONSIBLE FOR GROWTH OF HUMAN RIGHTS PRINCIPLES?

The interests of the allied victors of the Second World War in stigmatizing and penalizing their defeated enemies.

The interests of Cold Warriors in seeking to undermine each other's legitimacy.

The interests of superpowers in legitimizing intervention in the affairs of other states.

The interests of disadvantaged groups in claiming rights against the actions of the state.

Adapted from Waters (1996, p. 597).

---

interests. The point of a foundationalist ontology ... is to provide a universal basis for normative evaluation of human rights abuses.'

Whether or not sociology can provide a normative foundational justification for human rights is debatable, but we can say that Turner's arguments are persuasive and have been influential. The discipline is on far safer ground, however, when it focuses on the social construction of rights and their indeterminacy and when it provides us with the theoretical and conceptual tools to answer the questions of 'how rights came into social being', how they 'operate in social practice', 'whose purposes' rights serve and whose 'interests they protect', and finally, how far they are 'guaranteed or constrained by the letter and practice of the law' (Morris, 2006, p. 11). Social constructionist sociology can show that 'few rights are absolutes and most are in some way limited or conditional' (Morris, 2006, p. 11). Thus, sociology should declare an interest in the *indeterminacy* of rights (Morris, 2006, p. 25).

From a social constructionist perspective, *universal* human rights should be seen as 'historically and socially contingent, the product of a particular time, place, and set of circumstances, and a work in permanent progress' (Morris, 2006, p. 26). A sociological approach to rights discourses, practices, and struggles is necessary to identify the mechanisms that translate social phenomena into rights disputes. A social constructionist perspective views rights as an artefact produced through social processes of framing and construction, and in this sense, as Ken Plummer (2006) states, 'sociologists view rights as inventions'. Yet, viewing rights this way suggests that we must pay due attention to the social actors involved in their invention/construction if we are to understand rights regimes fully.

Indeed, Stammers suggests that we cannot ignore the link between **social movements**—networks of people who organize efforts to bring or resist change—and claims for human rights (see Chapter 9). It may be better to use a 'triadic relationship between human rights, social movements and power as an organizing focus for analysis' (Stammers, 1999, p. 981). This would provide a different understanding of rights from the prevailing dominant discourses, which focus on political power, the origins and development of human rights, and the potentials and limits of human rights (Stammers, 1999, p. 982). Like Turner, however, Stammers emphasizes the context of globalization, the changing role of nation states, and the misplaced view of the nation state as the 'principal duty bearer' of all human rights (Stammers, 1999, p. 1003). Indeed, given abuse of economic and social rights by private economic institutions, we should not look for a solution from the nation state. Alternatively, 'it might prove rather more useful to consider how *social movements* could renew and re-invigorate the challenge to economic power' (Stammers, 1999, p. 1003). The construction of social movements and the use of rights discourses have played a vital positive role in challenging relations and structures of power in respect of concentrated 'sites' of power and in terms of the way that power is embedded in everyday social relations (Stammers, 1999, pp. 987–8).

Power

Within this broad social constructionist sociology we can see an important dimension of sociological enquiry begin to emerge, i.e. the role of *power* in the domain of human rights. Human rights scholar Michael Freeman, in a major interdisciplinary contribution to the area (Freeman, 2002), identifies rights *institutionalization* as a social process, and he also displays an acute awareness of the role of power in that process, which he sees as perhaps the major sociological contribution. He writes:

The institutionalisation of human rights may ... lead, not to their more secure protection but to their protection in a form that is less threatening to the existing system of power. The *sociological* point is not that human rights should never be institutionalised, but, rather, that institutionalisation is a social process, involving power, and that it should be analysed and not assumed to be beneficial.

(Freeman, 2002, p. 85)

Freeman further argues that the social sciences have been 'excessively legalistic' and have overemphasized the UN system while neglecting to look deeper into the role of powerful global institutions and global power politics—most notably the G7, the **Bretton Woods institutions**, and the foreign policy of the US—in both the violation and construction of human rights (Freeman, 2002, p. 177). The discipline of sociology is well placed to investigate the role of *power* in this regard (see Box 6.2).

Social Structure

Up to this point we have seen that sociology views rights as a socially constructed phenomenon and we have discussed the importance of social actors—such as social movements—and power relations in the

---

BOX 6.2 DECONSTRUCTING: RIGHTS AND POWER

i. Rights and the law can be viewed primarily as instruments of governments, but instruments that take on their own autonomy and become channels of power in their own right. Contrary to Lockean political philosophy, 'rights' and 'freedom' were *not* in existence before 'power', but rather are the products of the 'new mode of social life' that is modern capitalism. (Woodiwiss, 2005, p. 32)

ii. Rights have a paradoxical nature in that they contribute to the production of social divisions, while at the same time they provide the language to 'discuss and contest such inequalities'. (Woodiwiss, 2005, p. 32)

iii. Rights and the law in general should be viewed as 'products of discursive formations', but with the emancipatory potential to generate power in order to 'serve the global majority'. (Woodiwiss, 2005, pp. 32, 136)

iv. Rights are constructed within existing power structures and hence there is a danger that their institutionalisation may lead to a substantive maintenance of the status quo.

---

construction of these rights. One aspect of sociological enquiry that we have not discussed so far is the role of **social structure**—that is, the ordered interrelationships between elements of society such as the different kinships, religious, economic, political, legal, and other institutions of a society—in the *violation* of rights. In the final section of this chapter we will discuss the role of *colonial structures* in the violation of Indigenous peoples' rights, and see how, following Indigenous political mobilization, these same structures also restricted the institutionalization of Indigenous land rights so as not to include de-colonizing political rights such as the right to self-determination and recognition of Indigenous sovereignty. At this point, however, it is worth noting that one of the few sociologists to engage with the role of social structures in a study of human rights violations was Rhoda Howard back in 1988.

Perhaps the main reason for Howard's focus more on the role of social structure was her injunction to view human rights as a normative concept, as 'entitlements' and not 'privileges' or benefits obtained through social struggle. Thus she was not exploring the uses of human rights talk or the socially constructed nature of legal rights. She based her structural analysis on Western and Central Africa, claiming that these societies have gone through such significant social change at a structural level that their cultural 'uniqueness' has all but ceased to exist, while the 'modern individual' has flourished (Howard, 1986, pp. 16, 33). Accordingly, she contended that '"culture" must not be used as a defence of human rights abuses' (Howard, 1986, pp. 16, 33), but it could be used 'as a check to radical universalism in carefully defined circumstances'. She was very wary of most claims for cultural relativity, which she viewed as an 'ideological tool to serve the interests of powerful and emergent groups in Commonwealth African society' (Howard, 1986, p. 17), and thus commonly result in withholding human rights from 'other' members of the same society (Howard, 1986, p. 34). For Howard, then, human rights are a truly universal normative concept that should be applicable to all peoples, regardless of the material and cultural conditions within which they exist.

From the above discussion we can identify key sociological questions (see Box 6.3).

Sociological Research

So how have these sociological insights informed social research into rights issues? Some researchers have focused sociological enquiry on the question of *how access to rights is operationalized*. Since rights are related to the circumstances in which they emerge, it is the task of the sociologists to understand those circumstances, and to show that claims for the universality of given rights should be replaced by a thorough analysis of the 'variability in why, when, how, and under what circumstances' rights are likely or not to emerge as a

demand (Glucksmann, 2006). Others have focused on the conditions that trigger a turn towards universalistic human rights claims by, for example, women's rights campaigners. Elson (2006) has shown how the adoption of human rights talk, as what social movement theorists term a mobilizing master frame, can be explained in the light of the opportunities generated by existing institutional arrangements at an international level. Indeed, sociological research has also drawn attention to how rights claims and rights talk has instrumental use value for many actors.

Social research has shown how rights should be viewed as instrumentally useful strategic resources invoked by social actors in competition for power in domestic and international arenas (Ruzza, 2006). Rights can be constructed through the interplay of domestic and international forces, and will be reinforced as long as otherwise powerless social actors find no other alternative but to engage in rights talk. Sociology may be the discipline best equipped to discuss the social forces that underline the genesis of such rights and the social struggles from which they materialize (Plummer, 2006). A primary 'task for sociologists is to become intimately familiar with the crusaders, their claims, and the social processes through which rights emerge' (Plummer, 2006), while being careful to balance claims for universality with the reality of societal and cultural diversity. Sociological researchers are also well placed to examine the 'considerable gap between the recognition of the need for protection and its achievements in practice' (Morris, 2006, p. 3). In summary, the discipline of sociology is well equipped to expose, discuss, and possibly amend obvious limitations in existing conceptions of rights, especially the formal legalistic dimensions, the limitations of which, as we shall see later, are something that social anthropologist Richard Wilson is also concerned to 'move beyond'. Such sociological research is now gathering pace. Indeed, the British Sociological Association now has a 'Sociology of Rights' study group, from which has already emerged a major contribution to the subfield entitled 'Sociology and Human Rights: New Engagements' (Hynes et al., 2011).

The issue of cultural relativism has of course influenced both sociological and anthropological perspectives on human rights. It was a major factor that led sociology to take such a long time to engage with the phenomenon at all; anthropology, on the other hand, was an influential voice at the outset of the international codification of human rights norms.

BOX 6.3 KEY SOCIOLOGICAL QUESTIONS

How have rights come into social being?

How are rights socially constructed—by whom, for whom, and in what social context?

How and why do particular social actors and groups claim and access rights?

How are rights affected by the social, political, and economic context in which they emerge and operate?

What role is played by social structures—are they enabling, constraining, or both?

To what extent are rights guaranteed or limited by the law?

Have power relations affected the construction and functionality of rights?

Whose interests do rights actually work to protect?

Anthropology of Human Rights

The discipline of anthropology has evolved to be concerned with the study of the entire range of cultures and societies in the world. Given such scope, there are significant points of convergence between anthropology and sociology. Yet in the early stages of its development anthropology tended to focus on non-Western 'primitive' societies, which led to important differences between the two disciplines. Indeed, sociology historically tended to focus on Western societies, which consequently generated methodological and theoretical differences between sociology and anthropology. For example, when Western sociologists studied their own society they could take much context for granted before hypothesizing about their data, while anthropologists studying other cultures could make few safe assumptions and consequently developed a holistic methodology which emphasized that each social entity or group has its own identity that is *distinct* and not reducible to individual constituent parts. Thus, anthropology would not assume that all cultures shared the same values, which is the fundamental ontological position that guided the discipline's early attitude towards the notion of universal human rights.

The discipline of anthropology's first, most notable, engagement with human rights can be traced back to December 1947 and Melville Herskovits's 'Statement on Human Rights' published in the *American Anthropologist* (*AA*) journal (AAA, 1947). During what sociologists would call the social construction of the UDHR, formal representations were sought from academics, public intellectuals, and non-government actors on the proposed text in order to make it as fair and unbiased, and hence legitimate, as possible. Herskovits's statement was quickly adopted by the American Anthropological Association Executive Board and consequently published as the lead article in the ultimate *AA* issue of that year (see Box 6.4).

The bad news for the UN was that the statement refused to endorse the proposed Universal Declaration. The rejection was based on the following three arguments.

1. Anthropology, as the social 'science of mankind', had shown that moral systems varied considerably in form and content, and thus any assertion of universality that had a moral flavour would always be prescriptive and certainly not descriptive of a social reality.

2. Given the scientific, **empirical ethnographic methodology** of the discipline, which seeks to describe and then explain social phenomena, it could not contribute to a normative endeavour that implicitly makes moral judgements, based on a set of universal rights, about cultural practices. Quite simply, the point being made was that anthropology as a discipline was fundamentally inimical to the nature of the proposed project.

3. If the proposed Universal Declaration was being designed as an aspirational text for the international community, in an attempt to universally operationalize this particular set of moral values, then the likely consequences of this would surely include the *denial* of freedom to those people whose view of the 'good life' may differ considerably from the prescribed priorities of a Universal Declaration. For example, some cultures may exhibit more collective value systems that emphasize things like collective ownership of land rather than the individual private property rights.[1]

For anthropology, these objections stood as a metaphorical disciplinary wall, blocking engagement with human rights for a very long time. Indeed, following a short-lived exchange of views on the subject of human rights after the publication of the American Anthropological Association (AAA) Statement (Barnett, 1948; Steward, 1948), there was virtually no anthropological interest in the phenomenon of human rights *as a specific subject of inquiry* until the mid-1980s (see Goodale, 2006a, p. 2). However, in the years following the publication of the 1947 Statement anthropologists nonetheless continued to practise 'public anthropology', reflecting the discipline's long-standing concern with creating linkages between anthropological research and projects for social justice (see Goodale, 2006a, p. 2). Moreover, anthropologists obviously encountered human rights issues and concerns in their work.[2] The same was true of sociologists during their period of non-engagement, but they did not study this intersection, or the specific human rights dimensions, *in its own right*. When anthropologists did finally seek to investigate and analyse human rights specifically, they did so against the backdrop of this previous indirect engagement. Yet the relativistic thrust of the Statement reflected the prevailing attitude of anthropology to

human rights for quite some time despite this indirect engagement.

Emancipatory Cultural Politics

Anthropology's relativistic perspective was born out of a detached scientific methodology that frequently observed a plethora of value systems in its research 'subjects'. This 'detached' approach, however, did not last as the dominant perspective. While many anthropologists were able to maintain an 'objective' detachment from their research subjects, increasingly this approach gave way to immersion and empathy, which in turn led to political activism on behalf of the subjects. It was this political engagement, with its implicit moral dimension, that eventually led to a reorientation of anthropological perspectives on human rights. Perhaps the pivotal moment in this new normative turn came from Clifford Geertz and his 1983 AAA Distinguished Lecture 'Anti Anti-Relativism', which confronted head-on the most commonly cited anthropological objection to the notion of universal human rights. In 1990 a Special Commission was created by the AAA to investigate human rights violations against the Yanomami by the Brazilian state—a quite remarkable turnaround when one considers the AAA's prior disciplinary detachment and relativistic stance. This engagement was taken even further in 1992 with the establishment of an AAA Commission for Human Rights. In 1994 the AAA solidified its commitment to engagement with human rights issues by making anthropology and human rights a thematic priority in its annual meetings, while in 1995 it converted the Commission for Human Rights into a permanent Committee for Human Rights. Finally, in 1999 that same Committee wrote a 'Declaration on Anthropology and Human Rights' that confirmed a significant disciplinary realignment since the AAA adopted Herskovits's 1947 Statement.

In 1997 a special issue of the *Journal of Anthropological Research* (*JAR*) sought to develop a distinct vision for a disciplinary engagement with human rights. The arguments contained therein suggested that anthropological understandings of specific cultural processes, which are embedded in wider (what sociologists would term 'structural') social power relationships, should be used to bolster specific endeavours for social change and/or to assist specific marginalized peoples, populations, or groups in resisting threats to their survival. This approach views human rights as a useful tool for serving an ethical commitment towards threatened peoples and cultures. The effectiveness of human rights as a tool in this sense can be greatly improved through more expansive and inclusive definition.[3] Thus, there is a normative suggestion in this approach that anthropologists *should* work to expand the definitions of *human rights* so as to increase their effectiveness for marginalized groups and cultures— an approach termed 'emancipatory cultural politics' (Turner, 1997). This approach (see Box 6.5), which encourages anthropological engagement with human rights discourse as a political strategy for the protection of threatened populations, was perhaps the first major disciplinary current to emerge in the anthropology of human rights.[4] Perhaps the most notable recent research within this broad approach is that of Shannon Speed, which she has termed 'critically engaged activist research' (Speed, 2006). This approach is concerned to embrace the issues raised by the social actors, not shy away from engagement and commentary, and in fact warns against an *overly detached* anthropology of human rights (Speed, 2006). The focus of the research is not just about *research on* human rights in the particular site—Chiapas, Mexico—but also *advocacy for* human rights there. Consequently, it could be suggested that such research does not fall into the trap of forgetting the 'human' in human rights. For the social actors suffering injustice, human rights are much more than an academic curiosity.

The Ethnographic Turn

Thus, as with the discipline of sociology, the 1990s was the decade when anthropologists from around the globe truly began taking the issue of human rights seriously enough to conduct significant research. From about the mid-1990s, mirroring the reorientation in the AAA, anthropologists from outside the USA began to see merit in the 'social practice of rights' as a worthy *object* of anthropological investigation. The perspectives that emerged from this endeavour were collected in several important edited volumes (Wilson, 1997; Cowan, Dembour, and Wilson, 2001; Wilson and Mitchell, 2003) and through several monographs (e.g. Riles, 2000; Wilson, 2001; Merry, 2005; Slyomovics, 2005). These contributions evolved into a second major current in the contemporary anthropology of rights, which can be identified as the 'ethnographic' approach (Goodale, 2006a, p. 3). This second disciplinary thread in the anthropology of human rights seeks to use the discipline's ethnographic methodology to explore and investigate the 'social practice of human rights' or, as Richard Wilson puts it, 'the social life of rights'. Wilson, a social anthropologist, agrees with the main thrust of the sociological approaches that we discussed earlier, arguing that social scientists should be primarily concerned with analysing rights as socially constructed phenomena. He writes:

The intellectual efforts of those seeking to develop a framework for understanding the social life of rights would be better directed not towards foreclosing their ontological status, but instead by exploring their meaning and use. What is needed are more detailed studies of human rights according to the actions and intentions of social actors, within wider historical constraints of institutionalized power.

(Wilson, 1997, pp. 3–4)

Taking up this call, researchers began to focus on an increase in negotiations and claims made by various social groups *in a language of 'rights'*. A trend began to emerge in which long-established theoretical debates about concepts such as rights, justice, and citizenship began to engage with empirical 'data' that contextualizes rights-claiming processes (Cowan, Dembour, and Wilson, 2001). Anthropologists started to advocate the need to explore how exactly universal concepts were being used in local struggles. In essence, the relationship between culture and rights was seen as an issue to be studied *empirically*. The thrust of this approach is thus descriptive

---

BOX 6.5 'EMANCIPATORY CULTURAL POLITICS': CORE ELEMENTS

Anthropological understandings should be used to reinforce specific endeavours to assist threatened peoples, populations, or groups.

Human rights are a useful tool for serving an ethical commitment toward this endeavour.

BUT, anthropologists should work towards *more expansive and inclusive definitions* of human rights so as to increase their effectiveness for marginalized groups and cultures.

and makes no claim to endorse the universality of human rights. It is an effort to uncover how human rights actually function in an empirical sense, to uncover what they mean to different social actors in different social contexts. More attention was gradually being paid to empirical, contextual analyses of specific rights struggles. This intellectual strategy sought to record how individuals, groups, communities, and states use rights discourse in the pursuit of particular ends, and how they become enmeshed in its logic (Cowan, Dembour, and Wilson, 2001, p. 21). Thus, in contrast to the first disciplinary thread to engage with human rights, that of 'emancipatory cultural politics' (see Goodale, 2006a) which is inherently normative, the ethnographic approach is more *a study of normativity*.

One of the main issues investigated by this approach is the relationship between culture and rights (see Cowan, Dembour, and Wilson, 2001). Anthropologists interested in this relationship have sought answers to questions such as: How do transnational ideas such as human rights approaches to violence against women become meaningful in local social settings? How do they move across the gap between a cosmopolitan awareness of human rights and local sociocultural understandings of gender and family? (Merry, 2006, pp. 38–51.) In exploring these questions, anthropologists have sought to construct theoretical frameworks that seek to explain the different ways in which human rights are viewed instrumentally and also experienced by transnational social actors. While theorizing processes of translation, anthropological analysis of translators helps to explain how 'human rights ideas and interventions circulate around the world and transform social life' (Merry, 2006, p. 38).

Anthropological studies in this area often highlight the inherent risks to culture of a hegemonic human rights regime and accordingly advocate an approach to human rights that firmly scrutinizes how rights regimes actually function, and in particular their functional impact on culture. Such an approach will not anchor political projects or movements for cultural autonomy based on claims for cultural rights; rather, it is an anthropology of interrogation that is pluralist, sceptical, and penetrating (Goodale, 2006a). This sceptical approach to rights, as we shall see in the later section of this chapter, can be evidenced by recent, more sociological, writings on Indigenous rights.

A sceptical pluralist view of rights is now a dominant feature of the ethnographic current. It is a view that recognizes the 'plural and fragmentary nature of the international rights regime and the ideological promiscuity of rights talk' (Wilson, 2006, p. 77). Its focus is on the performative dimensions of human rights, social mobilization dynamics, and the attitudinal changes of elite and non-elite social actors toward the formulations of 'rights' and 'justice' inside and outside legal processes (see Wilson, 2006, p. 77). By ethnographically studying the *'social life of rights'* we can move beyond the tired universalism versus relativism debate to examine what actors 'actually do with human rights in specific fields of political contestation' (Wilson, 2006, p. 78).

Thus the essence of the ethnographic approach is the careful documentation of the social life of rights (see Box 6.6). This may involve examining phenomena such as 'the dynamics of social mobilisations in rights-based social movements, or the performative dimensions of rights movements including marches, vigils, funerals, and so forth' (see Wilson, 2006) or, as we shall see in the next section, examining how power politics impacts upon rights construction—often to the detriment of the ultimate rights-holders (see Short, 2007). In following this approach we can locate the foundations of human rights in 'everyday human sociality', rather than through complex philosophizing or the 'rational actor and positive law' (Wilson, 2006). (See also Box 6.7 for a critique of both ethnographic and emancipatory cultural politics.)

BOX 6.6 THE ETHNOGRAPHIC APPROACH: CORE ELEMENTS

The relationship between culture and rights is an issue to be studied *empirically*.

The approach is descriptive and does not implicitly endorse the universality of human rights.

It seeks to uncover how human rights *actually function* and what they mean to different social actors in different social contexts.

It seeks to document and record how social actors use 'rights talk' in the pursuit of particular ends.

Its overarching concern is to ethnographically explore the 'social life of rights'.

The foundation of human rights is *human social activity*, not a universal morality.

BOX 6.7 ALTERNATIVE POINTS OF VIEW: ECUMENICAL ANTHROPOLOGY?

i. Mark Goodale (2006b, 2008) has advanced an influential argument that critiques both the ethnographic and emancipatory cultural politics strands and argues for an expanded object of inquiry *beyond human rights* to a slightly larger set of normative processes in which human rights are nonetheless embedded (Goodale, 2006b). This study of 'ethical theory as social practice' involves anthropologists engaging ethnographically with social actors and processes through which human rights encounter *other normative phenomena*.

ii. This approach sees anthropologists participating in 'co-theorizing' with social actors as they attempt to make sense of human rights through interpretation and reinterpretation (Goodale, 2006b).

iii. This engagement with interlocutors distinguishes Goodale's approach from a straight 'ethnographic' methodology. It is a distinction he sees as necessary 'because of both the conceptual demands that human rights processes place on social actors (including anthropologists) and the fact that human rights discourse links social actors to transnational

regimes whose scope and meanings can only partially be captured ethnographically' (Goodale, 2006a, p. 5).

iv. Goodale (2006a) describes such an approach as representing, broadly speaking, an '*ecumenical anthropology of human rights*' (Goodale, 2006a). It is an anthropology that tolerates and encourages research that is *fundamentally critical of contemporary human rights regimes* but also research that is *politically or ethically committed to these same regimes*.

v. An 'ecumenical anthropology of human rights is one that draws from an internal epistemological pluralism to better understand the pluralism—whether irreducible or not—that characterizes contemporary human rights practice' (Goodale, 2006a). This approach aimed to take the anthropology of human rights *beyond what had come before*; nevertheless, much of this recent research could still, broadly speaking, fit within the twofold classification of anthropological approaches to human rights—the 'emancipatory cultural politics' and the 'ethnographic' strands.

KEY POINTS

The 1947 *AAA* Statement set out objections, based on the scientific, empirical methodology of the discipline, which blocked engagement with human rights for a very long time.

Over time, 'objective' detachment gave way to immersion and empathy, which in turn led to political activism on behalf of the subjects.

An 'emancipatory cultural politics' thread emerged, that saw human rights as a useful tool for serving an ethical commitment toward threatened peoples and cultures.

This was followed by the 'ethnographic' turn, which sought to understand 'the social life of rights', the meaning and use of rights according to the actions and intentions of social actors working within constraints of institutionalized power.

In 2006, an important argument emerged that attempted to frame anew the anthropology of human rights with an 'ecumenical anthropology of human rights'—an anthropology that tolerates and encourages approaches that are both fundamentally critical of contemporary human rights regimes and politically or ethically committed to these same regimes.

Critical Thinking Questions:

What are the ethical reasons for anthropological analysis of human rights issues going beyond observation and reportage? What are the pros and cons of such an approach, and how would you navigate these in your own work?

A Common Thread: The Social Construction of Rights

As we have seen, despite the initial scepticism towards human rights and the resultant reluctance to engage with the concept, there is now a growing body of research emerging from both sociology and anthropology that analyses the 'social life of rights'. However, we can see that the sociological engagement tended to begin with broad structural observations about human ontology, the capitalist mode of production, or the role of international power politics in the construction of the UDHR and the like. Anthropology, by contrast, usually began with a more microethnographic methodology, only subsequently invoking contextualizing social structural insights that would draw attention to broader, more sociological issues such as the role of 'institutionalized power' (see Wilson, 1997). While the two disciplines display somewhat different points of origin in their study of human rights, they share one common and very important perspective, which can be called a 'social constructionist' view of human rights. It is a view of human rights (see Box 6.8) that shows that such 'rights' are not simply givens, but products of human social interaction, with all its imbalances and imperfections. Thus a common disciplinary lesson is that we should not assume that the rights that emerge on local environments (Samson and Short, 2006). Global activism of hitherto separate groups of Indigenous peoples has developed in response to these destructive homogenizing forces. Indigenous groups such as the Wirajuri, Ngunnawall, Nahuatl, Ogiek, Blackfoot, Tuareg, and Innu are now intimately involved in the construction of their rights through the United Nations system (Samson and Short, 2006). This quest through the UN system is born out of frustration at the extreme social and political disadvantage suffered by many Indigenous peoples worldwide, and frequently out of disillusionment with the rights conferred on them by the settler states in which they live.

One such domestic rights regime is the so-called 'native title' land rights that have emerged in Australia. Recent research (see Short, 2007, 2008) has shown that in the Australian context the domestic institutionalization of international human rights standards as they pertain to Indigenous peoples is best understood sociologically as a product of the balance of power between political interests, taking place within a settler colonial social and political structure. In 1992 the High Court of Australia in the *Mabo* case finally acknowledged that to deny Indigenous rights to land would be unjust and contrary to contemporary international human rights standards, especially the principle of racial equality. The court was aware of, in sociologist Bryan Turner's (2006, p. 25) terms, the 'vulnerability' of dispossessed Indigenous people and did not seek to worsen their plight by flouting the international moral code that prohibits racial discrimination. Yet, when the government responded to the landmark case, the interests of vulnerable Indigenous groups were ignored in favour of powerful commercial interests. The net result was legalization that sought to *limit* Indigenous rights behind a veneer of agrarian reform. Thus, as Freeman (2002, p. 85) warned, 'the institutionalisation of human rights may ... lead, not to their more secure protection but to their protection in a form that is less threatening to the existing system of power'. The research examined the trajectory of Indigenous rights to land in a manner that went beyond the formal, legalistic dimensions of such rights, where, as Wilson (2001, p. xvii) pointed out, they always appear to be a 'good thing'. In contrast to such perspectives, this research's social constructionist approach showed how the institutionalization of 'native title' land rights was

from such interaction are necessarily beneficial to the rights-holders. A particularly striking illustration of this key observation is highlighted by recent research into Indigenous peoples' land rights in Australia (see Short, 2007, 2008), to which we shall turn later in this section. Indeed, the study of Indigenous rights in general is an excellent example of how these two disciplines can offer complementary insights: the anthropological interest in non-Western cultures and a rigorous ethnographic methodology, coupled with sociological structural appreciation, can combine to help us more fully understand the social life of these particular rights.

As we have seen, the discipline of sociology was slow to engage with human rights, yet it has been even slower to engage with the specific case of Indigenous rights. Historians, anthropologists (not surprising given the discipline's interest in non-Western cultures), and political and legal theorists have all made commentaries and undertaken significant research on Indigenous peoples and their rights (see Chapter 19), yet only a few sociologists have taken an interest in a subject that is now truly global in its ramifications (Samson and Short, 2006). In the face of the homogenizing forces of economic globalization and strong nation states, it is becoming increasingly clear that the affluence produced by international capitalism comes at the expense of both the ecosystem (see Chapter 23) and the cultural vitality of small peoples whose ways of life depend a social process bound by colonial structures and ultimately intertwined with power, elites, privilege, and the actions, intentions, and interests of the social actors involved. The research placed the institutionalization of native title rights in the context of political battles for control of resources that pitted Indigenous peoples against powerful commercial lobby groups. It showed how, through the social construction of a discourse of crisis, industry 'uncertainty', and the deliberate generation of unfounded public fear, commercial lobby groups and their political and media supporters successfully pressured the government to severely limit Indigenous land rights (see Short, 2007, 2008).

In short, this research showed that seemingly beneficial Indigenous land rights were in fact constructed in such a way as to actually *maintain* existing social, political, and economic inequalities and perpetuate the colonial status quo. In this sense the work highlighted a gulf between settler state-granted Indigenous rights and their normative benchmark: the United Nations *Declaration on the Rights of Indigenous Peoples* (the Declaration). Indeed, the Indigenous land rights debate in Australia is an example of, in Turner and Rojek's (2001, p. 127) terms, 'the frequent tension between national systems of rights and international human rights'. Yet, of course, it must also be stated that the 'normative benchmark' of Indigenous rights, the UDHR, is itself a social construction. The significant difference between the Declaration and settler state-granted Indigenous rights, however, is that, despite the inequalities in bargaining power between states and Indigenous representatives in the UN, Indigenous peoples were nonetheless a major force in the construction of the Declaration (see Niezen, 2003; Morgan, 2004). Thus, the international Indigenous peoples' movement has accepted the 2007 United Nations Declaration on the Rights of Indigenous Peoples as a more just articulation of their rights than those imposed on them by 'settler' states. This position is based on the Declaration's inclusion of **self-determination**, which is seen as a remedial *politicalright* of distinct dispossessed 'peoples' and 'nations'; this political right contrasts with the individual citizenship rights, or limited rights to land occupation, conferred on them by colonial nation states. The broad interpretation of self-determination in this context refers to the right to political autonomy, the freedom to determine political status, and the right freely to pursue economic, social, and cultural development.

Consequently, the right is viewed as central to a 'just' response to colonial dispossession and the resultant political and social subordination of Indigenous peoples. Indigenous calls for self-determination derive from the fact that they were self-governing political entities or 'sovereign nations', and in spite of colonization many Indigenous groups still claim such status (see Short, 2008).

In a notable recent development, sociologists and anthropologists have turned their attention to exploring the social and environmental harms and rights violations associated with the wave of new high-risk 'unconventional energy' extraction technologies sweeping the globe. Indeed, in our growth-driven global economy, as conventional reserves are depleted and demand for energy rises, there is increasing pressure to exploit unconventional energy sources. Michael Klare first coined the term 'extreme energy' (see Short et al., 2015) to describe a range of relatively new, higher-risk, non-renewable resource extraction processes that have become more attractive to the conventional energy industry as the more easily accessible supplies dwindle. In the countries where such development has taken place, it has been controversial and divisive. Supporters of unconventional gas development often claim that it reduces gas prices, creates employment opportunities, and provides 'energy security', all while producing lower carbon emissions than coal. Its detractors often contest all of these claims, usually pointing to contrary data emerging from the USA and Australia. Indeed, in numerous studies from both countries, local communities most affected by developments often cite considerable negative impacts on the environment and human health, including groundwater contamination, air pollution, radioactive and toxic waste, water usage, earthquakes, methane migration, and the industrialization of rural landscapes, the cumulative effect of which has led to calls for the United Nations Human Rights Council (HRC) to condemn unconventional techniques as a threat to basic human rights, particularly the rights to water and health (Short et al., 2015). The United Nations Environment Programme (UNEP) has issued a 'Global Alert' on the issue of unconventional gas and oil development, warning of significant environmental risks to the air, soil, and water (contamination and usage competition); ecosystem damage; habitat and biodiversity impacts; and fugitive gas emissions—which will endanger carbon reduction targets. In terms of public health, UNEP warned of risks of pipeline explosions, release of toxins into air, soil, and water, and competition for land and water resources needed for food production, and that unconventional gas would be likely to be used 'in addition to coal rather than being a substitute' and would thus pose a threat to the development of sustainable economies.

In a recent paper, anthropologist Kim de Rijke (see Short et al., 2015) noted that:

'the extraordinary expansion of the unconventional gas industry has ... led to questions about social power and the rights of individuals and local communities, the role of multinational corporations in politics and rural service provision, as well as related questions regarding fundamental processes of democracy, capitalist economies and social justice', while the 'close relationship between governments and powerful multinational corporations brings to the fore questions about political influence and human rights'.

Thus, to address these 'important conundrums', de Rijke advocated further academic research into unconventional resource extraction, from multiple perspectives. This new field of study will be yet another domain where sociological and anthropological insights into human rights issues may well prove vital to protecting the interests of vulnerable local communities and populations (Short et al., 2015).

KEY POINTS

Despite the initial scepticism toward human rights of both disciplines, there is now a growing body of research that analyses the 'social life of rights'.

In approaching human rights, however, the two disciplines begin from different positions—sociology with broad structural observations, anthropology with a microethnographic methodology.

The disciplines, however, share one common and very important perspective that can be labelled 'social constructionist'.

Rights are seen as products of human social interaction and, most significantly, power relations. Consequently, we should not assume them to be beneficial.

The case of Indigenous land rights in Australia is a prime example of the importance of a social constructionist perspective.

Extreme energy production raises numerous questions about human and environmental well-being, which sociological and anthropological approaches to human rights may be well positioned to address.

Critical Thinking Question:

Can you think of examples, analogous to the native land rights issue discussed here, in which the institutionalization of rights actually results in limitations on people's enjoyment of their rights?

Conclusion

We have seen how anthropologists and sociologists were historically sceptical of human rights due to the dominant positivistic and relativistic disciplinary biases, and how each discipline eventually moved away from this position towards an engagement with human rights that sought to explore rigorously the nuances, contingencies, contestations, and meanings that are part and parcel of the 'social life of rights'. Indeed, we have seen that there is now a growing body of research emerging from both sociology and anthropology that seeks to go beyond legal positivism and abstract political philosophy, the hitherto dominant avenues of enquiry into human rights, in order to explore the meaning and use of rights. While both disciplines share a social constructionist view of rights, which is acutely aware of contingencies,

contestations, and differing meanings, and also of political power and social structures, they differ in their methodological 'point of origin' and consequently on the relative emphasis placed on these factors. We have seen that sociology sought to emphasize the effect that broad structural factors, such as the capitalist mode of production, international political structures, or the colonial nation state, had on the construction of specific rights, while anthropologists usually began with a more microethnographic exploration of the lived experience of rights before seeking to contextualize more broadly with structural insights such as the role of institutionalized power in rights struggles. Yet, despite the different methodological 'points of origin', the disciplines share a common 'social constructionist' view of human rights. As

Plummer suggested earlier, 'the task for sociologists is to become intimately familiar with the crusaders, their claims and the social processes through which rights emerge', a view that echoes social anthropologist Richard Wilson's desire for more research into the 'social life of rights'. Such a social constructionist approach to human rights will delve deeper than legal perspectives where, as Wilson warns, rights are seen as inherently a 'good thing'.

Through a brief summary of recent 'social constructionist' research into Indigenous land rights, we have seen that this is certainly not the case with the seemingly beneficial 'native title' rights in Australia. Such 'rights' have actually functioned to dispossess

Indigenous peoples further, which has compounded the tragedy of colonial dispossession and its legacy of extreme social, political, and economic disadvantage (see Short, 2008). Thus, in addition to the knowledge gleaned from legal, philosophical, and political approaches to the study of human rights, we should embrace anthropological and sociological studies that explore the 'social life of rights', since it is only through such studies that we can hope to understand fully the *practice* of human rights in the modern world. Such perspectives will be invaluable when facing new challenges to the enjoyment of universal human rights such as those posed by unconventional energy extraction.

QUESTIONS

Individual Study Questions

1. Why did it take the discipline of sociology so long to engage with human rights?
2. On what grounds did Turner defend the universality of human rights? Is this compatible with a social constructionist view?
3. Are the insights of the classical sociological theorists relevant to the study of human rights?
4. What broad insights can we attribute to the sociology of human rights?
5. What were the main objections of the discipline of anthropology to the idea of universal human rights, and were they overcome?
6. What are the two main currents of the anthropology of human rights and how do they differ?
7. What are the similarities and differences in sociological and anthropological approaches to human rights?
8. How do such approaches aid our understanding of human rights?

Group Discussion Questions

1. Do we need a 'foundational ontology' to study and research human rights?
2. Are the interests that Waters identifies as responsible for the growth of human rights convincing (see Box 6.1)?
3. What precisely is meant by the 'social life of rights'?
4. If you were to choose an anthropological methodology to research a rights issue, which of the two main anthropological approaches would you choose to use, and why?

FURTHER READING

American Anthropologist (2006). In focus: Anthropology and human rights in a new key, **108**/1.

An excellent collection of anthropological theorizing and research on the topic of human rights by leading scholars in the field.

Goodale, M. (2008). *Human Rights: An Anthropological Reader.* Blackwell Readers in Anthropology. Chichester: Blackwell.

A useful guide for students wishing to further their understanding of the broad range of anthropological work on human rights.

Goodale, M. and **Merry, S. E.**   (2007). *The Practice of Human Rights: Tracking Law Between the Global and the Local.* Cambridge Studies in Law and Society. Cambridge: Cambridge University Press.

Building from their contributions to the *AA* 'In focus', the authors focus on the 'practice' of human rights, which fills a significant gap in theoretical and empirical understanding.

Hynes, P., Lamb, M., Short, D., and **Waites, M.**   (2011). *Sociology and Human Rights: New Engagements.* London: Routledge.

This book was published as a special issue of the *International Journal of Human Rights* in 2010, which was the first publication to emerge out of the recently formed British Sociological Association's 'Sociology of Rights' Study Group (see http://www.britsoc.co.uk/specialisms/socrights.aspx). The collection includes a range of new sociological work addressing issues such as genocide in relation to Indigenous peoples, rights-based approaches in development work, trafficking of children, and children's rights in relation to political struggles for the decriminalization of same-sex sexual activity in India. It examines contexts ranging from Rwanda and South Korea to Northern Ireland and the city of Barcelona.

Morris, L. (ed.) (2006). *Rights: Sociological Perspectives.* Abingdon: Routledge.

The first book to publish essays specifically geared towards exploring rights issues sociologically. Students should pay special attention to the Introduction for a fuller examination of the relevance of classical sociology to the study of contemporary human rights, and to Chapter 9 for a fuller discussion of what sociology can offer the study of Indigenous peoples' rights.

Short, D. (2008). *Reconciliation and Colonial Power: Indigenous Rights in Australia.* Aldershot: Ashgate.

Students should pay special attention to Chapters 3 and 21 of this text for an example of a social constructionist approach to understanding Indigenous land rights.

Short, D., Elliot, J., Norder, K., Lloyd-Davies, E., and **Morley, J.** (2015). Extreme energy, fracking and human rights: A new field for impact assessments? *International Journal of Human Rights*, **19**/6, 697–736. DOI: http://dx.doi.org/10.1080/13642987.2015.1019219

This article examines sociological work on human rights and 'fracking'.

Turner, B. S. (2006). *Vulnerability and Human Rights.* University Park, PA: The Pennsylvania State University Press.

This book is Turner's definitive work on human rights, which encapsulates and builds on the main arguments of his breakthrough work in the early 1990s. Turner's work is still perhaps the most plausible foundationalist account of human rights to have emerged from the discipline of sociology.

WEB LINKS

http://www.asanet.org/advocacy/statement_on_human_rights.cfm   As evidence of the discipline of sociology's significant reorientation towards human rights, see this link. The American Sociological Association (ASA) took the celebration of its centenary (1905–2005) as an opportunity to reiterate its strongest support for the basic civil and political freedoms of peoples of all nations as articulated by the Universal Declaration of Human Rights (UDHR).

http://www.asanet.org/footnotes/septoct04/indextwo.html   Mary Robinson's important address on sociology and human rights at the 99th annual meeting of the American Sociological Association. http://www.sociologistswithoutborders.com/

http://ssfinternacional.blogspot.com/2008/02/sociology-and-human-rights.html   An initiative that began in Madrid in 2001, *Sociologists without Borders/Sociólogos Sin Fronteras* (SSF) is a non-governmental organization that advances a cosmopolitan sociology with a specific commitment to human rights. The group advances human rights by working with, and in, communities, societies, workplaces, and other social institutions. The second web link explains their specific human rights approach.

http://franke.uchicago.edu/aaa1947.pdf   June 1999 Declaration on Anthropology and Human Rights defines the basis for the involvement of the American Anthropological Association, and, more generally, of the profession of Anthropology in human rights. http://extremeenergy.org

An academic forum that focuses on the social and environmental impacts of unconventional energy extraction, and includes numerous contributions from anthropologists and sociologists of human rights.

NOTES

1. See Goodale (2006a) for an excellent detailed discussion of these objections.

2. Goodale (2006a, p. 2) cites some obvious examples, including the work of 'forensic anthropologists in collating evidence for international human rights investigations, linguistic and political anthropologists studying the problem of linguistic minorities' attempts to find protection through a discourse of marginalization that is supported by international human rights instruments'.

3. At this point we can see how such an ethical commitment can act as a more idealist counterpoint to the 'social constructionist' approach of sociologist Malcolm Waters—as discussed. Indeed, viewing human rights as socially constructed phenomena, subject to power politics, does not preclude their construction by marginalized groups—it just makes it more difficult.

4. See Goodale (2006a, p. 4) on this.

 Visit the Online Resource Centre that accompanies this book for updates and a range of other resources: www.oxfordtextbooks.co.uk/orc/goodhart3e/

7

Contemporary Critiques of Human Rights

David Chandler

Chapter Contents

Reader's Guide

This chapter seeks to explain why human rights claims, which assert the need to empower the poor and excluded, often appear to enforce the power of dominant Western states and international institutions. It will demonstrate that there is a paradox at the heart of the human rights discourse, which enables claims made on behalf of victims, the marginalized, and excluded to become a mechanism for the creation of new frameworks for the exercise of power. It will suggest that, rather than understanding human rights frameworks in the international sphere as a challenge to power relations, it would be more accurate to describe them in terms of a challenge to the existing formal international legal order. It will clarify that there is nothing progressive or empowering about human rights claims in themselves and that, if the enforcement and protection of these claims relies on external and unaccountable actors, then existing informal hierarchies of power will become increasingly formalized, while formal protections of the rights of self-determination and self-government will be undermined.

Introduction

Many commentators have observed the fact that human rights frameworks have become an integral part of a new, more hierarchical, international order, undermining UN Charter restrictions on the use of military force and justifying new, more coercive forms of international regulation and intervention in the post-colonial world. To view these consequences of human rights claims and discourses as the ideological 'misuse' or 'abuse' of human rights would already be to approach the question of understanding human rights with a certain set of assumptions. These assumptions would be based on an idea that human rights claims necessarily challenge entrenched power relations and are an important mechanism of advocacy on behalf of the victims of abuses or those excluded from traditional frameworks of representation. This chapter will suggest that these prior assumptions, of the 'purity' of human rights claims and of their 'abuse' by powerful actors, are themselves problematic.

Human rights claims cannot in themselves be accurately seen as either enforcing or challenging the existing relations of power. The one thing that can be asserted with confidence is that human rights claims conflate an ethical or moral claim with a legal and political one. The discourse of the 'human' belongs to the sphere of abstract universal ethics, while that of 'rights' belongs to the framework of a concretely constituted legal and political sphere. In conflating the two spheres, human rights claims pose a challenge to rights as they are legally constituted. The content of this challenge, whether it has any consequences, and if it does have consequences what these consequences are, is a matter for concrete analysis. To suggest that any challenge to the framework of legally constituted rights is necessarily an effective one, or necessarily a good or progressive one, would clearly be naive.

In fact, it was the challenge of naivety that was famously articulated by Jeremy Bentham, the **utilitarian** philosopher, when he denounced the idea of human rights as 'nonsense on stilts' (see Chapter 1). He had nothing but contempt for the new-fangled universal 'rights of man' proclaimed at the end of the eighteenth century. For Bentham, rights meant nothing unless they were enforceable with clear contractual obligations and backed by law. Declarations of the 'rights of man' were no more than rhetorical fancies and collections of pious wishes that were not worth the paper they were written on. The idea that we were born with universal equal rights simply because we were human made no sense to Bentham. First, we are born into a relationship of dependency rather than equality, and are not considered as moral or legal equals until we reach maturity (children are not born with criminal liability as they are not responsible for their actions). Second, it was clear that there could be no universal human equality: the opportunities we have depend fundamentally on the societies we live in and our position within those societies.

However, few people would have the confidence to argue in Bentham's dismissive terms today. It would appear to be undeniable that our understandings of and respect for human rights are central to the way we and our governments make policy and act in international affairs. Yet, despite today's consensus on the fact that 'human rights are a good thing', there is still the nagging sense that Bentham may have a point, that human rights may sound very nice on paper but be much more ephemeral when it comes to giving these aspirations meaning and content, and that, nice as these claims sound, they may be open to abuse.

Claims to anything can be abused and all claims to rights can be misused. However, it is vital to appreciate that it is inherent in human rights claims that they are more open to abuse or misuse than other claims—those of democratic and civil rights, for example. The reason for this, in the words of Norman Lewis, is quite simply because human rights are not derived from 'socially constituted legal subjects' (Lewis, 1998, p. 85). Where Bentham saw abstract rights claims as merely childish or superstitious thinking, much as the 'belief in witches or unicorns', their abstract nature—the fact that they can reflect radical and progressive aspirations rather than merely legally enshrined rights—is held to be a major factor in their use and support across the globe.

This chapter is tasked with focusing on the downside of human rights claims—what is commonly understood by advocates of human rights to be the 'misuse' or 'abuse' of human rights. It will be demonstrated that the ambiguous and abstract nature of human rights claims is at the same time their point of attraction, but equally makes the opportunity for 'abuse' a constant one. Unfortunately for the advocates of human rights frameworks, their openness to abuse is not incidental but is intrinsic to the concept of human rights themselves.

Human Rights and the Legal Subject

The discourse of human rights has a pre-history in terms of the claims of **natural rights** from the **Enlightenment** onwards, where claims of a universal human nature were an essentialist grounding for ideas of individual equality and self-determination, which challenged the aristocratic and feudal social and political hierarchies (see Box 7.1). Natural rights claims are therefore seen at the centre of the revolutionary movements of liberal modernity: the Declaration of the Rights of Man and of the Citizen of the French Revolution and the Declaration of Independence and the Bill of Rights of the American Revolution.

With the development of more social and historical frameworks of thinking, expounded by theorists such as Emile Durkheim, Max Weber, and Karl Marx, the idea of natural rights was discredited (see Chapter 6). In its place was a consensus of understanding that rights were social and political products, dependent on the state and society in which the individual lived. Concrete rights of citizenship replaced the abstract conception of natural rights.

Twentieth-Century Critiques

For the leading political theorists of the twentieth century, the idea of human rights as universal claims

---

BOX 7.1 SOPHOCLES'S ANTIGONE: ETHICS VS LAW

The conception of human rights can be dated back to ancient Greece and the work of the famous playwright Sophocles. To quote the US State Department pamphlet, 'Human Rights and US Foreign Policy', published in 1978:

The idea of human rights is almost as old as its ancient enemy, despotism . . . When Sophocles' heroine Antigone cries out to the autocratic King Creus: 'all your strength is weakness itself against [t]he immortal unrecorded laws of God' she makes a deeply revolutionary assertion. There are laws, she claims, higher than the laws made by any King; as an individual she has certain rights under those higher laws; and kings and armies—while they may violate her rights by force—can never cancel them or take them away.

(Cited in Sellars, 2002, p. vii)

This is an excellent example of the essence of human rights claims: legal rights are equated with power and oppression and challenged in the name of a non-legally constituted rights subject.

---

made no more sense than it did to Jeremy Bentham. Writing in 1950, in the aftermath of the Second World War, Hannah Arendt remarked that the Holocaust demonstrated the abstract and meaningless nature of the concept of human rights (see Box 7.2). When Jews were denied the rights of citizenship—their political status—they were forced to fall back on the abstract claims of human rights. In doing so, their status was transformed from active, decision-making political subjects to objects of the charity or benevolence of others. For Arendt, what makes us human and rights-bearing subjects is not our bare humanity but our capacity to create rights-bearing and rights-giving political communities. The lesson of the Holocaust, for the Jews, was not the need to give more attention to human rights, but the need to ensure the political rights of citizenship, achieved through the struggle to establish and safeguard the state of Israel.

Arendt makes the point here that human rights are 'fictional' rights: they are rights that are not dependent on the collective agency of their subject (Chandler, 2003). Individuals 'freed' from the political process of collective decision making no longer have an active say in what their rights are or should be; at most they are lobbying or begging others for favours, and place themselves in a situation of dependency. For Arendt, the rights of the 'human' are much less than the rights of the 'citizen'. The bearer of merely 'human' rights is subordinate, dependent, and in a position of supplicant to others. The response to these rights claims is therefore an arbitrary one. Arendt argues that it may result in 'privileges in some cases, injustices in most' because 'blessings and doom are meted out to them [bearers of human rights] according to accident and without any relation whatsoever to what they do, did, or may do' (Arendt, 1973, p. 296).

For Arendt, human rights frameworks, in separating the rights bearer from the agent capable of enacting these rights, legitimize a framework that is in fact worse than that suggested by Bentham's view of pious wishes and utopian dreaming. Arendt suggests that a field of fictitious 'rights' is opened up that is inherently open to abuse and arbitrary interpretation and enforcement.

Carl Schmitt, a German legal and political theorist, writing at the same time as Arendt, was also critical of the idea of universal human rights. Schmitt approached the subject from the opposite end of the spectrum (not from the viewpoint of the human rights subject—the individual claiming human rights—but

---

BOX 7.2 HANNAH ARENDT AND CARL SCHMITT ON HUMAN RIGHTS

Hannah Arendt on Human Rights

. . . the public sphere is as consistently based on the law of equality as the private sphere is based on the law of universal difference and differentiation. Equality, in contrast to all that is involved in mere existence, is not given us, but is the result of human organization insofar as it is guided by the principle of justice. We are not born equal; we become equal as members of a group on the strength of our decision to guarantee ourselves mutually equal rights.

(Arendt, 1973, p. 301)

Carl Schmitt on Human Rights

Humanity as such cannot wage war because it has no enemy, at least not on this planet . . . When a state fights its political enemy in the name of humanity, it is not a war for the sake of humanity, but a war wherein a particular state seeks to usurp a universal concept against a military opponent . . . The concept of humanity is an especially useful ideological instrument of imperialist expansion, and in its ethical-humanitarian form it is a specific vehicle of economic imperialism. Here one is reminded of a somewhat modified expression of Proudhon's: whoever invokes humanity wants to cheat. To confiscate the word humanity, to invoke and monopolize such a term probably has certain incalculable effects, such as denying the enemy the quality of being human and declaring him to be an outlaw of humanity; and a war can thereby be driven to the most extreme inhumanity.

(Schmitt, 1996, p. 54)

---

that of the external actor deemed to be responsible for enforcing human rights). He argued that claiming to intervene militarily on behalf of universal human rights was an act of power rather than principle, stating famously that 'whoever invokes humanity wants to cheat' (see Box 7.2).

Schmitt makes similar points to Arendt in arguing that the concepts of 'humanity' and of 'human rights' are empty abstractions, i.e. that they do not correspond to any political reality of constituted rights and duties. Schmitt argues that the concept of human rights may well have had a useful polemical appeal at the end of the eighteenth century as a rallying cry against the then existing aristocratic feudal system and the inequalities and privileges associated with it. However, this did not mean that the era of universal human rights had arrived. The fact that the world is divided into different and distinct political societies or states means that universal rights-bearing individuals do not exist. If they did exist then we would have a universal government, giving political and legal form to those universal rights (Schmitt, 1996, p. 55).

For Schmitt, in the absence of a unified world government that could constitute the universal human being as a rights-bearing subject in reality, human rights claims will have no clear court of adjudication or mechanism of enforcement. Schmitt argued that humanitarian action could be unproblematic if it was based on inter-state agreement and administered through a non-political body, such as the **International Committee of the Red Cross (ICRC)**. His point was that if abstract human rights claims were set against the agreed constituted rights framework, then they threatened conflict and instability. This was because the subject of these claims was separate from the agency enforcing them. The enforcement of claims of non-socially constituted legal subjects is necessarily an arbitrary one, decided by questions of power rather than principle. Schmitt feared that universal claims to judge the needs or interests of 'humanity' were not just illegitimate acts of power rather than law per se, but that they were also dangerous and destabilizing in a politically divided world (Schmitt, 1996, pp. 53–8).

The Paradox of Human Rights

The points made by Hannah Arendt and Carl Schmitt get to the heart of the paradox of human rights. Their capacity for challenging power as well as for being mechanisms of the exercise of power (unrestrained by law) stem from the fact that human rights claims are made on behalf of non-legally constituted subjects. Human rights claims may reflect the imminent revolutionary overthrow of the established order or they may reflect the oppressive use of governing power to rule beyond the limits of the law. By separating the holder of rights from the agency of enforcement of these claims, human rights claims reflect merely the challenge to the legal order. Without a consideration of the context in which a discourse of human rights arises, it is impossible to make a normative judgement as to whether this challenge to the legal order of constituted rights is something to be supported or opposed.

KEY POINTS

Human rights claims conflate ethical and legal claims because the subject of rights is not a socially constituted legal subject.

For this reason, human rights claims challenge the existing legal framework (whether it is authoritarian or democratic).

Human rights claims express a **capacity gap**—where the rights-holder is held to lack the capability of acting on their own behalf. Therefore an external agent is held to be required to enforce these rights. The dependency on an unaccountable external actor therefore makes enforcement indeterminate and contingent on the relations (and interests) of power.

Critical Thinking Questions:

This chapter is concerned with critiques of human rights on the basis of their distinction from democratic and civil rights, which presuppose the formal equality and autonomy of all people. Do we all have equal rights in reality, no matter if we are rich or poor, men or women, adults or children? What other aspects do liberal rights frameworks exclude? What about the rights of the environment, future generations, non-humans, etc?

The Rise of Human Rights

Natural rights, in terms of human rights, were revived in the sphere of international politics only during the Second World War. The modern government-led human rights movement could be seen to have been born during the War, with US President Franklin D. Roosevelt's famous 'Four Freedoms' speech of 1941 or H. G. Wells's publication *The Rights of Man, or, What are we Fighting For?* of 1940. The defence of 'essential liberties and freedoms' helped to cohere the Allied war effort against Germany and Japan, but it is important not to confuse the declaration of abstract universal values with the intention (or capability) of enforcing a framework of universal rights in the international sphere.

The gap between human rights as abstract rhetoric and as legally constituted and enforceable rights is illustrated well by the **Universal Declaration of Human Rights** (UDHR) agreed by the *United Nations General Assembly* (UNGA) in December 1948. There was agreement on thirty human rights expressed as a set of abstract moral claims or aspirations; these rights were abstracted from political questions of concrete societies' priorities and concerns and therefore could be signed up to by states with market or

state-regulated economic systems. There could be common agreement precisely because the UN did not claim to be describing rights that were universally recognized in every state, nor did it attempt to enact or enforce these rights in a legal form.

The Post-War Order

Human rights frameworks can therefore be read back into the formative legal and political moments of the post-War international order. However, if we were to read this focus on universal human rights as either a challenge to sovereignty or a challenge to the dominant framework of international order, we would be reading history backwards from the vantage point of today. It is important to appreciate that the Nuremberg Tribunal, the UDHR, and even the 1949 **Genocide Convention** were seen as enforcing the framework of equal **sovereign** rights and the principle of non-intervention.

The post-War order was constituted by the establishment of sovereign states as the only rights-bearing subjects of international law (see Chapter 4). This was made explicitly clear in the great power deliberations and international conferences in preparation of the UN Charter. There was no contradiction between state sovereignty and human rights (between the rights of states and the rights of individuals) because the international order did not recognize individuals as legal subjects. Therefore, as US Secretary of State Edward R. Stettinius stated, the legal situation was clear: 'The provisions proposed in the Charter will not, of course, ensure by themselves the realization of human rights and fundamental freedoms for all the people. The provisions are not made enforceable by any international machinery. The responsibility rests with the member governments to carry them out.' (Cited in Lewis, 1998, p. 88.)

Second, natural rights were brought into international relations through the **Nuremberg Tribunal**. Many human rights advocates argue today that the trial marked a fundamental legal break in the undermining of the rights of sovereign state authorities. This claim makes little sense as, with Germany's unconditional surrender in 1945, the Allied states who organized the military tribunal at Nuremberg did this explicitly as occupying powers with sovereign authority rather than as a supranational authority (see Laughland, 2007, pp. 53–68). Where the tribunal broke new legal ground was in using natural law to overrule *positivist* law, to argue that the laws in force at the time in Germany were no defence against the retrospective crime of 'waging an aggressive war'. This was justified on the grounds that certain acts were held to be such heinous crimes that they were banned by universal principles of humanity (Douzinas, 2007, pp. 21–2). Human rights frameworks were used to undermine positivist law, to cast the winners of the War as moral, not merely military, victors.

Human rights frameworks emerged during and at the close of the Second World War in an attempt to give moral legitimacy both to the Allies' actions during the War and to the post-War international order. While today the UDHR and the Nuremberg Tribunal are understood to have raised a challenge to the rights of state sovereignty, this was not the case at the time. The preparatory discussions for the UN Declaration and the deliberations of the Nuremberg judges both made it absolutely clear that the sovereign state was the subject of international law and that sovereignty was not challenged by any transnational legal authority. States were held to be the upholders and enforcers of both the moral and political order.

Human Rights and the Cold War

The habit of reading the rise of human rights consciousness back to 1945 as a story of the teleological march of universal ethics and values is one that unfortunately underplays the radical shift in the importance of human rights after the end of the **Cold War**. The strong consensus today that universal human rights are a guide to international policy making is, in fact, a relatively recent development. For the first twenty years after the Second World War, one of the major journals on international relations, *Foreign Affairs*, did not carry one article on human rights (Korey, 1999, p. 151). During the bulk of the Cold War era there was little concern with the implications of the UDHR for state policy or practice. Until the 1980s, the majority of academic commentators and policy makers were not convinced that human rights concerns or ethical considerations were an appropriate subject of study when assessing a state's foreign policy.

This is not surprising as human rights claims were understood to be particular rather than universal (see Box 7.3). In the West, human rights claims were interpreted as largely synonymous with democracy and the free market. The US Government and the human rights organizations that it funded consistently played

down the economic and social aspirations of the UDHR. As a propaganda weapon against the Soviet states, Western governments focused on political and civil freedoms, such as freedom of movement and information and the right to leave and return to one's country. Human rights aspirations were part of the international agenda, but they were a constituent part of the Cold War framework and understood as subordinate to the rights of sovereignty.

Their subordination to the geopolitical division of the Cold War was highlighted by the lack of consensus on moving forward the aspirations of the 1948 Universal Declaration. In the 1950s, two separate UN committees were established. These produced two separate international covenants in 1966: one dealing with civil and political rights and the other with economic, social, and cultural rights. The opposition of leading Western states to rights in the economic and social sphere was highlighted in 1986 when the UNGA adopted the *Declaration on the Right to Development*, and the USA, UK, Germany, and Japan either voted against or abstained (Mutua, 1996, pp. 606–7).

It was through attempts to overcome divisions within the US establishment and the need to address the decline of US credibility abroad, following defeat in Vietnam and the US-backed overthrow of Salvador Allende's government in Chile in 1973, that human rights concerns were put back on the international agenda (Sellars, 2002). Human rights became the mechanism by which America's reputation was to be redeemed. In 1974 the Congressional report *Human Rights in the World Community: A Call for US Leadership* set the tone for Gerald Ford's inclusion of human rights provisions into the East–West **Helsinki Agreement** of

---

BOX 7.3 CHALLENGING ASSUMPTIONS: QUESTIONING THE 'HUMAN' IN HUMAN RIGHTS

Human rights assumptions presume a universal abstract understanding of the human. This position has been challenged by those who stress the social, historical, and economic specificity of what it might mean to be human, and the oppressions and exclusions which can be obscured in universal framings of human rights—for example, post-colonial, feminist, and Marxist perspectives, which highlight the power, gender, and class assumptions behind universal rights.

How does each of these positions challenge your assumptions about what human rights are or how they work?

1975—signed by the United States, Canada, the Soviet Union, and most European states including Turkey—and for President Carter's declaration in his 1977 inaugural speech that 'our commitment to human rights must be absolute' (Sellars, 2002, p. 118). Human rights were on the agenda, but there was still little understanding of them as universal norms, rather than as a weapon in Cold War geopolitics.

From 1975 onwards, human rights were institutionalized as part of Cold War political exchanges through the establishment of the Organization for Security and Co-operation in Europe (OSCE). The Helsinki process of East–West negotiations gradually institutionalized mechanisms of human rights monitoring and information provision under the **Human Dimension Mechanism**—which allowed OSCE member states to raise issues of human rights concern with other member states. This process was used on over a hundred occasions, but, on all but one (Hungary's use against Romania over disturbances in Transylvania), the raising of human rights concerns was directly linked to geopolitical divisions (Bloed, 1993; Brett, 1993). As long as the Cold War persisted and human rights issues were used as weapons in the geopolitical divide, it was clear that there would be no support for the idea that human rights concerns could undermine sovereignty. Only in the 1990s did human rights appear to be a subject of concern in their own right, so important as to challenge the rights of states and existing frameworks of diplomatic relations and policy-making priorities.

KEY POINTS

Universal human rights claims could help provide moral legitimacy to international institutions, but do not undermine or challenge the state-based international order.

Because human rights claims had no socially constituted legal subject they empowered nation states as their agents, deciding on the content of these rights and the means of their enforcement.

During the Cold War, human rights claims were heavily politicized and subordinate to the interests of power, used by both the US and the Soviet Union to achieve instrumental ends.

Human rights were equated for ideological reasons with civil and political rights in the West and with social and economic rights by Soviet states.

Critical Thinking Questions:

This chapter charts the increasing dominance of human rights in international discourses after the end of the Cold War. Do you think that the resonance of human rights is still as strong today as it was in the 1990s and early 2000s? Have the international treaties and domestic legislative reforms privileging human rights been successful? Or is more necessary than formal legal agreements and legislative reforms? If so, what else is required to make human rights effective?

Human Rights and International Intervention

With the end of the Cold War, human rights concerns shifted from the margins to the mainstream of international concerns as universal humanitarianism appeared to be a feasible possibility. Western states and international institutions had much greater freedom to act in the international sphere with the attenuation of Cold War rivalries freeing policy from narrow geostrategic concerns. The new possibilities for intervention and aspirations for a more universal framework of policy making were increasingly expressed through the expanding discourse of human rights. There were relatively few critical voices until the 1999 Kosovo war—waged unilaterally (without UN Security Council support) by NATO states against Serbia—brought to a head concerns about the potential misuse or abuse of concerns of humanitarianism and human rights. In particular, there was concern about the idea of 'humanitarian war' tying human rights advocacy with the preponderant use of US military power. In the following sections, the relationship between human rights claims, humanitarian advocacy, international law, and military intervention will be examined, with a particular focus on the ethical, legal, and political questions raised by the Kosovo war.

Human Rights and Humanitarianism

It was in the humanitarian sphere that the shift from formal views of rights, based on rational autonomous subjects, to ethical views of rights, based on a lack of capacity and the need for external advocacy and intervention, became a major factor in international relations. The introduction of the human rights-based approach into traditional humanitarian practices reflected two trends: first, the increased penetration of external actors and agencies into post-colonial states and societies; and second, the transformation of the content of traditional humanitarian principles.

As Western humanitarian **non-governmental organizations** (NGOs) acquired greater powers and authority in post-colonial states, they redefined the central concepts guiding their work. Universality and neutrality came to be redefined, not on the basis of a universal view of humanity as being equally moral and autonomous, but on the basis of end goals or aspirations. This expansion of external power, through redefining the 'human' as lacking autonomy, effectively set up a hierarchy of the 'helper' and the 'helpless'. Through the ethic of responsibility to assist the 'helpless'—those without autonomy—this discourse reframed political choices as ethical questions. In this way, external NGO actors maintained a 'non-political' stance of neutrality at the same time as claiming extended rights to intervene in domestic political processes. From the late 1960s onwards, international humanitarian NGOs used the discourse of human rights to rewrite the boundaries of their authority through expanding the sphere of ethics into the sphere of political decision making.

The debate within the NGO community, from the late 1960s, over differing approaches to universal humanitarian ethics, counterposed two views of universality. The former 'rights equality' view espoused by the ICRC was based on the Enlightenment understanding that the recipients of aid were autonomous capable moral beings, and therefore made no judgement regarding the actions or political choices of

recipients (see Ignatieff, 1998, pp. 109–63). The human rights-based approach saw the recipients of aid in more judgemental terms: this universality was based on ends-based outcomes of peace, development, justice, etc. The importance of the shift from a universal 'rights equality' approach to that of a 'human rights-based' approach is rarely clarified; one exception is Michael Ignatieff's discussion of ICRC 'impartiality' in his book *Warrior's Honor* (Ignatieff, 1998) (see Box 7.4).

The human rights-based discourse of humanitarianism enabled NGOs to blur the distinction between politics and ethics. Central to this conflation of politics and ethics was the development of new codes of practice based around redefining neutrality. Neutrality no longer meant equal respect for parties to conflict or for locally instituted authorities, but was redefined as neutrality with respect to human rights frameworks and outcomes. In this way, NGOs claimed decision-making powers over who deserved aid and which practices of development were more appropriate. NGOs accrued more authority through the human rights discourse because they were held to be acting on behalf of rights subjects unable or incapable of acting on their own behalf.

The extension of the power and authority of humanitarian non-state actors took place in relation to changes in approaches to both conflict and to development. First, through the extension of assistance to victims of war, there was a shift from the ICRC approach of aid to casualties and assistance to prisoners regardless of political affiliation, to a more engaged, 'solidarity' approach advocated by agencies such as Doctors without Borders, who argued that there was a need to discriminate between abusers and victims and to

---

BOX 7.4 ALTERNATIVE POINTS OF VIEW: HUMANITARIANISM

Michael Ignatieff on Humanitarianism

[The ICRC's] doctrine of neutrality is called into question by organizations like Médecins sans Frontières [Doctors Without Borders], which maintains that humanitarian intervention cannot be impartial between the Serb militiaman and the Muslim civilian, or the machete-wielding Hutu and the Tutsi victim . . . [T]his leaves the ICRC wondering whether [its] insistence that all victims are equal, whatever the justice of their cause, makes sense in the bitter conflicts where one ethnic group is now seeking to obliterate the other.

(Ignatieff, 1998, p. 124)

James Orbinski (MSF) on Humanitarianism

The moral intention of the humanitarian act must be confronted with its actual result. And it is here where any form of moral neutrality about what is good must be rejected. The result can be the use of the humanitarian in 1985 to support forced migration in Ethiopia, or the use in 1996 of the humanitarian to support a genocidal regime in the refugee camps of Goma. Abstention is sometimes necessary so that the humanitarian is not used against a population in crisis.

(Orbinski, 1999)

intervene in conflict with a view to rights-based outcomes (see Box 7.4). Second, there was a shift in NGO approaches to emergency relief, and an increased understanding that famines and natural disasters could be better addressed by long-term developmental approaches rather than short-term palliative ones (see further Chandler, 2001).

It now appeared that humanitarian NGOs were duty bound to intervene in much more direct and lasting ways. However, this approach of solidarity and education and training meant that the relationship between NGOs and their beneficiaries changed from one of charity between ostensible equals to one of dependency and empowerment. The humanitarian NGOs shifted from a traditional liberal rights-based approach of equality to an instrumentalized political approach of human rights that facilitated the inequality of treatment. This has resulted in humanitarian NGOs opposing the provision of aid in cases where it was felt that human rights outcomes could be undermined (Leader, 1998; Fox, 2001).

By the end of the Cold War, the discourse of humanitarian universalism had become a highly interventionist one, transformed through the modern discourse of human rights values and assumptions. Once the barriers to state actors intervening were diminished, this discourse was increasingly taken over by leading states and international institutions, and NGOs boomed in numbers and authority as new frameworks of intervention were instituted. According to Mark Duffield, the 'petty sovereignty' of NGOs—their increasing assumption of political, decision-making powers in regions where they intervened—was 'governmentalized' in the 1990s: integrated in a growing web of interventionist institutions and practices associated with external intervention and regulation (Duffield, 2007).

Human Rights and International Law

Human rights claims, the ethico-juridical claims of a non-constituted legal subject—the human—tend to conflict with formal international legal frameworks, which necessarily operate on the basis of constituted legal subjects—sovereign states. Over the course of the 1990s and the early 2000s the understanding of this conflict has changed. Key to the changing nature of the discussion of human rights and international law have been debates on the redefinition of the meaning and relevance of the legal subject in international law, i.e. the meaning of sovereignty.

The discussion of the meaning of sovereignty reflects the discussions of neutrality and universality, highlighted in the previous subsection. The universal essence of sovereign equality was not the power or capacity of states, which clearly varied tremendously. The quality of equality was that of moral and political autonomy, the equality of the right of self-government. Since the end of the Cold War, this framework of sovereign equality has been challenged through the framework of human rights, which asserts that formal juridical frameworks are inadequate to address the needs of people living in many states where governments are held to be 'unable or unwilling' to protect their rights (International Commission on Intervention and State Sovereignty (ICISS), 2001).

At the most basic level, sovereign autonomy or self-government is seen as increasingly problematic on its own terms. The possession of formal democracy is no longer seen as adequate to safeguard the rights and interests of individuals. Many commentators follow Fareed Zakaria in his view of the post-Cold War rise of 'illiberal democracies' (Zakaria, 2003). Democracy without liberal cultures and frameworks of rights protections is held to be as likely to be a licence for tyranny as for freedom. In order to prevent the 'tyranny of the majority' or the arbitrariness of democratic mandates (Mill, 1972, p. 73; Guinier, 1994), international human rights enforcements have been increasingly demanded as part of the agenda of 'good governance' and the 'rule of law'.

There is also a second approach of human rights advocacy that undermines the rights of sovereignty, not on the basis of the problems of the formal political framework of citizenship rights, but on the basis of economic and social provisions. This is the discourse of the 'failed' or 'failing' state, where it is asserted that problems with social welfare provision or with economic development indicate that many post-colonial states need external assistance to enhance their 'functional' sovereignty (see Ghani, Lockhart, and Carnahan, 2005). Here the ethico-juridical framework of human rights redefines sovereignty on the basis of social and economic capacities, creating a sliding scale of sovereignty and marginalizing the importance of a juridical framework based on autonomy and sovereign equality.

Critical commentators are increasingly suggesting that human rights approaches have succeeded in redefining sovereignty so that it lacks any distinct legal meaning and that, in this way, external intervention is no longer seen as conflicting with or undermining sovereignty. Mark Duffield suggests that sovereignty has been redefined in terms of the **biopolitical**— based on the needs of the population rather than the needs of the ruler or government—to justify intervention in the cause of enhancing the standards of human development or human security (Duffield, 2007). Graham Harrison's work on the 'governance state' has highlighted how sovereign institutions of government have become transmission belts for external governance (Harrison, 2004; see also Chandler, 2006). On the basis of human rights frameworks, the claims of sovereign states to legal equality have been weakened, as they have been judged to be often less capable of ensuring that human rights are protected than alternative human rights-based frameworks of international regulation and intervention.

On the basis of the undermining of claims of sovereignty, it is increasingly argued that international law is becoming 'domesticated'—i.e. that it is becoming more like domestic law, enshrining the individual as its legal subject. It is often suggested that the prioritizing of individual human rights above the rights of state sovereignty can be understood as the creation of a new international moral legal order, highlighted in the conviction of state leaders for war crimes through the establishment of ad hoc international tribunals for former Yugoslavia and Rwanda, the prosecution of Chilean dictator Augusto Pinochet, the establishment of the **International Criminal Court** (ICC), and the development of ideas of **universal jurisdiction**. For human rights advocates, this new international order is one that is capable of institutionalizing the legal and political equality of individuals in place of the UN Charter framework of the equality of sovereign states.

It is in the area of international law, therefore, that the problematic fact that the individual subject of human rights is not a legally constituted subject becomes clearly highlighted. Rather than extending international law on the basis of reconstituting the formal nature of the international sphere, international law is being transformed into a 'moral–legal order', where the spheres of ethics and of law are becoming blurred (Douzinas, 2007, p. 148). The sphere of law is formally one of equality, where under equal circumstances the punishment is the same. However, the rise of human rights frameworks has introduced an ethical component into international law that, according to Costas Douzinas, 'reconstitutes the structure, subjects and core values of the international system' (Douzinas, 2007, p. 183).

This change reflects and institutionalizes the shifting nature of power relations in the international sphere

in the aftermath of the end of the Cold War. During the Cold War, there was a balance of power between the US and the Soviet Union. Although the sides may not have been exactly equal, the key point is that minor disputes or conflicts risked escalating into a nuclear superpower confrontation. For this reason, smaller states found that their sovereignty and independence were safeguarded, not so much because of the letter of international law, but because the maintenance of the status quo and restriction on the use of force to challenge sovereign borders was seen to be vital for world peace and international order. Weak states maintained their sovereignty against more powerful external rivals because of the constitution of the international order (see Jackson, 1990). With the end of this *balance of power*, a new more hegemonic and 'unipolar' world order came into existence, which has been reflected in the renegotiation and overcoming of Cold War formal and informal limits to external intervention.

The human rights framework has facilitated and smoothed the transition away from the formally constituted international order of the Cold War. The ethical challenge of human rights has helped to legitimize the downgrading of the formal legal subjects of the previous order—equal sovereign states—and in their place sets up the more flexible framework based on the claims of non-constituted legal subjects. In the 1990s the contradictions between the two approaches to framing international order seemed transparent in the debate between the formal 'right of sovereignty' and the emerging 'right of intervention' on behalf of universal human rights claims. This polarization was highlighted in relation to the NATO war over Kosovo in 1999, where human rights were held to trump sovereignty. The problem was that, for many, it was clear that the agency empowered by human rights claims was not the Kosovo victims so much as NATO powers, who claimed the right of intervention without UN Security Council permission.

Following Kosovo, the UN established an independent commission, the International Commission on Intervention and State Sovereignty, which, with some success, attempted to overcome the problem of clashing rights. In its report, *The Responsibility to Protect* (ICISS, 2001), the Commission suggested reframing the meaning of sovereignty to include the respect for human rights, enabling external intervention to be presented as supporting or enhancing sovereignty, rather than undermining it. At the same time, the report advocated the revival of Just War justifications for military intervention if the UN Security Council was not able to agree to interventions to protect human rights. The Commission's report smoothed the transition away from the formal framework of the UN Charter towards a more flexible moral–legal framework, which inevitably gave more rights to power (Simpson, 2004).

Critical commentators suggest that rights-based approaches shift sovereignty towards a new global centre, but one which is not formally or legally constituted. For many critics, the work of Carl Schmitt (1996) and the more recent work of Giorgio Agamben (2005) highlight that sovereignty, understood as the decision-making power over the exception, has shifted to give Western states, specifically the USA, greater sovereign decision-making power, at the expense of the loss of sovereignty of post-colonial states.

For these critics, the key examples of the shift away from formal equality of sovereignty can be found in the overturning of the principle of non-intervention in Kosovo and Iraq. They highlight the inequalities created by this process: while the USA refuses to be bound by international treaties that are held to limit its powers of sovereign decision making—for example, being the only state (apart from Somalia and South Sudan) not to sign up to the *International Convention on the Rights of the Child*, its refusal to submit to the ICC, etc.—other states have been forced to admit external intervention into their affairs.

For Douzinas, human rights discourses constitute a challenge to the UN Charter legal order, but one that seeks to constitute a hierarchy of unequal rights rather than a more universal order based on the equality of rights (see Box 7.5). The rights of sovereignty and self-determination for smaller or more peripheral states have been removed: 'Lost sovereignty has not disappeared. It has been absorbed and condensed into a super-sovereign centre' (Douzinas, 2007, p. 271; see also Jabri, 2007). For Douzinas, the collapse of traditional restrictions on military intervention and the projection of Western power undermine plural relations of equal sovereignty and reveal that 'In a historical reversal, an emperor is emerging but the empire is still under construction' (Douzinas, 2007, p. 257).

Human Rights and Military Intervention

The privileging of human rights as individual rights above the sovereign rights of states has altered traditional international practices, especially with regard to international law and the use of force. The human

BOX 7.5 COSMOPOLITANISM: A NEW HIERARCHY OR A NEW UNIVERSALISM?

Costas Douzinas on Cosmopolitanism

The alleged cosmopolitan character of contemporary politics does not derive from their global subjection to universal rules. The reverse is true: universal rules are created as ideal accompaniments of global phenomena by those who can exercise world policy. Domestic considerations have always played an important role in the calculation of the great powers and determine the ways in which foreign relations are exercised. This leads to a crucial distinction between globalisation and universalisation, which has been almost totally elided in the debate on human rights.

(Douzinas, 2007, pp. 180–1)

Vivienne Jabri on Cosmopolitanism

The consequences of what may be referred to as cosmopolitan war are profound, for they suggest . . . a wholesale transformation of social and political relations both domestically and internationally . . . [and] in Foucaultian terms . . . relations of power that seek to discipline conflict and dissent emerging from other societies . . . What emerges from discourses that seek to modernise, civilise, or democratise, is a conception of a world rendered in hierarchical terms, those that can claim the right of judgement and others who cannot, those within the law and those located beyond the law, those worthy of protection and others not so deserving; all suggesting a hierarchy of worthiness the remit of which is hegemonic domination.

(Jabri, 2007, pp. 96–7)

rights-based justification for military intervention is often posed in terms of the revival of pre-modern Just War thinking, which is concerned with the moral and ethical basis of war rather than with its legal grounding. Here the clash between the universal ethics of human rights and the legal framework of international society as it is currently situated comes into stark clarity.

The Kosovo war is often seen as marking the high point for human rights internationalism. Jürgen Habermas supported the Kosovo war, despite the fact that it was illegal under UN Charter rules, on the basis that in going to war for human rights NATO was pushing the boundaries of international law into a cosmopolitan, universal direction (Habermas, 1999). The war, alleged to be in the 'grey area' between legality and morality, illustrated the essence of human rights claims as an ethical challenge to law (IICK, 2000). To some commentators, using ethical arguments of human rights to undermine UN Charter law against war was dangerous or an 'abuse' of ethics; for others, as outlined with respect to Habermas, on the contrary, this was a valuable 'use' of ethics.

However, the rights of the 'human' (of 'human security' or of human rights) that are enforced are not the rights of legally constituted subjects—they are not the rights of states, the subjects of international law. As the rights being enforced are not those of legal subjects, the content and enforcement of human rights is dependent on the ad hoc agency of states willing to shoulder the burden of paying for and participating in intervention. The ad hoc nature of human rights enforcement means that the ethico-juridical undermining of UN Charter law cannot take a universal form, but is inevitably dependent on a case-by-case approach, with the decision making dictated more by the interests and concerns of the powerful than the needs of the powerless.[1] For some critics, such as Danilo Zolo (2002), it is the global hegemon, the United States, that is empowered by more informal and ad hoc decision making, but for others, such as Michael Hardt and Antonio Negri, it is global **neoliberal** capitalism itself, taking the post-national form of *Empire* (Hardt and Negri, 2001).

Whether the case of Kosovo, where human rights were held to trump sovereignty and international law (HRW, 1999), is understood as a positive step towards a more universal order or as a reactionary step towards a more hierarchical order may be a matter of normative choice. What is beyond dispute is that the existing legal order was challenged and undermined by states powerful enough to take the decision to wage war against the Serbian state. The US and most of the European powers, which backed the war, unilaterally decided to wage war outside the legal restrictions of the UN Charter order. In doing this they claimed that they were waging war on behalf of the rights of the Kosovo Albanians. But the nature of human rights claims is that, while Kosovo Albanians were the subjects of these rights, the active agents in enforcing them were the NATO powers, who in doing so accrued or claimed the right to wage war independently of the UN.

Today, human rights, the rule of law, and good governance provide the key framework of international institutional policy practices. However, when it comes to the international sphere, the lack of mechanisms to generate global consensus, the increased power

inequalities, and the limited safeguards make any attempts to institutionalize human rights regimes outside the mutual agreement of sovereign states much more problematic. The problem with constituting frameworks of sanction, intervention, and war on the basis of non-socially constituted legal subjects is that it leaves wide open the problem, raised by Schmitt, of 'who decides?' (Schmitt, 1996, 2003). Whether the intention is to (mis)use human rights ideologically or genuinely to do good in the world, the outcome is the same: ultimately, greater decision-making power and authority accrue to the states (or, some would argue, to the USA as the sole remaining great power) that have the capacity to take on the responsibilities of deciding and enforcing.

KEY POINTS

The human rights-based approach has facilitated humanitarian aid being denied in some circumstances and in support for more militarized humanitarianism—for example, the NATO war over Kosovo.

Human rights approaches appeared to directly challenge sovereignty in the 1990s, but in the 2000s have sought to redefine sovereignty as being compatible with international human rights protections. Central to this shift has been the ICISS report, *The Responsibility to Protect* (ICISS, 2001).

Human rights approaches tend to redefine war fought in the post-colonial world as a matter of human rights crimes and human rights victims; they also tend to redefine war fought by Western powers, seeing intervention in the cause of human rights as more akin to police action than war making.

Human rights approaches have facilitated a more flexible and positive framework for military intervention, shifting away from UN Charter approaches that saw war as the 'scourge of humanity'.

Critical Thinking Questions:

Have the disappointing outcomes of international intervention led to disillusionment with the enforcement of universal human rights?

It is increasingly argued that human rights should not be seen in formal terms and that human rights can be progressed through enabling processes of empowerment rather than through the external provision of formal legal frameworks; do you agree?

If human rights are increasingly being seen less in legal terms and more in terms of processes of empowerment and capacity building, does international intervention still undermine rights to sovereignty?

Human Rights and the Search for Meaning

Michael Ignatieff has emphasized that the universalism of human rights and humanitarianism represents a very different type of universalism than that traditionally associated with human rights as a progressive demand based on human rationality, autonomy, and self-determination. Rather than expressing human aspirations for a better future, the modern universal ethic of human rights tends to view humanity itself as problematic. Here, what draws humanity together as a universal is our capacity to commit crime and to suffer it. He argues that 'Modern moral universalism is built upon the experience of a new kind of crime: the crime against humanity' (Ignatieff, 1998, p. 19). The universal human subject is the victim: 'genocide and famine create a new human subject—the pure victim stripped of social identity' (Ignatieff, 1998, p. 20).

Human Rights and Political Disillusionment

Rather than universal discourses of human rights expressing a new progressive political era, Ignatieff highlights that the focus on human rights expresses disillusionment with political engagement and social change: the concern that 'there are no good causes left—only victims of bad causes' (Ignatieff, 1998, p. 23). He notes the danger of this modern moral universalism, which 'has taken the form of an anti-ideological and anti-political ethic of siding with the victim; the moral risk entailed by this ethic is misanthropy' (Ignatieff, 1998, p. 250).

There is a danger that our modern anti-political sentiments and disillusionment with progress and collective aspirations may take the form of a misanthropic view of humanity rather than a critique of economic and social relations in which our political lives are constructed and constrained. This misanthropic view is universalist, but also extremely divisive and self-comforting. Ignatieff (1998, p. 95) suggests that in seeking to rationalize the problems of the world, a depoliticized human rights perspective finds it easy to blame non-Western societies and governments and, in so doing, portray better off Western society as blameless and morally superior. In fact, it is often difficult to separate our concern for others and the construction of our own self-image or

identity. As people and politicians in the West lack a sense of mission and purpose and strong shared or collective self-image, there is a danger that we seek personal and collective affirmation in our relationship to the non-Western world: '. . . when policy was driven by moral motives, it was often driven by narcissism. We intervened not only to save others, but to save ourselves, or rather an image of ourselves as defenders of universal decencies. We wanted to show that the West "meant" something.'

The view that the shift towards framing international politics through the lens of human rights reflects the fact that major Western states and societies lack positive political goals or a strong sense of their own social cohesion gives a different angle to the (mis)use of human rights from the one we have discussed. Rather than an assertion of Western (or neo-imperial) interests and power and global aspirations of domination, the human rights discourse expresses a post-Cold War loss of confidence and lack of clear aims among leading Western and international policy actors.

Alain Badiou (2001, p. 31) suggests that citizens' rights and the domestic political process no longer provide individuals or societies with a sense of meaning or purpose: 'Parliamentary politics as practiced today does not in any way consist of setting objectives inspired by principles and of inventing the means to attain them.' Rather than representing a new social collectivity, for Badiou the focus on consensual ethics reflects the 'end of ideology' and political contestation and the lack of instrumental aims or social goals of state leaders (see Box 7.6).

Human Rights and the Lack of a Political Project

The work of Zaki Laïdi (1998) provides some valuable insights into how to tie together the themes of loss of instrumental goals and collective meaning with the search for social cohesion and legitimating 'mission' through the international discourse of human rights activism. Ethics and moral values can be seen to have displaced instrumental national interests because governments have little sense of themselves as representatives of a collective social project. Human rights claims, because of their ungrounded and abstract nature, fill the vacuum by providing an ethical purpose or set of 'values' that no longer need to be strategically acted upon. The lack of clear instrumental

BOX 7.6 THE PESSIMISM OF HUMAN RIGHTS

Michael Ignatieff on Universal Humanitarianism

In the twentieth century, the idea of human universality rests less on hope than on fear, less on optimism about the human capacity for good than on dread of human capacity for evil, less on a vision of man as maker of his history than of man the wolf toward his own kind.

(Ignatieff, 1998, p. 18)

Alain Badiou on Ethics

Whether we think of it as the consensual representation of Evil or as concern for the other, ethics designates above all the incapacity, so typical of the contemporary world, to name and strive for a Good . . . For from the beginning it confirms the absence of any project, of any emancipatory politics, or any genuinely collective cause . . . 'concern for the other' signifies that it is not a matter—that it is never a matter—of prescribing hitherto unexplored possibilities for our situation, and ultimately for ourselves.

(Badiou, 2001, pp. 30, 33)

or strategic political goals becomes repackaged as an asset rather than a problem. Human rights abuses (like the threat of terrorism) are held to be issues of urgency, crisis, or emergency, where strategic thinking and long-term planning are no longer called for (see Chandler, 2007b).

The shift from national or collective political interests to global or ethical values indicates a fundamental shift in both the meaning and practice of politics. The importance of this shift is indicated in Max Weber's essay on 'Politics as a Vocation'. Here he argued that there were 'two fundamentally different, irredeemably incompatible maxims': the 'ethics of conviction' and the 'ethics of responsibility' (Weber, 2004, p. 83). The former is about being judged on intention, the expression of values as a statement about

oneself; the latter is about being judged on outcomes, the expression of political action as a strategic and instrumental engagement in the world. It would appear that, in the framework discussed in this section, the shift from strategic interests to ethical values is not primarily about the recasting of interests in an ideological form, but more a rejection of the responsibilities of power. In the new world order of human rights and universal humanity it would seem, states Laïdi, that 'there is no longer any distance between what one does and what one aspires to', with human rights acting as the discursive framework through which political programmes and long-term projects can be side-stepped.

Ironically, the search for values and meaning in the discursive frameworks of human rights and humanitarianism exposes the lack of strategic interests behind military interventions and other forms of human rights conditionality and regulation. Acting on behalf of the 'ethics of conviction' exposes the lack of genuine conviction or strategic concern behind international interventions under the banner of 'human rights', and, for that matter, the 'war on terror'. Interventions and the use of the international arena to find a sense of mission and shared values exposes Western intervention as merely an act of power without meaning (Laïdi, 1998, p. 109). For Laïdi, attempts by Western states and, through them, international institutions, to project their power in order to generate meaning are doomed to failure. This can be understood as a failure in a double sense. First, because the intervention itself is not primarily concerned with the object of intervention, there is therefore little strategic or instrumental concern with regard to final outcomes. Second, there is failure with regard to the attempt to use intervention, or the international sphere more broadly, to generate meaning and purpose. This is because the problem of meaning is an internal one, based on the lack of connection between governing elites and their societies (see Chandler, 2007a, 2007b).

KEY POINTS

Human rights discourses and practices of intervention do not necessarily have to be critically understood as problematic because of their instrumentalism: the narrow projection of traditional great power or imperial interests.

The asymmetries of power—of Western domination—allow the international sphere to be used as an arena for the creation of meaning or purpose, for both governments and individuals.

The use of the international sphere to generate a sense of 'mission' leads to the projection of Western power with little strategic or instrumental consideration. This can be highly destabilizing.

Critical Thinking Questions:

Do you think that the attraction of ethical foreign policy, cosmopolitan political understandings, and universal human rights frameworks in the 1990s and 2000s succeeded in providing a new coherence to international policy making and international institutions? If not, why not?

It seems a lot easier to criticize human rights understandings today. Do you think this is because human rights claims were misused or abused in the interests of power? Or is it precisely because human rights claims led to universalist understandings and one-size-fits-all approaches to problems? Do you think the increased criticism of human rights approaches results from disillusionment with international policy interventions or from a deeper disillusionment with liberal universalism?

Conclusion

There can be no clear line of demarcation between the ideological use and (mis)use of human rights frameworks in international politics. Because human rights involve a separation between the agent of protection and the rights subject, there is no formal legal and political framework to judge whether claims of human rights at an international level are abused. The question is a normative one. Where there can be a greater level of consensus is at the empirical level: the rise of human rights approaches reflects the declining importance of the UN Charter order of international law, and the development of more ad hoc and informal mechanisms of international regulation and intervention.

Thus it has been argued that the demand to bring forward claims in the terminology of human rights reflects a world in which the international legal order oriented around the constitutive rights of sovereign states is under challenge. This challenge takes the form of a shift from rights taking a purely legal form, the 'black and white' wording of the UN Charter, to an ethico-juridical form. This shift away from formal legal rights to more informal expressions of rights and duties could be described as a shift towards the dominance of human rights above the rights of states, or as emerging cosmopolitan legal norms. The shift away from legal rights, framed in terms of autonomy, self-determination, and non-intervention, to ethico-juridical rights reflects a more hierarchical and interventionist order, in which issues that were previously considered to be the domestic affairs of states have become internationalized—from peace processes to issues of internal governance.

Human rights provide the framework for this internationalization. As we have considered, the dynamic behind intervention and internationalization is not straightforward, whether this is seen as a matter of reasserting imperialist power or as a reflection of domestic concerns of self-identity, mission, and purpose—or positively as a confluence of self-interest and altruism, or even an act of selfless altruism—the fact remains that human rights frameworks reflect a world in which the enforcement of rights is an unequal and contingent one and where international relations are more open to ad hoc and arbitrary policy responses. However we choose to understand the drive behind growing human rights regimes of regulation and intervention, it would be wrong to see the abuse or misuse of power as being an exception rather than the rule.

? QUESTIONS

Individual Study Questions

1. What is the difference between the subject of human rights and the subject of democratic and civil rights? Does it make a difference whether we claim rights as 'humans' or as 'citizens'?

2. How do human rights claims challenge the framework of law? Does this make these claims progressive? If not, why not?

3. How did the framework of human rights help to legitimize the post-Second World War order based on state sovereignty? Did human rights clash with sovereignty during the Cold War? If not, why not?

4. Why do human rights approaches challenge the legitimacy of state sovereignty and of international law?

5. How has the debate on the relationship between human rights and sovereignty changed between the 1990s and the 2000s?

6. What happens when state sovereignty is undermined? Does sovereignty go elsewhere? If so, where?

7. In what ways do human rights approaches challenge traditional understandings of war? Is war more or less permissible under human rights frameworks?

8. Are human rights interventions subject to the same strategic and instrumental processes of guidance as more interest-based or traditional policy interventions?

Group Discussion Questions

1. How can we explain the rise of human rights frameworks and understandings? Is this purely the exercise of power interests? Does it reflect the congruence of interests and ethical outlooks?

2. Will human rights approaches result in a more ethical or a more peaceful or a more equal world?

3. Do human rights constrain power or facilitate power?

FURTHER READING

Chandler, D. (2006). *From Kosovo to Kabul: Human Rights and International Intervention* (2nd edn). London: Pluto.

A study of human rights approaches as a challenge to universal frameworks of formal rights protection.

Douzinas, C. (2007). *Human Rights and Empire: The Political Philosophy of Cosmopolitanism.* London: Routledge Cavendish.

An analysis of the double-edged nature of human rights as a tool, both to challenge power and to enforce it.

Duffield, M. (2007). *Development, Security and Unending War: Governing the World of Peoples.* Cambridge: Polity.

An analysis of human rights frameworks in relation to the use of development interventions as mechanisms of international domination.

Ignatieff, M. (1998). *The Warrior's Honor: Ethnic War and the Modern Conscience.* New York: Chatto & Windus.

A study of the challenge that human rights approaches pose for the traditional humanitarianism of the ICRC.

Laïdi, Z. (1998). *A World without Meaning: The Crisis of Meaning in International Relations.* London: Routledge.

An analysis of the problems that Western governments have in developing clear foreign policy goals and the shift from interests to ethics.

Sellars, K. (2002). *The Rise and Rise of Human Rights.* Stroud: Sutton.

A history of the development of human rights approaches during the Second World War and the US-led revival of human rights concerns in the 1970s.

Zolo, D. (2002). *Invoking Humanity: War, Law and Global Order.* London: Continuum.

An analysis of the challenge that human rights approaches pose to international law and the restrictions on war.

WEB LINKS

http://www.counterpunch.org   *CounterPunch*. An online newsletter of c'ritical journalism and comment.

http://www.dissentmagazine.org   *Dissent*. A quarterly magazine of politics and culture.

http://www.newleftreview.org   *New Left Review*. A bi-monthly independent journal.

http://www.spiked-online.com   *Spiked*. An independent website with journalistic commentary and analysis.

http://www.zcommunications.org/zmag   *Z Magazine*. An independent monthly magazine with critical analysis.

 NOTE

1.   Note the defence of case-by-case approaches in the work of normative theorists, such as Chris Brown (2007) and Richard Devetak (2007); for a critique, see Chandler (2008).

Visit the Online Resource Centre that accompanies this book for updates and a range of other resources: www.oxfordtextbooks.co.uk/orc/goodhart3e/

8

Measuring and Monitoring Human Rights

Todd Landman and Larissa C. S. K. Kersten

Chapter Contents

Reader's Guide

This chapter provides a general overview of the purpose, challenges, and types of human rights measures. It covers the main content of human rights that ought to be measured, including the different categories (civil, political, economic, social, and cultural) and dimensions (respect, protect, and fulfil) of human rights. It outlines the different ways that human rights have been measured using different kinds of data and measurement strategies, including events data, standards data, survey data, and socio-economic and administrative statistics. It examines new trends in human rights measurement, with a focus on new ways to measure economic and social rights, 'open source', and 'big' data, and the mapping and visualization of human rights data. It concludes by identifying the remaining challenges for this sub-tradition in the field of human rights, including biased reporting, incomplete source material, and the need for continued dialogue between different academic disciplines on the need for measurement.

Introduction

The measurement and monitoring of human rights has been a mainstay activity of human rights **non-governmental organizations** (NGOs), primarily for advocacy purposes, and has become increasingly important among political scientists and social scientists more generally. Human rights NGOs such as Amnesty International and Human Rights Watch use monitoring systems to track the degree to which international human rights treaties have been implemented, to alert the international community about egregious violations of human rights, to mobilize different constituencies around particular human rights issues, and to advocate for additional standard setting in the international law of human rights. Political science, particularly since the **behavioural revolution** (see Box 8.1), has sought to measure and analyse political *violence* from state and non-state actors—an effort that has since the 1980s turned to systematic analysis on the *causes and consequences of cross-national variation in human rights protection around the world* (e.g. McCamant, 1981; Mitchell and McCormick, 1988; Landman, 2005a). Complementing these developments, scholars have published collections and reviews of human rights measures produced by academics and non-governmental organizations (Claude, 1976; Jabine and Claude, 1992), and efforts to collate and assess the quality of human rights measures continue to be carried out (e.g. see Green, 2001; Landman and Häusermann, 2003; Landman, 2004, 2006b; Landman and Carvalho, 2009; Landman, Kernohan, and Gohdes, 2012; Fariss, 2014). Increasingly, human rights concerns

and measures are entering the world of business with the advent of the 2011 UN Guiding Principles on Business and Human Rights (UNGPs) endorsed by the UN Human Rights Council (UNHRC). Multinational corporations (MNCs) are increasingly carrying out due diligence assessments of country human rights conditions, which are informed by human rights measures.

Since the publication of *Human Rights and Statistics* (Jabine and Claude, 1992), there have been an increasing number of efforts to measure more and different categories of human rights (e.g. the Cingranelli and Richards Human Rights Data Project and the Social and Economic Rights Fulfilment Index), and there have been a variety of international conferences and workshops on human rights measurement sponsored by professional academic organizations (e.g. the 2004 Chicago workshop organized by the Human Rights Section of the American Political Science Association, and the 2005 conference on economic and social rights organized by the Human Rights Institute at the University of Connecticut in Storrs) and organizations at the international level (e.g. the 2000 conference on human rights and statistics in Montreux, followed by similar summits in ensuing years in Merida, Munich, and Brussels, leading to the Metagora project, and the 2010, 2011, and 2012 meetings of the International Network on Quantitative Methods for Human Rights and Development—Metrics for Human Rights in Oslo, New York, and Madrid) and regional level (e.g. the annual conferences organized by the European Union Agency for Fundamental Rights, and the 2015 science and human rights coalition meeting on big data and human rights organized by the American Association

---

BOX 8.1 THE BEHAVIOURAL REVOLUTION

The behavioural revolution began in the 1930s and 1940s, primarily in the United States, and putatively moved political science away from normative questions and 'value-based' research, and concentrated on *observable* and *measurable* attributes of human beings and human societies in an effort to uncover empirical regularities and provide 'law-like' generalizations that had universal applicability. Research in this tradition involves hypothesis testing using **quantitative** measures on individuals and states, and the research design in such studies is one very much beholden to the natural science model of knowledge accumulation typically found in books such as Hempel's (1966) *The Philosophy of Natural Science*. Where human rights featured in the early years of this research tradition, if at all,

was in the focus on political violence and state repression, as found for example in Ted Robert Gurr's (1970) seminal book, *Why Men Rebel*. But this research did not adopt the language of rights to frame its research questions or its policy implications. It did, however, initiate the attempt to measure state and non-state violence in ways that would prove crucial to the development in human rights measures in the years to come. For example, Steven Poe and Neal Tate (1994) used standard measures of human rights and built models to explain their variation across a large number of countries and time. Since this study, political science and social science more generally have carried out increasingly complex analyses of human rights violations that remain wedded to this tradition of research.

for the Advancement of Science).[1] The most cutting-edge advances in human rights measurement, however, have come from the non-governmental sector, particularly from organizations working with truth commissions around the world. In particular, the work of the Human Rights Data Analysis Group (HRDAG), a non-profit organization based in San Francisco, California, has been instrumental in developing systematic techniques for the measurement and analysis of large-scale human rights violations across a range of different country contexts. HRDAG's approach focuses on the violation of civil rights primarily, and the ways in which statistical techniques can be used to document, count, and estimate the number of casualties that occur during periods of conflict, occupation, authoritarian rule, and other periods of violent political contestation (see Ball, Spirer, and Spirer, 2000; Seybolt, Aronson, and Fischoff, 2013).

The increasing provision and availability of human rights measures has led to a new demand in the international human rights and **donor** communities—such as the United Nations, the World Bank, the European Union, and the aid ministries in the US (USAID), UK (DFID), Sweden (SIDA), Canada (CIDA), and Denmark (DANIDA)—to integrate human rights assessment into overall policy formulation and aid allocation strategies. Donors such as the Department for International Development (DFID) in the UK use human rights assessment in their aid programming to find ways in which different aid modalities can address particular needs in partner countries to improve the human rights situation while at the same time addressing larger questions of poverty reduction. In contrast, the Millennium Challenge Corporation (USA) uses human rights measures as an incentive to allocate aid to countries that can demonstrate improvements in their human rights performance. In addition, the Office of the High Commissioner for Human Rights in Geneva published its *Human Rights Indicators: A Guide to Measurement and Implementation* in 2012, after engaging in a long-term process of consultation with international experts to provide matrices of human rights indicators for use in state party reports to the treaty monitoring bodies. The United Nations Development Programme's (UNDP) Oslo Governance Centre has produced guides on measures of good governance and human rights for use in their own country offices, as well as across the donor community more generally (see UNDP 2004, 2006).

In addition, the developments at the international level have led to country reporting on human rights

that moves beyond UN treaty obligations and includes national-level projects for the collection and analysis of human rights data. For example, the Equalities and Human Rights Commission in the United Kingdom has been developing a series of eighty indicators across ten human rights found in the European Convention on Human Rights and domesticated through the 1998 Human Rights Act. In Mexico, the Office of the High Commissioner for Human Rights, in partnership with local academics and NGOs, is collecting indicators for a wide range of different human rights, while the Ministry of the Interior (SEGOB) has commissioned work to assess the implementation of national human rights and anti-trafficking legislation. These and other national projects for monitoring, measuring, and analysing human rights demonstrate that human rights measurement is very much on the political agenda.

This chapter locates and discusses these developments in the context of broader historical shifts in the discipline of political science and shows that at present significant progress has been made in providing different kinds of measures of human rights for an increasingly larger collection of rights. It does so through consideration of (1) the purpose of measurement, (2) the challenges to measurement, (3) the types of measures, (4) new developments, and (5) the remaining gaps in the field. The discussion is cautious in its approach since much of human rights practice remains 'hidden' and thus difficult to measure; there remain significant issues that relate to source information, verification, validity, and reliability in a field for which all these issues are vitally important. It is clear from this chapter that the measurement and monitoring of human rights has established itself as a distinct subfield within the discipline of political science, as well as an increasingly important activity among international and domestic governmental and non-governmental organizations, and business and private sector organizations.

The Purpose of Measuring Human Rights

Human rights measures serve a variety of important and interrelated functions across the academic and non-academic sectors of the human rights community. First, they allow for *contextual description and documentation*, which provide the raw information for the monitoring carried out primarily by non-governmental organizations, as well as for developing and deriving standardized measures of human rights. Second, they help efforts at *classification*, which allow for the differentiation of rights violations across their different categories and dimensions, and for grouping states and regimes into different categories, such as authoritarian, personal dictatorship, fragile states, unconsolidated or weak democracies, and one-party dominant regimes. Third, they can be used for *monitoring* the degree to which states respect, protect, and fulfil the various rights set out in the different treaties to which they may be a party. Fourth, they can be used for *mapping and pattern recognition*, which provide time-series and spatial information on the broad patterns of violations within and across different countries, as well as within different groups of countries (e.g. human rights performance in less-developed countries). Fifth, they are essential for *secondary analysis*, including hypothesis testing, prediction, and impact assessment, the inferences from which can be fed into the policy-making process. Finally, human rights measures can serve as *important advocacy tools* at the domestic and international level by showing the improvement or deterioration in rights practices around the world. The accumulation of information on human rights protection in the world and the results of systematic analysis can serve as the basis for the continued development of human rights policy, advocacy, and education (Rubin and Newberg, 1980, p. 268; Claude and Jabine, 1992, pp. 5–34; Landman and Carvalho, 2009).

Traditionally, organizations such as Amnesty International and Human Rights Watch have used various indicators for depicting the human rights situation in different countries, which provide in-depth information on developments with respect to particular rights problems. Human rights measures add weight to an assessment of a country situation and enhance efforts to persuade the international community to take action on behalf of individuals or groups that are suffering. Increasingly, human rights organizations are using more sophisticated forms of measurement and analysis to enhance the types of international argument and dialogue needed to bring about progressive change in human rights. For example, the Centre for Economic and Social Rights has been working on comparisons of the relative ability and effort of states for the progressive realization of social and economic rights; the World Organization Against Torture carried out a large-scale project that analysed the causes of violence using cross-national human rights measures; and the International Council for Human Rights Policy carried out a project and consultation that examined the causes and consequences of corruption and their implication for human rights policy and advocacy (ICHRP, 2009).

In the academic world, the use of human rights measures has allowed social scientists to compare and contrast the human rights performance of countries over time and across space, in an effort to explain why some countries have a better record at protecting human rights than others (see Chapter 5). The analysis has concentrated on social and political variables such as the level of economic development, the level of democracy, and involvement in civil war and international war, and various international factors such as trade with other countries, the level of interdependence, and the degree to which a country takes part in the international regime for the protection of human rights. These studies are important in identifying the underlying reasons why countries have different levels of human rights protection and provide guidance to political leaders, international governmental organizations, and international non-governmental organizations for the types of issues that need to be addressed in order to improve the protection of human rights. For example, one seminal study carried out by Steve Poe and Neal C. Tate (1994) argued that the three issue areas that most needed attention from the international community in order to reduce human rights violations were the promotion of economic development, democracy, and conflict resolution. In this way, results from global statistical analysis have policy implications that can be implemented through different foreign policy tools, such as overseas development assistance, support for civil society and political parties, and strengthening state capacity in different areas of governance.

Private and business organizations have started to incorporate human rights due diligence into their risk-management processes and general risk assessment, with regards to the latter by assessing the human rights conditions in countries of potential investment. A small but gradually increasing number of MNCs has started to assess the actual and potential impact of their business operations on human rights in order to address and prevent human rights violations. The 2011 UN Guiding Principles on Business and Human Rights provide some guidance on how human rights due diligence should be conducted. To guide and support the practice of conducting human rights due diligence that includes the application of human rights measures, non-profit organizations have been developing tools for assessing management processes (e.g. the Human Rights Compliance Assessment Tool by the Danish Institute for Human Rights) and human rights impact (e.g. the Human Rights Impact Assessment Toolkit by NomoGaia).

KEY POINTS

Human rights can and should be measured.

The measurement of human rights has six main purposes:

- contextual description and documentation
- classification
- monitoring
- mapping and pattern recognition
- secondary analysis
- advocacy tools and political dialogue.

Analysis of human rights measures helps increase their protection worldwide.

Critical Thinking Question:

In what way does the measurement of human rights contribute to improvement in their protection?

Challenges to Measuring Human Rights

There are significant theoretical and methodological challenges to measuring human rights. Theoretically, there is both an absence of agreed philosophical foundations for human rights and the ongoing contestation over the meaning of human rights and the core content of human rights (see Chapter 1). Together these make the *operationalization* (or translation of these definitions into measurable concepts) for political science research problematic. Many of the methodological challenges to human rights measurement are related to the theoretical challenges in the sense that efforts to measure rights necessarily draw on theoretical attempts to define human rights in general terms and to provide 'systematized' definitions that can be operationalized for political science research (see Adcock and Collier, 2001). There are additional methodological challenges relating to the extent to which human rights problems can be observed

and then measured in any systematic fashion since information about human rights is often biased, uneven, and highly incomplete (see Bollen, 1992, p. 198).

At a theoretical level there are two broad sets of responses to the absence of agreed philosophical foundations. *Legal responses* cite the growth and proliferation in human rights norms, instruments, and declarations as evidence that there is an emerging global consensus on the need to promote and protect human rights (Freeman, 2001), as well as a 'language of commitment' from state and non-state actors in the international community (Boyle, 1995, p. 81). *Social and political responses* argue that rights 'made' initially through domestically based struggles in the eighteenth, nineteenth, and early twentieth centuries have been joined by international advocacy efforts at standard setting and implementation to create the international human rights system as we now know it (see e.g. Marshall, 1965; Tilly, Tilly, and Tilly, 1975; Claude, 1976; Barbalet, 1988; Foweraker and Landman, 1997; Ishay, 2004; Landman, 2013, 2015). Current research shows that indeed a justice cascade is taking place in which human rights norms developed at the international level are finding leverage at the domestic level, particularly in countries emerging from long periods of conflict and authoritarianism (see Sikkink, 2011; Landman, 2013). This 'making' of rights has led to more general and pragmatic claims that human rights represent 'bulwarks against the permanent threat of human evil' (Mendus, 1995, pp. 23–4), 'necessary legal guarantees for the exercise of human agency' (Ignatieff, 2001), or an 'important political lever for the realization of global justice' (Falk, 2000). And it is these pragmatic functions and dimensions of human rights that have provided important starting points for their measurement.

Categories and Dimensions of Human Rights

But even if the legal and socio-political arguments hold, there remains considerable disagreement on the meaning of different types of human rights that continues to complicate attempts to measure them. It is probably unfair to say that human rights are 'essentially contested' (Gallie, 1956), since the international law of human rights and its associated jurisprudence have made great strides in clarifying the content of human rights in ways that have not been done for other contested concepts (see Chapter 4). Still, for purposes of social scientific research, there remain definitional problems that present significant obstacles for their operationalization. The international instruments have in many ways established both *categories* and *dimensions* of human rights that ought to be protected. The categories are well known and range across civil, political, economic, social, and cultural rights. The notion of human rights *dimensions* has evolved from understanding human rights in 'positive' and 'negative' terms to 'generations' of rights, to a more useful formulation that comprises the separate dimensions of respect, protection, and fulfilment arising from the legal obligations of states that are party to international human rights instruments (e.g. E/C.12/1999/5).

The obligation to *respect* human rights requires the state and all its organs and agents to abstain from carrying out, sponsoring, or tolerating any practice, policy, or legal measure violating the integrity of individuals or impinging on their freedom to access resources to satisfy their needs. It also requires that legislative and administrative codes take account of guaranteed rights. The obligation to *protect* requires the state and its agents to prevent the violation of rights by other individuals or non-state actors. Where violations do occur, the state must guarantee access to legal remedies.

The obligation to *fulfil* involves issues of advocacy, public expenditure, governmental regulation of the economy, provision of basic services and related infrastructure, and redistributive measures. The duty of fulfilment comprises those active measures necessary for guaranteeing opportunities to access entitlements (see UNDP, 2006, p. 4).

Combining these categories and dimensions produces a simple matrix of the scope of human rights, and provides a good starting point from which to operationalize human rights for social science analysis (see Table 8.1). To date in the social sciences, more attention has been given to civil and political rights across the two dimensions of respect and protect. Such attempts can be seen as a function of larger ideological and methodological reasons that go beyond the scope of this chapter (but see Landman, 2005a). The table shows that all rights have these different dimensions and that the realization of all rights relies on the provision of state resources, as well as the state refraining from violation and protecting individuals from third party violations. Such a depiction of human rights transcends the dichotomy (false in my view) between so-called 'positive rights' and 'negative rights', and suggests that all rights have positive and negative dimensions.

Table 8.1 The categories and dimensions of human rights

		Dimensions of human rights		
		Respect No interference in the exercise of the right	**Protect** Prevent violations from third parties	**Fulfil** Provision of resources and outcomes of policies
Categories of human rights	Civil and political	1 The extent to which the state does not engage in torture, extrajudicial killings, arbitrary detention, electoral intimidation, disenfranchisement, etc.	2 Measures to prevent non-state actors from committing violations, such as militias, uncivil movements, or private sector firms or organizations.	3 Public investment in judiciaries, prisons, police forces, electoral authorities, and resource allocations to ability.
	Economic, social, and cultural	4 The extent to which the state engages in ethnic, racial, gender, or linguistic discrimination in health, education, and welfare, and resource allocations below ability.	5 Measures to prevent non-state actors from engaging in discriminatory behaviour that limits access to services and conditions.	6 Progressive realization; investment in health, education, and welfare, and resource allocations to ability.

Source: Adapted from UNDP (2006, p. 5)

Other Methodological Challenges

While this matrix provides a good overview of what is to be measured in terms of the different categories and dimensions of human rights, there are many remaining methodological challenges to providing *valid* (i.e. the measure measures what it purports to measure), *meaningful* (i.e. it actually measures something that matters), and *reliable* (i.e. that the measure can be produced in other contexts and by other people consistently) measures that fill the different cells in the matrix. Human rights are a class of social phenomena that are often unreported, misreported, under-reported, or over-reported in ways that make their systematic measurement highly problematic. In addition, analysis has shown that the raised awareness about human rights can produce systematic changes in the ways in which human rights are reported and documented, which in turn affects the kinds of measures that are produced (see Fariss, 2014). Over the years, political science has moved away from straight *event counting* (i.e. counting how often particular rights are violated) based on a select number of newspapers, to the use of multiple sources of information that are coded more systematically and reliably (and, as we shall see, the use of increasingly available 'open data' and 'big data' sources online). But there remain significant trade-offs in the types of data available that measure human rights directly and the types of political science analysis that can be carried out with them. On the one hand, there are very good but limited collections of highly **disaggregated** forms of human rights events data available for a handful of countries that have experienced prolonged authoritarianism, foreign occupation, or civil war (see Jabine and Claude, 1992; Ball, Spirer, and Spirer, 2000; Ball et al., 2003; Landman, 2006b; Landman and Carvalho, 2009; Seybolt, Aronson, and Fischoff, 2013). These data are on gross violations and are coded using multiple sources of information, such as statements collected by official truth commissions, monitoring systems developed by non-governmental organizations, analysis of morgue records (e.g. Haiti) and cemeteries (e.g. East Timor), or some form of retrospective survey instrument (e.g. East Timor) (see Landman, 2006b, pp. 107–25).

On the other hand, there are more extensive collections of human rights data for many countries (150 < N < 194) over time (25 < T < 36) that are of a more general nature and capture broad trends in the protection of certain human rights (see Jabine and Claude, 1992; Landman, 2002, 2006b; Landman and Carvalho, 2009). These data are coded from a variety of sources (some of which are not explicitly reported[2]) in which some form of a standardized scale is derived from a deep reading of narrative accounts on general trends in different categories of human rights, and which have by and large relied on the country reports produced by either the US State Department or Amnesty International (as we shall see). So-called 'official statistics' and the use of socio-economic and administrative data can involve problems of validity and reliability, since government agencies may not have the capacity to collect data, and the data may not have been collected in ways that are useful for human rights analysis.

There are methodological challenges with the use of survey instruments that ask random samples of individual respondents different sets of questions about perceptions of human rights or actual experiences of human rights violations. Issues include: disagreement around the type of sample and sampling strategy; the design of the survey instrument; the types of question that are used; and the sensitivities around using such a 'blunt' instrument for acquiring detailed information about something as tragic as a human rights violation. The design of a survey, before starting to ask questions, needs to take into account the nature and extent of the human rights problem that is being investigated, the affected communities, and any linguistic and cultural factors that may make the use of surveys problematic. Moreover, any one of the steps involved in survey research, if not addressed adequately, can bias the results of the survey and lead to incorrect conclusions about the human rights situation under investigation (see Landman and Carvalho, 2009, pp. 91–106).

Like other trade-offs in political science, scholars are thus faced with engaging in research using different forms of data, while recognizing the different types of inferences made possible through the analysis of different samples of countries. To date, the published political science literature engages in either the statistical analysis of pooled cross-national time-series (PCTS) data sets or small-N comparative and single case studies that make little use of available events data. PCTS data sets comprise measures of human rights and other variables across a large number of countries and over long periods of time. Events data are simply not yet available for many countries in the world, which precludes this kind of analysis from being carried out. For those countries where these kinds of data have been gathered, it is possible to conduct a comparative analysis that seeks to explain the similarities and differences that are present across a selection of countries, such as Brockett's (2005) comparison of human rights data in El Salvador and Guatemala. While events data on human rights are most suited for single-country analyses that focus in much greater detail on the specific features of countries, few studies have yet to take full advantage of these data.

Overall, efforts to develop systems for human rights measurement have advanced both within the discipline of political science and among other human rights scholars and practitioners, covering more categories and dimensions of human rights using a variety of measurement strategies. It is to these different types of human rights measures that the discussion now turns.

KEY POINTS

Human rights have different categories and dimensions that can be measured.

Some categories and dimensions have been measured more than others.

There are many methodological challenges to measuring human rights that are being overcome.

Political scientists use measures to compare many countries, few countries, and to carry out analysis of single countries.

Critical Thinking Question:

How does greater awareness about the promotion and protection of human rights affect the ways in which they are measured and how the state of human rights in the world is assessed?

Types of Human Rights Measures

Despite the continued problems with definition and operationalization, five main types of measures have been developed that serve as direct measures of human rights or as significant proxy measures for different dimensions of human rights. *Events-based* data count and chart the reported acts of violation committed against groups and individuals. *Standards-based* data establish how often and to what degree violations occur and then translate such judgements into quantitative indicators that are designed to achieve commensurability by **coding** narrative information on human rights conditions into a standardized scale.

Survey-based data use random samples of country populations to ask a series of standard questions on the perception of rights protection and/or experiences with human rights violations. Increasingly, *socio-economic and administrative statistics* have been used to measure, in a more indirect fashion, states' efforts to respect, protect, and fulfil human rights. Finally, some efforts at measurement have combined different types of data to measure human rights or compare human perceptions to human rights performance of different countries (e.g. see Anderson et al., 2005; Richards, 2006) (see Box 8.2).

Events-Based Data

Events-based data answer the important questions of what happened, when it happened, and who was involved, and then report descriptive and numerical summaries of the events. Counting such events and violations involves identifying the various acts of commission and omission that constitute or lead to human rights violations, such as extra-judicial killings, arbitrary arrest, or torture. Such data tend to be disaggregated to the level of the violation itself, which may have related data units such as the perpetrator, the victim, and the witness (Ball, Spirer, and Spirer, 2000; Landman, 2006b, pp. 82–3; Seybolt, Aronson, and Fischoff, 2013). Events-based data analysis has a long tradition, where one of the first applications of statistics to the study of violence analysed the distribution of more than 15,000 'quasi-judicial' executions carried out during the height of the Reign of Terror (March 1793 to August 1794) after the French Revolution. Using the archived documents of the tribunals that sentenced people to death, Greer (1935) analysed the patterns of sentencing and executions over time, space, and by social class (nobles, upper middle class, lower middle class, clergy, working class, and peasants). Similar analyses have been carried out for the more contemporary cases of Guatemala (Ball, 2000), Peru (Ball et al., 2003), Kosovo (Ball and Asher, 2002), Colombia (Guzmán et al., 2007), and Syria (Price, Gohdes, and Ball, 2014). In each study, highly disaggregated forms of violations data are used to estimate the total number of violations that have occurred or that have been reported (usually extra-judicial killings and disappearances), the temporal and spatial patterns in the data, and any ethno-political dimensions that might demonstrate that particular groups suffered disproportionately. In his comparison

BOX 8.2 COMBINING MEASURES OF HUMAN RIGHTS

The World Bank has devised measures of 'good governance' that maximize the use of a broad range of available indicators on good governance through a data-reduction technique that combines up to 300 disparate indicators of good governance into six separate indices.

These separate indices include:

1. voice and accountability;
2. political instability and violence;
3. government effectiveness;
4. regulatory burden;
5. rule of law;
6. graft.

Many of these categories of good governance have significant overlap with many human rights principles and standards, and focus almost exclusively on the protection of civil and political rights. The governance measures are now available for a large number of countries for over a ten-year period. See http://www.govindicators.org.

The Social Progress Index is an example of combining indicators based on different types of data into one aggregate measure. The index, which measures social progress, is composed of three dimensions (see 1 to 3) each consisting of four underlying components (see a to d). Each component is an aggregate of three to six relevant indicators measuring different

aspects of the relevant component (fifty-four indicators in total).

1.	Basic human needs:	a) nutrition and basic medical care
		b) water and sanitation
		c) shelter
		d) personal safety
2.	Foundations of well-being:	a) access to basic knowledge
		b) access to information and communications
		c) health and wellness
		d) ecosystem sustainability
3.	Opportunity:	a) personal rights
		b) personal freedom and choice
		c) tolerance and inclusion
		d) access to advanced education

The indicators under the *opportunity* dimension are mostly proxy measures for civil and political rights, and the indicators under the *basic human needs* dimension include proxies for economic and social rights. Under the *foundations of well-being* dimension the Social Progress Index takes into account further aspects of human well-being including, for example, environmental sustainability. See http://www.socialprogressimperative.org.

of El Salvador with Guatemala, for example, Brockett (2005) uses time-series events data on social protest and patterns of state repression to show how state violence in Guatemala virtually eliminated a popular rural movement, while in El Salvador similar levels of state violence did not.

Standards-Based Measures

Standards-based measures of human rights are one level removed from event counting and violation reporting, and merely apply an ordinal scale to qualitative information, where the resulting scale is derived from determining whether the reported human rights situation reaches particular threshold conditions. The most prominent examples include the Freedom House scales of civil and political liberties (Gastil, 1978, 1980, 1988, 1990; http://www.freedomhouse.org), the 'political terror scale' (Mitchell et al., 1986;

Poe and Tate, 1994; Gibney and Stohl, 1988), a scale of torture (Hathaway, 2002), and a series of seventeen different rights measures collected by Cingranelli and Richards (http://www.humanrightsdata.com). Freedom House has a standard checklist it uses to code civil and political rights based on press reports and country sources about state practices and then derives two separate scales for each category of rights that range from 1 (full protection) to 7 (full violation). The political terror scale ranges from 1 (full protection) to 5 (full violation) for state practices that include torture, political imprisonment, unlawful killing, and disappearance. Information for these scales comes from the US State Department and Amnesty International country reports. In similar fashion, Hathaway (2002) measures torture on a 1 to 5 scale using information from the US State Department. The Cingranelli and Richards human rights data codes similar sets of rights on scales from 0 to 2, and 0 to 3, with some combined indices ranging from 0 to 8, where higher scores denote better rights protections. In addition to a series of civil and political rights, Cingranelli and Richards also provide measures for such rights as women's economic, social, and political rights, workers' rights, and religious rights.

While these scales have been primarily developed to measure the *de facto* realization of human rights, other scholars have used standards-based measures to code the *de jure* commitment of states to the promotion and protection of human rights. In this application, the scale denotes the degree to which a state signs, ratifies, and files reservations to the various international human rights treaties that have been passed since the 1948 Universal Declaration of Human Rights. In these coding schemes, countries are rewarded for treaty ratification and punished for the degree to which their reservations undermine the object and purpose of the treaty. Camp Keith (1999), Hathaway (2002), Neumayer (2005), and Hafner-Burton and Tsutsui (2005, 2007) use a simple dummy variable for ratification, while Landman (2005b) and Simmons (2009) use variables that take into account state signature and combine them with variables that also measure the reservations states make, at the time of ratification and subsequently.

Survey Data

Survey data have been less widely used in social scientific research on human rights than either events-based or standards-based measures. They have usually featured more often in research on the support for democracy (e.g. Kaase and Newton, 1995), trust and social capital (e.g. Whiteley, 1999, 2000), patterns of corruption (http://www.transparency.org), or as components of larger indices of 'post-material' values (see Inglehart, 1997). But increasingly, household surveys have been used to provide measures for popular attitudes about rights and to uncover direct and indirect experiences of human rights violations. Some of the most notable work has been carried out by the NGO Physicians for Human Rights, which conducts surveys of 'at risk' populations (e.g. internally displaced people or women in conflict) to determine the nature and degree of human rights violations. The 'minorities at risk' project certainly captures the degree to which communal groups and other national minorities suffer different forms of discrimination. In addition, the truth commission in East Timor carried out a retrospective household mortality survey on all deaths and illnesses in the country during the period of Indonesian occupation between 1974 and 1999. The survey data were then matched with other kinds of data collected from statements given to the truth commission and from a census of all graveyards. These multiple sources of data were then used to estimate the total number of people who had died during the occupation using a log-linear method of estimation common in biological and epidemiological research (see International Working Group for Disease Monitoring and Forecasting, 1995; Ball et al., 2003).

Survey analysis and public opinion research have also begun to explore the degree to which citizens' attitudes and perceptions about human rights are in line with the actual human rights situation in countries. This research combines these standards-based indicators of human rights with random sample surveys that ask questions about respect for human rights, where typical response categories include such terms as 'a lot', 'some respect', 'not much respect', and 'no respect at all' (see Anderson et al., 2005; Richards, 2006). The research effort goes on to compare the perceptions of the human rights situation to the general trends in the protection of different categories of human rights, either for the world (Richards, 2006), or broken down for particular regions (Anderson et al., 2005; Richards, 2006). The global comparisons reveal that citizens have multiple rights referents when they formulate assessments of the human rights situation in their own countries, and that there is a moderate congruence between public opinion about the human rights situation and the actual human rights situation, which is further differentiated across regions (Richards, 2006, pp. 28–31). Across the post-communist states of Central and Eastern Europe, there is a high congruence between perceptions of human rights and actual human rights practices, but this congruence tends to be stronger for more highly educated citizens (Anderson et al., 2005). Both studies represent the application of cross-cultural analysis using perceptions as a main subjective variable of interest as it relates to more objective human rights conditions.

Administrative and Socio-Economic Statistics

Administrative and socio-economic statistics produced by national statistical offices or recognized international governmental organizations have been increasingly seen as useful sources of data for the indirect measure of human rights, or as indicators for rights-based approaches to different sectors, such as justice, health, education, and welfare. Government statistical agencies and intergovernmental organizations produce a variety of socio-economic statistics that can be used to approximate measures of human rights. For example, academic and policy research has used aggregate measures of development as proxy measures for the progressive realization of social and economic rights. Such aggregate measures include the **Physical Quality of Life Index** (PQLI), the Human Development Index (HDI), and the Social Economic Rights Fulfilment Index (SERF Index).[3]

The PQLI is a 0 to 100 scale derived from combining equally weighted measures of the literacy rate, infant mortality, and life expectancy. In similar fashion, the HDI is a 0 to 1 scale that combines differently weighted measures of life expectancy, literacy rate, gross enrolment ratio, and per capita Gross National Income (GNI). These two measures are highly correlated with each other and with per capita Gross Domestic Product (GDP), where the HDI has a higher correlation since per capita GNI is one of its components.

In both cases, the indices have been used to track both the level of development and the change in development, which are then linked to the notion of *fulfilling* social and economic rights. The PQLI represents a measure of subsistence rights (Milner, Poe, and Leblang, 1999) since it captures the fundamental aspects of an individual's life and those basic requirements for human existence. For Cingranelli and Richards (2007) the PQLI can be compared with other measures in ways that capture a state's achievement in the area of economic and social rights. Accordingly, they regress the PQLI onto per capita GDP (a rough measure of ability to fulfil these rights) and Landman's (2005b) standards-based scale of ratification for the **International Covenant on Economic, Social and Cultural Rights** (ICESCR), and then save the residual, which reflects the overall level of achievement on these rights as a function of ability and willingness. Their measure is thus derived from a socio-economic statistic and a standards-based measure, which captures the idea of 'government effort to respect economic rights' (Cingranelli and Richards, 2007, p. 224).

In contrast, the SERF Index (http://www.serfindex.org) measures on a 0 to 100 scale the extent to which states fulfil their obligations under the right to food (infant height and weight), the right to education (primary school completion, gross school enrolment, average maths and science PISA score), the right to health (contraceptive prevalence, life expectancy, infant mortality), the right to housing (improved access to sanitation and water), and the right to work (poverty headcount, long-term unemployment, relative poverty) in relation to countries' maximum available resources. Resource capacity is estimated using per capita GDP, which is compared with the measures of the various substantive rights across countries and time (1990–2006). The curve fitted through the outer region of the scatter plot is called the Achievement Possibilities Frontier (APF), and it defines the benchmark level of obligation for a state given its per capita GDP (see Figure 8.1). Comparing each country's actual performance on each right with its APF benchmark level for that right indicates how well the country is doing in light of its feasible levels of achievement.

The Social Progress Index (SPI) combines proxy measures for economic and social rights (see Box 8.2 for details) and takes into account measures for gender parity in secondary enrolment (under component access to basic knowledge), women treated with respect, tolerance for immigrants, tolerance for homosexuals, discrimination and violence against minorities, and religious tolerance (all under component tolerance and inclusion). The SPI provides a more complete picture of the human rights situation of marginalized and excluded groups and minorities than the PQLI, HDI, or SERF Index. Even though the SPI explicitly focuses on non-economic aspects, and does not take into account per capita GDP or GNI as such, the measure is very strongly correlated with the HDI—partly due to similar or same input variables—and with per capita GDP.

In any such application, however, these measures are imperfect since they provide too little information on the degree to which different groups in society enjoy the benefits of development. There are aggregate measures of macro-economic performance, and in the absence of a breakdown by gender, ethnicity, religion, and other social categories traditionally associated with exclusion, such measures do not yet capture a full picture of the human rights situation. Other measures, such as the percentage of minority groups in society that achieve levels of literacy and/or education, or the breakdown of households with access to available housing, health, and other social welfare services, can serve as indicators for the presence of possible discrimination against certain groups

Figure 8.1   Achievement Possibilities Frontier for infant survival rate for non-OECD countries

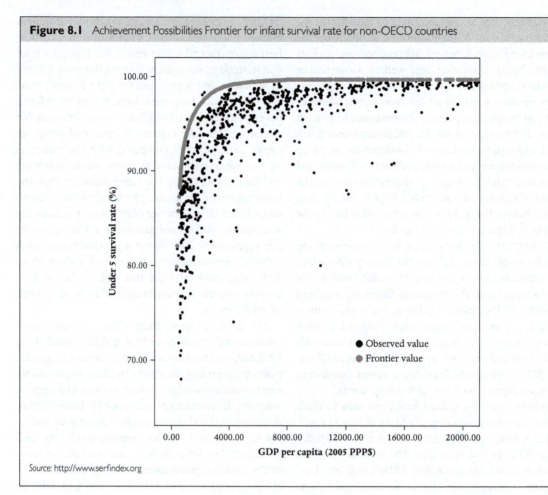

Source: http://www.serfindex.org

in the exercise of their social and economic rights. It is typical of national statistical offices to collect on an annual basis a variety of socio-economic indicators that, in principle, should be disaggregated by gender, age, income, and geography in ways that can provide proxy indicators for economic and social rights. However, owing to capacity issues and limited resources, sample sizes make it difficult to disaggregate the data. See Box 8.3 for more discussion on measures for economic and social rights.

New Developments

Alongside the continued development and refinement of these existing measurement strategies, there are new trends in data collection that make use of the

'democratization of technology' that has taken place more or less during the first decade of the twenty-first century. The rise of social media, and the increasing availability of smartphones and other mobile devices has led to a revolution in the ability of individual people to have a voice in ways that were hitherto not possible. User-generated content on the Internet, in the form of 'tweets', YouTube videos, SMS alert networks, and other platforms of information dissemination, have created a volume of information on country conditions that is beginning to transform the ability of political scientists and other researchers to study human rights. The information that is now available is 'double edged': on the one hand, it provides the ability for grassroots reporting and narrative accounts of real time events as they unfold, and on

BOX 8.3 CHALLENGING ASSUMPTIONS: MEASURES FOR ECONOMIC AND SOCIAL RIGHTS

The PQLI, HDI, and SPI utilize similar indicators that cover key aspects of economic and social rights. The authors of these indices do not explicitly apply the language of human rights, but provide measurements for life quality, human development, and social progress respectively. In contrast, the SERF Index measures the fulfilment of economic and social rights by taking into account countries' maximum available resources. Given that all four indices strongly correlate with each other and thereby indicate similar trends, what would be the value added of a SERF Index over the other three indicators? Figure 8.2 shows the SERF Index for selected Latin American countries, averaged for the years 2000 to 2010. Is the SERF Index a better measure for cross-country comparison? Is an index that refers explicitly to the normative content of economic and social rights more effective in contributing to the protection of human rights?

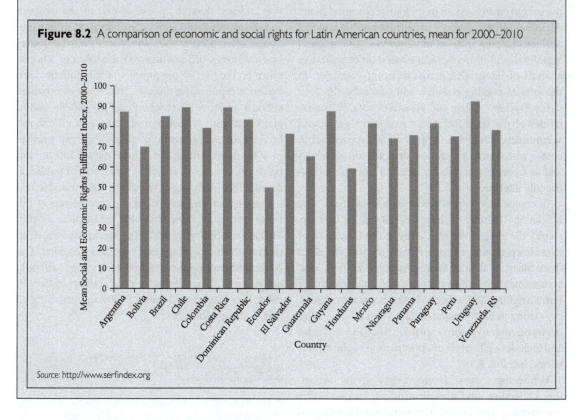

Figure 8.2 A comparison of economic and social rights for Latin American countries, mean for 2000–2010

Source: http://www.serfindex.org

the other hand, it provides 'meta data' on the events themselves, as smart technology often contains automatic functions that include the date, time, and location that something has happened (typically through embedded 'global positioning system' technology, or GPS).

The combination of real time data and meta data allows for collection, fusion, and visualization of human rights events across space and time, often at the 'street corner' level of accuracy. The collection of these kinds of data occurs in two ways: (1) 'crowd sourcing' through specialized data-collection 'portals' such as the platform made available through Usha-hidi (http://www.ushahidi.com), or (2) collection of data from already existing 'open data' sources, such as Facebook, Twitter, news media, and NGO reporting, among others. In their raw form, the data are not particularly useful, but, through fusing different sources into well-structured databases that conform to the 'who did what to whom' understanding of human rights violations, they can be used for human rights assessments of countries. Moreover, since the meta data may contain additional information about date, time, and location of events, it is possible to map violations on publicly available mapping programs such as Google Maps.

There have also been some interesting developments in the area of human rights data visualization. For example, the Migrant Integration Policy Index (MIPEX) contains data on the degree to which migrants are integrated into recipient countries. The data resource codes country integration policies and allows the user to create custom maps for the countries in the database. MIPEX (http://www.mipex.eu) is a useful tool for mapping migrant integration at a formal and legal level, and allows advocacy based on comparative analysis of integration across different countries. In the area of conflict research and advocacy, the LRA Crisis Tracker collects and visualizes data on the activities of the Lord Resistance Army in Uganda and surrounding countries (http://www.lracrisistracker.com), where events data are depicted on timelines and as frequency counts by location through a user-friendly interface.

In conjunction with a private sector company, The Mackman Group (http://www.mackmangroup.co.uk), the Human Rights Centre at the University of Essex has produced a *Human Rights Atlas* that visualizes three pillars of data on basic country indicators, legal commitments to human rights treaties, and measures of human rights practice (http://www.humanrightsatlas.org) using publicly available data sources. The Atlas draws on Andrew Fagan's (2010) *Atlas of Human Rights* and includes a global set of countries over a thirty-year period (see Box 8.4).

While these new developments in the reporting, collection, and visualization of human rights are exciting and useful, the same methodological issues arise across all these examples. Crowdsourcing and open data mining carry with them the same problems of representativeness and over- and under-reporting that we saw in our discussion of events-based data earlier in this chapter. Crowds and open data are 'convenience' samples, which is to say, people and organizations choose to report issues that they have seen and/or experienced. Such data are analogous to crime reporting data collected by law enforcement authorities (as opposed to crime surveys). Any data collected in this fashion will only ever reflect the population that has chosen to report it, while many violations remain hidden and simply unknown. But the geospatial aspects of this

work can begin to show the subnational variation in human rights violations, even if the records are incomplete and the patterns that are identified invite closer scrutiny.

Moreover, technology now allows for the collection of narratives about human rights violations that are 'triangulated' with photographs, videos, and other forms of data that carry with them the additional meta data. For example, in the United Kingdom on 1 April 2009, a newspaper seller named Ian Tomlinson was knocked down by police as part of the violence and chaos associated with G20 protests in London. Ian Tomlinson died very soon afterwards. Initial inquiries into the event did not uncover evidence of malfeasance on the part of the police, but subsequent video evidence captured on multiple smartphones provided enough evidence to charge Police Constable Simon Harwood with manslaughter. This example shows how the democratization of technology can provide new kinds of data about human rights and human rights-related events, as well as new forms of public accountability. Such use of technology has transformed the perception and analysis of the massive sets of political transformations that have taken place as part of the Arab Spring in 2011. The world has witnessed real time video coverage as events have unfolded. The continued development of new technology will only enhance the ability of analysts and activists to harvest valid, meaningful, and reliable data on human rights events around the world.

KEY POINTS

The democratization of technology means there is more information about human rights in the public domain.

Ordinary individuals and groups have used new social media technology to challenge governments and mobilize protest movements.

Analysts can capture new forms of human rights information and map it using readily available tools.

The power of new technology has led to a new form of accountability that is vital for promotion and protection of human rights.

Critical Thinking Question:

What are the risks of using 'open source' and 'big' data for measuring human rights?

BOX 8.4 VISUALIZING HUMAN RIGHTS DATA

All of the different types of human rights measures discussed in this chapter can be visualized in increasingly imaginative ways with the development of more and more online tools. These tools allow for visualization, moving beyond mere tables, bar charts, and scatter plots to the use of maps and interactive online tools. For example, the combined 'physical integrity rights' measure from the Cingranelli and Richards data resource can be visualized on a global map (http://www.humanrightsatlas.org). Figure 8.3 shows the measure (the 9-point scale has been adjusted to a 5-point scale) for 2010 on a global map. Countries that are shaded darker have better records of physical integrity rights protection. Alongside the mapping of the score itself, additional country information can be added that 'pops up' when a user moves his or her mouse over a country, which for the example of Argentina includes additional information on population, per capita GDP, the Human Development Index, and the ratification status of the 1966 International Covenant on Civil and Political Rights.

Figure 8.3 A mapping of physical integrity rights and an example of basic country statistics for Argentina, 2010

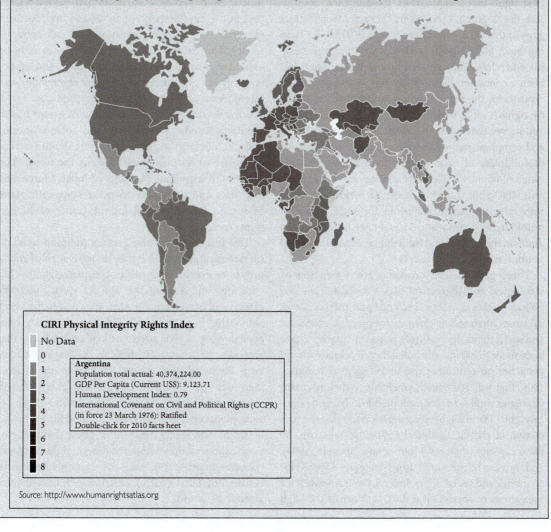

CIRI Physical Integrity Rights Index

No Data
0
1
2
3
4
5
6
7
8

Argentina
Population total actual: 40,374,224.00
GDP Per Capita (Current US$): 9,123.71
Human Development Index: 0.79
International Covenant on Civil and Political Rights (CCPR)
(in force 23 March 1976): Ratified
Double-click for 2010 facts heet

Source: http://www.humanrightsatlas.org

Conclusion

This brief overview of the purpose, challenges, and examples of human rights measurement and monitoring shows that human rights scholars and practitioners have made great advances since the measurement community first turned its attention to human rights. Political scientists, sociologists, statisticians, geographers, demographers, health professionals, and economists as well as activists from non-governmental organizations have all contributed to the general increase in the availability of human rights measures or indicators that can be used to support rights-based approaches. Despite these impressive developments, however, there remain distinct gaps in this field. The different cells in Table 8.1 have not been filled equally with sets of valid, meaningful, and reliable indicators of human rights. There has been a continued bias towards the production of indicators for the respect dimension of civil and political rights (Cell 1), with events-based, standards-based, and survey-based data that cover a wide geographical and temporal range. There are aggregate measures of fulfilment of economic rights that cover a wide range of countries (Cell 6) (e.g. Cingranelli and Richards, 2007), but there is a dearth of measures for the respect and protect dimensions for social and economic rights (Cells 4 and 5), and very little has been done on the protect and fulfil dimensions of civil and political rights (Cells 2 and 3).

These gaps in data provision are a function of ideological and theoretical biases towards civil and political rights in political science and methodological issues surrounding the measurement of economic and social rights. Increasingly, however, attempts have been made to explore the possibility of '**violations approaches**' to economic and social rights (Chapman, 1996) that will make them amenable to measurement strategies similar to those adopted for civil and political rights. There has been recognition too that the protection of civil and political rights also relies on the fiscal capacity of states (Holmes and Sunstein, 1999), and thus can be measured using strategies adopted for economic and social rights. Indeed, the framework for measurement developed at the UN Office of the High Commissioner for Human Rights includes notions of 'structure', 'process', and 'outcome' to define ideal sets of indicators, many of which are operationalized using socio-economic and administrative statistics related to civil and political rights (see Landman and Carvalho, 2009).

There is now an increasing demand for the provision of human rights measures from within both the academic and policy communities. It also appears that there is an increasing supply of innovative and more reliable measures for a growing number of human rights. Political scientists have played a large part in the development, analysis, and improvement of these human rights measures and will continue to do so in the future—an effort that can only be enhanced through the exchange of ideas and experiences from governmental, non-governmental, and intergovernmental organizations around the world. Work will continue on the provision of events-based, standards-based, survey-based, and socio-economic and administrative statistics to capture the full picture of human rights in countries around the world. The addition of increasing amounts of 'open source' and 'big' data and the ability to make systematic sense of these data bodes well for the future of human rights measurement.

This future will involve greater attention to *all* dimensions of all human rights, *disaggregation* of measures to assess the enjoyment of human rights within countries and among the world's most *vulnerable groups*, and more *open communication and transparency* about the ways in which different measures have been developed. The advent of new technologies that empower ordinary individuals in the ways that have been discussed here suggest that there are increasingly rich veins of data on human rights that will serve political scientists well in the future. These developments and the continued demand for more and better human rights measures suggest that this particular sub-tradition within the human rights field will continue to prosper in ways that can only be fruitful to the long-term goal of enhancing human dignity around the world.

QUESTIONS

Individual Study Questions

1.   Why is it important to measure human rights, and what are the challenges associated with different measures?

2.   What are the strengths and weaknesses of events-based, standards-based, and survey-based measures of human rights?

3.   In what ways can socio-economic and administrative statistics be used for measuring human rights?

Group Discussion Questions

1.   Is it good to have human rights violations reported publicly?

2.   Why is it important to take into account the different categories and dimensions of human rights?

3.   In what ways does the visualization of human rights data affect the ways in which they are promoted and protected?

FURTHER READING

Ball, P. B., Asher, J., Sulmont, D., and **Manrique, D.** (2003). *How many Peruvians have died?* Washington, DC: American Association for the Advancement of Science (AAAS).

The best example of the estimation of events-based human rights data using the case of Peru 1980–2000.

Green, M. (2001). What we Talk About when we Talk About Indicators: Current Approaches to Human Rights Measurement. *Human Rights Quarterly,* **23**/4, 1062–97.

A good overview of conceptual and methodological issues surrounding the measurement of human rights.

Hafner-Burton, E. and **Ron, J.** (2007). Special Issue on Human Rights. *Journal of Peace Research,* **44**/4.

An excellent illustration of the use of standards-based measures of human rights in political science research.

Hertel, S. and **Minkler, L.** (eds) (2007). *Economic Rights: Conceptual, Measurement and Policy Issues.* Cambridge: Cambridge University Press.

An excellent review of the conceptual and methodological issues surrounding the measurement of economic and social rights.

Jabine T. B. and **Claude, R. P.** (eds) (1992). *Human Rights and Statistics: Getting the Record Straight.* Philadelphia: University of Pennsylvania Press.

A great overview of human rights measurement, including theoretical and methodological issues.

Landman, T. and **Carvalho, E.** (2009). *Measuring Human Rights.* London and Oxford: Routledge.

State of the art review and discussion of human rights measurement.

WEB LINKS

http://www.freedomhouse.org   Freedom House: two standards-based scales on civil and political rights from 1972, updated annually.

http://www.humanrightsatlas.org   Human Rights Atlas: an interactive map-based website with data on country conditions, legal commitments, and human rights practices.

http://www.humanrightsdata.com   Cingranelli and Richards Human Rights Data: a large collection of standards-based data on seventeen different human rights from 1980 to 2006, updated occasionally.

http://www.hrdag.org   Human Rights Data Analysis Group: world-leading organization in the production and analysis of event-based data on human rights.

http://www.politicalterrorscale.org   Political Terror Scale: a standards-based scale on personal integrity rights from 1976 to 2006, updated occasionally.

 NOTES

1. For more information including podcasts on the Science and Human Rights Coalition Meeting: Big Data & Human Rights by AAAS, see http://www.aaas.org/event/science-human-rights-coalition-meeting-big-data-human-rights.

2. For example, Freedom House relies on a large number of sources, but does not list which ones in particular are used for the production of its two scales of civil and political rights. This is also true of Maplecroft, a private human rights and business risk company based in the United Kingdom.

3. There is no single source for the PQLI as it is derived from other measures available from various international sources. In contrast, the UNDP provides annual HDI figures; see http://hdr.undp.org/en/statistics. See also the statistical databases available from the United Nations: http://unstats.un.org/unsd.

 Visit the Online Resource Centre that accompanies this book for updates and a range of other resources: www.oxfordtextbooks.co.uk/orc/goodhart3e/

PART II
Human Rights in Practice

9

Global Civil Society and Human Rights

Marlies Glasius and Doutje Lettinga

Chapter Contents

Reader's Guide

This chapter explores the relationship between global civil society (GCS), understood as 'people organizing to influence their world', and the normative ideal of a 'global rule-bound society'. After an introduction on the concept of GCS, the chapter surveys some of the GCS actors involved in human rights issues and focuses on their background, methods, and influence. The activities of individuals and organizations in civil society in relation to human rights can be divided into three kinds, which can be considered as related to three different phases: shifting norms; making law; and monitoring implementation. The three types of activities will be illustrated with two brief case studies: norm-shifting activities in relation to economic and social rights, and lawmaking and monitoring activities in relation to the International Criminal Court.

What is Global Civil Society?

Civil society, let alone **global civil society** (**GCS**), is a confusing term. There are as many definitions of civil society and GCS as there are authors (see for instance: Howell and Pearce, 2001, pp. 13–37; D. Lewis, 2002; Kaldor, 2003, pp. 6–12). Nevertheless, this chapter quite intentionally uses this term, rather than other current ones such as 'global social movements' (Cohen and Rai, 2000), 'transnational advocacy networks' (Keck and Sikkink, 1998), or 'global citizen action' (Edwards and Gaventa, 2001).

Its history is bound up with the notion of rules to protect citizens—i.e. civil rights. The term goes back to ancient Rome (*societas civilis*), but was used particularly in the **Enlightenment** to express opposition to the idea that a ruler could treat his subjects as he pleased. Civil society referred to a voluntary association, based on a hypothetical social contract that outlined the rights and obligations of citizens (see Seligman, 1992). With the exception of Kant, Enlightenment thinkers conceived this rule-bound society in national terms.

Some authors still prefer terms like 'transnational' or 'international' civil society, arguing that 'global' sounds too grandiose (Smith, Chatfield, and Pagnucco, 1997; Keck and Sikkink, 1998; Florini, 2000). However, while 'global' may overstate the situation, 'transnational' understates it. A single border crossing counts as transnational; hence, the term does not capture the revolution in travel and communications and the opening up of many formerly closed societies of the last decades. Moreover, only 'global civil society' can be posed as a complement as well as a counterweight to the process now universally called **globalization**.

Finally, the term GCS has a normative aspiration that 'transnational civil society' does not. Just as the term 'human rights' has a universalistic intent that 'civil rights' lacks, GCS can be seen as an aspiration to reach and include citizens everywhere and to enable them to think and act as global citizens. Some of the literature on globalization stresses the emergence of a global consciousness, an 'imagined community of mankind' (Shaw, 2000). GCS is an expression of that consciousness, even if some participants cannot travel or even use the telephone (Anheier, Glasius, and Kaldor, 2001, pp. 16–17). At the same time, the post-War notion of universal human rights, coupled with a thickening network of international rules directly affecting citizens, has given birth to the dream of a global rule-bound society. As we illustrate, GCS in the modern sense of the whole of border-crossing, non-profit, non-governmental entities remains intimately connected with human rights law.

So what exactly *is* this GCS? In the *Global Civil Society Yearbook*, we developed the following working definition: 'global civil society is the sphere of ideas, values, institutions, organizations, networks, and individuals located *between* the family, the state, and the market, and operating *beyond* the confines of national societies, polities, and economies' (Anheier, Glasius, and Kaldor, 2001, p. 17). Here, we adopt a definition that is a little narrower and much simpler: GCS consists of people organizing to influence their world. Hence, it involves some sort of deliberate get-together. It is a political definition, excluding people who organize to play darts or make money. It does include those who attempt to influence their world in undesirable directions, or by unpalatable means (see Box 9.1). The subjective 'their world' suggests people concerned with

---

BOX 9.1 DECONSTRUCTING: THE 'CIVIL'

What is 'civil' about global civil society? While many civil society actors indeed aim to 'civilize' the state or the public, not all of them do this in a particularly 'civil' and peaceful way, or with progressive, liberal, and democratic ideals in mind. GCS is very heterogeneous, hence it also encompasses movements that are racist, sexist, or violent. But deciding what norms or what groups count as civil is problematic for many reasons. First, historically, colonial projects were often justified in terms of 'civilizing' the natives, even as the methods of subjugation were allowed to be uncivil. Second, to some extent all civil society manifestations are in some sense exclusivist: they claim the moral high ground for

their own position in opposition to all others. Third, civil—for instance democratic—aims do not necessarily coincide with civil—for instance democratic—behaviour. Uncivil movements may have civil outcomes and vice versa. Finally, civility is not the same as rule-following: adherence to existing legal or even societal norms is far from desirable in non-democratic societies, and proscribes challenges to the status quo even in democratic ones. Hence, GCS is best approached with a flexible concept of the 'civil' element, acknowledging that what constitutes civility is eternally contested (see Kopecky and Mudde, 2003, and Glasius, forthcoming for a longer discussion).

the world they see themselves living in, their *life-world*, not necessarily that they have planetary ambitions. That life-world is increasingly shaped by the forces of globalization. This definition, finally, suggests that (global) civil society is a contested terrain (Howell and Pearce, 2001, p. 234), populated by value-driven actors who do not necessarily share harmonious value systems: indeed, their values sometimes clash.

As an empirical concept with strong normative implications, the concept of GCS is not without its critics. We will outline four types of critique. The first is that lack of protection prevents the effective functioning of GCS. According to Chris Brown, 'there are major "law and order" problems in the international system, and these problems severely restrict the functioning of global civil society ... [non-governmental agencies] need the protection of a police force, and at the moment the only such bodies are provided by the individual states, and in many parts of the world are, at best, extremely ineffective, at worst, wholly corrupt' (Brown 2001). This view, however, takes a rather passive, 'hothouse plant' view of what GCS is. It may be intuitive that the emergence of a GCS depends on the development and observance of the international rule of law, but the opposite connection is missed: the history of humanitarian and human rights law (see Chapter 4) has been much more a product of the activities of people outside government than is commonly accepted. Almost every significant treaty in international humanitarian law originates with the **International Committee of the Red Cross** (ICRC). The idea for a Universal Declaration came from a small group of lawyers, some of whom had themselves been political refugees; the insertion of human rights provisions in the UN Charter was the work of **non-governmental organizations** (NGOs); and a post-War treaty like the **Convention Against Torture** was almost solely the brainchild of human rights NGOs (see Burgers, 1992; Keck and Sikkink, 1998, p. 85; A. M. Clark, 2001, pp. 55–67). It would be naive to believe that international law could emerge without the backing of states or overcome the opposition of a majority of states. However, those parts of international law that protect the interests of humanity, rather than the interests of states, rely heavily on the involvement of GCS.

A second critique is normative, and claims that while GCS actors claim to call to account states or corporate power-holders, they actually support a larger neoliberal global order. Working within the confines of the existing global economic and political

system, GCS organizations choose to tinker in the margins with the rules of the game rather than fundamentally challenge the game itself. GCS, by offering regulatory band-aids, actually legitimizes the global capitalist order, and (no longer) functions as a counter-hegemonic force. Ronnie Lipschutz (Lipschutz and Rowe, 2005, p. 202), for instance, has argued that 'the arrangement of rules, regulations and practices characteristic of contemporary capitalist states operating under and through global neoliberalism do not and cannot address more than a fraction of the "welfare of populations". Much of the remainder of this function is increasingly being provided through civil society, some of which has been drawn into existence in order to address these lacunae ... much of what appears to be opposition—by civil society organizations in particular—is better understood as integral to governmentality.' Undoubtedly, different GCS actors at different times both challenge and support centres of power. It is for social scientists to study empirically when they confront, collaborate with, or are co-opted by state and other actors.

A third strand critiques the dominant, secular, and Western understanding of GCS. According to Raouf Ezzat (2004), 'Religious devotion is a fundamental motive for many social movements in the South, from Latin America to Africa and South Asia. In many of these countries, grassroots politics, whether local or global, depend heavily on sacred notions, images and principles, and the religious dimension is mixed with public mobilization.' This is really a critique of certain blind spots of Western social science and Western public opinion rather than a critique of the concept of GCS as such, and could be countered with better research.

The fourth critique relates directly to human rights advocacy: the notion that with their border-transcending, norm-setting aspirations, international NGOs (INGOs), giving themselves the grander title of global civil society, are doing something essentially undemocratic. Ken Anderson for instance argues: 'international NGOs are "international civil society", international civil society is the voice of the people of the globe, the voice of "world opinion", and so states and international organizations must make a place for these NGOs at the negotiating tables, in the halls of power, because if they do not, these states—even, once again, democratic ones—and international institutions risk illegitimacy' (Anderson and Rieff, 2000, p. 111). This raises the question to what extent INGOs can legitimately claim to represent the needs and interests of smaller, local groups, and eventually of marginalized constituencies, at state and inter-state meetings. This tension between human rights advocacy and democratic representation will be revisited in the conclusion to this chapter.

This chapter explores the relationship between the empirical 'people organizing to influence their world' and the normative ideal of a 'global rule-bound society'. To avoid confusion, we use the term GCS only in the former sense to refer to 'actually existing civil society'. The next sections will introduce some of the GCS actors involved in human rights issues, focusing on their background, methods, and influence.

Global Civil Society Actors and Human Rights

The mother of international human rights organizations is Amnesty International, founded in 1961. It now claims to have more than 2 million members and supporters in over 150 countries. Its particular features continue to be its large membership base, especially in the Western world, and its emphasis on political neutrality. Human Rights Watch has a very different structure, with no broad-based membership. Instead, it draws strength from the research expertise of its staff. International Federation for Human Rights (FIDH) presents a third model: comprising 178 local organizations throughout the world as members, its

international presence services and draws legitimacy from its grassroots human rights groups, especially in countries where there are severe violations. Next to these three giants, there are many international thematic groups (some of which, on food, health, and housing, are featured in this chapter) and thousands of national and local human rights groups.

The growth of human rights groups reflects and perhaps even exceeds the general growth of non-governmental organizations between 1990 and 2010. The biggest recent areas of growth have been in the areas of economic, social, and cultural rights (as we describe) and transitional justice. Then there are organizations and movements that represent a cross-over between human rights and other issues (such as Global Witness, which focuses on the relation between environmental exploitation and human rights abuse), or that do not identify themselves first and foremost with human rights but nevertheless draw on human rights frames, such as solidarity campaigns, Indigenous peoples' movements, or women's movements. But global civil society in the realm of human rights should not by any means be thought of as the sole domain of organized, let alone professional, groups. Journalists, academics and students, religious leaders, barristers, and, perhaps more controversially, even businessmen and government officials in their personal capacity can all at times be 'people organizing to influence their world' in the field of human rights. (See also Box 9.2 for a discussion of who has legitimacy to talk about human rights.)

BOX 9.2 CHALLENGING ASSUMPTIONS: WHO HAS LEGITIMACY TO TALK ABOUT HUMAN RIGHTS?

Not only the 'civil' in GCS is problematic, so is the 'global'. Does it mean working on global issues, having global goals, or working in global networks? (See Williams (2005, pp. 350–1), cited from Bob et al., 2008.) With respect to the latter, there turns out to be an important imbalance between the West, where the majority of international NGOs are headquartered (see Table 9.1), and the rest of the world, which relies on less formal, more diverse, and usually less internationally influential forms of civil society. International organizations, with well-paid staff members trained in European or North American universities, are sometimes considered as too Western, elitist, and unrepresentative to speak on behalf of rights-holders. Local partners engaged in democracy and rights work are often perceived locally as self-serving and as more accountable to foreign donors than to local communities, giving governments an excuse to restrict their access to foreign funding.

Engagement with local civil society is seen as imperative for the accountability, legitimacy, and effectiveness of international human rights groups. But which civil society? Not all locally embedded civil society groups aim for progressive social change. As became clear in the so-called Arab Spring, some participants in the uprisings advocated for conservative values and discriminated against or harassed women and black Muslims joining the protests. International human rights organizations will defend the human rights of these people as a matter of principle, but should they also engage, partner, and campaign with them? Can they collaborate with those parts of civil society that are committed to the value of human rights, or at least to some human rights (e.g. to religious freedom yet not to sexual equality), but use non-peaceful means to reach their goals? Or should they only strengthen and cooperate with civil society groups that defend universal human rights and that reject violence, just like themselves?

Table 9.1 International NGOs per continent: Western bias?

Continents	International NGOs as counted by the Union of International Associations**	NGOs with consultative status, UN Economic and Social Council*
Africa	2,396	524
Asia	3,836	612
Latin America and Caribbean	1,859	181
Oceania	1,049 (Australia=819)	74 (Australia=41)
North America (Canada and US)	10,257	979
Europe	21,276	1,193
Not specified	–	4
Total	**40,673**	**3,567**

* Number of all NGOs with consultative status (general, specific, and on the roster) at the UN Economic and Social Council.

Source: NGO Branch. United Nations Department of Economic and Social Affairs. Available at: http://esango.un.org/civilsociety/display AdvancedSearch.do?method=search&sessionCheck=false (accessed 19 February 2015).

** Different types of NGOs: 'International organizations, Dependent organizations, Organizational substitutes, National organizations and Dead, inactive and unconfirmed bodies'.

Source: Union of International Association (ed.) (2014). Countries in which international non-governmental organization headquarters are located, ranked by continent, *Yearbook of International Organizations 2014–2015: Guide to Global Civil Society Networks,* 51/5, Statistics, Visualizations and Patterns. Leiden: Koninklijke Brill NV, p. 119. © Union of International Associations 1997–present.

While the impact of human rights activism should not be overstated, there are many positive examples where human rights groups and defenders in GCS have been crucial in pushing for progressive social, legal, and policy change. Human rights actors have not only managed to generate a wide acceptance of international human rights norms as valid and binding (*norm commitment*), but also play a key role in ensuring that states actually conform to them (*norm compliance*).

Global or transnational networks of human rights groups and defenders play a crucial role as 'norm entrepreneurs' in the processes leading from norm evaluation (translating, or **framing**, an issue into legally enforceable human rights), via norm commitment, to norm compliance. Their human rights advocacy helps swaying states and international organizations to endorse a norm and to codify it in domestic, regional, and international law. If the norm obtains a critical mass of supporters, it implies a 'tipping point' has been reached, and the norm can 'cascade' through the population. It then becomes internalized by a range of actors who will eventually take the norm for granted. If the norm fails to obtain a broad international consensus, the particular issue will not materialize into binding legislation, let alone normalize (Keck and Sikkink, 1998; Risse-Kappen, Ropp, and Sikkink, 1999).

But even an internationally accepted and institutionalized human rights norm does not immediately start guiding actual policy and programmes. Before states and other powerful actors start complying with human rights law and change their (corporate) behaviour, much ongoing pressure, coercion, persuasion, and support is needed by both state and non-state actors. The effectiveness of such pressure depends, in turn, on various conditions, including the degree of statehood and the regime type of the target state, the degree of centralization of rule implementation, and the state or other powerful actor's social and material vulnerability to such pressure (Risse, Ropp, and Sikkink, 2013).

Human rights actors, as part of GCS, make use of various strategies and methods to induce norm compliance. Chong (2010, pp. 42–4) observes two dominant and often jointly used strategies of international human rights organizations. The first consists of research into human rights violations and 'naming and shaming' recalcitrant governments through mass media and petitions, accompanied by advocacy. The target of shaming actions is a violation of international law with a clear perpetrator and a legal remedy. A second strategy is court-based, involving (quasi-) judicial proceedings, and consists of methods like strategic litigation, representing victims of human rights violations in courts or similar arenas, and submitting opinions known as *amicus curiae briefs*. Finally, global civil society impacts *inter-state* behaviour, campaigning for instance for sanctions against (Murdie and Peksen, 2013), or humanitarian intervention in (Murdie and Peksen, 2014), states that commit severe human rights violations.

KEY POINTS

GCS can be considered as a part and even a driver of globalization, but also as a potential counterweight to aspects of globalization.

GCS is populated by value-driven actors, organizing to influence their world, but they do not all have the same values. GCS is therefore also an arena of contestation.

GCS actors in the area of human rights engage in norm-entrepreneurship and framing to get new rules adopted and implemented, and in naming and shaming and legal strategies to monitor compliance.

Critical Thinking Questions:

Do you consider multinational corporations like Shell or transnational politico-religious movements like the Muslim Brotherhood as part of GCS? Why or why not? What are the pros and cons of including them as part of GCS? Can individual members or employees of such organizations be potential allies of international human rights organizations? Why or why not?

Case Study: GCS as Paradigm-Shifters: Economic and Social Rights

From Dead Letter to Activist Tool

Economic and social rights, despite being enshrined in international law via the **Universal Declaration of Human Rights** (UDHR) and the **International Covenant on Economic, Social and Cultural Rights** (ICESCR), had few civil society champions on either side of the political divide for most of the twentieth century, caught as they were in the crossfire between **liberal** and **socialist** ideologies (Glasius, 2012).

This began to change in the early 1980s, when small groups of activists and academics separately but simultaneously began to rediscover the most compelling of all economic and social rights, the right to food. Two

seminal texts advanced novel arguments. Amartya Sen's *Poverty and Famines* (Sen, 1981) challenged the consensus among developmental economists that famines were caused by a general decline in the availability of food. Instead, he argued, access to food depends on entitlements that are governed by socio-economic relations (Sen, 1981, pp. 154–5). 'The focus on entitlements', Sen concluded his essay, 'has the effect of emphasizing legal rights' (Sen, 1981, pp. 165–6).

Political philosopher Henry Shue (1980) attacked the distinction between civil and political rights, constructed mainly as *negative rights* requiring only a duty of non-interference, and economic and social rights, constructed as *positive rights* requiring active intervention (see Chapter 1). Instead, Shue distinguished three types of duties governing both types of rights: to avoid depriving people of their rights, to protect them against such deprivation by others, and to aid those whose rights have already been deprived (Shue, 1980, pp. 35–64). This categorization of obligations, later adapted to 'respect/protect/fulfil', has been a tremendous inspiration to subsequent generations of legal scholars.

At the same time, some grassroots membership groups of Amnesty International, frustrated with the organization's limited mandate, started networking with development and solidarity groups focused on the right to food. After three years, the network was transformed into a formal human rights organization, the Food First Information and Action Network (FIAN). Inspired by the Amnesty approach, it focused on blatant violations such as famines related to forced relocation, and undertook urgent actions, writing letters to governments, 'Even though we did not quite know what was a violation of the right to food, we were finding that out as we were doing it.'[1]

Finally, international lawyers began to take notice of economic and social rights, formulating the **Limburg Principles on the Implementation of the International Covenant on Economic, Social and Cultural Rights** as a point of reference for interpreting the sometimes obscure and contradictory legal text of the ICESCR (see Chapter 14). This sparked innumerable articles and a spate of doctoral dissertations, constituting a new field of expertise within human rights scholarship. The literature began to address objections against economic and social rights as 'too vague', 'too costly', or 'not amenable to judicial review'.

In the NGO field, the foundation of FIAN was followed in 1987 by Habitat International Coalition, in

1992 by the Centre on Housing Rights and Evictions (COHRE), and in 1993 by the Center for Economic and Social Rights (CESR) in New York. All have grown from kitchen-table initiatives into medium-sized international NGOs, and have since been joined by hundreds of other, mainly domestic organizations working specifically in the area of economic and social rights. Many are now part of ESCR-Net (International Network of Economic, Social, and Cultural Rights), a civil society network founded in 2003.[2]

Between them, the philosophers, the lawyers, and the grassroots activists promoted a new way of thinking that considered issues such as hunger, homelessness, and ill health not just as personal tragedies or social problems, but as violations of human rights. But mainstream organizations, both non-governmental and intergovernmental, took some convincing of this human rights norm.

Elevation into International Politics

Mainstream global human rights organizations slowly and gingerly began to take up economic and social rights from the mid-1990s. Some, such as the International Commission of Jurists, have always supported them in principle but devote relatively little attention to them. In 2001 Amnesty International broadened its mandate to enable it to work on all human rights, starting with 'respect' violations directly connected to earlier campaigns on civil and political rights (Amnesty International, 2005, 2014). While the vast majority of human rights organizations now recognize work on economic and social rights as a legitimate part of their mandate, there remains confusion and controversy on what that means in practice. Such differences of opinion were highlighted by a series of exchanges between Ken Roth, Executive Director of Human Rights Watch (see Box 9.3), and Leonard Rubenstein of Physicians for Human Rights (see Box 9.4), and more recently on OpenDemocracy.net between Aryeh Neier, President Emeritus of the Open Society Foundation, and Margot Salomon of the London School of Economics (see 'Web Links' at the end of the chapter).

Within the United Nations human rights apparatus, too, economic and social rights remained something of a backwater until the second High Commissioner for Human Rights, the vocal Mary Robinson, committed herself to redressing the imbalance. She famously emphasized that extreme poverty was the worst kind of human rights abuse. This constituted a paradigm shift. Most human rights experts at that time, and perhaps still, would have identified situations of **genocide** or **ethnic cleansing** as the worst form of human rights abuse. Most development experts would have been

BOX 9.3 KENNETH ROTH ON HOW INTERNATIONAL HUMAN RIGHTS NGOS SHOULD APPROACH ECONOMIC AND SOCIAL RIGHTS

Kenneth Roth contends that what international human rights organizations do best is 'investigate, expose, and shame', and that they can only effectively do so when there is relative clarity about violation, violator, and remedy. While progress has been made on documenting violations of economic and social rights, there is much less clarity on who the violator is, and what the remedy should be, than in the case of civil and political rights.

Therefore, international human rights organizations should restrict their work on economic and social rights to cases where governments are guilty of arbitrary or discriminatory conduct: for instance, South Africa's initial ideologically based denial of anti-retroviral treatment to HIV-infected mothers, or the US exclusion of child farm workers from general child labour regulations. International human rights organizations should stay away from economic and social rights issues that primarily concern allocation of resources. On the contrary, they need to move the public away from seeing economic and social rights purely as a matter of distributive justice.

Some developing countries simply lack the means to meet even the 'minimum core' standards set by the Covenant and its implementing Committee. In such cases, residents of the country in question have the clearest standing on how to allocate resources, and international human rights organizations are poorly placed to comment on government action plans. They cannot legitimately insist on trade-offs between different legitimate government investments.

Even when it comes to pressuring a Northern government or an international financial institution, international human rights organizations are not (yet) in a position to mobilize domestic human rights constituencies in Western states simply to demand more resources. Stigmatization on the basis of arbitrary or discriminatory spending is more likely to be successful.

(Roth, 2004a, 2004b)

BOX 9.4 LEONARD RUBENSTEIN ON HOW INTERNATIONAL HUMAN RIGHTS NGOS SHOULD APPROACH ECONOMIC AND SOCIAL RIGHTS

Rubenstein argues that human rights organizations must not rely on naming and shaming alone. They can collaborate with partner organizations in developing countries in lobbying for service delivery systems that respect economic and social rights, monitoring compliance of all states with the increasingly explicit legal obligations that they have in relation to these rights, and advocating for more resources from wealthy countries to be dedicated to economic and social rights.

International human rights organizations have decades of experience in making policy recommendations, including those with resource implications, in the area of civil and political rights, building up detailed knowledge on, for instance, weapons capabilities or designing an effective court system. If human rights organizations are not yet very good at identifying rights aspects of health or education policies, they will just need to get better at it. 'By the time bad social programs are designed and in place and the naming and shaming occurs, resources will have been misspent and human rights violated in a way that is not easily undone.' It is not necessary to restrict advocacy of economic and social rights to situations where there is a single identifiable villain: dealing with multiple layers of responsibility is the bread and butter of human rights organizations. Moreover, such a frame will have more resonance with the communities affected: HIV/AIDS victims who are being denied treatment want to demand anti-retrovirals on the basis of their right to survive, not on the basis of arbitrary government conduct.

The ICESCR stipulates that a state must spend on economic and social rights 'to the maximum of its available resources', and that other states have a duty of 'international assistance and cooperation'. It is therefore legitimate for human rights organizations to advocate for more resources. Moreover, advocating for resources is not a zero-sum game. Both at the domestic level, where international human rights organizations may play a support role to local ones, and at the international level, pressure for resources tends to increase the pot.

(Rubenstein, 2004a, 2004b)

inclined to think of extreme poverty as an intractable problem, not a human rights violation. Also at the UN, a campaign to create an individual complaints procedure through an 'optional protocol' to the ICESCR has been a priority for human rights advocates since the 1990s. After years of deliberation, the Optional Protocol was approved by the **Human Rights Council** in 2008 and came into force in May 2013.

The international financial and trade organizations remain unconverted to the cause of economic and social rights, however. Despite protests, civil society has not challenged them effectively, as shall be discussed. Nonetheless, an important concession to the right to health was made, as the result of massive civil society pressure, at the **World Trade Organization** (WTO) negotiations in Doha: developing countries are allowed 'flexibility' in producing, importing, and exporting generic drugs when they can demonstrate that a national health crisis requires it (WTO, 2003).

National and Regional Successes and their Limits

Perhaps the greatest (or at least most visible) advances in economic and social rights have been made at the national level. Parliaments have adopted laws and constitutional changes that directly recognize economic and social rights and attendant state obligations. Courts have begun interpreting national and international law in ways that require state redress of violations. Mostly, these new laws, legal judgments, and changes in policy have come about after sustained civil society campaigns.

In South Africa, the landmark 'Grootboom' decision on the right to housing demonstrated that a judicial court could review and enforce even the 'obligation to fulfil' economic and social rights, using a standard of 'reasonableness' that is familiar in many legal systems (Pieterse, 2004). But the case also raises questions about how much lawsuits can do: the urgent housing needs of the South African poor have not been substantially alleviated since the judgment, which, in fact, was inconclusive on *how* the right should be enforced (Landau, 2012).

In response to a series of civil society-instigated lawsuits, India's Supreme Court has issued interim orders requiring improvements in state food distribution systems (Birchfield and Corsi, 2010). In Ecuador, civil society groups concerned over the implications of a Free Trade Agreement with the USA for access to affordable medicine succeeded in convincing their national trade delegation to take into consideration the constitutionally protected right to health (Ecuador, 2004).

Even in the United States—historically one of the staunchest opponents of economic and social rights, and one of only a handful of states that have not ratified the ICESCR—economic and social rights are gaining friends and prominence in civil society against relatively little resistance. The US government too has modified its rejectionist stance. The Obama administration recognized the interdependence of human rights and joined the international consensus on some resolutions promoting economic, social, and cultural rights at the UN Human Rights Council and General Assembly (Amnesty International, 2014, p. 28).

There is no doubt that a 'tipping point' has been reached: a majority of relevant state and non-state actors now consider economic, social, and cultural rights as legal entitlements, rather than mere 'aspirations' or 'goals'. Moreover, human rights norms are now accepted as '**guiding principles**' for corporations and taken into account in WTO negotiations. But many countries still fail to enforce economic, social, and cultural rights domestically, and there are even larger challenges regarding international (financial or development) organizations and multinational corporations that disregard these human rights in their policy and practice abroad, leading Professor Samuel Moyn to regard economic and social rights as a failure (see Box 9.5).

Limited Convergence

Initially, due to ignorance or mutual suspicion, there was little contact or overlap between the anti-capitalist or social justice movement and the much smaller economic and social rights community. Recently, this has

begun to change somewhat. The 2005 **World Social Forum**, a global gathering of civil society activists founded in reaction to the World Economic Forum in Davos, made human rights one of its themes. Approximately one-third of the human rights events concerned economic and social rights topics (Forum Social Mundial, 2005).

One of the biggest areas of convergence has been over the right to health. One notable success was the South African Treatment Action Campaign's triumph in persuading the South African Supreme Court that the right to health required national roll-out of a particular anti-retroviral drug, and then, in coalition with international NGOs, in persuading the WTO to allow more flexibility in the manufacture and trade of drugs. Other successes include HIV/AIDS treatment in Thailand, Brazil, and other countries (Seckinelgin, 2002, pp. 123–5). Patients (especially people with AIDS), health professionals, human rights lawyers, development organizations, and anti-privatization activists are all part of this growing movement. Another momentous area of synergy is the right to water. Like food, water is so vital to human life that to claim it as a right has intuitive appeal. This issue appeals to development organizations, anti-dam campaigns, groups focused on political conflicts such as that between Palestine and Israel, and to anti-privatization campaigns (Dicke and Holland, 2007, p. 126).

It is uncertain to what extent these convergences result in lasting coalitions between human rights and global justice activists. Economic and social rights framing has not been prominent in the global social justice movements of the past decade, and it has been

---

BOX 9.5 ALTERNATIVE POINTS OF VIEW: THE FAILURE OF ECONOMIC AND SOCIAL RIGHTS

Some critics question the counter-hegemonic force of human rights to tame economic globalization: the integration of the global economy, trade and investment liberalization, and initiatives to privatize the provision of core public services (definition from Amnesty International, 2014, p. 33). Samuel Moyn (2014), for instance, calls human rights 'a powerless companion in the age of neoliberalism'. Even though he rejects the claim that human rights are complicit per se in the success of neoliberalism, he questions the effectiveness of economic and social rights norms to tame or counteract economic globalization. Human rights, he argues, do not purport to provide an egalitarian agenda, at least not in the sense of distributive or substantive equality. Human rights oblige states to

prioritize 'minimum core obligations'—to ensure minimum essential levels of protection for particularly the most marginalized and excluded—but they say nothing about the *maximum* level of inequalities in wealth and other primary goods that is permissible. Especially in the arenas of international trade law and policy, on the one hand, and corporate social responsibility, on the other, Moyn argues that 'human rights have proved distressingly ineffective, and their record does not seem likely to change'. Moyn believes that they have failed to deliver real outcomes in the socio-economic domain. For him, human rights 'need to be supplemented by both new frameworks of analysis and new modes of intra- and transnational activism' to address rising inequalities related to economic globalization.

conspicuously absent from the anti-austerity and de-mocracy protests of 2011 (Glasius, 2012). Doubts re-main about the usefulness of human rights to attain economic justice, because they are neither aimed at nor made for the radical system change that the pro-testors seek (S. Burke, 2014). The human rights move-ment must do better in convincing others of the added value of its approach, and simultaneously explore new methods and frames to be able to create new synergies.

KEY POINTS

The economic and social rights movement has succeeded in generating a wide acceptance of these rights as valid, but has not succeeded well in ensuring that states and corporations comply with their obligations.

The International Monetary Fund (IMF), the WTO, and the private sector remain unconverted to the idea of economic and social rights.

Lately, the movement has seen the emergence of new synergies with other movements, but discursive and strategic differences with the global justice movement remain.

Critical Thinking Questions:

How effective do you think that economic and social rights are today, both in discourse and in methods, to address rising socio-economic inequalities and precariousness related to economic globalization and the financial crisis? What are the potentials and pitfalls of using a rights approach for (re)distributive agendas?

Case Study: GCS as Lawmakers and Monitors: The International Criminal Court

The Idea of an International Criminal Court

The idea that there are certain moral standards for the treatment of any human being is a touchstone of in-ternational human rights law. International criminal law and the **International Criminal Court** (ICC) go a step further, establishing enforceable penalties for rulers or other individuals who commit or condone crimes against a population. These steps embed norms in an international system of enforcement, seeking to end the impunity of war criminals and perpetrators of crimes against humanity.

The idea of such a Court was first mooted by Gus-tave Moynier, founding member of the ICRC, in 1872, and was widely supported by civil society organiza-tions in the 1920s. It came under consideration im-mediately after the Second World War, but the **Cold War** foreclosed this opportunity. A draft code of inter-national crimes languished in the UN's International Law Commission as ethnic cleansing in Yugoslavia and genocide in Rwanda prompted the Security Council to establish ad hoc tribunals (see Glasius, 2006, pp. 6–14). The ad hoc tribunals provided proof that international criminal courts could work despite the lack of prec-edent and conflicting legal systems. They also formed a valuable training ground for those in GCS who were pushing for a permanent international criminal court.

The Campaign

The Coalition for an International Criminal Court (CICC) was founded in 1995. By the time of the final negotiations on the ICC Statute in Rome in 1998, it had grown into a network of over 800 organizations, 236 of which sent one or more representatives to Rome (Glasius, 2006, pp. 35–7).

Drafting the rules of the ICC was a delicate but fascinating task from a strictly legal point of view: different areas of domestic and international law all converged in new ways in the Statute. But human rights groups had particular reasons to take an interest in the ICC. After decades of working to build regional and global human rights mechanisms, human rights experts began to realize that, while the body of human rights law had become substantial, human rights vio-lations in the world were not actually declining. The emphasis therefore shifted towards implementation and the punishment of individual perpetrators as it became increasingly clear that the exclusive focus on states and their responsibility for violations obscured the complexities of power structures and interfered with human rights enforcement.

The large international human rights organizations dominated the ICC negotiations, devoting full-time staff and writing key advocacy documents. They also dominated the CICC Steering Committee, with reper-cussions for the wider campaign. Other groups work-ing for the ICC included many women's organizations, peace and conflict resolution organizations, groups focused on global governance and strengthening the

United Nations, and representatives of churches and religious organizations. Active members of the Coalition engaged in lobbying, produced expert documents, convened conferences, and strengthened state delegations with legal experts and interns. There were remarkably few adversarial or media-oriented actions, such as demonstrations (Glasius, 2006, pp. 27–44).

Despite the loose formal structure of the CICC and its members' varied interests, it was extremely effective in its coordinating role, particularly at the Rome Conference. In order to be as effective as possible, it split up into three types of subgroups—regional caucuses, who lobbied state representatives of their own regions, issue-based caucuses on gender justice, victims, children, peace, and a caucus of faith-based organizations, and twelve working groups, which shadowed the working groups of state representatives and made daily reports available to NGOs and state delegates (Pace and Thieroff, 1999, p. 394).

The level of recognition of the Coalition's role by state representatives and United Nations officials was probably unprecedented. Various committee chairs as well as many other official delegates took the participation of NGOs in the proceedings for granted, and the Coalition was their first point of contact (see, for instance, Bos, 1999, pp. 45–6). It was also asked by the United Nations to organize the accreditation of NGOs to the Rome Conference, a unique form of self-regulation (Pace, 1999, p. 209).

Achievements of GCS

Many state representatives in the ICC negotiations, including the successive chairs of the negotiations, have remarked on the strong involvement and influence of GCS in negotiating the Statute (Bos, 1999, p. 45; Kirsch and Holmes, 1999, pp. 11, 37). Perhaps the strongest expression of this sentiment came from a diplomat who did not belong to the **like-minded group** of states in favour of a strong independent Court. Israeli Chief Counsel Alan Baker acknowledged: 'In all my years of international work, I've never seen the NGOs play a more powerful role ... They were in on nearly every meeting. They were in on everything' (from the *Wall Street Journal*, quoted in Pace, 1999, p. 201). Taking a broader view, it can be considered the achievement of GCS that there should be a Court at all. The idea was first conceived, kept alive, developed, and advocated in international legal associations for 125 years. Even a few years before the adoption of the Statute, CICC

coordinator Bill Pace was told by a leading expert in international affairs to 'keep working on this, but don't get your hopes up too high for it isn't going to happen in your lifetime, or your children's lifetime, or your grandchildren's lifetime' (Pace, 1999, p. 193).

In terms of the content of the Statute, undoubtedly the most important achievement was the prosecutor's authority to choose his or her own cases. By the admission of the key diplomats involved, this could not have been achieved without sustained and overwhelming NGO pressure. Beyond NGOs, the active involvement of the prosecutors of the Yugoslavia and Rwanda tribunals was central in legitimizing the idea of an independent prosecutor. Within a few years, GCS succeeded in persuading a majority of states— though not the USA, which has remained reluctant to sign the Rome Statute—that independent authority of the prosecutor was desirable and achievable (Glasius, 2006, pp. 47–60). Another achievement is the requirement that states automatically accept the Court's full jurisdiction for all the crimes in the Statute upon ratification, instead of the 'à la carte' jurisdiction regime originally proposed. Automatic jurisdiction was the consistent and unanimous position of civil society actors, and, like the prosecutor, gradually came to be accepted by states (Glasius, 2006, pp. 63–6).

Largely through the advocacy of a very large, active, and expert Gender Caucus, the Rome Statute greatly advances the gender-sensitiveness of international law (see Bedont and Hall Martinez, 1999; Oosterveld, 1999). On the other hand, partly due to pressure from North American anti-abortion or 'pro-family' groups not affiliated with the CICC, the terms *gender* and *forced pregnancy* were defined so as not to pose obstacles to any state's ratification, regardless of its policies on gender (Glasius, 2006, pp. 28–35).

Intense pressure from civil society ensured the inclusion of war crimes committed in internal conflict situations. A special Victims Rights Group played an important role in forging rules that balance the need for fair and effective prosecutions with protection, sensitive treatment, and rights of victims and witnesses. The Child Rights Caucus played a role in the criminalization of conscription of children under 15, a new element in humanitarian law.

Controversies Within GCS

While the ICC negotiations were largely characterized by mutual respect and camaraderie, they were also the scene of a confrontation between two civil society groupings with diametrically opposed interests: the women's movement and the pro-family movement. The surfacing of two social movements with contradictory aims at the same venue highlights recurring questions about GCS participation in international forums: Who is legitimate? Who is representative? Who has a right to be there? Women's groups have been confronted with diverse voices from within the movement, but they still tend collectively to consider themselves as the sole representatives of women's concerns. Self-identified 'pro-family' groups explicitly question this notion.[3]

The clashes between the two movements focused on two issues: the use of the word 'gender' and the crime of 'forced pregnancy'. Pro-family groups objected to gender as potentially providing 'protection for "other genders" including homosexuals, lesbians, bisexuals, transgendered, etc.' (REAL Women of Canada, 1998), whereas women's groups insisted on the relevance of the socially constructed behaviour of men and women (see Chapter 11). Forced pregnancy was experienced in Bosnia, where Muslim women were not only raped but subsequently forced to carry their babies to full term. However, the Vatican and pro-family groups argued that defining forced pregnancy as a crime would make it illegal for states to prohibit abortion.

In both cases, narrow definitions were finally negotiated that took the sting out of the controversy. In the ICC Statute, 'the term gender refers to the two sexes, male and female, within the context of society. The term gender does not indicate any meaning different from the above' (Steains, 1999, pp. 374–5). Forced pregnancy remained a crime in the Statute, but defined only as 'the unlawful confinement of a woman forcibly made pregnant, with the intent of affecting the ethnic composition of any population or carrying out other grave violations of international law. This definition shall not in any way be interpreted as affecting national laws relating to pregnancy' (Steains, 1999, pp. 366–8). On the basis of these definitions, both groups could interpret the outcome of the negotiations as a qualified victory (Glasius, 2006, pp. 91–2).

African civil society groups played an important part in the establishment of the ICC (see Figure 9.1). But fifteen years on, the ICC is under attack, not only from states but also from African civil society groups, for focusing almost exclusively on African cases, for prioritizing criminal justice over other, more local transitional justice mechanisms, and for prioritizing justice over peace processes (see Chapter 22 and also:

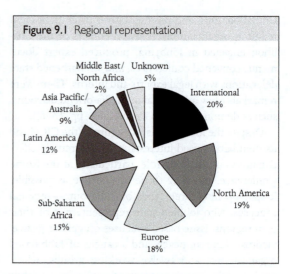

Figure 9.1 Regional representation

Middle East/North Africa 2% · Unknown 5% · International 20% · Asia Pacific/Australia 9% · Latin America 12% · North America 19% · Sub-Saharan Africa 15% · Europe 18%

T. Allen, 2005b; Branch, 2007; Flint and de Waal, 2009; Du Plessis, Maluwa, and O'Reilly, 2013; Refugee Law Project, 2015). Indeed, all of the twenty-one cases currently before the court are African.

Advocates and activists in favour of the Court, including many African NGOs, in turn have emphasized the *universal* aspirations of the court, ensuring justice and accountability for victims in countries across the globe where domestic legal systems reflect an unwillingness or inability of local authorities to prosecute the perpetrators, as well as the important role that African countries have played in its creation. Africans have filled prominent positions, including now that of the Chief Prosecutor. For these reasons, Archbishop Desmond Tutu of South Africa has called the ICC 'Africa's court' (Letter on the ICC to AU delegates in 2013, cited in Lamony, 2014, p. 70). Nonetheless, the resonance of the ICC's alleged double standards against Africa puts NGOs seeking justice and accountability in a difficult position in the societies where they work. 'The ICC backlash has created a major dilemma for us, no doubt about it. Deciding the appropriate course of action has become a very difficult question', one human rights worker told *Foreign Policy* (15 July 2014).

These examples show that GCS is not a harmonious entity with a single set of shared values. It is populated by actors with strongly held values, 'organizing to influence their world', but these strongly held values differ; they may diverge or even clash. Plurality and even discord are part and parcel of GCS. But the case of the Gender Caucus and the pro-family movement shows that compromises can in fact be found in multilateral negotiations, while the Africa controversy makes clear that the universal aspirations of human rights and transitional justice groups in GCS will not be taken for granted by other civil society groups in a world marked by unequal power relations.

KEY POINTS

The International Criminal Court is a civil society achievement: the idea was first developed in civil society, was kept alive in international legal associations, and would not exist in its current form without the civil society campaign of the 1990s.

The influence of civil society on the Rome Statute was in part based on the close alignment in expertise and values between the civil society activists and a majority of state representatives.

Civil society does not have a common view as regards to the role of the ICC or its functioning. Nonetheless, its engagement with the ICC may serve both to unmask state hypocrisy and to actually nudge the ICC towards being more responsive to the concerns of local communities affected by its work.

Critical Thinking Questions:

Are you in favour of consulting GCS when it is advocating for conservative social change? Should, for instance, anti-gay marriage advocates have a voice at UN negotiations on non-discrimination and equality legislation? Why or why not?

Conclusion

This chapter has attempted through two brief case studies to demonstrate the interdependence between the emergence of GCS and the development of human rights law. GCS in relation to human rights plays a key role in shifting norms through what Keck and Sikkink (1998, pp. 16–23) have called 'information politics' and 'symbolic politics'. At the global and domestic levels, civil society's right to inform, debate, and persuade on the basis of particular ethical convictions is not generally questioned. In the latter half of the twentieth century, the project of increasing the popularity of human rights had been incredibly successful. Not only politicians, but also corporate and religious leaders now routinely invoke human rights values, and outright rejection of human rights by any kind of public figure has become almost unthinkable. Because of GCS' ongoing human rights activism and advocacy, many human rights have been accepted as valid and binding. They are no longer marginal, but have become mainstream (Hopgood, 2014, p. 12). Like any frame, however, human rights are susceptible to instrumentalization by power-holders. There is also the risk of co-option. The more human rights become institutionalized, the more they lose their counter-hegemonic force and may serve power rather than confront and challenge it. This raises the question how subversive human rights movements should be in order to remain effective (see Neil Stammers on Opendemocracy.net— see 'Web Links' at the end of this chapter).

Moreover, human rights are not the only ethical frame prevalent in GCS. In the early twenty-first century, at least two other significant ideological master frames can be discerned: the social justice frame, more overtly concerned with power relations and re-distribution than with human rights, and religiously informed frames, above all the frame of the 'Umma', the Islamic brotherhood of mankind. Adherents to all three of these frames have in common a global project and a belief that their frame alone offers solutions for the marginalized and downtrodden of the world. Yet all three have been open to abuse by power-holders. A fourth frame, of renewed importance with the advance of climate change, may be that of environmentalism (see Chapter 23). None of these frames is necessarily entirely incompatible with any of the others. Historic separation and suspicion tend to accentuate the areas of conflict, but the search for common ground is urgent if there is to be one (pluralist) GCS instead of several separated and opposing strands.

In addition to adding new issues as human rights norms on the agenda (of both news media and legislatures or intergovernmental policy-making bodies), GCS in relation to human rights also aims to influence policy formulation by helping to codify norms in laws and regulations. Its participation in lawmaking is, however, contested. A remarkable feature of the negotiations on the ICC was that leading state delegates appeared to take this participation for granted. As Adriaan Bos noted, GCS involvement 'fills in gaps arising from a **democratic deficit** in the international decision-making process' (Bos, 1999, pp. 44–5). That there is such a deficit is generally acknowledged, but can GCS really fill the democratic gap?

There are two issues at play here: the unevenness of GCS representation in global decision-making forums and the problem of representation within GCS itself. First, whereas the UN has created various inclusive and effective consultative mechanisms, GCS is neither officially represented at **international financial institutions** (IFIs) like the IMF, the WTO, or the World Bank, nor at important informal forums such as the various G+ summits. Decision making affecting the distribution of wealth and resources happens far away from the communities affected by economic globalization. It is important that GCS acquires a stronger voice in international decision making in financial–economic realms and monitors IFIs' policies and practices more closely from a human rights perspective.

Second, while it can be argued on the basis of the ICC case that GCS can greatly strengthen certain features of democratic procedure, in particular transparency, equality, and deliberation (Glasius, 2006, pp. 114–27), GCS cannot be seen as offering a form of representation of the global *demos*, or at least not representation in its traditional form. It could be conceptualized as a form of participation ('a voice not a vote' (Edwards, 2003)), but in practice this participation is so limited and so uneven (see Table 9.1) that GCS cannot entirely be considered to be an adequate 'functional equivalent' (Rosenau, 1998) or 'alternative mechanism' (Scholte, 2001) to parliamentary democracy operating at the global level.

Even if it is accepted that GCS moves states towards appreciating, or at least appearing to appreciate, 'ethical' or 'common good' arguments over national interest arguments, the question remains which ethical projects make it to those forums and get taken up. In the ICC negotiations, while there was some open and some muted contestation, there was clearly a dominant

civil society project: to prise away from states the power to punish perpetrators of genocide, war crimes, and crimes against humanity. But if multilateral institutions like the United Nations are serious and sincere about being 'open to civil society', they should be open to all civil society representation, not just representation that reflects their own values. If human rights groups have a right to be active at forums such as the ICC negotiations—and they have fought hard for that right—then so do other groups. It is only on the basis of such ethical pluralism that GCS participation in international lawmaking can be defended.

Finally, GCS aims to affect the implementation of human rights law and policy by monitoring its effectiveness and influencing governments to commit the necessary resources. This form of GCS activism in the field of human rights compliance monitoring raises yet another democratic question. Civil society activists take personal risks in order to bear witness to violations of human rights of which we might not otherwise be aware. But what typically characterizes these efforts, whether in Tibet, Syria, or Mali, is that the population cannot speak freely about its own political aspirations. Therefore, human rights activists end up making recommendations for these populations without any mandate, save their own consciences. This is a necessary function of GCS in an imperfect world, but it should at the same time be recognized as a problem.

GCS cannot be artificially insulated from money, violence, or existing power structures, but what sets GCS apart from other international actors is that it operates on a different logic: the logic of persuasion. Human rights activism has been characterized by courage and determination, but this must be combined with humility and openness to other civil society perspectives for the human rights paradigm to remain persuasive.

? QUESTIONS

Individual Study Questions

1. In what ways are GCS and the international rule of law interdependent?

2. Why were the civil society actors engaged in negotiations on the ICC relatively successful?

3. Is there a danger of civil society actors being co-opted when they are close to power-holders? Where would you see yourself as a human rights activist: outside protesting or inside negotiating?

4. Does participation of GCS in international negotiations, such as on the ICC or on a complaints procedure for economic and social rights, make such negotiations more democratic? If so, in what ways?

5. What could human rights organizations do to hold international financial institutions accountable?

Group Discussion Questions

1. What is GCS according to you? Is it really global?

2. If you were a social justice activist concerned with rising inequalities in income and wealth related to economic globalization, would you campaign on economic and social rights? Why or why not?

3. Should civil society groups be given a role in the deliberations of an intergovernmental body such as the Human Rights Council? If so, on what basis?

4. Which recommendations do you have for global civil society organizations to increase their accountability to the communities in which they operate? What about for human rights organizations in particular?

5. Is it possible to distinguish between legitimate criticism of the Northern and elitist character of GCS, and the instrumentalization of these kinds of arguments by governments to deflect attention from their own human rights record?

6. Do you believe that the Office of the Prosecutor (OTP) of the ICC should consult civil society and victim groups before deciding whether to prosecute someone? Why or why not? Should it interfere in situations where local civil society cannot freely deliberate, for instance because of social conflict or intimidation?

FURTHER READING

Bell, D. and **Coicaud, J.-M.** (eds) (2007). *Ethics in Action: The Ethical Challenges of International Human Rights Nongovernmental Organizations*. New York: Cambridge University Press.

This edited volume is the result of a project bringing together leaders of human rights NGOs and political theorists to discuss ethical dilemmas.

Glasius, M. (2005). *The International Criminal Court: A GCS Achievement*. London: Routledge.

A detailed account of the role of GCS in the establishment of the ICC, with some wider considerations about the role of GCS in global governance.

GCS Yearbook Series (2001). For 2001–3 published by Oxford University Press, Oxford; 2004 onwards by Sage, London.

The most exhaustive resource on all aspects of GCS. Each book contains a section on concepts, on issues, on infrastructure, and a data programme. From 2007/8, the books are themed.

Ishay, M. (2004). *The History of Human Rights: From Ancient Times to the Globalization Era*. Berkeley, CA: University of California Press.

This history of human rights is at the same time an accessible history of the human rights movement.

Kaldor, M. (2003). *Global Civil Society: An Answer to War*. Cambridge: Polity Press.

A readable yet insightful introduction to the concept of GCS.

Keck, M. and **Sikkink, K.** (1998). *Activists Beyond Borders: Advocacy Networks in International Politics*. Ithaca, NY: Cornell University Press.

Groundbreaking work on the emergence of transnational advocacy networks, with an emphasis on human rights networks.

Murdie, M. (2014). *Help or Harm: The Human Security Effects of International NGOs*. Stanford: Stanford University Press.

Discusses, based on quantitative analysis, to what extent international NGOs act in a purely principled manner, and if they do, under what conditions they are able to impact human rights and development outcomes.

Willetts, P. (2011). *Non-Governmental Organizations in World Politics: The Construction of Global Governance*. London and New York: Routledge.

An accessible and informative textbook on the role and participation of NGOs in global policy making.

WEB LINKS

http://www.civicus.org   CIVICUS is a large general alliance of civil society organizations dedicated to strengthening citizen action and civil society throughout the world.

http://www.escr-net.org   ESCR-Net is an international network of groups and individuals around the world that aims to advance social justice through human rights.

http://www.opendemocracy.net/openglobalrights   A multilingual online forum for debating human rights movements worldwide.

http://www2.lse.ac.uk/globalGovernance/research/globalCivilSociety/publications.aspx   Free downloads of chapters from older editions of the *GCS Yearbook* (as mentioned in 'Further Reading').

 NOTES

1.   From a telephone interview with Rolf Kuennemann, founding Director of FIAN, 15 December 2005.

2.   See the ESCR-Net website: http://www.escr-net.org/.

3.   See the REAL Women of Canada website: http://www.realwomenofcanada.ca.

Visit the Online Resource Centre that accompanies this book for updates and a range of other resources: www.oxfordtextbooks.co.uk/orc/goodhart3e/

10

Human Rights and Religion

Roja Fazaeli

Chapter Contents

Reader's Guide

This chapter will address the ways in which theoretical and practical relationships between religion and human rights are constructed and understood. The many complex links between the fields of religion and human rights have developed historically and are continually evolving. The relationships between these two fields of study are also highly dependent on cultural and political contexts of practice. Questions about the proper relationship between religion and human rights are particularly obvious and urgent in relation to women, children, minority groups, and the environment. Attention should be paid to how religion and human rights interact and influence issues that may seem further removed, such as economic globalization.

Introduction

Religion and human rights have rich and connected histories, which often share the same philosophical currents. Both religion and human rights represent complex and diverse normative systems that should not be treated as homogeneous or immutable, but rather as varied and evolving. Oversimplification of the complexity of both systems and their relationship leads to the reductive classification of religion and human rights as oppositional systems. This chapter will highlight the multifaceted correlation between human rights and religion, which cannot be discussed without taking context and history into account.

Often, religious and human rights claims can seem to compete for the same normative and theoretical spaces. For instance, they both might appeal to what is natural, right, or good. The challenge of studying religion and human rights is to be able to distinguish their separate strands of logic and put them in conversation with one another. This can be especially tricky when they seem to share vocabularies, particularly around concepts such as justice, equality, and dignity. For this reason, it is important to understand that religion may be a potential source of human rights, but also a potential threat to human rights, and although it is less often considered, the reverse may hold true as well.

To understand the many relationships between religion and human rights we need context, historical understanding, and appreciation of the potential for both fields to change. Also, consider how you think about human rights and religion in categorical terms. Human rights is usually, though not always, deployed as a more discrete category, while the term religion is often applied very broadly. This chapter conceptualizes human rights primarily through public and positive structural expressions, such as the declarations, conventions, committees, and councils that form part of the broader United Nations (UN) system (see Chapter 3), as well as regional systems of human rights. Religion is conceptualized in sociological fashion as an umbrella term describing many overlapping qualities of transcendent experience and their functional expressions in human community. However, when specific issues of conflict or coherence between religion and human rights arise, these neat categories can sometimes become blurred.

The Historical Context of the Relationship

Religion and human rights have rich and intersecting histories. The current international human rights system is often seen as a bespoke project undertaken as part of the construction of the UN system. However, discussions of rights can be traced back through many complex social, intellectual, and religious histories (see Chapter 1). While human rights may be a relatively new coinage, human rights discourses have inherited, as well as rejected, ideas developed in many religious traditions. One of the more prominent of these traditions is that of **natural rights**, which was debated throughout the **Enlightenment**, a time when the working out of good and just relationships between rights and duties became a more fully acknowledged part of a shared global responsibility (Perry, 1998; R. K. M. Smith, 2003).

Many people hope that individuals and groups will be able to coalescence around shared, co-created, and distinctly international ideas of human rights. Yet some critics, ranging from narrowly sectarian religious voices to Third World Approaches to International Law (TWAIL) scholars, raise concerns that the current international system of human rights is misshapen and inaccessible. Some of these critics contend that the idea of human rights has been rooted too deeply in a European tradition shot through with colonial influences (see Chapters 1 and 2). Other critics question the compatibility of human rights and religious claims, and do not think there can be institutional cooperation or intellectual coherence, without first prioritizing one field over the other. The conflation of European and Christian traditions in many of these critiques is one place where concerns about the current form of the international human rights system are often raised.

Another unresolved area in institutional terms is the question of who controls, or frames, the historical narrative of human rights. For instance, do some rights historically emanate from arguments around particular religious systems? If so, contemporary rights discourses should acknowledge this while also maintaining an openness to the historic trends and emerging claims of alternative systems of belief and non-belief (Lauren, 1998). As globalization continues to impact human rights systems as well as religious movements, ideas, and identities, the relationship between human rights norms and religious practices requires even greater attention. Globalization in this sense entails the dynamic movement of people, resources, and ideas around the world through new technologies of transport and information, and the results of interdependency and influence. In the crossing of territorial boundaries, the role of the state, its authority and sovereignty with regard to both religion and human rights, may be challenged. Individuals, and international and transnational organizations can act as violators of rights, and advocates for rights, across boundaries. For example, secular international human rights organizations such as Amnesty International promote human rights, including the right to freedom of religion or belief, through their global movements, as does the Catholic organization Caritas Internationalis, whose mission is to promote charity and justice throughout the world.

The Enlightenment

Many visions of what human rights are stem from philosophical and religious discussions over how best to order human life. In this way human rights claims have historically drawn from thought in government, jurisprudence, and theology, among other areas of intellectual work. The ethics of how individuals ought to treat one another, the proper limits of political power, and the just treatment of minorities are all examples of sites or subjects where rights claims have coalesced, if not been fully worked out or resolved. The Enlightenment was a particularly fertile time for the advancement of modern human rights, especially with reference to religious and philosophical discourses on the concept of liberty (see Chapter 1). In this genealogy, the **Magna Carta** (1215) is an important link in the evolutionary chain.[1] With the 800th anniversary of the Magna Carta, there is currently a critical reappraisal of this document and particularly its influence on religious and legal environments shaped by the common law tradition it helped to anchor. By asserting regulatory power over the divine right of kings, the Magna Carta opened the way to the thinking of subsequent Christian humanists and reformers in the fifteenth and sixteenth centuries, such as Erasmus and Bartolome de las Casas (Ishay, 1997, p. 14; Skilling, 1981).

The writings of Hugo Grotius (1583–1645), a central figure in early international law theory, mark another major shift in thinking about natural rights,

which many regard as precursors to, or foundations for, human rights. Although still removed from the shape and form of contemporary human rights discourse, there are recognizable moves during the Enlightenment, some of which flew in the face of religious traditions at the time, toward the ideas of universality and non-discrimination that continue to influence the contemporary international human rights movement (Lauren, 1998, p. 12). Enlightenment era thinkers, such as David Hume, John Locke, Mary Wollstonecraft, Jean-Jacques Rousseau, and others, contributed to a burgeoning rights discourse that encompassed the American Declaration of Independence (1776) and Bill of Rights (1791) and the French **Declaration of the Rights of Man and of the Citizen** (1789). These documents figure significantly in the history of human rights up to and beyond the formation of the United Nations, and their answers to questions about the role of religion in society and the proper place of government in relation to religion, which both the American Revolution and the French Revolution were grappling with, have continued to have significant influence on the way the international community addresses questions of religion and human rights.

The Formation of the International Human Rights System

While it draws from and is shaped by a long line of historical influences, the contemporary system of international human rights still clearly remains the product of a particular post-conflict environment in the mid-twentieth century. Therefore, the socio-economic and political landscape at the inception of the post-War order is an important factor in examining the relationship between religion and human rights. The power hierarchies among member states of the UN, both contemporary and historical, should be considered. For instance, at the time of the drafting of the Universal Declaration of Human Rights (UDHR), large portions of the world were still colonized. This included many Muslim majority territories. Although the claims it makes with regard to the universality of rights have become increasingly accepted, partially through the international movement of ideas that is a part of globalization, it is nonetheless important to recognize that the language of the UDHR was not a descriptive assessment of the socio-political realities of the post-War order. The tensions between the aspirational language in the document and the socio-political and legal realities of the world continue today. They are evident, among other places, in religiously linked conflicts that continue to impede human rights advancement. Examples of these conflicts include the emerging Shi'a–Sunni tensions (see Box 10.1) in Iraq, and the historical violence in Mindanao, Philippines between Muslim and Christian communities, especially since the latter is framed around questions of separatism and autonomy.

The drafting committee for the Universal Declaration of Human Rights, which many locate as a guide for subsequent conceptions of international human rights, reflected an attempt to realize some representational diversity. The committee included Charles Malik (Lebanon) and Peng-chun Chang (China). René Cassin (France) also brought a voice of Jewish experience to the table. However, regional representation at the drafting of the UDHR was not even or proportionate. At the same time, attempts to achieve diversity did not necessarily translate into religious diversity. For instance, while Charles Malik did bring a Middle-Eastern voice to the table, his was a Greek Orthodox Christian perspective. As a consequence, Abdullahi An-Na'im (1999, p. 315) asserts, 'the initial conception and formulation of the UDHR, as the essential normative and institutional framework of all subsequent instruments and developments, was "negotiated" between delegates of primarily Western powers, with minimal representation from African and Asian countries'. This resulted in a central document of the international human rights movement shaped significantly, if indirectly, by regionally bound traditions of Christian humanism. As a result, a related criticism of the UDHR is that it lacks influences from, and points of access for, a variety of widespread and Indigenous religious traditions. It is important to consider whether North/South or West/East dichotomies established a geographical and thought bias at the inception of the modern human rights system (Cossman, 2003, p. 86). Such types of original bias may influence considerations of whether human rights instruments are acknowledged as universally applicable or coherent with various iterations of world religions in normative terms. (See Box 10.2 for information on key documents relating to religion in international human rights.)

Understanding the Evolution of Rights

From early religious texts, through medieval events such as the signing of the Magna Carta, and past Enlightenment advances to the contemporary international project, ideas about human rights have continued to evolve and grow. A portion of this evolution has involved engaging and adapting the internal logic of some religious narratives surrounding rights and duties. In contemporary human rights discourse, claims of rights and duties are linked. For example, the state, a duty bearer, must protect the rights of its citizens, who are rights-holders. In a similar way, the Jewish tradition of benevolence or charity, the Islamic pillar of *zakat* (alms giving), and the Christian injunction to love one's neighbour can all be understood in terms of how the rights of the poor and the duties of the privileged relate to one another. Concepts of rights and duties have also become more generally incorporated into the broad arguments that undergird the work of international human rights and aid organizations—both secular in character, like the International

BOX 10.1 SUNNI AND SHI'A ISLAM

The split of the Muslim *umma*, or community, into Sunnis and Shi'as was caused by a dispute over the identity of the rightful successor of the Prophet Muhammad after his death in 632 CE. The term 'Sunni' stems from the Arabic term *ahl al-sunna wa al-jama'a* (the people of tradition and community of believers). The Sunnis gave their allegiance to Abu Bakr, father-in-law of the Prophet, as the first leader (Caliph) of the *umma* after Muhammad.

The Arabic word 'Shi'a' means 'party', 'followers', 'group', 'associates', 'partisans', or in a rather looser sense 'supporters'. 'Shi'at Ali' consequently means 'Ali's party' or 'Ali's followers'. This was the name given to the followers and supporters of Ali ibn Abi Talib, cousin and son-in-law of the prophet Muhammad, whom they believed was named successor by Prophet Muhammad before his death.

Given this historical split, the Muslim population of the world consists of two main schools (*madhhab*). The majority are Sunnis, and a minority, 10–15 per cent of all Muslims, are Shi'as. Iran, Iraq, Bahrain, and Azarbaijan have the largest Shi'a populations. There are also significant Shi'a populations in Afghanistan, Kuwait, Lebanon, Pakistan, Saudi Arabia, Syria, and Yemen.

BOX 10.2 KEY DOCUMENTS RELATING TO RELIGION IN INTERNATIONAL HUMAN RIGHTS

Universal Declaration of Human Rights

Adopted and proclaimed by the United Nations General Assembly on 10 December 1948.

Relevant sections: Preamble (enjoyment of freedom of speech, belief and freedom from fear by all human beings); Article 2.1 (non-discrimination on basis of race, colour, sex, language, religion, political or other opinion, national or social origin, property, birth, or other status); Article 18 (freedom of thought, conscience, and religion).

Convention Relating to the Status of Refugees

Adopted on 28 July 1951 by the United Nations Conference of Plenipotentiaries on the Status of Refugees and Stateless Persons convened under General Assembly Resolution 429 (V) of 14 December 1950. It entered into force on 22 April 1954.

Relevant sections: Article 1 (2) (definition of a refugee originates in a 'well-founded fear of being persecuted for reasons of race, religion, nationality, membership of a particular social group or political opinion' that drives a person outside the country of his or her nationality and (because of that fear) is unable or unwilling to avail him or herself of the protection of that country); Article 3 (non-discrimination on the basis of race, religion, or country of origin); Article 4 (respect for freedom of religion and freedom as regards the religious education of their children); Article 33 (prohibition of expulsion or return ('refoulement')).

International Convention on the Elimination of All Forms of Racial Discrimination

Adopted and opened for signature and ratification by the United Nations General Assembly in Resolution 2106 (XX) of 21 December 1965. It entered into force on 4 January 1969.

Relevant section: Article 5 (non-discrimination and enjoyment of rights ... (d.vii) The right to freedom of thought, conscience, and religion).

International Covenant on Civil and Political Rights

The International Covenant on Civil and Political Rights was adopted and opened for signature, ratification, and accession by the United Nations General Assembly in Resolution 2200A (XXI) of 16 December 1966. It entered into force on 23 March 1976.

Relevant sections: Article 18 (1. right to freedom of thought, conscience, and religion; 2. non-coercion of religion and belief; 3.

freedom to manifest one's religion or beliefs subject to limitations as are prescribed by law and are necessary to protect public safety, order, health, or morals or the fundamental rights and freedoms of others; 4. respect for the liberty of parents and, when applicable, legal guardians to ensure the religious and moral education of their children in conformity with their own convictions); Article 24 (non-discrimination); Article 26 (equality before the law); Article 27 (protection of ethnic, religious, or linguistic minorities).

Declaration on the Elimination of All Forms of Intolerance and of Discrimination Based on Religion or Belief

Proclaimed by General Assembly resolution 36/55 of 25 November 1981. It is the result of three decades of discussion on religious rights, primarily within the Sub-Commission on the Prevention of Discrimination and Protection of Minorities, and has been considered a major international standard-setting instrument pertaining to the freedom of religion or belief.

The Declaration on the Human Rights of Individuals who are not Nationals of the Country in Which They Live

Adopted by the United Nations General Assembly Resolution A/RES/40/144 on 13 December 1985.

Relevant sections: Article 5; Article 7.

The Convention on the Rights of the Child

Adopted by the United Nations General Assembly in Resolution 44/25 on 20 November 1989 and entered into force on 2 September 1990. It incorporates Article 27 of the Covenant for Civil and Political Rights.

Relevant sections: Article 2; Article 14; Article 20; Article 29; Article 30.

International Convention on the Protection of the Rights of all Migrant Workers and Members of their Families

The International Convention on the Protection of the Rights of all Migrant Workers and Members of their Families was adopted by the United Nations General Assembly in Resolution 45/158 on 18 December 1990.

Relevant sections: Article 1; Article 7; Article 12 ; Article 13.

Declaration on the Rights of Persons Belonging to National or Ethnic, Religious or Linguistic Minorities

Adopted by the United Nations General Assembly in Resolution 47/135 of 18 December 1992.

Relevant sections: Article 1; Article 2; Article 4.

European Convention for Protection of Human Rights and Fundamental Freedoms

Adopted by the Council of Europe on 4 November 1950 and entered into force on 3 September 1953.

Relevant sections: Article 9; Article 14.

Human Rights Committee, General Comment 22, Article 18 (Forty-eighth session, 1993)

Compilation of General Comments and General Recommendations Adopted by Human Rights Treaty Bodies, UN Doc HRI/GEN/1/Rev.1 at 35 (1994).

Relevant sections: §1–11.

American Declaration of the Rights and Duties of Man

The American Declaration of the Rights and Duties of Man was adopted by the Ninth International Conference of American States of the Organization of American States in Bogota, Columbia, on 2 May 1948.

Relevant sections: Chapter one, Article III; Article XXII.

African Charter on Human and Peoples' Rights

The African Charter on Human and Peoples' Rights was adopted by African States members of the Organization of African Unity meeting in Banjul, Gambia, on 27 June 1981. It entered into force on 21 October 1986.

Relevant sections: Article 2; Article 8; Article 12.

Rescue Committee, and religious, like World Vision International.

Today, human rights are sometimes viewed as a form of secular humanism that is opposed to religion, but it is important to recognize common points of reference and shared histories as a way of complicating this oversimplified dichotomy. Alongside positive endowments—such as shared concerns for questions of equality, justice, and dignity—the histories of human rights and religion are also connected by a more pernicious patrimony of patriarchy. Historically, men have dominated religious realms as well as the political spaces in which human rights have been constructed. This has prompted some important critiques of the universality of human rights from women's perspectives (see Chapters 2 and 11). At the same time, human rights have also been used to challenge religiously based norms surrounding the role and status of women in many societies (see 'CEDAW and Reservations: An Illustration').

As understandings of rights developed, one vein of scholarship also began retrospectively to identify different generations of rights. First generation rights were understood to encompass the earliest advances in civil and political rights that are still most closely associated with the core protection of freedom of religion or belief. Second generation rights were grouped around economic, social, and cultural concerns that were increasingly articulated alongside the processes of industrialization and development, as more attention was paid to the question of disparity and inequality in these areas. Third generation rights, also sometimes styled solidarity rights, came into focus with increased attention to, and visibility of, environmental concerns; these rights seek, among other things, to make explicit connections between human communities and the natural environment. (Many of these third generation rights have been codified only in newer human rights instruments such as the African Charter on Human and Peoples' Rights.) Some have argued for the recognition of a fourth generation of human rights dealing with questions of **intergenerational justice**, which relates to the rights of future generations, and particularly issues of information, technology, and the environment. For example, the issue of climate change has serious consequences for future generations. This is one reason that the United Kingdom passed a climate change act (2008) with specific targets in order to enforce the reduction of greenhouse gases.

It is important to remember that while issues of religion are often pegged to the so-called first generation (civil and political) rights, there is no restriction on the ways in which religious considerations may affect, engage with, or inform any part of the spectrum of rights. Rights are interdependent and interrelated. For example, the fact that Jehovah's Witnesses do not allow for blood transfusions brings the right to religious freedom and the right to health and life together on competing grounds. Another helpful aspect of this generational analysis is that in grouping rights broadly it tends to break down the categories of geographical focus that sometimes restrict analysis of rights to a particular political, religious, or philosophical line of thought. As Sally Engle Merry argues, the international human rights system 'is now deeply transnational'. She continues, 'Vulnerable people take up human rights ideas in a wide variety of local contexts because they offer hope to subordinated groups' (Merry, 2006, p. 2). This correlation between vulnerability and hope is yet another point of potential intersection between human rights and many religious traditions. Systems of human rights offer very real hope for people around the world. Both Soile Lautsi and Leyla Şahin (see the case studies later in this chapter) turned to the regional European human rights body (the European Court of Human Rights) to seek remedies to felt injustices. While they were not guaranteed outcomes, this did provide a structured space in which to exercise agency and argue their cases.

Historically, people have also turned to religion in situations of injustice and hopelessness. Houses of religion and religious bodies have also provided places where people can feel they are heard and where their concerns are taken seriously, by a gathered community or before a religious, or divine, authority. This is not to disregard the fact that religion and religious actors can themselves also be violators of rights. The example of slavery in the United States illustrates this. Many enslaved men and women in the US took solace in religious traditions, particularly forms of Christianity. This gave them a sense of hope through narratives of liberation and empowerment through communion with God and each other. Christian churches were

also leaders in the movement to abolish slavery. Nonetheless, although some religious groups opposed slavery, some others used religious texts and pretexts to argue that a master had the right to be obeyed by his or her slave. In these instances concepts of rights and duties were taken out of a larger human rights framework and made subject to a religious and social ethic that did not value human equality. This injustice was corrected, in part, by US President Abraham Lincoln's 1863 Emancipation Proclamation, a human rights document, which in its reservation of full emancipation to specific geographic areas also demonstrates the highly political nature of many human rights claims and processes, whether linked to religious rationales or not.

KEY POINTS

Religion and human rights often operate in many of the same normative and theoretical spaces. It is important to distinguish how terms such as equality, justice, and dignity are used similarly and differently across these two fields.

The concepts of rights and duties are central to religions as well as to the human rights normative system.

To grasp the many relationships between religion and human rights we need context and historical understanding. In this, it is important to raise questions about who frames the historical narrative of human rights with regard to religious traditions.

Regional representation at the drafting of the UDHR was not even or proportional. As a result, a related criticism of the UDHR is that it lacks influences from, and points of access for, a variety of dominant and Indigenous religious traditions.

Globalization continues to impact the human rights system as well as religious movements, ideas, and identities. Therefore any study of the relationship between human rights norms and religious practices requires an appreciation of the potential for both fields to change.

Critical Thinking Question:

The 1948 Universal Declaration of Human Rights is a significant document in the history of human rights. Do you think it is easier for some religious groups to engage with the UDHR than others? Why is it important that there be a central human rights declaration that is universally accepted across diverse religious communities?

Contemporary Concerns

Questions around religion and human rights occupy a significant space in many contemporary social, political, and legal conversations. One idea that has received a great deal of attention is that some societies, primarily among developed states in the global North, are undergoing a steady process of secularization—that is, they are moving away from religious practice and belief as ethical guidelines and points of **normative** orientation. The debate over secularization is often contentious: some question its definition, others whether it is in fact occurring. Those who acknowledge secularization as a real phenomenon are also divided between those who welcome the move toward secularization as the natural and logical progression of rational human advancement rooted in Enlightenment-era ideas and those who deplore it as a misguided movement to destabilize traditional religious teachings. Frequently secularization is mistakenly used as a placeholder for human rights concerns and practice, although the two are distinct. For example, in the case of Leyla Şahin (which will be discussed later) the ruling of the European Court of Human Rights regards secularization as a placeholder for human rights and a democratic society. In this formulation, the headscarf—as a religious symbol—is seen as having the potential to undermine the secular political order of Europe, and of Turkey in particular.

At the same time that questions are being raised about secularization in certain parts of the world, in other places the strength of political and popular religious movements dominates public discourse and life. The rise, or resurgence, of religion as a political force is particularly visible throughout the global South—particularly in the greater Middle East, throughout the African continent, the Indian subcontinent, and Southeast Asia. This intensification can be identified amongst multiple religious groups, including Hindu, Jewish, Christian, Muslim, and Indigenous groups. Scholars who study these trends have raised questions about the compatibility of some expressions of religion with international human rights norms.

The Treatment of Women

Some of the questions raised in this context pertain to violence against women, including sexual harassment, and cultures of patriarchy. Women's rights are often violated in the name of religion. For example, in some Muslim majority communities, women are often regarded as bearers of their families' honour. In national contexts, the pious woman sometimes becomes an emblem of a nation. As carriers of culture, women's bodies can become sites of contestation, as well as forms of protest. In particular, they are often caught up in ongoing arguments about authority and interpretation, both of religious doctrines and rights claims. Often challenges to traditional discriminatory religious formulations of women's identities are made in the form of human rights claims and arguments grounded in an egalitarian ethos—for instance a woman's right to health or education. Such claims and arguments can be formal or legal in nature, but may also be advanced through public protest, social advocacy, or religious reform movements.

The apparent tensions between religion and human rights, as they pertain to women, stem in part from the fact that women's rights are not universally implemented. This is true across a wide variety of socio-religious environments. Yet debates around the compatibility of human rights—specifically, women's rights—and religion have been particularly strident recently with reference to some forms of Islam. For example, most Islamic schools of law (Box 10.1) give men considerably more rights in divorce proceedings, where at times a man has a unilateral right to divorce. At a global level, human rights documents such as the UN Convention on the Elimination of All Forms of Discrimination Against Women (CEDAW) seek to protect women's rights against encroachment, but at the same time have allowed for reservations to be lodged on religious grounds. In some instances, national and local legislation linked to a religious system can violate international norms for women's rights, while in other instances it can provide stronger and more enforceable protection of women's rights than international documents are able to do.

Religious Expression and Rights Claims in Multicultural Contexts

In today's world, local contexts are becoming increasingly diverse, and this diversity sometimes presents challenges when different religious, cultural, and value systems interact in new ways. As we have seen, one regular space of challenge is the conflict between religious expressions and human rights claims. As a response to this, Martha Nussbaum argues for accommodations to be made for religious particularism on the grounds of conscience. For Nussbaum (2012, p. 311), equal liberty of conscience strikes out a path between *anti-religionism*, which she terms a total rejection of religion from the public square, and *establishmentarianism*, that is, commitment to religious orthodoxy as the basis for good order and public safety. W. Cole Durham agrees that an 'accommodationist' model like Nussbaum's is 'the most optimal for religious freedom'. Kevin Boyle (2004, p. 16) describes the accommodationist model as one in which 'the intent of the State is neither to marginalise religion, nor to insist it retreat from any domains that the state decides to occupy, nor interfere with its internal life'. At the extreme ends of the spectrum, the accommodationist model may be attacked by secular fundamentalists, who do not see why they should have to bend to accommodate a religious rationale they do not share or understand. At the other end, some religious fundamentalists may chafe at a diversity of religious truth claims being accommodated equally. In fact, both may feel morally compelled, or politically empowered, to try to shape their surrounding society to fit their own perspectives with regard to human rights and religion.

The Significance of Symbols

Physical objects such as headscarves and crucifixes that serve as symbols of religious identities, expressions, and commitments are often objects of accommodation, and equally objects of contention. In both France and Turkey the headscarf is a regular source of tension with state-backed understandings of secular republican identity. Some attempts have been made to negotiate the expression of this identity in ways consonant with egalitarian principles. This negotiation has been pursued largely though the division and politicization of space into public and private spheres, with religion largely relegated to the private. However, in both countries there has been some marked antipathy to religious, particularly Islamic, subjects. The headscarf as a constructed symbol of Islam has assumed a certain place in both national narratives as antithetical to women's liberty. The religious response to this antipathy is complex, with some Muslim women claiming the headscarf as a religious symbol that is religious in its own right, while others have rejected the reduction of a complex faith structure to a singular, gendered object. In both instances, international politics has influenced national debates, with concerns over transnational, religiously motivated violence linked to interpretations of Islam being read—mistakenly or wilfully—as interchangeable with non-violent, domestic, and historical strands of practice.

Questions of Toleration

Intolerance encompasses exclusion, violence, discrimination, and marginalization, all of which lead to violation of human rights. Intolerance of the 'other', whether linguistic, religious, cultural, or ethnic, has historically been a pretext for conflict. Accommodationism can be seen as a subset or species of toleration. While toleration is a minimum passive requirement of coexistence, accommodation goes a step beyond in requiring some sort of positive action. Recent examples of intolerance and human rights abuses rooted in a religious world view include: the 2015 killings in Paris at the Charlie Hebdo office and a kosher supermarket, violent acts perpetrated by the self-proclaimed Islamic State across the Middle East and North Africa, kidnappings by the group Boko Haram in Nigeria, and the persecution of and forced migration of Rohingya Muslims by Rakhine Buddhists in Myanmar. There are also examples of intolerance and human rights abuses rooted in anti-religious world views, such as a 2012 shooting at a Sikh temple in Wisconsin, USA, where Sikhs were attacked in an apparent case of mistaken identity emerging from anti-Muslim animus. All of these events have an eventual effect on social and political ideas and practices of freedom, including freedom of speech, freedom of movement, freedom of the press, and freedom of religion. The human rights claims and religious understandings that overlap and ground these freedoms are both undermined by turns toward violence and practices of intolerance. Both the former and latter cases demonstrate how ill-informed religious and anti-religious world views can lead to violence and human rights violations.

As the movement of people across boundaries continues, both older and newly formed multicultural societies find themselves faced with new rights challenges. Often those related to religion and human rights are the most divisive. In part this is because religion is often inextricably woven into the larger cultural fabric of a society.

A Complex Relationship

Human rights and religion often occupy the same normative spaces. Religion can both promote and hamper human rights. Violations of human rights occur in the name of religion, but often religions promote concepts of dignity, equality, and justice that are also central to the human rights ethos. Human rights advocates and human rights violators hail from the full continuum extending between religious and secular camps, and into the territory beyond. Therefore the tension emanating from the relationship between religion and human rights is best addressed in context, and is often helped by way of comparative assessments.

Dignity and the Responsibility to Act on Behalf of Others

Paul Gordon Lauren offers one such comparative assessment in his work on human rights visionaries and religious visionaries. Lauren contends that there are important socio-historical connections between these types of visionary individuals. He is concerned in particular with the way that both challenge the status quo through the articulation of normative standards and exploration of the dignity of human beings. Lauren is also concerned with the ways in which religion and human rights share a 'concept of responsibility to act on behalf of others' Lauren, 1998, p. 6). The visions Lauren traces cohere in an ideal world without 'any discrimination, or persecution on the basis of gender, race, caste or class, religion, political belief, ethnicity, or nationality, or any other form of difference' (ibid.). This generalized field of vision emerges from across a wide array of cultures, societies, political systems, and religions.

Tensions Between Religion and Human Rights

However, lived expressions of such visions are necessarily bounded by place and time. It is particularly important to recognize this when looking at the history of the international systematization of human rights. Current debates over the origins of human rights display significant discrepancy and dissent regarding the creation narratives around the international system (Moyn, 2010; Bowring, 2008). Simultaneously, alternatively styled human rights documents, such as the Cairo Declaration on Human Rights (see Box 10.3),

> **BOX 10.3 ALTERNATIVE POINTS OF VIEW: THE CAIRO DECLARATION**
>
> The Cairo Declaration on Human Rights in Islam was agreed on by the member states of the Organisation of Islamic Conference (OIC) in Cairo, August 1990. The OIC, now renamed the Organisation of Islamic Cooperation, is an intergovernmental organization with fifty-seven member states, established in 1969. The Cairo Declaration can be seen as an 'Islamic' response to the UDHR. Where the UDHR document claims a universalist and secular language, the Cairo declaration affirms the primacy of Shari'a. This stems from the belief by some that Shari'a alone provides sufficient discourse for rights and therefore there is no need to adopt what is seen as a Western rights model and which fails to encompass the relevant religio-cultural contexts of Muslim majority communities.

both mediate between international human rights, Islamic faith claims, and the politics arising between them, and at the same time threaten to undermine the authoritative force of an international human rights framework that is in many instances already beleaguered.

Balancing Protection of Religious Freedom and Expression with Protection of other Human Rights

An examination of state reservations to international conventions made on the basis of religious rationale similar to that found in the Cairo Declaration raises the specific spectre and challenge of *à la carte* rights. Such reservations may call into question the integrity of the international system of rights. These types of reservations may also undermine national recourses to justice by enabling legal discrimination rooted in forms of religious logic. The right to religious expression and freedom should not trump other human rights, as human rights form an interdependent and indivisible system. At the same time there is an essential and inherent tension in the human rights enterprise as questions of derogation arise when rights come into conflict with one another (see Chapter 3). For this reason, human rights norms often coalesce slowly into the forms of international conventions and declarations only after being tested extensively by way of policy instruments, political platforms, and public discourse. As Abdullahi An-Na'im (2011, p. 275) asserts, 'the quality of being a universal norm can therefore only be achieved through a global consensus building, and neither assumed nor imposed through the hegemony of universalizing claims from one relativist perspective or another'. This type of time-intensive consensus building, while it may be contentious and conflicted, is not achieved by dint of force or turning to authoritarianism.

Questions of Authoritative Interpretation

Global consensus building around questions of religion and human rights is often forced to assess questions of religious authority. In the case of Islam, for example, the Qur'an is a primary source of Shari'a. However, there are many interpretations of the Qur'an and they may focus on different principles. Charles Kurzman boils Shari'a interpretations down to three types with respect to human rights. He identifies a 'liberal Shari'ah', which treats Islam and human rights as inherently compatible. Adherents of this liberal Shari'a believe that the rights scheme in Islam predates the so-called modern human rights scheme. Therefore, while sympathetic to rights claims, they may also often ignore existing discrimination that is culturally or religiously embedded. The second type of interpretation Kurzman proposes is 'silent Shari'ah', which holds that Islam and human rights may work in tandem, but only where certain human rights provisions are not mentioned in or derivable from Shari'a. In this category, there is little room left to challenge violations of rights that stem from primary sources of Islamic law. The third category, 'interpretive Shari'ah', regards Shari'a as being the divine law of God, but one that is open to various human interpretations (Kurzman, 1998, 1999; Mokhtari, 2004). Kurzman concludes that the 'interpretations of Islamic law that incorporate international human rights norms are just as authentic as traditional interpretations' (Mokhtari, 2004, p. 472). However, this is a not a universally accepted position—nor is the issue unique to Islam. Other religious authorities also take different stands on how to engage with questions of human rights. Therefore, if one tries to assess the status within, or compatibility of human rights with, some particular religious tradition, one cannot avoid the question of who counts as an authority qualified to interpret that tradition. These are contentious and

difficult questions that rarely have simple answers. They can be particularly vexing in international forums where certain voices are called upon, or assert themselves as speaking broadly for large and diverse religious communities, sometimes without democratic mandates or structures of accountability.

CEDAW and Reservations: An Illustration

One place where questions of authoritative interpretation and the treatment of women intersect when looking at human rights and religion is the review process used by the UN Committee on the Elimination of Discrimination Against Women. This committee is the custodian of the UN Convention on the Elimination of All Forms of Discrimination Against Women (CEDAW). Like the UDHR, CEDAW was negotiated in an era of confrontations between global superpowers and ideologies. Some vestiges of this oppositional friction between world views are still present in contemporary discussions around CEDAW (Rehof, 1993, p. 2; see also Box 10.4 for a discussion of religious objections to CEDAW). One example is found in the reservations that Muslim majority states regularly make when they ratify CEDAW. Since they tend to restrict national capacities for legal reforms to advance women's rights, these reservations often raise criticism from human rights communities. Such reservations demonstrate that even as the language of rights becomes legitimized through global consensus, it is still often used only in rhetorical terms, and is sometimes subject to reservations on religious grounds.

For example, Saudi Arabia ratified CEDAW on 7 September 2000. Yet women in Saudi Arabia still suffer a range of public and private discrimination, both at the workplace and at home. Saudi laws on gender-based segregation and dress codes restrict freedom of movement for women. Women in Saudi Arabia are not permitted to travel, work, or study without the permission of a male relative, and they are prohibited from driving. At the same time, following the ratification of CEDAW there have been advances in women's status in Saudi Arabia. A labour law passed in late September 2005 led to the expansion of professional fields where women are eligible to work, and King Abdullah declared that women would have the right to vote in Saudi's municipal elections in 2015 (Human Rights Watch, 2012). Saudi Arabia's ratification of CEDAW exemplifies the way that Muslim majority states may

BOX 10.4 CHALLENGING ASSUMPTIONS: RELIGIOUS OBJECTIONS TO CEDAW

As of July 2015, 189 countries have ratified CEDAW. The United States is one of the few states alongside Iran and Sudan that has not ratified this treaty. Although President Jimmy Carter signed the treaty on behalf of the US in 1980, indicating the intention to ratify, thirty-five years have passed without ratification. In order for CEDAW to be ratified it needs to come to the Senate, which it has never done, despite the recommendation made by the Senate Foreign Relations Committee in 2002. Although there are many domestic arguments in favour, there are many who are against ratification. The reason for non-ratification of CEDAW by the US is couched in religious rhetoric, similar to reservations made on articles of CEDAW by Muslim majority states such as Saudi Arabia. Those opposed to CEDAW insist that ratification of the Convention is a threat to US sovereignty and that the Convention aims 'to implement a radical agenda that would undermine "traditional" moral and social values, including marriage, motherhood, family structure, and even Mother's Day' (UNA-USA, 2001).

The proponents of CEDAW see ratification as a great benefit to the protection and promotion of women's rights in the US. In particular they contend it will enhance the legal efforts in the US to end violence against women.

coherence. However, reservations raise the question of how authentic or robust such coherence is, particularly when religious claims often go uncontested and are allowed a parallel normative status within the international framework.

All Muslim majority countries (referring here to members of the OIC) apart from Iran, Sudan, and Somalia, have ratified CEDAW. Yet it is striking to see the sheer number and similarity of reservations these countries have made to CEDAW on the grounds of religion. Ann Elizabeth Mayer asserts that many of these reservations help to encourage a false view that there is an inherent incompatibility between Islam and human rights (Mayer, 2007, p. 5). Of course from some Muslim perspectives there is such an incompatibility. In these cases, CEDAW is seen as a product of Western imperialism imposed on the Muslim world. Yet again, Mayer contends that very often the reservations are dressed up in religious rationale, but are staunchly political in calculation. For instance, Muslim majority countries might pursue reservations to CEDAW due to 'worry that reforms expanding women's rights could fuel a fundamentalist backlash; a concern to maintain regime legitimacy by demonstrating fidelity to Islamic law; and, the desire to win favour with rich donor nations, like Saudi Arabia, that sponsor a reactionary version of Islam' (ibid.). In these instances, many of the gender-discriminatory laws that are legitimated in the name of Islam, and protected through reservations to international human rights norms, are in fact products of power politics between states and disputes over religious authority and representation.

engage international human rights instruments as a route towards synchronization with international human rights norms, while at the same time issuing reservations to protect aspects of what they deem an essential religious identity. Ratification often leads to political rewards in an international system that values

KEY POINTS

There are dual trends—towards secularization in certain parts of the world, and towards popular religious movements in other parts of the world—that dominate public discourse and life. These trends demonstrate the diversity of experience encompassed by questions of human rights and religion, as well as the constant need to contextualize questions of human rights and religion.

When religious tenets and human rights norms come into conflict, or seem unresolvable, this need not be understood in terms of a zero-sum game. Instead, consider the argument made by some scholars that particular claims should be accommodated as a best practice on the grounds of equal liberty of conscience.

The complex relationship between religion and human rights may manifest itself in positive and symbiotic work toward the full realization of human dignity, and equally may be shaped by conflict around questions of intolerance and violence.

Neither the advancement of dignity nor the exacerbation of intolerance is an attribute exclusive to any community. Various human rights communities and various religious communities, where they diverge from each other, may each be responsible for these social and political forces in their own way.

Human rights form an interdependent and indivisible system. The right to religious expression and freedom should not trump other human rights.

Human rights norms often coalesce slowly, following political negotiations and social movements, into recognizable forms such as international conventions and declarations. During this process the question of who, or which groups, hold some form of authority to negotiate on behalf of religious communities becomes an important question that is often contested and sometimes unresolved.

Critical Thinking Question:

For different reasons both the US and a small number of Muslim majority countries remain among a few countries worldwide that have not ratified CEDAW. Discuss whether objections to the ratification of CEDAW are justifiable on the basis of religion.

The Lautsi Case

Lautsi v. Italy (2011) is a case that arrived at the European Court of Human Rights (ECHR) as an application by Ms Soile Lautsi against the Italian Republic. The case was brought under Article 34 of the Convention for the Protection of Human Rights and Fundamental Freedoms. Acting in her own name and on behalf of her two children, the Finnish born Lautsi pressed a case concerning the presence of a crucifix in each room of the Italian state school her children attended, to which she objected on the grounds of religious indoctrination. The case ended up at the ECHR after Lautsi pursued the matter with the school governors, an Italian Administrative Court, the Constitutional Court, and finally appealed to the Italian Supreme Administrative Court. The *Lautsi* case emerges from a complicated Italian social and legal context in which the political history of Italy, as well as its unique relationship with the Vatican, factor prominently. Initially, a Chamber (panel) of the Court ruled that the presence of the crucifix in the classroom was a human rights violation. Specifically, it held that there had been a violation of the right to education, as well as rights related to freedom of thought, conscience, or religion. Subsequently, the Italian government asked for the case to be referred to the Grand Chamber of the Court. In 2011, the Grand Chamber (the full Court) reversed this decision and held that there had been no violation of these rights. This means that at the end of the legal process the crucifix stayed on the wall of the classroom and the Court held that neither the human rights of Lautsi or her children had been violated (see Box 10.5).

Issues in Lautsi

The Lautsi case exemplifies the tension between an understanding of neutrality often associated with secularism and traditional values often rooted in a historical religious framework. Did the school community have a duty to accommodate the Lautsi family in its discomfort with the crucifix? Or alternatively, should the Lautsi family be expected to make accommodations to fit into the history and present ethos of the school community? This type of tension gets worked out differently in different types of contexts; as the Lautsi case shows, tensions get worked out differently through a legal system than they would be in other ethical or social systems. Sometimes legal judgments such as this may seem as if they are missing important components of lived human experience. For instance, we do not know what initial conversations between Lautsi and school administrators sounded like. We don't know exactly the ways the Lautsi children felt or how they were affected when they were in the presence of the crucifix. We also don't know what kinds of unsupervised conversations about religion and related questions of identity and influence occurred between the schoolchildren themselves in the classroom. With that said, as human rights becomes increasingly instrumentalized through law, legal judgments often become significant determinants for questions of human rights and religion.

One of the criticisms of the ECHR's ruling in the case was a lack of nuance in dealing with the presenting question as it related to religion. For instance, Malcolm Evans observed: '[i]t is a pity that the Court did not address directly the argument that the principle of neutrality does not demand the absence of religious symbolism in the educational setting on the grounds that such a response in fact privileges secularist views and is just "not neutral"' (M. D. Evans, 2011, p. 243). One of the reasons for this may be, as Sylvie Langlaude argues, that the rights of religious associations are slowly developing within the framework of international law, 'at the very least before the OSCE and the Council of Europe' (Langlaude, 2011, p. 529). As social stakeholders, religious associations should of course be included in any consideration of the mechanics

BOX 10.5 JUDGE BONELLO ON THE LAUTSI CASE

Selected sections from the concurring opinion of Judge Bonello (a Maltese Judge of the European Court of Human Rights) to the Lautsi case:

12.6 It must be emphasised that the symbol of the crucifix, thus understood, now possesses, through its references to the values of tolerance, a particular scope in consideration of the fact that at present Italian state schools are attended by numerous pupils from outside the European Union, to whom it is relatively important to transmit the principles of openness to diversity and the refusal of any form of fundamentalism—whether religious or secular—which permeate our system. Our era is marked by the ferment resulting from the meeting of different cultures with our own, and to prevent that meeting from turning into a collision it is indispensable to reaffirm our identity, even symbolically, especially as it is characterised precisely by the values of respect for the dignity of each human being and of universal solidarity ...

13.2 In fact, religious symbols in general imply a logical exclusion mechanism, as the point of departure of any religious faith is precisely the belief in a superior entity, which is why its adherents, the faithful, see themselves by definition and by conviction as part of the truth. Consequently, and inevitably, the attitude of the believer, faced with someone who does not believe, and who is therefore implicitly opposed to the supreme being, is an attitude of exclusion ...

13.3 The logical mechanism of exclusion of the unbeliever is inherent in any religious conviction, even if those concerned are not aware of it, the sole exception being Christianity—where it is properly understood, which of course has not always been and still is not always the case, not even thanks to those who call themselves Christian. In Christianity even the faith in an omniscient god is secondary in relation to charity, meaning respect for one's fellow human beings. It follows that the rejection of a non-Christian by a Christian implies a radical negation of Christianity itself, a substantive abjuration; but that is not true of other religious faiths, for which such an attitude amounts at most to the infringement of an important precept.

13.4 The cross, as the symbol of Christianity, can therefore not exclude anyone without denying itself; it even constitutes in a sense the universal sign of the acceptance of and respect for every human being as such, irrespective of any belief, religious or other, which he or she may hold ...

of justice, with no more, or less, privilege than any other group. But neither religion nor secularism, as categories of human practice, are thoroughly coherent. Each contains, and inspires, a range of diversity. As T. J. Gunn observes, '[a]lthough many international and regional human rights instruments guarantee rights related to freedom of religion or belief, none attempts to define the term "religion"' (Gunn, 2003, pp. 189–90). As cases like Lautsi demonstrate, a growing edge for questions of human rights and religion is for increased conversation between the rights guaranteed in international instruments and the specifics of how religion is practised and understood in local contexts.

The Impact of the Lautsi Decision

In its Grand Chamber decision, the ECHR protected states' **margin of appreciation,**[2] including state-sponsored interpretations of a majority religion. This means the Court decided to let states have a good deal of discretion as to how they would regulate religion. It demonstrates a logic operative among the European states that individual governments know their own national context best and that their own legal judgments should be deferred to in the first instance. However, the Lautsi case is interesting in that the first judgment of the Court contradicted the Italian position. It is particularly notable that the final decision in Lautsi represented a stark reversal of position between Chamber and Grand Chamber judgments. In the first instance, the ECHR Chamber judgment protected a 'neutral', 'secular' space. It would have taken down the crucifix. Upon referral, the ECHR Grand Chamber changed position and safeguarded an understanding of the 'European tradition' as being historically and essentially linked to Christianity. As a result, the crucifix stayed on the classroom wall. The final outcome of Lautsi complicates the question of how appeals to universal values and rights, whether couched in religious or secular language, can be squared with accommodation of difference claims. The scope of the Lautsi case also illustrates some of the fundamental concerns religious groups have about human rights systems (e.g. that human rights will be used to eradicate religion from public life), as well as some of the concerns human rights advocates have about the power and historical sway of religious identities (e.g. that tradition justifies the violation of human rights).

The Şahin Case

Like the Lautsi case, the case of Leyla Şahin deals with questions raised by the social effects of material religious culture. Leyla Şahin enrolled in the Faculty of Medicine at the University of Istanbul in 1997 following medical studies at the University of Bursa. Şahin wore the headscarf during her studies at Bursa. However, while at the University of Istanbul, the examination supervisors denied her access to a written examination because she was wearing the headscarf. Subsequently she was refused access to a course, a lecture, and another written examination. The repeated denial of access to courses, lectures, and examinations at the university were justified by reference to a document issued by the Vice-Chancellor of Istanbul University, which stated, 'students whose "heads are covered" (wearing the Islamic headscarf) and students (including overseas students) with beards must not be admitted to lectures, courses, or tutorials' (*Layla Şahin v. Turkey* 2005). Disciplinary actions were taken against Şahin due to her alleged failure to comply with dress rules.

It is important to note that in the Turkish context, secularism (*laiklik*) may be best explained in terms of the state's attempts to control religion. Since the establishment of the republic in 1923, a Kemalist line of secular nationalism has long pushed the headscarf out of the Turkish public square. However, the Regulation Concerning the Dress of Personnel Employed in the Public Institutions was not passed until 1980 and not implemented in any pronounced way until 1998. Consequently, Şahin was given a warning, and later suspended for one semester, for taking part in 'an unauthorised assembly'. Although she was later granted an 'amnesty', releasing her from all the disciplinary penalties and their effects, allowing her to complete her medical studies, Şahin moved her studies to Vienna University in September 1999.

While this transfer resolved educational access issues on a practical level, Şahin continued to pursue the question of justice in courts of law. After exhausting national remedies, Şahin lodged an application against the Republic of Turkey with the European Commission of Human Rights. In doing so, Şahin made it clear that she regarded wearing the headscarf as her religious duty as a Muslim woman and insisted that this religious obligation 'was neither ostentatious nor intended as a means of protest and did not constitute a form of pressure, provocation or proselytism' (Ibid.,

para. 85). Şahin also noted qualms that 'the restriction on wearing religious symbols was not applied uniformly'. For example, there was no evidence to suggest similar restrictions on Christian and Jewish students (Ibid., para. 88). Şahin therefore reasoned that 'a ban on wearing the Islamic headscarf in higher education institutions violated her rights and freedoms under Articles 8, 9, 10, and 14 of the Convention for the Protection of Human Rights and Fundamental Freedoms on 21 July 1998' (Ibid., para.102).

Issues Linking Şahin and Lautsi

In arriving at its decision, the Court acknowledged the history and influence of religiously aligned political movements in Turkey, as well as the degree to which foundational social realignment and the imposition of religious precepts remained a concern for Turkey. The Court also referred to precedent by which states were afforded leeway to guard against groups. *Refah Partisi* (The Welfare Party) *and others v. Turkey* (2001) and *Dahlab v. Switzerland* (2001) formed part of this precedent, the latter being a case in which a primary school teacher was prohibited from wearing the headscarf. In the Dahlab case, the headscarf was deemed to be a 'powerful external symbol' (*Layla Şahin v. Turkey*, 2005). Ultimately, the Court maintained 'that in a democratic society the State was entitled to place restrictions on the wearing of the Islamic headscarf if it was incompatible with the pursued aim of protecting the rights and freedoms of others, public order and public safety'. Therefore, it held that in prohibiting Şahin from access to aspects of her university course of study while she wore the headscarf, Turkey was pursuing the legitimate aim of preserving, rather than dampening, pluralism in the university and the state.

In reviewing the jurisprudence of the ECHR through Lautsi and Şahin, the contrasting language used in relation to religious symbols is striking. In the Lautsi case the crucifix is referred to as an 'essentially passive symbol', while in the Şahin case the headscarf is referred to as a 'powerful external symbol'. Differing applications of a gender lens may be one reason for this disparity. Similar to questions around the relationship between CEDAW and Muslim majority states, a concern with the politics of gender equality and religious claims can be located in ECHR jurisprudence. However, in understanding the headscarf as a symbol that appears 'to be imposed on women by a precept laid down in the Koran' and that is 'hard to reconcile with the principle of gender equality', the Court did not give appropriate attention to questions of women's agency. By framing the headscarf as 'a compulsory religious duty', the Court discounted the real possibility that Şahin made a voluntary and independent choice in wearing it.

In reading the scarf as a constant affront to gender equality, the Court left little room for religious freedom arguments, especially if that freedom is understood as freedom to manifest divergent views within an established socio-religious tradition. The Court argued that in Şahin, 'the issues at stake include the protection of the "rights and freedoms of others" and the "maintenance of public order" in a country in which the majority of the population, while professing a strong attachment to the rights of women and a secular way of life, adhere to the Islamic faith' (*Layla Şahin v. Turkey*, 2005, para. 115). Yet the singularity of that religion in the Turkish context remains an open question. Between the years 1998 and 2002, a headscarf ban in Turkey led to the dismissal of some five thousand female civil servants and the forced resignation of another ten thousand (Bottoni, 2013, p. 187).

In this context, the Şahin case raises the question of whether the margin of appreciation afforded to states by the ECHR protects a principle of neutrality or a political ideology. In other words, the ECHR deference to states' knowledge and expertise with regard to their own national context may at times empower a majoritarian, or dominant, political order to consolidate itself against minority claims. As the Şahin case demonstrates, this can have significant implications for the rights of religious minorities, or minority interpretations of majority religious traditions.

Effects of the Şahin Decision

In the Şahin case and the Lautsi case, by protecting a state's margin of appreciation, the ECHR preserved state-sponsored interpretations of a majority religion. Jeroen Temperman identifies a thematic link between the 'crucifixes put on school walls by public authorities as per a state law' considered in Lautsi and the prohibition of 'Islamic headscarves worn by individuals in educational premises' protected by *Leyla Şahin v. Turkey*. Temperman observes that the Court found that headscarves 'might have some proselytizing effect', while the crucifix is not understood as having a didactic influence. For Temperman, and for anyone

concerned with the relationship between religion and human rights, a comparison of the outcomes of these two cases raises questions around the ECHR's understanding of the state as a 'neutral and impartial organiser of the exercise of various religions', as well as how majoritarian traditions are best interfaced with minority interests, concerns, and rights. Both Lautsi and Şahin offer an invitation to examine critically the relationship between neutrality and ideology, whether political or religious. In this regard, these cases serve as bellwethers for ECHR and help tether overarching questions about the ongoing relationship between democratic values, religion, and human rights to a specific time and place. In the European context, and the larger international context, this relationship continues to draw, and deserves, significant and sustained attention.

KEY POINTS

Cases like Lautsi and Şahin demonstrate growing edges for questions of human rights and religion. One of these is for increased understanding between the legal dimensions of rights guaranteed in international instruments and the social specifics of how religion is lived and experienced in human communities.

Cases like Lautsi and Şahin help us to understand how appeals to universal values and rights, whether couched in religious or secular language, can come into conflict with accommodation of difference claims as mediated by a state. The ECHR has tended to side with and support a state's margin of appreciation to adjudicate such difference claims.

Both the Lautsi and Şahin cases demonstrate that there are a variety of ideas as to how the value of pluralism is best assessed or advanced when it comes to questions of religion.

Critical Thinking Question:

Imagine that some of the material facts in the Lautsi and Şahin cases were reversed so that in Italy children regularly attended schools in which a symbol of Islam was regularly and prominently visible, while in Turkey a student was denied access to aspects of higher education due to public adherence to a form of Christian dress or ritual. Do you think the cases would have been decided in the same ways? What difference does context make to the ECHR judgments, or to your own assessment of the normative questions of rights in each case?

Conclusion

Religion and human rights are normative systems of thought and social order that occupy similar philosophical and theoretical spaces. Taking into account context and history is essential when studying religion and human rights. The human rights system, as enshrined in the UDHR, the UN core treaties, and the regional instruments such as the European Convention on Human Rights, is regarded by some as having universal applicability, whereas others see it as lacking influence from diverse religions and cultures across the globe. Even so, the general rights to freedom of religion or belief, and non-discrimination on the basis of religion, are embedded in human rights law. While religion itself remains undefined in this context, both religion and human rights may be said to concern themselves on the whole with multifaceted concepts such as peace, duty, equality, dignity, and justice. Sometimes religion and human rights compete with one another over these concepts and sometimes they form alliances around them. There are instances where certain interpretations of religious tenets may be incompatible with human rights norms. However, differing interpretations of the same tenets and norms may yield no incompatibility. One place this is particularly visible is around women's rights and religion. In such instances, the question of authority—religious, legal, and social— becomes central to problems of human rights and religion. It is undeniable that human rights violations are at times perpetrated in the name of religion, but they may also be understood to emanate from broader spaces of intolerance that exceed the limits of any specific religious system. Such violations are often compounded by mitigating factors such as war and violence.

Human rights violations committed in the name of religion, or using a religious logic, stand in stark contrast to many of the universalizing idealistic visions and protections advanced by religious systems with regard to human nature and community. The prospect of partnership and coherence between human rights and religion and the reality of significant tensions between human rights and religion contributes to a paradoxical relationship between these two systems. Therefore, even as the relationship between religion and human rights norms becomes more regularized, the rich and diverse history of religion and rights is still open to, and in need of, systematic reform and reinterpretation As some movements toward ideas of secularization and some continued expressions of religious fundamentalism draw religion and human rights apart in exclusive terms, there is a need for individuals and organizations who are able to consider religion and human rights in integral ways, and who can help shape their future relationships in new and contextual terms.

? QUESTIONS

Individual Study Questions

1. To what degree should religion be a factor in determining and making human rights legislation?

2. Is the European Court of Human Rights biased in terms of religion?

3. How should conflicts between religious rights and other rights be mediated?

4. Is it always possible to distinguish religious discrimination from other related forms of discrimination?

Group Discussion Questions

1. Are the ECHR decisions on *Lautsi* and *Şahin* coherent or in conflict with each other in terms of the Court's jurisprudence on religion and human rights?

2. Discuss whether human rights can exist without religion.

3. Is a secular state necessary in order for human rights protections to be fully implemented?

FURTHER READING

Banchoff, T. and **Wuthnow, R.** (eds) (2011). *Religion and the Global Politics of Human Rights*. New York: Oxford University Press.

This book represents a major survey of the religious politics of human rights across various religious traditions and political systems.

Perry, M. J. (2006). *Toward a Theory of Human Rights: Religion, Law, Courts*. New York: Cambridge University Press.

In this book, Michael Perry addresses a number of questions around the morality of human rights and religion while engaging a range of topics including capital punishment, abortion, and same-sex unions.

Taylor, P. M. (2005). *Freedom of Religion: UN and European Human Rights Law*. Cambridge: Cambridge University Press.

This book is a comparative study of European and UN development of the laws of religious freedom.

Witte, J. Jr and **Green, M. C.** (eds) (2012). *Religion and Human Rights: An Introduction*. New York: Oxford University Press.

This book offers a comprehensive survey of religion and human rights which includes a broad spectrum of perspectives and traditions.

WEB LINKS

http://www.ohchr.org/EN/Issues/FreedomReligion/Pages/FreedomReligionIndex.aspx   This website provides information on the work of the Special Rapporteur on freedom of religion or belief, an independent expert appointed by the UN Human Rights Council.

http://www.strasbourgconsortium.org   The Strasbourg Consortium gathers the work of several academic institutions with interest in freedom of religion or belief and makes electronic resources available where these issues touch the work of the European Court of Human Rights.

https://scholarblogs.emory.edu/aannaim/   Professor Abdullahi An-Na'im is the Charles Howard Candler Professor of Law at Emory Law School. This website features Professor An-Na'im's scholarship on religion and human rights, in particular the relationship between human rights and Islam.

http://www1.umn.edu/humanrts/edumat/studyguides/religion.html   The University of Minnesota Human Rights Library provides a study guide on freedom of religion or belief.

https://www.opendemocracy.net/openglobalrights/religion-and-human-rights   Open Democracy is an online not-for-profit independent discussion forum, which has published a series of invited articles on the subject of collaboration between religion and human rights.

NOTES

1. The Magna Carta 'Great Charter' was signed by King John in Runnymede, England under pressure after a rebellion by a group of barons. The document asserts the rule of law, and places the king beneath the law. Some of its clauses remain part of British statutory law today, including the first clause that 'the English Church shall be free, and shall have its rights undiminished, and its liberties unimpaired'.

2. Margin of appreciation in the broadest terms refers to the degree of freedom accorded to national authorities in fulfilling their obligations under the European Convention on Human Rights. For more details see Steven Greer, *The*

Margin of Appreciation: Interpretation and Discretion under the European Convention on Human Rights, Human rights files No. 17, Strasbourg: Council of Europe Publishing, available online at http://www.echr.coe.int/LibraryDocs/DG2/HRFILES/DG2-EN-HRFILES-17(2000).pdf

 Visit the Online Resource Centre that accompanies this book for updates and a range of other resources: www.oxfordtextbooks.co.uk/orc/goodhart3e/

11

Sexual Orientation, Gender Identity, and Human Rights

Christine (Cricket) Keating and Cynthia Burack

Chapter Contents

Reader's Guide

This chapter explores the issue of the human rights of lesbian, gay, bisexual, transgender, intersex, and queer people (often abbreviated to LGBTI). In recent years, LGBTI groups have turned to the language and frameworks of human rights in order to organize against state, civil society, religious, and interpersonal violence and discrimination. This chapter addresses the following questions: What are the central human rights issues for LGBTI people, and how have these groups organized to address these challenges through a human rights framework? What are the challenges faced by LGBTI human rights advocates and what successes have they had? In addition to tracing the struggle for human rights of LGBTI people, this chapter examines critiques of human rights approaches to sexual orientation and gender identity justice struggles.

Introduction

Human rights language and discourses have been powerful tools to address the discrimination, marginalization, and persecution of oppressed people. LGBTI people and their allies have used and adapted human rights discourse, organized in local contexts, and engaged in coalitions with other groups at national and transnational levels to work on issues of rights in relationship to sexual orientation, sexual practice, and gender identity. The widening of the human rights framework to address issues of sexual orientation and gender identity has been an important development in both the human rights movement and the LGBTI movement. It involves the linked struggles to ensure that the human rights of LGBTI people are protected and recognized as well as to expand the concept of human rights to include freedom of gender identity and sexual orientation.

Sexual Orientation and Gender Identity Rights as Human Rights

Many scholars, lawyers, activists, and professionals who work in the area of human rights related to sexuality and gender use the term '**sexual orientation and gender identity**', abbreviated as SOGI, to refer to the basis of forms of discrimination aimed at people of minority sexuality and/or gender identity. Amnesty International (2015a) defines sexual orientation as pertaining to one's 'sexual desires, feelings, practices and identification'. For example, one might be primarily attracted to one's same sex (gay or lesbian), to the opposite sex (heterosexual or 'straight'), or to both sexes (bisexual). Distinct from sexual orientation, gender identity refers to 'a person's experience of self expression in relation to social categories of masculinity or femininity'; one's psychological identification with these categories is referred to as one's 'felt gender' (Amnesty International, 2015a). People are considered 'cisgender' when their felt gender is in congruence with their sex or physiological characteristics. When their felt gender is different from their sex or physiological characteristics, they are considered 'transgender'. When people have indeterminate or mixed sex characteristics, they are considered 'intersex'. A related term is 'gender expression', which refers to the ways in which people express their gender identities (see Table 11.1 for further discussion of these terms).

In this chapter, we will use the acronym SOGI in reference to struggles for sexual orientation and gender identity human rights and the acronym LGBTI (lesbian, gay, bisexual, transgender, and intersex) to refer to people who are likely to be targeted for their minority sexuality or gender identity. There are two main advantages of the use of the term SOGI in reference to human rights struggles for LGBTI people. The first is that this terminology focuses attention on sexual and gender diversity in general and the threats and forms of stigma that have often attached to minority sexual and gender identities. Secondly, the terminology avoids reinforcing particular categories of sexual and gender identity or names that people in global communities may not embrace. For example, using identity terms such as 'lesbian', 'gay', 'bisexual', 'transgender', and 'intersex', which have emerged in specific contexts, in a universal human rights discourse might serve to erase cultural and linguistic variation of sexual and gender identity and practice and reinforce Western cultural and linguistic dominance.

Why are LGBTI People Vulnerable?

All too often, LGBTI people face political persecution, violence, discrimination, and marginalization. In the words of the International Lesbian and Gay Association (ILGA), LGBTI people are often considered 'illegal, immoral and criminals, and deemed not to deserve the legal protections enjoyed by the rest' (ILGA, 2015c, p. 6). LGBTI people are vulnerable in particular because of social and political processes linked to heteronormativity and homophobia. Heteronormativity is a belief that being heterosexual, in an opposite-sex relationship, or cisgender is 'normal' and other modes of sexual orientation, gender identity, and gender expression are unnatural, immoral, or wrong. Heteronormativity contributes to these human rights violations by creating the impression that LGBTI people are somehow deviant or abnormal and that violence and discrimination directed towards them is thus somehow deserved or justified. Homophobia is closely linked to heteronormativity and refers to a fear of or an aversion towards people who either are or are perceived as being non-heterosexual or non-gender conforming. The term 'internalized homophobia' refers to anxiety about or aversion to one's own non-normative sexuality or gender identity. Internalized homophobia has been linked to low self-esteem and suicide in LGBTI individuals.

Table 11.1 LGBTI terms and definitions

	Sexual orientation	Gender identity	Gender expression
Heterosexual	Predominant or exclusive attraction to the opposite sex	May or may not be an issue	May or may not deviate from dominant norms of gender expression
Homosexual (men are referred to as gays, women as lesbians)	Predominant or exclusive attraction to the same sex	May or may not be an issue	May or may not deviate from dominant norms of gender expression
Bisexual (women and men)	Attraction to the opposite and to the same sex	May or may not be an issue	May or may not deviate from dominant norms of gender expression
Transgender (women and men)	May or may not be an issue	Rejects the gender identity that was assigned at birth	May or may not change appearance and/or anatomy
Cisgender (women and men)	May or may not be an issue	Accepts the gender identity that was assigned at birth	May or may not deviate from dominant norms of gender expression
Intersex	May or may not be an issue	May or may not be an issue	May or may not change anatomy, but experiences social pressure to possess physical anatomy, particularly genitalia, that match male or female standards

Adapted from Corrales and Pecheny (2010, p. 4).

In political contexts across the world, homophobia is often propagated by the state. The criminalization of homosexual practices as well as the use of anti-LGBTI rhetoric and policy by politicians or political officials is often referred to as state homophobia or state-sponsored homophobia. As of 2015, according to the ILGA, same-sex sexual practice is criminalized in seventy-five countries and is subject to the death penalty in five countries (ILGA, 2015c, p. 9). In addition to criminalization, LGBTI people are particularly vulnerable to rights violations in the form of harassment; social exclusion; employment, housing, and healthcare discrimination; denial and/or restriction of parental or adoptive rights; and violence. (See Figure 11.1 for information about the shifting legal context for SOGI human rights.)

Three Features of SOGI Human Rights Violations

In order to understand ways that people of minority sexual orientation or gender identity are vulnerable to human rights violations (see Box 11.1 on the relationship between rights and sexuality), it is important to keep three features of these violations in mind. The first feature is that people may experience SOGI violations explicitly or implicitly. In explicit instances of SOGI rights violations, people are targeted for violence, discrimination, or persecution expressly or explicitly because of their sexuality or gender identity. In addition to explicit violations, however, LGBTI people are vulnerable to human rights violations that are overlooked (or not investigated or enforced) because of their minority sexual orientation or gender identity. Human rights activists are working to address both explicit and implicit SOGI rights violations.

A second important aspect of SOGI human rights violations is that they are committed by states, in civil society, and interpersonally. Laws that target people of minority sexual orientation and gender identity are examples of state-level SOGI rights violations. On the civil society level, human rights in the areas of employment, healthcare, and housing are often in jeopardy for LGBTI people around the world. For example, when there are no protections in place in the workplace, LGBTI people can be subject to employment discrimination, dismissal, and harassment because of

Figure 11.1 The changing SOGI legal context: persecution, protection, and recognition

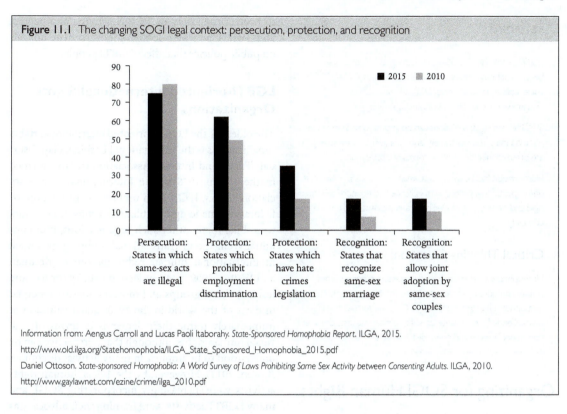

Information from: Aengus Carroll and Lucas Paoli Itaborahy. *State-Sponsored Homophobia Report*. ILGA, 2015.

http://www.old.ilga.org/Statehomophobia/ILGA_State_Sponsored_Homophobia_2015.pdf

Daniel Ottoson. *State-sponsored Homophobia: A World Survey of Laws Prohibiting Same Sex Activity between Consenting Adults*. ILGA, 2010.

http://www.gaylawnet.com/ezine/crime/ilga_2010.pdf

their sexual orientation or gender identity. LGBTI people also face issues such as the denial of healthcare, the restriction of visiting rights in hospitals and nursing homes, housing discrimination, and bullying at school by both teachers and other students. On the interpersonal level, people of minority sexual orientation and gender identity are subject to homophobic violence and intimidation by acquaintances and strangers, such as rape, bullying, harassment, torture, and murder. For example, an important focus of SOGI rights work is putting an end to so-called '**corrective rapes**' of lesbians and transgender people.

A third feature of SOGI/LGBTI human rights jeopardies is that they are often closely linked to other human rights concerns. Indeed, feminist scholar and activist Suzanne Pharr calls homophobia 'a weapon of sexism' in that it is one important way, along with violence and economics, that rigid and hierarchical gender roles are imposed and enforced in society. For example, in many parts of the world, women organizing for women's rights are often labelled 'lesbian' as a way of discrediting or delegitimizing them and their work (Pharr, 1997). When the human rights of sexual minorities are not protected, such a label brings with it the threat of violence, marginalization,

and exclusion, and works as a powerful disincentive to challenge sexism.

BOX 11.1 DECONSTRUCTING THE RELATIONSHIP BETWEEN RIGHTS AND SEXUALITY

To lay claim to rights protection under the human rights framework, one must show that one is a member of the category in question and that one has been injured because of it. Indeed, a rights-bearing subject assumes certain stable features, either in identity or in behaviour. A tension arises here because in using a rights framework to gain greater sexual freedom or more fluid gender identity, one must accept a certain definition of minority sexuality, which sometimes itself can be quite rigid. That is, one must fit one's sexuality into pre-existing sexual categories. For example, in order to apply for asylum, one must first prove that one is lesbian or gay. If one has been married, is bisexual, or does not 'look gay', one's application is often suspect (Immigration Equality, 2015). A question arises out of this tension: how might it be possible for oppressed individuals persecuted by governments for their sexual behaviour to challenge such persecution without solidifying or making more rigid identity categories?

Organizing for SOGI Human Rights

Human rights activism aims to (1) end the political persecution of people on the basis of sexual orientation and gender identity; (2) to implement measures that would protect people of minority sexual orientation and gender identity from violence, discrimination, and harassment; and (3) to foster the recognition of same-sex relationships and non-normative gender identities. As Figure 11.1 highlights, during the past five years, significant progress has been made towards these goals.

Advocacy work takes many different forms across multiple institutional and cultural contexts. Prominent national human rights groups—as well as smaller, sometimes local, groups—cooperate and coordinate with each other, with national governments, with local and regional LGBTI organizations throughout the world, and with multilateral international organizations. The specific forms of activism have varied widely. They include: encouraging more informed and realistic representations of LGBTI people; educating and engaging with fellow citizens and social, political, and religious opinion leaders on LGBTI issues; building the capacity of LGBTI and a variety of other civil society organizations; creating coalitions with non-SOGI groups and organizations; developing ways

to protect the safety of LGBTI activists and people; and—when possible—lobbying government officials on public policies that affect LGBTI people.

LGBTI-oriented International Rights Organizations

The oldest of the LGBTI-oriented international rights organizations is the International Lesbian, Gay, Bisexual, Trans, and Intersex Association (ILGA), formed in the UK in 1978 as the International Gay Association. Today, ILGA is an umbrella organization, or federation, made up of affiliated groups in 110 countries. Like many other such organizations, it did not initially engage in transnational lobbying grounded in international human rights discourse (Kollman and Waites, 2009, p. 4). Indeed, most gay (or gay and lesbian) rights groups and movements that emerged in parts of the world in the 1970s and 1980s did not immediately frame their demands in terms of universal human rights, although that perspective can be understood to be implicit in many activist discourses (Loftin, 2012). However, by the 1990s, human rights activists were increasingly incorporating SOGI, and many LGBTI activists were framing their advocacy as human rights. Claiming human rights reinforced the reality that what LGBTI people were seeking was not 'special rights', as their opponents often suggested, but fundamental freedoms of which they had often been deprived.

The turn of international LGBTI organizations came in 1990, when the International Gay and Lesbian Human Rights Commission (IGLHRC) was founded with the motto 'Human Rights for Everyone. Everywhere.' IGLHRC concentrates its work at multiple levels: 'improving the lives' of people harmed because of their sexuality or gender identity or expression, 'strengthening the capacity' of the global LGBTI human rights movement, and 'engaging in human rights advocacy' with a broad set of partners that includes the UN, governments, NGOs, and civil society groups (IGLHRC, 2014). IGLHRC holds consultative status at the UN as a recognized NGO and documents its activist work in a variety of ways, including through videos such as 'In Their Own Words: Documenting Violence and Discrimination against Lesbians, Bisexual Women, and Transgender People in Asia' and Country Reports that detail the situation of LGBT people in particular states (IGLHRC, 2013).

In the global history of the juxtaposition of human rights with same-sex sexuality, another key development occurred when mainstream human rights organizations formally incorporated discrimination and human rights violations based on sexuality, sexual orientation, and gender identity into their missions. The first of these organizations to do so was Amnesty International, founded in the UK in the early 1960s. Amnesty is a mass-membership human rights organization that bills itself as 'the world's largest grassroots human rights organization', a 'global movement of people fighting injustice and promoting human rights'. Although it engages in many other activities, Amnesty is best known for its targeted mobilizing of publicity and support for individuals who suffer human rights deprivations around the world.

In 1991, Amnesty took a position on judicial detention or imprisonment based on same-sex sexual behaviour, calling these acts of governments 'a grave violation of human rights' (Amnesty International, 2012). This development was not uncontested; some constituencies disagreed that people of non-normative sexual orientation and those who engaged in same-sex sexuality were proper candidates for human rights protection (Baehr, 2001, pp. 12, 121). However, internal disagreements were settled in favour of the organization taking a position in support of SOGI human rights. Today, Amnesty calls for the decriminalization of same-sex sexual relations, civil marriage equality, judicial recourse for human rights violations based on same-sex sexual identity and gender identity and expression, equality for LGBTI people in the administration of justice, and protections for those who defend the human rights of LGBTI people.

Soon other international human rights organizations embraced the human rights of LGBTI people. Human Rights Watch came into existence in 1978 as Helsinki Watch and extended its network of 'Watch Committees' throughout the world in the 1980s. Human Rights Watch engages in investigation, monitoring, documentation, analysis, and reporting of human rights violations worldwide, and it presses governments to address and resolve categories of human rights violation it identifies. Human Rights Watch targets a wide range of categories of human rights abuses and campaigns that include rape as a war crime, women's human rights, landmine abolition, workers' human rights, human trafficking, and use of child soldiers. The organization has integrated its concern with LGBTI human rights into its operations in the form of a human rights programme that is concerned with a range of anti-LGBTI abuses from discrimination to arrest, torture, and execution (HRW, 2014a).

International Law

One of the challenges facing SOGI human rights activists is that international law, as traditionally formulated, including the Universal Declaration of Human Rights, is silent on SOGI rights. As a result, there has been a lacuna in international law when it comes to addressing SOGI human rights abuses, though some have argued that rights related to sexual orientation and gender identity can be inferred from the Universal Declaration of Human Rights. As a result, human rights activists and organizations throughout the world at local, regional, and international levels have been working on creating a legal framework to address human rights issues related to gender and sexuality.

The Yogyakarta Principles

A key intervention in SOGI transnational organizing and advocacy with implications for international law and transnational human rights norms occurred in November 2006. Human rights professionals, activists, scholars, and leaders from around the world—including members of the International Commission of Jurists and the International Service for Human Rights—convened a conference at Gadjah Mada University on the island of Java, Indonesia to draft a document that would address the application of human rights law to questions of sexual orientation and gender identity. In their work, the representatives set out to articulate a set of human rights principles and state obligations with regard to sexuality, sexual orientation, and gender identity. They developed twenty-nine principles, known collectively as the 'Yogyakarta Principles on the Application of International Human Rights Law in Relation to Sexual Orientation and Gender Identity' (see Box 11.2).

The Yogyakarta Principles were developed to serve as 'a universal guide to human rights which affirm binding international legal standards with which all States must comply. They promise a different future where all people born free and equal in dignity and rights can fulfill that precious birthright.' These principles are divided into eight broad categories: rights to universal enjoyment of human rights,

BOX 11.2 EXCERPT FROM THE YOGYAKARTA PRINCIPLES

PRINCIPLE 1. The Right to the Universal Enjoyment of Human Rights

All human beings are born free and equal in dignity and rights. Human beings of all sexual orientations and gender identities are entitled to the full enjoyment of all human rights.

States shall:

a) Embody the principles of the universality, interrelatedness, interdependence and indivisibility of all human rights in their national constitutions or other appropriate legislation and ensure the practical realization of the universal enjoyment of all human rights;

b) Amend any legislation, including criminal law, to ensure its consistency with the universal enjoyment of all human rights;

c) Undertake programmes of education and awareness to promote and enhance the full enjoyment of all human rights by all persons, irrespective of sexual orientation or gender identity;

d) Integrate within State policy and decision-making a pluralistic approach that recognizes and affirms the interrelatedness and indivisibility of all aspects of human identity including sexual orientation and gender identity.

non-discrimination, and recognition before the law; rights to human and personal security; economic, social, and cultural rights; rights to expression, opinion, and association; freedom of movement and asylum; rights of participation in cultural and family life; rights of human rights defenders; and rights of redress and accountability.

Signatories to the Principles constitute a 'who's who' of human rights service and advocacy from across the world, including the former President of Ireland (and former UN High Commissioner for Human Rights) Mary Robinson, and with strong representation from the global South. Those who met to develop and finalize the Principles intended them to serve as a set of standards that should guide states and national communities regardless of the differences that might prevail between those states and communities. On the website constructed to disseminate the final document, the Yogyakarta Principles are translated into the six official languages of the United Nations: English, Spanish, French, Russian, Arabic, and Chinese. Although controversial, the Yogyakarta Principles have been influential

in debates and advocacy regarding those who may suffer harm on the basis of sexual orientation and gender identity (International Commission of Jurists and the International Service for Human Rights, no date).

The United Nations Human Rights Council Resolution on Human Rights, Sexual Orientation, and Gender Identity

The United Nations Human Rights Council has been increasingly vocal in its support of SOGI human rights initiatives. In 2011, for example, the United Nations Human Rights Council placed the imprimatur of the UN on the pursuit of the human rights of those persecuted or prosecuted on the basis of sexuality, sexual identity, or gender identity, by passing Resolution 17/19 that addresses 'specifically and explicitly the issue of human rights violations based on sexual orientation and gender identity' (IGLHRC, 2012). For members of the international human rights community, the resolution was a 'moment' because it was the 'first U.N. resolution to bring specific focus on human rights violations based on sexual orientation and gender identity' (Reid, 2012). Passage of the resolution was widely praised by organizations and advocates in the global human rights community, and seventeen human rights organizations issued a joint statement recognizing the 'groundbreaking achievement' and its 'signal of support to human rights defenders'. The joint statement recorded the votes of nations' representatives in four categories: states voting in support of the resolution (twenty-three), states voting against the resolution (nineteen), abstentions (three), and states co-sponsoring the resolution (HRW, 2011).[1] In 2012, the United Nations Office of the High Commissioner on Human Rights published a booklet, *Born Free and Equal*, that outlined the 'core legal obligations of states with respect to protecting the human rights of LGBT persons' (see Box 11.3). In this document, Navi Pillay, the then UN Commissioner for Human Rights, argued that 'ending violence and discrimination against individuals on the basis of their sexual orientation and gender identity is a great human rights challenge' (OHCHR, 2012, p. 7.)

The United States and SOGI Human Rights

The United States has played a complicated and often contradictory role in SOGI human rights struggles.

BOX 11.3 UN HUMAN RIGHTS COMMISSION: FIVE CORE LEGAL OBLIGATIONS OF STATES WITH RESPECT TO PROTECTING THE HUMAN RIGHTS OF LGBT PERSONS

1. **Protect** people from homophobic and transphobic violence. Include sexual orientation and gender identity as protected characteristics in hate crime laws. Establish effective systems to record and report hate-motivated acts of violence. Ensure effective investigation and prosecution of perpetrators and redress for victims of such violence. Asylum laws and policies should recognize that persecution on account of one's sexual orientation or gender identity may be a valid basis for an asylum claim.

2. **Prevent** the torture and cruel, inhuman and degrading treatment of LGBT persons in detention by prohibiting and punishing such acts and ensuring that victims are provided with redress. Investigate all acts of mistreatment by State agents and bring those responsible to justice. Provide appropriate training to law enforcement officers and ensure effective monitoring of places of detention.

3. **Repeal** laws criminalizing homosexuality, including all laws that prohibit private sexual conduct between consenting adults of the same sex. Ensure that individuals are not arrested or detained on the basis of their sexual orientation or gender identity, and are not subjected to baseless and

degrading physical examinations intended to determine their sexual orientation.

4. **Prohibit** discrimination on the basis of sexual orientation and gender identity. Enact comprehensive laws that include sexual orientation and gender identity as prohibited grounds of discrimination. In particular, ensure non-discriminatory access to basic services, including in the context of employment and health care. Provide education and training to prevent discrimination and stigmatization of LGBT and intersex people.

5. **Safeguard** freedom of expression, association and peaceful assembly for LGBT and intersex people. Any limitations on these rights must be compatible with international law and must not be discriminatory. Protect individuals who exercise their rights to freedom of expression, association and freedom of assembly from acts of violence and intimidation by private parties.

From United Nations Office of the High Commissioner on Human Rights (2012). *Born Free and Equal: Sexual Orientation and Gender Identity in International Human Rights Law*. New York and Geneva: UN. http://www.ohchr.org/Documents/Publications/BornFreeAndEqualLowRes.pdf

---

Issues of SOGI rights are extremely politically salient in the US and both advocates and opponents have engaged in transnational organizing. On the one hand, US Christian right groups have been extremely active in anti-LGBTI organizing worldwide, both funding and inspiring anti-SOGI groups. In response, progressive faith-based communities have worked to promote SOGI rights both nationally and internationally. Further, since the election of Barack Obama in 2008, the US government has pursued several foreign policy initiatives geared to the promotion of SOGI human rights worldwide.

The US Christian Conservative Right and Anti-LGBTI Organizing

The US Christian conservative right has been at the forefront of anti-SOGI human rights activism, driving opposition worldwide, either directly or indirectly. The Christian right movement rejects many contemporary tenets of human rights approaches more generally, including those that incorporate 'second generation' social and economic rights. The

movement also repudiates applications of human rights doctrine to many particular categories of identity, including, but not limited to, non-heterosexual sexual identities, and variations of sexual behaviour and gender identity that are inconsistent with the movement's heteronormative ideal of the 'natural family'. For Christian conservatives who oppose characterizing SOGI rights as civil and human rights, the inclusion of LGBTI people in categories populated by members of racial, ethnic, religious, and other groups of what they regard as genuine victims of oppression is an insult to the dignity of these groups.

Christian conservatives have organized locally, nationally, and transnationally to not only block the adoption of new civil and human rights protections for LGBTI people but also to fight the erosion of social stigma related to non-normative sexualities and genders. The activism of Christian conservative organizations, such as the USA-based World Congress of Families, and churches such as Kansas City's International House of Prayer, has a global reach. Further, coalitions between groups bring into existence a worldwide Christian conservative movement that operates in multilateral organizations such as the UN as well as in communities worldwide.

SOGI Human Rights Work in US Faith-based Communities

Many faith communities, organizations, and churches have been galvanized to participate in SOGI human rights advocacy, in part in response to the anti-LGBTI activism of Christian conservative churches, organizations, and leaders. While US Christian conservative anti-LGBTI advocacy has been well documented in scholarship as well as in films such as *God Loves Uganda*, the pro-LGBTI human rights work of more progressive faith communities has not yet received as much attention (Williams, 2013). Two examples of sustained advocacy on behalf of SOGI human rights, both within the US and in international forums, are the work of the General Synod of the United Church of Christ and the Unitarian Universalist Association of Congregations. The Unitarian Universalist (UU) faith community and individual congregations are 'welcoming' to LGBTI people, but the commitment to LGBTI 'welcome and equality' extends beyond the inclusion of LGBTI people into UU fellowship and even the operation of UU LGBTI Ministries.[2] Unitarian Universalists understand themselves as 'called to advocate for international human rights; to be a voice for the voiceless by promoting the inherent worth and dignity of all living things'. Through its membership in the Conference of NGOs in Consultative Relationship with the United Nations (CoNGO), the Unitarian Universalist UN Office (UU-UNO) engages in educational programmes and other activities on behalf of LGBTI, women's, and other groups' human rights around the world (Unitarian Universalist Association, 2014).

On a smaller scale, church-based faith groups have formed in recent years to advocate for people vulnerable to human rights violations based on sexuality or gender identity. One of these is the Friends New Underground Railroad (FNUR) of the Olympia Friends Meeting in Olympia, Washington, named for the role of northern Quakers in US anti-slavery activism in the nineteenth century, and especially for Quaker assistance to enslaved African Americans escaping from the American south. Launched in 2014, the FNUR is a grassroots effort to coordinate with Ugandan allies to fund the departure of imperilled LGBTI people from Uganda to safe asylum in other countries. Through mailings and email to supporters, the FNUR advertises its activities and solicits funds through accounts of successful asylum cases and first-person LGBTI 'Testimonies from the Field' (Olympia Monthly Meeting of the Religious Society of Friends, 2014).

US Foreign Policy and SOGI Human Rights

In contemporary politics, the US government has begun to play a larger role in the promotion of SOGI rights worldwide Although agents and agencies of the US government engaged in some isolated international projects and cooperation before 2008, the majority of these interventions have been developed and executed after 2008 by the Department of State's Bureau of Democracy, Human Rights and Labor (DRL), whose official mandate is 'protecting freedom and democracy and protecting human rights around the world'.[3] There have been several indicators of the growing salience of SOGI human rights to US foreign policy. One is a revision to the State Department's annual Country Reports on Human Rights Practices of nations throughout the world. In recent years, human rights violations perpetrated against LGBTI people have been noted in the Country Reports under the miscellaneous category 'other societal abuses and discrimination'. However, for the reports that examined the state of human rights in 2009—produced by State Department officials in early 2010—the category was expanded to denote explicitly the targeting of LGBTI people. Through 2011, the most significant programme of the US federal government aimed at protecting the human rights of LGBTI people outside the US was the extension of an emergency assistance programme, developed to provide 'legal representation, security, and, when necessary, relocation support' to human rights defenders, to LGBTI activists abroad. Between 2010 and the end of 2011, DRL provided assistance to LGBTI human rights defenders in Africa, Asia, and the Middle East (US Department of State, 2011).

In December 2011, then US Secretary of State Hillary Clinton delivered a speech in Geneva, Switzerland in honour of **International Human Rights Day**. In her speech, Clinton pledged US commitment to SOGI human rights worldwide and asserted that 'gay rights are human rights, and human rights are gay rights'. In tandem with Clinton's speech, President Barack Obama issued a 'presidential memorandum' which called on US government foreign affairs agencies to confront the 'global challenge' posed by egregious violations of SOGI human rights.

A key feature of the US government's public declaration of support for SOGI human rights was the implementation of the Global Equality Fund in 2011. The fund is an umbrella programme that provides emergency funds, advocacy support, and security assistance to human rights defenders, civil society organizations, or LGBTI individuals under threat or attack due to their work on behalf of LGBTI human rights (US Department of State, no date). Long-term capacity-building and technical assistance grants fund partnerships between international and local in-country organizations to perform a variety of tasks, including helping to enhance the capacity of pro-LGBTI civil society groups to support their constituencies and fostering the ability of civil society groups to monitor, document, and respond to human rights violations. The fund also disburses small grants to local organizations through US embassies. 'Embassy engagement' has been one prong of official US support for LGBTI human rights in recent years, and US embassy officials work with LGBTI advocates and grassroots organizations to support vulnerable populations.

In 2015, the US government announced the appointment of a US Special Envoy for Human Rights of LGBT People. For some time before the appointment, US-based LGBTI organizations had collectively lobbied members of Congress and pressed the State Department to appoint a special envoy or representative, whom they hoped would focus and enhance the US government's efforts to support LGBTI human rights. Although the move has been hailed by many LGBTI activists and organizations, not all SOGI human rights defenders support the position. For example, Nigerian gay rights advocate Adebisi Alimi reiterates a frequent concern about the appointment of special envoys for geographic regions or issues: that special envoys can function as symbolic substitutes for political commitment (see Lyman and Beecroft, 2014). Alimi also criticizes the appointment of a white man to such a post, pointing out the possibility that the choice could reinforce conceptions of same-sex sexuality as a Western practice at odds with non-Western cultures (Alimi, 2015).

KEY POINTS

The past twenty-five years have seen the growth of SOGI human rights advocacy work in both LGBTI and human rights organizations.

Claiming a human rights framework in struggles for SOGI rights reinforced the reality that what LGBTI people were seeking was not 'special rights', as their opponents often suggested, but fundamental freedoms of which they had often been deprived.

Goals of SOGI human rights organizing include decriminalization, an end to bias-motivated violence, civil marriage equality, judicial recourse for human rights violations based on same-sex sexual identity and gender identity and expression, equality for LGBTI people in the administration of justice, and protections for those who defend the human rights of LGBTI people.

Human rights activists and organizations have been working on creating an international legal framework to address human rights issues related to gender and sexuality. The Yogyakarta Principles serves as an important document to guide such work.

Faith-based communities, organizations, and churches participate in both anti- and pro-SOGI human rights discourse, organizing, and advocacy.

The United States has played a complicated and often contradictory role in SOGI human rights struggles. In recent years, the US government has pursued several foreign policy initiatives geared to the promotion of SOGI human rights worldwide.

Critical Thinking Question:

In what ways is the struggle for human rights for those of minority sexual and gender identity similar to the other struggles that you have learned about in this volume? In what ways is it different? How might the struggle for SOGI human rights link to these other struggles?

Critiques of SOGI Human Rights Activism

SOGI Rights and the Question of Cultural Imposition

One challenge to a human rights approach to issues of sexual orientation and gender identity is the argument that LGBTI identities and mobilization are 'foreign'— i.e. the result of cultural imposition or contamination generated by and in neocolonial political and legal frameworks, Western cultural hegemony, and/or international donor-driven agendas. Within this 'cultural imposition' framing, state actors characterize their repression of LGBTI mobilization and their policing of same-sex intimacy as efforts to protect morality and national cultural identities. SOGI human rights scholars and activists have worked to disrupt this justificatory framework by turning the homophobia-as-cultural-protection narrative on its head, holding that it is political homophobia that is the foreign import, not LGBTI identities and mobilizations. In order to do so, they call attention to the long history of tolerance for—and sometimes even celebration of—sexual and gender identity diversity in non-Western contexts. They argue that historically, Western colonial powers introduced, exacerbated, and/or consolidated homophobia in the global South by introducing legal frameworks that criminalized same-sex sexuality. They further note that the export of cultural and political homophobia continues to the present, pointing to the ways that a 'modular' form of political homophobia is funded and promoted by actors originating in the global North, and most especially from the US (Bosia and Weis, 2013).

LGBTI Critiques of Human Rights Approaches to SOGI Activism

Within LGBTI groups, there are also critiques of a human rights approach to SOGI activism. Some argue, for example, that human rights-based approaches to organizing are deeply Eurocentric and that they obscure other modes of LGBTI existence and resistance. Further, some activists worry that LGBTI human rights discourse and policies may be used by states to 'pinkwash' other human rights offences. Activists such as Sarah Schulman have argued, for example, that Israel has deliberately deployed a message of Israeli progressivism with regard to sexuality to 'rebrand' the nation and deflect attention from human rights violations perpetrated by the state against Palestinians in Israel and in occupied territories (Schulman, 2011). Others have worried that strategies of representation that highlight those LGBTI people and relationships that are closest to the mainstream, as well as the push for same-sex marriage, combine to produce a form of 'homonormativity' that leaves many people out and that can serve to restrict people's sexual and relational freedom. As Lisa Duggan explains, 'homonormativity

is a politics that does not contest dominant heteronormative assumptions and institutions—such as marriage, and its call for monogamy and reproduction—but upholds and sustains them while promising the possibility of a demobilized gay constituency and a privatized, depoliticized gay culture anchored in domesticity and consumption' (Duggan, 2002, p. 179). Rather than rejecting the right of LGBTI people to safety, inclusion, and recognition, however, these critics argue that struggles for sexual and gender identity diversity must be linked to struggles for racial, gender, and economic justice within nations and geopolitical justice between them.

The Question of the State in SOGI Human Rights Activism

Another critique is of the state-centredness of SOGI human rights activism. Human rights discourse and organizing faces a conundrum: on the one hand, many states perpetrate or accommodate human rights abuses; on the other hand, states possess many existing legal and institutional remedies for human rights abuses. As such, a human rights-based approach to organizing often entails turning to states for remedies even while criticizing them for their abuses. Indeed, some human rights activists and scholars worry that such rights-based approaches to LGBTI organizing can strengthen repressive institutions of the state—especially the criminal justice system and the military—that are loci of forms of state repression and violence related to racism, sexism, homophobia, and other forms of oppression (Spade and Willse, 2014; Keating, 2013). In the words of activist Wendy Somerson, 'mainstream GLBT rights organizations increasingly clamor for GLBT folks to be let into heteronormative mainstream institutions by pouring their energy and resources into legalizing gay marriage, passing hate crimes legislation, and insisting on our "right" to serve in the military'. She explains that approaches such as hate crimes laws are ineffective deterrents and 'subject perpetrators to higher mandatory sentences and thus increase the power of the prison industrial complex, which has never been known for its fair treatment of queers or other marginalized groups'. Instead of pursuing strategies that rely on state institutions for protection and intervention, she recommends building 'alternative systems of accountability and justice in our communities that do not rely on prisons and policing'

(Somerson, 2010). For example, one of the central organizational missions of FIERCE, an organization of LGBTI youth of colour in New York City, is to fight against police brutality. Noting that they are 'tired of our bodies constantly being targeted by police', the group has organized a police accountability committee and is working in coalition with other groups on a police reform campaign as well as on community empowerment projects (Fierce, no date). In addition to organizing on issues of police reform and accountability, other groups engage in building communities' capacities to address questions of harm from within. For example, some groups have advocated creating 'harm-free zones' that seek to foster, in the words of the Harm Free Zone project of Durham, NC, 'independent and self directing community autonomy' to diminish the need for communities to depend on the state for redress and protection (Spirit House, no date).

KEY POINTS

SOGI human rights proponents have responded to the critique that SOGI human rights are being culturally and politically imposed or are foreign by examining the historical links between homophobia and colonialism as well as the contemporary geopolitics of homophobia.

Progressive critiques of SOGI human rights approaches include a critique that human rights-based approaches to organizing are Eurocentric and obscure other modes of LGBTI organizing, that some states' embrace of SOGI rights can deflect attention from other human rights abuses, and that using the state to address SOGI rights violations can strengthen institutions that are responsible for state repression and violence.

Forms of SOGI human rights advocacy that address some of these concerns include intersectional approaches that link SOGI human rights struggles to struggles for racial, gender, economic, and geopolitical justice, and efforts to build alternative systems of recognition, justice, and accountability that do not rely on the state.

Critical Thinking Question:

In your opinion, is it preferable to (1) use the institutions and resources of the state to combat homophobia; (2) work to reform these state institutions; or (3) bypass these institutions and work instead to build strong communities that can address homophobia from within?

Case Study: Uganda

Uganda is an African nation that was colonized and administered by the British Empire as a British protectorate from 1894 to 1962. One feature of British law the Empire imposed on colonies was the criminalization of same-sex sexuality, and this prohibition remained law after the contemporary nation of Uganda was established. Uganda is not the only former British colony that was subjected to colonial-era laws prohibiting same-sex sexuality and then retained those laws after achieving independence. However, in recent years, Uganda has attracted international attention because of a surge of anti-LGBTI bias and human rights violations related to the promulgation of a new anti-gay law.

In tracing the provenance of that law, called the Anti-Homosexuality Bill, human rights defenders implicate a set of lectures delivered in Uganda's capital, Kampala, in early 2009. Three US anti-gay activists—attorney and minister Scott Lively, and two associates—presented themselves as experts and spoke to audiences of attorneys, ministers, teachers, and policy makers on the theme of 'The Gay Agenda'. Lively also delivered an address on that theme to the Ugandan Parliament. All three have disclaimed responsibility for the bill that quickly followed, though Lively is currently being sued in the US by a Ugandan LGBTI rights group for inciting the persecution of gay men and lesbians in Uganda. Within a few months after the 'Gay Agenda' presentations, a member of Parliament introduced the Anti-Homosexuality Bill and urged its passage. The original version of the Bill mandated enhanced criminal penalties for same-sex sexuality and provided for the death penalty for 'aggravated homosexuality' (a category that included having sex while HIV positive) or being a 'serial offender' (defined as multiple prosecutions for committing acts of same-sex sexuality). In addition, the Bill broadened the scope of criminalized behaviour by providing criminal penalties for failing to report another person's homosexuality and for promoting homosexuality. By including 'promoting homosexuality', the law's drafter intended to criminalize any public advocacy on behalf of LGBTI people's civil or human rights. Because the Bill made homosexuality a capital offence, international critics of the Bill began referring to it as the 'Kill the Gays Bill'.

Both international and Ugandan human rights communities began to protest the intended law soon after it was introduced in Parliament. Although the

Bill did not become law until 2014, public discourse about the immorality of same-sex sexuality and the charge that gay men and lesbians recruit children to same-sex sexuality encouraged violence and discrimination against LGBTI people. One example of anti-LGBTI public discourse was a 2010 issue of *Rolling Stone*, a Ugandan tabloid newspaper, publishing the names and addresses of LGBT activists with the front-page headline: '100 Pictures of Uganda's Top Homos Leak' and the exhortation inside the paper to 'Hang Them: They Are After Our Kids!!' Featured in that article was David Kato, a co-founder of the LGBT advocacy organization Sexual Minorities Uganda (SMUG). After Kato successfully challenged the newspaper in court to force its publishers to stop publishing the names and addresses of Ugandan LGBTI people, he was beaten to death. News outlets around the world reported Kato's murder in the context of ongoing anti-LGBTI attitudes and acts in Uganda.

A version of the Anti-Homosexuality Bill was passed and signed into law by President Yoweri Museveni in 2014. Although Museveni had voiced some reservations about the Bill between 2009 and 2014, he did support and sign the Bill. Human rights advocates point out that the Anti-Homosexuality Bill—and later the Act—served the President's political interests. At the same time that critics were challenging his regime's corruption and human rights violations, Museveni shored up domestic support by casting himself as a Christian leader concerned with spiritual threats to the nation and using LGBTI people as scapegoats.

By the time the Act was passed, several US Christian conservative leaders who had professed agreement with the anti-LGBTI attitudes of President Museveni and other Ugandans had been forced to distance themselves from the Bill and especially from its death penalty provision. The Bill that became law did not include the death penalty, and after it was challenged by critics was quickly overturned by Uganda's Constitutional Court. However, the Court did not annul the Anti-Homosexuality Act because the Act violated the human rights of LGBTI people; it did so because of a procedural technicality of its passage in the Parliament. Policy makers associated with it remain in favour of a law that would punish people who engage in same-sex relations. Even though the Anti-Homosexuality Act is no longer law, the human rights situation of LGBTI people in Uganda continues to be dire, and many LGBTI people and activists have been forced into hiding to protect themselves from threats, physical violence, and arrest.

Although every individual case of SOGI human rights peril is unique, Uganda's anti-LGBTI public policies share two characteristics with many other cases around the world. First is the role of politicized religious belief in stigmatizing LGBTI people and intensifying negative attitudes against them. The second characteristic Uganda shares with other nations where LGBTI people are imperilled is political figures who have discovered that they can build political support by scapegoating LGBTI people, and thus deflecting attention from their own failures and abuses of power. Uganda has attracted much attention because US Christian conservatives have been very active in helping to create the SOGI human rights situation that prevails there. However, in international SOGI human rights forums, activists point out that terrible conditions for LGBTI people and SOGI advocacy exist in many parts of the world, and that Uganda is far from unique in its persecution of LGBTI people.

Conclusion

Given that SOGI human rights violations occur on a variety of interconnected levels, SOGI human rights advocates must focus their efforts on multiple fronts. Families, neighbourhoods, workplaces, and schools are all critically important sites of SOGI human rights struggles, as are courtrooms, legislatures, and bodies of international governance. Such a multiplicity of sites of struggles means that people working in any of these arenas can be considered SOGI human rights activists, serving to deepen and extend both the LGBTI and the human rights activist traditions (see Box 11.5).

As this volume attests, human rights have been a dynamic and productive tool for those facing marginalization, domination, discrimination, or violence. SOGI human rights struggles are often closely linked to other human rights struggles, such as struggles for women's rights and struggles against political repression. A human rights framework has proven adaptable to these interlocking forms of injustice, offering powerful discursive and institutional mechanisms to protect those who bear the brunt of inequities within and between nations. Yet SOGI human rights struggles

BOX 11.4 ALTERNATIVE POINTS OF VIEW: SEXUAL RIGHTS AS HUMAN RIGHTS

The SOGI human rights perspective focuses on the rights of LGBTI people as human beings who share with others a right to a life free from violence, from state persecution, and from discrimination in housing, work, and medical care. In this framing, one's sexual practices, gender identity, or gender expression should not be grounds for the denial of these basic social goods. An alternative framing—perhaps a more capacious one—is the notion of sexual rights as human rights, in which sexuality is understood as a basic human good itself. Such a frame calls attention to the problem of what feminist and sexuality studies scholar Josephine Ho calls 'sexual deprivation'. According to Ho, sexual intimacy is a basic human entitlement, like education, work, healthcare, food and water, that should 'be placed in the context of a wider range of social goods which people should be entitled to but of which they are often deprived' (Bedford and Jakobsen, 2008, p. 28). Indeed, she notes that social norms and laws combine to 'virtually guarantee' sexual deprivation for some groups (Bedford and Jakobsen,

2008, p. 27). For example, laws that penalize same-sex sexual practice starkly enforce sexual deprivation for gays and lesbians. Disability rights activists have emphasized that people with disabilities are particularly at risk for sexual deprivation as well, and that 'the denial of sexual intimacy and knowledge about sexuality can be a devastating form of oppression' (Bedford and Jakobsen, 2008, p. 27). The notion of sexual rights as human rights is a concept that can link both of these groups' work towards sexual justice to struggles for reproductive rights, for access to knowledge and information about safe-sex practices, and against practices of sexual exploitation and violence. In the words of Claudia Hinojosa, 'our point of departure is a dominant sexual culture in which all sexual practices, particularly if they are pleasurable or not linked to reproduction, are guilty, unless proven innocent. The development of a new ethical framework in this regard could possibly lay out the vision of a political culture in which we can revisit sexuality as a practice of freedom' (Bedford and Jakobsen, 2008, p. 29).

also address distinct questions of personal liberty that have to do with sexual intimacy and love as well as gender identity and expression (see Box 11.4). As such, SOGI human rights struggles have the potential to expand the meaning and practice of freedom—not just for LGBTI people, but for all. Incorporating sexual orientation, gender identity, and gender expression into human rights law and discourse has been an important step in the development of the human rights framework, one that points to the possibility of advancing contemporary movements for justice, equality, and non-domination.

BOX 11.5 AN ACTIVIST'S GUIDE TO THE YOGYAKARTA PRINCIPLES

There is an inconsistency between the rights identified in international human rights documents, such as those in the Yogyakarta Principles, and the rights actually enjoyed by individuals. While international standards may grant us rights, discrimination, stigma, violence, and fear pose real threats to people of diverse sexual orientations and gender identities. Activists, human rights defenders, and individual members of

our many communities are the driving force behind closing this gap between our rights and our reality.

Sonia Onufer Corrêa and Vitit Muntarbhorn (2010). Foreword. *An Activist's Guide to The Yogyakarta Principles* (ed. Sheila Quinn). http://www.ypinaction.org/files/02/85/Activists_Guide_English_nov_14_2010.pdf, p. 6.

? QUESTIONS

Individual Study Questions

1. What is the difference between sexual orientation, gender identity, and gender expression?

2. Why do some people prefer the acronym SOGI over LGBTI human rights?

3. What is the difference between heteronormativity and homophobia? What are examples of both?

4. What are ways in which people of minority sexual orientation, gender identity, or gender expression are vulnerable to human rights violations on the state, civil society, and interpersonal levels?

5. What are the three main aspects of SOGI human rights advocacy?

Group Discussion Questions

1. While 'SOGI human rights' calls attention to categories of human rights abuse on the basis of sexual orientation and gender identity, 'LGBTI human rights' calls attention to the forms of identity and behaviour of those who are most likely to find themselves stigmatized and harmed by human rights abuses based on sexual orientation and gender identity. Which term do you think is more useful in struggles for human rights?

2. The Yogyakarta Principles direct states to 'recognize and affirm the interrelatedness and indivisibility of all aspects of human identity including sexual orientation and gender identity'. What are some examples of ways in which your sexual orientation and gender identity are central to your human identity?

3. In her landmark speech on SOGI human rights in 2011, Hillary Clinton opened her remarks by noting that she speaks on the subject 'knowing that my own country's record on human rights for gay people is far from perfect'. In your opinion, is it important for the US government to take a leading international role in advancing human rights even when the US human rights record is 'far from perfect'? Why or why not?

4. Homonormativity is a concept that calls attention to what kinds of people and relationships are most culturally and politically visible and valued in the LGBTI movement. What are some examples of homonormativity, either in cultural life or in policy making? Who is left out by these representations or these policies? What might a non-homonormative politics look like?

5. In a landmark essay on social movement building, Audre Lorde warned that 'the master's tools will never dismantle the master's house'. In what ways might this phrase apply or not to human rights struggles, including struggles for SOGI rights?

FURTHER READING

Brown, D. (2009–10) Making room for sexual orientation and gender identity in international human rights law: An introduction to the Yogyakarta Principles. *Michigan Journal of International Law*, **31**, 821–80.

An assessment of the impact of the Yogyakarta Principles on international law and the practice of SOGI activism. The author argues that the Principles do not merely interpret, but substantively extend international law to encompass SOGI human rights.

Buss, D. and **Herman, D.** (2003). *Globalizing Family Values: The Christian Right in International Politics*. Minneapolis: University of Minnesota Press.

An in-depth analysis of US Christian conservative global anti-feminist and anti-SOGI activism in international arenas, especially the United Nations.

Kollman, K. and **Waites, M.** (2011). *The Global Politics of LGBT Human Rights*. Oxford: Routledge.

A volume of articles from the 2009 special issue of the journal *Contemporary Politics*, on 'The Global Politics of LGBT Human Rights'.

O'Flaherty, M. and **Fisher, J.** (2008). Sexual orientation and gender identity in international human rights law: Contextualising the Yogyakarta Principles. *Human Rights Law Review*, **8**/2, 207–48.

A critical commentary on the Principles and their promulgation, and an assessment of their impact on SOGI human rights, co-authored by the Rapporteur for the development of the Yogyakarta Principles (O'Flaherty).

Weiss, M. L. and **Bosia, M. J.** (eds) (2013). *Global Homophobia: States, Movements, and the Politics of Oppression*. Urbana: University of Illinois Press.

A collection of articles, most by political scientists, that analyses the transnational phenomenon of 'political homophobia' in diverse global contexts.

WEB LINKS

http://www.amnestyusa.org/our-work/issues/lgbt-rights/about-lgbt-human-rights Amnesty International is an international organization that promotes human rights and exposes human rights violations. Amnesty supports SOGI human rights, including the decriminalization of minority sexual and gender identities worldwide.

http://www.hrw.org/topic/lgbt-rights Human Rights Watch is an international human rights organization that exposes human rights violations, documents abuses, and lobbies governments and the United Nations. Their LGBT human rights programme publicizes SOGI human rights violations as well as pro-LGBT human rights reforms.

http://iglhrc.org/ The International Gay and Lesbian Human Rights Commission (IGLHRC) is an international LGBTQI human rights advocacy organization that builds partnerships with other organizations and governing bodies. IGLHRC works to eliminate policies and practices that discriminate based on SOGI.

http://www.yogyakartaprinciples.org/ The Yogyakarta Principles are the most comprehensive effort to date to apply international human rights law to SOGI. Published in 2007, the Principles consist of twenty-nine human rights standards and their application to SOGI, along with specific recommendations to states for the implementation of these standards.

http://www.ypinaction.org/files/02/85/Activists_Guide_English_nov_14_2010.pdf An Activist's Guide to the Yogyakarta Principles was developed by a group of international SOGI human rights advocates that included members of the committee that drafted the Yogyakarta Principles. The Activist's Guide is intended to be used by SOGI activists in conjunction with the text of the Yogyakarta Principles.

http://www.publiceye.org/publications/globalizing-the-culture-wars/pdf/africa-full-report.pdf Globalizing the Culture Wars: U.S. Conservatives, African Churches and Homophobia: a report on Christian conservative anti-SOGI activism in Africa by Political Research Associates Senior Religion and Sexuality Researcher, Kapya Kaoma.

NOTES

1. Recorded as absent from the voting were Kyrgyzstan and Libya.

2. 'Welcoming', 'affirming', and 'reconciling' are common terms used by churches and faith communities in the US to denote pro-LGBTI solidarity. Churches and faith communities that reject such solidarity and affirm 'traditional' sexual and gender norms and identities sometimes call themselves 'transforming'.

3. As 'the lead U.S. Government agency that works to end extreme global poverty and enable resilient, democratic societies to realize their potential', the US Agency for International Development (USAID) has also participated in SOGI human rights programming, especially related to integrating SOGI human rights into development policy. See USAID, 'Who we are' (USAID website): http://www.usaid.gov/who-we-are (accessed 23 February 2015).

 Visit the Online Resource Centre that accompanies this book for updates and a range of other resources: www.oxfordtextbooks.co.uk/orc/goodhart3e/

12

Human Rights and Politics in Development

Sakiko Fukuda-Parr

Chapter Contents

Reader's Guide

This chapter addresses the importance of politics to the relationship between human rights and development. It presents the two major ways in which human rights struggles have focused on development processes in the last two decades: the right to development, the struggles of poor countries for a better deal in the global economic system; and the human rights-based approach to development, the struggles of poor people for development to realize their rights. The chapter begins by exploring the links between human rights, politics, and development. It then presents the concepts and debates surrounding the right to development and the human rights-based approach to development. A case study on the Millennium Development Goals and the successor, Sustainable Development, provides a critique from the human rights perspective to highlight how human rights principles are raised in contemporary debates on development priorities.

Introduction

This chapter is about how human rights are part of development and development is part of human rights as social challenges, theoretical concepts, and practice.

The objectives of development overlap considerably with the enjoyment of human rights—especially, though not exclusively, economic and social rights such as the rights to health, education, housing, and decent work. These two fields have evolved separately, but recently human rights activists began to address poverty as a human rights challenge and development practitioners began to adopt human rights principles in their work. Theorists in both fields began to develop concepts, measures, and analyses. Because this is a new area of theory and practice, it is still 'in the making' and basic ideas are evolving.

Politics are central to the relationship between human rights and development because development can be a process to realize human rights, but often poor people—both individually and collectively as communities and states—have to struggle to claim their rights.

The chapter presents the two major ways in which human rights struggles have focused on development processes in the last two decades: the **right to development** (RTD), the struggles of poor countries for a better deal in the global economic system; and the **human rights-based approach to development** (HRBA), the struggles of poor people for development to realize their rights.

The chapter is in four parts. The first part explains the nexus of human rights and development. It explains how development can promote the fulfilment of human rights and why politics are an important aspect of this nexus. The second and third sections review RTD and HRBA, respectively. These sections include the basic concepts and some of the current issues being debated, the context in which they emerged, and how they evolved in practice, with attention to the political factors that shaped the evolution. The fourth section looks at the case of the **Millennium Development Goals** (MDGs) and their successor, **Sustainable Development Goals (SDGs)**, to be adopted by the UN General Assembly in September 2015, the current consensus development priorities of the international community, and presents a human rights critique to illustrate the conceptual points made in the chapter. Because this is an emerging area of study and practice, there are many controversies, which makes it an exciting new way that human rights is engaging with contemporary challenges that people face in their lives.

Development and the Struggles for Human Rights

Politics and Human Rights

Human rights is an idea that 'empowers' the weak and vulnerable, protecting them from abuse of their rights to a life of dignity and freedom. Education, for example, may be a developmental goal for a Planning Ministry economist, or an aid agency programme officer. But it is an entitlement for a girl that she claims when denied schooling because there is no school provided by the state, or because the teacher does not turn up to teach, or because the parents do not value schooling for girls. In such a situation, social institutions have failed to ensure that she can enjoy her right to education. The language of rights is important in this case as the girl struggles to claim her right to education, the right to non-discrimination, and the right to equality. Her cause is helped if she can build alliances with others struggling for the same rights.

These struggles are part of claims being reaffirmed as human rights.[1] In explaining the emergence of human rights, philosopher and economist Amartya Sen (2006) explains that human rights are ethical norms that are a product of 'social ethics and public reasoning', while political scientist Jack Donnelly (2006) refers to their development through a history of 'social learning'. Human rights norms develop because people claim that certain conditions of life are entitlements and demand that they become recognized as human rights. These norms also emerge because people confront various threats to their survival as human beings and claim security against such threats (Shue, 1996).

People-Centred Approaches to Development

The concept of development is defined in many different ways, and human rights overlap with development defined as a people-centred process. Conventional economists, who have dominated the development field, focus on aggregate economic growth as an objective and production activities as the means. But this is not the only perspective on development. For decades, other perspectives, more compatible with human rights, have emphasized people as the purpose of development and its essential drivers. They include community development that emerged in the 1960s, the world employment programme of the 1970s, the basic needs approach of the 1970s and early 1980s, and, since the 1990s, the **human development and capability approach** (HD/CA) advocated by Sen and the UNDP Human Development Reports. Sen (1988, 1989, 1999a) has articulated the most theoretically grounded human-centred approach. He argues that development is essentially about expanding human capabilities that enable people to be and do the things that they value, an idea most widely known under the title of his 1999 book *Development as Freedom*, and among scholars as the capabilities approach. Mahbub ul Haq, who introduced the term *human development* (HD), expresses the same idea in a different way with different words: that development is a process that creates an enabling environment that expands opportunities for people, and that expands the capabilities that people have to lead lives that they value (UNDP, 1990; Haq, 1995).

In this broader perspective, struggles for human rights are also part of the process of development. Development is not only about national economic growth but also about how the benefits of economic growth are distributed among people—income groups, ethnic groups, racial groups, women and men, young and old, regional populations, rural and urban populations, workers in different occupations, and so on. It is also about how the resources generated by economic growth are put to use by government. How budgets are allocated among different sectors and uses has important consequences. Some uses are more likely to contribute directly to the fulfilment of human rights, such as supporting primary education, primary healthcare, social security, the judicial system and legal aid for people who cannot afford private legal services, or rural roads, while uses such as mining or military spending are less likely to contribute to the realization of human rights and may even have negative consequences.

The struggles of poor people for their rights are at least in part about those government policies and legal institutions that would advance the realization of their human rights—economic, social, cultural, political, and civil. Human rights are interdependent and indivisible; human dignity and freedom depend on the realization of all of these rights, and these rights are reinforcing. The plight of poor people illustrates this point: poor people are often denied their human rights in all of these five areas, and the denial of one right can reinforce the denial of another. For example, a woman who is a victim of human trafficking for prostitution is denied her rights to bodily integrity, to security, and to freedom of movement; she is likely to have been vulnerable because she came from a low-income family, had no access to protection from the courts and the police, and was perhaps illiterate and

unable to access information. These multiple denials of civil, political, economic, and social rights combine to leave her vulnerable. Moreover, the discrimination she may suffer on account of her gender, ethnicity, religion, or race may compound her vulnerability and explain why she was exploited by traffickers. Poor people from politically marginalized communities are vulnerable because their human rights are not guaranteed.

In these ways, development and human rights are inherently intertwined. Development is a process that can help to fulfil human rights, but not all types of development can do so. The struggle for human rights must therefore include a struggle for a process of development that can be positive for the promotion of human rights and not one that takes human rights backwards. This is the central point in linking human rights and development.

Linking Human Rights and Development: Right to Development and Human Rights-Based Approach to Development

Two important initiatives have brought together the fields of human rights and of development: the RTD initiative to recognize development as a human right, and the HRBA initiative to introduce human rights into development programmes. The Declaration on the Right to Development was adopted in 1986 and defines development as a human-centred process that leads to the realization of human rights. Promoted by Third World countries in the UN, it is particularly concerned with the obligations of international cooperation to create an enabling international environment necessary for development. HRBA was an initiative of development agencies and civil society groups to promote development programmes based on human rights principles.

Both RTD and HRBA are driven by a concern with global poverty as an affront to human freedom and dignity, and as a matter of injustice. Unlike the economic analysis of poverty, which looks to poor economic performance, inadequate resources, or inadequate policies as the causes of poverty, human rights is concerned with unequal distribution of power and wealth within and between countries as poverty's root cause.

The Right to Development (RTD)

Emergence of RTD and its Context

The right to development originated in the context of human rights debates of the Cold War and the development discourse of the **New International Economic Order (NIEO)**. It was formulated as a claim by less-developed countries to an international economic system that would create a more favourable—or enabling—environment for development. It emphasized issues in the global economic systems, many of which were legacies of colonialism, such as self-determination and international obligations of states to formulate appropriate policies and to provide international

cooperation (Beetham, 2006). These ideas are rooted in the *dependencia* theory that emerged in the 1960s, which traced the origins of underdevelopment to the persistence of colonial economic systems. Dependency theorists such as Frank, Furtado, and Prebisch argued that developing countries would remain underdeveloped even when colonization ended because they continued to be periphery countries in an economic system supplying primary commodities to the metropolis. Moreover, some of the major themes of the 1970s in international economic relations related to issues of declines in terms of trade, instability of commodity market prices, the terms of foreign investment in natural resource exploitation, the role of multinational corporations, and access to concessionary finance for public investments. With the economic crisis of the late 1970s and the adoption of liberalization policies in the late 1980s, these international economic issues retreated in prominence in international economic debates. But today RTD is perhaps even more relevant (Fukuda-Parr, 2006). Because of globalization, there is a greater need for states to act collectively to ensure that human rights are not threatened by the vagaries of the international economic system, such as the global financial crisis and economic recession, or food price spikes experienced in 2008.

Conceptual Issues

RTD marks a major conceptual and legal advance that links development and human rights (Sengupta, 2006). It defines a right to development as a right to a particular process of development that is 'people-centred', requiring: free, active, and meaningful participation; non-discrimination; fair distribution of benefits; respect for self-determination and sovereignty over natural resources; and a process that advances other human rights. This definition overlaps closely with Sen's concept of development as freedom and with the human development and capability perspective on development. The Declaration highlights the international dimensions of development, notably the obligations of states to act collectively as well as individually (Article 3), and for international development policies (Article 4).

The right to development implies a collective right, a right belonging to a group rather than an individual. Beetham (2006) argues that individuals can only enjoy human rights through a guarantee of the collective right to development. Both he and Sengupta (2006) argue that the right to development is therefore a right to a particular kind of development that would contribute to the fulfilment of human rights—for example, one where the benefits of development are widely shared. The right to development cannot be consistent with development where the state does not respect, protect, and fulfil human rights in the process. For example, investing in mineral exploration and exploitation by giving contracts to foreign multinationals that would primarily benefit the investors and political elites, while dislocating people from their homes, polluting the rivers, and clearing forests that provide an essential livelihood for the local population is hardly a kind of development consistent with human rights.

The concept of RTD is controversial among human rights scholars.[2] Quite apart from the challenges to economic and social rights in general, legal scholars have challenged the RTD as being too vague a concept to be useful (Ghai cited in Bunn, 2000), and characterized it as pure rhetoric that was motivated by political and ideological aims. In response to these critiques, a literature has developed to define the normative content of the right. Much of this literature was motivated by the work of the UN human rights system.

Implementation

RTD was debated for many years before it was finally proclaimed in 1986 in the *Declaration on the Right to Development*. Development as a human right was recognized in the Declaration and was reaffirmed in the **Vienna Declaration** of the 1993 World Conference on Human Rights, which recognized it as a universal and inalienable right and an integral part of fundamental human rights. But attempts to develop a **treaty** that would bind states legally have not advanced. Since then, the developing countries bloc in the UN, 'the Non-Aligned Movement (NAM)', has promoted a legally binding instrument on the RTD. This has met with the consistent opposition of the developed country bloc, the 'Western Group'. Within the UN, the Human Rights Commission created an Open Ended Working Group on the Right to Development in 1998 to promote the implementation of this right. To help in this process through analysis of key issues, the Commission appointed an Independent Expert on the Right to Development for the period 1999–2004, and a High-Level Task Force on the Right to Development for the period 2005–12. While these processes contributed to developing a better understanding of

the content of the RTD and to exploring some key international economic policy issues, political negotiations have progressed little.

However, RTD remains relevant in other UN norm-setting processes. For example, it is a part of the commitments of the 2000 Millennium Declaration, arguably one of the strongest consensus documents to emerge on development in recent decades. On the other hand, there is little mobilization for this right on the part of civil society. While international non-governmental organization (NGO) networks have actively advocated reforms in international economic policies to pursue a fairer distribution of the benefits of globalization, they rarely if ever make reference to the RTD.

The Right to Development is particularly important in the context of the globally integrated world of the twenty-first century because it addresses the need for collective action amongst states. RTD challenges the limits of the state-centric structure of human rights obligations where states are primarily responsible for their own citizens and residents, leaving ambiguity about the responsibilities for people outside their territories. Yet, increasingly, many pressing problems that obstruct the enjoyment of rights relate to actions of one state that have international repercussions on the enjoyment of rights—such as trade agreements on patents that raise prices of life-saving medicines to levels out of reach for poor people and poor countries, or environmental hazards created by foreign investors that negatively impact people's health. Important debates, advocacy, and initiatives have emerged on the international dimensions of human rights, especially responsibility for global poverty. An important step forward was the initiative by a group of leading scholars and activists to spell out the global responsibilities of states, and the 2011 publication of the Maastricht Principles on the Extra-Territorial Obligations of States in the Areas of Economic, Social and Cultural Rights (ETO Consortium).

> **KEY POINTS**
>
> The 1986 Declaration on RTD has not moved forward into a legally binding covenant or a convention.
>
> The content of RTD is controversial: some argue that it is vague and ideological; others argue that it is relevant to the realities of international economic relations. Yet there is little civil society mobilization to claim the right.

RTD is an entitlement to a particular kind of development that would fulfil human rights of individuals.

RTD imposes obligations on countries to cooperate to put in place policies conducive to Third World development.

Critical Thinking Questions:

In the state-centric system of accountability, while the current institutional arrangements for human rights hold states accountable, corporations and other 'non-state actors' often have an important role in people's enjoyment of rights. Consider further the case of access to life-saving medicines. What are the arguments for and against limiting human rights accountability to states?

Deconstructing the right to development:

(i) Consider the RTD as politics. Who are the key actors claiming the right to development? Who is resisting? What has been the role of international human rights networks and local civil society? How has the end of the Cold War and the onset of globalization shifted these politics?

(ii) Consider RTD as international law. How is the RTD different from other rights? What are the criticisms of RTD as international law?

(iii) Consider RTD as state obligations. How does RTD address collective obligations for obstacles to the enjoyment of human rights that cannot be fulfilled by a state for its residents?

(iv) Consider RTD as a contemporary challenge. Why is RTD relevant for globalization?

Human Rights-Based Approach to Development (HRBA)

Origins of HRBA and its Context

HRBA—also referred to as 'human rights in development' or 'rights-based development'—as a development approach originated in the international development aid community in the 1990s. HRBA aims to reorient the theory and practice of development. It argues that development and human rights pursue the same objectives—the realization of human rights and the respect of human rights principles in the process of development. HRBA often refers to programme approaches adopted by development

cooperation agencies that have introduced new priorities and activities. But these approaches are embedded in a broader 'discourse' that sees the realization of rights—economic, social, cultural as well as civil and political—as a goal of development. HRBA was also a reaction to neoliberal economic policies that led to the neglect of many social and equity priorities (Nelson and Dorsey, 2003; Darrow and Tomas, 2005). It builds on the alliance formed between the human rights and development communities in the 1980s to campaign for the *Convention to Eliminate All Forms of Discrimination against Women* (CEDAW), and the *Convention on the Rights of the Child* (CRC).

Cold War politics had driven a divide between civil and political rights, on the one hand, and economic and social rights on the other. Separate covenants developed, and civil and political rights became a tool of the West against the Eastern bloc countries and their Third World allies. Western human rights communities neglected, and many scholars and activists rejected, economic and social rights. Leading activists such as Aryeh Neier (2003) argued that they were excessive claims that could not be held up in a court of law; Kenneth Roth (2004a), President of **Human Rights Watch**, recognized economic and social rights but argued that international human rights organizations were ill-equipped to advocate for them. On the other side, some Third World leaders such as Singapore President Lee Kwan Yew argued that social and economic rights had to be fulfilled before political and civil rights could be promoted. These views have been countered by major theorists such as Sen (2004, 2005, 2006), who argue that justiciability is not a criterion for human rights and that law is the 'child of human rights', not the other way round. Pogge (2007) argues that global poverty is a massive human rights violation.

The end of the Cold War cleared the political obstacles for the development community to engage with human rights and for the human rights community to give attention to economic and social rights and the challenges of poverty. It opened the way for new political dynamics in international agendas for both human rights and for development. Leading advocates, starting with Mary Robinson as UN High Commissioner for Human Rights, began to champion economic, social, and cultural rights, and the **indivisibility** and interdependence of all human rights. Robinson also put global poverty on the human rights agenda, and human rights on the development agenda (UNDP, 2003; Robinson, 2005). Her successors have continued these efforts; Louise Arbour (2007, p. iii) stated, for example, that 'Poverty and inequities between and within countries are now the gravest human rights concerns that we face.' The human rights community began to embrace global poverty and development as human rights challenges. The decision by **Amnesty International**, which had historically focused exclusively on civil and political rights, to devote its 2010 campaign to global poverty is an important milestone in this shift.

The spread of HRBA was also facilitated by the rise of social movements in developing countries and international networks that championed human rights, especially economic and social rights, such as the right to food in Brazil and in India. These movements were facilitated by democratization across the world and by the growth of **global civil society** (see Chapter 9). Throughout Latin America, Africa, and Asia, authoritarian regimes gave way to multi-party democracies in what is called the 'third wave' of democratization. NGOs concerned with human rights and development began to proliferate in countries where authoritarian regimes had suppressed them, often taking up the cause of poverty. These organizations formed global advocacy networks. Just as globalization integrated markets and intensified the exchange of goods, it integrated social movements and intensified the flow of ideas and advocacy (UNDP, 1999, 2002).

HRBA was also facilitated by changes in the development field. When a people-centred discourse on development emerged as a strong intellectual countercurrent to the growth-centred discourse, development and human rights could be conceptualized as mutually supporting and compatible. In the early 1990s, HD/CA emerged, arguing that the ultimate end of development was improvement in human lives, in particular the expansion of capabilities—or choices to be and do what an individual values—rather than expansion of material output or economic growth. Economic growth is important, but only as a means, not the end (Sen, 1989, 1999a; UNDP, 1990). Such concerns were long-standing, but it was in the 1990s that they became prominent in international development debates. Defined in this way, development was no longer seen as antagonistic to human rights, but rather as a process supporting their fulfilment.

In 2000 the UNDP *Human Development Report* argued that these two concepts shared a common motivation: the pursuit of a life of freedom and dignity as the central concern. The two concepts also share

policy priorities that emphasize equality, participation, and agency. The tools of analysis and implementation approaches differ but are complementary and reinforcing. These arguments (UNDP, 2000; Sen, 2004, 2005) contributed to the conceptual framework of HRBA.

The HRBA Concept—Key Elements and Comparison with Human Development/ Capabilities and Neoliberal Approaches

While HRBA is a conceptual discourse, it is also a practice with methods and tools that apply human rights norms and principles based on international standards. These principles regarding rights include: (1) equality and non-discrimination; (2) true participation; and (3) indivisibility and interdependence of all human rights. From the perspective of the duty bearer (principally the state), the principles include the obligations: (1) to respect, protect, and fulfil rights—to refrain from violating, but also prevent others from violating, and taking active steps to ensure the realization of rights by all citizens; (2) to achieve progressive realization subject to maximum available resources—to make sustained efforts to achieve full realization of rights including allocating budgetary resources, legislation, and other measures.

How does HRBA differ from other approaches to development, particularly the neoliberal market approach and the HD/CA approach that is also widely endorsed by many practitioners?[3] As has been explained, HRBA emerged in part as a reaction against the neoliberal discourse on development. So there are important contrasts with that approach, but similarities with HD/CA (see Table 12.1).

The similarities between HRBA and HD/CA are grounded in a common motivation to enhance human dignity and freedoms. HRBA conceptualizes this in terms of human rights, HD/CA in terms of capabilities, but these are complementary if not overlapping concepts (Vizard, Fukuda-Parr, and Elson, 2011). Both contrast with the neoliberal approach, which seeks to maximize economic welfare, not the full range of human welfare, and which conceptualizes human well-being in terms of utility (Jolly, 1999). Sen (1981) has long critiqued the utility approach to welfare because it focuses on material means and consumption rather than on what people can be and do (their capabilities and functioning). Thus HD/CA and HRBA have compatible and consistent philosophical foundations, at odds with the neoliberal approach.

Table 12.1 Comparing key features of three approaches to development: human rights, human development, and neoliberalism[a]

Approach	Human rights	Human development	Neoliberalism
Conceptual framework			
Objectives of development	Realization of human rights	Expansion of choices, capabilities, and freedom	Maximization of economic welfare
Concept of human well-being	Dignity and freedom	Capabilities as freedom	Utility
Focus of concern	Individual as rights bearer and state conduct as duty bearer	Individuals and people	Markets
Guiding principle	International human rights law norms and standards	Equity, justice, and expansion of choice	Economic efficiency
Operational approaches **Evaluation of progress:**			
Main criteria for evaluating development progress	Right holder perspective: enjoyment of all rights; equality; non-discrimination	Human capabilities; equality of outcomes, fairness, and justice in institutional arrangements	Economic impacts
	Duty bearer perspective: accountability for legal obligations to respect, protect, and fulfil; subject to progressive realization; non-retrogression	Assessment of human impact of development policies	Assessment of policy choice on grounds of efficiency and effectiveness
Measurement and evidence base	Cases of rights denials documenting individuals' rights violated and duty bearer's failure to comply with obligations	Progress in human outcomes (e.g. literacy, child mortality)	Economic activity and condition
		Average, deprivational, and distributional measures; disaggregated measures	Averages and aggregate measures
Key indicators	No indicator sets in widespread use	Social and economic indicators: **Human Development Index (HDI), Gender-related Development Index (GDI), Gender Empowerment Measure (GEM), and Human Poverty Index (HPI)**	GNP per capita; GNP growth; headcount measure of income poverty incidence
Human agency in development:			
People as ends and/or means	Ends: beneficiaries with focus on the poorest and excluded	Ends: beneficiaries	Ends: not explicit
	Means: agents of change—claiming rights	Means: agents of change—taking charge to make their lives better	Means: human resources for economic activity
Mobilizing agency	Individual action through the courts; collective social action	Individual action and collective action	Individual action as entrepreneurs
Locus of action	Civil society and legal institutions	Civil society	Markets

Policy priorities			
Education, health, and nutrition	Ends in themselves as human rights; high priority for education and health of the least well off and excluded	Ends in themselves as expansion of capabilities	Important means—human resources—for improving productivity essential to economic growth
Ending gender, ethnic, and other discrimination, and reducing inequality	Central policy goal	A human right, an important priority	A social or ethical issue; concern with trade-off with efficiency
Economic growth	No position—little research on economic growth and human rights; widespread perception that fast growth often undermines human rights	Essential means to enhancing human capabilities and choices	Central policy objective of development policies
Governance	Strengthening state capacity to meet human rights obligations in economic, social, cultural, civil, and political domains—emphasis on access to justice for the poor and marginalized	Democratic and inclusive governance to democracy; enhance voice of people and accountability of the state—emphasis on state functions	Role of institutions necessary for efficient operation of the market—emphasis on rule of law, contracts, and eliminating corruption

a. Some of the elements are drawn from Jolly (2004), which compares the differences and overlaps between the human development approach and neoliberalism.

The similarities and contrasts among these approaches are more complex in the operational context. HRBA and HD/CA share common policy priorities but build on different tools. HD/CA and neoliberal approaches use the same tools but argue for different policy priorities.

Equality and participation are the two human rights principles that lead to the most striking policy contrasts. While mainstream international debates emphasize development and poverty reduction, the human rights approach is explicitly concerned with inequality. All three approaches share a commitment to policies to expand education, health, and nutrition, address gender and other inequalities, promote economic growth, and improve governance. The differences lie in the relative priorities and choices made about trade-offs among them. For example, in education and health policies, the neoliberal approach would justify education and health policies that would strengthen growth prospects, while the HRBA would emphasize education as an end in itself and stress the obligation to ensure equal access to all, with priority attention to the least well off and the marginalized. In the area of governance, HRBA would focus attention on those institutional arrangements that would enhance voice and participation of the poorest people in claiming their rights, while the neoliberal policy focus would be on those arrangements that facilitate investment and innovation. Such differences are apparent in the human rights critique of the MDGs, as the case study in this chapter will illustrate.

The Adoption of HRBA by Key Stakeholders

HRBA has been gaining momentum among development practitioners, particularly local and international NGOs, civil society groups, bilateral and multilateral donors, and think-tanks. Many leading national and international networks such as Oxfam, Care International, and Action Aid now work with HRBA principles. For example, Oxfam International[4] states: 'Our mission is a just world without poverty and our goal is to enable people to exercise their rights and manage their own lives.' Similarly, Action Aid states, 'We work with local partners to fight poverty and injustice worldwide, reaching over 13 million of the poorest and most vulnerable people over the last year alone, helping them fight for and gain their rights to food, shelter, work, education, healthcare and a voice in the decisions that affect their lives.' The United Nations has adopted a common policy—a 'common understanding'—across all agencies to base all of its development work on human rights principles (UNDG, 2003).

The United Nations Children's Fund (UNICEF) has been a pioneer in this approach, building on its commitment to children's human rights and its involvement in the 1980s with the formulation and passage of the CRC. It has developed many important programmes using the HRBA, such as budget analysis and monitoring in Ecuador (see Box 12.1). Among

---

BOX 12.1 UNICEF HRBA EXPERIENCE IN ECUADOR: THE PRINCIPLES OF UNIVERSALITY AND PARTICIPATION—A BUDGET FOR IMPLEMENTING SOCIAL RIGHTS IN ECUADOR

The following text is adapted from Elizabeth Gibbons (2006).

Ecuador experienced a serious macro-economic crisis during the late 1990s, which resulted in sharply decreased spending on social programmes, undermining the rights of children, as well as adults, to healthcare, education, and adequate nutrition. Concerned about these cuts, UNICEF began a dialogue with the Congress over the government's proposed budget. This led to an agreement with the Ministry of Finance under which UNICEF was authorized to have access to the Ministry's financial data to analyse the national budget, monitor its execution, and communicate its findings. Helping legislators and the public to understand how the budget functions and what priorities it reflects were the objectives of this exercise, whose goal was to encourage the creation of more equitable public policies based on a shared consensus regarding society's obligation to fulfil the human rights of all of its members.

Analysing, Monitoring, Communicating Budget Revenues and Expenditures

Analysis of the budget and spending patterns revealed that spending on social programmes was plummeting. For example, investment in education dropped from US$611 million in 1996 to US$331 million in 1999; and health spending fell from US$198 million to US$96 million. The budget analysis also revealed that spending for social sectors was disproportionately low (15 per cent for 2000) compared to allocations for debt repayment (60 per cent) and other non-social sectors. In addition, certain regions (the rural sector, Andean Highlands, and the Amazon)—particularly those with a majority Indigenous population—were not getting a fair share of social benefits.

Ecuadorian President Jamil Mahuad and UNICEF then agreed that UNICEF should track social expenditures and the key indicators of the national crisis. UNICEF created a series of visual tools—tables, bar graphs, pie charts, etc.—to make budget data accessible and comprehensible to ordinary Ecuadorians. Over time, this data became available online. UNICEF then undertook an ambitious outreach effort, sharing the information with a wide variety of partners, including legislators, business leaders, academics, media representatives, and Indigenous, religious, and trade union groups. The central issue during these meetings was how to make public spending more equitable. The key message of this advocacy effort was the universality of human rights translated into three goals: health and education for all and hunger for no one. It was a values-based message, offered in the spirit of overcoming a crisis felt by all, but seriously threatening the survival of the country's poor and Indigenous people.

UNICEF and government officials worked together to draft programmes consistent with the overriding goals of universality and equity, including: expanding existing school nutrition and income-support programmes; nutritional support for children under two, and pregnant and lactating mothers; and subsidies for poor families to send their children to school. All programmes were targeted to reach the most marginalized and impoverished segments of the population. In the following years, UNICEF's role expanded to include monitoring revenue as the government was preparing a proposal for tax reform. This information on tax reform was also shared widely; the tax issue received press coverage and was the topic of a national conference sponsored by the Ecuadorian Congress.

Impacts

In 2001, the percentage of total government spending devoted to social programmes rose to 22.1 per cent and then again to 23.2 per cent in 2002, exceeding the 1996 figure of 19.1 per cent. By 2002, *per capita* social spending had surpassed pre-crisis levels, although due to population growth, the poorest Ecuadorians were still receiving considerably less than in the past.

In addition, the need to reform the national tax structure and generate additional revenues resulted in important institutional changes. The capacity of the Internal Revenue Service was strengthened so that an additional four to five percentage points were collected in taxes, and a new Customs Service was created, which added a further two percentage points. Consequently, between 1999 and 2002, government revenue from taxes increased from 6.4 per cent to 13.7 per cent of GDP, although the underlying tax structure still relies mainly on indirect taxes, and efforts to modify the structure are ongoing.

Lessons for Building a Human Rights-Based Society

The results were also impressive for building a human rights-based society in Ecuador. A broad social consensus around the need for more just and equitable public spending policies clearly emerged during the first few years of UNICEF's public budget work. The leader of one of the country's largest Indigenous groups noted that the work had 'democratized budget information'. Previously, few Ecuadorians were aware of, or able to understand, the national budget.

In facilitating this process, Ecuador's political leaders made tremendous strides towards accountable and transparent governance. By increasing and targeting social sector investment in light of the discovery of critical inequities, the government took a human rights-based stance that placed priority on fulfilling the rights of the country's most vulnerable citizens.

Perhaps the most important lesson learned is that a human rights-based message can resonate and provoke change if it is based on widespread consensus and perceived as a positive contribution to society. Even in a historically inequitable society, most people share an underlying belief in human rights and social justice that, once tapped, can influence public policy making. Although Ecuador had ratified the CRC on 23 March 1990 and approved a Code for Children and Adolescents in 2002, it was less these legal instruments than the principles of universality and participation sustaining them that propelled the process forwards. At no time, whether analysing the budget or sharing its findings with wide sectors of society, did UNICEF encounter resistance to the underlying premise that rights must be universal. This experience, rooted in democratic institutions and processes, challenges contemporary assessments of exclusionary public policy in Latin America and offers a positive model of building solidarity for social inclusion, even in a context of extreme resource scarcity.

Reproduced with the permission of Canada's International Development Research Centre (http://www.idrc.ca) and of the author.

---

bilateral development agencies adoption has varied: the UK, Sweden, and Norway have prepared elaborate policies and guidelines, while others such as the USA have engaged little. But all have endorsed the principle of the importance of human rights under the Organisation for Economic Co-operation and Development's Development Assistance Committee policy of 1994. The most recent restatement of this policy recognizes human rights norms as 'an accepted normative framework reflecting global moral and political values'. It notes, 'there is growing consensus on the value of human rights principles—such as participation, nondiscrimination, and accountability—for good and sustainable development practice. The application of these principles builds on and strengthens good and sustainable development practice, with equal attention to process and outcomes' (OECD/DAC, 2007).

The human rights community has also increasingly engaged with poverty and development as priority concerns. Issues of poverty and development have long been a concern for human rights organizations in the South, though they have only recently become a priority for Northern NGOs, as discussed earlier. As for the UN machinery, a wealth of important new initiatives has been undertaken since the 1990s, such as the appointment of special rapporteurs on extreme poverty, and on the right to development, health, food, and other relevant issues. The Office of the High Commissioner for Human Rights (OHCHR) has also begun important substantive work to build up a battery of conceptual and analytical tools in this new area.

Within the international development cooperation, the language of rights has become widespread. For some organizations this was limited to a rhetorical adoption of the language, while for others it involved adoption of new methods and tools. For others it shifted programme priorities, particularly in the governance areas, to strengthen civil and political rights such as access to justice (Uvin, 2004; OECD/DAC, 2007; Piron, 2005). HRBA has contributed to shifting international development agendas, especially in raising issues of state–citizen linkages by use of the duty bearer–right holder and accountability perspectives, the structural roots of poverty, and focus on exclusion as an obstacle (OECD/DAC, 2007). Yet it remains at the margins of policy making and programme formulation for many development agencies that have adopted the approach rhetorically rather than in setting priorities or using specific tools. HRBA is not the dominant approach in national policy frameworks such as the **Poverty Reduction Strategy Papers** (PRSPs), which serve to set priorities for both the government and donors (Fukuda-Parr, 2008b), nor in the Millennium Development Goals (MDGs), which have come to define the consensus objective of international development (see case study).

The most effective use of HRBA has been in civil society advocacy. Civil society groups have mobilized across the world to claim the rights of women, children, and Indigenous people related to 'development' such as the negative consequences of investments in dams, mines, or gender discrimination in access to land, to name just a few examples. International NGO networks are advocating policy change to mobilization at local, national, and global levels on an increasingly broad range of issues including, for example, unjust taxation (see Chapter 9). These trends are particularly apparent in the UN Millennium Development Goals (MDGs) and the discussions over the successor Post-2015 Development Agenda and the Sustainable Development Goals (SDGs). (For a discussion of the conceptualization of development itself, see Box 12.2.)

KEY POINTS

HRBA is a development discourse that defines development as the realization of the human rights of all individuals. It emerged in the 1990s in response to the human consequences of neoliberal economic policy reforms.

HRBA is also the application of basic human rights principles, including participation, equality and non-discrimination, empowerment of people, and accountability of duty bearers for their obligations to respect, protect, and fulfil human rights. HRBA also explicitly makes use of international human rights norms.

HRBA shares much in common with other people-centred discourses on development, and contrasts with neoliberal approaches in critical ways, including the way development and human well-being are defined, the priorities for economic and social policy, and the role of people in the development process.

The HRBA has spread widely as an important discourse and practice but has not entered the mainstream approach to national policies and international agendas. It overlaps with but is not fully consistent with the consensus agenda, the MDGs launched in 2000. But there is increasing social mobilization to claim rights and international NGO advocacy for policy change.

Critical Thinking Questions:

What does the Ecuador case study (Box 12.1) show about the effectiveness of HRBA as a new method of development? Can you think of other similar cases where new types of projects can be introduced to advance human rights in development?

BOX 12.2 ALTERNATIVE POINTS OF VIEW: DEVELOPMENT

HRBA is an effort to bring international human rights norms and institutions into the practice of development by reconceptualizing development. Post-development theorists, such as Arturo Escobar (1995), Rahnema (1997), and others question the concept of development itself. They argue that development is a construct in which the countries of the **global North** impose their own paradigms of social organization, economic progress, and cultural values. Rooted in colonialism, development as an international economic and political project aims to continue the domination of the South by the North. Critical human rights scholars such as Mutua Makau (2013) argue that the dominant human rights practice is driven by Northern academics, governments, and NGOs, and focuses on human rights violations in the South. Their discourse can be characterized by the metaphor of 'savages-victims-saviours'; their role as 'saviours' is to defend people of the South, helpless 'victims', against the human rights violations committed by their own governments ('savages'). Other scholars, such as Eric Posner (2014) and Stephen Hopgood (2014) also see the international human rights project as one driven by the Western powers but criticize it as ineffective, politically outdated, and burdened with hypocritical posturing.

Case Study: The Millennium Development Goals (MDGs) and the Sustainable Development Goals (SDGs)

The MDGs—the targets to eradicate poverty by 2015—and their successor goals, the SDGs, have come to define the consensus agenda of the international development community. HRBA analysis of the MDGs and the SDGs helps to illustrate the continuing advocacy for human rights priorities in development strategies.

MDGs and SDGs—Concept, Origins, and Evolution

In September 2000, heads of state met at the Millennium Summit to commit their nations to 'doing their utmost' to end poverty. They vowed to work towards development along with peace, human rights, democracy, and environmental sustainability while respecting the principles of equality and solidarity. The resulting **Millennium Declaration** (the Declaration) contained some specific goals and timeframes for development, giving concrete meaning to these lofty objectives.[5] These were reconfigured in 2001 into a more coherent set of eight goals, eighteen associated targets, and forty-eight progress indicators—the MDGs—to be achieved by 2015 (see Box 12.3). In anticipation of the target date, a process for elaborating successor goals (Sustainable Development Goals or SDGs) and an agenda

(Post-2015 International Development Agenda) was begun in July 2012. A set of seventeen goals and 169 targets was proposed to the General Assembly in 2014 (see Box 12.4) and the final goals were adopted in 2015.

The SDGs differ in important ways from the MDGs, in both process of formulation and priority agenda. First, while the Millennium Declaration and the MDGs were elaborated by the UN Secretary General

---

BOX 12.3 HUMAN RIGHTS IN THE MDGs?

Each of the MDGs reflects a core human right, but not fully—as indicated in the note following each goal in brackets. There is no mention of the principles of equality, non-discrimination, or participation.

Goal 1. Eradicate extreme poverty and hunger [Relevant right: Right to adequate standard of living—*for all*]

- Target 1A: halve, between 1990 and 2015, the proportion of people whose income is less than $1 a day.
- Target 1B: achieve full and productive employment and decent work for all, including women and young people [Right to work].
- Target 1C: halve, between 1990 and 2015, the proportion of people who suffer from hunger [Right to food].

Goal 2. Achieve universal primary education [Relevant right: Right to free primary education]

- Target 2: ensure that, by 2015, children everywhere, boys and girls alike, will be able to complete a full course of primary schooling.

Goal 3. Promote gender equality and empower women [Relevant right: Women's right to equality—*in many more areas besides education*]

- Target 3: eliminate gender disparity in primary and secondary education, preferably by 2005, and in all levels of education no later than 2015.

Goal 4. Reduce child mortality [Relevant right: Right to life—*for all*]

- Target 4: reduce by two-thirds, between 1990 and 2015, the under-5 mortality rate.

Goal 5. Improve maternal health [Relevant right: Women's right to life and health—*for all*]

- Target 5A: reduce by three-quarters, between 1990 and 2015, the maternal mortality ratio.
- Target 5B: achieve, by 2015, universal access to reproductive health.

Goal 6. Combat HIV/AIDS, malaria, and other diseases [Relevant right: Right to health]

- Target 6A: have halted by 2015 and begun to reverse the spread of HIV/AIDS.
- Target 6B: achieve, by 2010, universal access to treatment for HIV/AIDS for all those who need it.
- Target 6C: have halted by 2015 and begun to reverse the incidence of malaria and other major diseases.

Goal 7. Ensure environmental sustainability [Relevant rights: Right to environmental health, Right to water and sanitation, Right to adequate housing—*for all*]

- Target 7A: integrate the principles of sustainable development into country policies and programmes and reverse the loss of environmental resources.
- Target 7B: reduce biodiversity loss, achieving, by 2010, a significant reduction in the rate of loss.
- Target 7C: halve, by 2015, the proportion of people without sustainable access to safe drinking water.
- Target 7D: have achieved by 2020 a significant improvement in the lives of at least 100 million slum dwellers.

Goal 8. Develop a global partnership for development [Relevant rights: Right to development, Obligations of assistance]

- Target 12: develop further an open, rule-based, predictable, non-discriminatory trading and financial system (includes a commitment to good governance, development, and poverty reduction—both nationally and internationally).
- Target 13: address the special needs of the least-developed countries.
- Target 14: address the special needs of landlocked countries and small island developing states.

- Target 15: deal comprehensively with the debt problem of developing countries through national and international measures in order to make debt sustainable in the long term.
- Target 16: in cooperation with developing countries, develop and implement strategies for decent and productive work for youth.
- Target 17: in cooperation with pharmaceutical companies, provide access to affordable essential drugs in developing countries.
- Target 18: in cooperation with the private sector, make available the benefits of new technologies, especially information and communications technologies.

and then negotiated for final adoption by states, the formulation of the SDGs from the beginning was led by an intergovernmental process of the UN General Assembly that constituted an 'open working group' (OWG) for this purpose. Their formulation has involved an intense process of multiple consultations. Alongside national governments and the UN, this involved a massive mobilization of civil society organizations, development agencies, and the private sector. Second, while the MDGs focused on poverty and implicitly addressed the needs of poor countries and partnerships of North–South development cooperation, the SDGs are broader, focusing on socially,

environmentally, and economically sustainable development, and are intended to apply to all countries, including middle- and high-income countries, in the context of multipolar partnerships.

The MDGs gained momentum as a consensus global framework for guiding international development. Global goals had been set before, but the impact of the MDGs was unprecedented in shaping policy discussions, assessing progress, and mobilizing support (UN Task Team on the Post-2015 UN Development Agenda, 2012). They are credited with having mobilized awareness on ending global poverty as an urgent priority that should be a concern for everyone in the

BOX 12.4 PROPOSED SDGs (2014)

In September 2014, the OWG submitted its report to the 2014 General Assembly (GA), proposing seventeen goals and 169 targets. The following goals were adopted in September 2015 by the GA. (https://sustainabledevelopment.un.org/index.php?page=view&type=400&nr=1579&menu=35)

Goal 1: End poverty in all its forms everywhere.
Goal 2: End hunger, achieve food security and improved nutrition and promote sustainable agriculture.
Goal 3: Ensure healthy lives and promote well-being for all at all ages.
Goal 4: Ensure inclusive and equitable quality education and promote lifelong learning for all at all ages.
Goal 5: Achieve gender equality and empower all women and girls.
Goal 6: Ensure availability and sustainable management of water and sanitation for all.
Goal 7: Ensure access to affordable, reliable, sustainable and modern energy for all.
Goal 8: Promote sustained, inclusive and sustainable economic growth, full and productive employment and decent work for all.

Goal 9: Build resilient infrastructure, promote inclusive and sustainable industrialization and foster innovation.
Goal 10: Reduce inequality within and among countries.
Goal 11: Make cities and human settlements inclusive, safe, resilient and sustainable.
Goal 12: Ensure sustainable production and consumption patterns.
Goal 13: Take urgent action to combat climate change and its impacts.
Goal 14: Conserve and sustainably use the oceans, seas and marine resources for sustainable development.
Goal 15: Protect, restore and promote the sustainable use of terrestrial ecosystems, sustainably manage forests, combat desertification, and halt and reverse land degradation and halt biodiversity loss.
Goal 16: Promote peaceful and inclusive societies for sustainable development, provide access to justice for all and build effective, accountable and inclusive institutions at all levels.
Goal 17: Strengthen the means of implementation and revitalize the global partnership for sustainable development.

world, not just in poor countries. Their strengths were quantification, simplicity, and targets that communicate a call to action. However, the MDGs also generated controversy for: (1) the lack of participation in the process of their elaboration; (2) the lack of attention to inequality; (3) the weak partnership goals without quantitative targets; (4) the narrowness of the agenda, which not only omitted many important priorities but also ignored the structural causes of poverty and inequality and lacked a transformative vision of development; (5) the mis-specification of targets; and (6) the application of global targets to all countries without adaptation to specific national priorities or acknowledging diverse starting points (see summary in UN Task Team on the Post-2015 UN Development Agenda, 2012). The human rights community was among the most critical voices in these controversies, as will be explained.

Human Rights in MDGs and SDGs

There is substantial overlap between MDGs and core economic and social rights (see Box 12.3), and they shift the focus of development from the economy to people, reflecting an important shift in development priorities. Human rights values frame the Millennium Declaration and its vision: freedom, dignity, solidarity, tolerance, and equity among people and nations.

Despite these overlaps, the MDGs were unsatisfactory and do not address the key human rights challenges of global poverty. The reality is that millions of people suffer from hunger, ill health, lack of access to education, and are denied these and other fundamental rights. Often this is due to discrimination on the basis of sex, race, ethnicity, sexual orientation, and the structures of power that maintain privilege for a few in the distribution of resources and voice in decision making. Yet the MDGs were silent on principles of non-discrimination and equality, participation and democratic governance.

A major constraint with global goals is that human rights goals are not quantifiable, starting with dignity and freedom, participation, and non-discrimination. They end up with a set of priorities that 'cherish what we measure' rather than 'measuring what we cherish'. MDGs are short and simple, leaving out many priorities. When (mis)used as programming and planning targets, global goals can distort priorities—for example to refocus efforts on primary school enrolment in a country where the greater challenges are in educational quality and in secondary and tertiary levels.

Furthermore, global goals frame debates by creating a simplified narrative of development as a target-driven process that neglects the root causes of poverty (Fukuda-Parr and Yamin, 2015).

The SDGs reflect learning from the MDGs and respond to many of these criticisms. The norms of inclusion and equity – 'let no one be left behind' – have been a core principle in elaborating the SDGs. The OWG proposals are framed in the HRBD perspective, intended to be goals for development that is human-centered, and 'to strive for a world that is just, equitable and inclusive' (UN 2015 p. 1). The SDGs are broader and less reductionist. They address the need for structural reforms including reducing inequality not only within but also between countries (goal 10), building just and accountable governance (goal 15), reproductive rights (target 5.5), participation (target 5.4), and more. The human rights community, including actors from civil society, UN agencies, and some national government offices, has been actively engaged in the process of SDG elaboration since 2012. As a result, the 2030 Agenda contains stronger human rights language, which states: 'this is an Agenda which seeks to respect, protect and fulfill all human rights. It will work to ensure that human rights and fundamental freedoms are enjoyed by all without discrimination'. It includes a much greater emphasis on reducing inequality, both within and between countries (goal 10), reflected in the overriding aim of 'leave no one behind', and for access to justice (goal 16).

KEY POINTS

The eight MDGs overlap with many social and economic rights but are unsatisfactory in addressing the root cause of poverty related to discrimination and unaccountable governance.

The SDGs can potentially be an improvement on the MDGs, but the transformative agenda of realizing human rights and HRBA go beyond what can be captured in a limited set of goals and numeric targets.

The human rights critique of the MDGs and engagement with SDGs illustrates how human rights concerns are influencing development agendas and how they remain controversial.

Critical Thinking Question:

Do you think the SDGs are likely to successfully address the criticisms made of the MDGs? Why or why not?

Conclusion

As most writers on the subject observe, the 'integration' of human rights in the practice of development has proven partial and difficult (Sano, 2000; Uvin, 2004; Robinson, 2005). Many development practitioners remain sceptical of the idea that human rights can provide useful tools for development, or that they should be adopted as the end goals of development (Ingram and Freestone, 2006). The difficulties of such integration can be explained by many factors, such as different traditions, analytical concepts, and implementation methods (Fukuda-Parr, 2008a). States, particularly the rich and powerful ones, resist the idea of having obligations to the world's poor or to redress injustices that keep people and countries poor. On the other hand, people are increasingly mobilizing to claim their rights in the spaces of development interventions, as illustrated by the civil society advocacy for human rights principles to be respected in setting the SDGs and the Post-2015 Development Agenda. The most important contribution of human rights in development is in the political process of people claiming their rights—the mobilization of advocacy for policy reforms to bring about development that ensures the realization of all rights of all people.

? QUESTIONS

Individual Study Questions

1. How did the Cold War influence the evolution of international human rights law and movements?

2. What are the different ways in which development is defined, and what are the main discourses on development today?

3. What is the difference between RTD and HRBA?

4. What are the key arguments for and against the RTD?

5. How does HRBA differ from the mainstream neoclassical approach and from the human development approach?

6. What is the political economy behind the arguments for and against HRBA, and RTD?

7. What are the key human rights principles in HRBA?

8. How do MDGs differ from SDGs, and do they reflect human rights principles more than the MDGs?

Group Discussion Questions on the MDGs and SDGs

1. If you were the head of an NGO for women's rights, what position would you have taken on the MDGs and what would be your organization's strategy—ignore them, criticize them, change them, or use them in your advocacy and action?

2. If you were a human rights activist, how would you revise the proposed SDG goals and targets? The devil is in the details—are the SDG goals and targets an improvement on the MDGs in advancing the human rights agenda?

≈ FURTHER READING

Andreassen, B. A. and **Marks, S. P.** (eds) (2006). *Development as a Human Right: Legal, Political and Economic Dimensions*. Cambridge, MA: Harvard School of Public Health. Distributed by Harvard University Press.

This volume collects some of the cutting-edge work on the theories of development as a human right and includes conceptual underpinnings, defining obligations, specific national challenges, and global processes. The contributors are leading thinkers on the issue and address some of the controversial issues on the right to development and on the human rights approach to development.

Balakrishnan, R. and **Elson, D.** (eds) (2011). *Economic Policy and Human Rights: Holding Governments to Account.* London: Zed Books.

This edited volume provides conceptual and empirical explanations for why economic policy choices are important for fulfilling human rights. It includes case studies of fiscal, monetary, and trade policies in the US and Mexico to illustrate those choices.

Donnelly, J. (2003). *Universal Human Rights in Theory and Practice* (2nd edn). Ithaca, NY: Cornell University Press.

This volume is an important theoretical work for exploring the relationship between human rights and development from political and other perspectives. It addresses the issue of universalism and the charge that human rights are a Western construct that may not apply to other parts of the world, especially the Third World.

Elson, D., Fukuda-Parr, S., and **Vizard, P.** (eds) (2012). *Capabilities and Rights: An Interdisciplinary Conversation.* London: Routledge. First issued as a special issue of the *Journal of Human Development and Capabilities,* **12/**1.

This collection explores the overlaps and complementarities between capabilities and human rights as theory and conceptual frameworks for development evaluation and promotion. It includes papers by leading theorists including Martha Nussbaum, and a substantive Foreword by Amartya Sen. The introduction provides an overview of the literature.

Farmer, P. (2005). *Pathologies of Power: Health, Human Rights and the New War on the Poor.*PL Berkeley:PN University of California Press.

This monograph provides a human rights analysis of the root causes of poverty and vulnerability to human rights abuses that can be traced to the structures of economic, political, and social power.

OHCHR (2004). *Human Rights and Poverty Reduction: A Conceptual Framework.* New York: United Nations. http://www. ohchr.org/Documents/Publications/PovertyReductionen.pdf

This short publication presents a useful conceptual framework for the links between human rights and poverty that is simple and up to date. It is useful for practitioners as a document on concept that complements more specific operational guidelines.

OHCHR (2006). *Frequently Asked Questions on Human Rights-Based Approach to Development Cooperation.* New York: United Nations. http://www.ohchr.org/Documents/Publications/FAQen.pdf

This short publication is an excellent document that clarifies basic concepts and definitions about the HRBA.

Sen, A.K. (1999). *Development as Freedom.* New York: Alfred A. Knopf, Anchor Books.

This is a classic text on the capability approach, which includes a chapter on human rights and elaborates on the relationship between human rights and capabilities.

Shue, H. (1980). *Basic Rights: Subsistence, Affluence and U.S. Foreign Policy.* Princeton, NJ: Princeton University Press.

This classic in the theory of human rights is an important foundation for exploring the relationship between human rights and development. It presents a theoretical defence of basic subsistence and survival rights, including economic rights that have been contested in the literature.

UNDP (2000). *Human Development Report 2000: Human Rights and Human Development.* New York: Oxford University Press.

Written from the human development perspective, this is a comprehensive text that clarifies the overlaps and complementarities between the HRBA and HD/CA. It includes chapters on concepts (written by Amartya Sen), history, democracy, the use of indicators, poverty, and a policy agenda.

Uvin, P. (2004). *Human Rights and Development.* Bloomfield, CT: Kumarian Press.

This book reviews the challenges of HRBA as a development practice. It provides a systematic analytical framework for this review, and sets the analysis in the context of divergent development discourses. It reflects on the obstacles and critiques of the HRBA approach without rejecting it.

WEB LINKS

http://www2.ohchr.org/   The official website of the OHCHR is a must-visit site for the study of human rights and development—in particular, the web pages on development, poverty, and MDGs.

http://www.ohchr.org/EN/Issues/Development/Pages/DevelopmentIndex.aspx   This page contains basic documents and information on current debates and activities of the working group on the right to development.

http://www.ohchr.org/EN/Issues/Poverty/Pages/SRExtremePovertyIndex.aspx   This page contains basic documents on poverty as a human rights issue. It provides information on current activities, reports of the independent expert on extreme poverty, and links to documents.

http://www.ohchr.org/EN/Issues/MDG/Pages/MDGIndex.aspx   This page on MDGs contains UN OHCHR perspectives on why MDGs are relevant to human rights, and documents on the subject.

http://www.chrgj.org/   The website of the Center for Human Rights and Global Justice of the New York University School of Law, a premier research centre on human rights and the consequences of globalization for poor people and poor countries. It contains a wealth of information and working papers on the latest research in this area.

http://www.cdhr.org.in/   The website of the Centre for Development and Human Rights located in New Delhi, India contains reflections on the right to development.

https://www.iidh.ed.cr/multic/DefaultIIDHEn.aspx   The website of the Inter-American Institute of Human Rights, a premier research and training institution in Latin America, provides a wealth of information on the human rights situation and analysis. The site provides information on specific rights and on current activities of the Institute.

NOTES

1. This is a common characterization of human rights, made particularly in the practice of human rights by advocates and defenders. See Chapter 3, which documents the history of human rights as global struggles. See particularly 'The Ongoing Global Struggle for Human Rights' (UNDP, 2000, pp. 27–9), which documents milestones and progress in the evolution of human rights in international legislation.

2. See Bunn (2000) for a review of these controversies.

3. There are many others, notably the sustainability approach, the 'local first' approach, or the post-development approach. These approaches are not all mutually exclusive. A full discussion of these approaches is beyond the scope of this paper, but Greig, Hume, and Turner (2007) provides a good summary review of these approaches.

4. See the Oxfam International website: http://www.oxfam.org/en/about.

5. The MDGs were not formulated overnight by the United Nations. They build on a global consensus reached in the 1990s among governments—a dialogue to which many civil society groups actively contributed (Emmerij, Jolly, and Weiss, 2001). All but two of the eight MDGs are, in fact, commitments outlined in the agendas negotiated and adopted at the UN development conferences of the 1990s, conferences which all involved a protracted preparatory process of country, regional, and global consultations. MDGs also build on the consensus of the rich countries of the world; the Development Assistance Committee of the Organisation for Economic Co-operation and Development (OECD) had earlier drawn up its own set of development goals (OECD, 1996).

 Visit the Online Resource Centre that accompanies this book for updates and a range of other resources: www.oxfordtextbooks.co.uk/orc/goodhart3e/

13

Economic Globalization and Human Rights

David L. Richards and Ronald D. Gelleny

Chapter Contents

Reader's Guide

This chapter uses statistical methods to examine the relationship between economic globalization and government respect for two subcategories of international human rights known as physical integrity rights and empowerment rights. First, an overview of different theoretical approaches regarding the relationship between economic globalization and government respect for human rights is provided. Then research findings from the quantitative literature examining this relationship are discussed. Finally, an original study using quantitative methods is conducted to examine whether a developing country's ability to attract foreign investment is affected by its level of governmental respect for human rights. We find that governments that respect their citizens' physical integrity and empowerment rights will be better able to attract foreign economic capital.

Introduction

In this chapter, we examine the relationship between economic **globalization** and government respect for human rights. First, we provide an overview of different theoretical approaches regarding the relationship between economic globalization and government respect for human rights. Second, we provide an assessment of the quantitative literature examining this relationship. Finally, we engage in a case study, including statistical tests, to examine whether a less developed country's (LDC) ability to attract foreign investment is affected by its level of governmental respect for human rights.

We define economic globalization as both the implementation of **neoliberal** economic policy reforms (e.g. deregulation and privatization policies) by governments and an increase in the worldwide flow of goods, services, labour, and capital (Richards and Gelleny, 2002, 2007). Increasingly, globalization has been viewed as the latest and, perhaps, final stage of the inevitable march of capitalism throughout the world. Countries that have been excluded from the process, owing perhaps to ideological policies, national policies of protectionism, or even self-imposed isolation from the world economy, are becoming entrenched in the international economic system. Governments view economic globalization as the principal means to develop economically and politically. In recent years, there have been surges of participation by Central and Eastern European countries in the world market and international organizations designed to promote and maintain the capitalist system, such as the **International Monetary Fund** (IMF), the **World Bank**, and the **World Trade Organization** (WTO). China and India, seeking to expand economic growth, likewise have become more integrated into the world market. Moreover, many countries in Africa—including Ghana, Kenya, Mauritania, and Tanzania—have begun to initiate free market policy reforms in an effort to attract more international investment (UNCTAD, 2007).

At the same time, the global community has become more focused on the relationship between globalization and human rights, questioning whether the process of globalization has enhanced or undercut government respect for human rights. Globalization is often imposed on a country's population from above, and those most adversely affected often have little or no input in its implementation. Indeed, much of the anti-globalization backlash hinges on the accusation that globalization permits **multinational corporations** (MNCs) to reap economic rewards at the expense of human rights. The media has spotlighted some of the notorious human rights violations associated with MNCs. The oil conglomerate Unocal, for example, was accused of involvement in forced labour, rape, and a murder allegedly carried out by soldiers along a natural gas pipeline route in Myanmar.[1] Shell and Chevron have also been accused of abusing

human rights in Nigeria. Wal-Mart suppliers in China and Honduras have been found in violation of numerous human rights. Furthermore, it was revealed that former talk-show host Kathie Lee Gifford's clothing line, sold by Wal-Mart stores, was produced by sweatshop workers in Honduras. Because of globalization's potential for harming human dignity, scholars must provide as transparent an understanding as possible of the consequences of the globalization process.

Economic Globalization and Government Respect for Human Rights: Two Opposing Views

The Optimistic View: Globalization and the Road to Development

Economic globalization can enter developing countries' economies in several ways. That is, MNCs and financial investors ensure their presence in economies worldwide through **foreign direct investment** (FDI) and portfolio investments. FDI consists of building plants in another country or acquiring a controlling interest (more than 10 per cent of outstanding stock) in an existing overseas company. Owing to the direct investment in buildings, machinery, and equipment, FDI is generally thought of as a long-term investment. **Portfolio investment** consists of the purchase of stocks and bonds of less than 10 per cent of the outstanding stock in foreign firms. Since portfolio investors have no controlling stake in the investment, these investments are of a much more fluid nature than FDI (see Kenen, 1994; Walther, 1997).

Countries that embrace globalization will raise their economic wealth, while countries that fail to join the movement will find themselves languishing in underdevelopment: studies have found a correlation between increased investment flows and a country's rate of economic growth and overall socio-economic welfare (see Box 13.1, Example A).

Many view MNC investment as the engine behind economic globalization. Developing countries that open their markets to FDI experience greater access to advanced technology, exposure to the most sophisticated management and marketing skills, stronger economic growth, and an expansion in the employment market. Moreover, MNC-generated jobs in developing countries tend to pay more than equivalent

---

BOX 13.1 EXAMPLES OF THE 'OPTIMISTIC VIEW'

(A) Access to global finance and export markets has enabled parts of China, such as the region of Zhejiang, to experience a boom in the expansion of many small and medium-sized enterprises, thereby raising the living standard for a large number of ordinary citizens (Eckholm, 2003). Since cutting barriers to trade and capital, India has begun to rival Chinese economic growth rates. India's economy surged by 9.2 per cent in 2006, and between 2002 and 2006 grew at a yearly rate of about 9 per cent (*The Economist*, 1 February 2007).

(B) British Petroleum has provided refrigerators in Zambia for the storage of anti-malaria vaccines and invested in computer technology in Vietnam for flood-related damage control, while Chevron has invested in Nigeria's water infrastructure to develop a more reliable water supply system for its citizens (Monshipouri, Welch, and Kennedy, 2003; Nwankwo, Phillips, and Tracey, 2007).

---

local employers (Harrison and Scorse, 2003; Bhagwati, 2004; Gray, Kittilson, and Sandholtz, 2006).

MNCs can also be seen as a driving force of change, diminishing the power of local elites, as well as altering traditional value systems and social attitudes in developing countries (Diebold, 1974; Biersteker, 1978). To attract and maintain MNC investment, governments may have to reshape traditional policies that benefit local interest groups at the expense of less affluent groups. Governments may be encouraged to establish and respect property rights, create a non-discriminatory hiring/employment environment, and invest in social services and infrastructure. Often, the MNCs export labour and hiring practices to their overseas operations that surpass local hiring requirements and worker safety conditions (Mears, 1995; Harrison and Scorse, 2003). Additionally, MNCs may exceed their corporate mandate and finance programmes supporting local infrastructure projects or invest in efforts to combat local social problems (see Box 13.1, Example B and Box 13.2). Consequently, MNCs can directly break down insular interests and stabilize internal relations in developing countries.

In addition to FDI, scholars point to portfolio investment as playing a critical role in promoting economic growth in LDCs. The liberalization of portfolio investment allows surplus assets (beyond the home market) to be funnelled to cash-impoverished borrowers in developing countries. A significant problem hindering economic growth in developing countries has been the lack of funds available to finance the expansion of domestic enterprises. Small and medium-sized enterprises, typically shut out of the financial market, are now presented with opportunities to finance expansion and technological improvements from international sources, thereby creating new local jobs and raising wages. Governments of developing countries are also less likely to carry out infrastructure projects. Instead, contracts are increasingly awarded to private companies that finance the infrastructure projects through international capital markets to garner a profit (Likosky, 2003). Proponents of this shift argue that infrastructure projects are completed more efficiently and at a lower cost to the taxpayer.

Another aspect of economic globalization is the liberalization of trade. The reduction and/or elimination of tariffs and non-tariff barriers have been a driving force behind globalization. Trade exposes domestic enterprises to international competition. To maintain high levels of national employment and income, local enterprises must be able to compete efficiently against foreign firms. With the decline of US trade dominance in the wake of globalization, many developing countries have marshalled their (limited) resources to create competitive advantage, thereby raising their citizens' standard of living. Frankel and Romer (1999) found that an increase of about one percentage point in the ratio of trade to *gross domestic product* (GDP) increases income by at least 0.5 per cent.

BOX 13.2 CHALLENGING ASSUMPTIONS: CORPORATE OBLIGATIONS

Consider the following common proposition: 'A corporation owes its highest obligation to its shareholders.' If this is the case, do corporations owe no obligation to non-shareholders? What about a corporation's non-share-owning workers? How does the fact that each human has the right to lead a life of dignity affect this logic of non-obligation, especially given how the size and power of corporations have changed since 1948?

For example, Morocco experienced a decline in the poverty rate from 26 per cent to 13 per cent of the population in just five years after trade was liberalized (Keller-Herzog, 1996).

A final aspect to consider is **structural adjustment policies** (SAPs). SAPs are lending policies of the IMF and the World Bank, designed to promote economic efficiency and growth in developing countries by minimizing the role of the state in the economy. Essentially, the IMF and World Bank provide loans to cash-strapped countries in exchange for the implementation of free market policies. These policies include slashing barriers to the flow of goods and capital, privatizing government enterprises, taming inflation, cutting government spending, and shrinking the government bureaucracy.

According to the pro-globalization school, economic growth owing to unfettered participation in the global trade and financial markets will translate into greater democracy and respect for human rights in LDCs. Specifically, as the economy grows and modernizes, the middle class will expand in size. The middle class generally represents a segment of society that will be more tolerant of others, challenge the status quo of the political elites, demand a greater voice in the political process for not only their own class, but also of those who are less fortunate, and progressively oppose political violence and repression (Lerner, 1958; Lipset, 1959; Nelson, 1987). The demand for government respect for political and human rights will grow and strengthen as long as the middle class continues to flourish. Thus, the globalization process generates economic growth that in turn creates a stable and tolerant political environment.

The Pessimistic View: Economic Globalization and the Race to the Bottom

The pessimistic, or anti-globalization model sees economic globalization as a threat to the well-being of developing countries. Critics of globalization assert that the implementation of neoliberal market ideology makes states less able or willing to carry out traditional societal tasks such as providing social safety nets and enforcing worker safety standards. That is, as a government decreases its role in the economy in order to promote global competitiveness and attract international investment, the state relinquishes its responsibilities for the provision of education, health, water,

and other social services to its citizens. Consequently, the economic globalization process exploits workers and citizens of developing countries.

MNCs, in contrast to the neoliberal view, are not seen as agents of beneficial change. Instead, they are seen as profit-seeking conglomerates that fail to consider the social welfare implications of their actions. MNCs extract more money from developing countries than they invest, displace local capital, and add to unemployment by promoting capital-intensive production rather than labour-intensive activities, and they use the threat of exit to extract other 'business-friendly' policies (see Burgoon, 2001; Burkhart, 2002; Frenkel and Kuruvilla, 2002; Arnold and Hartman, 2006). Hence, developing governments are progressively held captive to market principles if they wish to sustain high levels of MNC investment. The ensuing competitive environment created by the mobility of MNCs and financial firms encourages a *race to the bottom* between LDCs, in which different countries compete to lower tax, wage, labour, unionization, and social welfare standards.

Sceptics of economic globalization also argue that MNCs and foreign investment firms tend to invest in LDCs that exhibit political stability. Simply put, regime change increases the financial risk of these investors. Portfolio investment is particularly susceptible to internal political and economic shocks, thereby causing a swift and massive exit of financial capital. Domestic elites, often profiting from the prevailing economic situation, are usually willing to do what is necessary to maintain the political climate required to preserve foreign capital (Maxfield, 1998; McCorquodale and Fairbrother, 1999; Darrow and Tomas, 2005).

Critics of globalization also point out that the pay-offs from trade liberalization are not equally dispersed. Instead, the benefits of trade are skewed towards companies that can move swiftly and effortlessly across international borders. Thus, countries that embrace liberal trade policies are not guaranteed to experience greater economic growth (Rodrik, 1997; Aaronson and Zimmerman, 2006). Furthermore, workers for MNCs often find themselves working long hours in unsafe working conditions in order to minimize production costs (Rodriguez, 2004; Arnold and Hartman, 2006). Domestic firms that face intense international competition are often forced to cut jobs and lower work and safety standards to maintain their presence in the world economy. Those displaced from their jobs due to international competition are individuals with little education, who find it difficult to find a replacement job quickly (Moghadam, 1993; Cheng, 1999).

Finally, opponents of economic globalization see the imposition of SAPs by the IMF and the World Bank as detrimental to the economic and political development of LDCs. Some studies suggest that these policies fail to provide the promised economic conditions and can even impair economic growth (Przeworski and Vreeland, 2000; Vreeland, 2003). If economic growth declines, governments cut social programmes and eliminate public sector jobs due to an inability to raise necessary funds (see Box 13.3, Example A).

The result of maintaining a 'business-friendly' climate and the imposition of austerity policies on less developed countries has the effect of heightening societal tension. Governments must suppress threats to political and economic stability and move aggressively to suppress political opponents, union leaders, and other political activists who may challenge current policies. Similarly, opposing political party members, union members, and other political activists often respond to the imposition of SAPs with food riots, demonstrations, and violent protests. Ruling authorities respond by restricting citizens' political and civil liberties (Howard-Hassmann, 2005; see Box 13.3, Example B).

BOX 13.3 EXAMPLES OF THE 'PESSIMISTIC VIEW'

(A) Zimbabwe was forced to eliminate educational funding owing to an IMF-imposed structural adjustment policy (SAP) (McCorquodale and Fairbrother, 1999). For the first time since independence, tuition fees were charged for primary-level schooling and, while decentralizing education helped the government move towards meeting some SAP goals, it exacerbated the education gap between rich and poor (Kanyongo, 2005, p. 71).

(B) On 30 July 2006 over 100,000 individuals in Ordu, Turkey protested against the low prices of hazelnuts. Farmers were upset that the government refused to assist in the purchase of surplus hazelnuts from a bankrupt cooperative, thereby further depressing the price of the commodity. IMF austerity measures, imposed in 2003, required the Turkish government to suspend its policy of subsidizing hazelnut farmers by purchasing surplus supplies. Ensuing clashes with the police in Ordu resulted in about thirty-five arrests and fifty-one injuries. Interestingly, the chief of police was relieved of his position for being too lenient with the demonstrators (Akinci, 2006).

KEY POINTS

Financial and investment globalization enter developing countries primarily in two ways: foreign direct investment (FDI) and portfolio investments.

According to the pro-globalization school, economic growth owing to unfettered participation in the global trade and financial markets will translate into greater democracy and respect for human rights in LDCs.

Critics of globalization assert that the implementation of neoliberal market ideology makes states less able or willing to carry out traditional societal tasks such as providing social safety nets and enforcing worker safety standards.

Critical Thinking Questions:

How would the pro-globalization and anti-globalization viewpoints presented here be affected by the Great Recession of 2007–10?

How would the pro-globalization viewpoint respond to events in the Middle East since the Arab Spring uprisings that started in late 2010?

Globalization and Human Rights: Examining the Empirical Results

Scholars examine the relationship between globalization and human rights in several ways. **Quantitative studies** use statistical techniques to examine a number of countries together over a period of time in the search for generalizations that can be made from these countries' collective experiences. **Qualitative studies** tend to focus on an in-depth case analysis of a particular country or reference group such as women, or a particular ethnic group.[2] Qualitative studies have provided some of the most thoughtful theoretical critiques of globalization. (See Box 13.4 for a discussion of how both these traditions could be correct.)

The results of quantitative studies examining the relationship with economic globalization have been mixed, but lean towards implying that in many places and times economic globalization is associated with better respect for human rights. We will provide a short illustrative outline of this literature, incorporating findings from some major studies.

BOX 13.4 ALTERNATIVE POINTS OF VIEW

Earlier, we noted that the quantitative and qualitative research traditions have produced differing bodies of findings about the relationship between economic globalization and human rights, with the qualitative work being more pessimistic. It is worth entertaining the idea that both traditions could be correct. The common phrase 'exception to the rule' illustrates how this could be. While no true socio-political axioms exist, there indeed are regularities in socio-political behaviour that could be looked at as 'rules'. For example, in general, it is widely understood that citizens in democracies enjoy greater levels of government respect for their human rights than do people living under other types of regimes. The quantitative research method is very useful for identifying these types of regularities. However, for every rule there are exceptions—especially with regards to socio-political behaviour, since human behaviour is changeable. When it comes to respect for human rights, leaders do not always act consistently with the expectations of the regime type within which they operate.

With respect to economic globalization and human rights, it could indeed be true that investment money generally flows to more rights-respectful countries, while at the same time also being the case that in some times and places this investment goes to abusive states, for the very reason that their governments are abusive. It is important to understand both dynamics. In this case, the general rule may point towards institutional arrangements that increase the probability of respect for human rights in the face of foreign investment. The exception, on the other hand, may point towards shortcomings in the ability of such institutional arrangements to meet the challenges of certain situations.

Meyer (1996) found US-based FDI to be associated with better respect for human rights in recipient countries. However, Smith, Bolyard, and Ippolito (1999), using alternative globalization and human rights indicators, failed to replicate Meyer's findings. This is one peril of quantitative studies—that findings may be an artefact of the way the study is conducted. Other research supports Meyer's findings, however. There is evidence that trade liberalization, a mainstay of the globalization process, leads to greater government respect for human rights. For example, it has been found that governments of countries that traded more were less likely to violate a category of internationally recognized human rights known as **physical integrity rights** (summary execution, torture, disappearance, and political imprisonment) (Apodaca, 2001), and

that trade liberalization is associated with lower infant mortality rates in developing countries (Apodaca, 2002). A number of studies have also shown that trade liberalization is associated with greater *women's status*, defined as the extent to which women are able, both in an absolute and relative sense, to exercise precise rights codified in a large body of international human rights law and to enjoy the objectives of those rights (Richards and Gelleny, 2007). Trade liberalization has also been associated with improving female life expectancy and literacy rates (Gray, Kittilson, and Sandholtz, 2006).

The effect of FDI on government respect for human rights also seems to be generally helpful, judging from the quantitative literature on this relationship. Increases in MNC investment have been found to be reliably related to greater political rights and civil liberties, including the freedom from censorship and freedom of religion, political participation, travel, and unionization (Meyer, 1996, 1998; Richards, Gelleny, and Sacko, 2001). Apodaca (2001, 2002) found evidence that FDI improved government respect for physical integrity rights and reduced infant mortality rates in developing countries. That said, Tuman and Emmert (2004) found FDI to flow to Latin American and Caribbean countries with poorer human rights records. Results are also mixed in the area of women's status. While Richards and Gelleny (2007) found FDI to be generally related to higher scores on both the United Nations' Gender Empowerment Measure and Gender-Related Development Index, Gray, Kittilson, and Sandholtz (2006) found FDI to have a corrosive influence on female life expectancy and literacy.

The findings regarding the influence of portfolio investment on government respect for human rights have been less conclusive. Several studies have shown that developing countries that opened their markets to this type of investment have experienced greater respect for physical integrity rights and lower infant mortality rates (Richards, Gelleny, and Sacko, 2001; Apodaca, 2002). However, other findings suggest that portfolio investment has a corrosive influence on women's status (Richards and Gelleny, 2007). SAPs have not been shown to have a helpful influence on government respect for human rights. Abouharb and Cingranelli (2006) refute the neoliberal assertion that SAPs should improve economic performance, thereby creating better human rights practices. Instead, they find that World Bank adjustment policies have the effect of worsening government respect for physical integrity rights.

While physical integrity rights and women's rights are probably the most studied categories of rights in the quantitative globalization literature, there are studies of other types of rights and human rights environments. Burgoon (2001) found mixed results when examining the results of trade openness on welfare policies. Colonomos and Santiso (2005) found globalization carved an issue space in France, allowing for the adoption of human rights-based corporate social responsibility codes. Contrary to the race to the bottom logic, Kucera (2001) found that foreign investors favoured countries with higher labour standards rather than lower standards.

KEY POINTS

Scholars examine the relationship between globalization and human rights in several ways.

Quantitative studies use statistical techniques to examine a number of countries together over a period of time in the search for generalizations that can be made from these countries' collective experiences.

Qualitative studies tend to focus on an in-depth case analysis of a particular country or reference group such as women, or a particular ethnic group. Qualitative studies have provided some of the most thoughtful theoretical critiques of globalization.

The results of quantitative studies examining the relationship with economic globalization have been mixed, but lean towards implying that in many places and times economic globalization is associated with better respect for human rights.

Critical Thinking Questions:

Are some types of research questions always more appropriate for either a qualitative or a quantitative research design?

Why might it be that qualitative studies tend to be more critical of globalization than quantitative studies?

Case Study: Do MNCs Invest in Human Rights?

Traditionally, respect for human rights has not been considered a responsibility of multinational corporations. Instead, human rights have been considered

a domestic government issue (Skogly, 1993; Kinley and Joseph, 2002). In recent years, however, there has been an upsurge in the judgement that MNCs should also be held accountable for human rights violations. Clearly, MNCs are powerful international entities, and corporate decisions have a vast impact that stretches far beyond the boardroom. Yahoo! executives found themselves under scrutiny after handing over data to Chinese authorities that led to the arrest of two dissidents. In November 2007, Yahoo!'s chief executive and chief lawyer were denounced by US Congressman Tom Lantos as 'technology giants but moral pygmies' (*The Economist*, 17 January 2008). Such instances, combined with the growth in the number of MNCs that have created codes of corporate social responsibility, hint strongly that investing in countries that violate human rights is becoming an important matter for MNC executives. This raises the following question: are MNCs more likely to make future investments in countries where governments respect human rights than in countries that abuse them?

Human Rights Determinants of FDI

As we will see, MNCs and other international investors have varying incentives or disincentives to consider human rights when making investment decisions. We will survey these factors and conduct a statistical analysis to ascertain which factors are generally stronger.

Property Rights

Any MNC investment is a risk, since firms can never be certain of the eventual success of the project owing to both political and economic factors. However, property rights appear to be one of the most important factors in attracting FDI. Guaranteeing political and civil rights, such as independent judiciaries and a democratically functioning electoral system, further strengthens property rights.[3] Consequently, MNCs that invest where regimes respect the rule of law hope to find their investments protected from nationalization by predatory dictators.

Mozambique provides an example of an LDC reaping positive economic benefits as a consequence of establishing a political environment that is more respectful of human rights. Mozambique was plagued by internal strife for much of the 1980s and 1990s. Yet, by the mid-1990s, with the help of the United Nations,

Mozambique had held successful elections and largely ended its abuse of physical integrity rights. The result was a growing economy spurred forwards by an influx of foreign investment. About 6 billion dollars' worth of foreign investment was committed to Mozambique in projects ranging from mining to farming and tourism—twice the amount invested in the rest of sub-Saharan Africa (excluding South Africa; *The Economist*, 15 May 1997).

Zimbabwe provides an example where a government's lack of respect for political and civil rights hinders foreign investment. Compared to other African countries, Zimbabwe had experienced strong levels of FDI, education, and economic growth into the 1990s. However, the imposition of a messy political land reform policy, combined with increased political violence, chaotic economic policies, and soaring inflation rates, reduced foreign investment flows to a trickle. The passage of Zimbabwe's September 2007 Indigenisation and Empowerment Bill, giving the state a controlling interest in foreign-owned businesses (including banks and mines), only added to an already hostile investment environment. Business leaders warned that the legislation would prompt a further 30 per cent decline in foreign investment (*Financial Times*, 12 November 2007).

Concerns about stability may cause MNC disinvestment even for those companies whose foreign footprint is constrained by geology. Industrial firms, such as mining companies, must generally locate near sites where their raw materials exist. In 2001, Lukas Lundin of Lundin Petroleum AB noted, 'We go where the big resources are', and when asked about investing in war-torn Sudan (where Lundin has a history of investment) he added, 'There's 250 million barrels there' (Hasselback, 2001, C08). A year later, Ian Lundin, President of Lundin Petroleum, announced that his company was suspending operations in Sudan 'until there is a "sustainable" period of peace', and that 'We need some type of sustainable and peaceful environment for us to look at long-term investment.'[4] It is instructive to note, however, that as Sudan's conflict morphed into **genocide** (see Chapter 20), Lundin Petroleum was again operating in Sudan, earning a place on the Sudan Divestment Task Force's 'Highest Offenders' list of companies found to be 'unresponsive to engagement by shareholders or unwilling to alter problematic practices in Sudan' (Sudan Divestment Task Force, 2007, p. 7).

Labour Policies

Before expanding production facilities to LDCs, MNCs evaluate labour and wage policies. Policies of concern include the right of workers to organize, safety standards, social welfare policies, and wage rates. Firms that produce goods that do not require skilled labour or intense investments of capital are often attracted to countries that have a large number of low-waged, non-unionized labourers. Additionally, MNCs seek to increase profits by locating in countries where taxes, such as employer social security and unemployment contributions, are relatively low. Furthermore, as competition among countries increases for FDI, countries compete with each other to provide MNCs with a 'business-friendly' environment regarding the above policies.

Reputation

Companies may seek to improve their reputations by associating their product with improving human rights (Spar, 1998; Colonomos and Santiso, 2005). Otherwise, MNCs may run the risk of being exposed to an embarrassing media campaign highlighting their connections to regimes with human rights abuses. For example, in 2007 the British engine producer Rolls-Royce announced that it planned to withdraw from Sudan. The company cited its concerns about the worsening humanitarian condition in Darfur as the principal reason that it had chosen to leave (*Financial Times*, 19 April 2007).

One study of Fortune 500 companies showed that '36 percent of respondents "decided not to proceed with a proposed investment project because of concerns over human rights abuses" while 19 percent "have disinvested from a particular country because of human rights concerns"' (Cowell, 2000, C4). The same study found that 44 per cent of companies that have written codes of ethics mention human rights in those codes.[5] Major companies employing such codes include Shell, Reebok, and Levi Strauss.

Nevertheless, others maintain the traditional view that corporate policies based on human rights concerns, including image campaigns, are wrong-headed and dangerous; corporations should not be in the business of ethics, and should only be concerned with generating profits for their shareholders. Milton Friedman (1962, p. 133) aptly summed up this view by stating, 'there is one and only one social responsibility of business—to use its resources and engage in activities designed to increase its profits'.

Multinational corporations consider a number of other factors when deciding whether to invest capital overseas. We will outline these additional factors.

Market Conditions

Corporations are likely to invest in countries that have large populations and stable and growing economies, where sales potential is greater (E. Crenshaw, 1991; Asiedu, 2002; Bandelj, 2002; Tuman and Emmert, 2004). China, for example, has a large and growing market in which many MNCs are eager to establish a presence. India is another large market where MNCs have sought to increase their market share. Seeking to expand economic growth, Indian politicians reversed their long-standing opposition to foreign investment in the 1990s. Consequently, MNCs have reacted to these new policies enthusiastically and have significantly increased FDI investment in India.

Inflation rates have also been used as an indicator of LDC domestic macro-economic stability. High inflation is a disincentive for MNCs to invest in LDCs because it makes it difficult for multinational firms to accurately evaluate production costs and profits, thereby increasing the risk of foreign investment projects.

Tariff and Capital Barriers

Government economic policies directly targeted at attracting multinational foreign investment—including lower capital barriers, financial subsidies, and tariff rates—must also be considered by MNCs (Edwards, 1990; Gastanaga and Nugent, 1998; Asiedu, 2002). Governments may entice companies to relocate production facilities by implementing high tariff rates. Companies may find it cheaper to relocate to foreign markets to avoid the cost imposed on their products by high tariff rates. However, firms are more likely to search for regions to which they can profitably shift their subsidiary labour-intensive assembly and then export finished products back to the parent firm. Therefore, MNC subsidiaries must be able to import inputs and capital goods from the home market of the parent firm with a minimum of costs. As such, MNCs often prefer to invest where trade barriers are negligible and few restrictions limit the flow of capital. Consequently, the majority of FDI and other investment flows are likely to be a function of openness to foreign capital (Gilpin, 2001; Asiedu, 2002; Tuman and

Emmert, 2004). Decreased market regulation also provides MNCs with access to a variety of capital opportunities, and perhaps greater advantage over local domestic competition.

Political Risk and Stability

All investors are concerned with political risk, and may consider withdrawing their assets to less risky countries. Indeed, MNC executives report that political instability is one of the most critical factors influencing foreign investment assessments (Bandelj, 2002). Governments that are experiencing internal or external conflict may be more likely to implement repressive business policies than politically stable countries. In order to appease political allies or raise required resources quickly, fearful governments may implement policies that include restricting the movement of goods and capital, increasing corporate taxes, and the forced sale or seizure of foreign enterprises. Furthermore, constant civil strife increases the probability of government change, thereby heightening MNC anxiety regarding the stability of business policies. The possibility of continual regime instability increases the risk of changing business regulations, thus increasing the uncertainty of production costs and profits. Therefore, countries with stable regimes and respect for the rule of law are rewarded by increased flows of foreign investment.

Although we expect countries experiencing high amounts of internal and external conflict to attract lower amounts of FDI, studies have revealed mixed results regarding the relationship between political stability and FDI. Indeed, empirical research has reported findings about political stability and FDI ranging from no effect to both helpful and harmful effects (Asiedu, 2002; Bandelj, 2002).

Market Infrastructure and Skill Level

Others argue that foreign investors are attracted to countries that comprise a reasonably well-educated workforce and modern infrastructure (Gelleny and McCoy, 2001; Tuman and Emmert, 2004). That is, the combination of low wages and an educated workforce is a very attractive feature to a foreign investor. Furthermore, LDCs that are modernizing in the transport and communication sectors provide an environment that is appealing to multinational corporations. An educated workforce and a growing modern infrastructure are expected to increase productivity and profitability.

Protection of property rights through rule of law appears to be one of the most important factors in attracting FDI. MNCs that invest in regimes that respect property rights find their investment protected from nationalization by predatory dictators.

Multinational corporations seek to increase profits by locating in countries where taxes, such as employer social security and unemployment contributions, are relatively low, as are wages. Furthermore, as competition among countries increases for FDI, countries compete with each other to provide MNCs with a 'business-friendly' environment regarding these policies.

Companies may seek to improve their reputation by associating their product with improving human rights; otherwise, MNCs may run the risk of being exposed to an embarrassing media campaign highlighting their connections to regimes with human rights abuses.

Multinational corporations often prefer business environments with negligible trade barriers and few restrictions managing the flow of capital.

All investors are concerned with political risk, and may consider withdrawing their assets from more risky countries in favour of countries that are perceived to be stable, as regime instability increases the risk of changing business regulations, thus increasing the uncertainty of production costs and profits.

Some argue that foreign investors are attracted to countries that comprise a reasonably well-educated workforce and modern infrastructure. An educated workforce and a growing modern infrastructure are expected to increase productivity and profitability.

Critical Thinking Questions:

Should the two goals collide, would most corporations choose reputation or profit?

How does your answer to the previous question affect what behaviour one would expect to see from corporations with regard to their effect on government respect for human rights?

Data and Research Design

Sample

Our study examines LDCs for the years 1981 to 1999. We begin our study in 1981 as we believe that, because of source bias in human rights reports, information

about government respect for human rights is not reliable before this date. Our sample of LDCs encompasses all developing regions of the world, including Africa, Asia, the Caribbean, Eastern Europe, and Latin America. Since economic and political data for many LDCs are not systematically recorded, there are fewer cases than would be ideal because of missing data.

Model and Estimation Technique

Our general model of the relationship between foreign direct investment and government respect for human rights is illustrated in Table 13.1. The plus and minus signs indicate our hypotheses about the relationship between each of the independent variables (those to the right of the equal sign) in the model and our **dependent variable** (FDI).[6] A plus sign indicates that we expect a *positive* relationship: as the **independent variable** increases, FDI is expected to increase. A minus sign indicates that we expect a *negative* relationship: as the independent variable increases, FDI is expected to decrease. Where there is a '+/–', we are unsure what to expect.

Although in this section of the chapter we are chiefly interested in the effect that government respect for human rights has on FDI inflows, it has been shown (e.g. Meyer, 1998; Richards, Gelleny, and Sacko, 2001; Richards and Gelleny, 2002) that foreign economic investment can influence government respect for human rights. Thus our model must account for any influence that FDI may have on government respect for human rights, while at the same time investigating the effect of government respect for human rights on FDI. To accomplish this task we estimate two models simultaneously, thereby allowing us to test for reciprocal effects (i.e. where human rights and FDI influence one another at the same time). The bracketed variables in Table 13.1 show a second model, contained within our general model, that examines the relationship between FDI and government respect for human rights. This 'nested' model, where respect for human rights is the dependent variable and the variables in the brackets are the independent variables, is estimated simultaneously with the general model.

Dependent Variable

Foreign Direct Investment

While we discussed many ways in which the global economy can enter an LDC, for the purposes of this

Table 13.1 General model for statistical analyses

Foreign direct investment =	+/– Constant
	+/– Level of respect for human rights
	[= Foreign direct investment
	– Domestic conflict
	– Inter-state conflict
	+ Regime type
	+ Level of economic development
	– Population size]
	– Domestic conflict
	– Inter-state conflict
	– Capital controls
	+ Market wealth
	+ Trade openness
	+ Urbanization
	+ Infrastructure
	+ Literacy
	– Inflation

illustrative chapter we focus on one: foreign direct investment (FDI). Specifically, our dependent variable is a measure of FDI as a percentage of a country's GDP, which is the total amount of services and goods produced in a country in a given year. This measure of FDI is regularly used in globalization studies (Asiedu, 2002; Bandelj, 2002; Alderson, 2004; Truman and Emmert, 2004) and was drawn from the World Bank's *World Development Indicators on CD-ROM* (2005).

Independent Variables

We use a number of independent variables to help explain a country's level of FDI. We will list and explain these variables.

Government Respect for Human Rights

To measure the level of government respect for human rights, we use two indices from the CIRI Human Rights Dataset (Cingranelli and Richards, 2010).[7] These two indices represent the levels of government respect for physical integrity rights and **empowerment rights**, respectively, in a given year. Physical integrity rights include the rights to freedom

from torture, disappearance, extrajudicial killing, and political imprisonment. The CIRI physical integrity rights index is a nine-point scale ranging from zero (*no respect* for any of the four physical integrity rights) to eight (*full respect* for all four physical integrity rights). The CIRI empowerment rights index used is an eleven-point scale constructed from five indicators of government respect for political rights and civil liberties: open and free political participation, workers' rights, freedom of domestic travel, freedom of religion, and free media. This measure ranges from zero (*no respect* for any of these five empowerment rights) to ten (*full respect* for all five of these rights).

Trade and Capital Restrictions

Government policies regarding both trade and capital (investment) play an important role in a country's ability to attract and maintain foreign investment. Regarding trade policies, multinational corporations that engage in export-oriented ventures will prefer to invest in open (less regulated) economies. To measure policies relating to trade, we use what has become a standard measure of trade openness: the ratio of a country's trade exports and imports to its GDP. We obtained these data from the World Bank's *World Development Indicators on CD-ROM* (2005).

A country can similarly be described as open or closed, based on its capital control policies. We expect to see a negative relationship between the institution of capital controls and foreign investment in LDCs. In the early 1990s, countries became more open to foreign investment by attempting to attract foreign firms to invest directly in their markets (Spero and Hart, 1997; Gilpin, 2001; Cohn, 2003). To measure capital restrictions we use a variable from the International Monetary Fund's annual reports on exchange arrangements and exchange controls (IMF, various years). The variable is an index of state restrictions on foreign exchange and both current and capital accounts, ranging from zero to four and indicating which (if any) of the following existed in a given country and year: multiple exchange rates, current account restrictions, capital account restrictions, and export proceeds surrender requirements.[8] For example, a score of zero indicates no capital restrictions and a score of four indicates complete capital restrictions.

Domestic Economic Conditions

A country's macro-economic condition also needs to be considered when one is examining FDI. Thus, we include three measures accounting for LDC economic growth and market stability. First, we include GDP per capita (we use its logarithmic value to reduce the possibility that extreme values will interfere with the analysis) to measure a country's level of economic development or its market wealth. Some assert that foreign investors are attracted to growing and dynamic regions (E. Crenshaw, 1991; Bandelj, 2002; Cohn, 2003). To measure potential market size we turn to a country's degree of urbanization—the share of the total population living in areas defined as urban. Finally, we also include a country's inflation rate as a measure of its macro-economic stability. All three variables were obtained from the World Bank's *World Development Indicators on CD-ROM* (2005).

Political Risk and Stability

Our indicators of domestic and inter-state conflict are ordinal variables from version three of the PRIO Armed Conflict Dataset (Gleditsch et al., 2002). The domestic conflict measure indicates the highest level of conflict between a state and organized groups in that country in a given year. It ranges from 0 (no

conflict) to 3 (internal war). The inter-state conflict measure indicates the highest level of conflict in a given year between two or more states, and ranges from 0 (no conflict) to 3 (inter-state war).

Infrastructure and Skill Levels

Multinational companies are more likely to invest in LDCs that have skilled workers and a modernizing infrastructure. To measure the state of a country's infrastructure, we include in our models an indicator that is the number of telephones per thousand people in a country. Although this measure only considers one aspect of a country's infrastructure, it does have the advantage of being available for most LDCs (Asiedu, 2002). To measure the skill of a country's domestic labour force we turn to adult literacy rates. This indicator represents the percentage of people aged 15 and above who can, with understanding, read and write a simple account of their everyday life. Both variables were obtained from the World Bank's *World Development Indicators on CD-ROM* (2005).

KEY POINTS

Our study examines LDCs for the years 1981 to 1999. Our sample of LDCs encompasses all developing regions including Africa, Asia, the Caribbean, Eastern Europe, and Latin America.

Our dependent variable is a measure of FDI as a percentage of gross domestic product (GDP), which is the total amount of services and goods produced in a country in a given year.

We use a number of independent variables to help explain a country's level of FDI: government respect for human rights, domestic economic conditions, political risk and stability, infrastructure, and skill levels.

Critical Thinking Questions:

Are there other independent variables the authors might have done well to include in their models?

Why is FDI as a percentage of a country's GDP used in the author's model, instead of simply the total amount of FDI in a country?

Findings

To *estimate* (test) our models statistically, examining the relationship between government respect for two types of human rights and FDI, we used a statistical technique that allows us to account for the possibility that respect for human rights may be affecting FDI at the same time that FDI may be affecting respect for human rights. It also allows us to produce results that are not biased by the way we assembled our data (we did so in what is known as a 'pooled' form, where a single spreadsheet contains many years' worth of data for a large number of different countries).

Table 13.2 shows the result of models examining the relationship between government respect for physical integrity rights and FDI (Model 1), and for empowerment rights and FDI (Model 2). At the bottom of Table 13.2, 'N' stands for the number of cases of data that are used to estimate (test) each model. Each individual case, called a country-year, represents a single country in a single year (e.g. France in 1997 or Brazil in 1993). The more cases we have, the more we know about the world, so the more we can trust our results. The F-test values of 0.00 for both models in Table 13.2 tell us that we can predict FDI

levels with significantly better accuracy knowing a country's score on these independent variables than we could if we did not know that information (see Table 13.2).

One basic purpose of estimating these models is to discover whether each of these independent variables is reliably or unreliably associated with a country's FDI (expressed as a percentage of GDP). By 'reliable', we mean that we are confident to some degree that the relationship between an independent variable and FDI is not likely to have merely occurred due to chance, or luck. The '$P < 0.10$' at the bottom of Table 13.2 says that we need to be 90 per cent sure that a relationship is not merely due to chance to report it as being 'reliable'. We label any independent variable that we cannot be 90 per cent sure of as 'unreliable'. Note the letters P, p, N, and n at the bottom of Table 13.2. We use these to note whether a particular independent variable is reliably or unreliably associated with a country's FDI, and what direction—positive or negative—that relationship takes.[9]

Table 13.2 Results from two models of the relationship between foreign direct investment and government respect for human rights

	Model 1	Model 2
Lagged FDI (t—1)	P	P
Physical integrity rights	P	–
Empowerment rights	–	P
Domestic conflict	P	p
Inter-state conflict	P	p
Capital controls	N	N
Market wealth	N	P
Trade openness	p	P
Urbanization	n	p
Infrastructure	P	P
Literacy	P	P
Inflation	N	N
Constant	N	N
N	1204	1205
F-test	0.00	0.00
$P < 0.10$		

P = Statistically reliable positive relationship. p = Statistically unreliable positive relationship. N = Statistically reliable negative relationship. n = Statistically unreliable negative relationship.

For example, an independent variable receiving a P means that that particular variable has a relationship with FDI such that higher levels of that variable are associated with higher levels of FDI, and we can be at least 90 per cent sure that that association is not due to chance alone.

Model 1: Physical Integrity Rights

Model 1 in Table 13.2 shows that a government's level of respect for physical integrity rights is reliably and positively associated with a country's FDI intake. Because of the statistical technique we used, this is true, even controlling for any influence that FDI may simultaneously have on respect for human rights. At the very least, this tells us that those countries with better respect for physical integrity rights receive more FDI than do those countries with less respect for these rights. Further, we might expect FDI to increase in countries with greater respect for human rights. Were we to look at the actual numeric coefficients from the statistical analysis, they would show that, for each one-unit increase in government respect for physical integrity rights on the CIRI scale, we can expect a corresponding increase of about 1 per cent in FDI (as a percentage of a country's GDP).

Model 1 tells some other stories too. First, FDI has a positive relationship with domestic conflict. That may be the result of either (or both) of two stories. On the one hand, FDI may be going to places with respectable levels of domestic conflict. For example, Senegal simultaneously experienced greater FDI investment alongside domestic conflict in the late 1990s. On the other hand, countries such as Jamaica—which in the early to mid-1980s lost FDI despite having no significant domestic conflict—might also produce a positive relationship. Finally, as we expected, Model 1 shows that better infrastructure and greater literacy levels attract FDI, while more capital controls and higher inflation levels tend to reduce FDI. Also, as expected, past levels of FDI are strongly predictive of current levels.

Statistical analysis allows us to go beyond assessing merely whether the relationship between two variables is reliable. We can also determine the strength of these relationships. Figure 13.1 shows the relative strengths of the reliable relationships shown in Model 1 in Table 13.2. The higher the bar is above the 0.00 horizontal line, the greater the return (in terms of FDI investment) on increases in a particular variable. To the extent that a bar drops below the 0.00 line, higher levels of that variable are associated with losses in FDI (a negative relationship). We see that only a country's

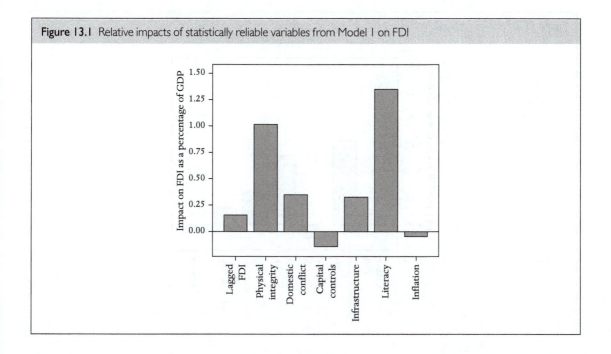

Figure 13.1 Relative impacts of statistically reliable variables from Model 1 on FDI

literacy rate has a greater impact on FDI than does government respect for physical integrity rights. A one-standard-deviation increase in respect for physical integrity rights leads to a one-standard-deviation increase in FDI as a percentage of GDP. The greatest negative impact is that of capital controls.

Model 2: Empowerment Rights

Model 2 in Table 13.2 examines the relationship between government respect for empowerment rights and FDI. We see that a government's level of respect for empowerment rights is a statistically significant predictor of the level of FDI for that country. Again, this is true, even controlling for any influence that FDI may simultaneously have on respect for human rights. As we saw with physical integrity rights, this tells us that those countries with better respect for empowerment rights receive more FDI than do countries with less respect for these rights. Further, we might well expect FDI to increase in countries with increased respect for human rights. The actual numeric coefficient from the statistical analysis would tell us that for each one-unit increase in government respect for empowerment rights on the CIRI scale, there is a corresponding increase of about 0.63 per cent in FDI (as a percentage of GDP).

However, Model 2 shows several things that are in contrast to the results from Model 1. First, there is no reliable relationship between either type of conflict and FDI. Second, market wealth and trade openness are found to be reliably associated with increased FDI. Finally, literacy was not found to be reliably associated with FDI in Model 2.

There were several factors (aside from the significance of the human rights variables) that proved to be consistent across Models 1 and 2. Capital controls and inflation were both reliably associated with decreases in FDI. Also, neither urbanization nor inter-state conflict was found in either model to be a reliable associate of FDI. Finally, past levels of FDI were strong predictors of current levels.

Figure 13.2 can be read in exactly the same manner as Figure 13.1, and shows the relative strengths of the statistically reliable coefficients on FDI. Unlike in Figure 13.1, we see that government respect for human rights (empowerment rights here) has the greatest impact on FDI. A one-standard-deviation increase in respect for empowerment rights leads to a 0.80-standard-deviation increase in FDI as a percentage of GDP. Only market wealth comes close to matching this impact. As in Figure 13.1, the greatest negative impact on FDI comes from capital controls.

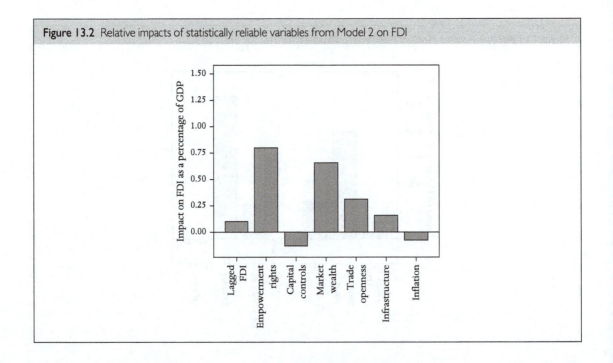

Figure 13.2 Relative impacts of statistically reliable variables from Model 2 on FDI

KEY POINTS

A government's level of respect for physical integrity rights is reliably and positively associated with a country's FDI intake. Further, FDI seemingly continues to go to places with respectable levels of domestic conflict.

A government's level of respect for empowerment rights is a statistically significant and positive predictor of the level of FDI for that country. However, there is no reliable relationship between either type of conflict and FDI regarding respect for empowerment rights.

Critical Thinking Questions

Why might levels of FDI be higher both in places where physical integrity violations are low and in places where domestic conflict is high?

Human rights are theorized as being interdependent. Looking at the physical integrity and empowerment results together, what can we learn about the interdependence of these two types of rights?

Conclusion

This case study has yielded some interesting findings relating to the relationship between government respect for human rights and foreign direct investment. First, we found that countries with greater levels of respect for the rights to freedom from torture, disappearance, extrajudicial killings, and political imprisonment seem better able to attract capital from foreign sources. A couple of things may account for this finding. Any foreign investment poses a considerable risk for private investors and companies doing business in countries where human rights are grievously abused, as they themselves may ultimately be exposed to charges of putting profits ahead of human dignity. For example, human rights groups may launch prominent media campaigns designed to damage the reputation of brand-name products. Continued abuse of physical integrity rights can heighten citizen resentment and can result in domestic conflict—possibly damaging or capturing private foreign-owned property and/or destabilizing an economy. Investors are often hesitant to expose their capital in such an environment, unless the potential pay-off is considerable.

Second, we found respect for empowerment rights to be strongly associated with greater levels of FDI. Countries where government respect exists for open political participation, an open media, the right to form unions, religious freedom, and the freedom to travel experience higher levels of FDI. Or, MNCs appear willing to invest in countries where political and civil rights are better respected. Countries with such an environment are more likely to follow the rule of law, thereby establishing a stable business environment for MNCs by reducing the risk of costly policy changes.

Together, these findings imply that governments that respect their citizens' physical integrity and empowerment rights will be better able to attract foreign economic capital. Thus such governments should be better placed to compete for and attract much-needed foreign investment. This is significant, as FDI is generally thought to be of critical importance for LDC economic development. Foreign investment not only provides new jobs, but it also introduces new technology and managerial skills that can be applied to other sectors of the host economy. Consequently, a growing economy can provide a government with additional economic resources that can be used to implement policies that enhance and maintain an attractive environment for FDI. Additional resources can be used to improve education and infrastructure, thereby increasing the probability of solidifying economic and political stability. At the very least, should a country not choose to make further human rights and infrastructure improvements in light of FDI-driven economic growth, it can no longer claim poverty as a reason, and the **naming and shaming** of the international human rights regime can begin to exert pressure for reform.

?   QUESTIONS

Individual Study Questions

1.   Describe two ways in which women, as a group, may be affected by economic globalization.

2.   What is the consensus finding from the quantitative literature investigating economic globalization's effect on respect for human rights? What questions about economic globalization and human rights remain that can be addressed by quantitative study?

3.   This chapter examines respect for physical integrity rights and empowerment rights in the light of economic globalization. How might other types of rights, such as economic, social, and cultural rights, be affected?

4.   What are the advantages and/or disadvantages of choosing to study the relationship between economic globalization and human rights using quantitative methods as opposed to qualitative methods?

5.   How connected to the global economy does a country's own economy have to be in order to be considered 'globalized'?

6.   Should one expect foreign investment originating in a developing country to affect human rights in a different way than would investment from a developed country?

7.   As developing countries become more industrialized and more integrated into the world economy, should we expect the relationship between FDI and human rights to change or stay the same? Why?

Group Discussion Questions

1.   Divide your group or class into two, with one representing the 'optimistic' view of globalization and the other representing the 'pessimistic' view of globalization. Choose a group or class member or the instructor as moderator and take turns arguing your side's take on how economic globalization will affect respect for human rights. Have the moderator choose as winner the group who makes their case most effectively.

2.   The timeframe of this study ends in 1999. Would significant world events since then change the findings if the study was updated through to 2016?

3.   Can the 'race to the bottom' hit bottom? That is, can wages and other labour standards become so low, worldwide, that there is nowhere cheaper for MNCs to relocate? If so, what will happen to economic globalization? Divide your group or class into two, representing the 'optimistic' and 'pessimistic' views and answer from those perspectives.

4.   Divide your group or class into two, with one representing the quantitative research tradition and one representing the qualitative research tradition. In these groups, have members discuss the strengths and weaknesses of their approach relating to studying government respect for human rights. Then have the class assemble as a whole and discuss as a group whether and/or how one might integrate aspects of both these research traditions in order to improve human rights research.

≋   FURTHER READING

Abouharb, M. R. and **Cingranelli, D. L.** (2008). *Human Rights and Structural Adjustment*. New York: Cambridge University Press.

A thorough empirical investigation of how structural adjustment policies have affected a variety of human rights.

Bennett, J. (2008). *Where Underpants Come From*. New York: Simon & Schuster.

By travelling to the sources of the story, the author uncovers some of the global economy's inner workings in his quest to trace the origins and path to market of a pack of 'Made in China' underwear he found available for inexpensive purchase at his local retailer.

Blanding, M. (2010). *The Coke Machine: The Dirty Truth Behind the World's Favorite Soft Drink*. New York: Avery.

This book contains stories from around the world about how the Coca-Cola company has affected a broad range of human rights, including economic rights, empowerment rights, and physical integrity rights.

Friedman, T. L. (2004). *The Lexus and the Olive Tree*. New York: Random House.

New York Times columnist (and proponent of globalization) Thomas L. Friedman examines globalization as a framework in which to understand the post-Cold War world in essays examining the reach and types of globalization, and how globalization affects tensions between the modern and the traditional elements both in and across societies around the world.

Lechner, F. J. and **Boli, J.** (eds) (2004). *The Globalization Reader*. Malden, MA: Blackwell.

This book provides a wide variety of contrasting points of view on what globalization is and how it affects societies.

Richards, D. L. and **Carbonetti, B.** (2012). Worth what we decide: A defense of the right to leisure. *The International Journal of Human Rights*, **17**/3, 329–49.

A historical analysis and defence of the right to leisure (UDHR Article 24) as a workers' right. While economic rights are not analysed in this chapter, it is crucial to understand how globalization might affect economic rights such workers' rights.

Stiglitz, J. (2002). *Globalization and its Discontents*. New York: W. W. Norton & Company.

Nobel Prize-winning economist Joseph Stiglitz examines how the policies of large intergovernmental economic institutions such as the IMF and the World Bank affect individual countries' economies and the global economy, and what the societal effects are of these policies.

Wallerstein, I. (2006). *World-Systems Analysis*. Durham, NC: Duke University Press.

This is an introduction to world-systems analysis, which provides a theoretical challenge to the neoliberal goal of the 'endless accumulation of capital'.

Yergin, D. and **Stanislaw, J.** (2002). *The Commanding Heights: The Battle for the World Economy*. New York: Touchstone.

This book examines the modern global economy's early twentieth-century roots, and weaves a story tracing the world economy's growth through the recent era of globalization.

WEB LINKS

http://www.humanrightsdata.com   The *Cingranelli–Richards (CIRI) Human Rights Data Project* provides standards-based quantitative information on government respect for a large number of internationally recognized human rights for 202 countries, from 1981 to 2011.

http://www.ohchr.org/Documents/Publications/GuidingPrinciplesBusinessHR_EN.pdf   The United Nations' *Guiding Principles on Business and Human Rights* outlines guidance on, among other things, the responsibility of corporations to respect human rights.

http://www.hrw.org/category/topic/business   Human Rights Watch's 'Business' website offers in-depth reports and news updates about how the global economy affects respect for human rights.

http://www.ohchr.org/EN/Issues/Business/Pages/BusinessIndex.aspx   The *Office of the United Nations High Commissioner for Human Rights* website, 'Business and Human Rights', offers information, original documents, and learning tools about how multinational companies interface with states regarding human rights.

NOTES

1.   In 2005 the company settled a lawsuit based on these charges.

2.   Examples of large quantitative macro-analysis studies include Apodaca (2001), Richards, Gelleny, and Sacko (2001), Hafner-Burton (2005), Hafner-Burton and Tsutsui (2005), Abouharb and Cingranelli (2006), and Gray, Kittilson, and Sandholtz (2006). Smaller quantitative studies have been conducted by Meyer (1996), Smith, Bolyard, and Ippolito (1999), Apodaca (2002), Burkhart (2002), and Tuman and Emmert (2004). For qualitative studies see Pollis and Schwab (2000), Monshipouri, Welch, and Kennedy (2003), Rodriguez (2004), Colonomos and Santiso (2005), Howard-Hassman (2005), and Arnold and Hartman (2006).

3.   See North (1990) and Olson (1993).

4.   See http://www.gasandoil.com/news/2002/04/cna21657.

5.   The University of Minnesota's online Human Rights Library provides access to business codes of conduct as well as industry initiatives and multilateral instruments—see http://www1.umn.edu/humanrts/links/allcodes.html.

6.   The dependent variable is the one whose variation is being explained (here, FDI), and the independent variables are the ones explaining variation in the dependent variable.

7.   Measurement schemes, coding details, and estimates of the inter-rater reliability for all of the human rights data used in this paper are available online at http://www.humanrightsdata.com.

8.   Many scholars apply similar scales (see Garrett, 1995, 1998; Li and Resnick, 2003).

9.   In actuality, all coefficients listed as either P or N in Table 13.2 are reliable with 95 per cent confidence, except inflation in Model 1, which is reliable at 90 per cent confidence. We report only $P < 0.10$ to avoid confusion.

Visit the Online Resource Centre that accompanies this book for updates and a range of other resources:
www.oxfordtextbooks.co.uk/orc/goodhart3e/

14

Political Democracy and State Repression

Christian Davenport

Chapter Contents

Reader's Guide

This chapter discusses the relationship between political democracy and state repression. Specifically, it evaluates what research has been conducted on the topic but also what has been ignored. Exploration of the United States and its treatment of African Americans is used as an example of how existing research in this field should change. This case emphasizes the importance of disaggregation (regarding institutions, actors, and actions). The chapter concludes with specific suggestions for further development.

Introduction

For hundreds of years, activists, policy makers, and ordinary citizens have been interested in reducing the amount and severity of state coercive behaviour directed against those subject to this power (e.g. restrictions on speech, association, assembly, and religion, as well as torture, **disappearances**, and mass killings). It was not until about thirty years ago, however, that this issue was examined systematically in dozens of articles and books. What do we now know about what diminishes state repression?

Research has revealed that only two variables diminish human rights violations: (1) political democracy—

political institutions that involve the governed in the process of governing, as well as diverse practices that subject leaders to some degree of oversight/account-ability; and (2) economic development—societies that produce greater amounts of wealth typically experience fewer human rights violations (e.g. Hibbs, 1973; Mitchell and McCormick, 1988; Henderson, 1991, 1993; Poe and Tate, 1994; Davenport, 1995, 1996, 1999, 2007a, 2007b; Poe, Tate, and Camp Keith, 1999; J. King, 2000; Zanger, 2000; Camp Keith, 2002; Bueno de Mesquita et al., 2005; Hill and Jones, 2014). Although similar in causal impact, there are some important differences between these factors. First, the impact of democracy has been far greater in magnitude compared to economic development: democracy is simply a more powerful determinant of state repression than the economy. Second, since the Second World War, it appears that the external 'imposability' and internal development of democracy around the world have been far more successful than efforts to spark economic development (Diamond, 2008). In short, it is easier to create and sustain democracy than economic development.[1] Third, most activists, policy makers, and ordinary citizens see democracy as the solution for repression, and they call for this outcome and mobilize people to achieve this objective in part for this reason (one can find examples for this from the French and Haitian revolutions through to the Arab Spring). Such a solution follows a relatively long tradition in political science, where democracy is viewed as a resolution to a wide variety of problems, but it also follows a relatively long tradition in policy making and non-governmental organization (NGO) communities as well. Indeed, it is only recently that such thinking has been challenged (e.g. Carothers, 2002; Diamond, 2002; Levitsky and Way, 2002).

Despite the sheer wealth of empirical and popular support for the pacifying influence of democracy on state repression, there are some important limitations with existing work. For example, while correlations are consistently statistically significant, the scholarly community is only just beginning to understand what causal mechanisms are involved, in what manner they function, and in what contexts they are most effective (Davenport, 2007a; Hill and Jones, 2014). As a consequence, there is a great need for further examination. This chapter provides an overview of existing research on the democracy–repression nexus, highlighting its strengths. It also outlines a more nuanced way of examining the topic, shedding light on the problems

with existing work—specifically, the failure to **disaggregate** democracy and repression across space and actors—and what could be done to address these limitations. These problems are illustrated through a brief discussion of the relationship between democracy and repression in the United States during the 1940s to 1980s. The final section suggests several areas of investigation that might prove to be fruitful.

Understanding the Democracy–Repression Nexus

To understand why governments ban, beat, torture, disappear, and kill their citizens takes some care. Adopting a version of rationalism, most researchers who study the topic highlight the centrality of government leadership (i.e. the executive) and they employ a simple decision calculus to understand when repressive behaviour will be undertaken (e.g. Dahl, 1966; Walter, 1969; Dallin and Breslauer, 1970; Gurr, 1986; Duvall and Stohl, 1988; Karklins and Peterson, 1993; Simon, 1994; Lichbach, 1995; Gartner and Regan, 1996; Bueno de Mesquita et al., 2005; Davenport, 2007a). In this work, coercive activity is expected when (1) the perceived benefits of repressing exceed the costs, (2) there are no viable alternatives for socio-political control, and (3) the probability of success from repressive action is high. Repression is not anticipated when benefits are low, costs are high, there are alternatives, and the probability of success is minimal.

Given this framework, exactly why does democracy matter? What is it about these political institutions that reduce state coercion? There are several reasons for a link between democracy and coercive pacification, all directly connected to what is meant by democracy and repressive behaviour—where I will begin.

Democracy and Repression

In existing research, 'democratic' political institutions generally refer to the minimalist conception of democracy advocated by scholars such as Schumpeter: i.e. competition among elites for electoral support. Here, a mechanism of governance is discussed rather than the end to which that mechanism is directed. Of course, there is some variation with regard to the means highlighted. For example, some focus on the constraints placed on political leaders, highlighting veto 'points' or 'players' and executive constraints (Tsebelis, 2002). Others focus on the participation of the citizenry in popular elections (Davenport, 1997; Richards, 1999a). Others focus on the representative and/or competitiveness of political parties (Richards, 1999b). Still others focus on combinations of these various elements. In all variations, however, the basic point is the same: there are ways of governing that are more 'democratic' than others. For example, a democracy is more likely to place greater constraints on its political leaders so that they will be less able to do what they wish and will consequently feel a greater degree of oversight/constraint. A democracy is more likely to involve more of its citizenry in the selection of its leadership so that those subject to rule can have a greater degree of control over who is guiding the political unit. Finally, a democracy is more likely to have diverse political parties, as well as highly competitive electoral contests between them, so that a wide variety of perspectives can find their way into the political system.

Similarly narrowed is the conception of repression (see Box 14.1). As conceived in the literature, this phenomenon involves the actual or threatened use of physical sanctions against an individual or organization within the territorial jurisdiction of the state, for the purposes of imposing a cost on the target and deterring specific activities and beliefs perceived as challenges to government personnel, practices, or institutions. Like other forms of coercion, repressive behaviour relies on threats and intimidation to compel targets, but it does not concern itself with all coercive applications (e.g. deterrence of violent crime and theft). Rather, it deals with applications of state power that violate rights concerning expression, due process in the enforcement and adjudication of law, and personal integrity or security (Davenport, 2007b, p. 2).[2]

Given these predominant definitions, there are several influences that democracy is expected to have on state repression (Davenport, 2007b, pp. 10–11). These are adopted by scholars, activists, advocates, and policy makers the world over:

1. Democratic institutions are believed to increase the costs of using repressive behaviour because authorities can be voted out of office if voters find their actions inappropriate.

2. Individuals in democracies generally accept specific values regarding toleration, communication, and deliberation—values that are challenged and undermined by the use of repression.

3. Democracies provide an alternative mechanism of control through participation and contestation. They also weaken the justification for coercive activity by reducing the likelihood for human conflict and facilitating the conveyance of grievances.

In the first scenario, democracy decreases repression because it frightens policy makers, making them aware that there are repercussions for hurting citizens. In the second, democracy decreases repression because it socializes leaders and citizens to embrace certain actions and beliefs and to reject others. In the third scenario, democracy decreases repression because it provides a different way to influence citizens. For example, by 'channelling' individuals into pre-existing institutions

---

BOX 14.1 DECONSTRUCTING REPRESSION

Repression is a very controversial concept, and even its label is problematic (others have used coercion, suppression, human rights violation, or domination to refer to the same thing). Some believe that what matters most is the coercive element, ignoring political objectives. Others focus on the political objectives, downplaying the coercion. Indeed, these latter individuals would highlight that there are a wide variety of non-coercive mechanisms of control which can be and are employed, such as controlling the school curriculum and firing teachers believed to be radical. The difficulty here is with how broadly one uses the term—not everything would be politically repressive. It is generally good that both the coercive and political elements be involved with any conception of repression.

There is also some confusion between the terms 'repression' (which concerns behaviour being enacted by political authorities against those within the relevant territorial domain espousing particular politically-oriented beliefs or behaviour) and 'oppression' (which concerns behaviour enacted by non-political authorities against individuals within the relevant territorial domain, with no specific concern about what they believe or do). These two terms are frequently used interchangeably, but this actually confuses several very different considerations. If women are poorly treated by corporations, owing to sexism or misogyny, and as a result receive poor health and wages, then it would be more appropriate to say that they are oppressed rather than repressed. If the particular women under discussion are also engaging in political behaviour which intends to alter the allocation of public resources, and if their ill-treatment is on this account, then it would be appropriate to say that they are being repressed.

and regulated behaviour, democratic political systems are able to reduce the need for employing other, more violent techniques.

It is with these relationships in mind that scholars analyse relationships between democracy and coercive state behaviour. They want to see if democratic political institutions could deliver on their promise to pacify state coercion. Of course, not all of these analyses are comparable—there have been some significant changes over time.

For example, the earliest examinations of the democracy–repression nexus adopted a large-N approach, where they attempted to identify how democracy (generally a composite index of diverse components such as the **polity index** (Gurr, 1974; Marshall and Jaggers, 2000)) influenced repression in the present across as many *nation-years* as they could obtain data for (e.g. Hibbs, 1973; Ziegenhagen, 1986). Here, it was assumed that movement up the scale of democracy led to movement down the scale of repression. The findings of this body of work were clear and consistent. Across time, space, measurements, and methodological techniques, almost all studies found that democratic political institutions and activities decreased state repressive behaviour. In earlier work I referred to this as a 'domestic democratic peace', mirroring the findings of international relations scholars (Davenport, 2007b, p. 11).

Over time, a few researchers began to speculate about the functional form of this relationship (Muller, 1985; Fein, 1995; Regan and Henderson, 2002; Davenport and Armstrong, 2004). Adopting the same large-N approach employed in earlier work, these scholars argued that democratic institutions did not influence repression in a linear fashion, with every increase in democracy leading to a decrease in repression. Instead, scholars began to suggest that the relationship and theoretical argument functioned in a very different manner, and that the domestic democratic peace might be a bit more optimistic than warranted.

For example, some maintained that it was not the degree of democratization that diminished repression, but rather the clarity or certainty with which political leaders governed. A distinctive lack of clarity and certainty characterized political systems in the middle of a democratic continuum, and these so-called 'hybrid' or 'anocratic' regimes prove to be the most repressive. This is commonly referred to as the 'more murder in the middle' (MMM) hypothesis (e.g. Fein, 1995), indicating that these regimes in the middle of the spectrum engage in the most repression (an inverted U-shaped relationship). Researchers examined this proposition by introducing democracy and its square into estimated models, consistently finding support for the argument.

Others maintained that it was not clarity or certainty but 'democraticness' that was crucial to understand. In this view, not all movements to democracy are comparable, and it is only when a certain threshold is passed that we should expect an influence (Davenport and Armstrong, 2004; Bueno de Mesquita et al., 2005). In order to examine these relationships and also to consider alternative specifications such as the inverted-U relationship of the MMM hypothesis, the methods adopted in this work were more sophisticated than any attempted earlier. For example, Davenport and Armstrong (2004) employed a variety of sophisticated statistical techniques (e.g. LOESS graphs, the binary decomposition model, and time-series cross-sectional analyses) to estimate relationships. The findings of this work have provided the most definitive results regarding the influence of democracy on repression. As found, the threshold model (where there is no impact until the highest values of democracy are reached) is far superior to any other. In short, there is no murder in the middle—at least nothing extraordinary.

The form of the relationship was not the only part of earlier scholarship questioned by later work. Researchers also began to speculate about exactly what aspect of political democracy wielded an influence on state repression. This question is extremely important, for it focuses discussion on determining which element of the political system needs to be modified to achieve reductions in repressive behaviour. On this point opinions differ, with researchers advocating and exploring diverse components of democratic regimes, including constitutional structure (Davenport, 1996; Camp Keith, 2002), elections (Davenport, 1997; Richards, 1999a), political party diversity (Richards, 1999b; Bueno de Mesquita et al., 2005), veto points (Davenport, 2007a), executive constraints (Davenport, 2004; Bueno de Mesquita et al., 2005), executive constraints weighted by participation (Davenport and Armstrong, 2004), and, more recently, freedom of the press (Davenport, Moore, and Armstrong, 2008).

To examine the relevant relationships, the basic approach used by earlier scholars was modified. In this case, researchers had to disaggregate measures of democracy and use indicators that *operationalized* the particular mechanisms of interest. This effort was made easier in part because these distinct components were always available; they had just been ignored because earlier applications lumped them together into indices. The findings of this research have been mixed. Most of these studies find statistically significant relationships, and thus support is generated for the proposition that there are specific aspects of democracy that influence repression. Unfortunately, there has not yet been an effort to examine all components against one another systematically and competitively. The best of this work has only compared a handful of rival explanations (Bueno de Mesquita et al., 2005; Davenport, 2007a). Additionally, there has not yet been an attempt to explore non-linear relationships within these disaggregated efforts. The validity of the threshold, as opposed to the MMM hypothesis, has not been examined at the subnational level.

The Future of the Democracy–Repression Nexus

This section identifies some important elements of what should be the next wave of **quantitative** research on the relationship between democracy and repression. Specifically, these elements address three limitations of previous work.

First, existing research has ignored the fact that the nation-year might not be the most appropriate unit of analysis. Research on political culture (Elazar, 1972; Putnam, 1994) as well as political violence (Ball, Kobrak, and Spirer, 1999; Davenport and Stam, 2003; Boudreau, 2004; Wilkinson, 2004; Kalyvas, 2006) has clearly established that important differences exist within countries in each of these areas. Indeed, the research has largely problematized all efforts to examine nation-years, showing that factors within countries are more important predictors of repression and that it is inappropriate to argue that whole territorial units are subject to similar influences or influenced similarly by the same factors. More directly relevant to the subject at hand, work by Kim Quaile Hill (1994) has revealed that the degree of democracy in a nation state (in this case the United States) varies significantly across space. Additionally, historical work by Frank Donner (1990) reveals significant variation in political repression across the USA.

Second, related to the last point, existing research has ignored the fact that different aspects of political democracy may exhibit distinct influences on different repressive agents (i.e. the military, the police, the court system, politicians, and non-state militias at local, state, and national levels). This acknowledges that not all actors engaged in coercive activity are similarly or equally influenced by the same factors.

Third, existing research has largely ignored the fact that repression might influence democracy. This influence is commonly addressed in literature on 'liberalization'—which refers to a 'relaxation' of political repression (Wood, 2000). Here, it is expected that relaxing or reducing repression provides an opening for diverse societal and political actors to promote democratic institutions and behaviour by putting into place diverse mechanisms (e.g. elections and constraints on policy making) that further reduce the likelihood of repression.

Why have these issues been ignored? There are several reasons. One of the most important is that the data used for analyses of the democracy–repression nexus are generally aggregated to the nation-year, and there was nothing that could be analysed at a more fine-grained level. This is beginning to change. Over the last few years, researchers have been disaggregating political and conflict processes with greater frequency. Another important factor is that democracy scholars have not been particularly interested in repression and have been more interested in economic development (e.g. Lipset, 1959; Burkhart and Lewis-Beck, 1994; Przeworski, 2000). Indeed, democracy scholars rarely use the word 'repression', focusing instead on 'liberalization'. In contrast, repression scholars have long been interested in political democracy.

To redirect scholarship and improve our understanding of what is taking place when repression is applied, therefore, it is imperative that researchers focus within states—paying close attention to who is engaging in repressive behaviour, where they are in the state, how they are connected to those in power, and what connection (if any) they have to relevant democratic institutions. To provide an example of how researchers might begin to think about these issues, a discussion is given in the next section of perhaps the most famous case of how varied quality in democracy within a country influenced the application of repressive action within that country: the coercion of African Americans in the American South between the 1940s and 1980s.

Case Study: Democracy and Repression in the United States: A Peculiar Story of African American Persecution and Freedom

Most people in the United States think of human rights violations as being something that takes place in authoritarian regimes or in democratic transitions—places far, far away. I could thus discuss the continued repression found in Tunisia after the minor increases in democracy resulting from the reforms of the Arab Spring of 2011 in connection with the threshold argument, or discuss the continued manifestation of state repressive action in South Africa after the fall of apartheid. I wish to alter this practice and argue that the same insights we have discussed apply to the US case. Indeed, I will go on to argue that this case allows us to explore several of the issues raised in this chapter with greater depth and nuance.

When most people think of the USA, they think of it as a democracy—perhaps *the* democracy. This is consistent with the views of some of the most prominent scholars of the topic (e.g. Dahl, 1966, 1971; Huntington, 1991; Held, 1996). It is also consistent with some of the most prominent measures of the concept. For example, considering 'the presence of institutions and procedures through which citizens can express effective preferences about alternative policies and leaders' and 'the existence of institutionalized constraints on the exercise of power by the executive' (Marshall and Jaggers, 2000, p. 22) between 1800 and 2004, the polity index indicates that, except for the earliest part of the 1800s, the United States has been in the highest categories of democracy for about two hundred years (see Figure 14.1 and Box 14.2). During the early 1800s there were significant restrictions on the regulation of parties, but these were changed in 1809 during James Madison's inaugural year—a point after which the USA would never return to a level below the highest two categories on the measure.

Disaggregating Nation States

Now, immediately someone will note that the quality of this democracy was limited for much of this history. For instance, women had not obtained the right to vote until 1920 (with the Nineteenth Amendment to the Constitution) and African Americans, the focus of this section, were effectively disenfranchised until 1965, when the **Voting Rights Act** was passed. The neglect of this point can be directly attributed to the measure being used. Polity does not include information on suffrage, and thus this issue would not (and has not) come up in most of the research relying on this indicator (which is the most popular indicator for democracy in the social sciences). This issue of neglect should not be levied against only polity. Given the similarities between this measure and others, it is likely that this would be the same for them as well (e.g. Munck and Verkuilen, 2002).

When one considers suffrage in the African American case, however, it is clear that there is variability

Figure 14.1 Democracy in the United States: The Polity Index, 1800–2004

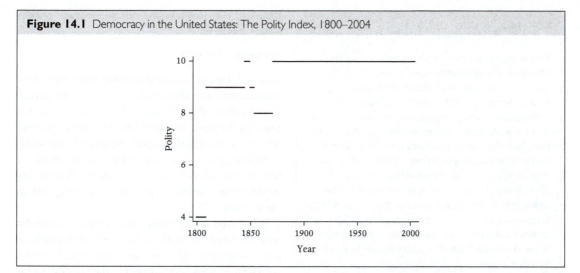

in democracy, especially in the southern part of the country. Indeed, it is generally understood that, from the period of slavery through to the late 1960s and early 1970s, extensive voting rights restrictions and other aspects of authoritarianism existed in the Deep South: Alabama, Arkansas, Florida, Georgia, Louisiana, Mississippi, North Carolina, South Carolina, Tennessee, Texas, and Virginia.[3] These restrictions were almost exclusively based on ethnicity. Historically, there is thus significant spatial variation within the United States regarding the quality of political democracy as gauged by one of its core components—the right to participate in the political process.[4]

Even after accepting this point, we should be careful not simply to view all of these states as comparable. Although uniformly less democratic (more authoritarian) in nature towards blacks, there was significant variation even among these southern states. For example, the percentage of voting age African Americans registered to vote was less than 0.5 in Alabama (where blacks make up 35 per cent of the total population), Louisiana (36 per cent), Mississippi (49 per cent), and South Carolina (43 per cent); the percentage of voting age African Americans registered to vote was between 2 and 9 per cent in Arkansas (25 per cent), Florida (27 per cent), Georgia (35 per cent), Texas (14 per cent), and Virginia (25 per cent); and the percentage of voting age African Americans registered to vote was between 10 and 16 per cent in North Carolina and Tennessee—where, respectively, blacks made up 27 per cent and 17 per cent of the total population (K. Hill, 1994, p. 29).

BOX 14.2 UNDERSTANDING THE POLITY MEASURE

Polity is conceived on a ten-point scale—with 10 as the highest value of 'democracy' and 'autocracy' that one could achieve. Different points are provided for distinct aspects of political democracy. In this project, a score of 10 represents the most developed democracy with no restrictions on political parties, significant restrictions on the executive, and no limitations on who could run for national-level leadership positions. A 0 score represents a situation where none of these exist. Source: Gurr et al. (2002). Additional source for polity project: http://www.systemicpeace.org/polity/polity4.htm.

Looking at party competition reveals similar patterns (K. Hill, 1994, p. 60). Here, we find that Georgia, Louisiana, Mississippi, South Carolina, Texas, Alabama, Arkansas, Florida, North Carolina, Virginia, and Tennessee were one-party (and thus less competitive) Democratic states in the 1940s. South Dakota, Vermont, and North Dakota were one-party Republican states. In contrast, Rhode Island, Missouri, Utah, Nevada, Washington, Massachusetts, Minnesota, Delaware, Montana, Nebraska, Colorado, Connecticut, and Illinois were two-party, competitive states.

While one could obviously extend a discussion of repressive activity directed against African Americans back to slavery and the slave codes (1619–1865) or the legal restrictions and activities of the black codes (1800–66), I focus on the period associated with *Jim*

BOX 14.3 JIM CROW LAWS

At diverse periods in time, the United States legal system established very specific restrictive (i.e. repressive) laws regarding the civil liberties of African Americans. During slavery (1619 to 1863) there were the 'slave codes'. These outlined a wide variety of limitations on what slaves could do, as well as what masters and ordinary whites could do against them. Later, there were 'black codes' in the South but also the North, which attempted to deal with African Americans after the ending of slavery (between 1866 and 1875). By 1876, however, there was a more detailed and formalized system of laws—the so-called Jim Crow laws—that emerged to separate blacks and whites throughout almost all dimensions of public as well as private life. These laws were largely found in the South, although some could be found in the North as well.

Crow (1876–1965; see Box 14.3). Although neglecting the worst horrors of the earlier periods (e.g. torture in the form of floggings and whippings as well as political terror in the form of lynchings), this period is of interest because it immediately precedes the efforts to desegregate (begun with *Brown v. Board of Education of Topeka, Kansas*), the civil rights movement (1955–68), and the so-called democratic revolution in the South (in the Civil and Voting Rights Acts). This period therefore establishes the context within which three of the most important events in US democratic history occur. It is also the period that has some of the most extensive documentation on relevant government activities, and it immediately follows the initial period of data collection undertaken by Hill (as discussed).

By far the most extensive effort to identify state authorized/required restrictions on African Americans during the Jim Crow era was undertaken by Pauli Murray (1951). This voluminous work identified all of the legislative controls that were imposed to enforce racial segregation across a wide variety of categories: amusements, public halls, education, employment, hospitals, penal institutions, welfare institutions, transportation, and miscellaneous. The work was intended to be as comprehensive as possible:

[t]he compilation includes segregation and anti-miscegenation statutes, laws relating to public accommodations and which are popularly called 'civil rights' laws, fair educational practice acts, fair employment practice acts, statutes directed against lynching and the activities of the Ku

Klux Klan, alien land laws, and miscellaneous anti-discrimination measures.

(P. Murray, 1951, p. 5)

This said, Murray was careful not to misrepresent the effort, stating that the compilation, while extensive, is not complete (ibid.). Additionally, she notes that her research does not interpret laws but rather presents what they say and draws out the direct implications of this language. The actual implementation of the laws is ignored, creating the possibility that the real world looked different from the one imagined by the statutes.

What type of repressiveness do we see when this work is considered? In the situation of relative political authoritarianism—that is, black disenfranchisement with white (ethnic) domination of the political, social, and economic systems—how were African Americans treated? Murray's summary table is replicated in Table 14.1.

What is perhaps most striking from the compiled information is the wide variety of restrictions that were placed on blacks. Moving through the table, one is able to see that races were segregated in pool rooms, race tracks, circuses, schools, facilities at work, medical care, prisons, housing, and even diverse forms of sports, such as boxing. Mirroring the discussion we have had about democracy, we also see significant variation across space. Directly in line with expectations, the least democratic states are the most restrictive on African Americans: Alabama (with 18 different types of restriction out of 51), Arkansas (20), Florida (19), Georgia (16—the low), Louisiana (19), Mississippi (21), North Carolina (26—the high), South Carolina (23), Tennessee (18), Texas (21), and Virginia (23). In these states one sees pervasive limitations across diverse aspects of life, reflecting a clear effort to keep blacks 'in their place' and to prevent racial mixing.

In contrast, there are no segregation restrictions authorized by law in the states that would traditionally be conceived as being the most democratic in the 1940s: e.g. Connecticut, Illinois, Maine, Massachusetts, Michigan, Pennsylvania, Rhode Island, New Hampshire, New Jersey, New York, and Vermont. Similarly, in states fairly high on a democracy scale there were a few or a single restriction: e.g. Washington, Indiana, Kansas, Minnesota, and Colorado.

Repression varied by category. For example, by far the largest number of restrictions existed in the realm of education. Not only were there extensive attempts made to prevent ordinary young children from coming together in public and private institutions, but there were also attempts made to separate those having trouble in school (juvenile delinquents), those who were challenged in some way (the deaf, blind, and dumb), as well as those seeking to improve themselves by learning a trade or pursuing higher education. The second most pervasive restriction, across states, existed in the realm of intermarriage. This particular category is interesting because this prohibition was adopted not only by all states in the South, but also in almost all other states at the time.

In line with existing literature, therefore, we find some preliminary support for the argument that the lowest levels of democracy, viewed at the subnational level, were associated with some of the highest levels of political repression. Interestingly, there is also some support for the linear argument when whole countries are disaggregated. For example, while West Virginia would normally be considered to be on the middle of a democratic continuum (K. Hill, 1994, p. 96), it is found at the mid-level of repression during the period in question, with fourteen restrictions being found. As West Virginia is generally considered to be part of the upper-South/mid-Atlantic (between what is traditionally considered the South and North—thus not subject to all of the cultural and political influences in either), this middle position makes sense. This argument also accounts for the orientation of Maryland (with twelve restrictions). In line with this, Oklahoma would normally be considered to be on the lower end of a democratic continuum—i.e. authoritarianism (K. Hill, 1994, p. 98). This accounts well for its relatively high level of repressiveness (with twenty-one restrictions).

From an evaluation of democracy (suffrage and party competitiveness) and repression (restrictions on civil liberties) across the states of the USA, therefore, it is clear that the basic argument of the domestic democratic peace is sustained at a lower-level aggregation below the nation state: more democratic states (i.e. states where blacks had the right to vote and where party competition was higher) tended to repress African Americans less (i.e. these states tended to have fewer restrictions on what blacks could do). This work suggests that it is not only possible but crucial to examine relationships within, and not just across, countries. National-level assessments of political democracy and state repression are simply too coarse to capture adequately the reality on the ground. The aggregation of these highly varied experiences might also result in misperceptions of causal relationships.

Aspects of Democracy and Repression

Within this brief chapter, I do not mean to suggest that all aspects of democracy are relevant for all aspects of repression. I have highlighted that two often-neglected aspects of US democracy, suffrage and party competition, were crucial for understanding exactly why repression was enacted against part of the American population: African American citizens did not have the ability to select less repressive leaders, nor did they have the opportunity to remove legally those who engaged in behaviour that they disliked. In this context, those interested in using repressive action were able to do so with **impunity**.

Another illustration from the American case concerns the existence of vigilantes and popular militias. After the *Brown* decision by the Supreme Court in 1954, which eliminated the legal justification for separate educational facilities, it was left for state authorities to enforce the ruling. This was extremely problematic in two ways. First, because some authorities, as well as diverse citizen organizations such as the Mississippi State Sovereignty Commission and White City Councils, did not support the ruling, those attempting to exercise their newly won rights were left unprotected. As a result, it was frequently the case that restrictive practices were allowed to continue for some time. Second, enforcement was problematic because African Americans and whites who attempted to adhere to the newly established federal law were hindered by local-level violence and repression enacted by mobs, Klansmen, and other whites—violence and repression abetted by police and political inactivity.

But the situation did not continue indefinitely.

After the beating of a white minister who was trying to help black students enter the school ... (U.S. Attorney General) Brownwell ... announced the federal government would prosecute persons who forcefully interfered with the integration of Clinton High. U.S. marshals then received orders to round up troublemakers, and on December 5, 1956, the Justice Department for the first time asserted its own authority to halt interference with a desegregation order.

(Belknap, 1987, p. 39)

Table 14.1 Segregation Authorized or Required by State Law (Murray, 1951, Chart III).

STATES → / DISCRIMINATORY PRACTICE IN ↓	AL	AK	AR	CA	CO	CT	DE	DC	FL	GA	ID	IL	IN	IA	KS	KY	LA	ME	MD	MA	MI	MN	MS
Amusement																							
Billiards										√													
Public halls																							
Parks																							
Public Halls																							
Racetracks		√																					
Circuses											√												
Education																							
Constitutional provision	√					√			√	√		√				√	√		√				√
Statutory provision—public school	√	√	√				√	√	√	√		√	√			√	√		√				√
Private school									√							√							
Schools for deaf				√				√	√							√							√
Schools for dumb																							
Schools for blind				√					√	√						√							
Reform schools	√		√	√				√	√	√						√	√		√				√
Trade schools	√	√							√	√						√	√						√
Higher education	√	√				√			√	√						√			√				√
Teacher's training	√	√				√			√	√						√			√				√
Separate schools—indians				√																			
Separate textbooks—black/white									√														
Separate libraries																							
Employment																							
Separate washrooms in mines				√																			
Separate toilets in manufacturing businesses																							
Segregation in cotton textile factories																							
Hospitals																							
Segregation generally																							√
Mental patients	√									√						√	√		√				√
Tubercular patients	√															√	√						
Nursing	√																						√
Penal institutions									√														

MO	MT	NE	NV	NH	NJ	NM	NY	NC	ND	OH	OK	OR	PA	RI	SC	SD	TN	TX	UT	VT	VA	WA	WV	WI	WY
															√										
√											√				√										
																	√				√				
															√										
√								√			√				√		√	√			√		√		
√						√		√			√				√		√				√		√		√
											√						√								
								√			√						√	√			√		√		
								√										√			√				
								√			√						√	√			√		√		
√								√			√			√			√	√			√		√		
√								√			√			√			√	√					√		
√								√			√			√			√	√				√	√		
√								√			√			√			√	√				√	√		
								√																	
								√																	
√								√											√						
											√						√	√							
								√																	
															√										
															√										
√								√			√				√		√				√		√		
											√							√					√		
															√										

Table 14.1. (*continued*)

STATES →

DISCRIMINATORY PRACTICE IN ↓	AL	AK	AR	CA	CO	CT	DE	DC	FL	GA	ID	IL	IN	IA	KS	KY	LA	ME	MD	MA	MI	MN	MS
Segregation generally	√	√							√	√						√						√	
Separate chain gangs	√	√							√														
Welfare institutions																							
Homes for ageing/orphans							√								√	√							
Paupers	√																						
Transportation																							
Buses	√	√							√	√							√					√	
Railroads	√	√							√	√					√	√			√			√	
Street cars, etc.		√							√								√			√		√	
Steamboats/ferries																				√			
Waiting rooms	√	√							√								√					√	
Sleeping compartments		√								√												√	
Miscellaneous																							
Mixed marriages																							
White–Negro/Mulatto	√	√	√	√	√		√		√	√	√	√				√	√		√			√	√
White–Indian																							
White–Asian			√	√						√	√								√			√	√
Cohabitation prohibited	√	√							√								√		√				
Adoption by persons of same race only																	√						
Separate army batallions													√										
White–Negro boxing prohibited																							
White–Negro fraternal organization prohibited																							
Cannot advocate social equality																					√		
Telephone booths																							
Voting lists, etc.	√	√								√		√											
Voting places		√																					
Housing																√							

MT	NE	NV	NH	NJ	NM	NY	NC	ND	OH	OK	OR	PA	RI	SC	SD	TN	TX	UT	VT	VA	WA	WV	WI	WY
						√								√		√				√				
						√																		
							√																	
							√										√ √							
										√									√					
						√			√															
						√			√					√		√ √ √				√				
						√			√					√										
							√		√					√										
√	√			√		√		√	√					√ √ √ √		√				√ √				
						√			√					√		√				√				
√								√						√						√				
√						√								√	√									
																				√				
						√																		
										√							√							
						√																		
														√		√								

National guardsmen, the US military, and agents of the Justice Department were used in similar situations throughout the South.

This development was important because local instability, caused by a lack of effective policing of a hostile part of the white population, compelled a response from higher-level political authorities as the unrest directly addressed the federal government's ability to enact laws and policies. In short, the violence not only threatened human life but directly challenged the **rule of law** and maintenance of order that were essential for the functioning of the political system. As an Eisenhower speechwriter recalled after the fact:

[t]he President, so slow to take firm federal action in support of civil rights, could and would respond with dispatch to a public challenge to presidential and constitutional authority.

(Belknap, 1987, p. 49)

As the President stated, '[f]ailure to act ... would be tantamount to acquiescence in anarchy and the dissolution of the union' (in Belknap, 1987, p. 49). In this context, it was revealed that democratic processes within certain aspects of government do not directly resonate with all aspects of the repressive apparatus. Indeed, they might be completely disconnected from one another.

Another example is provided by federal responses to the extensive bombing campaign undertaken by supporters of white supremacy in the mid to late 1950s and into the 1960s. By this time, African Americans were less likely to be targeted with the lynch rope. Rather, given the higher degree of mobilization, extremist whites used explosives to undermine black organizations and to intimidate those seeking an extension of democracy. Towards this end, the homes of religious leaders (such as Martin Luther King Jr) were targeted; meeting places (churches and education facilities) were also targeted.

Unlike the high degree of political complicity identified above, in this case local officials moved against white extremism. As stated by Belknap (1987, p. 55), 'most public officials in the South do seem to have made a sincere effort to stamp out the epidemic of dynamiting that was plaguing their region'. The evidence was clear.

In South Carolina the attorney general, the governor, and the chairman of the judiciary committees in both houses of the legislature all pressed for tougher laws against

bombing and bomb threats. Tennessee Governor Frank Clement and Alabama Governor James Folsom both offered rewards for information leading to the arrest of bombers. So did Montgomery's mayor and city commissioners. Perhaps the best evidence of how serious southern officials were about halting the terroristic use of explosives was their creation of the Southern Conference on Bombing (SCB). Initiated by Jacksonville Mayor Haydon Burns after dynamite ripped a black high school and a Jewish community center in his city, the SCB began with a meeting of seventy delegates in May 1958. The founders included ten mayors and law enforcement officers from twenty-one southern communities.

(Belknap, 1987, p. 55)

The reason for their willingness to act was not attributable merely to the fact that they felt that lethal violence was deemed unacceptable, and to popular fears of growing conflict. Rather, it was that they feared that if they could not control overt activity directed against African Americans attempting to exercise rights granted by higher political institutions, then others at the federal level would do so. Although initially federal authorities under President Eisenhower were hesitant about becoming involved, over time a variety of new laws or newly interpreted laws facilitated and enhanced federal involvement. For example, the intrastate nature of the violence was used to invoke federal authority in connection with the transportation of explosives and incitement to violence. The implications of these developments were significant but not too far-reaching—at least not in the short term. The **Civil Rights Act** of 1964 created new federal offences with significant punishments, but it represented simply another step along a continuum of increasing federal intrusion into the southern states. It would not be until the violence associated with the **Freedom Riders** and vicious attacks on non-violent demonstrations associated with the Southern Christian Leadership Conference a few years later that even greater strides would be made in this direction.

This element of the story is better known and will not be discussed here. What is important is that southern political actors eventually decided to enforce federal law and subdue those in their communities who were engaged in violent behaviour. This represented a sea change in the attitude and behaviour of local government authorities. It also paved the way for the development of democracy in the South.

Repression as a Determinant of Political Democracy

What is interesting about the case under discussion is that different actors engaged in different repressive acts, having important implications for the overall outcome. For example, in the South, legal and political restrictions as well as violence were enacted against African Americans. Some of these activities were undertaken by agents of the state (e.g. politicians, judges, and police officers) but some were not (e.g. White City Councils and Klansmen). In some cases, these were the same people. Whatever the case, those who were not favourably disposed toward African Americans were outmatched and outnumbered. Additionally, there was little possibility of any punishment being levied against the perpetrators of repressive activities. After changes at the federal level—in the realm of law as well as political sensibility—this situation changed. In this context, those who were against black persecution (particularly the more violent form, which was not popularly supported) had greater leverage for challenging the repressors. Additionally, there was a growing (albeit slow) possibility that the actions undertaken would be investigated and potentially prosecuted.

What becomes interesting is that repression that was once enacted or supported by local authorities became criminalized as political officials and diverse citizens attempted to distance themselves from what was taking place. At the same time, the federal government began increasingly to engage in repressive activity against the subset of the southern population that had been marginalized by its adoption of and commitment to racial violence—something that was viewed as disruptive and threatening to law and order, not to mention unconstitutional.

Between roughly 1960 and 1980, a literal revolution in political rights occurred, giving millions of previously disenfranchised citizens the right to vote and otherwise participate in the governmental process. That change was largely the product of federal government intervention in voting rights policy, with the express purpose of making our political processes more democratic. Doubtless, too, that intervention has made this a more democratic nation.

(K. Hill, 1994, p. 18)

Not all things had improved to the same degree, however. While the number of 'democratic' states increased dramatically over time (none would now

BOX 14.4 CHALLENGING ASSUMPTIONS: 'THE NEW JIM CROW'

Some have argued that the period of Jim Crow has not ended (Alexander, 2012); indeed, they maintain that all we have is the 'New Jim Crow'. Given the recent revelations of police violence against African Americans, as well as significant differences in arrests, sentencing, incarceration, parole, and stop/frisks (profiling), would you say that there has been a significant change from the policies described in Table 14.1? If so, in what ways?

be considered autocratic), the Deep South still falls at the bottom of any summary measure: Georgia, South Carolina, Mississippi, Texas, Alabama, Louisiana, and North Carolina remain the least democratic of the American states (K. Hill, 1994, pp. 96–8). (See Box 14.4 for discussion of the present day situation.)

The US case is somewhat at odds with existing democracy scholarship in numerous ways. First, it is an increase in repression and not its relaxation that appears to explain the movement to democracy in the American South. Or perhaps a certain degree of targeted repression precedes the relaxation that other scholars highlight, thus pushing the relevant time period for study backwards in time. This would seem to be similar to the South African case, as the African National Congress was subject to a significant amount of repression prior to the de-radicalization of its political programme and negotiation with the apartheid government. Second, the same acts are interpreted quite differently under different contexts. For example, what was earlier tolerated, supported, and sometimes enacted by government officials later became intolerable, unsupported, criminalized, and prosecuted. This leads us to focus on not only what is done but by whom, acknowledging that clear associations with political authorities may not always be possible (see Box 14.5 for a discussion of repressive institutions and anarchy).

KEY POINTS

Generally, researchers consider country-level assessments of democracy and repression, but this is problematic. For example, in the case of the United States and the treatment of African Americans, there was incredible variation in the quality of democracy and repression across states. Some states were quite democratic and treated African Americans quite well. Other states were quite autocratic in nature and treated blacks poorly. All of these states were found within the same country.

Perhaps the most important aspect of democracy regarding African Americans was the right to participate. For most of their existence in the US, blacks were not able to vote. Consequently, they were not able to hold authorities responsible for the coercive treatment they endured. In those states where blacks were able to vote, they tended to be treated better.

Repression can also facilitate political democracy. By eliminating those in the society who were coercively engaging with other citizens (e.g. local elites suppressing the freedom of African Americans), the federal government was able to facilitate the extension of democracy at the local level.

Critical Thinking Question:

Who should have the right to classify whether a country is democratic or not? Who should have the right to classify how much a country represses?

The Path to Peace: Directions for Future Research

This chapter has attempted to provide an overview of the existing literature on the relationship between democracy and repression as expressed in the quantitative research community—work extending back over approximately forty years. This review involved identifying the general approach and findings of this work, noting both strengths (rigour and consistency in results) and weaknesses (a failure to examine causal

BOX 14.5 ALTERNATIVE POINTS OF VIEW: COERCION AND REPRESSION

Anarchists like Peter Kropotkin and Errico Malatesta argued that there would always be repression as long as governments had control over the police, secret service, militias, militaries, and paramilitaries. If these institutions could be eliminated, however (i.e. if there were no police, no secret service, no militias, militaries, or paramilitaries), then (and only then) would state repression cease to exist—regardless of the type of political system that was in place. In short, for anarchists, it does not matter how much democracy there is, or how many trade unions and human rights NGOs. What matters is how many coercive institutions there are and who controls them.

mechanisms in greater detail, as well as a failure to disaggregate units of analysis). The historical case of the United States, with specific reference to the treatment of African Americans, was used as an example of exactly what is being missed in existing research. This section seeks to outline more precisely what subsequent examinations of the democracy–repression nexus must address in order for our understanding of the topic to improve.

Different Questions

The first shift in scholarship that I would recommend concerns a transformation in the type of questions that are asked. It is no longer necessary to ask if democracy influences state repression and human rights violations, or even to ask about the nature of the specific relationship. This issue has already been addressed. It is now important for researchers to pinpoint the causal mechanisms at work—to identify exactly which aspect of democracy is relevant and for what type of repression, as well as for which repressive agents. The latter issue is much less developed than the others. In following from this, it would also be valuable to explore how and why variation in democracy within a country leads to variation in repression within the same territorial jurisdiction. It is no longer appropriate to talk about democracy influencing human rights violations without acknowledging that the quality of democracy varies across relevant territorial units.

A different line of inquiry, one that is clearly emerging in the pages of newspapers around the world, is the issue of subcontracting. It has recently been discovered that many governments (including some democracies) send those whom they wish to be tortured or otherwise coerced to other countries to be dealt with (see Chapter 15). This is important, for it reveals that political leaders have a concern with the costs involved with relevant behaviour: they fear being discovered as it could cause them to lose legitimacy or office. At the same time, it reveals that political leaders are not deterred from repressive action as much as they are deterred from repressing in an obvious fashion. These issues need to be explored in greater detail. Related to this is the issue of non-lethal mechanisms of torture. It has recently been discovered (e.g. Rejali, 2007) that democracies have pioneered the use of repressive techniques that are less likely to leave trace evidence (such as marks on the victims). This again reveals that, while the costs of repression influence democracies, they may simply lead to shifts in tactics away from the most obvious/egregious forms of repression. Similar arguments could be made about the use of political surveillance.

Disaggregating Data

To explore the issues raised above, there would need to be a fundamental change in the way researchers conceptualize the relevant unit of analysis. While most literature in comparative politics and international relations examines nation-years, it is imperative that future analyses of the topic consider lower-level aggregations. It is becoming less reasonable to assume that one summary score captures well the degree of democracy in a country. There is significant variation within nation states regarding the role and influence of the mass population, as well as the type and magnitude of restraints on political authorities. In addition to this, the role and use of diverse repressive tactics in their efforts to establish and maintain socio-political order varies significantly within nation states. If researchers, policy makers, activists, and ordinary citizens are interested in understanding how repressive power is wielded by political authorities, it is incumbent upon them to explore the nuances of exactly how coercion is wielded.

Relevance

A third and final direction for future research concerns the connection between human rights scholarship, policy, and activism. For too long these areas have been held apart from one another—to the detriment of all. This is unfortunate because discussions and debates about the 'war on terror', counter-insurgency, and protest policing have taken place without being informed by an important branch of social science devoted to studying precisely these topics. This is also unfortunate because round tables, journal articles, and academic books on these subjects have been developed without any concern for their immediate and practical implications in the current context. For example, one area of research and policy that would be improved by explicit consideration of the democracy–repression nexus is democratic development and the effectiveness of counter-insurgency. In my recent

book examining 137 countries from 1976 to 1996, I find that, while certain aspects of democracy (measures of competition/participation and executive constraints) influence repression in the expected manner, some do not (suffrage and the number of veto players). Additionally, I find that the pacifying influence of democracy on repressive behaviour is increased in the context of inter-state war, decreased in the context of violent dissent, and mixed in the context of civil war. As Iraq has revealed all three contexts, it thus provides an interesting opportunity for the generalizability of this argument to be further explored. Unfortunately, the insights garnered from a human rights/repression approach have not yet been applied to this case; most individuals engaged in research on this topic have adopted approaches developed in the areas of inter-state and civil war (as well as the somewhat less rigorous work on counter-insurgency and counter-terrorism). Applying the democracy–repression nexus to this case and competitively evaluating it against arguments emerging within other disciplines and subfields of political science might prove to be useful as we attempt to understand how political violence is used and could be lessened in the world.

KEY POINTS

Researchers need to improve the way in which they think about the relationship between democracy and repression. For example, they need to ask different questions, moving to understand exactly how democracy influences repression and why.

Researchers need to modify how they gather information about democracy and repression, collecting information on a highly disaggregated level. This would allow examinations to be as accurate and as realistic as possible.

Researchers as well as policy makers and activists should attempt to overcome their differences and work together on the problems that concern all of them: the elimination or reduction of state repression.

Critical Thinking Questions:

Where can we go to get information about democracy and repression? Who should be asked? How can we get to these people?

Conclusion

This chapter discussed the relationship between political democracy and state repression—the democracy–repression nexus. It began with an evaluation of the diverse ways in which researchers have investigated the relationship, discussing dominant conceptualizations, consistent findings, and diverse puzzles that have emerged from this work: (1) disaggregating nation states and exploring within-country variation, (2) considering how different aspects of democracy influence different types of repression, and (3) considering how repressive behaviour influences political democracy. The chapter then explored these different puzzles in the context of the United States and its treatment of African Americans. The chapter ended with several suggestions for future research. These included: shifting the questions that are being asked from the general issue of whether and if democracy influences repression to how and where; improving the way that data is collected to facilitate an examination of relationships in a more disaggregated and nuanced fashion; and, finally, making a better connection between academic research and political activism and policy making that allows the discussions taking place in each venue to be receptive to and influenced by the other.

QUESTIONS

Individual Study Questions

1. What is democracy?

2. What is repression?

3. Why and how does democracy influence repression?

4. What are the common errors in existing scholarship?

5. What should be examined in the future?

Group Discussion Questions

1. Can democracy and repression be separated from one another conceptually?

2. Do you believe that democracy influences repression, that repression influences democracy, or both?

3. Do you believe that democracy or economic development is more important for reducing state repression?

FURTHER READING

Davenport, C. (2007). *State Repression and the Domestic Democratic Peace. New York*: Cambridge University Press.

This book discusses the impact of democracy on state repression/human rights violation, considering the important influence of political dissent and civil war.

Della Porta, D. and **Reiter, H.** (1998). *Policing Protest: The Control of Mass Demonstrations in Western Democracies.* Minneapolis, MA: University of Minnesota Press.

This book discusses general approaches to how dissent is repressed within political democracies.

Gibson, J. L. (1988). Political intolerance and political repression during the McCarthy Red Scare. *American Political Science Review,* **82**/2, 511–29.

This article provides an insightful analysis of the causal mechanisms involved with democratic applications of state repression.

Mitchell, N. (2012) *Democracy's Blameless Leaders: From Dresden to Abu Ghraib, How Leaders Evade Accountability for Abuse, Atrocity, and Killing*. New York: New York University Press.

Within this book, Mitchell maintains that against popular thinking leaders within political democracies are more than capable of avoiding responsibility for any wrong doing. Indeed, he argues that they are quite good at it.

Powell, G. B. (2000). *Elections as Instruments of Democracy: Majoritarian andProportional Visions*. New Haven, CT: Yale University Press.

This book explores how and to what degree democracy can function as a mechanism of popular will.

Reiter, D. and **Stam, A. C.** (2002). *Democracies at War*. Princeton, NJ: Princeton University Press.

This book explores exactly how and why democracies do what they do when conflict is under way—specifically when they enter wars and how they fight wars.

Stohl, M. (1976). *War and Domestic Political Violence: The American Capacity for Repression and Reaction*. Beverly Hills, CA: Sage.

This book explores the dynamics of how democracies use repression in situations of inter-state war.

WEB LINKS

http://staterepression.weebly.com/repression-data.html *Human rights and repression data*. This link provides information on all known human rights/repression databases.

http://www.state.gov/g/drl/ *US Bureau of Democracy, Human Rights and Labor*. This site provides information on human rights conditions in the United States and throughout the world. There are also links to US evaluations of their efforts to establish democracies around the world.

http://www.coginta.org/en/ *The World Database on Policing*. This site has information about policing institutions from around the world.

http://www.pbs.org/wnet/jimcrow/themap/map.html *The Rise and Fall of Jim Crow*. This site provides an interactive mapping program that allows the viewer to explore diverse aspects of the Jim Crow system (e.g. the laws, population movements associated with the relevant period, and violent activity directed against African Americans).

http://www.pbs.org/wnet/jimcrow/resources.html *The History of Jim Crow*. This site provides a variety of easily accessible resources on the topic.

http://www.inmotionaame.org/home.cfm?bhcp = 1 *In Motion: The African American Migration Experience*. This site links to a variety of maps from across US history that capture the physical movement of African Americans throughout the states.

NOTES

1. Since the invasion and occupation of Iraq, the opinions about imposing democracy have shifted, but that these political systems have been created with greater frequency is undeniable.

2. There is a new project that is working on this explicitly but it is not yet completed: https://v-dem.net/.

3. Although the Fifteenth Amendment made restrictions based on race illegal in 1870, there was still a wide variety of strategies employed to prevent African Americans from participating.

4. Many scholars also note that southern politics was not only about how whites would control blacks but also which whites would exercise this control (Woodward, 1951, p. 328).

 Visit the Online Resource Centre that accompanies this book for updates and a range of other resources: www.oxfordtextbooks.co.uk/orc/goodhart3e/

15
Torture

William F. Schulz

Chapter Contents

Reader's Guide

Torture is among the most common human rights crimes in the world. It is usually associated with interrogation procedures but is often inflicted to intimidate political opponents, reinforce cultural practices, or spread gratuitous violence. This chapter examines the use of torture in Western history and considers such questions as: Are all torturers sadists or can an average person be trained to be a torturer? Are some societies more prone to practise torture than others? And is torture ever justified? In respect to this last question, the chapter examines in detail the pro and con arguments of the hypothetical case in which a suspect is thought to know the location of a ticking bomb that is about to explode and may injure large numbers of people. It concludes that such a scenario is extremely rare and describes how far more common instances of torture may most successfully be diminished.

Introduction

Miguel Angel Estrella is one of the world's great pianists. In 1977 he was arrested and thrown into Uruguay's notorious Libertad prison for alleged 'subversive associations'. His case attracted international attention and the Queen of England herself intervened on his behalf, requesting the head of the Uruguayan military junta to allow Estrella, at the very least, access to a piano. The authorities agreed and the Queen sent a piano to be presented to him. What the great performer received, however, was merely the keyboard ripped out of the body of the instrument, making it therefore inoperable. 'Your playing will disturb the other prisoners', the musician was informed (Weschler, 1990).

When we think of torture, we customarily conjure up images of dark chambers and brutal physical treatment. Indeed, there is plenty of that. When Belgium's King Leopold ruled the Congo in the late nineteenth century, his minions were fond of punishing the Indigenous workers with whips made from raw, sun-dried hippopotamus hide cut into long, sharp-edged corkscrew strips. Twenty-five lashes brought unconsciousness and one hundred brought death (Hochschild, 1998, pp. 120–3). Beatings, electroshock, rape—all of these are common forms of torture. The United States has acknowledged using water-boarding (in which the victim's mouth is covered with cloth and water is poured over his face to simulate drowning) to extract information from terror suspects (Schoof, 2008; see Figure 15.1).

Figure 15.1 Water-boarding

Name: Water-boarding

Description: There are several different forms of water-boarding, but the most typical, depicted here, is to place a cloth or towel over the mouth and then pour a steady stream of water over it. This simulates the feeling of drowning, thus precipitating severe stress. Its use may be as old as the sixteenth century. The American CIA admitted using the technique on three al-Qaeda prisoners in 2002–3 and the administration of US President George W. Bush denied that water-boarding constituted torture. But the late journalist Christopher Hitchens, a strong supporter of President Bush's intervention in Iraq, underwent water-boarding himself and concluded that without a doubt it was a form of torture (Hitchens, 2008). (You can watch Hitchens undergo water-boarding at https://www.youtube.com/watch?v=Efh_6_-tHgY and judge for yourself, and read about his experience in Hitchens, 2008). The Convention Against Torture (CAT) prohibits 'any act by which severe pain or suffering, whether physical or mental, is intentionally inflicted on a person for such purposes as obtaining from him or a third person information or a confession …'. It would be hard to argue that water-boarding does not meet this definition and, indeed, in 2009 President Barack Obama banned its use by the US.

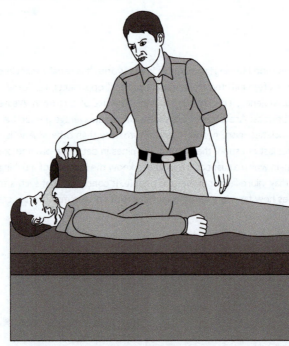

Adapted from Carter (2005)

Some torturers are fiendishly creative. I remember reading about the technique used by the *mujahedeen* (religious warriors) in Afghanistan. They would strap their captured enemies to corpses and let the two bodies, one dead, one alive, rot together in the sun. In Brazil during the 1970s, prisoners were stripped naked and left in a small concrete cell with only one other occupant—a boa constrictor (Dassin, 1986, pp. 16–17). In the Philippines at the turn of the twentieth century, American prisoners of war were buried up to their necks in manure, molasses was then poured over their heads, and fire ants let loose on their scalps (Schulz, 2003, p. 155).

The Americans got their revenge, however, by employing the popular 'water cure' against the Filipinos. One US soldier described it this way:

Lay them on their backs, a man standing on each hand and each foot, then put a round stick in the mouth and pour a pail of water in the mouth and nose, and if they don't give up pour in another. They swell up like toads.

(Kramer, 2008, p. 38)

But psychological torture, such as that employed against Estrella, has also been popular. The Soviets, for example, would frequently deceive a man in custody by informing him that the screams he heard in the next room were from his wife or daughter who were themselves being tortured. It was a sure-fire way to get him to talk (Solzhenitsyn, 1973, pp. 106–7).

It is hard to know how widespread the use of torture is today, but Amnesty International reports that it 'has documented torture in more than 150 countries … In more than 70 countries, it is widespread. People in 80 countries have died as a result …'. Among the countries where torture has been documented are some of the most populous, including China, Russia, and the United States.

No matter exactly how many people have been subjected to torture, we know it is one of the most common human rights violations. And while no respectable observer would defend wife-beating or terrorism, there are more than a few who can imagine circumstances in which torture is justified. That is one reason why it is so important to understand the phenomenon.

In this chapter we will look first at the history of torture in the Western world and then consider what it takes to turn someone into a torturer. We will explore whether some social conditions make the use of torture more likely and whether there are cases in which its employment is justified. Finally, we will describe what can be done to diminish, if not end, the

instances of torture and how those efforts complement other developments in the field of human rights.

Torture in Western History

Today the use of torture is largely hidden: conducted in secret locations, never advertised to the public. Most governments deny that they would even think of manhandling prisoners. Even those who defend the practice agree that it should be employed only rarely and within strict limits. But, interestingly enough, in ancient times people found the use of torture as natural as can be.

Torture of Slaves: 'I Cannot Tell a Lie'

Perhaps it is not surprising that the ancient Greeks and Romans felt little compunction about torturing slaves. Marginalized people, people with less power, are often more likely to be subjected to harsh treatment than those who possess political and economic might. But what is intriguing about the practice of torture in early Greek and Roman history is the *rationale* for slaves being subjected to torture. It was because slaves (in contrast to free citizens) lacked the quality of reason (what the Greeks called *logos*) and hence lacked the capacity to lie. Free citizens could tell the difference between truth and falsehood. But, not possessing *logos*, a slave could not think through the consequences of telling the truth or prevaricating. If forced, he had no choice but to tell the truth. Therefore, if public officials were trying to determine what *really* happened—who really stole the wine; who really killed the shepherdess—they had merely to torture a slave (DuBois, 1991, pp. 63–6).

Here is an early example of a common characteristic of victims of torture: they are regarded as somehow less than fully human, as missing some quality (in this case reason) that warrants their being treated with the same degree of respect as everyone else. They are therefore regarded as 'outsiders', different from 'us', and hence it is less heinous to abuse them. We will see this dynamic at work again and again.

But at least the Greek and Roman legal systems had an honourable motive for the torture of slaves (which is not to say, of course, that many slaves were not tortured for less than honourable reasons): they were seeking the truth. Eventually, however, the limitations of relying on slave testimony alone became obvious. There were only so many slaves, among other things, and not every crime was conveniently accompanied by a slave witness. Other means for ascertaining the facts in a criminal matter would have to be discovered. Fault could be decided by the reputation of the parties involved or the credibility of oaths that they were willing to swear. Physical tests (called 'ordeals') could be undertaken. If, for example, the accused could carry a hot piece of metal in his bare hand for nine feet without the hand blistering, he was judged not guilty; in contrast, the appearance of blisters was unimpeachable evidence of guilt. By the twelfth century, however, it was generally agreed that one means of telling truth from falsehood was superior to all others: a confession!

'The Queen of Proofs'

So reliable were confessions considered by the late Middle Ages that they came to be known as 'the Queen of Proofs'. And what was the most effective way to elicit a confession? Torture, of course. Torture therefore became a routine part of everyday criminal procedure and interrogation. Indeed, the very word *quaestio* (Latin for 'the question falls') came to be synonymous with torture.

The judicial system of the age adopted an elaborate series of 'safeguards' to govern the use of torture. If there were two witnesses to a crime, for example, a confession (and hence torture) was not necessary. Before someone could be tortured, there either had to be one witness to the offence or profound circumstantial evidence of guilt. Interrogators were forbidden to use suggestive questioning (Langbein, 1977). Despite these and other restrictions, though, many innocent people were brutalized, often in the most horrendous ways, as tales of medieval torture chambers readily attest.

It was difficult enough to decide likely guilt sufficient to warrant torture in civil cases. But when it came to religious questions like heresy (deviation from official church doctrine) and witchcraft, the matter became even more complicated. These were, after all, in large measure crimes of thought, not deed, and hence hard to prove. But that only reinforced the need to secure confessions. The Church itself undertook inquisitorial tribunals in which torture was commonplace.

From the standpoint of religious officials, of course, heretics and witches were even more dangerous than common thieves and murderers because they were thieves and murderers of the eternal soul. If their pernicious beliefs spread and were adopted by others, thousands of innocents would not just be deprived of earthly property or physical life, as was the case with common crimes, but would be subjected to eternal

torment. The torture of a few miscreants was a small price to pay to prevent such a tragedy.

But how could anyone know for certain that the right people were being punished? Under torture, victims confessed to all sorts of things. Most of those accused during the Salem, Massachusetts, witchcraft trials of 1692, for instance, eventually admitted that they were guilty even *before* they were tortured! Like the slaves of ancient times, theological deviants were categorized as less worthy of the legal protections that accrued to the rest of society. The result was that often those who were innocent suffered the same penalties as those who were guilty.

The Cry for Abolition

Gradually a reaction to such injustices set in. Five years after the Salem trials, one of the judges, Samuel Sewall, stood up in church and passed a piece of paper to his minister to read to the congregation. 'Samuel Sewall', the preacher read while Sewall bowed his head, '... being sensible ... as to the Guilt contracted, upon the opening of the late [court] at Salem ... Desires to take the Blame & Shame of it, asking pardon of Men, And especially desiring prayers that God ... would pardon that Sin ...' (Francis, 2005, p. 181).

In 1734 Sweden became the first country to abolish virtually all forms of torture, and a few years later Prussia did away with the practice altogether. Other countries followed. The French historian Michel Foucault suggested that the rejection of orthodoxy and 'superstition' that characterized the **Enlightenment**, along with the cruelty that accompanied them, accounts for the change. There was a vast repulsion at the public displays of brutality that had typified the Middle Ages. 'It was as if', Foucault (1977, p. 9) wrote, 'the punishment was thought to equal, if not exceed, in savagery the crime itself ... to make the tortured criminal an object of pity and admiration.'

Abolitionist sentiment, as expressed most popularly by the Italian economist Cesare Beccaria in his 1764 'An Essay on Crimes and Punishment' (Kramnick, 1995, pp. 525–32) and the French *philosophe* Voltaire in his 'On Torture and Capital Punishment' (Kramnick, 1995, pp. 532–5) the same year, was sweeping Europe. Lynn Hunt (2007), a historian, attributes this in large measure to empathy for other people's suffering occasioned by the popularity of eighteenth-century novels depicting the plight of heroines with whom the public identified. Coupled with growing personal modesty—an end to urinating in the street or blowing one's nose in one's hand—that signalled the advent of the self-contained and hence inviolable body, this trend helped to usher in new respect for human rights.

The eminent legal historian John Langbein (1977, pp. 10–12) offers a different theory. He contends that the trigger was not changing views occasioned by the Enlightenment but a shift in the way proof was established by the courts that occurred two centuries before, namely that judges began evaluating the evidence pro and con, based on its merits without the need for confession or torture. Whatever the case, by the turn of the nineteenth century cultural norms in Europe had turned sharply against torture—or at least the torture of fellow Europeans (we have seen that King Leopold had no hesitation about torturing Africans well into the twentieth century). Combined with growing opposition to slavery (the slave trade was abolished in Great Britain in 1833), there was reason to think a more humane form of civilization might be at hand. The early development of international **humanitarian law** (sometimes called 'the laws of war') reinforced such optimism. In 1863 the International Red Cross was formed and the next year sixteen European countries adopted the first of the **Geneva Conventions and Protocols** that mandated humane treatment of battlefield casualties and protection for the civilians who offered them aid. This in turn was followed by the **Hague Conventions** of 1899 and 1907 that sought to make warfare itself less brutal by banning such things as nerve gas and hollow point bullets, and the Third Geneva Convention of 1929 that offered protocols for the treatment of prisoners of war. It was not of course that torture and war crimes ceased altogether, but that no one could any longer claim official sanction for such atrocities.

Until, that is, the coming of the Holocaust. The crimes of the Nazis and their collaborators were not only unprecedented in ferocity and scale—the Second World War has been dubbed a 'total war' because, in addition to the customary attacks on troops, civilians and their property were indiscriminately targeted—but they were planned and executed by what had been regarded as the most cultured nation in Europe. In reaction to the catastrophe, both the United Nations and eventually the modern human rights movement were born. The 1948 **Universal Declaration of Human Rights** (UDHR) declared in Article 5 that 'No one shall be subjected to torture or to cruel, inhuman, or degrading treatment or punishment.' Adopted without dissent, the UDHR established norms and expectations not just for Europeans but for the entire world.

Since that time, dozens of other **treaties**, conventions, codes of conduct, and other international legal instruments have reiterated the prohibition of torture (see Box 15.1) until today it is regarded as **customary international law**—that is, law that is so fundamental and universal as to be beyond dispute and hence is applicable to, and the responsibility of, all governments; and torturers are considered *hostis humani generis* or enemies of all humankind. The most important of these international instruments is the **Convention Against Torture and Other Cruel, Inhuman, or Degrading Treatment or Punishment** (CAT), which entered into force in 1987 and has been ratified by more than 140 countries.

And yet, despite all this opprobrium, torture endures.

KEY POINTS

The ancient Greeks and Romans regarded slaves as incapable of telling a lie because they lacked the capacity to reason. It was therefore thought completely appropriate to torture a slave (as opposed to a free citizen) in order to ascertain the truth about a criminal matter.

In the medieval period, legal authorities considered a confession to be the 'queen of proofs', the most reliable way to resolve a question of guilt or innocence. Since torture was an efficient way of eliciting confessions, it was commonly used, albeit in accordance with a set of guidelines. The Church had little reticence about using torture to expose heretics and witches.

Gradually, whether because of new cultural norms ushered in by the Enlightenment or changes in the legal system, torture became prohibited throughout most of Europe. Coupled with codification of the laws of war and international humanitarian law, there appeared to be promise of a more civilized approach to international relations.

Such promise was badly set back by the Holocaust, though one of the consequences was the development of the modern human rights movement, including a now universal legal prohibition on the use of torture.

Critical Thinking Question:

We know that false confessions, even without torture, are not uncommon. What circumstances can you imagine in which you might confess to a crime you did not commit?

BOX 15.1 EXTRACTS FROM THE PRINCIPAL INTERNATIONAL INSTRUMENTS AGAINST TORTURE

Universal Declaration of Human Rights

'No one shall be subjected to torture or to cruel, inhuman or degrading treatment or punishment.' (Article 5)

Geneva Conventions and Protocols

'… the following acts are and shall remain prohibited at any time and in any place whatsoever with respect to the above-mentioned persons:

a. violence to life and person, in particular, mutilation, cruel treatment and torture …

c. outrages upon personal dignity, in particular humiliating and degrading treatment …'(Common Article 3)

International Covenant on Civil and Political Rights

'No one shall be subjected to torture or to cruel, inhuman or degrading treatment or punishment. In particular, no one shall be subjected without his free consent to medical or scientific experimentation.' (Article 7)

European Convention for the Protection of Human Rights and Fundamental Freedoms

'No one shall be subjected to torture or to inhuman or degrading treatment or punishment.' (Article 3)

American Convention on Human Rights

'No one shall be subjected to torture or to cruel, inhuman, or degrading punishment or treatment. All persons deprived of their liberty shall be treated with respect for the inherent dignity of the human person.' (Article 5)

African Charter on Human and Peoples' Rights

'Every individual shall have the right to the respect of the dignity inherent in a human being and to the recognition of his legal status. All forms of exploitation and degradation of man, particularly slavery, slave trade, torture, cruel, inhuman or degrading punishment and treatment, shall be prohibited.' (Article 5)

UN Convention against Torture and Other Cruel, Inhuman or Degrading Treatment or Punishment

'Each State Party shall take effective legislative, administrative, judicial or other measures to prevent acts of torture in any territory under its jurisdiction.' (Article 2)

Inter-American Convention to Prevent and Punish Torture

'The States Parties shall ensure that all acts of torture and attempts to commit torture are offenses under their criminal law and shall make such acts punishable by severe penalties that take into account their serious nature.' (Article 6)

UN Body of Principles for the Protection of All Persons under Any Form of Detention or Imprisonment

'No person under any form of detention or imprisonment shall be subjected to torture or to cruel, inhuman or degrading treatment or punishment.' (Principle 6)

Convention on the Rights of the Child

'No child shall be subjected to torture or other cruel, inhuman or degrading treatment or punishment …' (Article 37)

UN Declaration on the Elimination of Violence against Women

'Women are entitled to the equal enjoyment and protection of all human rights and fundamental freedoms in the political, economic, social, cultural, civil or any other field. These rights include, *inter alia*:
… (h) The right not to be subjected to torture, or other cruel, inhuman or degrading treatment or punishment.' (Article 3)

UN Code of Conduct for Law Enforcement Officials

'No law enforcement official may inflict, instigate or tolerate any act of torture or other cruel, inhuman or degrading treatment or punishment …' (Article 5)

How to Make a Torturer

Are torturers madmen? Deviants? Hardened criminals? Sexual predators? Almost never. In fact, most police and military units weed out the psychological misfits because they know such people have trouble taking orders. The horrible truth is that the vast majority of torturers are average Joes, like Jose Valle Lopez (see Box 15.2) or, on far rarer occasions, Janes.

The Psychology of Transformation

Turning Joe into a torturer is remarkably easy. You put him in a restricted environment, such as a police or military training camp, under the command of a vaunted authority figure. It helps if the recruit is young and impressionable but people of all ages are susceptible to the demands of authority under the right circumstances—even murderous demands, as the famous Milgram and Stanford prison experiments demonstrated (see Box 15.3).

BOX 15.2 THE CASE OF JOSE

Jose Valle Lopez did not think of himself as a bad man. He had joined the army of his native Honduras at 15; slowly gained more authority within its ranks; married, and fathered two children. Over the years Jose, who, because of his weight, was known as *El Gordo*, 'The Fat One', developed a kind of hardened attitude to prove that he could take the teasing, that he had *cojones*—manliness, courage. As a result, when word spread among the military authorities in the 1980s that the Honduran army would not allow the Communists to infiltrate Honduras as they had done in neighbouring Nicaragua and threatened to do in El Salvador, Jose was more than willing to do what he was told to protect his country.

At first he was assigned to surveillance, then to kidnapping. But the hours of the latter were erratic, so Jose was transferred to the torture division in order to have more regular time with his family. As a journalist who told his tale years later put it, 'he would kiss his wife and children goodbye, pick up his lunch and go off to work in the torture chambers'. There he would submerge his victims in water, suffocate them, and apply electroshock to their genitals.

Eventually he could no longer tolerate the screaming. But when he asked for a transfer, the ridicule began again: 'What's the matter, El Gordo? No *cojones*?' Still, Jose persisted: he wanted out. And that is when the threats began: 'The day you leave, Jose, we will cut your head off.' When he could no longer take the threats, Jose fled with his family to Canada and finally went public with his story. He wanted the world to know that he was not a monster. He wanted to make the case that, under similar circumstances, many others would have done the same thing.

Adapted from Atkinson (1989)

BOX 15.3 THE MILGRAM AND STANFORD PRISON EXPERIMENTS

Two experiments in social psychology have become classics in the field, often cited to illumine the motivations of those 'average citizens' who inflict cruelty on their fellow human beings. Each experiment has been criticized both as to its ethics and its methodology, but both also reflect at least a germ of truth that is worth exploring.

The experiments conducted by Yale psychologist Stanley Milgram beginning in 1961 involved an authority figure (the experimenter) instructing a subject who had been designated the 'teacher' to issue an electric shock to another person (designated 'the learner') every time the learner made an error in a word test. The voltage of the shock supposedly increased at a regular pace and, though the teachers could not see the learners, they could hear them expressing pain, screaming, and eventually begging the teacher to stop shocking them. (In reality, no shocks were being administered.) Despite hearing these pleas, a significant number of teachers, when instructed to do so by the authority figure (the experimenter), continued to issue the shocks. Milgram concluded that most people had a strong tendency to obey authority and that therefore ordinary people could be transformed into agents of destruction under the right circumstances (Milgram, 1974).

The Stanford prison experiment was led by Stanford University psychologist Philip Zimbardo in 1971. One group of university students was designated 'guards' and another 'prisoners' and they were then placed in a simulated prison environment in the basement of the Stanford psychology department building. Because the behaviour of many of the guards quickly took on a sadistic character—even though all participants knew the situation was no more than a simulation—Zimbardo stopped the experiment prematurely, concluding, like Milgram, that in certain situations otherwise well-balanced individuals will act in a cruel fashion towards others perceived to be weaker or different, especially when given sanction to do so (Haney, Banks, and Zimbardo, 1973).

You then subject your recruit to intense stress, harassment, and brutality. The Greek military police in the time of the Greek generals (1967–74), for example, were renowned for their torture squads. Each of the recruits to those squads was forced to go weeks without food and undergo severe beatings, sometimes not being permitted to defecate for up to fifteen days at a time (Haritos-Fatouros, 1988). Joan Golston (1993), a psychotherapist who has studied torturers, theorizes that the abuse heaped on trainees casts them in the 'victim' role and, in order to mitigate the shame of that experience and differentiate themselves in their own minds from 'real' victims, they in turn inflict abuse on others. This is what she calls *'the torturer's bind'*.

Be that as it may, once we have created an angry, desensitized, but obedient servant, the next steps are to train that servant in torture techniques—the object is to inflict enormous pain but not to kill—and to provide sanction for employing those techniques against a vulnerable but despised and dehumanized object: 'These are the people who are threatening our country.' 'This is the person who killed your comrade.'

One thing that virtually every victim of torture has in common is that he or she has been defined as alien to the dominant culture: one of 'them', not one of 'us'; in short, a 'barbarian', to use the word the novelist J. M. Coetzee chooses in his famous story, *Waiting for the Barbarians* (see Box 15.4). Those who are labelled outsiders, as having violated our most sacred values, can be thought to have sacrificed their claim to the protection of rights, including their right to be regarded as human.

In many cases the torturers, like Jose Valle Lopez, convince themselves that they are acting in a higher cause, that the questions they ask and the information they procure are essential to other people's welfare or the survival of a way of life. But all too often the motivation for torture is not so 'high-minded'. Often the real goal is intimidation of the prisoner or the members of his or her group or community. Unlike those earlier forms of torture that were prompted by a desire to solve crimes or save souls, modern-day torture often reflects little more than a sadistic character, a desire to display complete sovereignty over the will of another person. This is certainly the case, for example, when rape is used as an instrument of war, as it was in the war in the Balkans (Allen, 1996), or when prisoners are led around on leashes or forced to masturbate for the cameras, as they were at the US prison at Abu Ghraib, Iraq (Danner, 2004).

Whatever the motivation, there is one more characteristic shared by virtually all torturers: they believe they will get away with their crimes. Very few act on

BOX 15.4 WAITING FOR THE BARBARIANS

In his classic 1982 novel *Waiting for the Barbarians*, the South African novelist J. M. Coetzee captures the phenomenon of dehumanization concisely. He describes a large crowd that is awaiting the appearance of a group of prisoners—'Barbarians!'—who are tied to each other by a rope around their necks. In addition, a metal wire has been looped through a hole in each prisoner's cheek that connects in turn to a hole in his hand. 'It makes them meek as lambs', one soldier says, 'They think of nothing but how to keep very still.'

The prisoners are paraded in front of the crowd so that 'everyone has a chance … to prove to his children that the barbarians are real'. Then the Colonel of Police steps forward.

Stooping over each prisoner … he rubs a handful of dust into his naked back and writes a word with a stick of charcoal … 'ENEMY … ENEMY … ENEMY … ENEMY'. He steps back and folds his hands … Then the beating begins.

(Coetzee, 1982, pp. 102–5)

their own whim. Torture is rarely the case of 'a few bad apples' acting contrary to the wishes of their superiors. Whether they have received explicit orders or only 'a wink and a nod', most torturers believe that those to whom they are accountable will at least privately approve of what they do. Indeed, torture does not survive long without **impunity**, that is, the belief that the perpetrator will be exempt from any punishment or penalty.

And yet sometimes—again Jose is an example—the stress of the job itself begins to take its toll. Frantz Fanon (2004, p. 195), a psychiatrist who became a famous philosopher of anti-colonialism, tells of treating a police officer who came to him suffering from depression. 'The thing is, they never wanted to confess', the officer said of the people he had tortured.

Sometimes you feel like telling them that if they had any consideration for us, they'd cough up and not force us to spend hours on end squeezing the information out of them. But you might as well talk to the wall … So of course we had to give them the works. But they scream too much. At first it made me laugh. But then it began to unnerve me … Now I can hear those screams even at home. Especially the screams of the ones who died at police headquarters. Doctor, I'm sick of this job. If you can cure me, I'll request a transfer … If they refuse [to transfer me], I'll resign.

But getting out is not always easy, both because torturers have been taught psychologically to revere authority and obey it and because they are often threatened by their colleagues and supervisors if they try to leave.

Few systematic studies of the mental health of torturers have ever been undertaken—the universe of those willing to admit their guilt and subject themselves to testing is too small!—but it is not hard to believe that those who inflict brutality sustain emotional damage too. In a paradoxical way, then, the phenomenon of torture creates two sets of victims. See Box 15.5 for further discussion of torturers.

The Social Preconditions of Torture

If large numbers of 'average' people can be made into torturers, are all societies equally susceptible to resorting to the practice or are there some social conditions that make torture more likely?

In a broad sense, as we have seen, torture requires there to be a significant differential in power between torturer and victim. Based on his studies of Turkey during the years of the Armenian genocide (1914–18), Nazi Germany (1933–45), Pol Pot's Cambodia (1976–9), and Argentina in the period of the 'Dirty War' (1976–83), Erwin Staub (1990, pp. 49–50), one of the few social scientists to have studied the 'social indicators' of genocide and torture, identifies scapegoating of a subgroup as a social condition conducive to the rise of torture. Other characteristics of societies that resort readily to torture are: strong respect for authority and hence little questioning of leadership; a monolithic culture that militates against expression of conflicting views; widespread concepts of cultural superiority that may mask self-doubt or economic anxiety; and the presence of an ideology that rationalizes mistreatment of a minority or out-group.

All this is well and good. But we know that democracies—even robust democracies like the United States that sanction vigorous political debate and proclaim their commitment to equal treatment of all—can also succumb to the temptations of torture. Ronald Crelinsten (2005, pp. 76–7), a criminologist, has expanded on and reframed Staub's list based on contemporary examples associated with the post-9/11 'war on terror'. He, too, finds the dehumanizing of an out-group—in this case, Muslims—central to the institutionalization of torture. But he cites additional factors that make it more likely: a national emergency or perceived threat to security; the need to process large numbers of suspects; authorization to violate standard social norms (and here he does not limit that authorization to government or military officials but includes members of the media and academia who provide the rationale for brutality); and the presence of a 'sacred mission' in whose name anything is acceptable.

Suffice it to say that societies that feel themselves under threat are more likely to strike out at those whom they fear, and leaders of even the most open society can leverage that fear for unfortunate ends. But might there not indeed be circumstances where such fear is justified and the use of 'unusual methods', including torture, legitimate? We turn now to the hypothetical case of the 'ticking bomb'.

KEY POINTS

Many regimes have transformed average people into torturers by exposing them to authority figures who subject them to brutal training, teach them the techniques of torture, and then provide sanction for the mistreatment of some despised individual or group of people who are regarded as less than human.

Torture requires a sense of impunity. Few people will engage in the practice without the encouragement of their superiors.

Torture takes an immense toll on its victims, of course, but may also do damage to the mental health of its perpetrators, who may find it difficult to extract themselves from a torture regimen even if they want to.

Certain social conditions, including concepts of cultural superiority and exploitation of feelings of fear among a populace, may increase the likelihood of torture being practised, even in largely open, democratic societies.

Critical Thinking Question:

Consider Staub's and Crelinsten's respective lists of characteristics of societies that may be predisposed to sanction torture. Can you identify places in the world today in which you think those characteristics are evident and hence the use of torture a possibility?

BOX 15.5 CHALLENGING ASSUMPTIONS: ARE TORTURERS MADE OR BORN?

Through much of Western history, philosophers from Aristotle to Locke believed that human beings were born 'blank slates' (the Latin term is *tabula rasa*) when it came to the content of our minds, and characters, and that our behaviours for good or ill were formed largely by our experiences. More recently evidence has arisen that suggests some humans may be genetically predisposed to act in ways society is inclined to label 'evil'. What is your own take on this question? How easy do you think it would be for you to be persuaded to torture another human being? And if we are predisposed by our DNA to some forms of brutality, can we be held accountable for our actions?

Case Study: Ticking Bomb Torture

The Arguments for Torture

No respectable commentator has ever tried to defend torture inflicted for the sheer sadistic pleasure of it, but many noteworthy philosophers, including the great Jeremy Bentham (1748–1832), have argued that under a narrow set of circumstances torture is not only defensible but morally obligatory. The hypothetical case is usually put something like this: suppose that the authorities have in custody an individual whom they believe has information that, if they can procure it quickly, will help them prevent the detonation of a bomb that, if allowed to explode, will kill hundreds, if not thousands, of people. Would they not be justified in using whatever coercive means were necessary to force the revelations they seek? Indeed, could they not be accused of dereliction of duty if they allowed moral reservations to prevent them from doing so, thereby sacrificing the lives of many innocent people?

The argument for the use of torture under these circumstances is based on a pretty straightforward cost–benefit calculation: torture one suspect; save 1,000 (or however many) lives. It is hardly surprising that Bentham should favour torture, having been a thoroughgoing **utilitarian**—a system of ethics most simply explained as holding that the moral worth of an action can be determined by the degree to which it brings the greatest amount of happiness or pleasure to the greatest number of people. This is an example of what is called **consequentialism**, namely the notion that we ought to judge an act by its consequences (sometimes expressed simply as 'the ends justify the means'), in contrast to a **deontological** approach in which acts are considered intrinsically good or bad, no matter what their consequences.

On the face of it, the argument for 'ticking bomb torture' seems unassailable. It is not, however, without its weaknesses, and serious scholars who have advanced it have recognized that and tried to respond. One weakness is that it is not always easy to know who has the information we seek and who does not. No one believes that it is justifiable to torture an innocent person. So philosophers such as Michael Levin (1982), who argue for the legitimacy of ticking bomb torture, have agreed that we should 'torture only the obviously guilty', such as would be the case if '40 million people

see a group of masked gunmen seize an airplane on the evening news'.

Another potential weakness is the so-called 'slippery slope', the danger that, once we have allowed torture under very limited conditions, authorities will be tempted to expand on the number of people tortured or the circumstances in which it is allowed. Alan Dershowitz (2002), a well-known law professor, has proposed that if authorities wish to torture someone, they should be required to go to a judge and obtain a **torture warrant** that would limit the brutal treatment as to target, duration, intensity, etc. and have the additional virtue of placing responsibility squarely on the backs of higher authorities rather than on the low-level police or military officer who has to inflict the punishment directly.

In 1987 the Israeli government faced accusations that its security arm, Shin Bet, had been applying undue physical pressure to Palestinian prisoners, and a Commission of Inquiry headed by former Israeli Supreme Court Justice Moshe Landau was asked to investigate. The Landau Commission Report (1989) concluded that, faced with a ticking bomb situation, 'moderate physical pressure' (a detailed description of which was included in a secret annex to the report) could be applied as the lesser of two evils and could be legally defended under the **doctrine of necessity**, that is, the notion that one harmful act may be justifiable to prevent a second far more harmful act.[1]

The Arguments against Torture

To marshal the arguments against ticking bomb torture is a more complicated task than to argue the affirmative unless one feels comfortable relying on a strictly deontological stance and proclaiming, perhaps on the basis of religious doctrine or **natural law** philosophy, or simple illegality, that torture is intrinsically wrong under all circumstances. Exploration of such topics is beyond the bounds of this chapter, however, so we will restrict ourselves to arguments of a pragmatic or consequentialist nature.

As we have seen, the ticking bomb scenario looks like a situation in which torture is not only justified, but may even be morally imperative: we are certain that our suspect knows where the bomb is hidden; we must obtain that information quickly and we know that torture will be an effective means to pry accurate information out of him; we voluntarily limit our brutality to the suspect himself and limit the amount of pain we inflict to the minimum necessary to get him to talk; and more people will live as a result of our action than would otherwise die. This is what we will call the 'pure scenario' and, if this is the hypothesis we are faced with, it is difficult to bring persuasive consequentialist arguments to bear against it.

The problem is that in real life such a scenario is extraordinarily rare—we cannot say it has never arisen, but there are no documented cases of it having done so in exactly this form—and the last and most important calculation, namely that more people will live than die as a result of our use of torture, is, as we shall see, impossible to prove. So let us take the elements of the scenario one by one.

'We are certain that our suspect knows where the bomb is hidden.' But how certain do we have to be for torture to be justified? Levin appears to say that we must be 100 per cent certain. But how often are fallible human beings 100 per cent certain of anything? (And how do we measure degree of certainty anyway?) Even in the example that Levin gives—'40 million people see a group of masked gunmen seize a plane on the evening news'—there is room for doubt. The gunmen are, after all, 'masked'. And we know that television pictures can easily be altered to show just about anything. Moreover, the world in which torture interrogations take place is a world of shadows. Suspects are not paraded before the public or caught on camera; their bad deeds are rarely fully known. (Indeed, if they *were* known, we would have little reason to torture them.) So 100 per cent certainty seems like a pipe dream. What, then, if we were only 95 per cent certain? Should we refrain from torture then, even if we think coercion would save thousands of innocent lives? How about if we were only 50 per cent certain? If we had a fifty-fifty chance of saving people, would that not be worth the gamble? What if we only had a 1 per cent sense of certainty? Would it not be reasonable, even if we had only vague suspicions, to torture one individual if the consequences of not doing so might be the loss of thousands of innocents? And yet, if we were to follow that path, we would certainly end up torturing many suspects who had no relevant knowledge to share at all. You can see how quickly the 'limited circumstances' under which torture is justified morph into something much larger.[2]

'We must obtain the information quickly and we know that torture will be an effective means to pry it out of the suspect.' The vast majority of interrogations in which torture is used involve the quest for long-term information, the names of comrades, patterns of behaviour, and the structure of networks. The United States has acknowledged torturing many alleged terrorists in order ostensibly to prevent future 9 / 11s, but there is no reason to believe that those would-be attacks came within only minutes of being carried out but for the timely use of torture to prevent them. Moreover, there is good reason to believe that torture is an ineffective means of obtaining accurate information. Prisoners in excruciating pain are notorious for telling interrogators anything they want to hear. As a former FBI interrogation instructor put it,

Interrogation is an art form, not a street fight. It is built on guile, perseverance, and a keen understanding of how people respond to need. People will tell you anything if you present the questions in the proper context. You simply have to find the right way to ask.

(Whitcomb, 2002)

'We voluntarily limit our brutality to the suspect himself and limit the amount of pain we inflict to the minimum necessary to get him to talk.' But, under a consequentialist ethic, what possible reason is there for limiting our torture in any way? Why do we need to have any scruples at all about the techniques we employ? Furthermore, we know from reports of torture victims that it is often far more painful to see a loved one brutalized than to be subjected to harm oneself. If our initial acts of torture do not work, therefore, why are we not fully justified in torturing the suspect's spouse or teenage child or 2 year old baby to get him to talk? Would not harm even to a baby be morally justified if it saved the lives of hundreds of other people, including, no doubt, dozens of babies? What about torturing two babies to save four babies? Under the ticking bomb scenario, there is no good reason ever to stop. This is exactly why torture that is intended initially to be highly circumscribed so often ends up sliding down that slippery slope. Tens of thousands of people have been subjected to torture over the years. It is hard to believe that they all knew the whereabouts of a ticking time bomb.

'More people will live as a result of our action than would otherwise die.' This is, of course, the nub of the issue.

If we cannot show that torturing a prisoner ultimately does more good for more people than abstaining from torture would, we cannot make a defensible case for the practice, given all the problems we have raised thus far. Under the pure ticking bomb scenario, the cost–benefit calculation is self-evident. But in real life the consequences of torture may be far more complex. Let us assume that, by torturing a suspect, we manage to save 1,000 lives. How do we know that, on learning that their brother or comrade had been brutally tortured, other members of the suspect's community will not want to even the score by killing 2,000 people? What happens to our cost–benefit calculation then? We certainly know that many armed groups opposed to governments around the world often motivate their members by citing government atrocities. As the founder of the Israeli chapter of Physicians for Human Rights put it, those Palestinians subjected to torture by Israel 'are broken after their experience … Their families … want to take revenge' (*Village Voice*, 2001). And this is to say nothing about the damage done to the reputations of those governments that condone torture—damage that may very well make their citizens and property far more vulnerable targets of attack. As the former chief prosecutor for the US military commissions at Guantanamo Bay, Cuba, pointed out, one of the reasons the Iraqi army surrendered readily in the 1991 Persian Gulf war, thereby saving untold American lives, was because they believed that they would not be tortured by the American military (Davis, 2008). 'Would it have been different', he asked in 2008, 'if the perception of [Americans] as purveyors of torture and humiliation existed back then?' Even the strict utilitarian argument for ticking bomb torture may not stand up to scrutiny.

Twelve years after the Landau Commission Report, the Israeli Supreme Court struck down virtually all of the techniques of 'moderate physical pressure' that the Commission had allowed as 'not reasonable', 'not fall[ing] within the sphere of a "fair" interrogation' and 'impinge[ing] upon the suspect's dignity, his bodily integrity and his basic rights' (Supreme Court of Israel, 1999).[3] The Court did not rule out 'necessity' as a means of defence against the use of torture. But it said that necessity could not be cited *before the fact* as a rationale. It could only be called upon after an indictment had been brought against an alleged torturer to explain and excuse his acts.

Law professor Oren Gross (2004, pp. 229–53) has elaborated on this notion, arguing that torture

BOX 15.6 TORTURE AND THE CIA

In December of 2014, the US Senate Intelligence Committee released a heavily redacted executive summary of a report long in the making regarding the Central Intelligence Agency's use of 'enhanced interrogation' techniques against alleged terrorists (*The Senate Intelligence Committee Report on Torture: Committee Study of the Central Intelligence Agency's Detention and Interrogation Program* (http://www.feinstein.senate.gov/public/index.cfm?p=senate-intelligence-committee-study-on-cia-detention-and-interrogation-program).

Among its key points: the CIA's techniques, which included water-boarding, 'rectal feeding', and death threats, were more brutal than the agency had claimed; the CIA misled Congress and the White House about the extent of that brutality; and the CIA exaggerated the necessity and success of the programme.

The CIA fought relentlessly to prevent the release of the report and, once it was in the public domain, undertook a massive campaign to discredit it. But, importantly, the report is now on the public record, providing the kind of transparency that, while not sufficient by itself to stop the use of torture, is a key component of combating it.

should always be banned and hence its employment is always illegal, but that state agents, be they the torturers themselves or the higher authorities who directed them, might well seek *ex post facto* (retrospective) ratification of their acts either in a court of law or the court of public opinion. Such an approach presumably preserves the state's image (not least of all its self-image) as a righteous nation committed to the rule of law while recognizing the political and legal reality that, in the face of a pure ticking bomb scenario, authorities who resort to torture are unlikely to be punished. In contrast to Dershowitz's 'torture warrant' proposal, which codifies torture as a legitimate option *before* the fact, thereby offering certain impunity to officials and colouring the image of the society as one that tolerates cruelty, Gross's proposal forces authorities to commit civil disobedience and live with the knowledge that they may or may not be exonerated afterwards—knowledge that might discourage the kind of capricious use of torture that has been so common in the twentieth century and beyond. See Box 15.6 for a discussion of the CIA's use of torture.

KEY POINTS

Torture is often justified by its defenders with reference to a hypothetical situation in which a suspect has knowledge of a ticking time bomb that is about to go off and, if it does, will kill many people. Is it not justified to use torturous interrogation techniques against such a suspect under that limited circumstance to procure information necessary to avert an enormous tragedy?

This defence is based on a straightforward cost–benefit analysis: doing harm to one person in order to avoid harm to many more is a moral act.

Opponents of the use of torture argue that the pure hypothetical situation described in the ticking bomb scenario is not reflected in real life and that the calculations are far more complicated than they at first appear.

Israel has been one of the few countries that has regularly debated this issue in public and its experience may be useful.

Critical Thinking Question:

Which position makes most sense to you—Dershowitz's suggestion that torture may be legitimate under some circumstances but to be legal needs to be sanctioned by a court before it is used, or Gross's notion that torture should always be regarded as wrong or illegal though those who employ it, thereby breaking the law, may be exonerated afterwards if they can justify their actions to a court?

Putting an End to Torture: New Developments and High Promise

Regardless of one's opinion on the ticking bomb question, the fact is that it represents a tiny fraction of the instances in which torture is used. Far more common is the mistreatment meted out by police or military officials for political or religious reasons, to inflict retaliation, or to foster intimidation.

But what exactly constitutes torture? Where does cruel behaviour end and torture begin? The CAT requires torture to involve 'severe pain and suffering'. But what is the definition of severe? And is it not true that human pain thresholds vary and that what one person considers 'severe' pain another might consider relatively mild?

The **European Court of Human Rights** (ECHR) addressed this question in a landmark case, *Ireland* v. *United Kingdom* (1978), in which it ruled that five techniques—wall-standing; hooding; subjection to loud noise; deprivation of sleep; and deprivation of food and drink—used by British officials against Irish nationalists, while they 'did not occasion suffering of the particular intensity and cruelty implied by the word torture', did amount to 'a practice of inhuman and degrading treatment', and that in itself was a breach of the European Convention on Human Rights, which prohibited such practices. The point is that, while understandings of what constitutes torture may vary, even acts that do not rise to the level of torture are outlawed under most human rights conventions. Recall that the name of the most pertinent convention is the Convention Against Torture *and Other Cruel, Inhuman, and Degrading Treatment or Punishment.*[4]

The CAT defines torture, then, as:

any act by which severe pain or suffering, whether physical or mental, is intentionally inflicted on a person for such purposes as obtaining from him or a third person information or a confession, punishing him for an act he or a third person has committed or is suspected of having committed, or intimidating or coercing him or a third person, or for any reason based on discrimination of any kind, when such pain or suffering is inflicted by or at the instigation of or with the consent or acquiescence of a public official or other person acting in an official capacity.

Yet even this definition is incomplete. The ECHR ruled in *Aydin* v. *Turkey* (1997) that rape while in state custody constituted torture, thus expanding the category to include instances of gratuitous violence. Nor does it make sense to limit torture to acts involving public officials. After all, **non-state actors** (see Box 15.7), such as armed opposition groups, terrorist organizations, private security contractors hired by corporations, and tribal elders enforcing cultural traditions such as *female genital mutilation* (FGM), engage in practices that look very much like torture, even if they are not covered by the CAT definition. Many observers (Copelon, 1994) would now include severe forms of domestic violence and child abuse within the rubric too.

Once we have established the breadth of the problem, the final and most crucial question becomes: what can we do about it? We know that laws in and of themselves cannot stop criminal acts and that much international law goes unenforced. Over the past decade and a half, however, several important developments carry considerable promise that torture may be successfully combated, even if it is never eliminated.

'Non-state actors' is a revealing term when it is applied in a human rights context. In the first place it implies that traditional nations or states are the entities most fundamentally responsible for human rights violations, and historically that may well be true. Most human rights treaties are written in such a way as to hold governments accountable for human rights crimes. But as terrorist organizations and corporations have, in very different ways of course, both become more global in their scope and reach, it has become evident that they too need to be held responsible for violating human rights. Al-Qaeda and Islamic State are not 'governments' in any traditional sense but they are certainly responsible for serious human rights abuses.

Sometimes it is difficult to separate governments from non-state actors. Hezbollah, for example, is very closely aligned with the Syrian government and is suspected of often doing its bidding. China's government owns many large corporations and, though Western companies are usually at least theoretically independent of their home governments, corporate and state interests are often closely aligned. Eventually human rights law will need to catch up with the fact that non-state actors are often even more powerful than some governments and so need to be 'regulated' by human rights treaties and conventions, difficult as it may be to enforce such regulations.

In the first place, the vast majority of the world's nations have incorporated laws against torture into their own constitutions and legal statutes. This includes prohibitions against crimes that are often considered culturally sanctioned, such as burning the faces of brides who displease their husbands, dowry killings (the killing of brides whose dowries are not considered adequate), and female genital mutilation. While such laws are often sporadically enforced, they provide the legal basis for Indigenous human rights activists, whose numbers and sophistication have been growing rapidly, to challenge these practices, both legally and socially. Contrary to the old slogan 'You cannot legislate morality', the fact is that one of the ways to shift cultural norms is by declaring certain practices out of bounds legally and hence unacceptable to those who want to understand themselves as abiding by the rule of law. The more that torture is outlawed, the more it becomes socially deviant to practise or support it. The international community would not countenance today a debate

about whether slavery or piracy was an acceptable practice, and that is slowly becoming the case with torture as well.

But we need not rely on political pressure or social shaming alone. More and more torturers are being convicted of their crimes in courts of law, even years after their perpetration. One recent example is that of Duch, the Khmer Rouge commandant of the notorious S-21 Prison in Phnom Penh, Cambodia, where at least 17,000 people were tortured and died in the 1970s. In 2010 a joint international–Cambodia court found him guilty of crimes against humanity.

Perhaps the most important development of recent years has been the increasing vibrancy of the legal concept of **universal jurisdiction**, the doctrine that certain crimes are so serious that, regardless of where they were committed, any country on Earth may claim jurisdiction over them and seek prosecution of those alleged to have committed them. States party to the CAT are obligated either to prosecute those credibly accused of torture whom they find on their territory, even if the torture was committed elsewhere, or to extradite them to a country that will.

This doctrine has largely been honoured in the breach, but in 1999 the British Law Lords (the United Kingdom's highest court) ruled that General Augusto Pinochet, the former president of Chile who had come to Great Britain for medical treatment and hence was on British soil, could not claim **sovereign immunity**[5] and could be extradited to Spain to stand trial for the torture and murder of Spanish citizens even though those acts were alleged to have been committed in Chile. Pinochet was eventually judged too ill to stand trial and returned to Chile, where he later died, but the precedent that those accused of torture might legitimately be prosecuted anywhere in the world had been established by a highly respected court. Utilizing the doctrine of universal jurisdiction, Belgium in 2001 successfully prosecuted four Rwandan citizens accused of involvement in the 1994 Rwandan genocide. In principle, then, those who commit crimes against humanity, such as torture, need not only fear prosecution before such tribunals as the **International Criminal Court**, if it can claim jurisdiction, or various ad hoc tribunals, if they exist, but may also face indictment before national courts that are inclined to pursue them. Coupled with the burgeoning use of **truth commissions** (see Chapter 22) to sort out the facts of past human rights crimes and hold the appropriate people responsible for them, universal jurisdiction provides still one more way to effect a degree of accountability for crimes like torture.

In the United States such accountability is being pursued through the use of the **Alien Tort Statute (ATS)** of 1789 and the **Torture Victim Protection Act (TVPA)** of 1991. The ATS and the TVPA provide means through which US citizens and aliens (foreign nationals) can bring civil suits in US courts for torts (wrongs) committed overseas, either in violation of international law or of treaties to which the United States is a party. The ATS was originally intended as a mechanism to compensate those who had lost property to pirates, but in a historic case, *Filartiga* v. *Pena-Irala* (1980) (see Box 15.8), a US court ruled that torturers who have sought safe haven in the US could be sued for civil damages by their victims or their victims' families. Since then the Center for Justice and Accountability (CJA), among others, has successfully assisted a myriad of survivors of torture and other human rights abuses to bring such suits, most of which have been successful. In December 2005, for instance, a federal jury found a former El Salvador military colonel guilty of crimes against humanity and ordered him to pay US$6,000,000 to four people who had been tortured or had relatives killed by his security forces. In August 2012, a federal judge awarded US$21,000,000 million in compensatory and punitive damages to victims of atrocities committed by former Somali Minister of Defence, General Mohamed Ali Samantar. Plaintiffs do not always collect on these judgments but, even when they do not, they often feel that justice has been served because the guilt of the accused has been established publicly. Moreover, those found responsible for such crimes may well be subject to removal or deportation from the United States. The US Supreme Court has recently limited the reach of the TVPA in human rights cases against corporations (*Mohamed* v. *Palestinian Authority*, 132 S. Ct. 1702 (2012)) and of the ATS in both corporate and individual cases (*Kiobel* v. *Royal Dutch Shell Petroleum* 133 S. Ct. 1659 (2013)).

Though seldom used, the US also has criminal statutes which allow for the prosecution of torture and other human rights crimes committed overseas. In 2008, Chuckie Taylor, son of former Liberian president Charles Taylor, was the first person to be convicted under the federal criminal torture statute and sentenced to 97 months in prison.

Not one of these legal tools alone will put an end to torture. They must be supplemented by continuing vigilance on the part of international and Indigenous

> **BOX 15.8** *FILÁRTIGA V. PEÑA-IRALA*
>
> Joel Filártiga was a Paraguayan physician who ran a clinic for the poor and was an outspoken critic of the military dictatorship. In 1976 his son, Joelito, was kidnapped by a police official named Americo Peña-Irala, and others, and tortured to death. The Filártigas were unsuccessful in their attempts to have Peña-Irala held to account in Paraguay. In 1978 Peña-Irala, his mistress, and two relatives took up residence in Brooklyn, New York. When they were discovered, US officials arrested them for overstaying their visa and initiated deportation proceedings. But Dolly Filártiga, Joelito's sister, who was living in Washington, DC at the time, along with her father, filed a US$10 million civil suit against Peña-Irala under the Alien Tort Statute (ATS) for compensation for the death of Joelito. The suit was initially dismissed based on precedents that the application of international law in the US only applies to relations between states. But in June 1980 that judgment was reversed. Finding that customary international law forbade torture, a US federal appeals court ruled that the reach of such law extended everywhere and that therefore US courts *did* have jurisdiction over matters of this nature—when the defendant is found in the US—even though the abuses had occurred in another country (630 F. 2d 876 (2d Cir. 1980)). Since this precedent-setting decision, ATS and the TVPA have been used frequently to bring civil suits against alleged torturers who have taken up residence in the United States.
>
> (Claude, 1983)

human rights organizations, aided by: new forms of electronic communication, to bring torture out of the shadows; pressure from such bodies as the European Union, which has used Turkey's interest in joining the Union, for example, as a vehicle for encouraging that country to improve significantly its record on torture (Worden, 2005); and the systematic training of police and military officers in appropriate and effective methods of interrogation.

Torture will no doubt continue to claim its victims; fortunately, health professionals are establishing more and more treatment centres for victims of torture to ease the pain of the experience and help survivors rebuild their lives. But torturers can be less certain than in decades past that they will get away with their crimes. As the human rights movement matures and grows, that uncertainty will build and, just as nothing encourages torture to flourish more than impunity, so nothing will hasten its decline more readily than the sure knowledge that the use of such brutality will no longer go unpunished.

Conclusion

Why human beings so frequently inflict grievous injury in the form of torture upon one another is a complex scientific and perhaps theological question. One neuro-psychologist has suggested that the howls of pain that emanate from our fellow human beings are so appealing, especially to males, because they evoke the success of the hunt, hearkening back to the Palaeozoic era, and hence signal personal and social power (Nell, 2006). Other observers would attribute the appeal to the inherent human capacity for sin.

While we have dealt in this chapter with torture as it has occurred in the West, it is a worldwide phenomenon that has been found in virtually every region of the globe. As we have seen, the rationale for torture, dating back to the earliest eras of Western history, is often a perceived need to obtain information, but brutality has often been used for less 'reputable' reasons as well. It is not necessarily difficult to convince individuals to become torturers—a fairly standard process involving authority figures, isolation, brutalization, technical training, and assurances of impunity has been documented to work effectively. When such a process is introduced into a society that has identified a group of people as threatening outsiders and hence as people possessing fewer claims to rights or even to be considered human, torture is often almost inevitable.

Some have argued that a ticking time bomb scenario may warrant the use of torture, but such instances are extraordinarily rare and the question far more complex than it initially appears to be. The more common uses of torture, e.g. for political or social intimidation, may best be combated by strictly enforced laws against it, cultural norms that forbid it, and assurance that those who engage in it will pay a significant penalty.

It is said that Vladimir Lenin, one of the most brutal and hard-hearted men in the world, could not listen to Beethoven's *Appassionata* because it made him cry. It will take far more than beautiful music to rid the world of torture. Lenin's tears remind us that even the most corrupted soul may retain a spark of humanity to which we may appeal, but the far more important lesson that they teach is that tender thoughts can be misleading and that the only way truly to put an end to cruelty is to be vigilant in pursuit of its cessation.

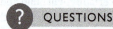 **QUESTIONS**

Individual Study Questions

1.   Why did the ancient Greeks and Romans think it appropriate to torture slaves to obtain information? Why was that practice ultimately considered inadequate as a way to solve crimes?

2. What is the 'Queen of Proofs'? Why were heretics considered to be even more dangerous than common thieves by the medieval church?

3. Describe two theories as to why European governments gradually came to abandon the use of torture as an official practice. Does one of these theories seem more plausible to you than another?

4. What is 'customary international law' and why does the prohibition of torture fall under its rubric? What are *hostis humani generis*?

5. Describe the general process by which police or military recruits are often transformed into torturers. Do you think that you yourself might be vulnerable to such a transformation?

6. Describe some of the characteristics of societies in which torture tends to be found.

7. What is 'universal jurisdiction' and why is it such an important tool in the fight against torture?

8. What is the Alien Tort Statute, and how has it been used against alleged torturers in the United States?

Group Discussion Questions

1. What is the 'ticking bomb scenario'? Describe the arguments in favour of the use of torture in such a situation and those against such use. Do you find one set of arguments more compelling than the other? Should torture be outlawed in all cases and those who engage in it forced to defend their use of it after the fact, or ought it to be possible to grant judicial permission for torture before it is employed?

2. What are the keys to diminishing the use of torture around the world? How do cultural norms change? Is it better to have laws on the books against torture even if they are not always adequately enforced, or do such 'sham laws' do damage to the integrity of the rule of law itself?

3. Is some amount of torture inevitable or do you believe it can be significantly reduced? What is your theory as to why brutality such as torture appears to be so frequently and commonly employed by human beings against one another?

FURTHER READING

Conroy, J. (2000). *Unspeakable Acts, Ordinary People: The Dynamics of Torture—An Examination of the Practice of Torture in Three Democracies*. New York: Knopf.

A gripping account based on first-hand interviews with torturers and their victims of the use of the practice in Northern Ireland, the United States, and Israel.

Danner, M. (2005). *Torture and Truth: America, Abu Ghraib, and the War on Terror*. London: Granta.

A comprehensive look at the United States' use of torture at the Abu Ghraib prison camp in Iraq by a prize-winning New York Times reporter.

Levinson, S. (ed.) (2004). *Torture: A Collection*. Oxford: Oxford University Press.

An excellent collection of essays on the philosophical and legal dimensions, with special attention to debate over whether torture is ever justified.

Peters, E. (1996). *Torture*. Philadelphia, PA: University of Pennsylvania Press.

Widely considered to be the definitive history of torture in the Greek, Roman, and medieval periods. It includes a superb appendix of documents.

Roth, K. and **Worden, M. (eds)** (2005). *Torture: Does it Make Us Safer? Is it Ever OK?* New York: New Press.

Largely original essays with special attention to the US' practice of torture.

Scarry, E. (1985). *The Body in Pain: The Making and Unmaking of the World*. Oxford: Oxford University Press.

A complex, highly sophisticated exploration of the experience and psychodynamics of torturing and being tortured.

Schulz, W. (ed.) (2007). *The Phenomenon of Torture: Readings and Commentary.* Philadelphia, PA: University of Pennsylvania Press.

An extensive digest of readings—some hard to find elsewhere—on all aspects of torture, from first-hand accounts of the experience to essays on the psychodynamics between torturer and victim, the ethics of its use, and the efforts to combat it.

Weschler, L. (1990). *A Miracle, A Universe: Settling Accounts with Torturers.* New York: Pantheon.

A moving, extraordinarily well-written account of torture in Latin America in the 1970s. Full of astonishing stories. A classic.

 ## WEB LINKS

http://www.amnesty.org   The world's oldest and largest international human rights organization, Amnesty International, carries updated information on torture in dozens of countries and what citizens can do about it.

http://www.cvt.org   The Center for Victims of Torture is one of the major organizations treating survivors of the experience.

http://www.hrw.org   Website of Human Rights Watch, a US-based human rights organization that tracks the use of torture around the world.

http://www.omct.org   Created in 1986, the World Organisation Against Torture (OMCT) is today the main coalition of international non-governmental organizations (NGOs) fighting against torture, summary executions, enforced disappearances, and all other cruel, inhuman, or degrading treatment.

http://www.kspope.com/torvic/torture.php   This website provides links to all major organizations working against torture.

NOTES

1. A commonly used example of the defence of necessity is the hypothetical situation in which one is asked by a would-be killer of a loved one to reveal the loved one's whereabouts. It is generally agreed that, while under most conditions lying is not morally defensible, under these circumstances the morally dubious act of lying is necessary and justifiable to prevent the far more morally egregious act of murder.

2. Germany, for example, was rocked some years ago by a case in which the police tortured a suspect to get him to reveal the location of a child he had kidnapped (Bernstein, 2003).

3. Justice Landau himself acknowledged publicly many years after the issue of his Report that he felt betrayed by Shin Bet for its having often exceeded the constraints that his Report had recommended (Felner, 2005, p. 39).

4. 'Cruel, inhuman, and degrading treatment' is sometimes referred to by its acronym, CID.

5. The legal principle that a head of government is immune from prosecution for acts committed in his official role as sovereign, as opposed to acts committed in pursuit of his/her own private interests. It is generally understood that, while a head of state could be prosecuted for such things as personal corruption or murder of a spouse, he/she could not be prosecuted for the consequences of state policies.

 Visit the Online Resource Centre that accompanies this book for updates and a range of other resources: www.oxfordtextbooks.co.uk/orc/goodhart3e/

16

Human Trafficking

Andrea M. Bertone

Chapter Contents

Reader's Guide

Human trafficking for sexual and labour exploitation is undoubtedly one of the major human rights concerns of our time, as it affects men, women, and children in nearly every country. Persons of any race, age, or socio-economic status can be trafficked, and a country may be a destination, transit, and/or origin for trafficking victims. Human trafficking, simultaneously defined as a process (recruitment and transportation) and a severely exploitative work situation (psychological and physical control), is not a new phenomenon. In fact, sexual and labour exploitation in their many forms have always been a part of the human condition. However, political leaders, activists, advocates, academics, and other concerned individuals have recently taken an intense interest in the issue of trafficking, due in part to the greater global awareness of human rights issues in general and the development of anti-trafficking advocacy networks across countries in particular.

Introduction

In 2004, Thai police and other Thai officials raided a makeshift garment factory producing jeans in Bangkok where eighteen girls—aged 11 to 14 years—from Lao People's Democratic Republic (PDR) were rescued. Police found the girls hidden in a space measuring 10 by 13 feet (3 x 3.9 meters) under the floor of a room that was padlocked. Several weeks earlier, two girls had escaped from the factory and told police that the girls had been dropped off at the factory by a Laotian recruiter who had promised them paid work. After six months they had not been paid at all; they were forced to work from 6 a.m. to midnight, were poorly fed, and were beaten. The Thai husband and wife running the factory were arrested and charged with human trafficking, unlawful detention, and illegally hiring migrant workers (Pearson, 2005).

Having been abandoned by her parents and sexually abused by the son of distant relatives, 16 year old Noi ran away to Bangkok to work as a prostitute. She then accepted an offer of a job as a waitress in Japan where she was told that she would not have to take clients if she did not wish to. In Japan, she was hired by a bar where she was told that she had to pay off a debt of one million yen (approximately US$9,500), and her food, rent, and other expenses would be added to this amount. Clients paid the *mama san* (a woman in charge of overseeing the girls and women in a sex establishment) directly for taking the women out during the debt repayment period, and Noi realized that the only way for her to pay off the debt was to go out with as many clients as possible. She lived with thirty other girls between the ages of 14 and 30. Sometimes the police would come in to check if there were overstayers of visas. A Japanese nun helped Noi to get back to Thailand, but she had savings of only 30,000 Thai baht (approximately US$900) after five years of struggle (adapted from Raymond et al., 2002).

A recruiter went to rural Thailand and convinced thirty Thai men to accept farming jobs in the United States. They were offered three years of work in North Carolina, to be paid US$8 an hour. However, they would have to pay US$11,000 in recruiters' fees to get there, money they probably acquired by selling family-owned property or borrowing from loan sharks in Thailand. When they arrived in the US, the labour contractor confiscated their passports and return plane tickets. The Thai men said that the owners stole their money, failed to pay them for their work, and held them captive with threats of violence. They got only two or three days of work a week on farms. They lived in a small storage unit behind the home of the president of their recruiting company, a native from Lao PDR, and they were not provided with adequate food or allowed to leave the property. When the work in North Carolina ran out, the workers were taken to New Orleans, where they spent a few weeks in a condemned hotel, damaged by Hurricane Katrina, without electricity or clean water. During the day they demolished parts of the hotel in which they lived. They were never paid for their work in New Orleans, so they trapped and ate pigeons. Finally, they escaped and were provided with assistance by social service organizations in the United States (Collins, 2007).

These stories capture the economic, social, and political complexities of what it means for men, women, and children to be trafficked across international borders for labour and sexual exploitation. The story of the Lao PDR girls in a Bangkok sweatshop reflects the problems of many Laotians who migrate to Thailand with incomplete information about working conditions. For Noi, her experience of sexual violence was a cumulative one that began during childhood and persisted through her adulthood. The characteristics that make this a trafficking case are not necessarily that she was taken to another country to be a prostitute per se, but that she was duped by the Thai broker and was told she would be a waitress. Instead, she became stuck in a debt bondage situation in Japan. For the Thai men in the United States, it is yet another story of being deceived and then finding themselves in an untenable situation of forced labour.

This chapter is concerned with two main issues: first, the ways that the international community has defined and framed the issue of human trafficking over the last century; second, the ways that the international community, and particularly the United States, has responded politically to the problem of human trafficking. Contemporary movements around international social issues can be traced to ideologically motivated precursor movements. There are striking similarities in the tactics, rhetoric, and framing strategies of earlier movements against sexual exploitation and the contemporary anti-trafficking movement. In fact, it is necessary to go back more than a century to understand current debates on trafficking. This chapter provides a critical examination of the strategies of the contemporary anti-trafficking movement by explaining the competing interpretations of trafficking and how they led to the development, acceptance, and implementation of anti-trafficking norms.

Definitions of Human Trafficking

Trafficking is a term that has been used to describe a broad spectrum of criminal acts encompassing sexual and labour exploitation. Most generally, it can be viewed as a process with multiple phases: the recruitment or transport of persons using some form of force, fraud, or coercion for an exploitative purpose (Chuang, 2006, p. 443). Other issues that are often subsumed under the umbrella term 'human trafficking' include sex tourism; child sex tourism; commercial sexual exploitation of children (CSEC); exploitation in domestic, restaurant, agricultural, factory, and sweatshop work; debt bondage; forced prostitution; forced begging; and servile marriage through the mail order bride industry. The word trafficking connotes movement of people, either across international borders or within a country, to circumstances of exploitation, and is often confused with people smuggling.

International law requires coerced or forced movement in order for a situation to constitute trafficking. Trafficking is also associated with the exploitative situation of the person's destination; for example, in the American legal context, movement is not required in order to constitute a situation of trafficking. Some

have sought to simplify the plethora of terms by calling trafficking a 'modern-day form of slavery' (US Department of Justice, 2007, p. 1). However, some argue that the term trafficking has been so overused that it should be 'jettisoned' (Kempadoo, 2005b, p. ix).

In the three cases cited above, the individuals made it out of the trafficking situations. However, since there are few reliable statistics about how many people are being trafficked around the world, it is also unknown how many escape and how many are forced to endure horrible conditions. The statistics provided in Table 16.1 show the range of estimates of the scope of human trafficking, although none of these numbers have been verified.

Trafficking was codified in international law several times in the first half of the twentieth century. However, the traffic in women and children for exploitation in prostitution was the primary focus; forced labour as a form of trafficking and men as trafficking victims were excluded from these definitions. In 2000, trafficking was codified in the Protocol to Prevent, Suppress, and Punish Trafficking in Persons, especially Women and Children (**Palermo Protocol**), supplementing the United Nations (UN) Convention against Transnational Organized Crime. Although

Table 16.1 Estimates of human trafficking worldwide

Estimate	Source
27,000,000 'slaves' globally	http://www.FreetheSlaves.net
20.9 million people in forced labour, bonded labour, forced child labour, and sexual servitude at any given time:	International Labour Organization 2012
— 1.5 million in North America and Western Europe	
— 1.8 million in Central and South America	
— 3.7 million in Africa	
— 600,000 in the Middle East	
— 1.6 million in the former Soviet Union	
— 11.7 million in South Asia and Southeast Asia	
Global estimates	International Labour Organization 2012
State-imposed forced labour: 2.2 million	
Sexual exploitation: 4.5 million	
Labour exploitation: 14.2 million	
55% of forced labour victims are women and girls	International Labour Organization 2012
98% of sex trafficking victims are women and girls	

the Palermo Protocol negotiations in Vienna, Austria, known as the **Vienna Process**, were extremely contentious, they marked the first time that the international community agreed on a comprehensive definition of human trafficking. The Palermo Protocol redefined the international norms on trafficking, in the sense that it acknowledged that people may be trafficked for purposes other than exploitation in prostitution and that anyone can be trafficked, including men and boys.

The internationally accepted definition of trafficking (see Box 16.1) does not describe a single act leading to one specific outcome, but rather refers to a process (recruitment, transportation, and control) that can be organized in many ways and involve a variety of actors and outcomes. The elements identified in the Palermo Protocol definition of trafficking themselves present definitional problems, however. For example, there is no international consensus regarding the definition of sexual exploitation—or even of exploitation—and abuses that come under the umbrella of trafficking can vary in severity, generating a spectrum of experiences (Anderson and O'Connell Davidson, 2002, p. 12).

The same year that the Protocol was signed in Palermo, Italy, the United States developed and passed its own **Trafficking Victims Protection Act** (TVPA). The TVPA is significant because it was at the time (and remains) one of the most progressive national-level anti-trafficking statutes in the world, and also because the law was written in such a way that it can be used (and has been used) as a foreign policy tool for the United States to export its own anti-trafficking norms to other countries (Chuang, 2006).

The greatest source of tension among the governments and organizations negotiating the Protocol in Vienna and among the US Congress and the organizations involved with writing the TVPA in Washington was the extent to which prostitution was considered inherently exploitative or just another form of work. Many feminist and conservative groups joined together to negotiate during the Vienna Process in the hope of resolving a century-old debate about whether trafficking comprised all forms of adult prostitution or only involuntary prostitution. Feminists split into two subgroups: those who advocated for the abolition of prostitution in all its forms (abolitionist feminists) and those who advocated for a focus on forced prostitution only (human rights feminists).

The distinction between sex trafficking and severe forms of sex trafficking is significant in the American legal context. The TVPA includes a definition for sex trafficking: 'the recruitment, harboring, transportation, provision, or obtaining of a person for the purpose of a commercial sex act' (United States Code, 2000), and a separate definition for severe forms of sex trafficking (see Box 16.1). The sex trafficking definition excludes the requirement of coercion contained in the Palermo Protocol and thus encompasses consensual migrant prostitution. However, the TVPA limits the operational application to severe forms of trafficking in persons—i.e. trafficking involving force, fraud, or coercion for the purpose of the inducement of a commercial sex act (Chuang, 2006, p. 450). Developing these two definitions signified the compromise between the two political camps.

BOX 16.1 DEFINITIONS OF HUMAN TRAFFICKING

Trafficking in persons is defined as:

Recruitment, transportation, transfer, harbouring or receipt of persons, by means of the threat or use of force or other forms of coercion, of abduction, of fraud, of deception, of the abuse of power or of a position of vulnerability or of the giving or receiving of payments or benefits to achieve the consent of a person having control over another person, for the purpose of exploitation. Exploitation shall include, at a minimum, the exploitation of the prostitution of others or other forms of sexual exploitation, forced labour or services, slavery or practices similar to slavery, servitude or the removal of organs.

(Palermo Protocol)

'Severe forms' of trafficking are defined as:

a. sex trafficking in which a commercial sex act is induced by force, fraud, or coercion, or in which the person induced to perform such act has not attained 18 years of age; or

b. the recruitment, harboring, transportation, provision, or obtaining of a person for labor or services, through the use of force, fraud, or coercion for the purpose of subjection to involuntary servitude, peonage, debt bondage, or slavery;

c. if the person is under 18 years of age, any commercial sex act, whether or not force, fraud or coercion is involved.

(United States Trafficking Victims Protection Act of 2000)

KEY POINTS

Trafficking was most recently codified in the Protocol to Prevent, Suppress, and Punish Trafficking in Persons, especially Women and Children, supplementing the United Nations Convention against Transnational Organized Crime (Palermo Protocol).

The internationally accepted definition of trafficking does not describe a single act leading to one specific outcome, but rather refers to a process (recruitment, transportation, and control) that can be organized in many ways and involve a range of actors and outcomes.

The same year that the UN agreed on the Palermo Protocol, the US government passed its own Trafficking Victims Protection Act.

The Vienna Process revived a long-running debate about whether all forms of prostitution should be considered instances of trafficking or exploitation.

Critical Thinking Question:

Why is it important for a definition of trafficking to be as comprehensive as possible?

The Anti-White Slavery Movement and the Rise in International Consciousness about the Traffic in Women

Contemporary concerns about trafficking can be traced back to a late nineteenth-century movement in the United States and Western Europe against a phenomenon known as **white slavery**. White slavery, or the white slave trade, was a term used to describe the kidnapping and transport of Caucasian girls and women for the purposes of prostitution (Doezema, 2002, p. 22). It was also used to describe the forced and voluntary movement of young white women from rural areas of the United States into houses of prostitution in large American cities at the turn of the twentieth century (E. Bell, 1910).

Thanks to somewhat sensational media coverage, many people in the United States and Europe fervently believed that large numbers of white girls and women were being abducted or lured into prostitution. However, contemporary historians question the extent of this trade, and most scholars now agree that the number of victims of white slavery was actually very small. There

was, however, an increase in migration from Southern and Eastern Europe to the United States and Latin America, and while some of those migrants may initially have been prostitutes (Doezema, 2002, Footnote 4), most were simply women travelling alone from countries in Europe with high levels of poverty and unemployment.

International and Domestic Responses to a Perceived Problem

The discourse on white slavery was neither monolithic nor consistent. For some, white slavery meant prostitution in general; others saw white slavery and prostitution as distinct but related phenomena. Many made a distinction between domestic prostitution and international migration of women for prostitution (Doezema, 2002).

The demographic and social trends at the turn of the twentieth century, combined with Victorian values, stoked fears—which escalated to a panic (Irwin, 1996)—about declining moral standards and racial purity.[1] David (1999, p. 4) argues that these fears engendered myths of innocent girls being forced into sexual slavery on a large scale, myths intended to discourage interracial relations, extra-marital sex, and travel by single women. The white slavery metaphor represented anxieties of the American and European middle classes, instead of factual accounts of women's experiences (Doezema, 2002, p. 26).

The rhetoric surrounding this panic hid or downplayed centuries of black slavery. Alfred Dyer, a Quaker who investigated forced prostitution of English girls in Continental Europe and who set up the London Committee for Suppressing the Traffic in British Girls, wrote in 1880 that the coercion into prostitution of white English girls was 'infinitely more cruel and revolting than negro servitude' because white slavery was 'not for labour but for lust; and more cowardly than Negro slavery' (Dyer, 1880, p. 6). Irwin (1996) argues that Dyer's assessment devalued the humanity of blacks and ignored the fact that black women experienced high levels of sexual exploitation and violence in their situation of slavery. Thus the use of white women as sexual slaves was afforded a form of moral disapprobation that the sexual exploitation of black women did not have.

Nonetheless, intense activism in Europe and the United States developed against white slavery, and national and international movements against the white slave trade had become quite extensive at the turn of the twentieth century. These campaigns must be analysed in the context of the European and American nineteenth-century discourses and narratives on prostitution. For example, Edwin A. Sims, the US District Attorney in Chicago, was concerned about the trafficking of white slaves, whom he depicted as innocent white girls from rural areas who were being exploited by Parisians and dark-skinned Mediterranean men (E. Bell, 1910, p. 261). E. A. Bell, Secretary of the Illinois Vigilance Association and a legislator, wrote that, while not all traffickers were French, Paris was an epicentre for systematizing commercial sex (E. Bell, 1910, p. 261). Sims and Bell never mention the Chicago businessmen who may have been just as involved in prostituting young girls as the dark-skinned Mediterranean men (Kraut, 1996).

In Britain, the issues of white slavery and child prostitution were linked in W. T. Stead's series of articles, 'The Maiden Tribute to Modern Babylon', which was published in the *Pall Mall Gazette* in 1885. In this sensational series, Stead claimed to have evidence of hundreds of English girls deceived, coerced, and sometimes drugged into prostitution, and he accused poor parents of selling their daughters to procurers (Doezema, 2002, p. 28). These stories helped to spark a fury among the middle classes in Europe. Stead did acknowledge that some women voluntarily migrated for prostitution, seeking more lucrative situations.

Early International Conventions

In 1895, the first international conference on traffic in women was held in Paris, followed by two other conferences in London and Budapest (Long, 2004, p. 20). In 1904, the first International Agreement for the Suppression of the White Slave Traffic was concluded in Paris by sixteen countries. Since some countries, such as France, regulated prostitution, the International Agreement did not make white slavery synonymous with prostitution. Instead, it addressed international recruitment for prostitution (Doezema, 2002, p. 23).

In 1910, the International Convention for Suppression of White Slave Traffic was expanded to include the recruitment for prostitution within national boundaries. In 1921, the International Convention for the Suppression of Traffic in Women and Children included trafficking in boys. These early agreements focused on recruitment and neglected the aspect of enslavement or conditions in prostitution. They distinguished between prostitution as a personal choice and slavery-like prostitution linked to coercion or traffic in persons. They banned the international traffic in persons but regarded prostitution as a human rights violation only when it involved overt coercion or exploitation. The agreements never acknowledged less

visible forms of economic, social, and psychological coercion, which critics claimed pushed girls and women into prostitution (Doezema, 2002).

The 1933 International Convention on the Suppression of Traffic in Women of Full Age made an explicit link between traffic in women and voluntary or involuntary prostitution, thus reflecting an abolitionist perspective in an international legal document (Doezema, 2002, p. 23). States were required to punish anyone who procured or enticed a woman, regardless of whether she had consented to work in prostitution in another country.

The 1949 Convention for the Suppression of the Traffic in Persons and of the Exploitation of the Prostitution of Others further solidified the connection between trafficking and prostitution while moving. There was a move away from gender- and race-specific language (Uçarer, 1999). Like the 1933 Convention, the 1949 Convention made sexual trafficking punishable even if a woman had consented, and for the first time in an international instrument it declared prostitution and trafficking to be 'incompatible with the dignity and worth of the human person and [to] endanger the welfare of the individual, family and the community'. The Convention made no distinction between forced and voluntary prostitution; it viewed prostitutes as victims and did not recognize the individual's right to choose to work as a prostitute (Lim, 1998, p. 15).

KEY POINTS

The contemporary anti-trafficking movement has its roots in a precursor movement against the white slave trade at the turn of the twentieth century.

'White slavery' and the 'white slave trade' are terms that were used to describe the abduction and transport of white women for prostitution out of, or within, the United States and Europe.

It is believed that stories and narratives about white slaves were triggered by the migration of young women from Europe.

A series of international conventions and agreements from 1905 to 1949 attempted to define and refine the international community's ideological position on prostitution.

Critical Thinking Questions:

Why was the white slave trade hyped in the media in the late nineteenth century?

Why did the international community in the early part of the twentieth century feel the need to continuously refine the definition of trafficking?

Origins of the Contemporary Anti-Trafficking Movement

Decades of Silence: 1950–79

After the 1949 Convention, the problem of trafficking in women did not disappear, but the political commitment to confront it nearly vanished. During the 1950s, 1960s, and early 1970s, the international community remained strangely silent on the issues of trafficking into prostitution, save for a few anti-slavery activists and feminists carrying the torch through the later mid-century. Very little discourse was written during or has been written about this time period, perhaps because the international political tensions of the Cold War eclipsed other international social issues. The only international instrument that was negotiated in the 1950s that related to trafficking was the 1956 Supplementary Convention on the Abolition of Slavery, which addresses 'selling women' and 'turning children over for exploitation and debt bondage schemes' (Farrior, 1997, p. 213).

National and international women's movements emerged in the 1970s and 1980s, and forums for discussions opened. At a global level, the UN International Decade for Women (1976–85) catalysed both activism and research on a range of issues affecting women around the world. For those interested in bringing the issues of international sexual slavery and forced prostitution back to the international agenda, there was hope in the 1970s when the United Nations Commission on the Status of Women was created, as well as the 1975 International Women's Year Conference in Mexico City (K. Barry, 1979, p. 64). The 1979 *Convention on the Elimination of All Forms of Discrimination Against Women* (CEDAW) directed states parties to take measures to prevent all forms of traffic in women, and prostitution of women (United Nations, 1979). However, the major thrust of CEDAW was to address problems of political discrimination, an emphasis reflecting the concerns of Western women more than those of women in non-Western countries.

In 1979, Kathleen Barry re-introduced the issue of sexual slavery to an academic audience in a book entitled *Female Sexual Slavery*. She argued that trafficking for prostitution was very much alive during the 1960s and 1970s, and provided evidence suggesting that high-level officials in certain countries were directly involved with trafficking women from developing countries for the purposes of commercial sexual exploitation. Barry shows that INTERPOL knew of these problems from

reports that the group made in the 1960s and 1970s. When the Anti-Slavery Society asked INTERPOL to release a particularly damning report to the public, INTERPOL refused. In fact, Barry argues that there was a concerted effort to suppress the evidence even in the UN, as countries did not want to implicate or embarrass other countries (K. Barry, 1979, pp. 58–62).

Women's Rights as Human Rights: 1980–95

The contemporary movement to combat trafficking benefited from precursor movements and the development of certain norms to push the notion that women's rights are human rights. Beginning in 1975, the United Nations held a number of international women's conferences, out of which came several key developments. First, states' attention was redirected to women's legal status and family practices that reinforced structures of gender inequality. Second, women's inequality was recognized to be global in nature. Third, several important women's human rights non-governmental organizations (NGOs) were formed (Brown Thompson, 2002, pp. 99–100). Beginning in the late 1980s, many women's rights organizations identified an important way to frame women's rights as an inseparable aspect of human rights (Brown Thompson, 2002, p. 102). Networks were formed by women, who came together in unprecedented numbers in the context of the UN conferences where they legitimized these issues (Keck and Sikkink, 1998, p. 169).

The discussions during the 1993 Vienna World Conference on Human Rights solidified the idea that women's rights are human rights (Brown Thompson, 2002, p. 107). At the Vienna conference, *violence against women* became a key issue among activists from all over the world. The issue of violence against women 'arrived late and dramatically in the [contemporary] international women's movement' (Keck and Sikkink, 1998, p. 166). The matter differed from the more classic problems of suffrage, equality, and discrimination, around which Western women had long mobilized. Many of the problems of Western women did not resonate with women from developing countries, who suffered from corrupt governments and Western economic policies that increased poverty, underdevelopment, and the commoditization of women (Keck and Sikkink, 1998, p. 166). Contemporary global activists tried to make the case that women anywhere in the world, regardless of age, ethnicity, and socio-economic status, could be victims of violence. Violence against women emerged as a common advocacy position around which women's organizations could agree and collaborate (Keck and Sikkink, 1998, p. 166). Keck and Sikkink (1998, p. 172) argue that violence against women was a category that served some key strategic purpose for activists trying to build a transnational campaign because it allowed them to attract allies and bridge cultural differences. This strategic focus forced transnational activists to search for a basic common denominator—the belief in the importance of the protection of bodily integrity of women and girls.

The networks built around the issue of violence against women could draw on pre-existing communication networks. The emergence of violence against women as a topic around which groups could advocate shows how separate transnational networks—human rights and women's rights—began to find a common language and transform one another (Keck and Sikkink, 1998, p. 166). Women's groups in developing countries pressed the issue of violence against women most forcefully, and, fortuitously, they found support among groups working on similar women's issues in the West (Brown Thompson, 2002). Though related, the contemporary shift to the frame of violence against women was a significant advance on the past efforts of the paranoia and the intensely racialized tone of the Victorian era. Women's groups refocused the human rights activism from campaigning around state-perpetrated violence in the public sphere to male-perpetrated violence against women in the private sphere. This was an advance in the global women's movement and it allowed separate campaigns to develop on specific practices of violence against women in a domestic context. For example, rape and domestic violence was an issue in the United States and Europe, female genital mutilation/cutting was relevant in Africa, commercial sexual exploitation was of concern in Europe and Asia, dowry deaths were in the media in India, and torture and rape of political prisoners were grave problems in Latin America (Keck and Sikkink, 1998, pp. 171–3).

The 1995 Fourth World Conference on Women in Beijing solidified the movement working to combat violence against women (see Box 16.2). After remaining in the background for a long time, the issue of trafficking for sexual exploitation rode the wave of the international women's movement into the mid-1990s. A broader view of trafficking that included forced marriage and forced labour emerged from this conference, along with the idea that governments bear

BOX 16.2 COMBATING TRAFFICKING FOR SEXUAL EXPLOITATION

The effective suppression of trafficking in women and girls for the sex trade is a matter of pressing international concern. Implementation of the 1949 Convention for the Suppression of the Traffic in Persons and of the Exploitation of the Prostitution of Others, as well as other relevant instruments, needs to be reviewed and strengthened. The use of women in international prostitution and trafficking networks has become a major focus of international organized crime. The Special Rapporteur of the Commission on Human Rights on violence against women … is invited to address, within her mandate and as a matter of urgency, the issue of international trafficking for the purposes of the sex trade, as well as the issues of forced prostitution, rape, sexual abuse and sex tourism.

(*Platform for Action* (1995), Fourth World Conference on Women, Beijing, China)

responsibility for the rights of women in the private sphere. Framing human trafficking as a human rights/women's rights issue helped to break down the public/private distinction that had long hobbled recognition of women's rights more generally, and it transformed private or 'women's' issues into human issues.

Contemporary Politics of Addressing Human Trafficking

Deep-seated disagreements in the women's human rights movement became evident during the negotiations for a new international instrument on human trafficking, which culminated in the Palermo Protocol. Contemporary, unresolved issues about the relationship between trafficking and prostitution that had been percolating since the late 1970s finally came to a boil in Vienna. The Palermo Protocol reflects only a weak international consensus on this transnational problem (Chuang, 2006, p. 438). During the Vienna Process, one group of states adopting the abolitionist perspective viewed any distinction between forced and voluntary prostitution as morally unacceptable. They opposed any definition of trafficking that would include a coercion requirement and argued that the definition should encompass all migration for sex work. Another group of states took the position that including non-coerced migration for sex work would make the trafficking definition over-broad and divert scarce resources away from the real problem (see Box 16.3).

BOX 16.3 ALTERNATIVE POINTS OF VIEW: ABOLITIONIST FEMINISTS AND HUMAN RIGHTS FEMINISTS

Two ideological camps have dominated the discourse on sex trafficking over the past decade and a half. The abolitionist feminists believe that prostitution, whether involuntary or voluntary, is exploitative. Trafficking is, by definition, the act of forcing or coercing an individual into a situation of sexual or labour exploitation. Therefore, those involved in prostitution are always in a trafficking situation. On the other hand, human rights feminists de-link prostitution and trafficking by arguing that some adult women and men are in prostitution voluntarily and should not be considered victims; only those who are forced or coerced to be prostitutes should be considered trafficking victims. While the vitriol between the two camps has diminished, the results of the rivalry are reflected in anti-trafficking policies throughout the world.

Although the Protocol does recognize the need to respect the human rights of trafficked persons, it is conspicuously not a human rights document. States insisted that they be permitted to enact measures to protect themselves against transnational organized crime, specifically the elements of organized crime that smuggle people across borders and/or exploit their labour after the movement across the border. The implicit purpose of the Protocol was to provide a mechanism for states to criminalize trafficking and, as a result, prosecute traffickers. Thus the Protocol has often been described as a protector of *states* rather than a protector of victims of human trafficking.

These debates underlined the complexity and divisiveness of the issue. However, in the end, the desire on the part of the states to come to a consensus outweighed their disagreements. There were two points of compromise evident in the final definition of trafficking. First, states excluded consensual migration for prostitution, thereby maintaining a distinction between migrant smuggling and trafficking (Chuang, 2006, p. 445). The *travaux préparatoires* (interpretive notes) indicate that the protocol addresses the issue of prostitution only in the context of trafficking, and that these references are without prejudice as to how states address this issue in their respective domestic laws (Gallagher, 2001, p. 986). One of the results of the compromises, however, was an international convention with few enforcement mechanisms and weak language directing states to improve their trafficking records.

The Palermo Protocol departed from its sister conventions earlier in the twentieth century by making elements of force or coercion essential parts of the definition of trafficking. This is a significant departure from the abolitionist stance of the 1949 Convention, and it left states free to recognize voluntary prostitution as labour and to regulate it. But while the Protocol makes an important distinction between coerced and non-coerced migration for prostitution, it does not offer many concrete human rights protections for trafficking victims (Chuang, 2006, p. 447).

KEY POINTS

The international community became relatively silent on the issue of trafficking between 1950 and 1979, largely due to the international political pressures of the Cold War.

Discussions began to open up in the 1970s, spearheaded by the UN, about issues affecting women all over the world, and by Kathleen Barry's seminal book *Female Sexual Slavery* in 1979.

The 1995 Fourth World Conference on Women in Beijing solidified the movement working to combat violence against women and strongly advocated the notion that women's rights are human rights.

Two ideological camps coalesced around the Protocol negotiations; they were focused nearly exclusively on the nature of prostitution.

Critical Thinking Questions:

What might the contemporary anti-trafficking movement look like if levels of activism had stayed high through the mid part of the twentieth century?

What is the effect on the broader fight against trafficking when so much emphasis is placed on sex trafficking?

The Ascendancy of Trafficking as a Global Issue in the 1990s

Few of the issues raised in contemporary forums to discuss human trafficking are unique to this time period. In fact, the reasons why this issue has gained ascendancy at the turn of the twenty-first century parallel those explaining its rise at the turn of the twentieth century. Doezema (2000, p. 24) aptly compares the trafficking victim from one century to another:

Recent research indicates that today's stereotypical 'trafficking victim' bears as little resemblance to women migrating for work in the sex industry as did her historical counterpart, the 'white slave'. The majority of trafficking victims are aware that the jobs offered them are in the sex industry, but are lied to about the conditions they will work under. Yet policies to eradicate 'trafficking' continue to be based on the notion of the 'innocent' unwilling victim, and often combine efforts designed to protect 'innocent' women with those designed to punish 'bad' women: i.e. prostitutes.

As this assessment suggests, the contemporary anti-trafficking movement has its roots firmly entrenched in debates going back as far as the late 1880s. The rhetoric has changed only slightly in over a century, and the abolitionist feminist/human rights feminist split with regard to the issue of trafficking as prostitution is still very much alive. The inability of these two camps to find common ground has contributed to the particular character of the current global anti-trafficking movement. There are several reasons why the contemporary global anti-trafficking movement has been able to sustain itself: a proliferation of national and international NGOs; hundreds of millions of dollars spent globally to combat trafficking since 2001; US unilateralism; sensational media coverage; and the facility with which organizations and people communicate across international borders in order to undertake transnational advocacy activities.

In 1991, the Soviet Union collapsed, destabilizing Central and Eastern Europe. The end of the Cold War precipitated an intense interest in the issue of trafficking in persons in Western countries, primarily because of the fear and concern about mass migration out of the former Soviet Union and Eastern Europe to Western Europe. Whereas a large number of people did make their way to Western Europe, an exodus did not materialize. But trafficking in women and children for sexual exploitation into the European Community came to the attention of a growing number of non-governmental organizations in Western Europe. Interestingly, some of these European NGOs had been working on related issues, with Asian activists, since the 1980s and

were aware of Southeast Asian women involved in forced and voluntary prostitution, as well as of abusive marriages between European men and Asian women.

However, Asian and African women in European brothels in the 1980s did not raise the same flags that the appearance of foreign, white women in the French, British, and German sex industries in the 1990s did. In much the same way that the white slavery panic of the early twentieth century was sparked by the migration of women out of Eastern Europe coupled with revulsion at the thought that white women were being enslaved sexually, an intense interest in the issue resurfaced with the end of the Cold War and the migration of women and men out of former Soviet countries and the belief that many of these (white) women were being enslaved sexually in Western European and American brothels. Jahic and Finckenauer (2005, p. 26) ask poignant questions about why there was a rise in interest in this issue in the 1990s:

Was the rise in concern for victims simply the result of a sudden increase in trafficking? Why did special interest groups, governments, and organizations suddenly become interested in a problem that had actually been present for decades? Was there something unusual about the new wave of trafficking from Eastern Europe and the former Soviet Union?

The answer they provide, which is in line with other findings, is that, unlike the women from Asia and Africa who were women of colour, the new trafficking victims were more recognizable to Western, particularly American, politicians and other middle-class do-gooders. The image of white slaves was unconsciously invoked, and this image resonated with activists and advocates in the West (Jahic and Finckenauer, 2005, p. 26).

Jahic and Finckenauer (2005, p. 27) also make a powerful argument about why trafficking has become such an important issue since the 1990s. The trafficking victims have been portrayed in the media as young, naive victims in need of protection. This portrait of a trafficking victim has made it easier to form anti-trafficking task forces. This is a particularly important point to make because, although transnational advocacy networks are the main facilitators of maintaining this issue on the international political agenda, Jahic and Finckenauer provide an

BOX 16.4 CHALLENGING ASSUMPTIONS: WHO GETS TRAFFICKED?

- Anyone can be a victim of sex or labour trafficking—men, women, and children.

- Women are primarily trafficked into forced sexual exploitation, domestic servitude, manufacturing, hospitality, and health and elder care.

- Men are primarily trafficked into the construction, fishing, agriculture, and mining industries.

- Children are primarily trafficked into sexual exploitation, domestic work, begging, manufacturing, agriculture, mining, and military conscription.

Who traffics?

- Both men and women, young and old, can traffic others. A trafficker might be a family member, an intimate partner,

a neighbour, or a complete stranger. Many traffickers are successful because they prey on and take advantage of people who are in vulnerable economic and social situations.

- The majority of traffickers work in small networks.

Where do people get trafficked?

- Nearly every country in the world is a source, transit, and/or destination country for trafficking, rendering it a truly global phenomenon.

- The top origin countries for people trafficked in the United States are Mexico, the Philippines, Thailand, Honduras, Guatemala, India, and El Salvador (US Department of State, 2014). There are also many American citizens who are victims of trafficking in the US.

---

explanation for the fuel for the advocacy networks. In addition to portraying prostitutes as victims to make anti-trafficking activities more palatable for public discourse, the issue that has also fuelled the activities of advocacy networks is the fact that those working on this issue do not have a clear sense of the scope of the problem (see Box 16.4). This has not stopped people from claiming that the problem is growing in magnitude. Most organizations and governments collect different kinds of data, which makes it difficult to reach meaningful conclusions about the scope of the trafficking (Jahic and Finckenauer, 2005, p. 27).

Root Causes of Trafficking

The accounts of women trafficked into exploitative prostitution have often been portrayed to justify a particular political, moral, and economic regime by governments and NGOs, particularly faith-based organizations. These accounts position women as victims who need the protection of powerful interests. By focusing only on the women's labour, sexuality, or mobility, these institutions fail to address the root causes of trafficking in the countries of origin, such as high rates of unemployment, abuse in families and other forms of gender-based violence, and limited opportunities for legal migration. Media accounts capitalize on the combination

of sexuality and exploitation to provoke public voyeurism by transforming the stories to be about the dehumanizing experience; the women are treated in the media as objects instead of subjects of their own histories. Long (2004, p. 7) argues that 'Contemporary sexual trafficking experiences remain largely invisible, reflecting in large part the particular interests and agenda of those defining trafficking for sexual exploitation rather than the lived experiences and perceptions of those who are trafficked.' Rarely in public discourse do people read about the economic, political, and social vulnerabilities that these girls and women face in their home countries. The rights and voices of women themselves are muffled and those in the West do not always have a clear understanding of the reasons why some women have to make the often difficult choice of migrating to other countries for various types of gendered work—prostitution, domestic service, childcare, for example. These women are faced with additional vulnerabilities after migration because of limited rights they may have as illegal immigrants, or being at risk of sexual violence and discrimination because they are female. Greater attention to human rights in general, including social and economic rights of women, would go a long way to addressing the vulnerability to coercion that underlies many of the reasons why girls and women become involved in prostitution.

Case Study: Human Trafficking in the United States

Brief Background of Trafficking Problems in the United States

The United States is a destination country for men, women, and children trafficked for the purposes of forced prostitution and forced labour. The full extent of trafficking in the US is not known as it is very difficult to determine the numbers of trafficking victims currently present in the US. Individuals are trafficked to and exploited in nearly every state of the United States; no community is immune, though the majority of trafficking cases have occurred in larger metropolitan areas and traditional ports of entry: New York, Miami/Florida, Texas, Los Angeles, San Francisco, Chicago, and Atlanta (US Department of Justice, 2007). People have been found trafficked in traditional and non-traditional sex industry establishments—brothels, bars, massage parlours—as well as in factories, sweatshops, farms, restaurants, private homes, even begging on the street. Young women are trafficked into sexual servitude from the former Soviet Union, Latin America, and Asia. Latin American and African women are also trafficked into domestic servitude. Latin American and Asian men are trafficked into forced labour or extremely exploitative labour situations in factories, farming, construction, agriculture, and landscaping.

It is unknown whether there are more situations of individuals in trafficking for forced prostitution than in labour trafficking. The US government maintains that 80 per cent of trafficking in the world is for sex trafficking—a figure that reflects its expansive view of sex trafficking—and that over 50 per cent of those trafficked are minors (US Department of State, 2008). The majority of prosecutions that the US Department of Justice has handled have been for forced prostitution (US Department of Justice, 2007). These figures contribute to a general assumption in the United States and elsewhere that sexual servitude is more prevalent than labour trafficking (US Department of State, 2006). However, other research has provided evidence to the contrary (Webber and Shirk, 2005).

It is not surprising that the United States is a magnet for migrants from all over the world. It is also not at all surprising that recruiters deceive many of these migrants in their home communities. Recruiters paint rosy pictures of what it is like to live and work in the United States. Because the routes for legal migration into the United States are limited, individuals increasingly turn to unscrupulous smugglers and traffickers.

Research has also shown that it is not the poorest of the poor who are trafficked or become trafficked in the United States, nor is it the least educated—though low levels of education and income do affect the likelihood of someone becoming exploited (Bales and Lize, 2005). In 2006, the *San Francisco Chronicle* ran a four-part story in which the reporter extensively interviewed one South Korean woman who came to the

US from a lower middle-class family in Korea. This young woman, in order to fit in with her friends in South Korea, had obtained a credit card and bought tens of thousands of dollars' worth of clothing and jewellery. When she was unable to pay off the credit card with her job as a waitress, she became desperate and agreed to pay money to a smuggler to bring her to the United States to work—she thought—as a waitress in California. She was unaware of the immigration and visa rules and allowed her smuggler to arrange the paperwork. Little did she know that she would first be flown to Mexico, smuggled illegally across the border into the United States, and then forced to work as a prostitute to pay off not only her credit card debts, but also the money she owed to her smuggler. After several months of working as a prostitute against her will, she had paid off enough of her smuggling debt that if she wanted to leave prostitution, she could. However, she chose to stay working as a prostitute for many more months to reduce her credit card debt in South Korea; besides, she did not know what her options were because she was an illegal alien. Eventually, after leaving the prostitution industry, her experiences came to the attention of an NGO. It was determined, by the group as well as by the US government, that she was a victim of trafficking, making her eligible for certain compensations under the TVPA (May, 2006). The details of this case illustrate the complexities of trafficking in the United States: not only can a person be smuggled then trafficked, but this woman chose to stay working in the sex industry after she could have exited because of her financial obligations in South Korea.

The situation of trafficking in the United States is distinctive because the majority of traffickers traffic people of their own ethnic/national groups. For example, Bales and Lize (2005, p. 27), in a report on human trafficking in the US, found that in eight of the twelve cases that they studied the victims were recruited by a person from their community of origin, meaning that someone from their neighbourhood, family, or ethnic group lured them to the United States. Forced labour is a phenomenon found within ethnic/national communities populated by a steady flow of migrants from the same geographic areas (Bales and Lize, 2005, p. 143). The fact that victims of trafficking are very often exploited within ethnic community enclaves in the United States is one of the factors that prevents local and federal law enforcement and non-governmental organizations from finding victims of trafficking throughout the United States. The psychological and physical coercion victims experience in exploitative situations is much more powerful when a trafficker knows the victim's family in her or his home country and can threaten to hurt those family members, especially children, left behind.

Development of US Norms to Combat Human Trafficking

In 1995, President Bill Clinton established the President's Inter-Agency Council on Women (PICW) within the Department of State in order to create a mechanism to carry out commitments that the US made in connection with the Beijing women's conference. The Chairperson of this Council was then-First Lady Hillary Rodham Clinton, who had been present at the Beijing conference and had given a stirring speech about women's rights as human rights. By early 1998, the ideological camps on the issue of prostitution's relationship with trafficking had already re-formed in the US. Abolitionist feminists sided with conservative social groups and a growing Christian conservative presence in the US Congress.

On 8 March 1998—International Women's Day—President Clinton issued an Executive Order on Trafficking in Women and Children that set out a comprehensive and integrated policy framework of domestic and foreign anti-trafficking initiatives. This Executive Order became the blueprint for US legislation on human trafficking. The Clinton administration established bilateral working relationships with several countries and spearheaded the drafting of the Palermo Protocol (Chuang, 2006, p. 449). The Executive Order also outlined an implicit normative framework for how the US Government and international organizations should address trafficking for the next decade, prescribing three important ways to combat trafficking: prevention of trafficking, protection of trafficking victims, and prosecution of traffickers (often referred to as the 3Ps). Congressional leaders introduced legislation in 1999 on sex trafficking, which was later broadened to include all forms of human trafficking, and in late 2000 President Clinton signed the Trafficking Victims Protection Act into law.

The motives underlying this legislation are interesting and important to understand. Several cases of human trafficking were brought before the US courts in the mid-1990s. Two large labour trafficking cases were discovered in 1995. Approximately a hundred deaf Mexicans were found being forced to peddle trinkets in New York City. In another case, approximately seventy Thais were found locked up in a sweatshop in El Monte, California, where some had been held for as long as seven years. Unfortunately, prosecutors did not have at their disposal statutes that addressed the specific problem of people being *psychologically coerced* and enslaved for work. Before the TVPA, US law recognized only physical coercion as part of slavery cases. These cases revealed that special attention was needed for people who might have agreed to be taken across the border but nonetheless ended up in situations of deception, coercion, and violence.

Although Chuang (2006) argues that these two cases prompted members of Congress to propose comprehensive anti-trafficking legislation, it is significant that legislation was not introduced in Congress until 1999. While the cases most certainly played a role in raising attention about worker exploitation, they were not the primary catalyst for Congress to pass anti-trafficking legislation. The years 1999 and 2000 were pivotal in the consolidation of US congressional and NGO support for action on the issue of trafficking. In addition to the several congressional hearings held about human trafficking—specifically trafficking for sexual exploitation—members of Congress introduced various bills on trafficking and sex trafficking (Hyland, 2001, pp. 60–1).

The Congressional co-sponsors of a developing policy on trafficking were greatly motivated by evidence presented by the now-defunct NGO, Global Survival Network (GSN), showing that a steady stream of girls and women from the former Soviet Union were being trafficked into prostitution in the US and Western Europe. On 28 June 1999, Congressman Chris Smith (R-NJ) held a hearing entitled 'The Sex Trade: Trafficking in Women and Children in Europe and the United States'. At that testimony, Congressman Smith stated (emphasis added):

Although trafficking has been a problem for many years in Asian countries, it was not until the end of communism in East-Central Europe and the break up of the Soviet Union that a sex trade in the OSCE [Organisation for Security and Co-operation in Europe] region began to develop. This appalling trade has grown exponentially over the ensuing decade. Trafficking rings exploit vulnerable women and children; and amidst the devastated economies of Eastern Europe and the newly independent states where women are unable to find jobs, traffickers have no shortage of potential victims.

Evidence provided by GSN sparked sentiments and compassion similar to those of the early abolitionists at the turn of the twentieth century of white slavery. US policy makers responded to advocacy about problems of forced prostitution of Eastern European and former Soviet nation women; they did not pay as much attention to the problem of labour trafficking, or human trafficking taking place in other areas of the world.

Moral Authority and Exporting US Norms Abroad

For well over a century, trafficking has been a problem that has evoked some moral obligation upon which to act—it concerns situations in which girls and women are being raped for the profit of others, women's and men's labour are being severely exploited, and children are being abused. Unique political alliances and debates between liberals—represented by human rights advocates and feminists—and conservatives—represented by abolitionist feminists and the conservative, religious right in the US—elevated human trafficking to a high place on the political agenda. The religious conservatives' and the abolitionist feminists' cooperation on the linkages between prostitution and trafficking was sufficient to maintain Congressional and Executive Branch interest in the issue of human trafficking, especially among the Republicans, years after the passage of the TVPA.

Early academic literature on the formation of transnational advocacy networks signifies an acceptance of the fact that people and organizations network because they perceive a moral obligation or urgency to act on issues such as human rights, environmental destruction, or women's human rights. However, others have challenged this view, arguing that activism is as much about politics and posturing as it is about morals. Clifford Bob (2005) asks why some issues get put on the global agenda while others are ignored. He offers several suggestions. First, local groups seek to transform their grievances into rights claims. Second, international human rights NGOs act as 'gatekeepers', screening such claims and deciding which to bring to the international level. Third, states and international organizations translate claims into rights by codifying and institutionalizing them (Hertel, 2006, p. 15).

After the UN adopted the Palermo Protocol and the US passed the TVPA, international campaigns such as the Global Alliance Against Traffic in Women (GAATW) and the Coalition Against Traffic in Women (CATW) set out to advocate their respective positions on trafficking and prostitution. The human rights camp was perceived to have won the debate after the passage of the Palermo Protocol, which empowered GAATW to organize its entire agenda around advocating governments' ratification of the Palermo Protocol. However, in 2001, almost immediately after the TVPA was passed, the US administration changed politically from Democratic to Republican. Even though a liberal president had signed it, the TVPA was implemented under a conservative administration.

Chuang (2006) argues that the TVPA has forced US norms into the international arena, potentially undermining 'the fragile international cooperation framework created' by the Palermo Protocol. The US took advantage of the fact that the UN would be unlikely to enforce the Protocol rigorously, due to insufficient funding and the lack of a central and powerful office at the UN tasked with the responsibility for its implementation. The international cooperation framework collapsed, creating a global leadership vacuum on the issue of trafficking, and the US slowly replaced the UN as the 'global sheriff' combating human trafficking (Chuang, 2006).

US confidence in this new enforcement role grew once it gauged the reaction of the international community to its tier designations of countries in the Trafficking in Persons Report (published by the US Department of State in 2001 and each subsequent year). Because the TVPA includes a sanctions regime, which is used as a foreign policy tool, it reaches beyond US borders to influence anti-trafficking policy abroad. This threat of sanctions elevated US norms above international norms by 'giving the former teeth that the latter so often lack' (Chuang, 2006, p. 439). The sanctions regime, along with normal US Government engagement with other governments, influenced many countries to develop laws and policies to combat human trafficking. What is interesting is that the US encouraged other governments to adopt and employ selective and sometimes ambiguous references to the norms of the Palermo Protocol (Chuang, 2006, pp. 439–40). The US supported nearly all of the norms delineated in the Palermo Protocol, with one crucial exception—the distinction between 'sex trafficking' as defined in the Protocol, and 'severe forms of sex trafficking' as defined in the TVPA

(Chuang, 2006). Although the overall outcome of the US engagement with other countries resulted in greater international attention to human trafficking and more national-level anti-human trafficking laws, the US Government's tactics were deemed imperialistic by many, as they undermined the tenuous consensus reached during the Vienna negotiations. The contemporary anti-trafficking movement spearheaded by the international community in the late 1990s has become a platform to keep the debate alive on the nature of prostitution in the 2000s. The site of the global debate on prostitution and its relationship to trafficking shifted to Washington, DC, where some US-based organizations, whose abolitionist ideology on prostitution has afforded them the political and financial support of the US Government, are located. US foreign policies on human trafficking have been viewed as both progressive and aggressive, and US-based organizations also took advantage of the global leadership vacuum mentioned above. While policies to engage aggressively with other countries have not changed dramatically, Obama administration officials are deemed to be more reasonable, less ideological, and more willing to see multiple sides of the debate.

KEY POINTS

Victims of trafficking are found in every corner of the United States.

There is an assumption that trafficking for sexual exploitation is more prevalent, but evidence has shown that labour trafficking may be a larger problem.

Under the Clinton administration, the US Government developed norms to combat trafficking: prevention, protection, and prosecution.

Despite prominent labour trafficking cases in the mid-1990s, US Congressional leaders were motivated to address human trafficking when it came to their attention that women from the former Soviet Union were being forced into prostitution.

The US has assumed the responsibility of global sheriff on enforcing anti-trafficking norms internationally.

Critical Thinking Question:

What are the pros and cons to the US exercising its power as a 'global sheriff' for human trafficking?

Conclusion

In the exploration of a historical perspective, similar patterns of political behaviour are evident across an entire century. It has been difficult for many organizations, activists, and advocates to transcend the emotive language that maintains stereotypes and influences narrowly conceived policies and projects around the world. Theoretically, it is important to examine the history of the anti-trafficking movement so that we understand the motivations of organizations and map their interaction with one another. Rhetoric and framing are important components in the development of alliances and networks. Under the Obama administration, the ideological camps are still evident, though drops in the funding available for combating human trafficking domestically and abroad have quieted some of the more virulent rhetoric audible during the Bush administration. However, we can anticipate a trajectory of continued debate on these complex issues.

? QUESTIONS

Individual Study Questions

1. What were some of the precursor international instruments to the Protocol to Prevent, Suppress, and Punish Trafficking in Persons, especially Women and Children (Palermo Protocol)?

2. What are the strengths and weaknesses of the Palermo Protocol?

3. What are the differences between the definition of trafficking in the Palermo Protocol and the United States Trafficking Victims Protection Act?

4. What was the most significant source of tension for those organizations and individuals negotiating the Protocol in Vienna?

5. How was the interest in trafficking rekindled for the international community in the 1990s?

6. What is the nature of the problem of human trafficking experienced by the United States?

Group Discussion Questions

1. What are the differences and similarities between the way that trafficking was framed at the turn of the twentieth century and then at the turn of the twenty-first century?

2. How were contemporary norms to combat human trafficking developed?

3. How was the international women's human rights movement connected to the global movement to combat human trafficking?

4. What role do the United States Government and organizations play in enforcing contemporary norms to combat human trafficking?

5. How has the rhetoric of slavery played a role in mobilizing activism against trafficking?

6. What were the motivations of US Congressional leaders to address human trafficking in the United States?

≋ FURTHER READING

Anderson, B. and **O'Connell Davidson, J.** (2002). *Trafficking—A Demand Led Problem?* Washington, DC: Save the Children.

The authors review current debates and research on the demand side of trafficking, arguing that the demand aspect of trafficking is problematized by the various definitional and political challenges that surround the issue, and that questions about supply and demand cannot be separated in the analysis of any given market.

Bales, K. and **Lize, S.** (2005). *Trafficking in Persons in the United States*. Washington, DC: National Institute of Justice.

Commissioned by the National Institute of Justice, the research by Bales and Lize opens a window on how people are trafficked into the United States and how the US Government is using the available legal tools to address this problem.

Barry, K. (1979). *Female Sexual Slavery*. New York: New York University Press.

Barry, considered to be an abolitionist feminist, argues that men are responsible for constructing social institutions that allow the exploitation and objectification of women to occur.

Chuang, J. (2006). The United States as global sheriff: Using unilateral sanctions to combat trafficking. *Michigan Journal of International Law*, **27**/2, 437–94.

Chuang argues that the United States Government has undermined and replaced the United Nations as the global enforcer of anti-trafficking norms. She questions the usefulness of the sanctions that the US Government can impose on other governments that do not comply with the norms defined by the Trafficking Victims Protection Act of 2000.

Doezema, J. (2002). Who gets to choose? Coercion, consent and the UN trafficking protocol. *Gender and Development*, **10**/1, 20–7.

Doezema argues that the vague way in which trafficking in persons is defined by the Palermo Protocol will serve to undermine future efforts to combat human trafficking at national levels. She is particularly concerned with the global norms to address prostitution as a form of trafficking and believes strongly that voluntary prostitution is not exploitative.

Keck, M. and **Sikkink, K.** (1998). *Activists Beyond Borders*. Ithaca, NY: Cornell University Press.

Keck and Sikkink examine networks of activists that form and operate transnationally. They focus on the impact that transnational activism has had on human rights, environmental politics, and the campaign around violence against women.

Kempadoo, K. (ed.) (2005). *Trafficking and Prostitution Reconsidered*. Boulder, CO: Paradigm Publishers.

Kempadoo and her colleagues argue against sensationalizing the issue of human trafficking. They provide alternative understandings of transnational migration, forced labour, sex work, and livelihood strategies in the context of globalization.

Lim, L. L. (ed.) (1998). *The Sex Sector*. Geneva: International Labour Office.

Lim and her colleagues show that the prostitution industry reflects other economic sectors because of its diversified structures. They also argue that prostitution is a social phenomenon related to unequal relations between men and women, and between children and parents.

 WEB LINKS

http://HumanTrafficking.org   An Internet resource on human trafficking in Southeast and East Asia, and the United States.

http://www.aaptip.org/   Australia–Asia Program to Combat Trafficking in Persons.

http://ChildTrafficking.com   A comprehensive library of articles related to human trafficking, maintained by Terre des Hommes Foundation

http://un-act.org/   A website of the United Nations Action for Cooperation against Trafficking in Persons.

http://www.ungift.org   Website of the United Nations Global Initiative to Fight Human Trafficking.

http://www.state.gov/j/tip   Website of the United States Department of State Office to Monitor and Combat Trafficking in Persons.

NOTES

1.   See Bristow (1977); Connelly (1980); Walkowitz (1980); Gibson (1986); Corbin (1990); Grittner (1990); Irwin (1996); Fisher (1997).

Visit the Online Resource Centre that accompanies this book for updates and a range of other resources: www.oxfordtextbooks.co.uk/orc/goodhart3e/

17

Children's Human Rights Advocacy

Vanessa Pupavac

Reader's Guide

This chapter explores some theoretical and practical problems in global children's rights advocacy. First, the chapter discusses the novelty of children's rights and the problem of identifying the moral agent of children's rights. Who determines what children's rights and interests are, and how they are interpreted, is not straightforward. Second, the chapter explores tensions between the universalism of human rights advocacy and the relativism of development advocacy. Children's rights research is influenced by **social constructivist** theories, which highlight the history of childhood and childhood norms. Early social constructivist approaches identified the concept of childhood underpinning the Convention on the Rights of the Child as a Western construction based on Western experiences and its exclusion of the experience of childhood in developing countries. Children's rights advocacy globalizes norms on childhood that arose during the industrial development of specific countries, without this economic development being universally shared or envisaged. More recent social constructivist approaches emphasize how childhood norms are constructed and therefore can be reconstructed. These approaches imply expanding global governance of international inequalities. Third, the chapter discusses the attempt to eradicate corporal punishment of children globally as a case study of global children's rights advocacy. The chapter indicates social and political problems with attempting to globalize childhood norms without globalizing material development.

Introduction

It is now more than two decades since the UN *Convention on the Rights of the Child* (CRC) came into force (United Nations General Assembly, 1989). Children born in the year of its creation are adults. The Convention's coming of age has encouraged children's rights advocates to take stock of its impact. The CRC is seen as creating a global geopolitical social contract for children and overcoming children's previous lack of international rights. Virtually all states have ratified the document: only the United States, Somalia, and South Sudan have yet to do so. Advocates want to move beyond law and address deep structural obstacles to children's rights and embed the CRC's provisions into cultures globally. To what extent might children globally be empowered by children's rights? What are children's interests and who should interpret them? How do legal norms become embedded as cultural norms in different social conditions globally? This chapter is concerned first with global children's rights advocacy and the problem of children's empowerment, and second with the tensions between global norms mobilized under the Convention and international development models. Analysis of children's rights raises problems relevant to global human rights advocacy more broadly.

International Children's Rights

Children's rights are a relatively recent idea historically. Accounts locate the origins of the children's rights movement in the beginning of the twentieth century; the state's expanding role in providing education and social welfare drew new attention to the impact of law on children and the family. Judges, lawyers, politicians, and civil servants took up the concerns of the earlier child protection movement led by religious organizations, charities, and welfare reformers (Parton, 1985). Children's rights advocacy has traditionally focused on children as victims, although ideas of child liberation appeared in the 1970s. Key concerns of children's rights advocates have been the legal status of children distinct from their parents and the problem of children's representation under the law.

Development of International Children's Rights

Internationally, the movement to recognize international children's rights arose in the aftermath of the First World War. A pioneering figure was Eglantyne Jebb, a pacifist whose experience as a nurse in that war and earlier conflicts left her appalled by war's impact on children. She contended that 'all wars are waged against children' (quoted in Van Bueren, 1998, p. 8). Her concerns led her to set up the Save the Children Fund in 1919 and to draft an international children's rights text. Jebb lobbied the newly formed League of Nations to take action. The League was reluctant to adopt an international human rights convention, although it was involved in monitoring minority rights provisions imposed on the newly independent Eastern European states. Still, in 1924 it adopted the Declaration of the Rights of the Child (see Box 17.1). The 1924 Declaration, with just five short points, actually represents the first human rights document adopted by the League (Van Bueren, 1998, pp. 6–7). It has a child welfare focus, and it symbolizes international hopes for children having safe and healthy childhoods, rather than embodying international law. Jebb lobbied on other matters, including making national sovereignty subject to human rights; though unsuccessful, her work anticipated the human rights advocacy of the 1990s.

The UN Declaration of the Rights of the Child (1959), with its ten points, is a little longer than the League declaration. The 1959 Declaration was linked to the UN Declaration of Human Rights and supplements its provisions, notably by recognizing protections for the disabled child and protections against neglect and employment detrimental to children's development (Van Bueren, 1998, pp. 10–11). Some of

---

BOX 17.1 DECLARATION OF THE RIGHTS OF THE CHILD 1924

1. The child must be given the means requisite for its normal development, both materially and spiritually.

2. The child that is hungry must be fed, the child that is sick must be nursed, the child that is backward must be helped, the delinquent child must be reclaimed, and the orphan and the waif must be sheltered and succoured.

3. The child must be the first to receive relief in times of distress.

4. The child must be put in a position to earn a livelihood, and must be protected against every form of exploitation.

5. The child must be brought up in the consciousness that its talents must be devoted to the service of its fellow men.

BOX 17.2 CONVENTION ON THE RIGHTS OF THE CHILD (CRC) 1989

'Broadly speaking, the Convention ... is concerned with the four 'P's: the participation of children in decisions affecting their own destiny; the protection of children against discrimination and all forms of neglect and exploitation; the prevention of harm to children; and the provision of assistance for their basic needs' (Van Bueren, 1998, p. 15).

It creates new rights under international law for children where no such rights existed, including the child's right to preserve his or her identity and the right of Indigenous children to practise their own culture. Secondly, [it] enshrines rights in a global treaty, which had until the Convention's adoption only been acknowledged or refined in case law under regional human rights treaties, for example a child's right to be heard either directly or indirectly in

any judicial or administrative proceedings affecting the child, and to have those views taken into account. Thirdly, the Convention also creates binding standards in areas which, until the Convention's entry into force, were only non-binding recommendations. These include safeguards in adoption procedures and the rights of mentally and physically disabled children.

The Convention also imposes new obligations in relation to the provision and protection of children. These include the obligation on a state to take effective measures to abolish traditional practices prejudicial to the health of children (although not mentioned expressly, this includes female circumcision) and to provide for rehabilitative measures for child victims of neglect, abuse, and exploitation (Van Bueren, 1998, p. 16).

its points are directly repeated from the earlier declaration. Commentaries highlight its recognition of the principle of special protection and the idea that the 'best interests of the children' are of 'paramount consideration' (Van Bueren, 1998, p. 11). These themes were taken up and developed in the drafting of the much more comprehensive Convention on the Rights of the Child 1989 (see Box 17.2).

UN Convention on the Rights of the Child 1989

The twentieth anniversary of the UN Declaration of the Rights of the Child in 1979, which was designated the Year of the Child, prompted Poland to call for an international convention on children's rights. Poland had been, since the 1950s, a proponent of a convention. Although the document it put forward was essentially the same as the 1959 Declaration (Van Bueren, 1998, p. 14), the final Convention on the Rights of the Child (CRC), agreed a decade later in 1989, was a much more comprehensive document, with fifty-four articles. Its drafting paralleled and reflected other human rights developments: it embodies a shift from negative freedoms to positive rights and goes beyond a simple synthesis of existing international or regional provisions and case law (Van Bueren, 1998, pp. 13–16; see Box 17.2). NGOs played a significant role in the drafting of the CRC and in building momentum behind it. This effort was helped by the fact that the issue of children represented a matter of shared global concern (Black,

1996; Detrick, 1992). The issue of children's rights was far less controversial culturally than, for example, women's rights—although children's rights have potentially equally far-reaching cultural implications, even if not immediately apparent. The process was not without controversy, including over the extent to which developing countries' perspectives were incorporated into the final document (Detrick, 1992). Poland, the original sponsor, also expressed some disquiet. Having just emerged from martial law, Poland was concerned about the implications of the new Convention's provisions empowering external intervention into family life.

The CRC was codified at the end of the **Cold War**, which witnessed the rising status of international human rights standards. In the three decades preceding the ratification of the two Covenants, the Universal Declaration of Human Rights (UDHR) was treated as merely aspirational in the international system (Henkin, 1981). There has only been significant international political will to consider human rights obligations binding under international law in the last two decades, although human rights advocates have argued that they were always binding.

Forgotten in today's consensus on children's rights is how the United Nations Children's Fund (UNICEF), as the key international children's organization, had been hostile to a children's rights convention and did not become involved in the drafting process until the mid-1980s (Black, 1996, p. 13). As UNICEF's commentary on the Convention explains, human rights agreements were 'not originally intended to have binding force' (UNICEF, undated). Yet, within a short period, UNICEF reversed its hostility to human rights approaches and now believes that they have 'gained binding character as customary law' (UNICEF, undated). Its commentary further considers that the term 'convention' as 'a formal agreement between States' is 'synonymous with the generic term treaty', although earlier international legal opinion saw them as distinct (see Chapter 4). Symbolically, the Secretary General's end-of-decade review, entitled *We the Children* (UN Secretary General, 2001), invited comparisons to the UN Charter's opening declaration, *We the Peoples* (United Nations General Assembly, 2001), illustrating international policy makers' greater will to recognize children's rights in international politics.

The CRC outlines a framework of responsibilities that goes far beyond the earlier League of Nations 1924 and the UN 1959 Declarations of the Rights of the Child. Moreover, the Convention has been accompanied by burgeoning supplementary international and regional norm-setting documents that take up the cause of children: the **International Labour Organization**'s (ILO) Convention Concerning the Prohibition and Immediate Action for the Elimination of the Worst Forms of Child Labour, the Organisation of African Unity's 'African Charter on the Rights and Welfare of the Child' (OAU, 1990), and the National Plans of Action arising from the 1990 World Summit for Children—to name just the most prominent documents. The reporting mechanisms of the Convention have been complemented by UNICEF's annual publication, *State of the World's Children*, or its various 'Progress of Nations' reports that expect countries to adopt global child rights policy approaches. Perhaps more significantly, UNICEF's concerns are being incorporated into the internationally guided national Poverty Reduction Strategy frameworks utilized by international financial institutions like the IMF and World Bank and integrated into global governance strategies—although advocates want stronger laws on children's rights (Pender, 2002, 2007; Duffield, 2007). In addition, the CRC has been invoked by the Security Council as part of the revised international security strategies. Through the Security Council's use of the Convention, children's rights have significance beyond child welfare related to international peace and security. Thus the potential scope of international children's rights in international politics is far-reaching.

KEY POINTS

Poland in the 1979 Year of the Child called for an international convention of children's rights.

UNICEF was originally opposed to the idea of a treaty and only became involved in its drafting from the mid-1980s.

The CRC came into being in 1989 at the end of the Cold War.

The CRC is a much more comprehensive document, with fifty-four articles, outlining a framework of responsibilities and reporting mechanisms.

Virtually all states have ratified the document.

Children's rights concerns are being incorporated into international development strategies.

The CRC has also been invoked by the UN Security Council.

Critical Thinking Question:

Why was UNICEF originally opposed to the CRC?

Special Challenges of Children's Rights

The idea of universal children's rights involves special challenges. First there is the meaning of recognizing children as autonomous rights-holders with their own rights. The Convention does not just recognize children as having protective welfare rights, but also enabling rights (N. Lewis, 1998, p. 92; Pupavac, 1998). Historically, the recognition of individuals as autonomous rights-holders has been associated with ideas of individual capacity for self-determination of one's own person and property (N. Lewis, 1998, p. 80). Modern democracies and citizenship rights are premised on the idea of citizens exercising equal rights. Yet, while children are recognized by the Convention as autonomous rights-holders, the meaning of their rights is problematic if they are not competent or able to exercise them (N. Lewis, 1998, p. 92). The codification of children's rights is therefore not the same as the recognition of the equal rights of earlier excluded groups like the emancipation of women, ethnic minorities, or the working classes, whose recognition simultaneously involved their capacity to exercise their rights themselves.

The model of children's enabling rights seeks to empower children, but does not recognize rights of autonomous self-determination. Indicatively, the CRC does not recognize children's equal political capacity to vote or stand in elections. Children's rights may draw on the ideals of equal rights, but how their rights are realized is dependent on third party determination of their interests. Tensions remain between the ideals of empowerment and the imperatives of protection, which do not escape forms of paternalism. In essence, children's rights are quasi-enabling rights whose exercise is decided by third parties.

Second, there is the meaning of universal children's rights in an unequal world where childhood is substantially different in developing and developed countries. Not least the CRC assumes a model of childhood to the age of 18 years old based on the normal experience in post-industrial countries where childhood is essentially a time of education and play, free from adult responsibilities. However, this model does not describe real-life experiences in many developing countries, where children have to become adults and take on adult responsibilities much earlier than the age of 18. In other words, the CRC excludes the norms of shorter childhoods in much of the globe. Hence there are questions over the relationship of the CRC with developing countries, the CRC's elevation of the norms of childhood in the global North, and its delegitimization of the norms of childhood in the **global South**. Here we come to broader questions of the relationship between the global North and the global South and the implications of expanding global governance for equality between states.

In summary, the special challenges of international children's rights involve fundamental questions of how we understand rights, how we understand progressive social change, and our visions of national and international politics.

Protective Rights to Enabling Rights

Traditionally children's rights were conceived as rights of protection and welfare. This model of rights is evident in the earlier 1924 and 1959 international children's rights documents.

Many critics see this traditional approach as old-fashioned and paternalistic, and seek to give children a greater voice. Here, those seeking to empower children have drawn on contemporary human rights and constructivist theories, which have criticized classic social contract understandings of rights and their model of rights-holders as rational, autonomous [male] individuals with the capacity to guarantee their rights (Santos, 1987, 1995, pp. 60–71; Mackinnon, 1987, 1993; Pateman, 1988; Milanović, 1992; Donnelly, 2003, pp. 16, 61). The classic model making rights contingent on capacity effectively disqualifies those weaker groups, who lack capacity and are most in need of rights protection, from having their interests recognized as rights.

Instead, constructivist human rights theories seek to go beyond a protectionist model and empower marginalized groups, overcoming the flaws of the classical approach. Its alternative, inclusive model of rights is consciously addressed to the moral claims of those who lack capacity. Advocates seek to entrench their interests as fundamental rights so that states cannot ignore their claims or treat them as discretionary. Rights are seen as empowering by signalling the moral worth of the rights-holders to themselves and the rest of society. Positive affirmation of the rights of particular marginal groups is seen as enhancing their self-esteem and social status. These ideas have been used to support children's enabling rights.

Children's incapacity bars them from acquiring rights at the same time that their vulnerability renders them in need of rights to defend their interests (Federle, 1994; Freeman, 1997). Opposing the classic conception of rights as exclusionary for making capacity a prerequisite, children's rights advocates seek to reconceptualize rights as 'not premised upon capacity but … powerlessness' (Federle, 1994, p. 366). They emphasize the socially constructed nature of childhood and the potential to empower children. They see the granting of rights as challenging the exclusion and powerlessness of children in which 'powerful elites decide which, if any, of the claims made by children they will recognize' (Federle, 1994, p. 344). Children's immaturity and need for special protection is not disputed. Nevertheless, recognition of children as distinct rights-holders is regarded as transforming attitudes towards children as well as children's views of themselves and their participation in society (Minow, 1990; McGillivray, 1994; Franklin, 1995). The legal philosopher Martha Minow (1990, pp. 297–8) argues that 'Including children as participants alters their stance in the community from things or outsiders to members … by signalling deserved attention, rights enable a challenge to unstated norms, to exclusion, and the exclusive perspectives.' CRC is distinct from earlier international children's rights approaches in codifying participatory rights, not just protective rights. Aspiring to treat children as rights-holders and to promote their

> ## BOX 17.3 EXTRACTS FROM INTERNATIONAL CHILDREN'S RIGHTS DOCUMENTS
>
> ### UN Declaration of the Rights of the Child 1959
>
> Principle 2: The child shall enjoy special protection, and shall be given opportunities and facilities, by law and by other means, to enable him to develop physically, mentally, morally, spiritually and socially in a healthy and normal manner and in conditions of freedom and dignity. In the enactment of laws for this purpose the best interests of the child shall be the paramount consideration.
>
> ### UN Convention on the Rights of the Child 1989
>
> Article 3 (1): In all actions concerning children, whether undertaken by public or private social welfare institutions, courts of law, administrative authorities or legislative bodies, the best interests of the child shall be a primary consideration.
>
> Article 17 (1): States Parties shall assure to the child who is capable of forming his or her own views the right to express those views freely in all matters affecting the child, the views of the child being given due weight in accordance with the age and maturity of the child.

voices, Article 17 (1) of the CRC gives children the right to express their views in matters affecting them and for their views to be taken into account according to their age and maturity (see Box 17.3).

Capacity Gap in Children's Rights

Yet do children's rights transcend a paternalistic model? Although the child is transformed into a rights-holder in children's rights discourse, the issue of powerful elites deciding 'which, if any, of the claims made by children they will recognize' (Federle, 1994, p. 344) is still pertinent. Childhood dependency may be artificially prolonged but it cannot be dismissed as a social construct (O. O'Neill, 1992, p. 38). The dependence of children on adults is biologically inevitable in their early years. For a period, 'Children have interests to protect before they have wills to assert', as the children's rights theorist Michael Freeman acknowledges (Freeman, 1997, p. 27). Since children lack the ability to assert their will, inherent to the notion of children's rights is the necessity of advocates acting on their behalf.

Children's enabling rights are therefore not the same as classic civil liberties in which the rights-holder and the moral agent of rights are one and the same person. The concept of children's rights leaves open the identity of the moral agent to act on the child's behalf, whereas the traditional approach regarded parents (or guardians) as representing the child's interests. As Freeman (1997, p. 27) has insightfully noted, 'Questions of "by whom?" and "how?" have not been satisfactorily answered.'

The dependent nature of children's rights is evident under the CRC, which makes 'the best interests of the child' under Article 3a the 'primary consideration', not children's views themselves (discussed in N. Lewis, 1998, pp. 77–104). Authorized advocates determine decisions affecting children and what they consider is in children's best interests, including how mature they consider children to be and what weight to give to their views under Article 17. In short, children's rights are interpreted and enforced by external advocates.

Who Should Represent the Child?

Who is to represent the child and define the child's best interests? How are potential conflicts of views and interests between professionals, or between the child and the child's appointed representative(s), resolved? Despite the inherent need for third party advocacy, the agent's accountability to the child is not addressed by children's rights advocates. Insofar as the question is addressed, it is in questioning the moral agency of parents. Indeed, the ultimate rationale for children's rights lies in the problematizing of parental moral agency. As Geraldine Van Bueren (1998, p. 46) observes, 'The Convention challenges the concept that family life is always in the best interests of the children and that parents are always capable of deciding what is the best interests of children.' Children's rights effectively empower officials in relation to parents, rather than empowering children. As such, children's rights advocacy, while often characterized as comparable to earlier civil rights movements, departs from the beliefs of these struggles. While classic civil liberties essentially embody freedoms from state interference, the expanding children's rights framework represents a trend towards external governance of interpersonal relations (Pupavac, 2002). Accordingly, children's rights advocacy is sceptical about the autonomy of the private sphere associated with classic civil liberties and about the ideal of the free and equal moral citizen (Arendt, 1959, p. 54; Rawls, 1973, pp. 161, 565; Mill, 1985; Habermas, 1996, p. 455). Critics warn that children's rights advocacy is empowering the state to discipline ordinary people for departing from preferred professional parenting norms, and risks giving a licence to repressive state powers and undermining human rights (N. Lewis, 1998; Pavlovic, 2007).

KEY POINTS

CRC is distinct from earlier international children's rights approaches in codifying participatory rights, not just protective rights.

Children's participatory rights in the CRC permit children a voice, but are subject to 'the best interests of the child', determined by authorized agents.

Children's rights as empowerment rights tend to challenge parental representation of children's interests, but the question of who is authorized to represent children's interests is not clear.

Children's rights express a **capacity gap**—children as rights-holders do not have the capacity to determine their best interests and enforce their rights. Therefore, children's rights depend on an externally authorized agent to do so. Their dependency means that children cannot hold the externally authorized agent accountable, so power relations remain.

Critical Thinking Question:

To what extent could the capacity gap of children's rights-holders be overcome?

Constructing and Reconstructing Childhood

The evolving international human rights framework emphasizes the interdependence and **indivisibility** of rights (Donnelly, 2003, pp. 27–33). Children's rights advocates also affirm the interdependence and indivisibility of rights under the CRC. At the same time, many

children's rights advocates, especially the more sophisticated, would identify themselves as social constructivists. Social constructivist approaches towards human rights have become more influential in the last couple of decades and have long informed children's rights thinking. Social constructivist approaches, pioneered by Ariès (1962), have sought to explore the historically or culturally contingent character of social norms and social organization. Ariès's own account documents French society's changing historical understanding of children in the early modern period, down to the very portraiture of children. Other studies have pursued both cross-country cultural and historical differences (Boyden, 1994; Burman, 1994; James and Prout, 1997). These build on earlier anthropological studies demonstrating the diverse forms of human ways of life and childhood (Mead and Wolfenstein, 1955).

Constructivist histories have also analysed the character of national and international advocacy movements for children (Platt, 1977; Parton, 1985; Cunningham, 1995). These histories identify a 'child-saving movement', which seeks to protect children, and a 'children's rights movement', which seeks to empower them. The latter needs to be distinguished from the more marginal idea of a child liberation programme, which was mooted in the early 1970s and argues for children's rights to self-determination and freedoms similar to those for adults. The child-saving approach dominated international organizations until the 1980s; since then, a rights-based approach has become more common. Nevertheless, the child-saving approach persists within the framework of rights and empowerment, as we will go on to discuss. Tensions between child-saving and enabling approaches are revealed in debates on prohibiting the recruitment of child soldiers or child labour (Hart, 2006). International child advocacy approaches have admitted distinctions between harmful exploitative child labour and non-exploitative incremental involvement of children in work. However, international child advocacy has been overwhelmingly opposed to child soldiers and viewed children's participation in armed forces as predominantly involving coercion (see Box 17.4). Research has also challenged the prevailing assumptions of children predominantly being forcibly recruited into armed forces (see Box 17.5).

The preamble of the CRC sets out a universal model of childhood embodying a space in which the child develops his or her personality 'in an atmosphere of happiness, love, understanding', protected

BOX 17.4 KEY INTERNATIONAL PROVISIONS ON CHILD SOLDIERS

1949 Geneva Conventions and the 1977 Additional Protocols

https://www.icrc.org/applic/ihl/ihl.nsf/vwTreaties1949.xsp

Additional Protocol I 1977

Article 77

Protection of children

1. The Parties to the conflict shall take all feasible measures in order that children who have not attained the age of fifteen years do not take a direct part in hostilities and, in particular, they shall refrain from recruiting them into their armed forces. In recruiting among those persons who have attained the age of fifteen years but who have not attained the age of eighteen years, the Parties to the conflict shall endeavour to give priority to those who are oldest.

2. If, in exceptional cases, despite the provisions of paragraph 2, children who have not attained the age of fifteen years take a direct part in hostilities and fall into the power of an adverse Party, they shall continue to benefit from the special protection accorded by this Article, whether or not they are prisoners of war.

3. If arrested, detained or interned for reasons related to the armed conflict, children shall be held in quarters separate from the quarters of adults, except where families are accommodated as family units as provided in Article 75, paragraph 5.

4. The death penalty for an offence related to the armed conflict shall not be executed on persons who had not attained the age of eighteen years at the time the offence was committed.

Convention on the Rights of the Child, 20 November 1989

Article 38

1. States Parties undertake to respect and to ensure respect for rules of international humanitarian law applicable to them in armed conflicts which are relevant to the child.

2. States Parties shall take all feasible measures to ensure that persons who have not attained the age of fifteen years do not take a direct part in hostilities.

3. States Parties shall refrain from recruiting any person who has not attained the age of fifteen years into their armed forces. In recruiting among those persons who have attained the age of fifteen years but who have not attained the age of eighteen years, States Parties shall endeavour to give priority to those who are oldest.

4. In accordance with their obligations under international humanitarian law to protect the civilian population in armed conflicts, States Parties shall take all feasible measures to ensure protection and care of children who are affected by an armed conflict.

Article 39

States Parties shall take all appropriate measures to promote physical and psychological recovery and social reintegration of a child victim of: any form of neglect, exploitation, or abuse; torture or any other form of cruel, inhuman or degrading treatment or punishment; or armed conflicts. Such recovery and reintegration shall take place in an environment which fosters the health, self-respect and dignity of the child.

http://www.unicef.org.uk/Documents/Publication-pdfs/UNCRC_PRESS200910web.pdf

Rome Statute of the International Criminal Court 1998

Article 8 categorizes as a war crime inter alia conscripting or enlisting children under the age of 15 years into armed forces or groups or using them to participate actively in hostilities.

http://www.icc-cpi.int/nr/rdonlyres/ea9aeff7-5752-4f84-be94-0a655eb30e16/0/rome_statute_english.pdf

International Labour Organization Convention No. 182 on the Prohibition and Immediate Action for the Elimination of the Worst Forms of Child Labour 1999.

Article 3 prohibits the forced or compulsory recruitment of children for use in armed conflict.

http://www.ilo.org/public/english/standards/relm/ilc/ilc87/com-chic.htm

Optional Protocol to the Convention on the Rights of the Child on the Involvement of Children in Armed Conflict 2000

States Parties shall take all feasible measures to ensure that members of their armed forces who have not attained the age of 18 years do not take a direct part in hostilities. (Article 1)

States Parties shall ensure that persons who have not attained the age of 18 years are not compulsorily recruited into their armed forces. (Article 2)

Armed groups that are distinct from the armed forces of a State should not, under any circumstances, recruit or use in hostilities persons under the age of 18 years. (Article 4)

(continued)

BOX 17.4 *(continued)*

Other key international initiatives

Cape Town Principles and Best Practices 1997

http://www.unicef.org/emerg/files/Cape_Town_Principles(1).pdf

Paris Commitments to Protect Children from Unlawful Recruitment or Use by Armed Forces or Armed Groups 2007

Paris Principles and Guidelines on Children Associated with Armed Forces or Armed Groups 2007

http://www.unicef.org/protection/files/Paris_Principles_EN.pdf

UN Integrated Disarmament, Demobilization, and Reintegration Standards (IDDRS)

http://www.unddr.org/

BOX 17.5 CHALLENGING ASSUMPTIONS: CHILD SOLDIERS

Historically, children's participation in armed forces has paralleled their other social responsibilities. Consequently in social conditions where children have to take on adult responsibilities at a younger age, they are also more likely to be mobilized into fighting roles (Hart, 2006, 2008). Nevertheless, the role of children in armed conflict is generally seen by children's rights advocacy as harmful and exploitative per se, even where some work children undertake may be accepted as non-exploitative. Furthermore it is feared that becoming a child soldier not only risks damaging the child's moral, social, and emotional development, but that child soldiers, because of their immaturity, risk becoming conditioned to violence and potentially more ready to commit atrocities (Goodwin-Gill and Cohn, 1994).

However, recruitment into the national armed forces has traditionally been a means of integration and mobility for socially marginal groups in society. Many states opposed a ban on recruiting 15–18 year olds in the UN Convention on the Rights of the Child. Instead, efforts have been concentrated on prohibiting compulsory recruitment of those under 18, or bans on those under 18 serving on the front line (see Box 17.4).

International campaigns on child soldiers have typically focused on the problem of child abduction and forced recruitment into armed groups such as the Lord's Resistance Army (LRA) in Uganda. The protection of children has become acute in wars in Syria, Iraq, and Yemen, as documented in international human rights reports such as the UN High Commissioner for Human Rights' 2015 report on the human rights situation in Iraq or Human Rights Watch's *'Maybe We Live and Maybe We Die': Recruitment and Use of Children by Armed Groups in Syria* (2014b). Terrorist groups such as ISIS openly display their recruitment of child soldiers and their readiness to commit atrocities in propaganda videos circulated on social media.

The abduction of over 250 girls from a boarding school in Chibok, northern Nigeria by the militant Islamist group, Boko Haram, in April 2014 galvanized international attention to its forced mobilization of children into their armed forces. In 2015, Amnesty International (2015b) estimated that over 5,500 civilians had been killed in the region by Boko Haram since 2014. Boko Haram specifically identifies itself in opposition to the international norms of children's rights—its unofficial name is a shorthand for the idea that Western education is sinful and forbidden (BBC, 2014). A high-profile international campaign was begun, with advocates including Michelle Obama, to raise awareness for the plight of the Chibok girls and to demand political action for their return. UNICEF's Missing Childhoods also seeks to bring the issue of child soldiers to the attention of young people through social media such as Facebook, Snapchat, Tumblr, and Twitter using the hashtag #bringbackourchildhood (UNICEF, 2014).

Global social media activism earlier galvanized around the *Kony 2012* video demanding the prosecution of the LRA's leader Joseph Kony for war crimes over the forcible mobilization of children. However, the campaign has been criticized for having a superficial, short-term impact (Drumbl, 2012a). Moreover, there has been some criticism of how international advocacy campaigns represent child soldiering: for example, social media activism has been accused of having a reductive understanding of the problem of child soldiers and overlooking measures such as amnesties which may be more useful in demobilizing child soldiers and facilitating their rehabilitation (Drumbl, 2012a). Mark Drumbl's *Re-Imagining Child Soldiers in International Law and Policy* (2012b) has challenged the common representations of child soldiers as forcibly recruited, highlighting the varied reasons why they might be attracted to joining armed forces.

Drumbl's analysis is helpful in exploring why increasing numbers of young people in the West are attracted to go abroad and join

(continued)

BOX 17.5 (*continued*)

al-Qaeda, ISIS, or other terrorist groups. Online recruitment to ISIS has been seen as analogous to other forms of online grooming, but we also need to account for how young people actually have to actively seek out jihadist websites. In other words, the teenage recruits are not simply passive victims, but willing and resourceful participants. Of the recent British recruits to ISIS, the growing number of teenagers is striking. For example, a 17 year old British ISIS recruit was killed in a suicide attack in Iraq in June 2015 (BBC, 2015b). Girls too are recruited: for example, in February 2015, three London girls aged 15 and 16 travelled to Syria to join ISIS and marry ISIS fighters, and various friends from their school were made wards of court and banned from travelling due to fears that they too might travel to Syria or Iraq to join ISIS (Boycott, 2015).

The lure of ISIS has been described as a mixture of religious-ideological conviction, anti-Western sentiment, a desire for excitement, glamour, and adventure against a risk-averse safety culture, and the thrill of becoming or marrying a daring, attractive fighter. The phenomenon has been equated to 'pop idols' and 'jihadimania' (Bunyan, 2015). Yet while a pop idol dimension is evident in the social media representations, the young recruits from Britain are not simply following pop idols, but groups publicly rejecting human rights (UN High Commissioner for Human Rights, 2015). The phenomenon therefore suggests these teenagers' profound sense of alienation not only from their own societies, but from the humanist beliefs and humanitarian concerns which underpin the idea of international human rights (Durodié, 2013).

from adult responsibilities and oriented towards 'an individual life in society'. Constructivist approaches show that a particular history underlies the norms of childhood and children's rights globalized through the CRC—namely, the industrialization of European and North American societies. Industrialization culminated in removing children from the workforce and incrementally extending childhood as a period of education and play, free from employment and other adult responsibilities (Berger, Berger, and Keller, 1974, pp. 171–4; Boyden, 1990; Cunningham, 1995; Cox, 1996).

Donnelly (2003, p. 71) has questioned the *genetic fallacy*, or the belief that because the concepts of human rights historically developed in Western societies they are therefore only relevant to Western societies. He and others rightly argue that the historical origins of a concept or product do not rule out its applicability for other societies, whether Arabic mathematics or Chinese fireworks (Donnelly, 2003, p. 71). But what happens when historical experiences are not shared?

Linking Material Improvement and Social Progress

Since the **Enlightenment,** moral improvement and social progress have been linked to material improvement. The importance of material improvement for other goods has been axiomatic to secular progressive thinking. 'All human progress, political, moral, or intellectual, is inseparable from material progression', wrote the sociologist Auguste Comte (1896, p. 222). Sociology's founding writers gave weight to the

relationship between material progress and cultural progress. Max Weber (1954) saw an 'elective affinity' between the rise of universal, impartial legal norms, the ideals of individual rights and equality before the law, and an impersonal public sphere and the modernizing institutions of the modern industrial economy and the state. Karl Marx (1990) specifically located the rise of universal legal norms in capitalist market relations. Notwithstanding the important distinctions between classic sociology and Marxist approaches, both emphasized the importance of advances in technological production (Berger, Berger, and Keller, 1974, pp. 29–43, 90–105).

Conversely, a society based around household production fosters particular communal obligations, kinship duties, and a personalized public sphere. The personalized character of social relations and obligations in traditional non-industrial societies circumscribe the operation of universal impartial legal norms and autonomous rights. A weak productive capacity limits the welfare resources available for societal redistribution, while a weak national infrastructure limits the ability to redistribute resources equitably and effectively. The traditional (non-industrial), semi-industrial, industrial, or post-industrial character of society fundamentally conditions childhood norms as well as the scope of law and its ability to influence childhood norms.

Law and Culture

Since Montesquieu's pioneering eighteenth-century work *The Spirit of Laws* (Montesquieu, 1949), comparative studies have observed a relationship between a country's legal norms and its social, economic, and cultural conditions and means of production (Weber, 1954, Arendt, 1972, pp. 63–6; Pashukanis, 1978; Glendon, Gordon, and Osakwe, 1982, p. 10; Geertz, 1983, p. 215). Accounts link development of individual rights to the social and political transformations from feudalism to modern capitalist societies (Dicey, 1959; Arendt, 1972, pp. 66–76; Pashukanis, 1978, Neumann, 1996, pp. 195–230; Miéville, 2005). Such studies raise questions over the translatability of law across different societies with different prevailing conditions. The relationship between modern human rights and developed capitalist relations assumed by earlier accounts suggests that rights enforcement will be strained under the traditional agricultural and patrimonial relations prevailing in many developing countries. Anthropological studies in particular have historically suggested the limits of law where social and cultural ways of life are at variance (Malinowski, 1945, p. 45). Put bluntly: 'law is culture and culture is law' (Grossfeld, 1990, p. 41). If older studies emphasize how law reflects social relations, later approaches emphasize law as shaping social relations (Geertz, 1983; Santos, 1987; Milanović, 1992). Idealist interpretations of legal social constructivism have informed expanding universal human rights since the 1990s. Cultures are not islands, and the Western origins of human rights concepts do not preclude their incorporation into other cultures or their use by oppressed groups (Wilson 1997, p. 10; Donnelly 2003, p. 71). Nevertheless, there are problems with globalizing legal norms where the historical conditions underpinning those norms have not been globalized. Predominantly agricultural societies and post-industrial societies have very different capabilities for realizing legal entitlements (Pupavac, 2011). Importantly, rights change their character where they have to be enforced against the prevailing social conditions. Problems complying with international human rights regimes in poorer, weaker countries legitimize more external governance, and its related unequal power relations (N. Lewis, 1998).

CRC Excluding Childhood of Developing Countries

Initially constructivists criticized the CRC for embodying a Western model of childhood and excluding the experience of children in developing countries who take on adult responsibilities much earlier than the age of 18 (Boyden, 1990, 1994; James and Prout, 1990; Burman, 1994, 1995; Franklin, 1995; Bar-On, 1996; N. Lewis, 1998). However, constructivist theories of children's rights are increasingly invoked by advocates to draw attention to how cultures are not fixed, as a prelude to discussing how the CRC can be mobilized to change cultural behaviour towards children.

Logically, particular historical experiences encourage particular childhood norms, and shared historical experiences encourage norms to converge. This points to a problem in global children's rights advocacy if the historical conditions that fostered the childhood norms embodied in the CRC are not universally enjoyed. The ambition to universalize these conditions was abandoned prior to the creation of the Convention, as we will go on to explore. Contemporary international development policy imagines a very different destiny for developing countries, involving substantial retention of traditional ways of rural survival (Pupavac, 2005; Duffield, 2007). Codifying a model of childhood derived from the social conditions of only part of the world delegitimizes other childhood experiences in different societies (Boyden, 1990, 1994; James and Prout, 1990; Burman, 1994, 1995; Franklin, 1995; Bar-On, 1996; N. Lewis, 1998; Hart, 2006).

Limits of Law to Improve Society

Previously, international policy saw legislation as having only a limited role in addressing the problems of children in poorer countries. As UNICEF argued in a 1963 report:

In the richer countries, much can be done to meet the needs of children through legislation, and substantial resources can be mobilized for aid through community or voluntary channels. Since the number of children with serious unfulfilled needs is relatively small, it is possible to mount very effective programmes of action to deal with these needs. In the least developed countries, on the other hand, where the needs of children are most extensive, it is difficult to improve the condition of children without raising the living standards of the population as a whole.

(UNICEF, 1963, p. 23)

This view clearly follows the classic sociological tradition.

An alternative strand of sociology views society as the sum of interpersonal relations and social change as the culmination of interpersonal change. Contemporary children's rights advocacy is closer to this idealist strand of sociology, which emphasizes the role of professional interventions and de-emphasizes the economic and social conditions (Boyden, 1994, 1997; M. King, 1997, pp. 7–8). Historically, Western social reform movements, including advocacy on behalf of children, as compared to mass political movements, have tended to emphasize moral/behavioural reform more than material goods (Williams, 1963; Parton, 1985). Social constructivist studies were previously closer to the classic strand of sociology in emphasizing the interrelationship between norms and material conditions. However, in recent years social constructivist approaches have become increasingly non-materialist and closer to the idealist strand of sociology in how they regard society as constructed through intersubjectivity.

Idealist and non-materialist interpretations are especially marked among professional children's rights advocates. Idealist interpretations present childhood norms as constructed and therefore open to being reconstructed. Yet they effectively end up disregarding the complex integral relationship of norms to the material conditions of a society highlighted in earlier constructivist studies, as they divorce normative transformation from material transformation. Contemporary approaches may acknowledge the earlier social constructivist studies, which trace distinct conceptions of childhood to the historical development from traditional to industrial to post-industrial society. But they overlook the implications of these studies for today's global children's rights advocacy when they divorce normative transformation from material transformation. Impediments to enforcing rights are commonly presented as problems of political will, even when references are made to the political economy (for example, Donnelly, 2003, p. 29).

Global advocacy believes in the universal applicability of human rights norms and wants to universalize the childhood norms arising in the post-industrial societies and embodied in the CRC, albeit with cultural modification. Conversely, international development thinking does not believe that developing countries should follow the same industrial development as the developed countries, and has evolved relativist models. Global advocacy emphasizes the interdependence and indivisibility of political, social, and economic rights, but paradoxically not the interdependence and indivisibility of political, social, and economic

conditions. Global policy invites the question of how childhood norms can be globalized if developing countries are envisaged as following distinct non-industrial development paths. In their decoupling of normative transformation from material transformation, global advocates echo classic philosopher-legislators, whose models of the good life focus on spiritual goods and disparage material wants. The rest of this chapter explores tensions between the universalism of human rights advocacy and the relativism of economic development.

KEY POINTS

Social constructivist studies show how childhoods have been constructed differently historically and cross-culturally.

CRC embodies a model of childhood to the age of 18 as a period of happiness, free from adult responsibilities, which is informed by the historical experiences of the advanced Western industrial countries.

The CRC attempts to globalize childhood norms without globalizing the historical conditions that fostered those norms—i.e. normative transformation is divorced from material transformation.

Previously, studies believed that legislation could only play a limited role in improving child welfare, especially in developing countries. However, doubt began to be cast on international modernization strategies in the late 1960s.

Global children's rights advocacy embodies an idealist, non-materialist approach to improving the condition of children.

Critical Thinking Question:

To what extent can law engender social change?

From Universal Development to Relative Development Models

Alarm over Urban Alienation and Street Children

International development policy originally regarded urban poverty as a step up from rural poverty, as urban life provided the poor with more employment opportunities and access to services, however inadequate, and viewed rural poverty as the most urgent problem

(Black, 1996, p. 119). Studies continued to suggest that urban migration offered poor families the chance of upward mobility that was not available in rural areas (Nelson, 1969). Gradually, however, urban poverty came to be seen as worse, particularly in its impact on the young (Black, 1996, p. 129). Early optimism that many urban problems were transitional eroded, and fears grew that urban life eroded family ties and left the young without appropriate parental guidance. The phenomenon of street children symbolized for many international policy makers how modernization strategies were threatening social cohesion and welfare (Black, 1996, pp. 128–30).

Social psychological approaches suggested that growing shanty towns and urban slums fostered social pathologies, producing maladjusted young people at risk of delinquency: 'social disorganization leads to the family's failure to ensure that the personality of young people develops satisfactorily, since, lacking the requisite norms, they are apt to indulge in all kinds of anti-social behaviour' (Hauser, 1961, p. 54).

Both official and radical critiques came to reject industrialization for the developing world, albeit from very different perspectives. Western policy makers feared that urbanization was promoting political radicalism—alarm grew that modernization strategies were politically destabilizing societies and exacerbating social problems rather than alleviating them (Huntington, 1968). Rapid urbanization, it was feared, was creating millions of displaced people and 'rising frustrations' (Lerner, 1967, p. 28). Radical circles had the opposite concern: that modern states created conformist individuals and that political opposition could only emerge from those outside the processes of the modern industrial state (Marcuse, 1964; Illich, 1997). Developing countries remained committed to industrialization and to the idea that states should play a primary role in development, in keeping with the idea of national independence struggles. Their critics wanted more resources devoted to people's basic needs and also saw the state playing a primary welfare role.

The decline of Third World nationalism and mass political movements through the 1970s and 1980s and the end of the Cold War allowed international development policies to abandon the idea of developing countries catching up with the advanced industrial countries.

Yet, while countries are expected to follow different development paths with different ways of life and standards of living, they are also expected to follow universal human rights. In other words, there are tensions between the promotion of relativist material development models and the promotion of universal human rights frameworks (Pupavac, 2005).

Crisis of Economic Development and the Rise of Children's Rights

Ironically, while universal development was abandoned in the 1970s, that decade witnessed a renewed movement to universalize human rights and expand normative reform programmes. There is not the space here to consider the international political context that fostered renewed international attention to human rights (T. Evans, 1996, 1998; Sellars, 2002). A catalyst for UNICEF adopting a children's rights approach was its growing alarm at the impact of urbanization, economic crisis, and **structural adjustment programmes** on families (Black, 1996). It hoped that a children's rights approach might help to prioritize the needs of children and mitigate effects of the 1980s world recession on children.

During the debt crisis of the 1980s, UNICEF pioneered crisis management strategies under the banner of 'adjustment with a human face' (Cornia, Jolly, and Stewart, 1987), selecting low-cost interventions that would have the greatest overall impact on child survival (Black, 1996, pp. 18–21). Similarly, UNICEF's Children in Extremely Difficult Circumstances programme targeted interventions at groups of children that were deemed particularly vulnerable. The selective interventions pioneered by UNICEF improved child survival rates but represented an international retreat from substantial material development. Moreover, the international retreat to selective welfare interventions designed to impact on the general survival rates of a population (Duffield, 2007) contradicts the CRC, which purports to address the rights of every individual child globally. This contradiction reflects a deeper tension in global children's rights advocacy.

Idealist Reconstructions of Childhood

There is a fundamental paradox in global children's rights advocacy, which seeks to globalize the childhood norms of post-industrial societies without globalizing the material conditions of childhood that fostered those norms. Consider how the 1990 African

Charter on the Rights and Welfare of the Child proclaims that children are to be protected from 'economic exploitation' and 'performing any work that is
likely to be hazardous or to interfere with the child's
physical, mental, spiritual, moral, or social development' (Article 15). Even international child poverty
models consciously seeing themselves as holistic and
highlighting the allocation of resources overlook
how the resources and means of allocation in societies organized around basic technological household production, as opposed to advanced industrial
production, are qualitatively different. Yet sustainable development envisages small-scale family farming based on low or medium technology to be the
backbone of the economies of developing countries.
The focus on redistribution tellingly overlooks how
the mode of production of predominantly agrarian
societies requires child labour. Whatever romantic
pastoral images sustainable development conjures
up, family farming without modern machinery involves intensive labour, including child labour. Some
insightful research has been conducted on the impact of the global political economy on children
and problems with global advocacy for children (N.
Lewis, 1998; Nieuwenhuys, 2000, 2001; Watson,
2006). However, the implications of the sustainable development model for children have been
under-explored.

Debates on universalism or relativism in human
rights have focused on contention over Asian values, but have not seriously asked whether universal
human rights promotion is compatible with relativist models of development. Donnelly suggests 'the
sharp break with traditional ways implicit in the idea
and practice of equal and inalienable rights' (Donnelly, 2003, p. 76). He is rare in asking whether a
rights approach requires particular social conditions
to flourish, but his analysis does not satisfactorily answer the problem of grounding rights that he raises.
He treats the uneven development caused by modernity as making human rights imperative rather
than unrealizable. Thus Donnelly writes of how
'the conditions created by modernization render the
individual too vulnerable in the absence of human
rights' (Donnelly, 2003, p. 85). The prevailing idealist
philosophy of human rights does not follow through
the contradictions of the international political economy that undermine individuals' rights highlighted
by the earlier underdevelopment theories (Frank,
1970, 1971; Amin, 1976).

KEY POINTS

International development policy originally promoted
economic industrialization models, which saw economic
modernization as encouraging the convergence of global
cultural, political, and social norms.

International policy makers feared that modernization was
causing political and social instability.

They feared urbanization was creating social problems such
as street children, who were represented both as victims and
as social threats.

International development policy shifted to non-industrial
sustainable development approaches.

Global advocacy is underpinned by universalist human rights
models but by relativist development models.

The CRC addresses the individual child, but international
policies targeting selective basic needs address problems at
the level of populations.

Non-industrial, low-technological household economies rely
on child labour, with consequences for childhood norms.

Critical Thinking Question:

What international development approaches best advance
the interests of children?

Case Study: Punishing Childhoods

Idealist Reconstruction of Cultural Norms

How does global children's rights advocacy understand culture and changing cultural norms? Children's
rights advocacy follows the idea that human rights are
universally relevant with cultural modifications (Donnelly, 2003). Advocates sympathize with relativist understandings of culture and tend to eschew universalist
definitions of culture as the highest achievements of
humanity. The term 'culture' is loosely used in global
advocacy, but nevertheless remains a core concept
underpinning interventions. Culture is sometimes
synonymous with a way of life or a people's identity,
or sometimes refers more narrowly to symbolic communication. In key respects children's rights advocacy
echoes anthropological and *behaviouralist* approaches
towards culture, whereby each people has a culture or
patterns of behaviour, and recognizes cultural identity

as important for a functional personality (Benedict, 1961). Thus the CRC's preamble states how the Convention takes 'due account of the importance of the traditions and cultural values of each people for the protection and harmonious development of the child'. In the same vein, it is commonly observed by advocates that the African Charter on the Rights and Welfare of the Child recognizes the responsibilities that children have towards their families as an example of how human rights advocacy does take into account regional differences (Article 31). In the text of the CRC, Articles, 8, 29, and 30 recognize as rights the preservation of identity and enjoyment of culture. They deny a hierarchy of cultures, although they identify certain cultural practices as illegitimate. At the same time, cultural norms are regarded as learned behaviour—and as learned behaviour, may be unlearned and reformed.

Here global children's rights advocacy diverges from the functionalist approach to culture, which had a strong influence on twentieth-century anthropology. Functionalism treats cultures as having an overall coherence, and proposes that the integral function of cultural norms and behaviour—customs or practices, which may seem bizarre, irrational, or harmful to outsiders—will, with more cultural insight and understanding, be recognized as functional. Human rights advocacy chimes more with an influential idealist strand of anthropology, which treats culture as distinct from social organization (A. Kuper, 1999). In this vein, human rights advocates refer to culture as a site of contestation (Donnelly, 2003, p. 102), made up of 'fluid complexes of intersubjective meanings and practices' (Donnelly, 2003, p. 86). But a model of indeterminate cultural flux over cultural coherence loses the social analytical understanding of the interdependence of cultural norms, ways of life, and material social conditions. Consequently there is a danger of failing to understand the problems of changing cultural norms, and realizing human rights and children's rights.

Paradox of International Cultural Reform Programmes

To what extent can the norms of behaviour towards children in traditional societies be changed while retaining their traditional economic organization around family labour? If childhood norms are to transform substantially, the underlying material social conditions also need to transform substantially. Global advocates want to respect traditional ways of life without sustaining their negative features, such as female genital mutilation or harsh corporal punishment. Thus the African Charter on the Rights and Welfare of the Child stresses 'the preservation and strengthening of positive African morals, traditional values and cultures' as part of children's education (Article 11), while stipulating that states discourage harmful practices (Article 3). Advocates want to use culture as a flexible resource, picking up those aspects of it that they like while rejecting its disturbing aspects. But how convincing is an *à la carte* approach to culture?

Global children's rights advocacy does not explain why people would or should make significant changes in their personal relationships and behaviour in the absence of broader social change. People's security in household subsistence farming is inherently precarious and subject to the forces of nature. Unable to rely on welfare support, they have to bear its hardships stoically and have little scope for error or experimentation. Why, if they are expected to continue their traditional way of life in its essentials, would they venture to adopt new family norms of behaviour? Embracing such an experiment only makes sense if their horizons are expanded, their social expectations are raised, and they see the younger generation preparing for a radically different way of life.

The problems of culture and development were familiar concerns to earlier international development thinkers, who sought to fire populations' enthusiasm for modernization. However, prior development research showing the limited impact of public programmes that did not address social expectations seems to be neglected in today's global rights advocacy. The conservative, anti-experimental character of traditional agricultural communities has long been observed by economists, anthropologists, and writers alike (Mead, 1953, pp. 185–6; Galbraith, 1964, 1977). To expect traditional communities to adopt radically different interpersonal norms is to expect them to undertake a huge social experiment. The very undertaking would involve them changing from an internally-oriented, tradition-based society to an externally-oriented, risk-taking society with wider expectations. Yet the rights-based sustainable development approach wants people to undertake this great social experiment of interpersonal norms while keeping them traditional in other respects.

External intervention in family relationships involves serious responsibilities, especially if global policy essentially expects families to look after their own material welfare. Past anthropological studies observed how even well-intentioned welfare interventions could disturb existing family relations and thereby unwittingly undermine family bonds, with overall negative consequences for the welfare of its members (Mead, 1953, pp. 181, 214–15). The disturbance of interdependencies and responsibilities risks making people's lives more insecure unless new sources of security are being created. International development thinking of fifty years ago aspired to build new national support systems and comprehensive universal public welfare services. Yet global children's rights advocacy involves trying to change adult–child relations fundamentally while expecting people to find material security in traditional relations.

Global advocates consciously want their programmes to accommodate existing cultures. However, global advocacy can end up displaying a rather superficial view of cultural change and culture as a way of life, isolating particular features of culture considered undesirable from the totality of relations.

The next section examines the current campaign for the universal prohibition of the physical punishment of children as a case study of the idealist character of global children's rights advocacy.

Campaign for the Universal Prohibition of the Physical Punishment of Children

The current campaign for the universal prohibition of the physical punishment of children usefully illustrates the idealist character of global children's rights advocacy.

Physical punishment has long been viewed as violent assault by children's rights advocates and is currently a major theme of global advocacy. However, earlier children's rights documents do not contain specific clauses prohibiting physical punishment. For example, under Article 20 on Parental Responsibilities in the African Charter on the Rights and Welfare of the Child, parents have the duty 'to ensure that the best interests of the child are their basic concern at all times', 'to secure, within their abilities and financial capacities, conditions of living necessary to the child's development', and 'to ensure that domestic discipline is administered with humanity and in a manner consistent with the inherent dignity of the child'. (See Box 17.6 for a discussion of the 'best interests' of the child.)

International children's rights advocates are seeking to extend both international and national provisions

---

BOX 17.6 ALTERNATIVE POINTS OF VIEW: WHO DETERMINES THE BEST INTERESTS OF THE CHILD?

The quality of parenting culture has become a key focus of social policy making, where parenting is seen as responsible for many social problems today (Vandenbroeck, Roose, and De Bie, 2011; Lee et al., 2014). The expanding state intervention is leading to tensions over who determines the best interests of the child.

Tensions between the authorities and migrant communities over children taken into state care have become apparent, with foreign governments making representations to the authorities on behalf of their nationals in various northern European countries including Britain, the Netherlands, Norway, and Sweden (Family Law Week, 2014). The Slovakian government has even threatened to take the UK to the European Court of Human Rights over various decisions whereby British authorities have removed children from Slovak parents living in the UK (Booker, 2012; Slovak Ministry of Justice, 2012).

However, such tensions do not just relate to those with different cultural backgrounds clashing with specific national professional views in their country of residence, but also to broader clashes between citizens and the authorities, with the parties invoking human rights. Consider, for example, Scotland's Named Person scheme, under which every child in Scotland will have a state-appointed guardian with an expanded remit to intervene to

ensure the well-being of the child. A campaign opposing the Named Person scheme (NO2NP) claims that the scheme breaches the European Convention on Human Rights in relation to the right to privacy and family, and has been gathering cases of conflicts between families and the authorities since the scheme began being trialled.

In these competing claims, families have increasingly been taking their concerns over professional decisions to the public via social media or the press, or covertly recording meetings with social workers fearing official misrepresentation in child proceedings (Medway Council, 2015; Tickle, 2015). Both concerns relating to a lack of official transparency and accountability, and parents' willingness to speak out have been reinforced by recent appalling failures of child protection by the authorities, such as the sexual exploitation of children in Rotherham and other UK cities, despite parents raising desperate concerns with officials (Jay, 2014). Strong public sympathy may be galvanized internationally where professionals are seen as overstepping their authority, such as in the case of the parents of Ashya King, who were issued with an international arrest warrant when they removed their 5 year old son with a brain tumour from a British hospital against its medical recommendations, in order to seek alternative medical treatment abroad.

to outlaw corporal punishment globally. Various campaigning organizations globally came together in 2001 under the Global Initiative to End All Corporal Punishment of Children (http://www.endcorporalpunishment.org/), which calls for a universal legal prohibition against all forms of corporal punishment, including smacking in the home. A number of individuals and organizations associated with the Global Initiative helped inform the UN Secretary General's study on violence against children (UN Secretary General, 2006), which supports universally outlawing corporal punishment, including in the home.

Global campaigns are beginning to influence national laws on corporal punishment of children, as the Global Initiative's 'Countdown to universal prohibition' indicates,[2] but professionals speak of difficulties in changing attitudes among ordinary people. The physical punishment of children has progressively softened in Western countries over the last century, although what is deemed acceptable punishment among ordinary people may still clash with the views of children's rights advocates. For example, the Scottish Children's Commissioner has repeatedly attempted to introduce a law in the Scottish Parliament banning parents from smacking their children (MacMahon, 2007), although smacking remains culturally acceptable among much of the population (Schofield, 2007).

The gulf between the norms on discipline espoused by global children's rights advocates and ordinary people is much wider in developing countries. Earlier studies were aware of how discipline norms, like childhood norms in general, have a social history. Discipline gradually softened in Western industrial countries as children were freed from work and their childhood became a period of education and play. Discipline over children has relaxed in post-industrial societies, only imposing minimal social responsibilities on children.

Earlier studies on modernization in developing countries emphasized that softened cultural norms of discipline followed a shift from a traditional way of life to a modern way of life and the growth of individualism under modernity (LeVine, Klein, and Owen, 1967, p. 223).

These studies saw cultural change as premised on a break with traditional ways of life. Yet the historical experiences, which fostered the gentler norms that advocates wish to enforce, are not shared globally. Effectively, global children's rights advocacy aims to globalize post-industrial professional norms of childhood discipline onto non-industrial conditions.

Punishing Experience of Child Labour

Forms of discipline need to be seen in the totality of social relations. Where children are allocated social responsibilities in the household division of labour, their community will have norms of discipline sufficient to ensure children fulfil their social roles. The persistence of rural household subsistence farming without advanced technology under international sustainable development models necessitates child labour and children disciplined to labour. The household security of all its members may be jeopardized if children do not carry out their allotted responsibilities properly. How do adults make their children consistently labour in tough conditions, irrespective of tiredness or boredom? The relentlessly demanding conditions of subsistence farming are a hard physical discipline over both adults and children, leaving little leeway for error. If children are careless, animals may be lost or crops damaged. Harsh conditions and high stakes make for tough discipline.

There is something disingenuous about condemning people to a hard way of life and condemning their rough norms of behaviour. Tough discipline is treated as superfluous to the physically onerous tasks demanded of children. In summary, past studies assumed that easing social conditions softened norms of behaviour, but present campaigns to prohibit physical punishment break the link between social conditions and cultural norms.

Delegitimizing the Developing World

Furthermore, international advocacy over punishing childhoods in the developing world has implications for the international legitimacy of developing states if the problems they face are constructed in normative terms divorced from the prevailing material conditions. Global children's rights campaigns claim moral legitimacy by isolating physical punishment from the harsh physical conditions of the developing world. The prevailing conditions in developing societies dictate that children take on difficult, hazardous adult responsibilities at a young age, which means that their childhood deviates from the model of safe childhood universalized as a right under the CRC. Contemporary children's rights advocacy tends to moralize the gap between the ideal of childhood under the CRC and the reality of many children's lives globally, rendering their societies in violation of their rights. As a consequence, developing countries are morally delegitimized as representatives of their children's best interests and become sites of extensive intervention under evolving relationships of global governance between the North and the South (N. Lewis, 1998; Pupavac, 2001).

Global children's rights advocacy, just as it mistrusts the private sphere domestically, regards the principles of sovereignty and non-interference in the internal affairs of states as cloaks for abuse. But democratic freedoms, whether of individual or national self-determination, risk being inverted in the name of children (N. Lewis, 1998; Pavlovic, 2007).

KEY POINTS

Global children's rights advocacy raises the question of whether cultural norms can be changed without substantial material change to a way of life.

Earlier studies concluded that it was difficult to change the cultural norms of communities in the absence of broader social change.

Global children's rights advocacy isolates cultural norms from the material social conditions of children's lives globally.

Historically, punishment of children in the post-industrial societies softened as children were withdrawn from labour responsibilities.

The global children's rights campaigns to eradicate physical punishment of children abstract the problem from the harsh social conditions prevailing in many developing countries and in the poorer communities' need to use child labour.

Critical Thinking Question:

How could the physical punishment of children be prevented or at least lessened globally?

Conclusion

The aspiration to improve children's lives globally is important. However, there are questions over whether children's rights are capable of empowering children and the extent to which legal approaches may address the problems faced by children globally. Selective moral campaigns based on a weak historical understanding risk distracting the development of analysis and action essential to realize a more humane world. Norms of a secure childhood cannot be globalized without universally transforming the material conditions of childhood. The fundamental interdependence between material advancement and social advancement needs to be re-established as a starting point for progressive thinking and practice that will substantially address the problems of children enduring punishing childhoods around the world.

? QUESTIONS

Individual Study Questions

1. How does the CRC differ from the earlier international children's rights documents?
2. How does the global children's rights advocacy movement compare to earlier political and civil rights movements?
3. Why was UNICEF initially opposed to the creation of a Convention on the Rights of the Child? What concerns led UNICEF to adopt a children's rights approach?
4. What is the model of childhood that underpins the CRC? How have social constructivist approaches influenced children's rights thinking? What criticisms have been made about the model of childhood in the CRC?
5. To what extent does the CRC empower children? What conceptual and practical problems exist? Consider the implications of Article 3 and Article 17.
6. Who is responsible for children's rights, and against whom may the rights under the CRC be claimed? Who should have the authority to speak on behalf of children domestically or globally?

7. How has international development policy changed over the decades? How does the CRC reflect changing international development policy?

8. To what extent are the social concerns of developing countries incorporated into the CRC? To what extent does the CRC recognize cultural differences? To what extent is it possible to realize the CRC norms in developing countries? What is the relationship between cultural norms and social conditions?

Group Discussion Questions

1. What is novel about the CRC's concept of children's rights?
2. Why do critics speak of the 'fallacy' of children's rights?
3. What are the implications of the CRC for international relations?
4. Why do children become soldiers?

FURTHER READING

Black, M. (1996). *Children First: The Story of UNICEF*. Oxford: Oxford University Press.

An informative account of UNICEF's changing child policies. Black explains why UNICEF was initially opposed to children's rights and why UNICEF came to adopt a children's rights approach.

Burman, E. (1994). Innocents abroad: Western fantasies of childhood and the iconography of emergencies. *Disasters*, **18**/3, 238–53.

One of various insightful articles by Burman, which discusses how Western disaster aid responses construct recipient countries as children and a form of 'disaster pornography'.

Detrick, S. (ed.) (1992). *The United Nations Convention on the Rights of the Child: A Guide to the 'Travaux Preparatoires'*. Dordrecht: Martinus Nijhoff.

This book provides very useful insights into the drafting process of the CRC and the concerns of developing countries with the CRC provisions.

Drumbl, M. (2012). *Reimaging Child Soldiers in International Law and Policy*. Oxford: Oxford University Press.

This study challenges the prevailing international thinking on child soldiers.

Freeman, M. (1997). *The Moral Status of Children: Essays on the Rights of the Child*. The Hague: Martinus Nijhoff.

One of the most sophisticated accounts of children's rights by an advocate of children's rights.

Hart, J. (2006). Saving children: What role for anthropology? *Anthropology Today*, **22**/1, 5–8.

An article usefully highlighting problems that arise for children whose lives deviate from children's rights or humanitarian models, such as child soldiers.

Lee, E., Bristow, J., Faircloth, C., and **Macvarish, J.** (2014). *Parenting Culture Studies*. Basingstoke: Palgrave.

This book explores how parenting has become central in social policy making.

Lewis, N. (1998). Human rights, law and democracy in an unfree world. *Human Rights Fifty Years On: A Reappraisal* (ed. T. Evans). Manchester: Manchester University Press.

An international relations critique of international children's rights. The chapter critically analyses international children's rights as an anti-democratic development, which undermines the legitimacy of developing countries and legitimizes the rights of the most powerful states over weaker states.

Nieuwenhuys, O. (2001). By the sweat of their brow? Street children, NGOs and children's rights in Addis Ababa. *Africa*, **71**/4, 539–57.

One of various insightful articles by Nieuwenhuys analysing problems with children's rights programmes in practice.

Pupavac, V. (2005). Human security and the rise of global therapeutic governance. *Conflict, Security and Development*, **5**/2, 161–81.

This article critically outlines how international development policies have changed over the decades from models linking material improvement and social progress to idealist models that have abandoned substantial material improvement.

Van Bueren, G. (1998). *The International Law on the Rights of the Child*. The Hague: Martinus Nijhoff.

An authoritative survey of international children's rights from a legal advocacy perspective.

 ## WEB LINKS

http://www.ilo.org/ipec/lang--en/index.htm   ILO International Programme on the Elimination of Child Labour (IPEC). IPEC gives insights into current international approaches to the problem of child labour, and includes useful papers and links.

http://www.ohchr.org/EN/HRBodies/CRC/Pages/CRCIndex.aspx   UN Committee on the Rights of the Child. The Committee reviews national implementation of the CRC, and its website includes national reports submitted to the Committee and the Committee's evaluations and recommendations.

http://www.unicef.org   UNICEF, as the leading international children's organization, is a core source of international children's rights policies and programmes.

http://www.unicef.org/protection/files/Paris_Principles_EN.pdf   Paris Principles and Guidelines on Children Associated with Armed Forces or Armed Groups, 2007.

 ## NOTES

1. *The Post-Development Reader* (Rahnema with Bawtree, 1997) has a useful selection of some of the key texts of relativist development thinking.

2. See http://www.endcorporalpunishment.org/progress/countdown.html.

Visit the Online Resource Centre that accompanies this book for updates and a range of other resources: www.oxfordtextbooks.co.uk/orc/goodhart3e/

18

Human Rights and Forced Migration

Gil Loescher

Chapter Contents

Reader's Guide

This chapter[1] outlines how the international community has prioritized the human rights protection needs of forced migrants and the difficulties that international organizations have in persuading states and non-state actors to observe their responsibilities to this group. It begins by identifying the human rights problems confronting forced migrants both during their flight and during their time in exile. It then outlines the differing definitions accorded refugees today and the difficulty in achieving a widely accepted definition. The chapter next explains the roles and functions of the Office of the UN High Commissioner for Refugees and the international refugee regime. In particular, it explores the tensions between the regime's normative agenda of promoting refugee protection and achieving solutions to refugee problems and the constraints and challenges of states' power and interests. It explains how the international refugee regime has institutionally adapted over time to respond to an ever-expanding and growing crisis of forced displacement. The case study of Myanmar/Burma illustrates many of the human rights features of a protracted refugee and internal displacement crisis. Finally, the chapter concludes by examining how the international community might respond to new and emerging challenges in forced migration and world politics, and better adapt to the ongoing tension between the power and interests of states and upholding refugees' rights.

Introduction

Human rights violations and refugee flows go hand in hand. Refugees are prima facie evidence of human rights abuses and vulnerability because people who are persecuted and deprived of their homes and communities and means of livelihood are frequently forced to flee across the borders of their home countries and seek safety abroad. Even larger numbers of people displaced by violence or persecution do not cross borders but remain within their country.

We live at a time when there is a global crisis of displacement. There are more forced migrants today than at any time since the Second World War, and the drivers of displacement are becoming ever more complex. Over 60 million people (half of whom are children) are victims of forced displacement caused by wars, violence, human rights abuse, and rising tensions over identity, ethnicity, religion, and politics. Many of them cross borders to seek safety and protection in the territory of another state and to become refugees. In some cases, they find the protection they need in a country of asylum, but they can suffer

further human rights violations while in exile. Many enter refugee camps or live on the margins of overcrowded cities in the developing world. Refugees are frequently deprived of their rights and abandoned to clandestinity and even death. At the end of 2014, there were 14.4 million refugees of concern to UNHCR—the highest number in twenty years. Many will remain refugees for years—even decades—trapped and without adequate resources, unable to return home and without a durable solution to their plight. Today 6.4 million refugees are in protracted refugee situations. The average length of major refugee situations has increased from nine years in 1993 to over twenty years today.

Forced migration is a human rights concern, but it also raises serious political, economic, and security issues. States have increasingly come to view the mass arrival and prolonged presence of refugees as a security concern and a burden on their local and national economies. Economic and security crises in the world have given rise to a new politics of xenophobia, fuelling new policies intended to restrict access to asylum. (See also Box 18.1 on the media and representations of

BOX 18.1 THE MEDIA AND REPRESENTATIONS OF REFUGEES

For many of us, our attitudes and assumptions about refugees are influenced by the ways in which they are represented in the media.

When reporting on humanitarian crises, the news media commonly portrays refugees in lurid terms as 'streams' and 'floods' and 'waves' of humanity fleeing ethnic slaughter, destitution, and despair. Rather than being allowed to speak for themselves, refugees are usually spoken about by reporters, non-governmental organizations (NGOs), or politicians. The aim is both to gain sympathy for the victims and to ensure financial contributions for assistance.

In other situations, particularly in reports and commentary about asylum seekers and migrants, the media coverage is different. Increasingly, today negative views of refugees as 'welfare cheats' and 'illegal aliens' overstaying their welcome fill the pages of newspapers and our television screens. These accounts emphasize the cultural and ethnic differences of the newcomers, and the political and security threats posed by these 'intruding' groups.

Public attitudes to asylum seekers in many Western countries are overwhelmingly negative, tending to see them as liars or bogus asylum applicants.

Throughout their time in exile, refugees are denied much of their agency and they are seldom allowed to speak for

themselves. When refugees are considered, they are treated as subjects of external intervention and as anonymous passive victims rather than resourceful and able-bodied individuals capable of speaking for themselves and contributing to their own future.

One hopeful sign of change is that new social media and other forms of technological innovation will in the future combine with more traditional media to present a more balanced and accurate view of refugees and give voice to their concerns. To a certain extent, this is already happening. For example, refugee communities in places like Texas, and in refugee camps in Kenya and along the Burma–Thailand border, are actively using new technology and the media to offer a new perspective on what refugees themselves think about their situations. It remains unclear whether this enhanced treatment of the refugee voice will actually lead to meaningful changes in policy towards forced migrants. What is clear is that refugee-run grassroots media outlets are a new factor in global refugee policy, empowering refugee communities through the use of technology, the Internet, mobile phones, and other means of communication.

Are there refugees at your university or in your local community? What do they think about how refugees are represented by the media?

refugees.) Refugees and migrants have been blamed for increased pressures on social cohesion and national identities, and are the focus of popular hostility in both poor and rich countries. A solution to the problems of forced migration requires not only humanitarian measures but also coordinated political, economic, and strategic responses.

Assessing the Problem

No continent is immune from mass displacement. While the refugee crisis is global, some regions of the world are more affected than others. The bulk of the burden of hosting refugees falls on some of the poorest states, which today host 86 per cent of the world's refugees compared to 70 per cent ten years ago. Refugee-hosting countries such as Bangladesh, Kenya, Lebanon, and Pakistan frequently note the heavy impact refugees have had on their economy, security, and environment. The great majority of forcibly displaced people remain within the borders of their own countries and are known as **internally displaced persons** (IDPs). IDPs are defined as 'persons in a refugee-like situation who have not crossed the borders of their country'. At the beginning of 2015, there were 38.2 million IDPs, up from 33.3 million the year before and the highest number ever recorded.

Causes of Refugee Flows

Forced migration is often closely related to the phenomenon of **failed and fragile states**. Most refugee movements and internal displacements are caused by war, persecution, ethnic strife, weak institutions, and sharp socio-economic inequalities, or a combination of these factors. The difficulty in building durable state structures in the context of deep ethnic divisions and economic underdevelopment often leads to the domestic conflict and political instability that developing states have experienced. In addition, forced migrations are generated by actions of both governments and non-state actors, ranging from decrees and overt use of force to more covert persecution, intimidation, discrimination, and inducement of an unwanted group to leave. Governments and non-state actors alike take steps to effect **ethnic cleansing** in their areas of control, forcing out perceived enemy social classes and ethnic groups in order to consolidate political control.

Forced migrants also frequently face a number of severe human rights problems in the countries to which they flee. By seeking asylum in another country, refugees no longer enjoy the legal protection of their home country. Refugees frequently face a precarious existence. As the world's urban population has grown, more refugees are moving to already overcrowded cities in the global South to escape the restrictions of camp life instituted by many host countries. Urban refugees lack documentation and formal legal status, and are forced to live on the margins of society. They often work for wages far below the local level, are subjected to widespread discrimination, and can be evicted from their homes and even expelled from their host country without recourse. Urban refugees without legal status typically do not have access to the education or health systems of the host country, and seldom receive adequate assistance from international or national agencies. In most instances, urban refugees and undocumented migrants do not benefit from international protection or assistance. In addition to settling in cities or remaining in camps, a significant proportion of refugees 'self-settle' within local populations. This typically occurs when refugees locate among members of their own ethnic group.

Encampment and Protracted Refugee Situations

Many host governments require refugees to live in designated camps, and place significant restrictions on refugees seeking to leave the camps, either for employment or educational purposes. This trend, recently termed the *warehousing* of refugees, has significant human rights and economic implications. The prolonged encampment of refugee populations (see Box 18.2) leads to the violation of a number of rights contained in the *1951 UN Refugee Convention*, including freedom of movement and the right to seek wage-earning employment. Restrictions on these rights deprive long-staying refugees of the freedom to pursue normal lives and to become productive members of their new societies. Faced with these restrictions, refugees become dependent on subsistence-level assistance, or less, and lead lives of poverty, frustration, and unrealized potential.

Prolonged exile, especially in confined camps, further compounds the vulnerability of certain categories of refugees, particularly refugee women and

BOX 18.2 PROTRACTED REFUGEE SITUATIONS

Recent decades have witnessed an important shift in the global refugee situation. In particular, the task of finding durable solutions to refugee problems has become increasingly difficult and refugees have consequently spent increasingly longer periods in exile. This has given rise to the phenomenon of *protracted refugee situations* where refugees are in exile for five or more years after their initial displacement, have no immediate prospect of a solution to their plight, and where their basic rights and essential economic, social, and psychological needs remain unfulfilled.

The grim reality is that protracted situations are now the norm for most refugees. UNHCR reported that at the beginning of 2015, some 6.4 million refugees (nearly half of the refugees under the Office's care) were in a protracted situation. These refugees are living in refugee camps or urban areas in twenty-six host countries, constituting an overall total of thirty-three protracted situations. For example, one in four inhabitants of Lebanon is a long-standing refugee. Other countries hosting the largest groups of protracted refugees include Pakistan, Iran, Jordan, Turkey, Kenya, Chad, Sudan, Central African Republic, Ethiopia, and Thailand. In addition, there are 5.1 million Palestinian refugees who are under the mandate of the **UN Relief and Works Agency for Palestine Refugees in the**

Near East (UNRWA) and are scattered throughout the Middle East. There are even Palestinian refugees who have been in exile for over six decades, as well as fourth-generation refugees.

It seems highly likely that the number of refugees trapped in prolonged exile will greatly increase in the future. The fighting in Syria and its spread into Iraq from 2014 has created the worst refugee crisis since the Second World War. Some 4.4 million Syrians have registered as refugees in neighbouring Lebanon, Turkey, Jordan, and Egypt, and many more are unregistered; these host countries have reached the limits of their capacity to cope. Many Syrians have set out for Europe as well—an estimated 1.1 million at press time. By 2016, long-staying Syrians in the region will be added to the overall number of protracted refugee situations in the world.

Despite the scale and importance of this issue, international responses to protracted refugee situations have been limited in their impact. While UNHCR has tried to encourage a more meaningful response through several initiatives in recent years, and while a number of individual governments have taken various steps to respond to individual protracted situations, the overall response to the global challenge of protracted refugee situations remains ineffective.

children. Significant increases in levels of domestic and sexual violence occur in situations where employment opportunities are restricted, freedom of movement curtailed, and where refugees are fully dependent on international assistance to survive over long periods of time. Likewise, prolonged exile and encampment can often lead to a breakdown of family structures, placing additional burdens on refugee women. Refugee children also face particular challenges. Opportunities for secondary or post-secondary education are often denied them. Many camps have strict control mechanisms administered by host government forces or by the refugees themselves to make certain that security is maintained. In some cases, armed groups among the exiled communities exert firm control over refugee populations and this leads to frequent instances of the forced recruitment of **child soldiers** from the camps. Finally, in situations where refugee youths lack opportunities and see no prospect for the future, they frequently turn to delinquency and petty crime. Prolonged exile also places disproportionate burdens on disabled and

medically vulnerable refugees, including elderly people. Programmes for social support, counselling, and rehabilitation are often among the first to have their funding cut.

Asylum Flows to Industrialized Countries

Refugees who do not find protection and safety in nearby host countries travel across continents to seek asylum in the industrialized countries. In 2015, over a million people applied for asylum in the industrialized countries, the highest number since 1992. Asylum applicants from Ukraine, Syria, Iraq, Afghanistan, Eritrea, the Democratic Republic of Congo, Serbia and Kosovo, Somalia, and Pakistan constituted the largest numbers. Russia, Germany, the United States, Turkey, and Sweden received the greatest numbers of asylum applicants.

In response to increasing numbers of **asylum seekers** trying to gain access to their territories, Western governments have installed a number of restrictive measures impeding and deterring entry. Human rights organizations such as Amnesty International and Human Rights Watch have documented numerous cases of asylum seekers, including vulnerable women and unaccompanied children, being routinely detained, maltreated, or sexually abused. Some governments deny asylum seekers work permits or meaningful social assistance while they await their claims being heard. At times, asylum seekers are forcibly returned to their home countries, despite the risk to their safety. To circumvent the strict border controls put in place by Northern governments, and in a desperate effort to seek safety, both asylum seekers and migrants are increasingly turning to illegal people **traffickers** to gain access to Western countries. Thus the travel arrangements of these transcontinental asylum seekers have become increasingly precarious and dangerous. International criminal syndicates make huge profits on the stealing and forging of travel documents, passports, and work and residence permits. The asylum seekers and migrants they traffic risk physical abuse and financial exploitation, and in the worst circumstances, death.

In recent years, record numbers of desperate men, women, and children from the Middle East, sub-Saharan Africa, and war-torn countries in Asia, in search of safety or a new beginning in Europe, have drowned in the Mediterranean and the Gulf of Aden as their flimsy boats have capsized and sunk. Many Haitians and others fleeing poverty and strife have faced a similar fate crossing the Caribbean. Similarly, in Southeast Asia during 2015, large numbers of Muslim Rohingya refugees and Bangladeshis trying to reach neighbouring Malaysia, Indonesia, and Thailand by boat have been refused entry and pushed out to sea where many were feared drowned. In 2015, networks of transit camps on the Thai–Malaysian border were uncovered where migrants had been penned, beaten, and ransomed until their families paid sums for their release. In several of the camps, mass graves holding the corpses of starved and beaten migrants were also discovered.

During the past several years, Australia has forcefully deterred boatloads of asylum seekers and migrants from landing on its shores and has sent them to the tiny South Pacific nation of Nauru and to Papa New Guinea's Manus Island for offshore processing of their asylum claims. Asylum seekers who arrive by air in Australia are routinely detained in remote centres where the processing of their asylum applications is frequently delayed. Across the world there has been a sharp backlash in receiving countries against the refugees and migrants who seek safety for themselves and their families.

Internally Displaced Persons

In addition to refugees and asylum seekers, the human rights plight of internally displaced persons or IDPs has risen on the international agenda. Internal displacement can be caused by conflict, environmental disaster, economic change, or large-scale development projects. Like refugees, IDPs have been displaced from their homes, suffer many of the same deprivations and human rights violations as refugees do, and are in need of protection. However, they do not receive the same rights and opportunities as refugees. While there has been a relatively clear legal and institutional framework regulating refugee protection, the IDP issue was rarely recognized or debated until the 1990s. The international regime governing IDP protection and assistance has only recently begun to take shape. Since the early 1990s, a Special Representative of the Secretary General for IDPs has been appointed, a set of Guiding Principles on Internal Displacement has been compiled and widely endorsed by states, and a new institutional framework has begun to emerge. For example, in recent years the African Union has adopted and entered into force the Kampala Convention on Internal Displacement. In addition, since 2005 UNHCR has acted as the lead international agency for protecting conflict-induced IDPs. Despite these positive developments, the implementation of the Guiding Principles in most countries hosting IDPs remains sporadic and ineffective.

The global crisis of forced migration confronts the international community with a range of urgent human rights and political challenges for which there are no easy answers. This chapter addresses the following questions: What defines a refugee and what factors account for the recent large and sudden movements of displaced people? What international organizations exist to protect refugees and other forced migrants? How can UNHCR reconcile its normative agenda of protecting refugees with the **realpolitik** interests of states? And how can the international refugee regime respond more effectively and more comprehensively to forced displacement?

KEY POINTS

Individuals fleeing persecution who cross borders to seek safety and protection in the territory of another state are considered to be refugees. IDPs are persons in a refugee-like situation who have remained in their home country.

Refugees are seldom allowed to speak for themselves and are frequently misrepresented by today's media.

The majority of refugee and IDP movements are caused by war, persecution and ethnic strife, weak institutions, and sharp socio-economic inequalities, or a combination of these factors.

In their search for safety and a more secure life, increasingly larger numbers of refugees and migrants are taking greater risks to reach countries of asylum in both the global North and global South.

Refugees can suffer further human rights violations while in exile through enforced encampment, discrimination, extortion, and exploitation, as well as other human rights violations.

As finding solutions for refugees has become more difficult, protracted refugee situations are the new norm for many displaced people.

Critical Thinking Question:

The global problem of forced displacement is growing out of control. What are the causes and many dimensions of this problem?

The Problem of Defining Refugees

The growth of an international refugee regime based on the idea that refugees should have international protection has been striking, and has been a prime example of the increasing importance of human rights in global affairs. International concern for refugees is centred on the concept of human rights protection and the need for regional and international stability. The origins of the modern refugee regime can be traced back to 1921. The League of Nations appointed Fridtjof Nansen as the first High Commissioner for Refugees to respond to the instability caused by the outflow of Russian refugees in the aftermath of the First World War. Over the next twenty years, the scope and functions of assistance programmes for refugees gradually expanded as efforts were made to regularize the status of stateless and denationalized

peoples. By the 1930s, however, international co-operation on refugees declined with the start of the Great Depression and the rise of fascism, which led to the rise of restrictive immigration policies everywhere. In response to the forced mass movements of people during and after the Second World War, the United Nations Relief and Rehabilitation Agency and the International Refugee Organization, each with a radically different mandate, further developed the international response to refugees.

The experience of persecution during the 1930s and 1940s—particularly the Holocaust, which resulted in the murder of millions of Jews, Gypsies, Slavs, and others in Europe—significantly shaped states' responses to victims of persecution after the Second World War. Consequently, human rights and justice emerged as central themes of post-War agreements and institutions. For example, Article 14 of the 1948 **Universal Declaration of Human Rights** (UDHR) provided that 'everyone has the right to seek and enjoy in other countries asylum from persecution'. While this so-called 'right to asylum' was not enshrined in future agreements, significant new steps were taken to improve refugee protection. The Office of the **UN High Commissioner for Refugees** (UNHCR) was created in 1950 to protect refugees and to ensure their eventual integration within either their country of origin or another country. The following year the international community formulated the **Convention Relating to the Status of Refugees** (see Box 18.3).

According to international legal norms, a refugee is a person who has fled across the physical borders of his homeland to seek refuge in another place and who, on being granted refugee status, receives certain rights not available to other international migrants. These rights include the right of **resettlement** and legal protection from **deportation** or forcible return to his country of origin (the so-called *non-refoulement* protection). People seeking international protection are referred to as asylum seekers. Most refugees seek asylum once they reach the country in which they seek protection, although it is possible to apply for asylum in an embassy or consulate.

Regional Widening of the Definition of Refugee

Since the early 1950s, usage of the term 'refugee' has expanded beyond the 1951 legal definition to cover people in diverse situations who need assistance and

BOX 18.3 UN AND REGIONAL REFUGEE DEFINITIONS

1951 UN Convention Relating to the Status of Refugees

Article 1 defines a refugee as a person who, 'owing to well-founded fear of being persecuted for reasons of race, religion, nationality, membership of a particular social group or political opinion, is outside the country of his nationality and is unable or, owing to such fear, is unwilling to avail himself of the protection of that country; or who, not having a nationality and being outside the country of his former habitual residence as a result of such events, is unable, or owing to such fear, is unwilling to return to it'.

The 1969 Organization of African Unity Convention Governing the Specific Aspects of Refugee Problems in Africa

In addition to the definition outlined in the 1951 UN Convention Relating to the Status of Refugees, the OAU

Convention states: 'The term "refugee" shall also apply to every person who, owing to external aggression, occupation, foreign domination or event seriously disturbing public order in either part or the whole of his country of origin or nationality, is compelled to leave his place of habitual residence in order to seek refuge in another place outside his country of origin or nationality.'

Cartagena Declaration of Refugees of 1984

The declaration, like the 1969 OAU Convention, broadens the definition of the term 'refugee' found in the 1951 UN Convention. Conclusion 3 includes in the refugee definition: 'those persons who have fled their country because their lives, safety, or freedom have been threatened by generalized violence, foreign aggression, internal conflicts, massive violation of human rights, or other circumstances that have seriously disturbed public order'.

---

protection. The most notable of these expansions is found in the **OAU Convention Governing Specific Aspects of Refugee Problems in Africa**, a regional instrument adopted by the Organization of African Unity in 1969, which includes as refugees people fleeing 'external aggression, internal civil strife, or events seriously disturbing public order' in African countries. The **Cartagena Declaration of 1984** covering Central American refugees also expands on the 1951 UN Convention by including 'persons who have fled their country because their lives, safety or freedom have been threatened by generalized violence, foreign aggression, internal conflicts, massive violation of human rights, or other circumstances that have seriously disturbed public order' (see Box 18.3).

These regional legal norms, particularly in Africa and Central America, are in fact much more inclusive and in keeping with the actual causes of flight throughout the global South than are those of the UN. They respond to the reality that many refugees in fact flee generalized violence and severe human rights violations that often make it impossible to generate the documented evidence of individual persecution required for refugee status by the 1951 Convention. While causes of specific refugee movements may differ in their effects on the direction, duration, and size of population displacements, most contemporary mass exoduses occur when political violence is of a

generalized nature, such as intrastate conflicts or severe repression rather than a direct individual threat.

Recognizing these realities, UNHCR has (in practice) broadened its protective umbrella beyond those categories of the persecuted listed in the 1951 Convention to include those who have been forcibly displaced from their countries because of internal ethnic or religious upheavals or armed conflicts. However, Western countries have strongly resisted this pragmatic expansion of the refugee definition and of UNHCR's mandate. In the global North, the 1951 definition, with its focus on individuals and on persecution, is used for resettlement and asylum purposes, although groups of people at risk of death or grave harm from violence if returned home are often given temporary protection.

Other Categories of Refugees and Forced Migrants

In addition to the variety of legal definitions of refugees, there are several other categories of uprooted people. For example, some 5.1 million Palestinians are registered with and assisted by the UN Relief and Works Agency for Palestine Refugees in the Near East in some sixty camps across the Middle East. Many Palestinians have been in exile for over 65 years and still hope for a return to their own homeland. There are also an estimated 10 million **stateless persons** today who have lost or are denied their nationality, are without citizenship or other documentation, and have few rights. They include, for example, the Biharis in Bangladesh, the Muslim populations of Burma/Myanmar, in particular the Rohingya who reside in or originate from the northern Rakhine state, the Bedouins throughout much of the Middle East, some Kurds in Syria, and in many populations across South and Southeast Asia. In the 1990s, the dissolution of the Soviet Union and the Yugoslav Federation caused migrations that left hundreds of thousands stateless throughout Eastern Europe and Central Asia. Twenty years later, tens of thousands of people in the region remain stateless or at risk of statelessness. The true scale of the problem remains obscure because of lack of awareness and inconsistent reporting, as few countries have procedures in place for their identification, registration, and documentation. While there exist two UN conventions on statelessness—the 1954 Convention relating to the status of stateless persons and the 1961 Convention on the reduction of statelessness—stateless persons experience widespread violation of their human rights. These include: lack of documentation, such as birth certificates, non-recognition of the right to reside in their country of birth and constant risk of expulsion, discrimination, human trafficking, and gender-based violence. Many also experience limited access to healthcare, education, and property ownership, among many other restrictions.

There are also 38.2 million IDPs who are uprooted within their own countries because of armed conflict, ethnic strife, and natural disaster, or because of forcible relocation by their governments or opposition movements, and who do not or cannot seek refuge across borders. Many IDPs are victims of the same civil wars or ethnic strife that produce refugees from countries in conflict.

The distinction between refugees and IDPs has been based on the principle of state **sovereignty**. As the central tenet of international law, sovereignty has been taken to imply the territorial integrity of states and the acceptance of the principle of non-intervention in the internal affairs of states. Consequently, border crossing has been a central distinguishing feature of refugee status for two main reasons. While for refugees, the protection of their home government is lost, for IDPs, the bond between citizen and state is never entirely severed. Consequently, the primary responsibility for protecting IDPs remains with the home state. Also, IDPs are not necessarily within reach of international assistance, creating a practical obstacle to their protection that does not exist for refugees (who cross borders).

As the number of IDPs grew from some 2 million in the early 1980s to about 25 million worldwide in the 1990s, the issue gained international significance (see Figure 18.1). Beginning in the late 1990s, the discussion about new international norms surrounding the **Responsibility to Protect** (R2P), coupled with renewed efforts at UN reform to coordinate international responses to IDP situations, led to calls for UNHCR to take a greater role in responding to the protection and assistance needs of IDPs. As a consequence of these developments UNHCR became increasingly involved, not only in IDP operations, but also in international responses to those displaced by natural disasters. UNHCR's expanded new role was finally formalized in September 2005 when the Office was assigned the lead role for protection, shelter, and camp management for IDPs displaced in conflict situations. At the start of 2015, UNHCR was conducting a wide range of protection and assistance activities for some 32.3 million out of 38.2 million IDPs worldwide. At the same time, extraordinary natural disasters—such as the Indian Ocean tsunami in December 2004, the Pakistan earthquake in October 2005, as well as flooding in Pakistan, and a devastating earthquake in Haiti in 2010, a typhoon in the Philippines and earthquakes in Nepal in 2015—generated massive numbers of displaced people in need of protection and assistance. UNHCR's responses to these natural disasters represent another significant expansion of its work.

Figure 18.1 traces the growth of both internally displaced persons and refugees (including both UNHCR mandate refugees and Palestinians under the care of UNRWA) since 1989. At the end of 2014, the global IDP total—38.2 million persons—was the highest estimated figure ever recorded, primarily as a result of the conflicts in Syria, Iraq, Afghanistan, Somalia, South Sudan, Ukraine, and other countries. The global IDP figure has risen dramatically in recent years, as well as the number of IDPs and refugees UNHCR assists.

In the future, IDPs and victims of natural disasters are likely to comprise an increasingly significant part of the international refugee regime. War and social disruption are likely as climate change erodes land, destroys farmlands, raises seas, melts glaciers, and increases storms and other natural disasters. Under such conditions, people will flee their homes and seek

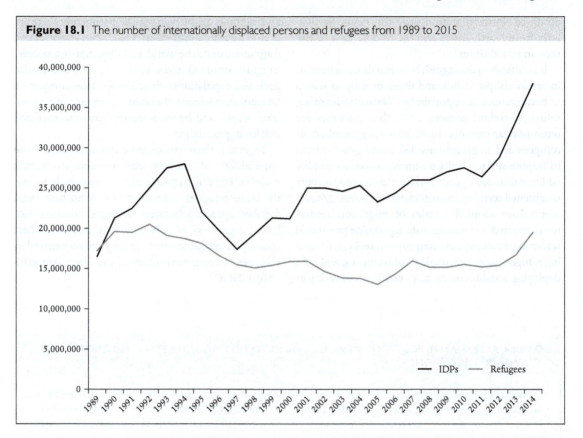

Figure 18.1 The number of internationally displaced persons and refugees from 1989 to 2015

shelter and protection in other communities or across borders. There remain serious gaps in international law regarding the protection and assistance of victims of natural disasters and climate change.

Another group in need of protection and assistance is former refugees who have repatriated to their countries of origin. Sometimes **returnees** go home under the auspices of UNHCR, from which they receive temporary assistance. But usually they go back without international sponsorship because they do not want to be publicly known as former refugees for fear of placing themselves in danger. Moreover, there are many constraints on providing protection and assistance to returnees, especially when the conditions in the countries of refugee origin that generated the exodus continue to exist.

Economic Migrants and the Asylum–Migration Nexus

There are also those who leave their countries because of economic factors: **economic migrants**. They do not qualify for UNHCR protection or assistance. However, in many developing countries that have few resources and weak government structures, economic hardships are generally exacerbated by political and criminal violence. While economic hardship is the proximate cause of flight, the root causes are often political. Therefore, it has become increasingly difficult to distinguish between refugees and economic migrants.

Furthermore, the nature of displacement is fundamentally changing during the twenty-first century. **Globalization** has created new opportunities and incentives for international migration. It has brought with it the development of improved transportation and telecommunications, including the expanding use of social media and network sites, new **diaspora** networks (comprising overseas immigrant communities with close links to their homelands), the dramatic growth of human trafficking and smuggling across dangerous sea and land routes, and the aspirations created by an increasingly global media. These trends have contributed to growing

South to North migration since the 1980s, particularly from North Africa and the Middle East to Europe in recent times.

It is difficult to distinguish between those in need of international protection and those moving in search of better economic opportunities. Distinctions among refugees, asylum seekers, and other migrants are often unclear (see Box 18.4). Increasing numbers of refugees and migrants have led many governments to impose stricter limits on immigration, to employ additional tactics to curb asylum claims, and to apply heightened scrutiny to such claims. Western governments have adopted a series of migration control measures to deter new arrivals, tightening pre-arrival screening, routinely detaining asylum seekers, deporting refugees to so-called safe third countries, and even deploying warships to intercept boatloads of refugees

and migrants on the high seas. Consequently, there are ever-expanding numbers of vulnerable and stranded migrants around the world, including stateless people, irregular, stranded, and survival migrants, urban refugees, and populations affected by food insecurity, state fragility, the violence of criminal gangs and other non-state actors, and by incompetent national, regional, and local governance.

Together, these trends raise questions about the applicability of conventional concepts to current realities. For the purposes of this chapter, however, the term refugees refers to people who have been forcibly uprooted because of persecution or violence, regardless of whether they have left their country of origin or whether they are recognized as refugees by the governments of their host countries or by UNHCR.

BOX 18.4 ALTERNATIVE POINTS OF VIEW: IS IT VALID TO DISTINGUISH BETWEEN 'FORCED' AND 'VOLUNTARY' MIGRATION?

Some academic researchers and most policy makers make a clear distinction between migrants and refugees. In their view, migrants cross international borders in search of employment, education, and other opportunities and a better life for themselves and their families. Refugees, on the other hand, have no choice and are forced to flee their home countries because of persecution or violence.

The separation of these two categories arises because there is a clearly defined international regime governing states' responses to refugees that permits states to accept some persons who flee their own countries as refugees and reject others. No such regime exists for economic migrants.

But is the distinction between 'forced' and 'voluntary' migration so clear-cut? Or in strictly distinguishing between the two categories of people on the move, do we risk ignoring the need for a more nuanced understanding of the often unjust social, political, and economic structures prompting people to migrate or to flee their home countries? In practice, many migrants and refugees are likely to move for a mixture of economic and political motives involving both coercion and volition. The 1951 Refugee Convention is not easily applicable in these situations and attempts to broaden or extend its coverage have failed so far.

Many people who are forced to flee their countries today are not fleeing direct state persecution but are instead fleeing state failure and incompetence. For example, between 2000 and 2010, several million Zimbabweans fled almost total economic and political collapse in their home country. There existed no

livelihood opportunities in that country to sustain even the most basic conditions of life. Yet because only a small minority had faced individualized persecution on political grounds, as required by the 1951 Refugee Convention, the vast majority were not accorded refugee status; many hundreds of thousands were detained in neighbouring countries, and many were deported back to Zimbabwe.

Similarly, in recent years large numbers of people in Central America, including unaccompanied children, have felt compelled to flee life-threatening situations such as starvation, incapacitating poverty, and unchecked violence by criminal gangs because their own governments are unwilling or unable to provide even minimal protection of their basic rights.

These examples of people fleeing serious human rights deprivations in fragile and failing states highlight important gaps in the current normative and institutional framework for refugees. In the future, new drivers of international migration—state failure, severe environmental distress, or widespread livelihood collapse—will require both a more complex understanding of human mobility and the revision or supplementation of the Refugee Convention and existing international refugee law.

For further discussion of some of the different approaches to these categories of migration see the books listed in the selected readings at the end of this chapter by Betts on survival migration, and by Goodwin-Gill and McAdam on international refugee law.

UNHCR, Human Rights, and the International Refugee Regime

Today, UNHCR is widely recognized as the UN's refugee agency. The Office's 1950 Statute set out a clear mandate focusing on two principal areas: ensuring refugees' access to protection and to a solution to their plight, usually involving their return to and reintegration in their home country or their integration in a new country.

In addition, the Refugee Convention defines a list of rights for refugees. Because refugees are individuals who have fled their home country and no longer enjoy the legal protections afforded to citizens of a state, the Convention stipulated that refugees should have access to national courts, the right to employment and education, and a host of other social, economic, and civil rights on a par with nationals of the host country. However, states decided not to grant refugees a right to asylum, notwithstanding the provisions of the UDHR.

Perhaps the most significant right granted to refugees by the 1951 Convention is *non-refoulement*: the right not to be returned to a country where a person risks persecution. *Non-refoulement* remains the cornerstone of international refugee protection. It would also become central to the later principle of voluntary repatriation, as states were prohibited from repatriating refugees until the dangers that confronted them in their home country had disappeared (see Box 18.5). Moreover, refugees themselves had the choice of deciding either to return to their home countries voluntarily or to remain in exile.

In addition to the 1951 Convention and international refugee law, sources of refugees' rights as well as states' obligations to refugees can be found embedded in other areas of law, including international human rights law. With only a few exceptions, forced migrants are entitled to the rights set out in international and regional human rights treaties and customary international law. In particular, human rights treaties such as the International Covenant on Civil and Political Rights and the Convention Against Torture provide protection against refugees being forcibly returned to situations where they would face a real risk of death, torture, or cruel, inhumane, or degrading treatment.

BOX 18.5 DURABLE SOLUTIONS

UNHCR is mandated to work with states and other actors to ensure that refugees find a solution to their plight. UNHCR's Statute outlines three possible 'durable solutions' for refugees: (1) they may repatriate voluntarily to their country of origin; (2) they may locally integrate in the host society; or (3) they may be resettled to a third country.

The role and relative importance of each of these solutions has changed over time. During the Cold War and the anti-colonial liberation struggles from the 1950s to the 1970s, those fleeing Communist regimes and colonial oppression were granted refugee status on the assumption that repatriation was not an immediately viable option. Consequently, until the 1980s,

(continued)

BOX 18.5 *(continued)*

resettlement by Northern states (for example, of Vietnamese boat people and Chileans fleeing the Pinochet regime), and local integration in some states in the global South (particularly in Africa) were the principal durable solutions. From the mid-1980s on, however, commitments to refugee resettlement by Northern states diminished considerably, particularly as immigration became an increasingly potent political issue. Meanwhile, in the context of structural adjustment, democratization, and diminishing international assistance, Southern states became increasingly reluctant to allow refugees to integrate locally.

From the late 1980s, repatriation emerged as 'the preferred durable solution' of states and UNHCR. However, where there are ongoing conflicts or human rights violations, the prospects for going home are often limited. During the 1990s, states and UNHCR sometimes attempted repatriation prematurely to countries like Afghanistan, Myanmar (Burma), Burundi, and Liberia in ways that proved both dangerous for refugees and unsustainable, as they often resulted in new refugee movements. In these situations, little was done to ensure that repatriation took place alongside peacebuilding and post-conflict reconstruction and long-term development to help ensure the sustainability of return. In 2014, as conflicts raged around the world, UNHCR recorded the lowest level of refugee returns in thirty-two years: only 126,800 refugees repatriated. The largest number of returned refugees included those from the Democratic Republic of the Congo, Iraq, Afghanistan, Somalia, Ivory Coast, Sudan, and Mali.

UNHCR also encouraged local integration as a durable solution through providing integrated community development assistance to both refugees and host communities. However, relatively few host states are prepared to allow refugees freedom of movement and the right to work, let alone provide them with the opportunity to integrate fully, acquire residency, and work towards citizenship. Nevertheless, there have been some recent cases of large-scale local integration of refugees by Southern states. For example, in recent years Sierra Leone, Liberia, and Tanzania initiated the process of naturalization and local integration of refugees. While encouraging, these initiatives have faced considerable challenges.

Resettlement efforts, too, have been disappointing in recent years, with states' willingness to resettle refugees declining. Total demand for resettlement always exceeds the available places. During 2014, a total of 105,200 refugees were admitted by twenty-seven resettlement countries, by far the largest of which are the United States, Canada, and Australia. The largest numbers of refugees who benefited from UNHCR-facilitated resettlement during 2014 were nationals of Iraq, Myanmar, Syria, Bhutan, Somalia, and the Democratic Republic of Congo. While these numbers are important, they pale in significance compared to the close to 4.4 million Syrians currently being given refuge by host countries in the Middle East. Only a small fraction of eligible refugees benefit from resettlement in any given year, and this important durable solution could be used to greater effect by the major resettlement countries.

At the same time, UNHCR has worked to consider how its current resettlement activities may be used to leverage additional solutions and better protection for refugees not resettled. For example, offers of resettlement may be used to convince host states to adopt more open policies towards refugees. This approach is known as the 'strategic use of resettlement'. In the past, states used resettlement strategically during the Indochinese refugee crisis in the 1980s and 1990s as part of their negotiations with host states in Southeast Asia to guarantee temporary asylum for those fleeing Vietnam, Laos, and Cambodia.

UNHCR's attempts to find solutions to long-term refugee situations have become more difficult. As a consequence, the average duration of protracted refugee situations has nearly doubled in the past decade to a staggering twenty years (see Box 18.2). In recent years, increasing numbers of Afghans, Eritreans, Iraqis, Somalis, Sri Lankan Tamils, Syrians, and others have sought their own solutions without UNHCR assistance, diversifying risks and maximizing their livelihood opportunities by moving around the world in search of security and economic well-being. In light of these developments, the international community needs to rethink its approach to durable solutions. In the future, ensuring the quality of asylum, opening up refugee migration possibilities, and adopting a more flexible approach to residency and citizenship rights will be key to solving refugee problems, especially long-standing ones.

UNHCR and the International Refugee Regime

Since its inception, UNHCR has been the central organization within the global refugee regime. **Regimes** comprise the norms, rules, principles, and decision-making procedures that regulate the behaviour of states. They are generally created by states in order to facilitate international cooperation in a particular issue area, such as trade or the environment. The centrepiece of the global refugee regime remains the 1951 Convention that defines states' obligations towards refugees. The Convention also explicitly identifies UNHCR as having supervisory responsibility for its implementation. The Office, therefore, has responsibility for monitoring and supporting states' compliance with its norms, rules, and decision-making procedures.

When UNHCR was established in the aftermath of the Second World War, principles of human rights and justice played a significant role in the establishment and shaping of global institutions. In recent years, however, the international refugee protection regime has struggled to persuade states to meet their obligations towards refugees in a changing international society. Power and interests rather than international refugee protection norms are increasingly the dominant influences in world politics. Consequently, the international refugee protection regime has been less successful in upholding its normative agenda than in previous decades.

In response to this changing international political context, UNHCR faces the challenge of upholding the regime while adapting its work to meet the new opportunities and constraints. The Office's core mandate has undergone numerous changes, and the scope of its work has expanded. In the 1960s and 1970s, for example, UNHCR shifted its focus from refugees in Europe and became increasingly involved in refugee situations in the global South. During the 1960s, violent decolonization and post-independence strife generated vast numbers of refugees, particularly in Africa. Refugee emergencies during the next decade emerged on all continents. Mass exoduses from East Pakistan, Uganda, and Indochina, highly politicized refugee crises in Chile and Argentina, and the repatriation of refugees and IDPs in southern Sudan expanded UNHCR's mission around the globe. The 1980s saw the Office shift away from its traditional focus on legal protection and assume a growing role in providing assistance to millions of refugees in camps in Southeast Asia, Central America and Mexico, South Asia, the Horn of Africa, and Southern Africa. With the collapse of the Soviet Union and the end of the Cold War, UNHCR assumed a wider role in providing massive humanitarian relief and engaging in repatriation operations across the Balkans, Africa, Asia, and Central America. The early twenty-first century has seen the UNHCR take on ever greater responsibility for the protection of conflict-induced IDPs and victims of natural disasters. The expansion of the Office's work to include these new areas has often been controversial, sparking concerns for some that UNHCR has been used by states in ways that may contradict or undermine its essential refugee protection mandate.

Constraints on UNHCR Action

Within this process of adaptation and expansion, UNHCR has had little political power of its own. Since its inception, the Office has faced the constraints of being dependent on the voluntary contributions of key **donor** states and reliant on host governments for permission to initiate operations on their territory. About 98 per cent of the Office's funding comes from such contributions, primarily from a small number of the major industrialized states, particularly the United States and the European Union (EU), who exercise a disproportionate amount of influence on the organization. These governments exert leverage on the Office by **earmarking** a high percentage of their funds for programmes that are of political or strategic interest to them, such as foreign policy, security, migration, and trade relations. It is not surprising therefore that the Office faces frequent funding crises. In 2015, UNHCR's budget stood at US$6.8 billion, the largest in its history. States also influence the UNHCR through their membership on the Office's **Executive Committee**, which oversees the agency's budget and advises it on policy issues.

The scope and extent of the High Commissioner's authority are further limited by states' insistence on norms of sovereignty and non-intervention in domestic affairs. UNHCR's Statute restricts the authority of the High Commissioner to assist refugees who have crossed international borders and expressly forbids the High Commissioner from involvement in political activities. Because the causes of refugee flows are considered to fall outside the organization's humanitarian and non-political mandate, UNHCR is reluctant to become involved in human rights monitoring in countries of asylum.

In addition to raising money from donor governments to support its programmes, UNHCR must secure permission from countries of asylum to operate within their territories. As a result, the world's principal refugee protection agency is reluctant to criticize publicly either host or donor governments' policies towards refugees. UNHCR officials are inclined to avoid raising delicate political questions when dealing with humanitarian issues for fear of overstepping their mandate or damaging relations with sensitive governments, most of whom would consider such intrusions to be interference in their internal affairs. UNHCR must navigate carefully between these states' interests and the norms that it seeks to uphold.

Human Rights and the Refugee Regime

Resolving refugee problems depends on a range of human rights activities. Establishing **civil societies** and pluralistic political systems, reinforcing legal and government structures, and empowering local grass-roots organizations remain central to establishing conditions for refugees to return to their home countries. However, neither ensuring good **governance** nor respect for human rights falls within UNHCR's domain.

The system of international refugee protection differs from the UN human rights mechanisms. No supranational authority exists to enforce the rules of the international refugee regime. There is no formal mechanism in international refugee law to receive individual or inter-state petitions or complaints. States parties to the 1951 Refugee Convention have not provided UNHCR with information and statistical data on the implementation of the Convention, as required. There is no system to review country practices, and thus no basis for formulating recommendations for government authorities. There are few, if any, safeguards to prevent abuse by states. Recently, many governments have circumvented some major provisions and exploited unregulated areas.

In the realm of asylum, states remain the final arbiters of refugees' fates. They retain the power to grant or to deny asylum. The international refugee instruments leave it up to governments to tailor refugee determination procedures to their administrative, judicial, and constitutional provisions. States regard these procedures as part of their national sovereignty and have been unwilling to transfer this authority to UNHCR or any other intergovernmental body.

In recent decades, this trend has been evident in the EU, where member states have greatly increased their cooperation with each other on asylum matters and have drawn up a number of treaties and agreements regulating European refugee and asylum policies. Many of these intergovernmental discussions have been closed to outside observers, including UNHCR and some other countries, reflecting the close link between sovereignty and control of borders in Europe and the growing trend towards restrictionism in the region. In the United States, apart from the possibility of contacting government authorities to express its views, UNHCR has no role in the **refugee determination process**. In developing countries, which host over 85 per cent of the world's refugees, the quality and quantity of asylum have also declined in recent years.

There is an urgent need to develop a coherent and integrated approach to the defence of human rights, the protection of the forcibly displaced, and the resolution of the global refugee problem. This will remain an uphill struggle as long as states guard their sovereignty and remain fundamentally opposed to international human rights monitoring and intervention. Most importantly, this will also involve a change in popular support for the cause of global refugees.

Refugees as a Political, Development, and Security Concern

In addition to being a human rights concern, refugee issues also play a central role in national, regional, and world politics. With growing political, religious, and economic volatility, an alarming expansion of armed violence, and new environmental pressures, states are increasingly concerned about movements of people within and across national borders. In some unstable regions, host governments fear that refugee camps on their territory will serve as bases and sanctuaries for armed insurgents, resistance, and terrorist movements. Refugee crises can also impact local economies and societies. Refugees' presence can exacerbate previously existing inter-communal tensions in the host country, shift the balance of power between communities, or cause grievances among local populations. Many host governments, in both the North and the South, now justify otherwise impermissible policy restrictions by presenting refugee populations as threats to national security and identity.

The international refugee regime's ability to protect refugees is related in complex ways to the contemporary nature of conflict. Since the end of the **Cold War**, the majority of the world's wars have been intrastate conflicts, often with a complex regional dimension. Instead of engaging with the underlying causes of these conflicts, states have often left humanitarian agencies to address the most visible symptoms of those conflicts. Yet UNHCR's ability to fulfil its mandate depends on the resolution of those conflicts. If the Office is to fulfil its responsibilities, states must do a better job at conflict resolution, post-conflict reconstruction and development, and sustainable peacebuilding.

Countries emerging from lengthy conflict receive too little financial and political support with rebuilding, despite a virtually universal consensus that peace agreements must be consolidated by investments that improve the security and economic well-being of former adversaries, victims of conflict, and returning refugees. International funding invariably declines soon after ceasefires are implemented and elections held. Assistance given to countries emerging from wars is conditioned in ways that emergency relief funds are not, hindering humanitarian and social initiatives. Greater resources must be devoted over longer periods of time to catalyse sustainable forms of development and to create conditions that will prevent refugee movements from reoccurring.

Despite greater efforts at coordination between the UNHCR and development and financial institutions such as the **UN Development Programme** (UNDP) and the **World Bank**, far more effective inter-agency planning, consultation, and implementation are required. There is a widespread perception within the UN system that refugees are UNHCR's 'problem'. Solutions to refugee situations have been more successful when they include the sustained engagement of a wide range of actors within the UN system, especially development actors, such as UNDP. However, the roles and responsibilities of refugee and development agencies in many refugee situations are determined on a situation-by-situation basis. In most countries, emergency relief aid is administratively and programmatically divorced from development concerns. Unlike refugee and relief-oriented organizations, development agencies usually work on the basis of long-term plans and programmes, making it difficult for them to respond to unexpected events such as refugee movements or repatriation programmes. So a *development gap* exists between short-term humanitarian relief assistance and long-term development programmes. The UNHCR is not a development agency; the overall rehabilitation after an emergency or conflict must be carried out by the UNDP, the World Bank, or by other UN agencies that can more appropriately deal with reconstruction and development. This requires a full transfer of responsibility from UNHCR to the development agencies after the immediate emergency relief phase is over. UNDP consistently resists such transfers because it views such programmes as emergency responses and therefore outside its mandate, which is long-term development. Inter-agency coordination is especially important in the large-scale repatriations after protracted conflicts. Political instability and new displacements are likely to occur without improved

economic prospects for returnees, and foreign aid and investment for rebuilding the physical infrastructure in these countries.

In countries where central government is weak or non-existent and unable to protect its citizens, the key issues include how to bring together contending groups and how to build institutions of governance. In such situations, economic development and social stability are inseparable. Rehabilitative relief and development activities must be accompanied by support in order for civil society to be effective. Sustainable progress can only be achieved if built on a strong civil foundation so that gains can be consolidated throughout society. Otherwise, relief and development activities will consume resources but generate little long-term change.

In an effort to make the UN system more coherent and collaborative, the **UN Peacebuilding Commission** was created in 2005. This new institution attempts to foster coordinated action by a broader range of UN actors in responding to the various consequences of conflict and to find solutions for refugees. With its focus on post-conflict recovery, the Commission could play an important role in drawing UN actors together to address the underlying causes of displacement and create the foundations for sustainable repatriation of refugees from neighbouring countries. At the same time, UNHCR should ensure that the Commission does not overlook the links between refugees and the regional dynamics of peacebuilding, especially given the importance of refugees in post-conflict reconstruction.

UNHCR's current work is also taking place in a changing international security environment. The global 'war on terror', the rise of Islamic radicalism, and the decline in states' observance of international norms have reinforced states' concerns with security. This has led to increasingly restrictionist asylum policies as states have attempted to assert more control over the entry of foreign nationals into their territory. Consequently, Northern states have reinvigorated policies such as **detention**, **interdiction**, limitations on asylum seekers' right of appeal, and proposals for **offshore processing** centres. Many Southern states, meanwhile, have used the same rhetoric as do Northern states to justify further restrictions of refugees' rights, leading to forcible repatriation and encampment as measures to control and restrict refugee movements on their own territories.

While UNHCR has tried to uphold its responsibilities, it has had little power other than moral authority and persuasion to fulfil this task. In an international political environment where power and interests dominate and define outcomes, the Office faces the question of how to reconcile its normative agenda with the self-interests of states in a rapidly changing world.

KEY POINTS

In addition to being the UN refugee agency, UNHCR is the central organization in the global refugee regime. For sixty-five years, in a changing international society, the Office has faced the fundamental challenge of persuading states to meet their human rights obligations towards refugees.

The international refugee regime is limited by a number of constraints. Reconciling the need to have an independent influence on states with being responsive to donor and host state interests has been a precarious balancing act for the Office. In addition to raising money from donor governments to support its programmes, UNHCR must secure permission from countries of asylum to operate within their territories.

While resolving refugee problems depends on a range of human rights activities, there does not yet exist a coherent and integrated approach to the defence of the human rights of the forcibly displaced and the resolution of the global refugee problem.

Solutions to refugee situations have been more successful when they include the sustained engagement of a wide range of actors within the UN system, especially development actors such as the UNDP. However, the roles and responsibilities of refugee and development agencies in many refugee situations continue to be determined on a situation-by-situation basis.

Refugee issues play a central role in national, regional, and world politics. The global 'war on terror', the rise of Islamic radicalism, and the decline in states' observance of international norms have reinforced states' concerns with security and have led to increasingly restrictive asylum policies in both the global North and global South, as well as to policies that aim to contain the refugee problem to the regions of refugee origin.

Critical Thinking Question:

What range of actors (humanitarian, political, development, and security) are necessary to respond effectively to global problems of forced migration?

Case Study: Forced Displacement in Myanmar

For over half a century, poor human rights and prolonged conflict in Myanmar (Burma) caused one of the most protracted refugee situations in Asia. Until recently, the Burmese military regime remained in power through a dual campaign of preventing democratic change and waging war against the country's numerous ethnic nationality parties and minority groups. As a consequence, the country experienced decades of political and minority group repression, conflict, poor governance, corruption, and the underdevelopment of remote ethnic nationality populated border areas.

The refugee rights group Refugees International estimates that 3 million people have been forcibly displaced in recent decades by these crises. The protracted conflict in Myanmar has produced huge numbers of internally displaced persons and created at least four separate but related protracted refugee situations in neighbouring Thailand, Bangladesh, India, and Malaysia. Over a hundred thousand Burmese are physically confined in camps in Thailand and Bangladesh, where they have no freedom of movement and are not permitted to work. Several generations of refugee children have now grown up in these camps and have little prospect for a decent future. In addition, over 2 million other Burmese eke out a meagre living in neighbouring countries as migrant workers or illegal aliens. Many of these migrants fled Myanmar for the same reasons as refugees and face discrimination, forced labour, and similar human rights problems.

For most of the past several decades there have been two principal causes of forced displacement. The first, most internationally recognized, cause was the long-standing suppression of the Burmese pro-democracy movement, led by the Nobel laureate Aung San Suu Kyi. The second, most significant, causes of displacement are the long-standing conflicts and counter-insurgency operations waged against the country's ethnic minority groups: the Karen, Karenni, Mon, Shan, Kachin, and others in the eastern borderlands and the Chin population along the border with India. In addition, the army and Buddhist militants have systematically suppressed the Muslim Rohingya population in northern Rakhine state in Myanmar.

Aung San Suu Kyi and her party, the National League for Democracy (NLD), were overwhelmingly elected to power in 1990. The Burmese army refused to honour the outcome and launched an intense nationwide campaign to crush civil protest and to exterminate support for the NLD. Aung San Suu Kyi was placed under house arrest and hundreds of NLD members were imprisoned. In fear for their lives, thousands of Burmese students and political activists fled to neighbouring countries. In 2007, more widespread demonstrations against the military's political repression broke out throughout Myanmar. The army responded with brutal force again, imprisoning and torturing large numbers of political activists, including Buddhist clergy who had led some of the demonstrations.

Finally, in November 2010, the military held a rigged election under an army-drafted constitution that guaranteed the military a central role in the politics of the nation and a quarter of all seats in the new parliament. The NLD boycotted the election and decried it as a sham. Shortly after the election, however, Aung San Suu Kyi was released from house arrest and the army handed power to a quasi-civilian government. The new government offered the possibility of national reconciliation and took initial steps towards partial democratic reform. Censorship was relaxed and the government released hundreds of political prisoners. In early 2012 Aung San Suu Kyi and other members of the NLD were elected to the new parliament in by-elections and the government initiated further reforms.

Despite these rapid moves towards partial political liberalization, sporadic clashes continued between government troops and ethnic militias fighting for greater autonomy, and thousands of new refugees have crossed over the borders with Thailand and China in recent years. For decades the military has sought to undermine ethnic minority political and military organizations by targeting their civilian support bases. Continuous armed conflict has impoverished large parts of the civilian population who have been displaced as a consequence of military occupation, social control, ethnic discrimination, and state-sponsored development activities. For decades also, the Burmese army forcibly confiscated villagers' lands and relocated civilians to new government-controlled villages as part of their counter-insurgency strategies and in an effort to obtain free labour and other resources.

In the eastern borderlands at least half a million Burmese ethnic minorities were forcibly displaced and deprived of significant international assistance. Liable to various taxes and extensive forced labour, many civilians were unable to support themselves. Food insecurity, lack of education and basic health services, and the outbreak of major health crises (malaria, cholera, HIV/AIDS) resulted in a major humanitarian crisis in Myanmar and left the civilian population extremely vulnerable to natural disasters, such as the cyclone that devastated the Irrawaddy delta region in southern Burma in May 2008.

The Burmese military's persecution of ethnic minority populations caused large refugee outflows to Thailand, where over 100,000 Karen, Karenni, and other national minority peoples still live in refugee camps. In addition, there are probably tens of thousands of refugees outside camps in Thailand plus at least 1.5 million Burmese migrants in Thai provincial towns and cities.

In recent years, preliminary ceasefire agreements between the Burmese military and the ethnic armies have led to a reduction in fighting. However, there has been no respite from continued militarization in the eastern borderlands. The Burmese military have seized territory in Shan state and have continued to intimidate Burmese ethnic minorities. Military skirmishes have continued, particularly against the Kachin, many of whom have fled across the border with China.

In northern Rakhine state near the border with Bangladesh, the Burmese army and Buddhist militants pursue a policy of harsh discrimination against the Muslim Rohingya population, leading to hundreds of deaths and forcing more than 140,000 into fetid and squalid camps. Religious intolerance, hate speech, and racial vilification against the Rohingya threaten the hope for a multicultural, rights-based, and plural society that many had hoped would underpin Myanmar's peace process. Government policy has not only rendered the Muslim Rohingyas stateless, but in many instances has systematically crushed the cultural, religious, and ethnic aspirations of the Rohingya and other minority peoples, such as the Chin who live in Chin state near the border of northeast India. Such policies have led to the destruction of community life, religious environments, and local cultures. These repressive measures contributed to the repeated waves of refugee flows to neighbouring states during the past several decades. In two separate refugee exoduses, in 1978 and in 1991, on each occasion over 250,000 Rohingyas fled their homes in northern Rakhine state to

Bangladesh. In 2015, thousands of Rohingyas remain in refugee camps, while an estimated 200,000 Rohingyas live outside the camps in Bangladesh. Another 80,000 Chin refugees have fled similar military repression and have taken refuge in India. Tens of thousands of Burmese refugees of all ethnic groups have also sought asylum in Malaysia during the past two decades.

In recent years, in a desperate attempt to reach Malaysia and other neighbouring countries, thousands of Rohingya have set sail in unsafe wooden trawlers from both Bangladesh and northern Rakhine state. Some of these journeys end in tragedy, with passengers dying from starvation, dehydration, and drowning. In mid-2015, thousands of Rohingya and Bangladeshis were abandoned on the high seas by people traffickers. When Malaysian and Indonesian authorities refused to rescue the migrants and towed the refugees' boats out to sea, many of the refugees died.

The plight of IDPs in Myanmar and the presence of Burmese refugees throughout South and Southeast Asia constitute one of the world's most difficult and complex protracted refugee situations. Most states in the region view refugees primarily as a security rather than a humanitarian concern and refuse to interfere in Myanmar's internal affairs by criticizing its treatment of the Rohingya. The majority of the region's states have not signed the UN Refugee Convention, and place restrictions on the protection and assistance roles that the UN and NGOs can play in their countries.

Western countries have resettled thousands of Burmese refugees from Thailand in recent years, but a resolution to the crisis depends ultimately on achieving a political solution to its causes. The conflict between the military and ethnic minorities, and the denial of citizenship and other fundamental rights to the Rohingyas and other minorities must be fully addressed before the Burmese protracted refugee situation can be resolved. Finally, before refugees and IDPs can return home, a meaningful peace process and comprehensive rehabilitation programme needs to be undertaken with the help of the international community. In late 2015, the NLD won a landslide parliamentary victory. There is no indication yet that this will lead to meaningful reform for the country's minority populations.

KEY POINTS

The protracted exile of Burmese refugees is a consequence of political repression, armed conflict, and military occupation in the border regions of Myanmar, and economic mismanagement.

The Muslim Rohingya's is one of the most vulnerable protracted refugee situations in the world.

In addition to the huge numbers of exiled populations in countries neighbouring Myanmar (Thailand, Bangladesh, Malaysia, India, and China), there are very large numbers of internally displaced people inside Myanmar.

Until a political solution is found for the ethnic conflicts, racial and religious discrimination, and other humanitarian crises in Myanmar, there will be no real political stability in Myanmar and no end in sight for Burmese forced migrants.

Critical Thinking Question:

How is the issue of human rights protection of national minorities a key factor in the future political stability of Myanmar?

The Way Forward: The Need for New Alliances and New Actors

In the current international political and economic environment, there is increasing recognition that solutions to forced migration cannot proceed solely within the mandate of international humanitarian organizations and the international refugee regime. In short, UNHCR cannot resolve the problems of refugees, IDPs, and other forced migrants single-handedly. The solutions to forced migrations cannot be separated from other areas of international concern such as human rights, international development, peace-building, and security. Because refugee problems are multi-dimensional in nature, UNHCR needs to build bridges between itself and organizations dealing with these other issues. This new approach to refugee problems involves an increase in the range of actors in the search for solutions, an increase in the range of issues that the refugee regime seeks to address, and an increase in the range of people it is designed to benefit.

UNHCR as a Catalyst in the UN System

In engaging more proactively with other organizations, UNHCR must guard against infinitely expanding its mandate and becoming a migration organization or a development organization. Rather, UNHCR should play a facilitative and catalytic role in mobilizing other international actors to fulfil their responsibilities with respect to refugees. In short, UNHCR may need to 'do more by doing less' and become more focused and strategic in the advocacy, coordination, and facilitation role that it plays.

Ensuring effective protection and access to solutions for refugees relies on a UN system-wide approach. Refugees should not be seen as exclusively UNHCR's responsibility. Rather, development actors, other humanitarian actors, the UN Peacebuilding Commission, and a possible future UN migration organization all need to recognize their role in refugee issues. UNHCR needs to develop clearly defined partnerships with these actors and draw upon their expertise. For such collaborative agreements to be effective, the Office of the Secretary General and the UN General Assembly must make other agencies aware of their responsibilities towards refugees and of the need to work cooperatively with UNHCR.

The Office also needs to become more aware of the highly politicized environment within which it works. This environment is largely determined by the interests and capacities of states. In the face of ever-growing refugee crises around the world, UNHCR must work with states to facilitate and encourage international cooperation and burden sharing that is appropriate in scale, scope, and duration in responding to the global refugee problem.

In the future, states should ensure that they engage fully in two forms of burden sharing. States may engage in financial burden sharing by providing the resources required by UNHCR and by host states to ensure effective protection and to find solutions. In the past, states' contributions to burden sharing have been limited and highly selective. States have historically contributed to the Office's annual budget or provided resettlement because they have had a perceived interest in a specific population or situation. Such interests are usually not related to refugee protection per se, but rather emerge from linked issue areas. In the Cold War context, for example, contributions were often

motivated by strategic or foreign policy interests. In the post-Cold War era, they are often motivated by concerns with security, migration, or development.

It is clear that the refugee regime cannot withdraw from recognizing and responding to world politics. Historically, UNHCR has been at its most effective when it has played a politically engaged role and has been willing to recognize and engage with states' wider interests. In contrast, UNHCR has been at its least effective when it has attempted to take on a passive and technocratic role. The challenge is to appeal to interests and engage with politics without being involuntarily shaped and moulded by political circumstances or inadvertently legitimizing the restrictionist policies of states.

KEY POINTS

UNHCR cannot resolve the problems of refugees, IDPs, and other forced migrants single-handedly. The solutions to forced migration cannot be separated from other areas of international concern such as human rights, international development, and security. The Office needs to build bridges to organizations dealing with issues such as human rights, sustainable development, and peacebuilding.

UNHCR should take on a facilitative and catalytic role in mobilizing other international actors to fulfil their responsibilities with respect to refugees.

UNHCR needs to become a more politically engaged actor and work with states to facilitate and encourage international cooperation and burden sharing.

States may engage in financial burden sharing by providing the resources required by the Office and host states to ensure effective protection and to find solutions. States may also engage in physical burden sharing by hosting refugees as a country of asylum, by allowing refugees to integrate locally, or by providing a solution to refugees through resettlement.

Critical Thinking Question:

Using a case study of a current refugee situation, outline how UNHCR could more effectively find a solution to the refugee issue at hand.

Conclusion

As the twenty-first century progresses, forced migration has become one of the world's most significant human rights concerns. UNHCR now works not only with refugees, but also with IDPs, returnees, stateless people, and other forced migrants. The rising number of persons displaced by natural disasters and a dramatic surge of both refugees fleeing conflict and other migrants fleeing failed states around the world—numbers predicted to rise further with continued conflict, state failure, global warming, and globalization—means that the challenge of forced migration is likely to increase in scale and complexity in the future. In practice, the definition of forced migrants incorporates many different kinds of displacement. However, there remain serious gaps in international law and inadequate institutional frameworks to deal with the range of forced migrants described in this chapter.

UNHCR's position highlights the challenges faced by an international organization vested with responsibility for upholding the human rights of refugees in the context of continuing conflicts and a changing international society. The scope and extent of the authority of the Office and the international refugee regime are limited by the continued importance attached by states to the pre-eminence of order over justice in international affairs and to international norms of state sovereignty and non-intervention in the domestic affairs of states. Perhaps most importantly, in the wake of globalization, the 'war on terror', the persistence of conflicts and inter-state rivalry around the world, states' perceptions of refugees have hardened in recent years. The future protection of forced migrants is endangered by the overriding concern of states with the threats of terrorism, organized crime, and illegal migration. Whereas refugees were once viewed as victims of persecution who had good cause to seek protection, today refugees and others in need of protection are frequently seen as illegitimate or even criminal, and are the object of active measures of exclusion. With these changing circumstances, therefore, states and some sections of the public seem unwilling to give international action in support of refugee protection the high priority it deserves.

The protection and assistance of forced migrants go far beyond the scope of the UNHCR and the contemporary international refugee regime. Addressing this problem in the future requires the creation of a UN-wide collaborative institutional framework that would incorporate a more intensive role for the Office of the Secretary General, development agencies, peace and security actors including the UN Peace-building Commission, and the Office of the High Commissioner for Human Rights, along with the support of NGOs, the media, and the concerned public.

? QUESTIONS

Individual Study Questions

1. How are forced migrants a human rights issue?

2. What is a refugee? Does the 1951 Refugee Convention adequately define a refugee? How has the term 'refugee' been widened over the past sixty-five years beyond its narrow legal definition?

3. What are the differences between the ways that refugees and internally displaced persons are treated by the international community? What special problems do IDPs present?

4. Should people who flee their home countries because of starvation and lack of livelihood opportunities be considered refugees? How far can the term 'refugee' be extended before it becomes too diffuse to be meaningful?

5. What are the major constraints facing UNHCR in fulfilling its role of protecting and assisting refugees? What does this tell us about the problems of governance in a world in which the interests of states dominate the global agenda?

6. How have the attitudes and policies of states, publics, and the media in the global North and the global South towards forced migrants changed in recent years?

7. How is the problem of refugees related to the prevalence of failed and fragile states?

8.   Why is the issue of refugees beyond the scope of any single UN agency? What range of actors needs to become involved in the search for solutions to the problems of forced migrants?

Group Discussion Questions

1.   From a human rights perspective, should economic migrants be entitled to the same protections as refugees?

2.   Should the term 'refugee' be replaced by the more inclusive term 'forced migrant'? Why or why not?

3.   The Refugee Convention does not explicitly cover people who have been persecuted on the basis of their sex or sexuality. Should protection be systematically offered to LGBTIQ persons who are persecuted and sometimes subject to death threats?

4.   How is the problem of finding solutions to refugees related to other global issues such as human rights, development, and peacebuilding?

5.   Should the systematic repression of a population that causes a massive refugee exodus to a neighbouring country be considered 'a threat to international security' and grounds for intervention by the international community?

6.   Is UNHCR an autonomous actor regarding refugee policy or is it mostly directed by state preferences and interests?

7.   Why is it so difficult for states to cooperate to resolve refugee problems, and under what conditions are states most likely to contribute to burden sharing and the protection of refugees at the national and global levels?

8.   How has the failure to achieve durable solutions for refugees contributed to the rise of protracted refugee situations?

FURTHER READING

Betts, A. (2009). *Forced Migration and Global Politics*. Oxford: Wiley-Blackwell.

This textbook systematically applies International Relations theory to the international politics of forced migration.

Betts, A. (2013). *Survival Migration: Failed Governance and the Crisis of Displacement*. Ithaca, NY: Cornell University Press.

This book argues that refugee international protection should be extended to those who flee countries where their own governments can no longer provide them with their basic rights to survival.

Betts, A. and **Loescher, G.** (eds) (2011). *Refugees in International Relations*. Oxford: Oxford University Press.

Some of the world's leading and emerging International Relations scholars consider what ideas from International Relations can offer our understanding of the international politics of forced migration.

Betts, A., Loescher, G., and **Milner, J.** (2016). *UNHCR: The Politics and Practice of Refugee Protection* (3rd rev. edn). Abingdon: Routledge.

Provides an up-to-date analysis of the major issues concerning refugee protection and the role of UNHCR.

Fiddian-Qasmiyeh, E., Loescher, G., Long, K., and **Sigona, N.** (eds) (2014). *The Oxford Handbook of Refugee and Forced Migration Studies*. Oxford: Oxford University Press.

An authoritative handbook comprising fifty-three state-of-the-art chapters by experts and practitioners of the key intellectual, political, social, and institutional challenges arising from refugees and forced migration today.

Gatrell, P. (2013). *The Making of the Modern Refugee*. Oxford: Oxford University Press.

A social and political history of global population displacement in the twentieth century.

Goodwin-Gill, G. and **McAdam, J.** (2007). *The Refugee in International Law*. Oxford: Oxford University Press.

The standard work on international refugee law.

Loescher, G. (2001). *The UNHCR and World Politics: A Perilous Path*. Oxford: Oxford University Press.

This book provides a comprehensive political history of the UNHCR and the refugee issue in international politics during the twentieth century.

Loescher, G., Milner, J., Newman, E., and **Troeller, G.** (eds) (2008). *Protracted Refugee Situations: Political, Security and Human Rights Implications.* Tokyo: United Nations University Press.

An overview and analysis of the political, security, and human rights implications of protracted exile.

Orchard, P. (2014). *A Right to Flee: Refugees, States and the Construction of International Cooperation.* Cambridge: Cambridge University Press.

A historical and political account of how patterns of international cooperation on refugee issues endure and adapt.

Orchard, P. (2016). *Protecting the Internally Displaced: Rhetoric and Reality.* Abingdon: Routledge.

A history of recent protection and assistance developments regarding internally displaced persons.

Phuong, C. (2005). *The International Protection of Internally Displaced Persons.* Cambridge: Cambridge University Press.

This book provides an analysis of the legal and political implications of protecting internally displaced persons.

UNHCR (2015). *Asylum Trends 2014.* Geneva: UNHCR.

A UNHCR publication outlining asylum statistics and trends.

UNHCR (2015). *Global Trends 2014.* Geneva: UNHCR.

Annual UNHCR publication outlining the statistics and trends for the previous year.

UNHCR (2016). *The State of the World's Refugees.* Oxford: Oxford University Press.

Leading experts discuss many of the major policy issues confronting UNHCR today.

WEB LINKS

http://www.fmreview.org/   Forced Migration Review is a quarterly magazine reviewing current policy issues in the field of forced migration.

http://www.forcedmigration.org/   Forced Migration Online is the most comprehensive website listing research sources on forced migration issues around the world.

http://www.internal-displacement.org/   The website of the Internal Displacement Monitoring Centre provides comprehensive information and analysis of the problem of internally displaced persons.

http://www.irinnews.org/   This international website provides humanitarian news and analysis from Africa, Asia, and the Middle East.

http://www.refugeesinternational.org/   The website of Refugees International, a leading NGO that provides up-to-date news, research, and advocacy on refugee situations across the globe.

http://www.unhcr.org/   The website of the UNHCR contains up-to-date information and statistics about the organization and the refugee populations it protects and assists globally.

NOTE

1. This chapter draws upon some of my earlier writings, including Loescher (2001) and Betts, Loescher, and Milner (2012).

Visit the Online Resource Centre that accompanies this book for updates and a range of other resources: www.oxfordtextbooks.co.uk/orc/goodhart3e/

19

Indigenous Peoples' Human Rights

Paul Havemann

Chapter Contents

Reader's Guide

For centuries, the powerful have simultaneously both acknowledged and denied the individual and group rights of Indigenous peoples, and still do. This ambivalence has dire consequences. The chapter begins by discussing who Indigenous peoples are; next, the historical evolution of Indigenous rights is outlined. The case study examines climate change and Indigenous peoples, highlighting the limited character of twenty-first-century human rights discourse for Indigenous peoples. The conclusion briefly examines the continuing ambivalence towards accommodating the group rights of Indigenous peoples and offers some principles that could inform stronger recognition.

Introduction

Indigenous peoples[1] are among the most vulnerable people on Earth, yet states are ambivalent about recognizing their rights. Several factors explain this: cultural, religious, political, and economic differences; profound differences in the relationship with nature; and the incompatibility of recognition with colonization. Today the individualistic premise of human rights regimes fails to secure Indigenous peoples' inextricably linked group rights to existence and self-determination. States still tend to regard self-determination for Indigenous peoples as a challenge to external sovereignty and internal stability that fundamentally threatens the state.

Three Types of Rights

Three broad, interrelated, and interdependent types of human rights inform the conceptual framework for this chapter: the right to existence, the right to **self-determination**, and individual human rights.

The right to existence is a group right inferred from the 1951 UN **Genocide Convention** (Thornberry, 1991), which established the right not to suffer **genocide**. The right to self-determination is a group right expressed in the 2007 UN Declaration on the Rights of Indigenous Peoples (UNDRIP), which emphasizes self-government, participatory development, and free, prior, and informed consent.

Individual human rights, developed in international law within the UN framework since 1945, are expressed in conventions and declarations emanating from the UN and its specialized agencies. These rights comprise: civil and political rights; social, cultural, and economic rights; and rights to development and to a healthy and sustainable environment. Most recently, Indigenous peoples organizations are calling for the recognition of the Rights of Mother Earth (Cochabamba Peoples Conference, 2010). In the 1993 **Vienna Declaration** the UN declared human rights to be 'universal, indivisible, interdependent and interrelated'.

Who are Indigenous Peoples According to International Law?

Modern law and policy constantly categorize and classify people to determine eligibility for certain rights or services. For this reason, definitions of the categories 'Indigenous people', 'minority', 'peoples', and 'tribal peoples' are hotly contested (Capotorti, 1977). Moreover, the categories overlap with respect to several salient characteristics. International law defines neither 'minorities' nor 'peoples' (Daes and Eide, 2000): international human rights norms accord Indigenous people a degree of autonomous development, whereas minorities are assumed to have a duty to participate actively in the larger society. The 1992 UN Minorities Declaration, unlike the then draft Indigenous Declaration, did not address rights to lands and natural resources. Finally, the Minorities Declaration referred to the rights of a 'person belonging to a minority', whereas the Indigenous Declaration refers to 'peoples'.

Gudmundar Alfredsson (2005, pp. 163, 165) estimates that altogether there are 12,000 to 19,000 Indigenous and minority groups in the world, who number 1.5 billion individuals and amount to about 25 per cent of the world population. Of these, Indigenous people make up a tiny fraction. The UN Permanent Forum for Indigenous Issues (PFII) (UNPFII, 2010) estimates that there are over 370 million Indigenous people in ninety states, occupying 20 per cent of the Earth's territory; they constitute only 5 per cent of the global population yet 15 per cent of the world's poor. Of 7,000 of the world's languages, 4,000 are spoken by Indigenous peoples, but by the end of the twenty-first century 90 per cent of these languages will be extinct.

Martin Scheinin (2005, p. 3) following Martinez-Cobo (1986), Special Rapporteur of the UN Sub-Commission on Prevention of Discrimination and Protection of Minorities, identifies several defining characteristics asserted by Indigenous peoples:

1. They are distinctive from the dominant society.

2. They self-identify as, and desire to be, different from that society.

3. They are uniquely connected to their lands, which form the central element in their history, culture, economy, and spirituality.

4. They assert that they are 'first in time'—that they have occupied their land and territories since 'time immemorial'. Now-dominant populations colonized them, dispossessing them of their land and usurping their sovereignty.

Indigenous peoples are under threat in all regions due to their subordination by dominant populations

(DESA, 2009; Lattimer, 2010) and due to climate change (UNPFII, 2010).

For Indigenous peoples, survival and sustained identity depends on rights to self-determination and existence. Self-determination includes the right to determine who members of an Indigenous people are. Descent from an Indigenous ancestor is the primary criterion, though in practice Indigenous peoples are more inclusive than this (Gover, 2010).

KEY POINTS

Every state has minority or Indigenous people who are not dominant and are consequently under cultural, economic, or physical threat.

International human rights law distinguishes among Indigenous peoples, tribal peoples, and minorities. Indigenous peoples are distinct in that their occupation of territory predated that of the majority of the state's present population.

The human rights of Indigenous peoples need to be considered in terms of their group rights to existence and self-determination as well as individual rights.

Critical Thinking Question:

Why do you think Indigenous people cling to their identity as members of a group, a people, instead of embracing assimilation and individualization as promoted by states and the dominant culture?

Centuries of Ambivalence about the Recognition of Indigenous Peoples

Explorers, colonists, states, multinationals, and international governmental organizations display deep ambivalence towards recognizing Indigenous people as human beings with rights to life, liberty, ownership of property, and self-determination. Denial of Indigenous people's rights makes it so much easier morally, politically, and legally to appropriate their land and resources and to deny their existence.

Denial of Individual and International Legal Personality

A basic organizing concept of law is *legal personality*. This concept allows legal orders to determine who

has standing within each system to sue and be sued; to own property; and to enjoy the protection of the state or be self-governing entities. States, citizens, and even corporations are deemed to have legal personality. Persons with standing have the capacity to exercise rights, perform duties, bear liabilities, and exercise powers, coupled with the competence to use their capacities rationally with an understanding of the consequences of their choices. Slaves, women, and Indigenous persons and peoples (overlapping categories) were deemed to lack standing or personality on the grounds of their lack of capacity. The Euro-American legal order privileged the sovereign state and the patriarchal authority of the individual and his right to property ownership among the bundle of individual rights accorded to citizens. Citizens are eligible to participate fully in the state political–legal order. In many states, citizenship was denied to Indigenous people until the late twentieth century. Initially, questions about their capacity turned on whether they were Christians and had souls and consciences to guide them (R. Williams, 2012). Later, states used **eugenics** (distorted Darwinian evolutionary theory) to label Indigenous peoples as not evolved enough to have sufficient capacity to be legal persons.

The concept of international legal personality evolved to identify which nations have standing as **sovereign** states. The Law of Nations that regulated the Westphalian model of inter-state relations from 1648 (Held, 1995) limited membership of the 'family of nations' to Christian sovereign states. Each had the right to make and enforce its own laws without interference from other states. Indigenous peoples did not qualify for international legal personality (Castro, 2007).

Much of the Westphalian model survived the creation of the UN in 1945. Only states have standing as members of the UN. International law sourced from UN activities reflects a compromise of state interests. Indigenous peoples, as peoples, have no standing due to the very limited enforceability of the self-determination right, and thus little way to assert their international legal personality (Meijknecht, 2001) despite the UN Declaration of the Rights of Indigenous Peoples 2007 (see Box 19.1). Instead, their entitlements are mostly expressed as duties imposed on states or principles for governance. In 2002 the PFII was set up to enhance indigenous participation in the UN—but half its membership is determined by states.

BOX 19.1 DECONSTRUCTING: INDIGENOUS SUSTAINABLE SELF-DETERMINATION VERSUS SOVEREIGNTY

Indigenous self-determination is not about sovereign statehood in the Westphalian model (Daes, 1993), involving illimitable power vis-à-vis other states. Official conflation of the two concepts handicaps Indigenous aspirations to self-determination by equating this with secession. Indigenous self-determination consists of a duty-based governance premised on maintaining sustainable intergenerational and inter-species interconnectedness with Mother Earth (Corntassel, 2008). Basic rights (and correlative duties) inherent in such self-determination are:

- to natural resource management;
- to ancestral land, territories, and resources, as a collective and individual right;
- to exercise control and management of their right to lands, territories, and resources;

- to self-government by their own institutions and authorities within their lands and territories;
- to self-development (meaning the right to their own decision making) on conservation and development options for their lands, territories, and resources;
- to fair and equitable benefit sharing from conservation and development actions involving their lands, territories, resources, and people;
- to conserve, develop, use, and protect their traditional knowledge (Collings, 2010, p. 86).

Such rights and duties can be secured within the state if the state honours their international human rights obligations (Primeau and Corntassel, 1995).

Centuries of Debate about Indigenous Rights

From the fifteenth century, territorial acquisition by European states through war, trade, and settlement profoundly affected Indigenous peoples and ecosystems all over the world (Keal, 2003). Acquisition gave the state sovereignty over the territory acquired, allowing for the imposition of extractive colonies, which exploited raw materials and cheap labour, and of settler colonies, where European states could send their surplus population. The Law of Nations authorized the following five modes of acquisition: **prescription**, the acquisition of territory based on its effective possession over a period of time; **cession**, the acquisition of the territory of another state through a treaty; **accession or accretion**, the acquisition of territory that emerged through natural processes; **conquest**, the acquisition of territory by the victor in a war (Robertson, 2005); and finally, **occupation or discovery**, the acquisition of territory not under the power of another sovereign. Such territories were sometimes described as *terra nullius* (Latin for 'land of no one', i.e. uninhabited).

Colonizing states often conflated the absence of an occupying sovereign with the absence of inhabitants with legal personality recognized by 'civilized' nations; they thus claimed to have discovered a *terra nullius*. The fact that people were already inhabiting territory acquired by occupation would otherwise have been highly problematic, morally and legally. But neither moral and legal niceties nor physical realities inhibited

the acquisition of the territories of Indigenous peoples by so-called discovery or occupation (Borrows, 1999; Miller et al., 2012; UNPFII, 2014;), conquest and genocide, or by legal sleight of hand concerning the validity of treaties of cession or peace made with Indigenous peoples (Gotkowitz, 2008; Foster, Raven, and Webber, 2008; Speed, 2008; Hitchcock and Totten, 2010).

Throughout the nineteenth and early twentieth centuries, settlers' rhetorical claims to liberal civilization clashed with their need to dispossess Indigenous peoples. The Law of Nations drew heavily on liberal legal ideology from the English-speaking world. This was exemplified by respect for sovereignty, property rights, and principles such as the **rule of law** to fetter the power of the state over individuals. However, the development of new political economies in the colonies was obstructed by the presence and rights claims of Indigenous peoples. The need to dispossess, disperse, or assimilate them led to coercion and genocidal practices, infantilization, and the denial of the legal personality of Indigenous people and nations on the basis of cultural differences. Despite instances of humanitarianism and fidelity to liberal principles, in this period the overwhelming practice of states, rationalized by the official jurisprudence, was to deny Indigenous people both legal personality as individuals and international legal personality as self-determining peoples.

Over the centuries, continuity rather than any doctrinal rupture marks debates over Indigenous peoples rights (see Box 19.2).

BOX 19.2 AMBIVALENCE TOWARDS INDIGENOUS LEGAL PERSONALITY

1492 Christopher Columbus found the periphery of the Americas, but claimed that he had discovered a new route to India.

1492 Pope Alexander VI's Papal Bull denied legal personality to Indigenous peoples in newly discovered Americas unless they converted to Christianity.

1514 Dominican priest Bartholemé de Las Casas advocated for the rights of the 'Indians' of the Spanish Indies.

1539 Theologian Franciscus de Victoria advocated for recognition of Indigenous peoples rights to life and property.

1550 The King of Spain set up a debate between de Las Casas and scholar Juan Gines de Sepulveda, who described 'Indians' as 'natural slaves' without rights.

1552 In *The Devastation of the Indies: A Brief Account*, Las Casas (1992) documents genocide and enslavement of Indians in the Spanish Indies (Cuba).

1604, 1625 Hugo Grotius advocated recognizing Indigenous peoples individual personality and international legal personality as peoples, and advocated restricting territorial acquisition under the doctrine of discovery or occupation to places that are truly unoccupied *terra nullius*.

1690 John Locke, in *Two Treatises of Government* (Locke, 1960), denied the individual and international legal personality of Indian people of North America because they lived in a primitive 'state of nature', lacked a recognizable political system, and did not cultivate the land as Europeans do.

1743 J. G. Heineccus equated international legal personality with the power to resist domination and exclude other states from territory.

1763 The King of England issued a *Royal Proclamation* to regulate settler behaviour in British North America and stabilize relations with Indian nations or tribes. It reserved lands west of the Appalachians for Indians and recognized their rights as property owners and as tribes, implying a collective legal personality. Since then Canada has made many treaties with Indigenous First Nations.

[The pre-existing Aboriginal title of First Nations was first recognized by the Supreme Court of Canada (SCC) decision *Calder* v. *The Queen* (1960) SCR 892. First Nations' distinct constitutional standing in Canada was first recognized by the Constitution Act 1982. In 2004 the SCC determined in *Haida* v. *British Columbia* 3 SCR 511 that the Crown had a duty to negotiate in good faith with First Nations. In *Tsilhqot'in Nation* v. *British Columbia* (2014) SCC 44 the Court amplified the meaning of Aboriginal title and imposed explicit burdens on governments to consult First Nations on resource developments and specifically justify any incursions on their territory.]

1765 William Blackstone stated in his *Commentaries on the Laws of England* (Blackstone, 1765–9) that Indigenous peoples lived in 'primeval simplicity' and therefore lacked individual or international legal personality.

1776 Captain James Cook of the British Royal Navy sailed out under orders to acquire 'with the consent of the natives' any territory found. Landing on the southeast coast of Australia, he found ample evidence of Indigenous people but claimed to have discovered an uninhabited continent (*terra nullius*).

[The High Court of Australia decision *Mabo* v. *Queensland* (No.2) (1992) 175CLR 1(HCA) repudiated the *terra nullius* assertion and recognized that Native Title pre-existed the British acquisition of territory.]

1787 The *Constitution of the United States* seemingly recognizes the international legal personality of Indian Tribes. The Commerce Clause (Article 1, section 8) states: 'The Congress shall have Power … to regulate Commerce with foreign Nations, and among the several States, and with the … Indian Tribes.'

1787 The United States Congress passed the *Northwest Ordinance*; Article III, concerning the government of territories northwest of the Ohio River, recognized the legal personality of Indians.

1823 The US Supreme Court, in *Johnson* v. *McIntosh*, rejected the power of Indian Chiefs to deal in land on behalf of the Tribes, thereby denying their individual and international legal personality.

1831 The US Supreme Court, in *Cherokee* v. *State of Georgia*, recognized the standing of Indian Tribes to have group rights in the form of limited self-government as 'dependent domestic nations', thus endowing them with partial legal personality as a group.

1835 The British Crown received a Declaration of Independence by Maori chiefs of Aotearoa/New Zealand.

1837 The British Parliament accepted a report from the Select Committee on Aborigines containing widespread evidence of massacres of Indigenous people in Australian colonies, and resolved that Indigenous peoples as British subjects be respected, protected, and assimilated, thereby endowing them with partial legal personality.

1840 The British Crown concluded the Treaty of Waitangi with the Maori chiefs. The Treaty purported to cede Maori sovereignty to the Crown and to grant Maori British subjecthood.

[In 2014, the Waitangi Tribunal found the Chiefs had not ceded sovereignty (*He Whakaputanga me te Tiriti: the Declaration and the Treaty* Waitangi Tribunal (2014, Wai 1040).]

(continued)

BOX 19.2 (*continued*)

1895 English legal scholar John Westlake asserted that treaties made with Indigenous peoples need not be honoured, as Indigenous peoples are uncivilized and therefore do not have legal personality.

1918 A. H. Snow's report on *The Question of Aborigines and the Practice of Nations* (1918) for the US State Department utilized the eugenicist dichotomy between 'backward races' and 'civilized nations' as that of ward and guardian. This justified treating 'treaties' with Indigenous peoples as not binding on states because 'backward peoples' had insufficient capacity as legal persons to enter into such binding international transactions.

1919 In *Re Southern Rhodesia* (AC 211), the Privy Council, highest court of appeal in the British Empire, was clearly influenced by the eugenics movement when it refused to acknowledge the legal personality of certain Indigenous peoples because they 'are so low on the scale of social organization that their usages and concepts of rights and duties are not

to be reconciled with the institutions and legal ideas of civilized society'.

1921 In *Amodu Tijani* v. *Secretary, Southern Nigeria*, the Privy Council held that the legal personality of peoples in conquered or ceded territory ought to be recognized.

1928 In the *Island of Palmas* case, the Permanent Court of International Arbitration dismissed Indigenous peoples standing, characterizing them as 'savage', semi-civilized peoples with no international legal personality.

1933 In *Legal Status of Eastern Greenland*, the Permanent Court of International Justice deemed Greenland to be a *terra nullius*; Indigenous Inuit peoples—the majority of the population—were not considered to have legal personality relevant to the case.

[In 1975 the International Court of Justice decided in the *Western Sahara* (1975) to repudiate doctrine of discovery/ occupation of an inhabited *terra nullius*].

After the First World War (1918), the **League of Nations** and the **International Labour Organization** (ILO) were established as state-based intergovernmental organizations (IGOs). The League principally focused on protecting national minorities as groups, but 'native' inhabitants were of concern too. It mandated some victorious states to ensure good government, including the supervision of the well-being of Indigenous peoples in the colonial territories of defeated European powers.[2]

The ILO was created, and still operates, as a tripartite organization representing states, employers, and employees in the setting and monitoring of labour standards. Until the 1950s it was the most prominent IGO to focus on Indigenous people. ILO conventions impose duties on states rather than recognize Indigenous rights.

KEY POINTS

Between the fifteenth and twentieth centuries the legal personality of Indigenous peoples was recognized in very limited forms, thereby justifying denial of their rights.

Indigenous peoples were denied standing as 'sovereign' states. Sovereign states were those European Christian states regulated by the Westphalian Law of Nations governing war and territorial acquisition.

Until 1975 territorial acquisition by discovery/occupation meant that territory not ruled by a sovereign state could be claimed as *terra nullius* and the rights of the Indigenous inhabitants could be ignored.

During the nineteenth and twentieth centuries, eugenics was used to characterize Indigenous peoples as 'backward' and

Europeans as 'civilized' to legitimate the non-recognition of Indigenous peoples rights.

Between 1919 and 1957 the ILO was the only IGO concerned about states' duties towards Indigenous peoples.

Critical Thinking Question:

The eugenics movement has been discredited as unscientific and justifying racism. Has the distinction between 'backward' and 'civilized' peoples actually been abandoned by states, international agencies, and corporations in their treatment of Indigenous peoples and citizens? Give reasons to support your view.

The United Nations and Indigenous Group Rights

The global character of the Second World War, the failure of the League of Nations, and the experience of the Holocaust precipitated a radical rethinking of the architecture of international governance. The ILO survived. In place of the League of Nations, the UN was created to address international peace, security, and well-being.

The Triumph of Individual Human Rights Discourse 1945–75

A new world order centred on the UN, and its specialized agencies took shape following the War. The UN Charter states that the 'peoples' (strangely, not the 'nations') of the UN reaffirm 'faith in fundamental human rights, in the dignity and worth of the human person, in the equal rights of men and women and of nations large and small'. The basic innovation of the UN-centred world order was the adoption of a platform of human rights for all human beings. The assumption was that the individual human rights regime would deliver equality and make group rights largely irrelevant, except in extreme circumstances. Group rights to freedom from genocide (right to existence) and to self-determination have major symbolic significance, yet yield little practical benefit to Indigenous peoples and minority groups (Thornberry, 2002). Perhaps the same can be said of human rights generally (Johansson Dahre, 2010).

Ignoring the Link Between Existence and Self-Determination

Indigenous peoples see their right to existence and their right to self-determination as being inextricably linked, while states regard their own sovereignty and territorial integrity as non-negotiable.

The Right to Existence

The 1951 Genocide Convention implies the right to existence as a group and the recognition of group rights under certain circumstances. Under Article 2, genocide involves specified acts 'committed with intent to destroy, in whole or in part, a national, ethnical, racial or religious group …'. This right is limited in three important ways. First, the Convention requires proof of intent. Intention has been hard to establish. Further, the Convention omits linguistic groups. Language is the basic nexus that binds the group into its culture

and distinguishes Indigenous and minority groups from the dominant population. Finally, the Convention eschews the broader concept of cultural genocide or ethnocide. The Convention has never been invoked to protect Indigenous peoples.

The 1957 ILO Convention on the Protection and Integration of Indigenous, Tribal, Semi-Tribal Peoples (No. 107) articulates standards in terms of individual and, for the first time, group rights. The Convention attempted to reconcile assimilationist versus cultural distinctiveness discourses surrounding Indigenous people. Only twenty-seven state parties ratified it. Indigenous peoples repudiated it on the grounds of its paternalism and perceived assimilationist objectives, which they regarded as undermining their right to existence as peoples, tribes, and nations.

The Right to Self-Determination

The group right to self-determination was first articulated in the 1960 UN Declaration on the Granting of Independence to Colonial Countries and Peoples. Self-determination was intended as the path to decolonization for peoples in the overseas colonies of European powers (the saltwater or blue water thesis), but not for minority or Indigenous peoples within these colonies or within other established states. Paragraphs 1 and 2 champion Indigenous peoples rights; yet paragraphs 6 and 7 severely qualify the circumstances in which the right to self-determination may be invoked, illustrating the tension between preserving the 'national unity and the territorial integrity of a country' while at the same time urging 'respect for the sovereign rights of all peoples and their territorial integrity'.

Similar ambivalence is clear in the 1965 UN Convention on the Elimination of All Forms of Racial Discrimination (CERD). This Convention reflects the international condemnation of apartheid in South Africa. It reiterates the right to equality and freedom from discrimination on the grounds of the race of individuals. Where CERD does acknowledge group rights through provision of special measures, such measures can only be temporary (Article 4). This implies that, once individual equality is achieved through the recognition of separate rights for the group, these special measures (for instance, self-government or the ownership of communal lands) would cease.

The **International Covenant on Civil and Political Rights** (ICCPR) and the **International Covenant on Economic, Social and Cultural Rights** (ICESCR) both recognize the right to self-determination in their first articles. Despite the plain language of the text, there is broad legal and diplomatic consensus that the right to self-determination does not apply to Indigenous peoples and minorities in the sense of secession from a state (Castellino, 2005), though it may imply self-government and limited autonomy within a state—i.e. internal self-government. Since 1977 the UN *Human Rights Committee*[3] has construed Article 27 of the ICESCR, which concerns the rights of persons 'in community with the other members of their group', as implicitly protecting group as well as individual rights (Orlin, Rosas, and Scheinin, 2000).

After 1975: Beginning to Link Existence with Self-Determination?

By the end of the 1970s, Indigenous people and supportive **non-governmental organizations** (NGOs) had become an effective lobby group in the UN system as well as in some states. Canada, New Zealand, the Nordic states, and some Latin American states gave some constitutional recognition to Indigenous rights to self-government. Incrementally, the UN has created mechanisms to allow Indigenous peoples to campaign for greater recognition of their rights in the international arenas.

For instance, in 1977 Indigenous participants at the UN NGO Committee on Human Rights and the Indigenous NGO Conference on Discrimination against Indigenous Populations framed a draft declaration that signalled the emergence of Indigenous activism that would ultimately lead to the 2007 UN Declaration on the Rights of Indigenous Peoples.

Throughout the 1980s the **World Bank** adopted new policies on involuntary resettlement in response to evidence of massive displacement of Indigenous people by Bank-financed projects such as dam building in Latin America. In 1982 the World Bank published *Tribal Peoples and Economic Development: Human Ecologic Considerations*. This report stressed the link between Indigenous people and the environment, and the risks that developments funded by the World Bank pose to them. However, rather than promoting self-determination, the report promoted the concept of reserves for some Indigenous people, as well as their 'acculturation' into the mainstream political economy. Such official policy statements operate as soft law. They illustrate the power of international financial institutions (IFIs) such as the World Bank to impact radically on the life chances of millions of people in the developing world (Eastwood, 2011).

The *UN Economic, Social, and Cultural Organization* (UNESCO) hosted a committee of experts who passed the San José Declaration Against Ethnocide in 1981. This defined **ethnocide** to mean that 'an ethnic group is denied the right to enjoy, develop, and transmit its own culture and its own language, whether collectively or individually' and declared it to be equivalent to genocide.

In 1982 the UN set up an expert Working Group on Indigenous Populations (WGIP). Until 2002 this was the sole mechanism available to Indigenous peoples in the UN context. The word 'populations' in its title carefully avoids recognizing Indigenous *peoples* as potentially self-determining peoples who could be the subjects of international law (i.e. like states, persons with standing in the international legal system). In 1986 UN Special Rapporteur Juan Martinez-Cobo delivered his major report, 'Study of the Problem of Discrimination Against Indigenous Populations', which highlighted the plight of Indigenous peoples as being among the least advantaged groups on Earth.

The ILO continued its work with a new Convention concerning Indigenous and Tribal Peoples in Independent Countries. The new Convention (No. 169), passed in 1989, made a modest shift in the direction of self-government for Indigenous peoples, but ambivalence about self-determination was expressed by the proviso in Article 1(3): 'The use of the term "peoples" in this Convention shall not be construed as having any implications as regards the rights which may attach to the term under international law.' The Convention nonetheless articulated the governance principle of free, prior, and informed consent as well as the right to free participation in all levels of decision making that impact on Indigenous and tribal peoples. Further, the Convention imposed on states a duty of consultation concerning any measures affecting Indigenous peoples (Articles 6 and 7).

Indigenous peoples rights achieved unprecedented recognition in 1992 at the UN Conference on Environment and Development in Rio de Janeiro, also known as the Earth Summit. Participation by states (172) and NGOs (2,400) was on a scale never seen before. Even an alternative summit attracted 17,000 people. Rio Earth Summit instruments identified the duty of states to respect the traditional environmental knowledge (TEK), closeness to nature, and stewardship duties of Indigenous peoples. Four instruments—Agenda 21, the Rio Declaration on Environment and Development, the Statement of Forest Principles, and the United Nations Convention on Biological Diversity—explicitly recognized Indigenous peoples rights, connectedness to the environment, and role in environmental conservation. One instrument, however, did not: the United Nations Framework Convention on Climate Change (UNFCCC). None of the instruments recognized that TEK is inextricably linked to self-determination, thereby enabling performance of Indigenous people's duty to live according to customary law (Tobin, 2014).

In 1993—the UN International Year of Indigenous People—the UN World Conference on Human Rights issued the **Vienna Declaration**, which, on the one hand, stressed the importance of the 'effective realization of this right' (of self-determination), but on the other stressed 'the territorial integrity or political unity of sovereign and independent States … possessed of a Government representing the whole people belonging to the territory without distinction of any kind'. The latter concern appears to be directed at discouraging outside interference from other states in the affairs of 'States conducting themselves in compliance with the principle of equal rights and self-determination of peoples'. Principle 20 of the Declaration exhorts states to honour their obligations to Indigenous peoples in 'recognizing the value and diversity of their distinct identities, cultures and social organization', but simultaneously assumes the absolute value of 'political and social stability', which seems to preclude rights of self-determination for Indigenous peoples.

Recognition that the right to existence is inextricably bound up with the right to self-determination—the viewpoint of Indigenous peoples' organizations—was not much evident in the UN-sponsored human rights discourse of the 1990s. The exception was the expert WGIP, which presented a draft Declaration on the Rights of Indigenous Peoples to the UN Sub-Commission on the Prevention of Discrimination and the Protection of Minorities in 1993. State parties, the WGIP, and Indigenous peoples' organizations worked continuously on successive drafts, but states remained adamant that the right to self-determination was not to be explicitly stated. In 2001 this unresolved tension led the UN to appoint a Special Rapporteur on the Situation of Human Rights and Freedoms of Indigenous Peoples, with a role complementary to that of the WGIP. A year later the UN created the PFII to supersede the WGIP.

The PFII reflects a shift from a state-centred world governance structure towards a somewhat more multi-actor, multi-centric, and multi-layered, networked form of global governance (Held, 2004; Slaughter, 2004) as no other non-state group as yet has permanent representation in the UN. The Permanent Forum serves as an advisory body to the Economic and Social Council of the UN (ECOSOC) concerning Indigenous issues such as economic and social development, culture, the environment, education, health, and human rights. Its mandate is: to provide expert advice and recommendations on Indigenous issues to the Council and, through the Council, to funds, agencies, and programmes of the United Nations; to raise awareness and promote the integration and coordination of activities related to Indigenous issues within the UN system; and to prepare and disseminate information on Indigenous issues.

Still, the very name given to this Permanent Forum, referring to 'Indigenous *Issues*' rather than '*Peoples*', signifies the continued wariness of state parties about self-determination claims. The state-centric model also remains explicit in the form and process of PFII membership. ECOSOC elects eight of the sixteen members from the nominees of states; the other eight are nominated by Indigenous organizations, but ultimately appointed by the President of ECOSOC. Members serve as individual experts and are not representatives of peoples. Membership reflects vast regions designated by the UN: Africa; Asia; Central and South America and the Caribbean; the Arctic; Central and Eastern Europe, Russian Federation, Central Asia, and Transcaucasia; North America; and the Pacific.

In 2007 the Declaration of the Rights of Indigenous Peoples was eventually adopted and the UN Expert Mechanism on the Rights of Indigenous Peoples was established. Notable among the opposing states were initially the African states as well as Canada, Australia, New Zealand, and the USA. The Declaration reflects compromises that attempt to address flaws in preceding drafts as well as the existing human rights regime from the differing perspectives of both states and Indigenous peoples. The Declaration does crystallize and highlight existing Indigenous rights under international law. So, for the first time, a UN instrument benchmarks specific Indigenous human rights standards for states, IGOs, multinational corporations (MNCs), IFIs, and NGOs to meet (Allen and Xanthaki, 2010; Charters and Stavenhagen, 2009).

Individual rights are reconciled with collective rights in Article 1. The right to existence as a group and as individuals is articulated in Article 7. This article, incidentally, subsumes the forcible removal of children under 'any act of genocide or any other act of violence', thus neatly skirting the issue of whether forcibly removing children (as in Australia) constitutes genocide. Article 3 leaves open the question of external self-determination; Articles 4 and 5 favour internal self-determination. Other articles concern: participatory development and other economic and social rights; the principle of free, prior, and informed consent; the right to consultation about activities on their lands; and the right to determine membership of, and to maintain, Indigenous institutions, as well as relations between and within states that affect Indigenous peoples.

Consequences of Denial of Rights

Indigenous peoples are among the most discriminated-against groups, regardless of recognition, in nearly all states. Evidence of the denial of group and individual rights is continuously reported by the Special Rapporteur on the Rights of Indigenous Peoples; UNPFII (UNPFII, 2010); the **UN High Commissioner for Refugees** (UNHCR, 2006); and NGOs, such as Forest Peoples Programme (FPP), Rights and Resources Initiative (RRI), Survival International, International Work Group on Indigenous Affairs (IWGIA). States frequently facilitate the dispossession of Indigenous people from their traditional lands and territories and their exclusion from access to natural resources fundamental to their way of life and survival. Genocide, persecution, and discrimination are the common experience of Indigenous and tribal peoples. Infrastructure developments frequently force their displacement within the

state or cause them to become economic, environmental, or political refugees elsewhere. Extractive industries take and pollute their lands and resources (Anaya, 2013; Franks et al., 2014; Alforte et al., 2014).

State policies promote coercive assimilation through education, child welfare, and market economics, leading to the loss of language, culture, and skills. Paternalist and non-inclusive governance and service delivery models perpetuate the denial of culture and the denial of the right to existence as self-determining groups, and exacerbate the participation deficit. Worldwide, dependency and disempowerment make the preservation of cultural, political, social, and economic integrity and social and economic development virtually impossible. Life expectancy, health, and well-being are markedly lower for Indigenous and tribal peoples than for the dominant population almost everywhere (DESA, 2009). Mental health suffers, too. After enduring centuries of colonization accompanied by a denial of rights by the dominant population, many Indigenous people suffer from 'historical trauma' or intergenerational post-traumatic stress disorder (Kirmayer and Valaskakis, 2009; Czyzewski, 2011).

Figure 19.1 links colonialism, **globalization**, and ethnocide to global warming and **ecocide** (the killing of ecosystems, including planet Earth), illustrating the multiple jeopardy suffered by Indigenous peoples.

KEY POINTS

After the Second World War, the UN established an individual human rights regime anchored in the Universal Declaration of Human Rights: the ICCPR and the ICESCR. The group right of self-determination is referred to in both covenants but applied only to the colonies of European powers.

A corresponding group right to existence is inferred from the prohibition and punishment of the crime of genocide, but the Genocide Convention has seldom been invoked against individuals or states, and never in the protection of Indigenous peoples.

Indigenous peoples became an effective lobby group in the 1970s. Agitation for a UN Declaration on the Rights of Indigenous Peoples started in 1977 but the meaning and implications of the rights to self-determination in drafts of the Declaration were to be a major stumbling block for states for thirty years.

In the 1980s, rights of consultation, participation, and prior informed consent emerged in various quarters, including the Earth Summit, the WGIP, and the ILO.

Set up in 2002, the PFII is the first UN body to give standing to peoples who are not states in the context of the UN's state-based system. The UN and states, however, control its membership. The 2007 Declaration on the Rights of Indigenous Peoples conferred the right of internal self-determination on Indigenous peoples but failed to establish a framework for relations involving Indigenous peoples as peoples, states, and the UN.

Genocide, dispossession of their territories, and the denial of their rights as legal persons and nations through colonization, globalization, and climate change make Indigenous people among the most vulnerable groups in the world.

Critical Thinking Question:

Has the rhetoric of human rights given Indigenous peoples voice and power, or have human rights actually been of little real value to them?

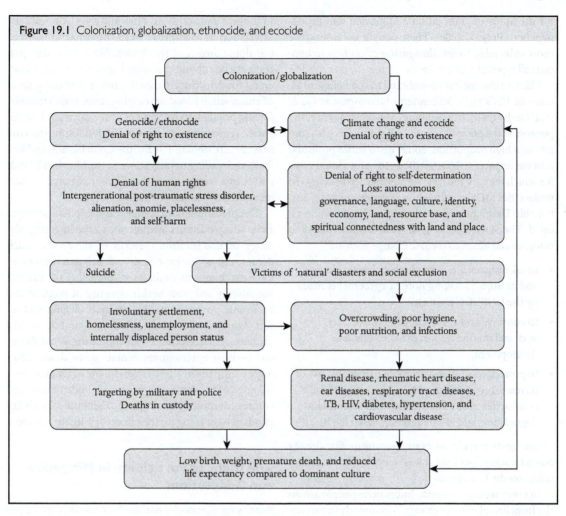

Figure 19.1 Colonization, globalization, ethnocide, and ecocide

Case Study: Indigenous Peoples and Climate Change

By the end of 2014, almost all states had unequivocally accepted a direct link between human activity and global climate change. The UN Intergovernmental Panel on Climate Change (IPCC) presented further compelling evidence for this link in its fifth report (IPCC, 2014). The UN Environment Programme and the World Meteorological Organization set up the IPCC in 1988 to assess relevant scientific, technical, and socio-economic information. Consensus in favour of urgent global human intervention to stop the growth of greenhouse gas emissions was reflected first in the 1992 UN Framework Convention on Climate Change and then in the 2005 Kyoto Protocol to the UNFCCC. The UNFCCC obliges states to reduce emissions and to take measures to mitigate and adapt to the profound ecological, economic (Stern, 2006), political, social, and cultural effects of climate change.

Climate change-precipitated disasters are on the rise in frequency and severity. These underline the importance of basic human rights for millions of poor people, many of them Indigenous (Tauli-Corpuz and Lynge, 2008). Indigenous peoples are among those already experiencing negative impacts of climate change that include loss of food security, sea level rise and coastal erosion, desertification, deforestation, intensification and frequency of 'natural' disasters, unprecedented species extinction, and the spread of vector-borne diseases. Further, climate change has already displaced 25 million people worldwide (Institute for the Study of International Migration and Brookings-Bern Project, 2008). These people are among the most vulnerable to the **abrogation** of (failure to honour) all types of human rights.

Climate change has contributed to the failure to attain the UN's eight Millennium Development Goals (MDGs) by their 2015 deadline. As a consequence, the poorest of the poor, of whom Indigenous peoples constitute a high proportion, continue to suffer profound adverse impacts (UNDP/RIIP, 2010) of a global crisis for which they are the least responsible (Ban, 2007). To replace the MDGs, a fifteen-year programme of Sustainable Development Goals (SDGs) has been developed. The SDGs include goals to enhance capacity to mitigate and adapt to climate change such as:

- to take urgent action to combat climate change and its impacts (taking note of agreements made by the UNFCCC forum);
- to conserve and sustainably use the oceans, seas, and marine resources for sustainable development;
- to protect, restore, and promote sustainable use of terrestrial ecosystems, sustainably manage forests, combat desertification and halt and reverse land degradation, and halt biodiversity loss (UNDP, 2015).

These goals merely reiterate commitments already made by states, but they at least elevate climate justice issues on the UN agenda.

In every region on Earth, Indigenous people are on the front line of climate change—frequently in parts of the developing world where the state is least equipped or willing to respond. In the Arctic region, very rapid climate change is fundamentally threatening the health and food security of Indigenous Inuit people at a speed and on a scale that makes mitigation and adaptation very difficult. In Southern Africa, drought and temperature rise leading to desertification are rendering 2.5 million hectares of the Kalahari area unusable for grazing or as a source of food for the Indigenous San people. In Asia, rising temperatures and decreased rainfall are leading to forest system collapse, crop failures, and mass fires. Coastal zones of Bangladesh and China are experiencing erosion, salt-water dilution of fresh water supplies, and population dislocation. In the Himalayas, glaciers are melting and high altitude ecosystems collapsing, while, downstream, flooding causes people to move from low-lying areas, increasing population pressures on Indigenous populations.

In Central and South America and the Caribbean, deforestation is widespread from the Amazon basin to the alpine forests of the Andes. Altered weather patterns are disrupting traditional agriculture and threatening food security. Coastal erosion is making areas of many small island developing states uninhabitable, forcing population movement onto scarce land. In the Pacific regions, coastal erosion, high tides, and stormy seas are threatening Tuvalu, the Cook Islands, and Kiribati, and leading to migrations in the Marshall Islands and Papua New Guinea that force traditional owners into conflict with newcomers.

The predicament of Indigenous peoples also stems from adverse factors attributable to the lingering ideology of colonization (Macchi et al., 2008), which denies rights to existence and self-determination. Climate change exacerbates vulnerability to continuing poverty and poor health. Absence of political and economic power limits the ability to defend and assert rights to land, natural resources, and diversified traditional livelihoods in an increasingly cut-throat competitive environment where trade deals seemingly trump the most essential climate agreement ever (Klein, 2014). Restricted access to information and communication technologies further limits the ability to adapt to or mitigate the effects of climate change.

The Right to Participate in Mitigation and Adaptation?

State party signatories to the UNFCCC are committed to formulating and implementing regional mitigation and adaptation programmes. These include irrigation and rainwater catchment, disaster planning, measures to address coastal erosion, and forest management schemes that intrude directly upon Indigenous peoples' existing way of life. Participation, prior informed consent, and consultation rights, as well as recognition of TEK and respect for land and natural resources rights, have long been areas of struggle between states and Indigenous peoples.

Until 2010, state parties to the UNFCCC ignored repeated requests from the International Forum of Indigenous Peoples on Climate Change (IFIPCC) to form an Expert Group on Indigenous People, though Indigenous Peoples Organizations (IPOs) have been allowed to attend and make statements, along with NGOs and industry lobbyists. The posture of states abrogates rights to participation, to prior informed consent, and to consultation, supposedly enshrined in international human rights law. While the UNFCCC and Kyoto Protocol oblige developed states to assist developing countries, these instruments do not yet acknowledge either the situation of Indigenous peoples or the contribution that TEK can make to successful adaptation. Indigenous peoples at present have no formal place in the work of expert bodies that advise the UNFCCC.

The IPCC, which neglected Indigenous people in its analysis of the data or presented them as 'helpless victims of changes beyond their control' (Salick and Byg, 2007), is now acknowledging the importance of TEK in assisting scientists and policy makers, as well as Indigenous and traditional communities, in adapting to climate change (Parry et al., 2007; IPCC, 2014, pp. 20, 29).

In May 2008 the UNPFII held its seventh session on 'Climate change, bio-cultural diversity and livelihoods: The stewardship role of Indigenous peoples and new challenges'. This session repeated the call for better recognition by the UNFCCC, inclusion of Indigenous peoples' issues in the work of the IPCC, and acceptance by states that the Declaration on the Rights of Indigenous Peoples should be the framework for further interaction between states and Indigenous peoples, nationally as well as internationally. Finally, in 2010 at the Cancun conference a subsidiary body of the UNFCCC conference of the parties (COP), the Ad hoc Working Group on Long-term Co-operative Action (AWG-LCA) (UNFCCC, 2010) acknowledged some of the UNPFII's concerns about the exclusion of Indigenous peoples. Recognizing the implications of the UNDRIP (2007), the AWG-LCA has undertaken to seek options for Indigenous participation in mitigation and adaptation schemes and for recognition of the importance of TEK. Whether this undertaking is gestural or authentic is yet to be seen.

A human rights and ecosystem-based approach to the participation of Indigenous peoples in the work of entities such as the UN, the World Bank, and NGOs is critically important as these bodies are designing and implementing global measures for climate change mitigation and adaptation that affect Indigenous people profoundly (Tauli-Corpuz et al, 2009; UNDP/ RIIP, 2010). For instance, under the Kyoto Protocol, three market-based mechanisms for reducing emissions have been introduced. These include 'clean development mechanisms', such as emissions trading and hydropower and dam building. Dams often cause involuntary resettlement that is likely to infringe rights. Indigenous leaders continue to argue that emissions trading is more about the commodification of nature than emissions reduction (Goodman, 2014). An offset industry promotes plantation crops such as oil palms for bio-fuels. Bio-fuel plantations contribute to the deforestation of vast areas of tropical rainforest and the decline in food security and biodiversity, and such plantations infringe Indigenous peoples' rights to forest and land tenure. 'Re-forestation' for voluntary carbon offset businesses in Europe has also infringed Indigenous rights through the forced eviction of peoples from their lands (Tauli-Corpuz and Tamang, 2007).

Meanwhile, high-emitting states such as Canada and the USA are still pursuing 'extreme energy' projects such as hydraulic fracturing or *fracking*, the ecocidal and genocidal tar sands extraction in Northern Alberta, and the associated Keystone XL pipeline initiative, all of which directly impact Indigenous peoples (Huseman and Short, 2012; Gonzalez and Goodman, 2014).

The World Bank's Forest Carbon Partnership Facility (FCPF) is a dominant player in the UN-sponsored emerging carbon market. Notably, the FCPF contributes millions of dollars to the UNFCCC programme of action for Reducing Emissions from Deforestation and Forest Degradation (REDD) (Barnsley, 2009). NGOs suggest that the approach is seriously flawed. Despite recent undertakings to build rights safeguards into the REDD scheme (REDD +), the FCPF neglects the Bank's own policies and obligations regarding respect for the participation, consultation, and informed consent rights of Indigenous peoples (Dooley et al., 2011) and their forest tenure rights (RRI, 2015).

Unfortunately, the reluctance of parties to the UNFCCC and the World Bank to recognize the standing of Indigenous peoples and to allow their active participation and consultation not only robs Indigenous peoples of their rights and increases their vulnerability, but also robs humanity as a whole of the contribution that Indigenous people stand ready to make.

Climate Change and the Human Rights of Persons Affected by Disasters

Because they are among the estimated 200 million people per year affected by so-called 'natural' disasters (many of them related to climate change) (Brookings-Bern Project on Internal Displacement,

---

BOX 19.3 CHALLENGING ASSUMPTIONS: CAN WE ASSUME THAT HUMAN RIGHTS ARE EFFECTIVE MEANS FOR SECURING THE EXISTENCE, SELF-DETERMINATION, AND WELL-BEING OF INDIGENOUS PEOPLES?

Human rights are premised on the 'myth of rights' (Scheingold, 2004). This myth is a dominant narrative in liberal, democratic sovereign states reliant on a capitalist mode of production for profit. This myth makes out that the individual's life, liberty, and private property are dependent on rights. Indigenous people have a very different way of thinking about their own well-being and their interactions with the natural environment. They focus on duties rather than rights, and have group-oriented cultures that assume interconnectedness with nature and all living things. They rely on a kin-based mode of production for sustainable use. Rights-based litigation and politics therefore compel Indigenous peoples to shed their values, customary laws, and governance systems, and to reframe their needs, duties, and entitlements into the language of, and to use the techniques of, their oppressors to produce outcomes often more functional to the latter (Medcalf, 1978; Corntassel, 2008; Borrows, 2010; and see Chapters 6, 7, and 23).

2007), Indigenous peoples are among those most in need of the human rights-based approach to disaster relief that the UN Inter-Agency Standing Committee advocates (Brookings-Bern Project on Internal Displacement, 2008). A human rights-based approach to reducing, mitigating, and adapting to climate change requires putting into practice the principle that all human rights are 'universal, indivisible, interdependent and interrelated' (see Chapter 23).

Basic to existence are rights to life, adequate food, water, health, shelter, and freedom from torture, found in the Universal Declaration on Human Rights and many other UN human rights instruments (Havemann, 2009). International law is weak in articulating an individual right to a healthy planetary ecosystem as a basic right of existence. The Rio Declaration's Principles suggest that rights derive from states' duties—for example: to consider environmental needs of future generations (Principle 3); to conserve, protect, and restore the health of the Earth's ecosystems (Principle 7—echoed in Article 29 of the Indigenous Peoples Rights Declaration); and to take a precautionary approach despite the absence of full scientific certainty where irreversible damage is threatened (Principle 15).

Self-determination is a fundamental dimension of disaster management. The bundle of rights associated with self-determination includes self-government, participation in mitigation planning, and access to information, found in the ILO Convention (No. 169); the UN Declaration on the Rights of Indigenous Peoples, Agenda 21; the Dublin Declaration on Access to Environmental Information; and the Aarhus Convention on Public Participation in Environmental Matters.

Linking rights to existence, self-determination, and individual human rights in an active rights and ecosystems-based approach to climate change will demand unprecedented and hitherto unachieved whole-of-system involvement in recognizing, respecting, and protecting all types of human rights (Tauli-Corpuz et al., 2009). See Box 19.3 for a discussion of whether human rights are effective means for securing the existence, self-determination, and well-being of Indigenous peoples.

KEY POINTS

Scientific evidence shows that Indigenous peoples are among those being hit hardest by climate change.

IPCC research supports the contention of Indigenous peoples that TEK can contribute to mitigation and adaptation measures.

After repeatedly denying requests from the IFIPCC and the UNPFII between 2000 and 2009, UNFCCC agreed in 2010 to recognize Indigenous peoples rights to participation in deliberations about mitigation and adaptation.

Some UN agencies advocate a human rights-based approach to climate change measures, including the use of the UNDRIP as a benchmark for standards.

Critical Thinking Question:

Is climate justice being done for Indigenous peoples?

Reconciling Indigenous Self-Determination with State Sovereignty?

Indigenous peoples conceive their right to existence as indivisible from, interconnected with, and interdependent upon their right to self-determination.

Consequently, Indigenous movements since the last quarter of the twentieth century have pursued self-determination.

Jorge Valadez (2000, pp. 185–234) categorizes three strands within these movements. *Accommodationists* will settle for a degree of self-determination within the structures of the state. **Autonomists** seek self-determination through autonomous institutional arrangements within the state. (The UNDRIP reinforces the legitimacy of rights to autonomous governance (Anaya, 2010)). *Secessionists* seek to form independent states. Among Indigenous peoples, secessionists are a minority. Even so, states have persistently interpreted Indigenous peoples' assertion of rights to self-determination as claims to external self-determination—tantamount to rights of secession. Most states perceive aspirations to self-determination as threats to their territorial integrity and sovereignty.

Many Indigenous leaders accept that the greatest gains are likely if self-determination is delimited as internal—ideally, along lines that 'autonomists' would accept. They recognize that self-determination can be a trap condemning peoples to long conflictual struggles with states (Weller, 2009). Indeed, Indigenous peoples have mostly pursued rights within the state, for instance to their own political–legal institutions, to participate in and be consulted about decisions concerning them, to benefit from sharing, and to give prior informed consent to the implementation of decisions by the state that concern or impact on them. As the country reports of the Special Rapporteur on Indigenous Rights attest, despite UNDRIP, states remain reluctant to respect these rights, even in the context of IGOs such as the UNFCCC that make decisions of direct and mortal relevance to Indigenous people (Special Rapporteur on Indigenous Rights, 2011).

Even recognizing a right to internal quasi-autonomous self-government that is not a claim to statehood presently appears to be beyond the scope of the traditional liberal model of the democratic state (Muehlebach, 2003), which is anchored in the non-Indigenous Westphalian concept of sovereignty (Primeau and Corntassel, 1995; Alfred, 2008; Corntassel, 2008). In such a state, citizenship is universal, equal, and individual. Democracy is majoritarian. There is one law, and one set of rights, for everyone. Introducing separate forms of autonomous self-government for Indigenous peoples challenges this model. States have mostly pursued the assimilation of Indigenous peoples as individual citizens, denying their claims

to group rights and autonomy. Modest exceptions to assimilationist institutions are found in Nordic states (Anaya, 2011b). Developments in Bolivia under its Indigenous president Evo Morales represent a radical attempt to depart from past state practices. There, the state has been redefined as plurinational, reflecting the fact that a large proportion of the population is Indigenous. This project is highly contentious and very much a work in progress (Gustafson, 2009; Webber, 2011). Attempting to counter the impact of untrammelled resource extraction and to reflect Indigenous rights, Bolivia has also enacted law recognizing the Rights of Mother Earth (Pachamama) (Vidal, 2011); fracking is nonetheless taking place (Hill, 2015).

Some liberal theorists and some democratic states do recognize that imposing one model on everyone, regardless of culture or history, may violate liberal values of tolerance and recognition of difference (Taylor, 1994). Furthermore, they accept that principles of good governance such as **inclusiveness, subsidiarity**, and **equivalence** require the authentic involvement of those whose life expectancies—let alone life choices and life chances (Held, 2005, pp. 258–9)—are most affected.

Liberal theorist Will Kymlicka (1995, pp. 6–8, 30–41) suggests a compromise between assimilation and separation, universalism and relativism. He suggests that liberalism requires three kinds of rights to accommodate Indigenous peoples and help them realize equal citizenship through recognition of differences. He proposes rights of self-government over internal affairs based on traditional mechanisms and institutions, such as in the Territory of Nunavut in Canada; polyethnic rights to protecting traditional religious practice, hunting and fishing, and stewardship of land and natural resources, such as some native title rights in Australia; and representation rights that would give groups a voice in state institutions when these deliberate matters directly affect the groups, such as the Saami Parliaments in the Nordic states. Differentiated citizenship can be justified in various contexts and on several grounds: in treaty obligations that bind the state to honour its historical undertakings; in special measures to assist those whose right to existence has been jeopardized by state practices; or, as a means of empowering Indigenous peoples' sustainable self-determination, allowing them to perform duties to the environment for the benefit of nature and all humankind.

The sticking point for liberal democratic states in recognizing differentiated citizenship arises when apparently universal, individual citizenship rights appear to be abrogated by the exercise of Indigenous self-government powers (Badger, 2011)—for example through rules discriminating against women or confining membership of the polity to descendants of a set of ancestors (Gover, 2010). For a state to condone a denial of the rights of a citizen would be to fail in the duty to protect and promote the human rights of all citizens equally. This would imply that citizenship rights are not universal but depend on one's identity or status—totally contradicting the idea of citizenship and the principle that human rights are interconnected, interrelated, and indivisible.

Seyla Benhabib (2002, pp. 18–19, 147–8) suggests that a resolution to the universalist versus relativist conundrum posed by differentiated citizenship could be guided by principles that protect the individual's rights from being sacrificed for the sake of the group without denying the right of the group to exist and govern itself within these limits. These principles recognize that state power should be shared by all, that minorities should not have fewer rights than the majority, that group membership must be voluntary and not imposed, and that group members should have a meaningful right of exit from the group (see also Chapter 2).

Another challenge—apparent in connection with issues such as climate change—is that the world increasingly has to be understood as a single place for governance purposes (Rosenau, 1997). Yet intensified globalization processes correlate with intensified secessionist pressures on states (Hechter, 2000) by peoples without states (Guibernau, 1999), such as Indigenous peoples.

> ## KEY POINTS
>
> Indigenous peoples conceive the right to existence as indivisible from, interconnected with, and interdependent upon their right to self-determination.
>
> States ascribe secessionist motives to Indigenous peoples' claims to self-determination.
>
> The accommodation of Indigenous peoples' self-determination with state sovereignty is possible when states recognize that internal self-determination is compatible with, as well as necessary for, good governance.
>
> Good governance requires the adoption of basic principles such as inclusiveness, subsidiarity, and equivalence to accommodate the rights and needs of distinct communities to differentiated citizenship within the state.
>
> ### Critical Thinking Question:
>
> Ought an Indigenous person to abandon explicit claims to self-determination despite having a right to them?

Conclusion

Much of the explanation for ambivalence about the rights of Indigenous peoples lies in the politics and economics of colonialism. Profit in the context of international competition depends on access to territory, raw materials, and cheap labour at the lowest compliance, and monetary costs. Even partial recognition of Indigenous peoples rights would have raised the cost and stalled the pace of growth. The neoliberal ideology driving much of globalization today perceives the same problem and overcomes it in much the same way, but with increasingly obvious ecocidal results (Havemann, 2005; Klein, 2014).

The Law of Nations, constituted from the coalescence of Euro-American, Judaeo-Christian, liberal legal, and capitalist ideologies, has rationalized, justified, and regulated territorial acquisition. Differences between Indigenous peoples and settlers (such as not being Christian, or farmers, or gardeners, and not having a European-style political society, or economy, or concept of individual private property) were used to justify the denial of recognition of legal personality to Indigenous peoples. This denial prevented Indigenous peoples from exercising or enjoying sovereignty and self-determination, as well as many other individual and group human rights associated with the right to existence. Despite the rhetoric of today's international law, for Indigenous peoples, deep ambivalence concerning the recognition of these rights remains evident at both national and international levels.

States and IGOs must work towards models of governance that provide both for Indigenous peoples rights to participation in the global arena and for the right to self-determination within the state. State recognition of Indigenous peoples rights in these ways is an expression of state sovereignty and not a restriction upon it, and ensures that local as well as global governance is inclusive, not exclusive, of those whose life choices and life chances are most affected by decisions.

QUESTIONS

Individual Study Questions

1. Are individual rights a necessary and sufficient type of right for the protection of Indigenous peoples' human rights?

2. How are Indigenous peoples officially distinguishable from minorities?

3. How is the crime of genocide defined? Why is it linked to the right to existence?

4. What is meant by the doctrine of discovery/occupation?

5. Why is the recognition of Indigenous peoples rights seemingly incompatible with governance principles of liberal sovereign states and capitalist economies?

6. Compare sovereignty with Indigenous sustainable self-determination.

7. How does traditional environmental knowledge (TEK) contribute to climate change adaptation?

8. Why are Indigenous peoples particularly vulnerable to climate change?

Group Discussion Questions

1. Debate the Indigenous case for, and the state case against, self-determination for Indigenous peoples.

2. Evaluate Indigenous people's claim that they ought to have a distinct place in climate change governance processes.

FURTHER READING

Allen, S. and **Xanthaki, A.** (eds) (2010). *Reflections on the UN Declaration on the Rights of Indigenous Peoples* (Studies in International Law). Oxford: Hart Publishing.

This is a collection of chapters by key players in the development of the Declaration. They offer a regional analysis of the possible reception of the Declaration and predict its future impact on state and IGO practice.

Anaya, S. J. (2004). *Indigenous Peoples in International Law* (2nd edn). Oxford: Oxford University Press.

The former UN Special Rapporteur on Indigenous rights offers a detailed historical overview of the emergence of Indigenous peoples rights, including an analysis of the right to self-determination and its changing meaning and attributes in the late twentieth century.

Kymlicka, W. (1995). *Multicultural Citizenship: A Liberal Theory of Minority Rights*. Oxford: Oxford University Press.

Kymlicka evaluates how the rights and status of minority cultures, such as Indigenous peoples, can be accommodated within liberal democracies. He argues that certain collective rights of minority cultures are consistent with liberal democratic principles, and that standard liberal objections to such rights can be answered.

Silverman, A. (2014). *Know Your Rights Related to REDD+: A Guide for Indigenous and Local Community Leaders*. Washington, DC: Tebtebba & Centre for International Environmental Law. http://theredddesk.org/resources/know-your-rights-related-redd-guide-indigenous-and-local-community-leaders

Silverman outlines which human rights are relevant to the struggles of Indigenous peoples in combating and negotiating Reducing Emissions from Deforestation and Forest Degradation (UN REDD+). REDD+ is market-based adaptation measures. REDD+ projects often involve land grabbing, loss of access, denial of tenure, relocation, and other threats to Indigenous and other forest peoples.

Tobin, B. (2014). *Indigenous Peoples, Customary Law and Human Rights: Why Living Law Matters*. London: Earthscan/Routledge.

Tobin links Indigenous human rights, self-determination, and customary law. He explains why recognition of Indigenous customary living law is intrinsic to governance based on principles of social justice and cultural equity in relation to land, resources, and cultural heritage, and other group and individual rights.

WEB LINKS

http://social.un.org/index/IndigenousPeoples.aspx   UN Permanent Forum on Indigenous Issues (PFII).

http://www.rightsandresources.org/   Rights and Resources Initiative (RRI) is an NGO, based in Washington, DC, that supports the developing world's Indigenous peoples and local communities in forests and other rural areas, helping them to secure and realize the rights to own, control, and benefit from the natural resources.

http://www.tebtebba.org   Website of Tebtebba Foundation (Indigenous Peoples' International Centre for Policy Research and Education): a Philippines-based Indigenous peoples' NGO advocating that the rights of Indigenous peoples are recognized, respected, and protected worldwide.

http://www.ohchr.org/EN/Issues/IPeoples/SRIndigenousPeoples/Pages/SRIPeoplesIndex.aspx   Special Rapporteur on the rights of Indigenous peoples in the Office of the UN High Commissioner for Human Rights. The Rapporteur conducts detailed and critical studies of the way Indigenous peoples' human rights are respected worldwide.

http://www.forestpeoples.org   Forest Peoples Programme (FPP) is a UK-based NGO whose mission is to bridge the gap between policy makers and forest peoples through advocacy, practical projects, and capacity building and research.

NOTES

1.   For brevity, the phrase 'Indigenous peoples rights' (with no apostrophe) refers to both Indigenous people's rights as individuals and Indigenous peoples' rights as groups—though most of this chapter concerns their group rights.

2.   For instance, the Dominion of South Africa's mandate in German Southwest Africa.

3.   *Chief Bernard Ominayak and the Lubicon Lake Band* v. *Canada* (Communication No. 167/1984). Views adopted 26 March 1990. Report of the Human Rights Committee, GAOR, 38th Session. Suppl. No. 40(A/38/40), 1–30.

Visit the Online Resource Centre that accompanies this book for updates and a range of other resources: www.oxfordtextbooks.co.uk/orc/goodhart3e/

20

Genocide and Human Rights

Scott Straus

Chapter Contents

Reader's Guide

Genocide is one of the most extreme forms of human rights violations and the subject of an early human rights treaty. However, the definition of genocide is contested, and the treaty's promise of prevention oversells the actual international mechanisms put in place to stop genocide. In recent years, there have been moves to relabel the field as one of 'atrocity' or 'mass atrocity' prevention, and there have been new efforts to develop a better policy on prevention. This chapter examines different definitions of genocide as well as some of the treaty's weak points, and outlines the major developments in recent years. Also explored in the chapter are theories of why genocide occurs. The chapter ends with case studies of Rwanda and Darfur. These case studies describe the background to the mass violence in both locations, as well as the international responses; the case studies also illustrate the conceptual and theoretical points raised earlier in the chapter.

Introduction

The problem of **genocide** has been and remains one of the most acute in the realm of international human rights. Frequently recognized as the 'crime of crimes' and one of the most extreme forms of human rights violation, genocide is the subject of an early and theoretically powerful treaty, the 1948 United Nations **Convention on the Punishment and Prevention of the Crime of Genocide** (Genocide Convention). The treaty obligates state parties to 'punish' and to 'prevent' genocide where it occurs. In recent years, international actors have intensified efforts to punish genocide perpetrators through international criminal justice mechanisms. Nonetheless, despite widespread ratification and recent developments, the overall record on genocide prevention during the past sixty-plus years has been dismal.

This chapter presents an overview of major topics in the scholarship on genocide. The first section focuses on the origins of the concept of genocide. The section introduces Raphael Lemkin, who coined the term in 1944, and subsequently became a leading advocate for an international treaty on the punishment and prevention of genocide. The section in turn discusses the resulting treaty, the Genocide Convention. Finally, the section presents some controversies and disagreements on how genocide is defined, some of which have spurred advocates to relabel the field as one of atrocity prevention. In the second section, the chapter focuses on social scientific theories of why genocide occurs. The section discusses both classic theories of genocide, as well as more recent scholarship. The third section focuses on two contemporary cases, Rwanda and Darfur. The section presents empirical overviews of the cases, historical background, and summaries of

the international response. The section also links the case studies to the conceptual and theoretical material introduced in the first two sections.

The Origins of the Concept of 'Genocide'

Raphael Lemkin and the Origins of Genocide

Few major human rights concepts have as clear a point of origin as the concept of genocide does (Courthoys and Docker, 2008). Although the Holocaust during the Second World War prodded the international community to recognize and pledge to prevent genocide, the term itself was coined by Raphael Lemkin, a Polish international lawyer (see Box 20.1). It combines the Greek 'genos' (meaning race, nation, or tribe) and the Latin 'cide' for 'killing'.

In his 1944 book and subsequent writings, Lemkin argued that the main idea of genocide was the destruction of human groups, specifically nations and ethnic groups (Lemkin, 1944, p. 79; 1947, p. 147). More specifically, Lemkin (1944, p. 79) defined genocide as 'a coordinated plan of different actions aiming at the destruction of the essential foundations of the life of national groups, with the aim of annihilating the groups themselves'. These statements form the core of the common notion of genocide as group annihilation. The contemporary Oxford English Dictionary, for example, defines genocide as 'The deliberate and systematic extermination of a national or ethnic group'.

Substantively, a key dimension of genocide is that the intent of the violence is to destroy groups.

BOX 20.1 RAPHAEL LEMKIN: A SHORT BIOGRAPHY

Prior to the Second World War, Raphael Lemkin, a Polish Jew and jurist, had been attracted to legal constructs as a way of protecting civilian social groups against mass violence. As a young legal scholar, Lemkin proposed the term 'barbarity' to outlaw the premeditated destruction of specific population categories. However, his proposal never gained much traction and effectively died before the outbreak of war. During the Holocaust, Lemkin's family was decimated, but he managed to survive by fleeing Poland in 1940. Lemkin eventually landed in the United States, where he first worked as a law professor at

Duke University, and later as an adviser to the US War Department. During the war, Lemkin amassed a collection of information about policy in Nazi-occupied territory and subsequently published a book on the topic. That book, *Axis Rule in Occupied Europe*, not only catalogued Nazi practices, but also coined the term 'genocide' to refer to the atrocities. Having given the crime a name, Lemkin did all he could to use the law to prevent and punish genocide.

(Power, 2002)

What distinguishes genocide from other crimes is the focus on group destruction; even though individuals suffer violence, genocide is defined by this special intent or purpose of annihilating groups. In Lemkin's words, 'The acts are directed against groups, as such, and individuals are selected for destruction only because they belong to these groups' (Lemkin, 1947, p. 147).

For Lemkin, genocide entailed not only killing, but also a range of different activities that prevented or substantially endangered the life of groups. That is, genocide included not just murder, but acts that destroyed the social, economic, cultural, religious, and moral foundations of a group. In his original formulation, Lemkin listed acts of genocide ranging from forced sterilization, abortion, artificial infection, deliberate separation of families, as well as replacing one nation's institutions with those of another nation (Lemkin, 1944). Genocide, Lemkin wrote, consisted of two phases: destroying a group and imposing the 'national pattern of the oppressor' (Lemkin, 1944, p. 79).

Genocide in International Law

Having coined the term, Lemkin worked tirelessly to promote it. The first official use of the term came in the indictments of twenty-four Nazi officials by the International Military Tribunal (IMT) at Nuremberg (the **Nuremberg Tribunal**). The IMT charged the Nazi defendants with crimes against peace, crimes against humanity, and war crimes; under the latter, the tribunal alleged that the defendants had 'conducted deliberate and systematic genocide, viz. the extermination of racial and national groups, against the civilian populations of certain occupied territories' (International Military Tribunal at Nuremberg, 1946, Section VIII A). However, the ultimate judgment from the IMT did not make reference to genocide.

The next major development was a 1946 Resolution from the United Nations General Assembly—a resolution that was indebted to Lemkin's lobbying effort. The resolution formally recognized genocide as a crime under international law and called for a draft convention on the prevention and punishment of genocide. The drafting process began about a year later, and, in a series of sessions, different state representatives debated exactly how genocide would be defined and incorporated into treaty form. The net result was the Genocide Convention, which the General Assembly adopted on 9 December 1948—a day before endorsing the **Universal Declaration of Human Rights**.

The topics of debate in the drafting process are instructive. Most famously, the Soviet Union objected to 'political groups' being included as a protected category. The Soviets worried that Communist policies could fall under the Convention if political groups were protected (L. Kuper, 1981). Lemkin similarly argued that political groups did not have the same permanency as racial, national, and ethnic groups (Schabas, 2000). For its part, the USA opposed a statement on 'cultural genocide' in the Convention—a position Lemkin opposed. Other debates focused on the place of intentionality, whether a group could suffer 'partial' destruction, how genocide related to **crimes against humanity**, how parties to the Convention should respond to genocide where it occurred, and how genocide should be prosecuted (Schabas, 2000). The debates were prescient: each of these issues in the nearly seventy years since the Convention was drafted has proven complex and at times confusing.

In the end, the drafters defined genocide as the 'intent to destroy, in whole or in part, a national, ethnical, racial or religious group, as such' (see Box 20.2). The definition's key dimensions are as follows:

1. There must be *intent* to destroy a group as such; in other words, to demonstrate genocide a deliberate, usually planned, campaign of violence with the express purpose of destroying a protected group must be in evidence.

2. Only national, ethnical, racial, or religious groups are protected—political, disabled, regional, gender, and other conceivable groups are not explicitly protected.

3. Genocide may be constituted by 'partial' destruction of a group, which courts have subsequently interpreted to mean that a 'substantial' part of the group must be destroyed.

No genocide ever succeeds in total extermination; at the same time, the standard for determining when 'substantial' group destruction indicates intent to destroy a group is murky.

In Article II, the treaty lists a number of different methods of genocide. These include killing, causing serious physical or mental harm, inflicting 'conditions of life calculated to bring about its physical destruction in whole or in part', preventing birth, and transferring children (see Box 20.2). Several ideas resonate with Lemkin's notion that genocide may take the form of preventing the reproduction of a group; however, the methods are indirect, making proof of the special intent to destroy groups difficult.

On the question of prevention, Article I of the Genocide Convention holds that contracting parties 'undertake to prevent' genocide. However, what 'undertaking to prevent' means is unclear, and the matter received comparatively little attention in the drafting process (Schabas, 2000). Article VIII holds that parties 'may call upon the competent organs' of the United Nations to take action under the Charter to prevent and suppress acts of genocide (see Box 20.2). In short, the treaty language implies that states may intervene, perhaps against the wishes of a sovereign state, to stop genocide. Many have interpreted the Convention this way. However, in reality the treaty language is fairly vague and weak as to specific mechanisms, policies, and procedures that states must take to prevent genocide. The example of Darfur is a case in point, as we will discuss.

By contrast, the Convention has considerably more on punishment. The treaty lists five specific charges and conditions for extradition. The law additionally states: that individuals may be punished whether or not they are public officials; that contracting parties must enact legislation outlawing genocide; and that persons charged with genocide must be tried by a domestic or international court. In recent years—more specifically, with regard to the crises in the former Yugoslavia, Rwanda, and Sudan—the Genocide Convention's punishment provisions have proven more

---

BOX 20.2 THE UNITED NATIONS GENOCIDE CONVENTION (SELECTED ARTICLES)

The Contracting Parties

Having considered the declaration made by the General Assembly of the United Nations in its resolution 96 (I) dated 11 December 1946 that genocide is a crime under international law, contrary to the spirit and aims of the United Nations and condemned by the civilized world;
Recognizing that at all periods of history genocide has inflicted great losses on humanity; and
Being convinced that, in order to liberate mankind from such an odious scourge, international co-operation is required,

Hereby agree as hereinafter provided

Article I

The Contracting Parties confirm that genocide, whether committed in time of peace or in time of war, is a crime under international law which they undertake to prevent and to punish.

Article II

In the present Convention, genocide means any of the following acts committed with intent to destroy, in whole or in part, a national, ethnical, racial or religious group, as such:

a. Killing members of the group;
b. Causing serious bodily or mental harm to members of the group;
c. Deliberately inflicting on the group conditions of life calculated to bring about its physical destruction in whole or in part;

d. Imposing measures intended to prevent births within the group;
e. Forcibly transferring children of the group to another group.

Article III

The following acts shall be punishable:

a. Genocide;
b. Conspiracy to commit genocide;
c. Direct and public incitement to commit genocide;
d. Attempt to commit genocide;
e. Complicity in genocide.

Article IV

Persons committing genocide or any of the other acts enumerated in article 3 shall be punished, whether they are constitutionally responsible rulers, public officials or private individuals.

Article VIII

Any Contracting Party may call upon the competent organs of the United Nations to take such action under the Charter of the United Nations as they consider appropriate for the prevention and suppression of acts of genocide or any of the other acts enumerated in article III.

effective than those on prevention. That reality is consistent with a general strengthening of international judicial mechanisms for the criminal punishment of mass violations of human rights. Today there are international or hybrid domestic–international courts for crimes committed in the former Yugoslavia, Rwanda, Cambodia, and Sierra Leone. The **International Criminal Court** has also come into existence in the past couple of decades. Nonetheless, embedded in the language of the 1948 Genocide Convention is clearly more specific language on punishment than on prevention.

The Genocide Convention came into force in January 1951. Today the treaty has 146 state parties and wide regional endorsement. Among the first states to ratify were Australia, Bulgaria, Cambodia, Costa Rica, Ecuador, El Salvador, Ethiopia, France, Guatemala, Iceland, Israel, Jordan, Laos, Liberia, Monaco, Panama, the Philippines, Korea, Saudi Arabia, Sri Lanka, and Turkey. The United States was one of the first to sign the treaty—President Truman's administration did so only two days after the General Assembly adopted the Convention. However, the treaty ran into a phalanx of opposition when the Senate considered ratification. The American Bar Association took aim at the ambiguities in the Convention: in particular, the potentially low threshold of 'causing mental harm' and the notion of group destruction 'in part'. Southern Senators, in particular, opposed ratification, worrying that discriminatory laws against African Americans could constitute genocide under the Convention. The treaty died in the Senate until William Proxmire (Wisconsin, D) took it up as a personal cause, making thousands of speeches on the Convention. Eventually, a controversy during Ronald Reagan's second term, in which the president visited a German cemetery where SS

officials had been buried, triggered a process that ultimately led to US ratification in 1988 (Power, 2002).

Enduring Controversies in the Definition of Genocide

The Genocide Convention is the first binding international human rights treaty to emerge from the post-War United Nations system. The law is theoretically one of the most powerful in its obligation to punish and prevent genocide where it occurs, and the treaty itself is testament to a rhetorical commitment to end one of the worst forms of human rights violation. Nonetheless, embedded in the concept of genocide and the Convention are issues that limit the power of the innovation. In particular, genocide is a contested concept with important ambiguities around the types of groups protected, the extent and means of violence that would constitute genocide, and the difficulty in demonstrating intent. Since the Convention, there have been numerous attempts to redefine genocide (Straus, 2001).

To account for the ambiguities, scholars have proposed other terms, such as *politicide* (the systematic destruction of political groups; Harff, 2003), *democide* (mass killings by governments; Rummel, 1994), and *mass killing* (the intentional killing of more than 50,000 civilians in a five-year period; Valentino, 2004). The net impact is that in the literature there is neither a set definition of genocide nor a settled list of cases. The literature veers between narrower definitions of genocide (as the extermination of racial, ethnic, or religious groups) and broader definitions (intentional mass killing on the basis of group membership). The differences in definitions have important consequences for what is counted as 'genocide' or a related term (see Table 20.1).

Table 20.1 Genocide cases in the twentieth century

Manus Midlarsky	Barbara Harff
The Killing Trap: Genocide in the Twentieth Century (2005, p. 23)	'No Lessons Learned from the Holocaust? Assessing Risks of Genocide and Political Mass Murder Since 1955' (2003, p. 60)
Narrow definition of genocide	Broad definition of genocide and politicide
Three genocide cases in twentieth century:	1955–97 cases include:
Armenian Genocide, 1915–16	Sudan, 1956–72
The Holocaust, 1941–5	China, 1959

Table 20.1 *(continued)*

Manus Midlarsky	Barbara Harff
The Rwandan Genocide, 1994	Algeria, 1962
	Iraq, 1963–75
	Rwanda, 1963–4
	Congo-Kinshasa, 1964–5
	Burundi, 1965–73
	Indonesia, 1965–6
	South Vietnam, 1965–75
	China, 1966–75
	Pakistan, 1971
	Philippines, 1972–6
	Uganda, 1972–9
	Chile, 1973–6
	Pakistan, 1973–7
	Angola, 1975–2001
	Cambodia, 1975–9
	Indonesia, 1975–92
	Argentina, 1976–80
	Ethiopia, 1976–9
	Congo–Kinshasa, 1977–9
	Afghanistan, 1978–92
	Burma, 1978
	Guatemala, 1978–96
	El Salvador, 1980–9
	Uganda, 1980–6
	Iran, 1981–92
	Syria, 1981–2
	Sudan, 1983–2001
	Burundi, 1988
	Iraq, 1988–91
	Somalia, 1988–91
	Sri Lanka, 1989–90
	Bosnia, 1992–5
	Burundi, 1993–4
	Rwanda, 1994
	Serbia, 1998–9

Moreover, despite the rhetorical international commitment to prevention and 'never again' to allow genocide to occur, the key international treaty lacks clear and specific enforcement mechanisms that could trigger collective action to stop genocide. The conceptual openness and the status of genocide as the crime of crimes ironically make the genocide label one that is attractive to diverse actors, who use the term to grab attention to their case. At the same time, the conceptual ambiguities and weak enforcement provisions make debates about whether acts constitute 'genocide' frequently irresolvable and often without dramatic practical consequences.

In recent years, some scholars and policy makers have advocated for developing a broader standard than genocide. One argument is that genocide is a specific type of large-scale violence against civilians—the attempted destruction of certain kinds of groups—but there are other types of mass violence that international actors should seek to prevent. This might include large-scale attacks against civilian populations but not necessarily attacks directed against groups. Another argument is that by the time a genocide determination can be made—that is, by the time the intent to destroy a group becomes clear—the violence has already been under way for some time. Some have argued that

the standard for responding to the situations should be broader so as to engage on policy at an earlier time. Lastly, given some of the weaknesses with the Genocide Convention and with the conceptual ambiguities around genocide, insisting on that term as the only one that would garner action is a weak policy strategy.

The most common alternative to genocide in the policy-making community is 'atrocities' or 'mass atrocities'. For example, in 2011, US President Barack Obama issued Presidential Studies Directive 10, which declared genocide and atrocity prevention to be in the national interests of the United States. The President later established an interagency Atrocities Prevention Board. The question then becomes what atrocities or mass atrocities are. In general, within the United Nations system and in much of the policy-making community, the answer usually refers to the crimes that are associated with the Responsibility to Protect and with the Rome Statute, which established the International Criminal Court (see Chapters 3, 4, and 21). In other words, atrocity prevention would include not just focusing on preventing genocide but also on preventing crimes against humanity, war crimes, and ethnic cleansing. Some critics worry that such a standard is too broad (see Box 20.3).

BOX 20.3 CHALLENGING ASSUMPTIONS: IS 'GENOCIDE' A RESTRICTED TERM?

Some scholars and practitioners have moved away from 'genocide' as the sole standard for seeking to prevent large-scale massacres against civilians. For them, the focus on genocide is too limiting. Genocide is restricted to the destruction of groups; in international law, genocide is restricted to the four protected groups listed in the Convention. Yet terrible, large-scale violence may take place that is not necessarily directed at groups but still results in massive human suffering. Genocide also requires the establishment of intent on the part of perpetrators. However, once such intent is manifest, the violence is often at a late stage, which undercuts any international effort to save civilian lives. Lastly, the Genocide Convention is not as powerful as some hoped it would be, so insisting on using the concept, with all its ambiguities, is counterproductive. On the other hand, some insist on the importance of the label. Genocide has name recognition, and usage of the term captures international attention in ways that alternatives do not. Moreover, the term is

associated with the Holocaust, on which there is broad international consensus.

Many scholars and practitioners consider alternative standards. The most common substitute is 'atrocities' or 'mass atrocities', by which practitioners often mean crimes against humanity, ethnic cleansing, and war crimes, in addition to genocide. Yet the conceptual boundaries of these three additional categories of crime can be fuzzy. War crimes and crimes against humanity include many different types of violence, and they do not necessarily imply the scale that genocide or ethnic cleansing do. Ethnic cleansing, for its part, does not have a definition in international law, even though elements of it can be construed as crimes against humanity. Moreover, a lower threshold for atrocity prevention that includes crimes against humanity and war crimes might lead policy makers to dilute their focus. The question thus remains: if genocide is too narrow a standard, what should the alternative be?

been a surge of research on genocide since the early 1990s.

Genocide is a big outcome and a quite complex phenomenon. Genocide involves multiple social dimensions and sometimes lasts many years. Different aspects of state and government frequently play a part, including—in different cases—the political elite, the military, a state-backed militia, the police, and administrative institutions. Private actors in the media and business are also often part of how genocide is perpetrated. On the victim side, genocide usually entails the loss of hundreds of thousands, if not millions, of lives, and how groups are targeted and how they survive are complicated stories. The literature on particular cases or on genocide in general reflects the macro-nature of genocide, as well as the diversity of topics that can be examined.

In this section, the focus is on studies that seek to explain the root causes of genocide. Broadly speaking, such studies emphasize either the macro-level conditions that shape why genocide occurs or micro-level dynamics that prompt individuals at the local level to perpetrate atrocity. Social scientists in various disciplines—anthropology, history, psychology, political science, and sociology—have addressed both sets of questions. For brevity's sake, the concentration here is on macro-level explanations.

Theories of Genocide

If one major question concerns the definition of genocide in and outside law, a separate major area of focus is explaining why genocide occurs. For many years, that question was marginal to the social sciences—for at least three reasons. First, some objected to the notion that genocide could be explained. To some, genocide is unimaginable violence; moreover, explaining genocide risks rationalizing it. Second, until the 1990s, the principal reference point for discussing genocide was the Holocaust, and to some that case was unique in the extent and method of violence. Comparison was thus discouraged. Third, genocide was not a matter for considerable discussion in the public domain. The key turning point was the mid-1990s—in particular, with the mass violence in the former Yugoslavia and Rwanda. Genocide became a matter of pressing concern as well as a political phenomenon that could and should be explained like other social outcomes. As a result, after a period of slow development, there has

Classic Theories of Genocide

The early scholarship on macro-level causes of genocide reflects three main lines of analysis, each importantly influenced by understandings of the Holocaust. One set of arguments focuses on inter-group antipathy. At the most general level, the insight is that genocide is more likely to occur in societies that exhibit deep misgivings between ethnic, racial, or religious groups. In one of the first formulations, Leo Kuper argued that the root of genocide is a divided society, one in which there are 'persistent and pervasive cleavages' between different groups, often created by colonial rule (L. Kuper, 1981, p. 57). In the extreme, deep divisions take the form of stratified, unequal groups where one group dominates another. Kuper argued that different genocides had different processes—some were more, some less organized—though all involved the state. Another constant was the dehumanization of the other (L. Kuper, 1981).

Kuper, a political scientist, is recognized as a pioneer of genocide studies. Another pioneer is sociologist

Helen Fein. In a 1979 book, as well as in subsequent publications, Fein contends that a precondition for genocide is a form of prejudice and dehumanization—namely, that a perpetrator group defines a victim group as 'outside the universe of obligation' (Fein, 1979, p. 9). The 1979 book is based on an innovative study of Jewish victimization rates in different countries during the Second World War; in the book, she proposes a four-part hypothesis. In addition to dehumanization, she argues that state decline, ideologies of group domination, and war all matter for shaping the calculus of genocide (Fein, 1979).

A second stream of argumentation pivots less on inter-group antipathy and more on state power and authoritarianism. Two theorists stand out here. The first is Irving Louis Horowitz, who in 1976 published *Genocide: State Power and Mass Murder*. Horowitz argued that genocide is connected to the absolute concentration of power. Genocide, Horowitz claims, is the 'operational handmaiden of a particular social system, the totalitarian system' (Horowitz, 1997, p. 36). The second author of note is Rudolph Rummel, who claims that 'absolute power kills absolutely' (Rummel, 1994, p. 19). For both Horowitz and Rummel, the institutionalization of democracy is the best bulwark against genocide. In Rummel's language, limits and restraints on power diminish the likelihood of democide.

A third stream of argumentation focuses on hardship and crisis. The causal logic here is that in the context of widespread social deprivation and deep social crisis—economic depression, starvation, war, even rapid social change and revolution—groups blame other groups for their suffering: they scapegoat. The argument is especially well articulated in the work of psychologist Ervin Staub. Staub claims that, in the context of 'difficult life conditions', human beings feel threatened and frustrated, which in turn gives rise to a feeling of hostility and a desire to blame others for their troubles. That desire to find an outlet for the anger is channelled through existing cultures: in particular, where certain groups are denigrated or where there exists a culture of obedience. The result can be genocide (Staub, 1989).

In many respects, these three streams of analysis—on inter-group antipathy, regime type, and widespread hardship—formed the core of a 'first generation' of macro-level analysis of the causes of genocide. To be sure, other influential research was conducted (e.g. Melson, 1992), but the three identified approaches were especially prominent.

Recent Theories of Genocide

In recent years, there has been a new surge of comparative research on genocide. The impetus was primarily the high-profile cases of the 1990s: in particular, the former Yugoslavia and Rwanda. As these cases captured scholars' attention, comparative social scientists began to ask what the cases had in common with historical cases of genocide. The result is a newly energized field of inquiry (Bloxham and Moses, 2010; Straus, 2007). The new research on genocide is diverse. Some is **quantitative** (Harff, 2003; Valentino, Huth, and Balch-Lindsay, 2004). The majority, however, is **qualitative**—country-case comparisons of different episodes of genocide in different regions of the world. The new work is exciting, broad, and rapidly expanding. To summarize the emerging scholarship, this section focuses on three emerging lines of argument and emphasis.

The first argues that *ideology* is in some way the root of genocide. To be sure, the importance of ideas was present in the earlier studies of genocide, but in the new wave of literature, ideology receives a new primacy and articulation. Historian Eric Weitz, for example, claims that genocide emerges from quests to achieve utopia. When leaders seek transcendence for their societies based on racial or nationalist ideals, Weitz argues, the idea of eliminating categories of people becomes thinkable (Weitz, 2003). In a similar vein, French political scientist Jacques Sémelin argues that quests to achieve purity in the context of acute crisis constitute the main origins of genocide (Sémelin, 2007). In a sweeping study of genocide through time, historian Ben Kiernan argues that there are several ideological pathways to genocide, including ideologies based on race or religion, agrarian romanticism, cults of past glory, and fears of biological contamination (Kiernan, 2007).

The second line of argument focuses on the strategic aims of leaders and state interests. The claim is most clearly articulated in the work of political scientist Benjamin Valentino (2004). He argues that leaders engage in mass killing and genocide when they believe that doing so is the best available means to achieve their most cherished political and military goals. Valentino identifies several principal scenarios in which elites will engage in mass killing and genocide: in particular, in the contexts of guerrilla war, Communist revolution, and ethnic conflict. A key insight for Valentino is that leaders who commit mass killing and genocide make calculated decisions; genocide is not the product of totalitarianism per se, deep social hatred, or even widespread deprivation. Fellow political scientist Manus Midlarsky similarly claims that leaders choose genocide from a decision-making calculus. But Midlarsky argues that the decision is less rational, more a product of 'imprudent' thinking after a state has lost territory in a war. Midlarsky also points to the importance of international allies who create a permissive environment for genocide to happen (Midlarsky, 2005).

The third major recent approach is to situate the genocide in the context of long-term political development. Two exemplars of this approach are sociologist Michael Mann and historian Mark Levene. Mann directly challenges the claim that genocide is the product of authoritarianism; rather, he argues that genocide is a perversion of democratic ideals. The key for Mann is organic nationalism—the idea that a state belongs to a core ethnic group. Mann contends that this idea is rooted in a democratic quest to establish a state in the name of the people. Organic nationalism arises when 'the people' is conceptualized as an ethnic group (Mann, 2005). Levene focuses more on the development of the modern nation state. Genocide, Levene argues, is rooted in the ways in which a modern state monopolizes violence, homogenizes populations, and aggregates power (Levene, 2005).

The above discussion of the determinants of genocide is not meant to be comprehensive, but rather indicative of some major ways of approaching the subject from a social scientific perspective. Two points should be especially clear. First, the literature is rich with different ideas about the causes of genocide. If micro-level theories and other theories were added to the mix, the literature on causes would appear even more diverse. Second, there is relatively little consensus on the determinants of genocide. Different scholars emphasize inter-group animosity, authoritarianism, deprivation, ideology, strategic objectives, and the historical development of nationalism and nation states. Theoretical consensus about the determinants of large-scale political and social phenomena eludes many topics. The field of genocide studies may have specific reasons for the lack of theoretical convergence (Straus, 2007). Nonetheless, given the importance of the outcome, the topic of what causes genocide is likely to remain a lively field of inquiry in years to come (see Box 20.4).

> **KEY POINTS**
>
> Since the 1990s, there has been a surge of scholarship on genocide.
>
> Classic theories of genocide emphasize inter-group antipathy, authoritarianism, and hardship.
>
> More recent theories emphasize ideology, strategic calculations and state interest, and political development.
>
> The literature lacks consensus on the primary causes of genocide.
>
> **Critical Thinking Questions:**
>
> Are the causes of genocide likely to be different from the causes of other types of atrocities?
>
> Can genocide be explained? By explaining such violence, are outsiders excusing it?

Case Studies: Rwanda and Darfur

Having addressed the history of the concept of genocide and macro-level theories of genocide, the chapter now turns to two cases to illustrate some of the points. In particular, the chapter focuses on the mass violence in Rwanda in 1994 and in Darfur from 2003 to 2006. Genocide occurs in all regions—indeed, the most famous case (the Holocaust) was in Europe, as was Bosnia in the mid-1990s, which some argue was a case of genocide. In Asia, genocide arguably occurred in Cambodia under Pol Pot during the late 1970s, and in Latin America some scholars argue that genocide occurred in Guatemala in the 1970s and 1980s (Sanford, 2008). Depending on one's definition, some argue that genocide took place in Indonesia, East Timor, Bangladesh, Nigeria, and Burundi, among other countries. In recent years, the large-scale violence in Syria as well as in Iraq—by both state actors and non-state actors—has earned significant attention. The Africa focus here is not to suggest that the continent is uniquely prone to genocide and mass atrocity. Rather, the focus on these two cases is because Rwanda and Darfur have received considerable scholarly attention in the past two decades, and because they are also critically important human rights cases not covered extensively elsewhere in this volume.

Systemic forms of deprivation and disenfranchisement arguably should be considered genocide. This raises the question: what counts, or should count, as genocide? Is colonialism therefore a form of genocide? Some argue that some forms of colonialism entailed the systematic destruction of Indigenous populations and Indigenous cultures. In the international legal definition of genocide, 'cultural destruction' is not genocide. Yet for many, colonialism was fundamentally about the destruction of group-specific ways of inhabiting the world, which is akin to genocide. In some cases, colonialism led to the wholesale destruction of native populations. In some instances, that destruction was not necessarily intended: native people suffered because of disease introduced by European settlers, for example. That said, native groups were also more vulnerable to disease because of the displacement and deprivation that they faced due to European settlement.

In the present day, we might consider the case of the high rates of incarceration of African American men in the contemporary United States. Does this constitute genocide? Recent data suggest that African American men are incarcerated at six times the rate of white men in the United States (Pew Research Center, 2013). The rates are particularly bad for African American men without a high school diploma. In 2010, nearly a third of all African American men between 25 and 29 without a high school diploma were in prison (Neal and Rick, 2014). This means that a substantial proportion of African Americans do not have liberty and face years of deprivation in prison. But are these high rates of incarceration evidence of an intent to destroy the group? Does such an intent have to be demonstrable? If so, do these examples suggest that racism is at the core of genocide?

Rwanda

The mass violence that occurred in Rwanda in Central Africa in 1994 is widely acknowledged today as an unambiguous case of genocide and one of the worst mass atrocities of the second half of the twentieth century. In approximately three months, Hutu hardliners in the government and military orchestrated a systematic campaign of violence against the Tutsi minority in that country. In a country of roughly 7 million persons, Hutus constituted a majority of 85–90 per cent, and Tutsis a minority of 10–14 per cent; Rwanda also had a third major group, the Twa, who comprised 1 per cent of the population. Estimates differ as to the total number killed during the genocide, but the most careful calculations put the toll at between 500,000 and 800,000 Tutsi civilians murdered by government forces (Des Forges, 1999; Verpooten, 2005). That number constitutes roughly three-quarters of the resident Tutsi population in Rwanda at the time of the genocide. In addition, rebel forces killed primarily Hutu civilians as the soldiers advanced. While the extent is not known, the rebel violence probably constituted crimes against humanity and war crimes, but was on a smaller scale in 1994 than the genocidal violence committed by government forces.

Historical Background

The immediate context in which the genocide occurred was twofold. On the one hand, Rwanda was

undergoing a democratic transition from one-party rule to multi-party elections. Rwanda's transition was part of a broader post-**Cold War** trend in Africa in which sub-Saharan states were pressured to end single-party dictatorships in favour of competitive, multi-party politics. In Rwanda, the ruling regime was headed by Juvénal Habyarimana, a Hutu military general who had been president since he took power in a coup in 1973. The main domestic opposition was composed of Hutu politicians, who drew support from people and regions of the country that were not well represented under Habyarimana.

On the other hand, the Habyarimana regime was in the middle of a civil war. The armed opponents were primarily Tutsi exiles who lived in neighbouring countries or who had joined the rebellion once it had started. The name of the rebel organization was the Rwandan Patriotic Front (RPF). The RPF had invaded northern Rwanda from Uganda in October 1990. Backed by the governments of France and Zaire, Rwandan government forces initially repelled the rebels, though later the rebels gained and held territory. In 1993, government forces, opposition politicians, and the rebels agreed to a ceasefire and power-sharing agreement known as the Arusha Accords (so-named after the city in Tanzania where they had been signed). The agreement was largely favourable to the rebels, apportioning them significant representation in a proposed new military and transitional government (B. Jones, 2001). As part of the agreement, the

United Nations would deploy a peacekeeping force to monitor the ceasefire agreement. That peacekeeping force would ultimately be headed by Canadian General Roméo Dallaire.

In short, on the eve of the genocide the elites in or with access to power faced two major challenges to their power: on the one hand, a domestic, largely Hutu political opposition and, on the other, a predominantly Tutsi rebel fighting force. In addition, a formal peace agreement that President Habyarimana had signed substantially eroded the power of the ruling party and the entrenched interests in the state. The genocide began on 6 April 1994, immediately after President Habyarimana was assassinated. The political and military officials who orchestrated the subsequent violence were largely those who had been threatened by the democratization and civil war processes.

In addition to the immediate context, Rwanda also has a deeper history of politicized and polarized ethnicity. To be brief, in the centuries immediately prior to colonial rule, a dynastic kingship governed Rwanda. Recognized as one of the most sophisticated monarchies in eastern Africa, the Rwandan kingdom was predicated on a status distinction between animal raisers and agriculturalists. By and large, animal raisers were of higher status and were often identified as 'Tutsi'. By contrast, agriculturalists were of a lower status and were often identified as 'Hutu'. The kingship was additionally dominated by Tutsis from particular clans. The social categories 'Tutsi' and 'Hutu' were thus largely based on status and economic activity in pre-colonial Rwanda. Social relations were nonetheless complex. Hutus and Tutsis were in the same clans; they spoke the same language; with enough cattle and status, a Hutu could become Tutsi and vice versa. The hierarchy was also codified through labour and land: some Hutus would exchange labour for access to land to grow crops (Chrétien, 2003). Pre-colonial Rwanda was neither harmonious nor simple; a strict hierarchy existed, but the main point is that the social categories Hutu and Tutsi were more complex than 'tribes' or 'races', which is how they would come to be interpreted.

European travellers first began exploring the region in the second half of the nineteenth century, and Rwanda (together with the neighbouring kingdom of Burundi) was eventually apportioned to Germany during the great colonial partitioning of Africa. Germany controlled Rwanda until just after the First World War, when Rwanda (and Burundi) was awarded to Belgium as part of a colonial trusteeship programme. The European intervention had many impacts, but one consistent theme is the way in which Europeans interpreted Rwanda's social categories and the effects of those interpretations.

On finding Rwanda's sophisticated governing system and social hierarchy, European travellers, and later colonialists, concluded that they were in the presence of two distinct races. The Tutsi, they concluded, were a superior race of 'Hamites' who had descended from northern Africa to subjugate the agricultural Hutu, who were seen as more typically negro 'Bantus'. Europeans referred to Tutsis as smarter, more elegant, and natural-born rulers. This interpretation of Rwanda's social categories was in step with then-current theories of race, and especially a theory called the 'Hamitic hypothesis'. That theory held that all civilization in black Africa was the product of Hamites who had descended from northern Africa or the Middle East (Mamdani, 2001; Chrétien, 2003).

As the Germans, but especially the Belgians, established their colonial authority, the racial interpretation had important implications. For one, the colonial powers backed not only the existing monarchy, but Tutsis more generally. Through a series of reforms, Tutsis came to occupy positions in the colonial administrative apparatus; Tutsis were sent to receive Western education; and literacy allowed them to participate in the new colonial governing system. In summary, under colonial rule Tutsis were systematically elevated to positions of authority and power. In addition, the colonial authorities entrenched and further racialized the social categories. National identity cards were introduced in the 1930s, and a person's 'race' was entered. During the colonial period, anthropologists and others sought to identify scientifically racial differences by measuring height, cranium, and noses of Hutus and Tutsis. The colonial intervention thus not only widened the power differential between Hutus and Tutsis, but also institutionalized and racialized the social categories (Newbury, 1988; Mamdani, 2001). All of these changes would have an effect as Rwanda's political history unfolded.

The Tutsi favouritism of the colonial period stayed in place until the heady period after the Second World War. For a mix of reasons in that period, the Belgian administration and clergy took steps to increase Hutus' power. Tutsi elites who had benefited under colonial rule resisted the change, leading the Belgians to lend further support to Hutu counter-elites. For their part, young Hutu intellectuals began espousing an ethnic nationalist position—namely, that since Hutus were the majority, and since democracy meant majority rule, Hutus should govern. All that set the stage for a rapid cascade of sometimes violent events known as the 'Hutu Revolution', during which the Belgians abolished the Rwandan monarchy, appointed a Hutu head of state, and oversaw the purging of Tutsis from positions in the administration. By the time independence was granted in 1962, there had been a near complete reversal of representation, with Hutus dominating the state and Tutsis largely out of power. The period also saw massacres of Tutsi civilians and the exile of many Tutsis, who sought refuge in neighbouring countries (Lemarchand, 1970). It would be the descendants of the early Tutsi exiles from the late 1950s and 1960s who formed the core of the RPF rebel movement that invaded in the 1990s (see Box 20.5 for discussion of RPF violence in the region).

Rwanda and Theories of Genocide

What does this brief history of the Rwandan case tell us about theories of genocide? When the violence started and the images and stories of massacres circulated, much of the initial commentary focused on antipathy. Many claimed that the genocide was the product of 'ancient tribal hatred' between Hutus and Tutsis. That idea remains somewhat popular but, as the brief history shows, the reality is considerably more complex. First, Hutus and Tutsis are not 'tribes'; they speak the same language, come from the same regions, intermarry, and the like. Moreover, the differences between the categories were originally based on status, and then the European encounter racialized the two identities. Second, the European intervention had a decisive impact, so the notion of tribes who have hated each other for centuries is misleading. Third, in Rwanda there exists an ethnic nationalist ideology that is predicated on European racial categories and that is similar to nationalist ideologies in other cases of genocide. Fourth, the notion of tribal fighting severely underplays the state-level, top-down orchestration of the violence.

Evidence from the Rwandan case in truth supports multiple theories. Even if 'ancient tribal hatreds' is a misleading cue, Rwanda had elements of a divided society that Kuper described. Even if Rwanda was undergoing a democratic transition at the time of the genocide, Rwanda had been an authoritarian state, and the country has a firmly entrenched hierarchical system of government. For those who emphasize deprivation (e.g. Uvin, 1998), Rwanda had widespread poverty and the country was at war. For those who emphasize ideology or ethnic nationalism, the Hutu hardliners who unleashed the genocide embraced a specific racial ideal that held that Hutus were the majority and should rule. For those who emphasize the strategic interests of leaders or statist calculations in the context of wartime territorial loss, the Rwandan case again provides support for the theory. And finally, the case may be interpreted to show the importance of a modern state and the ways in which modern ideas of race play a role. To be sure, different scholars emphasize different aspects of the Rwandan case to make their argument; nonetheless, to say that many theories fit the case also shows how difficult it is to evaluate theories of a relatively rare and complex macro-social event like genocide.

The International Response

This section turns to a more traditional human rights concern: the international response. As noted, the United Nations had deployed a small peacekeeping force to Rwanda as part of the peace agreement. Several months before the genocide, General Dallaire had received information about militia training to kill Tutsi civilians. However, when he sought authorization to use his troops to raid militia weapons caches, the UN Department of Peacekeeping Operations refused. The story was much the same once the genocide started. Quickly realizing that a major atrocity was unfolding, Dallaire requested reinforcements to

BOX 20.5 ALTERNATIVE POINTS OF VIEW: THE RWANDAN GENOCIDE AND THE RPF

One cannot see the Rwandan genocide in isolation. There is a history of violence against Hutus in neighbouring Burundi, and the RPF committed significant violence during the civil war in Rwanda and in later years in the Democratic Republic of Congo. How, if at all, does this information change your assessment of the genocide in Rwanda? In the Democratic Republic of Congo, millions of civilians died between 1996 and 2004, and the RPF-led Rwandan government was instrumental in starting and sustaining the wars in the Congo. Should we speak of the genocide in Rwanda without speaking of the violence and destruction in the Congo?

protect Rwandan civilians. However, the response from his superiors in New York, as well as from all of the most powerful international actors, was to avoid direct confrontation. Indeed, the international response from European states and the USA in the first weeks of the genocide was, first, to evacuate their nationals and, second, to neuter the UN peacekeeping force on the ground (Dallaire with Beardsley, 2003). In effect, then, the international response was to allow the genocide to unfold in Rwanda, despite widespread ratification of the Genocide Convention.

Several explanations of the international response are put forward in the literature. First, the Rwandan genocide unfolded less than a year after the debacle in Somalia in which eighteen American soldiers died. The Somalia violence was a foreign policy blow to the Clinton administration, as well as to UN peacekeeping operations, and neither the USA nor the UN had the appetite for a risky intervention in another African state (Barnett, 2002; Power, 2002). Second, Rwanda is a small, landlocked, francophone, coffee and tea exporting state in Central Africa. Rwanda had little name recognition in the Anglophone world and little strategic value to Northern powers. The European country with some of the strongest interests in Rwanda, Belgium, advocated for the withdrawal of UN forces shortly after Belgian peacekeepers were killed on the first day of the genocide. Third, the language of 'ancient tribal hatreds' that saturated the public coverage created little incentive to intervene. If Rwanda was composed of tribes that had hated each other for centuries, the international community would have poor odds in staunching the killing. Fourth, interviewed after the fact, Clinton administration officials acknowledged that there had been little public outcry for action (Power, 2002). Finally, the genocide happened quite quickly. Many commentators refer to Rwanda as the 'preventable genocide' given early warnings of escalation, the already existing presence of a peacekeeping force, the rudimentary means of violence used in the country, and finally the lack of ambiguity about genocide (OAU, 2000). Nonetheless, the sheer speed of the violence was a major obstacle to mobilizing an effective response (Kuperman, 2001).

If the international response was to avoid intervention, a corollary was to refuse to label unequivocally the events in Rwanda as 'genocide'. Within the Clinton administration, the concern was that if officials called the violence 'genocide' then they would be obligated to act to prevent the massacres under the Genocide Convention. Initially, US spokespeople were instructed to avoid the term; US officials also thwarted attempts at the United Nations to declare the violence 'genocide'. Eventually, the policy allowed US officials to speak of 'acts of genocide'. Nonetheless, the idea was to sidestep obligations under the terms of the Convention by refusing to label events in Rwanda definitively as 'genocide' (Power, 2002).

More than fifteen years after the Rwandan genocide happened, the case is frequently recognized as one of the most significant foreign policy and human rights failures of the late twentieth century. In many respects, lessons from this case shaped the international response to Darfur (as we will discuss). At the same time, despite the failure on the prevention side, the aftermath of the genocide has seen a flurry of activity on the punishment side. In late 1994, the United Nations established the International Criminal Tribunal for Rwanda to prosecute the major architects and planners of the genocide. Inside Rwanda, the victorious RPF initially established domestic courts to prosecute perpetrators. They later followed with a large experiment in 'community justice' called *gacaca*, in which ordinary Rwandans would judge perpetrators in open-air sessions (P. Clark, 2010). Each of the three justice mechanisms has its problems (ICG, 2001; Waldorf, 2006; Peskin, 2008; Rettig, 2011). These issues in **transitional justice** are beyond the purview of this chapter (see Chapter 22), but the level of activity around justice and punishment is consistent with other cases: the punishment provisions of the Genocide Convention have proven more influential than the prevention ones.

Darfur

The second major case discussed in this chapter concerns Darfur in western Sudan. Darfur is composed of three separate provinces, comprising an area roughly the size of France and home to some 6 million people prior to the latest conflict. The violence and mass human rights abuses that put the region on the international map began in mid-2003. The worst violence took place between 2003 and 2006, but low-level conflict and violence continue as of this writing in 2015. Estimates of the number killed vary, with the high-end estimate being around 450,000 and a more conservative estimate of about 200,000. In addition to those who have perished as a direct consequence of

KEY POINTS

The Rwandan genocide is one of the worst mass human rights atrocities of the late twentieth century.

In three months, at least 500,000 civilians were killed, mostly of the minority Tutsi group. The violence was systematic and government-led.

The proximate context was a transition to multi-party politics, civil war, and the assassination of President Juvénal Habyarimana.

Rwanda also has a history of racialized and politicized ethnicity in which European colonial intervention played a major role.

The international community failed to respond to early warnings of genocide and largely abandoned Rwanda as the genocide started.

Critical Thinking Questions:

What responsibility did colonialism have in shaping social identities in Rwanda?

Would the international response have been different in the absence of the Somalia experience?

If war was a driver of the genocide, what responsibility does the RPF have in the unfolding of events?

the fighting, some 2.5 million Darfurian civilians were displaced during the conflict. Less is known about the proximate and deep origins of the violence, in comparison to Rwanda. But from an international human rights perspective, the case is again instructive with regard to the difficulty of prevention.

Historical Background

Darfur is enormously complex demographically, with dozens of tribes and clans operating in the region. However, the contours of the conflict largely revolve around a cross-cutting cleavage between, on the one hand, farmers and herders, and, on the other hand, 'Arabs' and 'non-Arabs'. In Sudan, one of the enduring cleavages is between those who identify their origins as 'Arab' and who have a North African and Middle Eastern orientation, versus those who identify as 'non-Arab', with a more sub-Saharan African orientation (Deng, 1995; Lesch, 1998). In most of Sudan, the ethnic identity cleavage is overlaid with a religious

and regional one: most Northerners are Muslim and many identify as 'Arab', while most Southerners are Christian or Animist and identify as 'non-Arabs'. The North–South, Muslim–Christian, Arab–African cleavage was the source of two long civil wars in Sudan, one from 1955 to 1972 and one from 1983 to 2005. Darfur is unusual in at least two respects, vis-à-vis the rest of Sudan. First, Darfurians are uniformly Muslim. Second, the Arabs and non-Arabs are integrated within the region. Nonetheless, in Darfur, as in the rest of Sudan, there exists a cleavage between those claiming Arab identity and whose main economic activity is pastoralist herding, and those who identify as non-Arab and whose main economic activity is sedentary agriculture.

In most periods of time, differences between Arabs and non-Arabs were not a source of violence in Darfur. Indeed, there is evidence of much intermarriage in the region, and visitors to the region cannot tell apart physically an Arab from a non-Arab. Nonetheless, starting in the mid-1980s and proceeding to the early twenty-first century, relations between some Arab and some non-Arab tribes began to deteriorate in the region. This was the case for three main reasons. First, increased drought and desertification meant that competition for the most important resources in the region—water and arable land—increased. As a consequence, some herders encroached on farmers' lands, sometimes violently. In response, farmers formed self-protection units to protect their lands. Second, there was an influx of weaponry and Arab supremacist ideology. Both largely had to do with a spill-over war from neighbouring Chad. In the late 1980s, Chadian rebels used Darfur as a staging ground, receiving weapons from Libya. Third, when Arabs clashed with non-Arabs, successive Arab-dominated governments in the Sudanese capital Khartoum backed the local Arabs, and often appointed them to positions of local authority. All three changes upset pre-existing relations and increased tension and violence between groups in Darfur (Prunier, 2005; Daly, 2007; Flint and de Waal, 2008).

The conflict came to a head in 2002 and 2003 when two separate Darfur rebel groups formed and began attacking government positions in the region. The two groups, the Sudan Liberation Army and the Justice and Equality Movement, drew their support primarily from among Darfur's non-Arab populations: in particular, the Fur, Massaleit, and Zaghawa tribes. Initially, the government did not pay terrific attention to the rebel forces. The government had been focused on the twenty-year civil war between Northern and Southern forces. But in early 2003 the rebels scored a series of victories, including one spectacular attack on an air base in El Fasher. With that attack in particular, the Darfur emergency began.

Responding to the rebel attacks, the government's strategy was to target the rebels' purported civilian supporters and to fight the insurgency using a proxy militia force. The latter was recruited primarily from Darfur's Arab populations, including those who had come into conflict with non-Arabs during earlier land clashes. The government-backed militia in the latest crisis is widely referred to as the *janjawid*, which roughly translates as 'mean-spirited men on horseback'. Most research conducted on the patterns of violence indicates that government forces and militias have routinely been involved in joint attacks on non-Arab civilian populations. A common pattern is for government aircraft to bomb villages, followed by militias riding into the villages, killing stragglers, looting, setting buildings and homes on fire, and poisoning wells. Sexual violence has also been widespread (Askin, 2006). Many deaths are due to direct killing; many Darfurians have also died as a consequence of forced displacement from their homes.

Darfur and Theories of Genocide

What does Darfur say about theories of genocide? It should be noted that much of the in-depth research that has shaped an understanding of the Rwandan case is still in process for Darfur. Nonetheless, the evidence from the case lends itself to numerous theories. If one were to stress deep, etched visions, the Arab/non-Arab cleavage at the local and national levels is an important dimension (Hagan and Rymond-Richmond, 2009). As for regime type, during the Darfur conflict Sudan is going through a political opening: in particular, through the integration of Southerners as part of a peace deal from the North–South war. Nonetheless, the government in Sudan is largely authoritarian. At the national level, the deprivation argument is harder to make—though the North–South peace deal amounts to a significant change in society. Nonetheless, in Darfur the water and land shortages exacerbated by environmental factors are critical factors in the conflict. For those who point to ideology, the key points are the influx of Arab supremacist thinking in Darfur as well as a broader commitment

to Arab nationalism among Northerners in Sudan. Like Rwanda, Darfur is occurring in the midst of a civil war—and those who stress the wartime, strategic dimensions of genocide have a clear argument. Finally, with regard to political development, more research should be done, but an argument pointing to the ethnic purging and killing as part of a consolidation of power and identity would have a case to make. In short, different theories highlight different contributing dimensions of the violence, and more research and careful hypothesis testing will be in order to weigh the merits of the possible theoretical claims.

The International Response

On the international side, the Darfur crisis received relatively limited attention during the first year of violence. However, 2004 was the tenth anniversary of the Rwandan genocide, and as Rwanda was commemorated Darfur received a surge of new attention, especially in the USA. Much of the subsequent response to Darfur was driven by lessons from Rwanda. In particular, activists in the USA formed a diverse civil society coalition to put pressure on the Bush administration. Moreover, the initial focus was to have the administration label the violence 'genocide' under the theory that doing so would trigger action under the Genocide Convention. To cut a long story short, in historic moves both Congress and the administration ultimately called Darfur 'genocide', the latter doing so after an innovative study (Straus, 2005; Totten and Markusen, 2006). However, the administration interpreted the Convention's terms to indicate that the obligation meant taking the issue to the United Nations.

At the United Nations, the primary obstacles to intervention lay with the Security Council. China and Russia opposed non-consensual coercive action that would effectively 'prevent' genocide. Both countries generally oppose policies in which human rights issues are a pretext for armed intervention. Moreover, China has large oil interests in Sudan, and Russia sells military hardware to the Sudanese government. As Permanent Five members of the Security Council with veto power, China and Russia formed an initially insurmountable obstacle to forcible intervention. Moreover, given its commitments in Iraq and Afghanistan, the United States was not in a position to lead a mission.

Facing such realities, then-Secretary General Kofi Annan appointed a commission to study whether the violence in Darfur was genocide. In a 2005 report, the commissioners detailed the violence but concluded that they lacked evidence to indicate genocide. In particular, the commissioners did not find sufficient indicators of top-level intent to destroy the non-Arab population of Darfur (COI, 2005). The report recommended that the matter be referred to the International Criminal Court (ICC), a recommendation that the Security Council ultimately endorsed. In 2007, the ICC indicted two Sudanese, one a government official and the other a *janjawid* leader; then in 2009, the ICC issued the first of two arrest warrants for Sudanese President, Omar al-Bashir, which include charges of genocide. The move was the first time the ICC had issued an arrest warrant for a sitting head of state. As of this writing in 2015, none of those indicted has been arrested.

On the prevention side, the question of whether the United Nations would use military force to protect civilians simmered until mid-2006. In May, under significant international pressure, the government and one rebel faction signed a ceasefire agreement, which included a provision on accepting a UN peacekeeping mission. The Security Council subsequently agreed to send a large peacekeeping mission to Darfur with a robust mandate to protect civilians. However, the government of Sudan opposed different dimensions of the plan, especially the composition of the forces—Sudan wanted more African representation. There followed a new negotiation leading to a new Security Council resolution authorizing a hybrid United Nations/African Union force of nearly 20,000 uniformed peacekeepers, a number that has since grown. The mission was initially slow to deploy, and meanwhile the situation in Darfur has grown even more complicated, with rebel groups splintering into multiple factions and some fighting among themselves (ICG, 2007). As of this writing in 2015, the situation in the region remains unstable, and fighting continues in other parts of Sudan—notably in Southern Kordofan and the Blue Nile regions.

In short, in Darfur, the international community as represented by the United Nations was slow to put into place an effective civilian protection force. Despite the recognition that Rwanda was an international failure, a decade after Rwanda another case has shown how difficult prevention is and how limited the international commitments to prevent genocide are (see Hagan and Palloni, 2006).

KEY POINTS

During 2003–6, at least 200,000 civilians died, and 2.5 million were displaced from Darfur in western Sudan. A large UN peacekeeping force now exists but the situation in the region remains violent and unstable.

The worst episodes of violence were perpetrated primarily by government forces and state-backed Arab militias known as the '*janjawid*'. The victims primarily came from the non-Arab populations of Darfur.

The proximate context was a civil war and clashes over land and water.

The deeper context is a country with politicized ethnicity and cleavage between Arabs and non-Arabs.

The US has called Darfur 'genocide'; a UN Commission of Inquiry has not. Sudan's president has been indicted by the ICC on charges of genocide.

After years of negotiations, a large hybrid United Nations/African Union force was approved to deploy to Darfur to protect civilians.

Critical Thinking Questions:

What similarities and differences are there between the Rwanda and Darfur cases?

What are the main obstacles to effective international response to prevent genocide?

What are the advantages of studying genocide by comparing similar cases and by comparing cases in which genocide did and did not occur?

Conclusion

Since the Holocaust, international actors have regularly pledged 'never again' to allow genocide to happen. The landmark treaty on genocide, the United Nations Genocide Convention, is the law that embodies that promise. Measured against the pledge to prevent genocide, the rhetorical commitments and the Convention have proven weak and ineffective. Nonetheless, the problem of genocide is receiving greater and greater attention. Scholarship on the topic is rapidly expanding, and the hope of 'punishing' genocide is an increasing reality. As a major human rights violation—the 'crime of crimes' in one common formulation (Schabas, 2000)—genocide has a special place in the firmament of international human rights treaties. The question for the future is how and whether the promise to rid this 'odious scourge' (to cite the Convention's language) will come to pass.

? QUESTIONS

Individual Study Questions

1. In what ways do the discussions in the drafting of the Convention prefigure debates on what constitutes genocide?

2. What are the strengths and weaknesses of the United Nations Genocide Convention?

3. What are the most important points of difference about the definition of genocide, and why do they matter?

4. Using both the definitions in the United Nations Genocide Convention and Raphael Lemkin's original definition of genocide, what are the elements of the Darfur and Rwanda cases that do or do not indicate genocide?

5. What theories of genocide apply most clearly to the Rwanda case, and what theories apply most clearly to the Darfur case?

6. What are the important similarities and differences between the causal factors in Rwanda and Darfur?

7. In what ways did the international failures in Rwanda shape the international response to Darfur?

8. What does Darfur show the international community that Rwanda does not?

Group Discussion Questions

1. In what way is the history of the United Nations Genocide Convention similar to and different from the story of other major international human rights documents that emerged after the Second World War?

2. What do the Rwanda and Darfur cases reveal about the ambiguities in the definition of genocide and the weaknesses of the Genocide Convention?

3. In the chapter, it is argued that over time the punishment provisions of the Genocide Convention have proven stronger than the prevention ones. What does this say about international human rights more generally?

4. In what ways do the theories of genocide presented in the chapter conform to your own understanding of genocide? In what ways are they different?

5. In what ways is Rwanda similar to and different from the Holocaust?

6. What should be the takeaway lessons from Darfur, if any?

≋ FURTHER READING

Bloxham, D. and **Moses, A.** (2010). *The Oxford Handbook of Genocide Studies*. New York: Oxford University Press.

A comprehensive collection of essays on different dimensions of genocide.

Dallaire, R. with **Beardsley, B.** (2003). *Shake Hands with the Devil: The Failure of Humanity in Rwanda*. Toronto: Random House Canada.

An excellent memoir by the Canadian head of the peacekeeping mission to Rwanda.

Daly, M. (2007). *Darfur's Sorrow: A History of Destruction and Genocide*. New York: Cambridge University Press.

A comprehensive discussion of the history and politics of Darfur.

Flint, J. and **de Waal, A.** (2008). *Darfur: A New History of a Long War* (revised and updated). London: Zed Books.

A rich and thoughtful discussion of the crisis in Darfur and the proximate context.

Hagan, J. and **Rymond-Richmond, W.** (2009). *Darfur and the Crime of Genocide*. New York: Cambridge University Press.

A criminological account of the violence in Darfur, arguing that the case is genocide.

Power, S. (2002). *'A Problem from Hell': America and the Age of Genocide*. New York: Basic Books.

A Pulitzer-Prize winning account of international, especially US, failures to prevent genocide; also a good discussion of Raphael Lemkin.

Prunier, G. (1995). *The Rwanda Crisis: History of a Genocide*. New York: Columbia University Press.

An overview of Rwandan history and the genocide.

Schabas, W. (2000). *Genocide in International Law: The Crime of Crimes*. Cambridge: Cambridge University Press.

The definitive text on the drafting of the United Nations Genocide Convention and various legal dimensions of the treaty.

Stone, D. (ed.) (2008). *The Historiography of Genocide*. London: Palgrave Macmillan.

An overview of historical debates of more than a dozen cases.

Straus, S. (2006). *The Order of Genocide: Race, Power, and War in Rwanda*. Ithaca, NY: Cornell University Press.

A social scientific analysis of the dynamics of genocide in Rwanda, with an emphasis on local dynamics.

Valentino, B. (2004). *Final Solutions: Mass Killing and Genocide in the Twentieth Century*. Ithaca, NY: Cornell University Press.

A well-written, accessible, political science account of the causes of genocide and mass killing.

WEB LINKS

http://www.ushmm.org/genocide/   The Committee on Conscience website provides analysis and advocacy on contemporary genocides.

http://www.enoughproject.org/   The Enough website provides analysis and advocacy on ending genocide and crimes against humanity.

http://www.crisisgroup.org/home/index.cfm   The International Crisis Group website provides analysis of contemporary conflicts, including Darfur.

http://www.unictr.org   Website of the International Criminal Tribunal for Rwanda.

http://www.icc-cpi.int/Menus/ICC/Home   Website of the International Criminal Court provides information on prosecuting mass atrocities in Darfur and beyond.

http://genocidescholars.org/   Website of the International Associate of Genocide Scholars.

http://www.tandf.co.uk/journals/titles/14623528.asp   Website of the *Journal of Genocide Research*.

http://utpjournals.metapress.com/content/120325/   Website of the journal *Genocide Studies and Prevention*.

http://www.ushmm.org/genocide/taskforce/   Website of the Genocide Prevention Task Force, a US-based policy initiative to strengthen measures to prevent genocide.

Visit the Online Resource Centre that accompanies this book for updates and a range of other resources: www.oxfordtextbooks.co.uk/orc/goodhart3e/

21

Humanitarian Intervention

Alan J. Kuperman

Reader's Guide

This chapter explores humanitarian intervention and its relationship to the promotion of human rights. The first section examines the evolution of humanitarian intervention, especially in the wake of the Second World War and the Cold War, to include military force and the violation of traditional norms of neutrality and state sovereignty. The chapter then discusses some obstacles to effective intervention—including the speed of violence, delays in accurate information, logistical hurdles to military deployment, and insufficient political will. Next, it analyses unintended consequences, including how the 'moral hazard' of humanitarian intervention may inadvertently trigger and perpetuate civil conflict, thereby exacerbating civilian suffering. A detailed case study of humanitarian intervention in Bosnia—from 1992 to 1995 by the United States, European Community, United Nations, and NATO—illustrates many of these concepts. The conclusion offers recommendations to improve humanitarian intervention and to reconcile it with the promotion of human rights.

Introduction to Humanitarian Intervention

Humanitarian intervention is not identical to the promotion of human rights but is related to it—in ways that sometimes are obvious but also can be quite counter-intuitive. Strictly speaking, humanitarian intervention is the use of diplomatic, economic, and military resources by one or more states or international organizations intended primarily to protect civilians who are endangered in another state. These civilians may be at risk either from natural disaster or from political violence (including war) in which they are targeted deliberately or suffer from the resulting social disruption.

Because civil war may be both the cause and consequence of human rights violations, there is an intimate relationship between humanitarian intervention and the promotion of human rights. Persistent violations of a group's human rights may cause members of that group to feel so aggrieved and frustrated that they eventually take up arms and rebel, triggering a civil war. During the course of war, civilians may suffer both humanitarian deprivation—inadequate food, water, shelter, and medical care—and blatant violation of their human rights, including arbitrary detention, forced displacement, or summary violence. International action that is able to end the war may alleviate both problems, so that humanitarian intervention sometimes also promotes human rights.

But at other times, the two goals are contradictory. Efforts to promote human rights may exacerbate humanitarian suffering. Or humanitarian intervention may exacerbate violations of human rights. In such cases, advocates may have to decide which of these two worthy causes is their higher priority and temporarily sacrifice the other. Philosophers and social scientists label this the dilemma of, or trade-off between, 'peace and justice'.

Many of these dynamics are illustrated in Bosnia, a European country that suffered a bloody civil war from 1992 to 1995 and was subject to many forms of humanitarian intervention. The case of Bosnia will be detailed later in this chapter.

Evolving Concepts of Intervention

Humanitarian intervention was originally defined narrowly as the provision of vital materials to at-risk civilians, expressly avoiding any action or even commentary related to the possible political causes of civilian suffering. The prototypical humanitarian organization in this tradition is the **International Committee of the Red Cross** (ICRC), which originated in 1863 at the international conference that also gave rise the following year to the original version of the **Geneva Convention and Protocols** that assure wartime protection of medical care for civilians and soldiers. The ICRC philosophy is to eschew any political criticism of the states where it intervenes, in order to facilitate its humanitarian mandate. For example, if the ICRC were to criticize a government for intentionally harming its civilians, that government might bar the organization from entering the country to provide humanitarian aid, resulting in greater harm to the civilians. Thus, traditional humanitarian organizations such as the ICRC explicitly subordinate concern over human rights violations in order to facilitate their humanitarian objective. On several occasions, the ICRC has been harshly criticized for this strictly neutral stance—notably during the Holocaust, when it witnessed but did not report or condemn Nazi crimes.

A broader definition of humanitarian intervention has emerged over the last five decades. A key turning point was Nigeria's 1967–70 secessionist war in its Biafra region, when some ICRC employees rejected their organization's political neutrality. They believed that the government of Nigeria was intentionally inflicting humanitarian deprivation on the Biafra region in a ruthless attempt to compel the secessionists to abandon their aspirations of self-determination and independence. In their opinion, merely providing humanitarian aid to the victims, as ICRC was doing, did not address the root cause of the suffering. Accordingly, these frustrated humanitarians split from the ICRC and in 1971 formed their own organization, namely *Médecins Sans Frontières* (MSF; Doctors Without Borders), which would not only provide aid but also condemn state policies that they believed created suffering in the first place. MSF abandoned the ICRC's principle of political neutrality on the grounds that **naming and shaming** human rights violations was the best way to reduce humanitarian suffering in the long run, even if it might interfere with their ability to provide aid in the short term.

Impartial and Neutral

Humanitarians often claim to be both impartial and neutral in their interventions, but in practice it may be impossible to attain both goals simultaneously during a civil war. **Impartiality** denotes that aid is delivered solely on the basis of need, without consideration of the political or military allegiance of the recipient. **Neutrality** means that the intervention strives to avoid affecting the balance of power between the contending parties. The incompatibility of impartiality and neutrality stems from two facts: civil wars are usually lopsided rather than symmetrical, and humanitarian intervention also benefits combatants. At any point in a civil war, one of the sides is usually winning, in the sense of suffering less. Accordingly, when interveners deliver humanitarian aid impartially, they provide it mainly to the weaker party and often require the stronger party to halt hostilities to facilitate delivery. Both of these actions alter the balance of power in the conflict, strengthening the weaker party relative to the stronger, so that the intervention is not neutral. If interveners strive to be neutral, then they must provide equal aid to the side that is not suffering as much, which would violate the principle of impartiality.

In the 1990s, the concept of humanitarian intervention was expanded again to include the use of military force, not merely to protect delivery of aid, but in some cases to deter or defeat actors perceived as aggressors endangering civilians. The end of the **Cold War** broke the US–Soviet deadlock in the United Nations Security Council, enabling the authorization, on a case-by-case basis, of intervention using all necessary means, including military force, to protect civilians. Examples are discussed in the next section.

In 2001, following several such interventions, the ad hoc International Commission on Intervention and State Sovereignty (ICISS, 2001) concluded that there was a **Responsibility to Protect (R2P)**—that is, a generalized obligation of states to intervene through a variety of means to protect civilians on humanitarian grounds. These means included 'all forms of preventive measures, and coercive intervention measures— sanctions and criminal prosecutions', as well as 'military intervention'. In December 2004, a UN panel agreed: 'We endorse the emerging norm that there is a collective international responsibility to protect' (United Nations, 2004, p. 66). Finally, the UN General Assembly, at the 2005 World Summit, codified the 'responsibility to use appropriate diplomatic, humanitarian, and other peaceful means … to help protect populations from genocide, war crimes, ethnic cleansing, and crimes against humanity' and to authorize force 'on a case-by-case basis … should peaceful means be inadequate' (United Nations General Assembly, 2005, p. 30). The original formulation of the R2P declared that the international community was responsible for three types of intervention if civilians were threatened: prevention, protection, and rebuilding. When this was criticized as neocolonial, the R2P was reformulated to comprise three alternative responsibilities:

(1) states should protect their populations; (2) the international community should offer states assistance to do so; (3) if states nevertheless fail to protect their populations, the international community should intervene in accordance with the UN Charter (G. Evans, 2009).

Despite considerable support for this concept, sceptics in the developing world and on the political left, notably in Europe, criticize the emerging norm as a form of neo-imperialism in which ostensible humanitarianism disguises self-interested intervention—to impose regime change, exploit natural resources, or open markets to Western exporters. Some critics also complain that governments with histories of massive human rights abuses—such as in Rwanda, Burundi, and Ethiopia—whitewash their own crimes by contributing troops to humanitarian intervention in other countries, such as Sudan and Somalia.

KEY POINTS

Humanitarian intervention was traditionally the provision of vital materials to at-risk civilians.

Interveners traditionally avoided entanglement in politics, as when the ICRC refused to criticize even the Nazis.

Modern intervention often confronts the political root causes of civilian suffering: for example, by naming and shaming offenders who target civilians.

Impartiality is the delivery of aid solely on the basis of need. Neutrality is not altering a conflict's balance of power. The two goals are typically not compatible.

Since 1991, military force has been used increasingly in humanitarian intervention, both to protect the delivery of aid and to target perceived aggressors.

The United Nations, in 2005, acknowledged the responsibility to protect civilians through humanitarian intervention, including military force if authorized.

Critical Thinking Questions:

What should be done when there is a tension between the goals of humanitarianism and human rights? For example, under North Korea's dictatorship, the population suffers not only violations of its political rights but periodic famine. The humanitarian imperative dictates that the international community provide food for starving North Koreans. But alleviating famine could bolster domestic support for the dictatorship, thereby perpetuating its violation of political rights. Which concern should take precedence in this case— promoting humanitarianism or human rights—and why?

Military Intervention

During most of modern history, the norm of **sovereignty** prohibited states from intervening in the internal affairs of other recognized states (which typically excluded territories in the New World populated by Indigenous peoples; see Chapter 19). The norm was adopted to reduce the incidence of war and to promote international stability. It arose in response to the horribly bloody 'religious wars' between Catholics and Protestants in Europe during the sixteenth and seventeenth centuries that culminated in the 'Thirty Years War' of 1618–48. Such wars were fought largely over the internal behaviour of states—specifically, their religion—rather than their external behaviour. Wise statesmen and jurists realized that war could be frequent and particularly savage if it were permitted to be fought over such internal differences, in light of the inherent diversity of states and the intense passions aroused by disputes over ostensibly universal values.

Accordingly, a norm of sovereignty was established in 1648 by the Treaty of Westphalia, ending the Thirty Years War. Henceforth, war could legally be fought only over the external, not internal, behaviour of states. States would enjoy total sovereignty over their internal affairs, and no other state could intervene with force or otherwise. Although the norm was sometimes violated (Krasner, 1999), it stood as a pillar of international law for over 300 years. The principle was reiterated in the UN Charter of 1945, which in its first chapter (Articles 2.4 and 2.7) prohibits intervention by either the United Nations or its members in the internal affairs of states:

All Members shall refrain in their international relations from the threat or use of force against the territorial integrity or political independence of any state ... Nothing contained in the present Charter shall authorize the United Nations to intervene in matters which are essentially within the domestic jurisdiction of any state or shall require the Members to submit such matters to settlement under the present Charter.

These prohibitions hold unless the Security Council approves a resolution in a specific case under Chapter VII of the Charter, authorizing intervention in response to a threat to *international* peace and security, or unless a state is acting in self-defence against international aggression under Article 51 of the Charter.

Eroding the Norm of Sovereignty

The first modern, legal intrusion on the norm of sovereignty was the UN's 1948 Convention on the Prevention and Punishment of the Crime of Genocide, adopted in the wake of the Holocaust. In the Convention, signers 'undertake to prevent and to punish' the crime of genocide. Given that genocide may be committed by a state against its own citizens, the convention thus commits signers to intervene in another state, based solely on the internal behaviour of that state. The responsibility to protect further erodes the norm of sovereignty, endorsing intervention to prevent not only genocide but other massive violations of human rights that occur within a state, including **war crimes**, **ethnic cleansing**, and **crimes against humanity**. To remain consistent with the UN Charter, intervention proponents argue that the widespread violation of human rights in a country is no longer 'essentially within the domestic jurisdiction of any state'. In this way, the norm is gradually evolving to privilege some individual human rights over state sovereignty, although the ultimate extent of that evolution is still to be determined (see also Box 21.1).

Even prior to the formal erosion of the sovereignty norm, states occasionally intervened in the internal affairs of other states on humanitarian or human rights grounds. In the late nineteenth century, for example, some European states intervened with diplomatic pressure and threats against the Ottoman Empire over

BOX 21.1 CHALLENGING ASSUMPTIONS

Humanitarian intervention is based on the assumption that the highest priority of the international community during a civil war should be protecting civilians from harm. But is that always true? Are other goals, such as freedom or democracy, important enough that the international community should prioritize them above the protection of civilians? Moreover, is it possible that the opposing groups in a domestic conflict have the right to settle their dispute by force, if they so choose, without outside interference? What gives outsiders the right to intervene in other countries, especially ones that are far away and may have very different cultures? Think back to the US Civil War in which more than half a million Americans died before the Union defeated the Confederacy, unifying the country and ending slavery. In retrospect, would it have been preferable for interveners to stop the violence on humanitarian grounds, even if that preserved the slave-holding Confederacy?

treatment of its Christian peoples, including Armenians, who were seeking greater rights. In the late 1960s, several states intervened in Nigeria on behalf of ethnic Ibos, who were suffering from the government's response to the armed secession of their Biafra region.

Military Force

The widespread advent of humanitarian intervention with military force emerged after the Cold War. The model was established in 1991, following the Gulf War that expelled Iraqi troops from Kuwait. In March of that year, in northern Iraq, ethnic Kurd separatists launched a rebellion against the Baghdad regime of Saddam Hussein. The Iraqi army responded with brutal suppression, compelling ethnic Kurds to flee northwards towards the mountains bordering Turkey, creating a humanitarian emergency. In April 1991, the United States launched Operation Provide Comfort, a military intervention justified on humanitarian grounds. The United Nations (in Security Council Resolution 688) quickly urged its members to contribute to the humanitarian effort, and a coalition of states then helped the United States to protect the Kurds, establish displacement camps, provide humanitarian aid, and assist with resettlement. The United States also spearheaded a **no-fly zone** over the Kurdish area of Iraq, conducting missions from bases in Turkey to patrol and shoot down any Iraqi aircraft operating in that airspace. The intervention thus provided not merely emergency humanitarian aid, but long-term military assistance that shifted the balance of power in Iraq, effectively rewarding the Kurds with political autonomy that also promoted their human rights.

The use of military force in humanitarian intervention has since become widespread. Such action is sometimes carried out with the consent of the target state, typically authorized under Chapter VI of the UN Charter. In other cases it is non-consensual, authorized either under Chapter VII of the UN Charter or outside the legal bounds of that charter, as in Kosovo where intervention controversially was authorized by NATO —a US–European military alliance—rather than the UN. Since 1991, interveners have deployed forces to protect civilians in at least twenty-four countries: Afghanistan, Albania, Bosnia, Burundi, Central African Republic, Chad, Croatia, Democratic Republic of Congo, East Timor, Georgia, Haiti, Iraq, Ivory Coast, Kosovo, Liberia, Libya, Macedonia, Mali, Rwanda, Sierra Leone, Somalia, South Sudan, Sudan, and

Tajikistan—some on multiple occasions. During the same period, interveners have also deployed troops or monitors to support peace processes in another sixteen countries (not counting pre-existing operations): Cambodia, Chad, Comoros, El Salvador, Eritrea, Ethiopia, Guatemala, Guinea Bissau, Kuwait, Lebanon, Moldova, Mozambique, Papua New Guinea, Peru, Solomon Islands, and Western Sahara. Although the latter missions are not explicitly authorized to protect civilians, they are motivated heavily by the desire to shield civilians from renewed violence. In some cases, such as Sudan's north–south civil war of 1983 to 2005, the international community has also applied sanctions against states or provided covert aid to rebels in an attempt to coerce a halt to violence.

The increased frequency and extent of humanitarian intervention has spurred rapid growth in both government spending and the number of **non-governmental organizations** (NGOs) devoted to this mission. Annual spending on official humanitarian assistance, excluding military costs, increased from US$3.4 billion to US$13.3 billion during 1990–2010.[1] Such increased spending has triggered a proliferation of humanitarian organizations, so that aid delivery often involves literally hundreds of NGOs for a single emergency.

Major Interventions

After the Cold War, several cases of humanitarian military intervention have been especially prominent. In 1992, the United Nations and the United States deployed troops to Somalia to facilitate the delivery of humanitarian aid to civilians who had been cut off, sometimes deliberately, by factions in a long-running civil war. Although impartial, the intervention was not neutral in that it diminished the power of a Somali warlord, Mohammad Farrah Aideed, who retaliated by killing UN troops from Pakistan. The United States responded by targeting the warlord, who again retaliated by killing eighteen US troops in a single battle in October 1993, an engagement immortalized in the film *Blackhawk Down*. The interveners withdrew during the next eighteen months, after they had alleviated the immediate humanitarian emergency. However, the underlying conflicts soon exploded in renewed war, triggering further civilian suffering and intervention that continues as of early-2016.

From 1992 to 1995, the United Nations and NATO conducted a complex humanitarian military intervention in Bosnia, as detailed later in this chapter.

Soon after, in neighbouring Serbia's Kosovo province, ethnic Albanian militants of the Kosovo Liberation Army responded to government oppression by launching a secessionist rebellion. Serbian leader Slobodan Milošević retaliated with a harsh counterinsurgency that targeted the rebels but also killed several hundred civilians and displaced hundreds of thousands more during 1998. The United States first intervened to protect Kosovo's civilians by threatening Serbia with NATO air strikes, compelling Milošević in October 1998 to withdraw many Serbian forces and permit international monitors. But the ethnic Albanian rebels renewed attacks, reigniting a war that again displaced civilians. The United States then drafted a peace agreement that promised Kosovo an independence referendum after three years, and demanded in February 1999 that Milošević sign it or face NATO attack. This time Milošević refused, so NATO commenced bombing in late March 1999. Serbian forces responded by quickly expelling from Kosovo some 850,000 ethnic Albanians, approximately half their population in the province, and killing about 10,000. After eleven weeks of NATO bombing, Milošević relented, signing a peace agreement to remove all his forces from Kosovo and to permit international peacekeepers. As the ethnic Albanian refugees returned, they forcibly displaced about half of the 200,000 Serbs in the province, and killed hundreds more, despite the presence of peacekeepers. Proponents of the intervention claim that it prevented even more Serb violence against Albanian civilians, while critics say it backfired, amplifying this violence and failing to prevent vengeance against Serb civilians.

In early 2011, Libyan security forces killed approximately two hundred protesters in three days, which provoked escalation of an armed uprising. The militants initially made progress, but after a month Libya's security forces were poised to capture the last rebel stronghold of Benghazi to end the war. To coerce the rebels to surrender or retreat, Libya's government threatened to show no mercy to any who remained defiant. The rebels responded by persuading the international community that a bloodbath against *civilians* was imminent, which some Western critics in retrospect have labelled a false pretence, given the fact that during the preceding month the government had targeted mainly rebels.[2] Nevertheless, the United Nations authorized the imposition of a no-fly zone, an arms embargo, and 'all necessary measures ... to protect civilians and civilian populated areas'. NATO

then exceeded this mandate, pursuing regime change by bombing government targets including retreating forces for seven months while enforcing the embargo only against the government, not the rebels.

The intervention almost surely averted some violence in Benghazi, but it also perpetuated war and civilian suffering in the rest of the country, thereby increasing the death toll up to tenfold. After eight months, the rebels finally captured power, executed former leader Muammar Gaddafi, and took vengeance against his suspected supporters. The victorious rebel factions then refused to disarm or merge into a national security force, which created anarchy and a safe haven for radical Islamist terrorists, who in 2012 killed the US ambassador to Libya. Also due to the intervention, the regime's forces leaked out of Libya, triggering regional proliferation of weapons and a civil war in Mali, which created that country's worst ever humanitarian disaster and yet another terrorist safe haven. In 2014, Libya's civil war reignited, pitting Islamist against secular forces, and shutting down the oil industry that is the country's lifeblood. By the next year, the Islamic State terrorist group had established a foothold in Libya and executed some Christians. Libya is thus a clear example of well-intentioned intervention that backfired by exacerbating civilian suffering (Kuperman, 2013, 2015).

Failure to Intervene

The failure to intervene has been harshly criticized in several recent cases of large-scale violence against civilians. In Rwanda, ethnic Tutsi rebels invaded in 1990 and fought for three years against a government controlled by members of the ethnic Hutu majority (see also Chapter 20). In 1993, a peace agreement permitted the deployment of 2,500 UN peacekeepers. But in April 1994, the Hutu president was assassinated, and Hutu extremists immediately launched a genocidal campaign that killed half a million Tutsi (three-quarters of their population in the country) in just three months. Tens of thousands of Hutu were also killed. Most of the UN peacekeepers were withdrawn upon the renewal of violence, although 500 remained and protected several thousand civilians. After the first month of violence, the UN authorized a humanitarian military intervention in May 1994, but international reinforcements did not arrive in Rwanda until late June 1994, by which time the genocide was virtually over. In retrospect, many advocates of intervention have claimed that a quick UN reinforcement could have prevented the genocide, although this is disputed in the next section (Kuperman, 2001).

In Sudan's northwest region of Darfur, militant members of African tribes launched a rebellion in 2003, complaining of neglect and discrimination by the Arab-dominated regime in Khartoum (see Chapter 20). Sudan's government retaliated using security forces, indiscriminate air strikes, and the arming of local Arab militias, who conducted a scorched-earth counter-insurgency against African villages. These attacks displaced two million civilians, resulting in tens of thousands of deaths. In 2004, the African Union (AU) authorized a small military intervention to monitor the situation and to facilitate humanitarian aid—a force that grew to 7,000 troops over the next three years. Violence diminished, but most of the affected civilians remained displaced, vulnerable, and dependent on humanitarian aid, which spurred international activists to demand more forceful intervention. In 2007, the United Nations authorized an expanded, hybrid UN–AU force of 26,000 troops and police, most of whom deployed gradually over the next several years. In 2009, based on crimes in Darfur, the International Criminal Court issued an arrest warrant for Sudan's president, who responded by expelling humanitarian organizations that he accused of collaborating with the court, thereby triggering a temporary humanitarian emergency until other groups filled the aid gap. As of early 2016, violence has diminished between Arab and African tribes, but low-level fighting continues—among rebels, security forces, and some tribes—and widespread displacement persists.

In Syria, government forces began attacking peaceful protesters in early 2011 at the same time that NATO intervened in Libya ostensibly to stop similar violence. In the case of Syria, however, the international community declined to intervene. This failure to implement the responsibility to protect was explained on several grounds: Syria's army was too strong; the UN Security Council was blocked by the opposition of Russia and China; and intervention might help radical Islamists and spread war to neighbouring states. The estimated death toll in Syria climbed above 250,000 during the first five years of conflict (United Nations, 2015). Ironically, the international community had launched a humanitarian intervention in Libya, where the government targeted mainly rebels, but failed to intervene in Syria where the government initially targeted mainly civilians.

KEY POINTS

The norm of sovereignty was adopted in 1648 to promote peace by prohibiting inter-state war over domestic matters.

The UN Charter of 1945 reiterates non-interference in internal affairs.

Some individual human rights trump state sovereignty under the Genocide Convention and the responsibility to protect.

After the Cold War, humanitarian military intervention became more common, triggering increases in spending and a proliferation of humanitarian NGOs.

In Iraq, starting in 1991, humanitarian intervention also aided the self-determination movement of Kurds by altering the balance of power in the country.

In Somalia, starting in 1992, intervention alleviated the immediate humanitarian emergency but failed to resolve the underlying conflicts, which soon reignited, triggering further civilian suffering and intervention.

In both Kosovo and Libya, intervention amplified greatly the violence against civilians.

In Rwanda, Darfur, and Syria, the absence of forceful intervention has been harshly criticized by some humanitarians.

Critical Thinking Questions:

How, if at all, should the international community intervene in Syria to protect civilians? Intervention against the government could bring to power the main opposition group, the Islamic State, which has an even worse track record of mass murder and human rights violations. One alternative might be to deploy more than 100,000 occupation forces. But in Afghanistan and Iraq that proved unpopular in troop-contributing countries, which suffered tens of thousands of casualties. *Do you personally care enough about protecting Syria's civilians to risk your own life there? If not, do you support your government ordering your fellow citizens in the armed forces to attempt that dangerous mission?*

Obstacles to Effective Intervention

Several factors can impede timely humanitarian intervention in civil conflicts. Perhaps most obvious is the lack of *political will* by potential interveners, as discussed by Samantha Power (2002) in her book *'A Problem from Hell'*. She argues that powerful states could intervene fairly easily, including with military force, to prevent genocide, but they do not because they give low priority to humanitarian concerns in comparison to their traditional national interests of security and prosperity. Undoubtedly, states do relegate humanitarian concerns to a lower priority and this is one reason why they sometimes fail to intervene, or do so belatedly and inadequately, as in Rwanda and Darfur.

But there are also practical obstacles to a timely response, as discussed in my book, *The Limits of Humanitarian Intervention: Genocide in Rwanda* (Kuperman, 2001). That study identifies three common obstacles to effective intervention: the rapid pace of violence against civilians; the delay in accurate information reaching potential interveners; and the logistical hurdles to deploying an adequate force. In Rwanda, for example, I found that most of the Tutsi victims were killed in the first three weeks, but even regional experts did not realize what was happening for two weeks, while it would have required more than a month to deploy an adequate force urgently by air to stop the genocide. Thus, even if potential interveners had possessed the political will, they could not have intervened quickly enough to protect most of the targeted civilians.

These obstacles to timely intervention are not universal but are common in humanitarian crises resulting from war. Violence against civilians has often been very quick: Croatia in 1995, where more than 100,000 ethnic Serbs were expelled from the Krajina region in less than a week; Kosovo in 1999, where most ethnic Albanians were expelled in less than two weeks; and East Timor in 1999, where most of the infrastructure was destroyed and most of the population displaced in less than a week. In Darfur, the period of peak violence against civilians lasted considerably longer, perhaps a year, but it was not widely reported in the Western media until spring 2004, by which time the displacement and killing were already tapering off.

The deployment of intervention forces also confronts some physical limitations that cannot be overcome by political will. Transporting forces by sea from Western military bases to conflict zones typically requires at least a month to load, travel, and unload. Air transport is quicker for bringing in initial intervention forces, but another month or more is required to deploy essential weapons, equipment, and supplies by air because of logistical obstacles such as the small payload of transport aircraft, the limited throughput capacity of regional airfields, and the considerable mass of modern military forces. Even if humanitarian advocates could generate sufficient political will for military intervention, the forces would often arrive too late to protect most at-risk civilians. To actually prevent civilian suffering, humanitarians need to

contemplate less forceful strategies that can avert the outbreak or escalation of violence in the first place.

KEY POINTS

Timely military intervention can be inhibited by a lack of political will among powerful states, which prioritize traditional interests, such as their own security and prosperity.

But practical obstacles also inhibit timely intervention.

For example, large-scale violence against civilians is often perpetrated very quickly, sometimes within a week.

Due to delays in obtaining accurate information, violence may be mostly completed before Western media or intelligence agencies report it.

Deploying an adequate number of properly equipped military forces for humanitarian intervention typically requires at least a month, whether by air or by sea.

Thus, even with sufficient political will, it may be impossible to deploy military forces in time to protect most at-risk civilians.

Humanitarians should expand their focus to include non-military strategies that can avert the outbreak or escalation of civil war, which causes most violence against civilians.

Critical Thinking Question:

Given these obstacles to timely military intervention, how can the responsibility to protect best be implemented?

Unintended Consequences of Intervention

Humanitarian intervention can have a wide range of unintended consequences contrary to its intent of protecting civilians. These perverse consequences sometimes arise simply from the delivery of subsistence commodities, as documented by John Prendergast (1996), Alex de Waal (1998), Mary Anderson (1999), and Fiona Terry (2002). Since militants often intermingle with civilians in places such as refugee camps, humanitarian aid may provide sustenance to rebels, enabling them to fight longer. The camps may also inhibit repatriation, thereby perpetuating grievance and rebel mobilization that prolong or renew war. Combatants may also intercept aid and resell it, or charge a tax for its safe delivery, acquiring funds for their war effort. In some cases, combatants may even fight each other to control the delivery of aid, so that humanitarian assistance creates an extra incentive for war.

Humanitarian aid can also undermine local economies and governance in several ways. First, the provision of free commodities may make it impossible for local farmers and businessmen to sell their goods, hindering economic development and potentially compelling them to turn to war to make a living. International aid organizations also siphon off local talent by employing skilled individuals as translators, drivers, and office workers, diminishing the human capital for domestic entrepreneurship and good government. Moreover, as long as essential social services are provided by external actors, local government may be deprived of the legitimacy that is essential for successful peacebuilding. Finally, because international humanitarian NGOs engage in fierce competition to win government contracts, they may concentrate more on the rapid delivery of aid than on preventing such unintended consequences.

Military force on humanitarian grounds may also backfire. Richard Betts (1994) observes that military intervention can vary in two ways—being either biased or impartial, and either limited or overwhelming—which yields four potential combinations. One effective combination is limited–biased intervention on behalf of the stronger party, enabling it to attain victory and thereby end the violence. Two other effective combinations are overwhelming intervention in either a biased or impartial manner, so that a powerful intervener simply imposes a settlement. But, regrettably, Betts says the most common combination in humanitarian military intervention is limited–impartial, which assists the weaker party just enough to prolong the fighting but not to end it (see Table 21.1). Similarly, Edward Luttwak (1999) has noted that well-intentioned intervention backfires by prolonging war and the resulting humanitarian suffering. The better way to promote stability and

humanitarianism, he argues, is not to intervene but instead to let the war burn out more quickly by victory of the stronger side.

Moral Hazard

My own research warns of a systemic *moral hazard* problem whereby the responsibility to protect may perversely increase the human suffering that it intends to alleviate (Crawford and Kuperman, 2006; Kuperman, 2008). The root of the problem is that civilian suffering often stems from state retaliation against a sub-state group for rebellion (such as armed secession) by some of its members. Humanitarian intervention not only protects at-risk civilians but often facilitates, intentionally or not, the political objectives of the rebels. The expectation of intervention can therefore encourage rebellion by lowering its anticipated cost and increasing its likelihood of success. Some militants even deliberately provoke state retaliation against civilians in order to attract intervention. Although humanitarian intervention may help rebels attain their political goals, it usually comes too late or is inadequate to avert retaliation against civilians. Thus, the responsibility to protect resembles an imperfect insurance policy against genocidal violence. It creates moral hazard that encourages the excessively risky or fraudulent behaviour of rebellion by members of groups that are vulnerable to retaliation, but it cannot fully protect the group's civilians against the violent backlash. As a result, the emerging norm of humanitarian intervention may cause some civilian suffering that otherwise would not occur. The most commonly cited examples of the **moral hazard of humanitarian**

Table 21.1 Four strategies of humanitarian military intervention

	Limited force	Overwhelming force
Impartial	Most common. Saves lives in short term, but may prolong war and resultant humanitarian suffering. (Bosnia: UN peacekeepers, 1992–5)	Rare. Can end violence quickly, but at cost of major military commitment and entanglement in renewed violence if perceived as non-neutral. (Somalia: US peacekeepers, 1992–5)
Biased	Less common. Works faster if biased towards stronger party. Or can end violence gradually by helping weaker side to win, but at risk of short-term backlash against civilians. (Kosovo: NATO bombing of Serbia, 1999)	Rare. Can end violence by quickly helping one side to win, but at cost of major military commitment and loss of neutrality. (Iraq: US-led intervention and no-fly zone in Kurd region, 1991–2003)

Adapted from R. Betts (1994).

intervention are Kosovo, Darfur, and Bosnia—the last of which is detailed in the following section.

The moral hazard problem can arise from any international action that is primarily motivated by the humanitarian desire to protect civilian targets of state violence but that also helps rebels. The spectrum of such action is wide, ranging from low-cost measures that respect traditional state sovereignty to high-cost ones that impinge on it, including: rhetorical condemnation, threats or imposition of economic sanctions, recognizing the independence of secessionist entities, air strikes on military or economic assets, military assistance to or coordination with rebels perceived as defending at-risk civilians, consensual deployment of peacekeepers, and non-consensual deployment of troops for peace enforcement. Possible ways to overcome the moral hazard problem are discussed in the conclusion of this chapter.

KEY POINTS

Humanitarian provision of subsistence commodities may exacerbate violence if it sustains combatants, is stolen by them and sold, or becomes the object of fighting.

Such purely humanitarian aid may also undermine local economies and governance by making redundant the roles of farmers, businessmen, and government institutions.

An international aid organization usually hires the most talented local residents, reducing their potential contribution to entrepreneurship and government.

Humanitarian NGOs often focus on winning contracts and delivering aid, rather than preventing unintended consequences.

Humanitarian military intervention is typically limited and impartial, which bolsters weaker parties just enough to prolong fighting and civilian suffering.

'Moral hazard' arises because humanitarian intervention may help rebels attain their political goals, thereby encouraging rebellion that provokes retaliatory violence against civilians.

Moral hazard can stem from any international action, motivated by the humanitarian desire to protect civilian targets of state violence, if it also helps rebels.

Critical Thinking Question:

The quickest way to protect civilians in civil war is to end the fighting, and the quickest way to end the fighting is to help the strongest side, typically the government, to win. But government crimes may be the cause of the war in the first place. Which is more important: ending the violence to protect civilians, or helping to overthrow a criminal government?

Case Study of Intervention: Bosnia

The dynamics of humanitarian intervention are well illustrated by Bosnia's war of 1992–5. This war stemmed from the break-up of Yugoslavia—a formerly stable, communist country that had been the most prosperous in Eastern Europe from the Second World War until the late 1980s. The demise of Yugoslavia had multiple causes. Its population comprised multiple ethnic groups, several of which had histories of large-scale violence against each other. The country was divided territorially, mainly along ethnic lines, into six autonomous republics—Bosnia, Croatia, Macedonia, Montenegro, Serbia, and Slovenia—and two autonomous Serbian provinces, Kosovo and Vojvodina (see Figure 21.1). Its leader after the Second World War, Marshal Josip Broz Tito, was able to suppress ethnic rivalries, but he died in 1980. Economic decline during the 1980s exacerbated tensions, especially among the richer republics of Slovenia and Croatia, which resented the drain of the poorer ones. The fall of the Berlin Wall in the late 1980s inspired democratization in Yugoslavia that revived nationalist tendencies. Serbia's leader Slobodan Milošević accused ethnic Albanians in Kosovo of discriminating against ethnic Serbs, revoked the province's autonomy, and instituted a police state. This fostered secessionism in Slovenia and Croatia, the latter of which also adopted nationalist constitutional reforms that frightened its ethnic Serb minority. Both of these republics seceded from Yugoslavia in June 1991. The Serb-dominated Yugoslav army fought a short, unsuccessful war in Slovenia, where there were few Serbs. But in Croatia, the Yugoslav army and Serb paramilitaries fought a bloody six-month war to retain control of Serb-populated territories and expel Croats from them. The war in Croatia killed thousands and displaced hundreds of thousands.

Bosnia remained largely peaceful during this time, but soon confronted a fateful decision. Its population comprised three main ethnic groups: Muslims (> 40 per cent), Serbs (> 30 per cent), and Croats (< 20 per cent). Serbs ideally wanted Bosnia to stay part of Yugoslavia, but, if Bosnia were to become independent, they insisted it first be divided internally along ethnic lines into autonomous cantons, so that Serbs could rule areas where they predominated. The Muslims, sometimes known as 'Bosniaks', were the largest group and wanted Bosnia to become independent as a unitary state without ethnic division. Croats chose to ally temporarily with the Muslims in favour of independence,

Figure 21.1 Ethnic demography of pre-war Yugoslavia, 1991

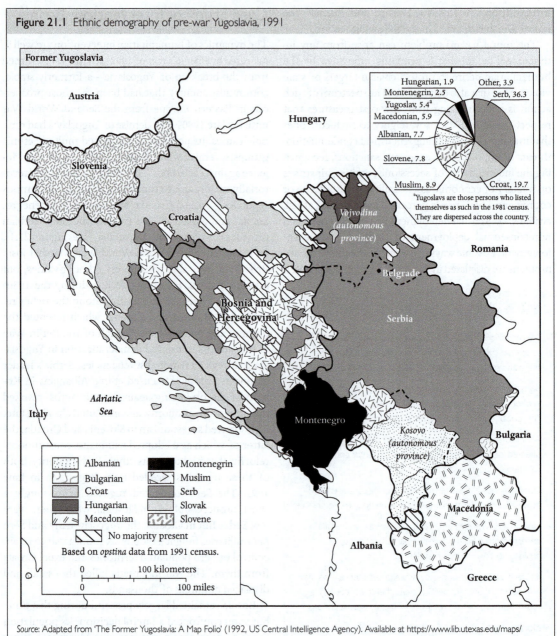

Source: Adapted from 'The Former Yugoslavia: A Map Folio' (1992, US Central Intelligence Agency). Available at https://www.lib.utexas.edu/maps/europe/yugoslav.jpg

but secretly planned for most of their areas to be annexed by neighbouring Croatia.

Some Muslim leaders were concerned by the prospect of war if Bosnia declared independence, so in August 1991 they explored a deal to remain within Yugoslavia, but popular Muslim sentiment rejected that option. The Serbs reiterated that they would not accept peacefully the independence of a unitary Bosnia, and the Yugoslav army redeployed to Bosnia those Serb troops who originated from the republic. At the end of February 1992, Muslim and Croat leaders insisted on holding a referendum on independence, which their ethnic groups approved overwhelmingly, while virtually all Serbs boycotted it.

Preventive Diplomacy Backfires

International diplomacy towards Bosnia was driven heavily by the humanitarian desire to avoid another war like the recent one in Croatia. The lead negotiator of the European Community (EC), Portuguese diplomat José Cutileiro, insisted that Bosnia's independence should not be recognized until the three groups agreed to an internal territorial division along ethnic lines. Briefly, leaders of the three groups agreed to such a plan in February 1992, based on a patchwork of non-contiguous ethnic cantons, and Cutileiro believed that war had been averted. But US diplomats argued that human rights and humanitarian interests could better be protected by recognizing the independence of a unitary Bosnia, to deter the Serbs from resorting to violence. After the United States convinced European officials to recognize Bosnia even without an agreement on internal ethnic division, the Muslims and Croats withdrew their approval for the Cutileiro plan. This exemplifies moral hazard: the United States intended to deter Serb violence, but instead emboldened the Muslims and Croats to reject a compromise and declare independence of a unitary Bosnia, despite Serb warnings that this would provoke war.

The decision by the United States and the EC to recognize the independence of a unitary Bosnia on 6–7 April 1992 failed to deter the Serbs as hoped and instead spurred them to violence, as they had warned. The Yugoslav army quickly seized control of territory, while Serb paramilitary groups engaged in killings, rapes, and forced expulsions (ethnic cleansing) to remove non-Serbs from Serb-dominated and ethnically mixed areas. Within three months, Serb forces controlled 70 per cent of Bosnia and had imposed a siege on the capital Sarajevo, attempting to compel the surrender of the Muslim and Croat leaders and the new Bosnian army that had been cobbled together from Muslim militias. By the end of June, 10,000 Muslim civilians had been killed, hundreds of thousands of Bosnians had been displaced, and Serb forces had established camps in which suspected militants were interrogated, tortured, or killed, and some women were raped. The war, lasting three and a half years, ultimately killed 97,000 Bosnians—including 64,000 Muslims, 25,000 Serbs, and 8,000 Croats. Among these were 40,000 civilian victims, of whom 33,000 (82 per cent) were Muslim. The war and the forced expulsions by each ethnic group caused the displacement of 2 million Bosnians, representing half the population.

Humanitarian intervention formally began in June 1992, when the UN Security Council voted to reopen Sarajevo airport for humanitarian deliveries and French president François Mitterand flew in to break the siege. The UN peacekeeping mission for the former Yugoslavia, originally created for Croatia in early 1992, was expanded to ensure the delivery of aid to Sarajevo and (as of September 1992) the rest of Bosnia. For the next three years, the main focus of UN troops in Bosnia was to assure the delivery of humanitarian aid to those suffering deprivation due to the fighting. Serb forces continued to surround Sarajevo (and other Muslim enclaves) and attack them with artillery and sniper fire, but they permitted sufficient aid deliveries to alleviate humanitarian suffering, which also enabled the Bosnian army to fight on. The Serb forces apparently hoped to preclude more decisive intervention against themselves by permitting the humanitarian deliveries. At the time, the United Nations maintained an arms embargo on the former Yugoslavia that perpetuated the Serb superiority in heavy weapons. As Richard Betts (1994) argues, this 'limited impartial' humanitarian military intervention helped the weaker Muslims just enough to continue fighting but not to prevail, and so had the unintended effect of perpetuating the war and its consequent humanitarian suffering, albeit mitigated by the provision of aid.

Forceful Intervention

The UN and NATO tried to use military threats and force, and diplomatic pressure, to prevent or deter the Bosnian Serbs and their supporters in Yugoslavia from continuing the war and endangering civilians. In May 1992, the UN expanded its limited arms embargo on combatants to a comprehensive arms embargo on Yugoslavia's two remaining republics, Serbia and Montenegro, on the grounds that they supported the Bosnian Serbs. In November 1992, NATO also began enforcing a UN-authorized naval blockade on these two republics. The sanctions compelled Serbia's leader Milošević to reduce military aid to the Bosnian Serbs to pressure them to make peace, but for domestic political reasons he could not cut them off entirely, so they refused to relent. This demonstrates that sanctions as a coercive tool of humanitarian intervention are not as toothless as some detractors claim, but neither can they force officials to take actions tantamount to political suicide.

In March 1993, the United Nations imposed a no-fly zone over Bosnia, and two months later authorized NATO air patrols to shoot down violators—both steps clearly targeted against Serbs, given that

Figure 21.2 Ethnic cleansing and 'safe areas' in Bosnia, 1994

Source: Adapted from *Balkan Battlegrounds: A Military History of the Yugoslav Conflict 1990–1995* (2002–3, Washington, DC: Central Intelligence Agency). Available at http://commons.wikimedia.org/wiki/Image:Bosnia_areas_of_control_Sep_94.jpg

the Bosnian government had no military aircraft. In April and May 1993, the UN Security Council also declared **safe areas** in six Bosnian Muslim enclaves: Bihac, Gorazde, Sarajevo, Srebrenica, Tuzla, and Zepa (see Figure 21.2). This meant that Serb forces were prohibited from attacking these cities that they surrounded, even though Muslim forces used the cities as bases for attacks against Serbs. Both the no-fly zone and the safe areas illustrate how ostensibly impartial humanitarian intervention to protect civilians

is often not neutral because it alters the balance of military power.

By 1993, the Muslim–Croat alliance had fractured, so that the most intense fighting and targeting of civilians during the summer was between these erstwhile allies. The United States still sought to reverse previous Serb gains in Bosnia, which required repairing the Muslim–Croat alliance. Through intense diplomacy and pledges of military assistance, the United States succeeded in March 1994 in forging the Washington

Agreement: a new alliance among Bosnia's Muslims and Croats and neighbouring Croatia. Retired US military officers began training the Croatian Army, and the United States stopped enforcing the arms embargo against Croatia, in return for it transferring a portion of imported weapons to Bosnia's Muslims and Croats. Such steps were all but certain to fuel renewed fighting, and, indeed, were intended to. This reveals that the human rights imperative of reversing aggression and displacement took precedence over the humanitarian imperative of minimizing harm to civilians.

Escalation of Intervention

Starting in 1994, NATO threatened and employed a variety of air strikes against the Serbs on humanitarian grounds, authorized initially under the previous year's UN Resolution 836 that called for 'all necessary measures, through the use of air power, in and around the safe areas'. In January, NATO threatened to bomb Serb forces near Sarajevo, compelling them to turn over heavy weapons to UN peacekeepers and withdraw further from the city. In February, NATO's governing council declared that it would use air strikes to enforce a heavy-weapon exclusion zone of 20 kilometres (12 miles) around Sarajevo. In March, NATO launched close-air-support strikes to help UN peacekeepers confronting Serb forces. In April, NATO bombed Serb forces surrounding Gorazde, compelling them to withdraw and permit the entry of UN peacekeepers. In August, NATO bombed Serb forces in retaliation for their retaking weapons from UN custody, persuading the Serbs to return the weapons. In September, NATO bombed Serb forces for violating the Sarajevo exclusion zone. In November, the Muslim-led Bosnian army launched an offensive from the Bihać safe area; Serb forces counter-attacked, and NATO responded by bombing a Serb-controlled air base in Croatia. Throughout 1994, these small-scale air strikes succeeded in compelling the Serbs to permit humanitarian deliveries and not to crush the safe areas that they surrounded, but air power could not end the war or compel Serb forces to surrender territory. This demonstrates the limits of small-scale air strikes as a tool of humanitarian intervention, at least in the absence of coordination with capable ground forces. Advocates of more robust military intervention against the Serbs derided the 1994 air strikes as mere 'pinpricks'.

The moral hazard arising from anticipated humanitarian intervention also exacerbated the fighting.

Bosnia's Muslim-controlled government and army repeatedly resisted ceasefires, even though the main victims of continued fighting were fellow Muslims, because of the expectation that such suffering would attract humanitarian military intervention sufficient to help them win the war. The UN's first commander of peacekeepers in Bosnia, Canadian General Lewis MacKenzie (1993, pp. 159, 308), declared that the Muslim-led 'Bosnian Presidency was committed to coercing the international community into intervening militarily'. A successor, British General Michael Rose (1998, p. 141), likewise reported that the Muslims rejected ceasefires because 'if the Bosnian Army attacked and lost, the resulting images of war and suffering guaranteed support in the West for the "victim State"'. Even James Gow (1997, p. 96), an academic overtly sympathetic to the Muslims, concedes that the Bosnian army broke ceasefires 'in the hope of provoking a U.S. intervention'. A senior Bosnian Muslim official, Omer Behmen, later admitted that the strategy had been to 'put up a fight for long enough to bring in the international community' (Kuperman, 2008). If not for this expectation of humanitarian military intervention, the Muslims might well have agreed to an early ceasefire, truncating the war and the resultant civilian suffering.

Peace Plans Rejected

Diplomatic efforts failed for three years to end the war because the proposed peace deals did not adequately reflect the military facts on the ground. In January 1993, the UN and the EC proposed the Vance–Owen peace plan: an internal division of Bosnia into a patchwork of ethnic cantons. This was similar to the pre-war Cutileiro plan, which had been proposed by the EC and accepted by the Serbs but rejected by the Muslims, the Croats, and the United States. During the first months of 1993, the Vance–Owen plan overcame initial resistance from the United States, Bosnia's Muslims and Croats, and Serbia's leader Slobodan Milošević. In spring 1993, however, Bosnia's Serbs rejected the proposal on grounds that, in light of the onset of war, security concerns now dictated a single contiguous Serb territory, not a patchwork.

The second diplomatic attempt by the UN and the EC, in August 1993, was the Owen–Stoltenberg plan, which responded to the Serbs' complaint by granting them a single, contiguous territory comprising 52 per cent of the republic, and dividing the rest into Muslim and Croat zones. This proposal was initially opposed by the Muslims, on grounds that it represented an ethnic 'partition' of Bosnia, and later by the Serbs who were loath to give back so much of the 70 per cent of the republic's territory that they still controlled militarily.

The third diplomatic effort was sponsored by a new transatlantic coalition, the 'Contact Group', initially including the United States, Russia, France, Britain, and Germany. Its July 1994 peace plan built on the renewed Croat–Muslim alliance by proposing a two-way partition of Bosnia into a contiguous Serb entity, comprising 49 per cent of the republic, and a Muslim–Croat entity in the remainder. But the Serbs again refused to surrender peacefully the territory that they had captured in war.

A Double-Edged Sword

The double-edged nature of humanitarian military intervention is well illustrated by the events of 1995. Since the previous year, the United States had facilitated the arming of Bosnia's Muslim–Croat alliance and Croatia to reverse the military advantage of the Serbs and thereby compel them to surrender territory and end the war. In May 1995, Croatia demonstrated its new-found strength by recapturing western Slavonia (see 'UN Western Zone' in Figure 21.2), an area of its country that since 1991 had been controlled by Serbs, who now fled in terror, creating a new refugee crisis.

Bosnian Serb leaders realized that humanitarian intervention had tilted the military balance against them—via aid, sanctions, air strikes, the no-fly zone, and especially the arming and training of their Croat and Muslim adversaries—so they moved to consolidate their territorial gains. For three years, the Serbs had been deterred from capturing the Muslim enclaves that they surrounded in eastern Bosnia (designated as safe areas by the UN in 1993), hoping to avoid triggering a more robust humanitarian military intervention. But now such intervention was upon them anyway, which removed their incentive for restraint. In May 1995, Serb forces violated the Sarajevo exclusion zone, prompting NATO air strikes, which the Serbs responded to by shelling safe areas and seizing 370 UN peacekeepers as hostages. More consequentially, in July 1995, Bosnian Serb forces seized the safe areas of Srebrenica and Zepa. In Srebrenica, Serb forces killed an estimated 8,000 Muslim men—the single largest crime of the war—in a savage revenge for the Muslims previously having used the safe area as a base for attacks. A small battalion of Dutch UN peacekeepers was present in Srebrenica but chose not to confront the better-armed

Serb forces. This illustrates the danger of attempting to deter humanitarian crimes with only air power and under-equipped ground forces, which offer a false sense of security that may actually increase the vulnerability of the populace. The events also demonstrate that, when humanitarian intervention is not neutral, it can provoke a violent backlash from those who perceive the interveners as being biased against them.

Decisive Intervention

The Srebrenica massacre and the seizure of UN hostages galvanized international support for more robust humanitarian military intervention against the Serbs. UN peacekeepers were consolidated in defensible areas to reduce their vulnerability, and a NATO rapid-reaction force was deployed to Mt Igman near Sarajevo. Ironically, the next major war crime in the region was committed not by Serbs but by Croatia's army, which in August 1995 seized control of its country's main Serb enclave, Krajina (see Figure 21.2), and expelled more than 100,000 Serbs. This represented another unintended consequence of humanitarian intervention: military aid intended to help the Croats and Muslims rectify past humanitarian offences inadvertently facilitated revenge crimes. The United States did not intervene against the Croatian troops—indeed, it had helped to arm and train them—which spurred criticism by the Serbs of a double standard. The Croatian army then proceeded to assist Bosnia's Croat and Muslim forces to reverse Serb gains in western Bosnia, causing further displacement of civilians.

The final escalation of humanitarian military intervention came in late August 1995, in response to an alleged Serb attack on a marketplace in Sarajevo. The next day, NATO initiated Operation Deliberate Force, a two-week bombing campaign against Serb military targets in Bosnia. The air strikes facilitated a renewed Croat–Muslim offensive in western Bosnia that rapidly diminished Serb control of the republic's territory from 70 per cent to less than 50 per cent. A ceasefire was agreed in October, and the following month the United States convened a peace conference in Dayton, Ohio. The Dayton Peace Accords, modelled on the Contact Group plan, were initialled in November and then signed in Paris in December 1995. These accords divided Bosnia internally into a contiguous 'Serb Republic' in 49 per cent of the territory, a contiguous Muslim–Croat Federation in most of the rest, and a sliver of land in the north whose sovereignty was still to be determined. Bosnia's Serb leaders, who had rejected the offer of 49 per cent of the territory when they controlled much more, now willingly accepted it in light of their abject retreat. Operation Deliberate Force illustrates that air power can be an effective tool of humanitarian intervention, at least when coordinated with capable ground forces.

Looking back over the entire episode, Bosnia demonstrates several dilemmas of humanitarian intervention. During the war, the provision of subsistence commodities reduced some civilian suffering. But this aid also enabled the Muslims to break the siege of Sarajevo in summer 1992, and thereby perpetuated a war that might otherwise have ended quickly. The militarization of humanitarian intervention in Bosnia had even more complex consequences. Prior to the war, expectations of such intervention convinced the Muslim leadership to reject the Cutileiro plan and declare the independence of Bosnia as a unitary state, despite Serb threats to respond with violence, as soon transpired. After the fighting started, even though Muslim civilians were the main victims of the war, the Muslim leadership resisted ceasefires because it hoped that humanitarian suffering would attract military intervention on its behalf. These events demonstrate that the prospect of intervention contributed to both the outbreak and perpetuation of war. (See Box 21.2 for a discussion of whether humanitarian intervention does more harm than good.)

Military intervention—including weapons supply, training, a no-fly zone, and air strikes—gradually enabled the Muslims and Croats to reverse Serb military

gains. But, by changing the balance of power, such intervention also unintentionally spurred humanitarian crimes, including the ethnic cleansing by Croatia of Serbs in Krajina and the slaughter by Serb forces of Muslims in Srebrenica. Overall, it is difficult to determine whether humanitarian intervention did more good or harm in Bosnia. But the experience does suggest ways to improve humanitarian intervention, which are discussed in this chapter's final section.

BOX 21.2 ALTERNATIVE POINTS OF VIEW: DOES HUMANITARIAN INTERVENTION DO MORE GOOD THAN HARM?

This chapter suggests that humanitarian intervention is justified only in some conflicts that threaten civilians, and only if implemented in a manner likely to do more good than harm. Critics offer at least three contending views. Optimists claim that intervention almost always does more good than harm, especially as 'political will' grows for earlier and longer intervention. Proponents include Thomas G. Weiss (2012) and Alex J. Bellamy (2014).

Pessimists argue that intervention, even if well-intentioned, invariably does more harm than good for both the interveners and those they intend to help. Exponents include Barry R. Posen (2014). Sceptics contend that humanitarian intervention is merely a cover for imperialism. This perspective is applied to Bosnia by Diana Johnstone (2003), and more broadly by Jean Bricmont (2007).

KEY POINTS

Bosnia's war started because of distrust and disagreement among its three main ethnic groups. Serbs wanted Bosnia either to stay in Yugoslavia or to be divided internally along ethnic lines prior to independence. Muslims and Croats wanted Bosnia to become independent without internal ethnic division.

When the Muslims and Croats declared Bosnia independent as a unitary state, Serb forces responded by quickly capturing 70 per cent of Bosnia's territory and killing, expelling, or detaining many non-Serbs.

Humanitarian intervention alleviated some civilian suffering but also helped to perpetuate a war that eventually killed 97,000 Bosnians—including 40,000 civilians—and displaced two million.

Muslim leaders rejected ceasefires because they expected the suffering of their own civilians to attract humanitarian military intervention that would help them win the war—which illustrates the moral hazard of humanitarian intervention.

Economic sanctions compelled Serbian leader Slobodan Milošević to reduce military aid to Bosnia's Serbs but not to terminate it, because he faced domestic pressure to support fellow Serbs.

Non-neutral military intervention enabled the Croats and Muslims to reverse territorial losses and return to their homes, but also led to the ethnic cleansing of Croatia's Serbs and the massacre of Srebrenica's Muslims. These events illustrate that sometimes there is a trade-off between promoting human rights and humanitarian.

Limited humanitarian military intervention—including air strikes, a no-fly zone, and deployment of peacekeepers—proved inadequate to guarantee the protection of civilians, as demonstrated in Srebrenica.

Proposed peace plans failed for three years to end the war because they did not reflect the military facts on the ground, whereas the Dayton Accords succeeded by recognizing those facts, as they had been altered by intervention.

Conclusion: Lessons of Humanitarian Intervention

Some advocates of forceful intervention claim that it can simultaneously promote humanitarian and human rights objectives. In reality, there may be a trade-off between the two. This is most obvious for military intervention in support of 'freedom fighters'— militants who claim to be fighting for their group's human rights, as in Bosnia. Such intervention encourages the launching and perpetuation of rebellion or armed secession, which often provokes states to retaliate in a manner that inflicts suffering on the group's civilians. Forceful intervention to promote human rights thus often undermines humanitarian aims. In theory, a timely and robust military intervention might achieve both objectives, but logistical and political obstacles inhibit such an ideal use of force.

This dilemma can be overcome through less forceful and more precise intervention methods. Relief aid should be delivered in ways that benefit mainly civilians—for example, by distributing it at refugee and displacement camps that are policed to exclude rebels, or at least their weapons. Human rights may be supported by intervening diplomatically and economically on behalf of non-violent protest groups— for example, by offering trade and aid to states that address the legitimate grievances of such opposition movements. Threats of forceful intervention should be reserved for cases in which states either attack non-violent groups or respond disproportionately to rebellion by deliberately targeting civilians. Such an enlightened approach, aiming to discourage opposition groups from rebelling while raising the incentives for states to accommodate their demands, has the potential to promote both humanitarian and human rights objectives.

These lessons are illustrated by further investigation into the case of Kosovo (Kuperman, 2008). Starting in 1989, Serbia revoked the autonomy of this province, disenfranchised the local ethnic Albanian majority, banned public education in the Albanian language, dismissed most ethnic Albanian professionals from their jobs, and instituted repressive police patrols— a widespread and systematic violation of human rights. For the next eight years, the ethnic Albanians resisted by non-violent means, which provided an ideal window of opportunity for the international community to use diplomatic sticks and carrots to persuade Serbia to restore their human rights. Such international pressure would have been unlikely to provoke a genocidal backlash from the Serbs, because they faced little violent opposition in the province. Analogous non-violent movements, typically benefiting from international support, have succeeded in promoting human rights in many countries (Schock, 2005), including India, the United States, South Africa, the Philippines, the former Soviet Union and other communist states of Eastern Europe, Indonesia, Serbia, Lebanon, and—in the Arab Spring of 2011—Tunisia.

Regrettably, the international community devoted insufficient support to Kosovo's non-violent human rights movement. As a result, this pacifist resistance eventually gave way in 1997 to a rebellion by militant ethnic Albanians, who provoked a violent counter-insurgency by Serbian forces that also endangered Albanian civilians. Interveners might still have mitigated violence if they had targeted humanitarian aid mainly to the affected civilians. Instead, the United States coordinated with the rebels and threatened to attack Serbia, and then NATO followed through on that threat—which only fuelled the Albanian rebellion, exacerbated Serbian retaliation, and magnified several-fold the humanitarian suffering.

The Kosovo case demonstrates that, in order to promote both human rights and humanitarianism, the international community should focus its leverage to persuade oppressive states to meet the legitimate demands of non-violent groups. Failing that, if a rebellion breaks out, intervention should be aimed at helping civilians, not rebels, to avoid exacerbating rebellion and the resulting backlash against civilians.

The good news is that it is possible simultaneously to promote human rights and humanitarianism. The cautionary note is that, unless intervention is properly designed to avoid rewarding rebels, the promotion of one of these admirable goals could well undermine the other.

 ## QUESTIONS

Individual Study Questions

1. What is the traditional definition of humanitarian intervention, and how and why has it changed since the end of the Second World War?
2. What is the difference between humanitarian intervention and the promotion of human rights?
3. What is the responsibility to protect, and how does it differ from the traditional norm of sovereignty?
4. What is the difference between impartiality and neutrality?
5. How was military force used in humanitarian intervention in Iraq, Somalia, Kosovo, and Libya, and in what cases was it conspicuously absent?
6. Why did war break out in Bosnia?
7. What were the military aspects of humanitarian intervention in Bosnia?

Group Discussion Questions

1. When is humanitarian intervention compatible with the promotion of human rights, and when are they in tension?
2. What are the obstacles to effective humanitarian military intervention?
3. How and why does humanitarian intervention sometimes backfire, and what is the 'moral hazard' problem?
4. How did humanitarian intervention both reduce and increase civilian suffering in Bosnia?
5. What steps should be taken to improve humanitarian intervention?

 ## FURTHER READING

Anderson, M. (1999). *Do No Harm: How Aid Can Support Peace—Or War*. Boulder, CO: Lynne Rienner.

A simple guide for would-be humanitarians.

Betts, R. (1994). The Delusion of Impartial Intervention. *Foreign Affairs*, **73**/6, 20–33.

An argument for either taking sides or staying out.

Burg, S. and **Shoup, P.** (1999). *The War in Bosnia-Herzegovina*. New York: M. E. Sharpe.

The quintessential account of this case.

Crawford, T. and **Kuperman, A.** (eds) (2006). *Gambling on Humanitarian Intervention: Moral Hazard, Rebellion and Civil War*. New York: Routledge.

Scholars debate the moral hazard hypothesis, especially regarding Kosovo.

de Waal, A. (1998). *Famine Crimes: Politics and the Disaster Relief Industry in Africa*. Bloomington, IN: Indiana University Press.

De Waal explains how and why humanitarian NGOs veer off course.

Kuperman, A. (2001). *The Limits of Humanitarian Intervention: Genocide in Rwanda.* Washington, DC: Brookings Institution Press.

An explanation of why political will is not the only obstacle to timely and effective intervention.

Kuperman, A. (2008). The Moral Hazard of Humanitarian Intervention: Lessons from the Balkans. *International Studies Quarterly,* **52**/1, 49–80.

This article shows how expectations of intervention helped trigger and perpetuate violence in Bosnia and Kosovo.

Kuperman, A. (2015). Obama's Libya Debacle: How a Well-Meaning Intervention Ended in Failure. *Foreign Affairs,* **94**/2, 66–77.

An illustration of how intervention can backfire for both the target country and interveners.

Posen, B. (1996). Military responses to refugee disasters. *International Security,* **21**/1, 72–111.

A useful typology of intervention scenarios.

WEB LINKS

http://www.globalhumanitarianassistance.org   Website for Global Humanitarian Assistance.

http://www.crisisgroup.org   Website for the International Crisis Group.

http://www.nato.int/docu/handbook/2006/hb-en-2006.pdf   The NATO Handbook details NATO Intervention in Bosnia.

http://www.un.org/en/peacekeeping/missions/past/unprofor.htm   This website details the UN Intervention in Bosnia.

NOTES

1.   See http://www.globalhumanitarianassistance.org/data-guides/datastore.
2.   Kuperman (2011).

Visit the Online Resource Centre that accompanies this book for updates and a range of other resources: www.oxfordtextbooks.co.uk/orc/goodhart3e/

22

Transitional Justice

Joanna R. Quinn

Reader's Guide

In the months and years after atrocities such as genocide, disappearances, torture, civil conflict, and other gross violations of human rights have taken place, states are left with a puzzling and often difficult question: what to do with the perpetrators of such acts of violence? Such conflict leaves physical scars, evident in the destruction of hospitals and schools, for example. But it also leaves deep and lasting social scars. Transitional justice considers the social implications of this kind of brutal conflict. It is concerned with how to rebuild societies in the period after human rights violations, as well as with how such societies, and individuals within those societies, should be held to account for their actions. It is this past violation of human rights that forms the basis of transitional justice, and is the impetus that pushes the processes of transitional justice forward. How to deal appropriately with these kinds of past human rights violations makes the processes of transitional justice quite controversial.

Introduction

The idea that states can and should deal with the perpetrators of violent crime during a period of civil conflict, or repressive or authoritarian rule, is relatively new. For many years, leaders of rebel groups and states were simply left alone, without consideration of punishment or having to 'pay' for their deeds. Tyrants, such as Idi Amin of Uganda or Jean-Claude 'Baby Doc' Duvalier of Haiti simply left their own countries, moved to countries that were willing to house them, and faded into obscurity. It was only in the 1990s that scholars and practitioners began to sort out how to deal with their violent histories.

At that time, of course, there were many situations of violence and conflict under way, or just ending (see Box 22.1). Private property had been confiscated and secret government files maintained in former Soviet-bloc countries in Eastern Europe. The **genocides** of Rwanda and Bosnia were taking place. Bloody civil conflicts continued in countries such as Somalia, Sierra Leone, Liberia, Haiti, and Guatemala. Yet the perpetrators of even the most egregious human rights violations went free.

It was becoming clear that someone should be made to answer for such horrible crimes. Still, just who should be held to account, and for what, posed a dilemma. Should every single person who had committed a crime be punished and sent to jail? Should only the 'big fish', officials and officers of the former regime, be brought to trial? Or should those lower down the chain of command, the 'small fry', also be tried? Who should carry out such prosecutions? Should governments and their bureaucracies be 'purged' of officials who had helped to carry out such awful acts? How should victims be rehabilitated for the abuses and injuries, both emotional and physical, that they had suffered? Should

victims themselves be acknowledged for their suffering? **Transitional justice**, as it has come to be called, deals with all of these questions, and more.

These issues are intrinsically linked with the study of human rights for several reasons. First, the mechanisms of transitional justice deal explicitly with the gross human rights violations that have been committed. Second, transitional justice is an important tool for ending the cycle of **impunity**, and the kind of immunity from prosecution that is prevalent in states where the history of human rights abuses is in the not-so-distant past; justice itself is deeply related to human rights. Third, the mechanisms being utilized in the pursuit of transitional justice are increasingly established, sanctioned, or funded by parts of the United Nations—the main international organ concerned with the protection of human rights.

Transitional justice is also deeply intertwined with the principle of **universality**. In their ideal form, transitional justice mechanisms deal with all individuals equally in giving them an opportunity to participate. In its embrace of the values of universalism, transitional justice works to restore individuals back to their rightful place in society. And insofar as transitional justice also seeks to promote human rights, universality is also a central tenet.

The task, therefore, that confronts societies aiming towards transition from authoritarian or repressive regimes to democracy, or from conflict to peace, is daunting. Where to start? Obviously, changes need to take place in virtually every sector, and at virtually every level. Often, reforms are required in sectors including security, economics, healthcare, education, and infrastructure. Transitional justice focuses specifically on reforms to the justice sector, working towards the re-establishment of the rule of law and assisting in the rebuilding of the system of courts that is required in a functioning, democratic society.

Even so, it can be difficult for transitional societies to come to an agreement about just what this means, or how it will be carried out. One worry, of course, is that decisions about who should be punished will be made by the victorious party, and will not necessarily address the concerns of the population as a whole. In post-apartheid South Africa, for example, white supporters of the defeated National Party worried that they would be attacked by the newly victorious (and mostly black) African National Congress. A second worry is that, in the negotiation of peace settlements, or the handing over of power from one regime to the

---

BOX 22.1 WHAT ARE SOME SITUATIONS THAT COULD BENEFIT FROM MECHANISMS OF TRANSITIONAL JUSTICE?

- Genocide
- Civil conflict
- Racism
- Forced slavery
- Community violence
- Man-made famine
- Gross violations of human rights

BOX 22.2 THREE DIFFERENT APPROACHES TO TRANSITIONAL JUSTICE

Retributive Justice

Goal: to correct the perpetrator by means of prosecution and punishment.

Usual mechanisms: trials, tribunals.

Sample case: Cambodia: Extraordinary Chambers in the Courts of Cambodia established in 2001 by the Cambodian National Assembly to create a court to try serious crimes committed during the Khmer Rouge regime, 1975–9.

Restorative Justice

Goal: to restore the dignity of the victim; to restore the perpetrator back into society.

Usual mechanisms: truth commissions, healing circles.

Sample case: Guatemala: Commission for Historical Clarification (*Comisión para el Esclarecimiento Histórico*) established in 1994, during negotiations between the Guatemalan Government and leftist rebels under the Oslo Accord process, which ended more than thirty-five years of violence.

Reparative Justice

Goal: to repair the injury suffered by victims.

Usual mechanisms: restitution, apology.

Sample case: United States: $20,000 was awarded by Congress in 1988 to each American of Japanese ancestry who had been forcibly removed and detained in internment camps located throughout the country during the Second World War.

Adapted from Minow (1998).

more than 80 per cent of judges there did not hold law degrees, and many of those had never received formal education at all, let alone legal training.

No one solution will ever be acceptable to everyone. For victims of heinous crimes, no remedy can ever be enough. No court sentence can restore a missing limb. No amount of money will bring back a dead child. Similarly, for perpetrators—such as Nazi officers—whose actions were taken in an environment that condoned, rather than condemned, them, it may be difficult for society to try them. Still, common morality dictates that something must be done.

As the idea of coming to terms with past abuses has unfolded into practical application, different ways of dealing with both victims and perpetrators have developed (see Box 22.2). The types of mechanisms that states adopt tend to reflect the circumstances that arise from the particular crimes committed, and the social and political conditions that follow. They also correspond to particular ideas about how and why justice must be done, and must be seen to be done. Martha Minow (1998) has characterized these approaches as three distinct *paradigms* (philosophical or theoretical frameworks): retributive, restorative, and reparative justice. This typology is useful as a means of both explaining and understanding the different ways of approaching transitional justice.

Retributive Justice

Retributive justice is the kind of 'justice' that those in the 'West' are used to thinking about. In this paradigm, justice equates with legal prosecutions and the rule of law. This includes the kinds of court proceedings and sentencing that are common throughout much of the world today, all of which are based on the notion of retribution or punishment for crimes committed. Typically, a trial involves a person charged with the commission of a crime being brought before an arbitrator, if not a panel of his peers, whereupon his guilt and subsequent penalty are determined.

The rationale behind retributive justice is at least fourfold. First, if a person has done something wrong, those actions need to be publicly acknowledged. During the process of a trial, details about specific crimes committed are openly discussed, often being revealed for the first time. Second, a perpetrator needs to be punished for his actions. The objective of punishment is both to remove the perpetrator from the

next, the perpetrators of heinous crimes will be given some kind of **amnesty**, or immunity from prosecution. In Chile, for example, General Pinochet simply granted himself and his accomplices lifetime immunity, insulating himself and them from possible criminal charges. Third, the capacity of the legal system may have been badly compromised during the conflict, and/or may find itself unable to cope with the large numbers of prosecutions that will be required. More than 120,000 people were identified as perpetrators of the Rwandan genocide, for example, which placed an enormous burden on the court system there; it was estimated that it would take nearly 180 years to prosecute all of them. And in Cambodia, the court system was weak to begin with. It has been reported that circumstances in which he committed the crime and to rehabilitate him before his release into the community. Third, by disciplining someone for his actions, there is a wider, educative effect for the public. That is, if others see that someone is being punished for committing particular crimes, they will be deterred from committing the same crimes. And fourth, the ability to conduct a trial demonstrates and reinforces that the justice system is both capable of carrying out retributive actions and is viable as an institution. If a trial takes place, it must be the case that the justice system is fully functioning, and able to transmit the full authority of the law of the land.

National Trials

And so, a number of societies in transition have opted to utilize mechanisms of retributive justice, mostly in the form of trials, to deal with the perpetrators of past crimes. In most parts of the world, this is the remedy that would be expected. Under normal circumstances, in fact, it is the main forum for such resolution.

Such was the case in Greece, which experienced a *coup d'état* (violent overthrow) by a military *junta* (pronounced HOON-ta) in April 1967. The constitution was suspended and martial law was declared. In 1973, thousands of students were arrested, injured, or killed in a

---

BOX 22.3 TIMELINE OF MODERN INTERNATIONAL MECHANISMS OF TRANSITIONAL JUSTICE

1945 *Nuremberg Trials* **established by victorious Allies in post-War Germany**

- Tribunal located in Nuremberg, Germany.
- Four justices and four alternates from the four Allied countries adjudicated cases.
- Charges of crimes against peace, crimes against humanity—crimes that did not exist at the time of commission.
- More than 200 Nazi officials tried, excluding most senior decision makers.

1946 *Tokyo Trial* **established by victorious Allies in post-War Japan**

- Tribunal located in Tokyo, Japan.
- Eleven justices from ten countries adjudicated cases.
- Charges of crimes against peace, crimes against humanity, and conventional war crimes.
- Twenty-eight top Japanese officials tried.

1993 *International Criminal Tribunal for the Former Yugoslavia* (ICTY) **established by the UN Security Council to try top officials from the conflict in the Balkans**

- Tribunal located in The Hague, Netherlands.
- Sixteen justices elected to four-year terms by the UN General Assembly, and twelve *ad litem* justices (appointed only for specific cases) adjudicated cases.
- Charges included grave breaches of Geneva Conventions and Protocols, violations of laws of war, genocide, and crimes against humanity.

- Most 'big fish' eluded capture and escaped prosecution.
- Tribunal intended as ad hoc or temporary, to be disbanded when mandate met.

2002 *Special Court for Sierra Leone* (SCSL) **established between the United Nations and Sierra Leone as the first hybrid national/international tribunal to try criminals from Sierra Leone's brutal civil war**

- Tribunal located in Freetown, Sierra Leone (except Charles Taylor, who was tried in The Hague under SCSL auspices).
- Eleven judges appointed from ten countries, from across Africa and the West.
- Charges included war crimes and crimes against humanity committed in Sierra Leone.
- 'Big fish' including Charles Taylor charged, detained, and tried.

2002 *International Criminal Court* (ICC) **established by states parties to the Rome Statute**

- Tribunal located in The Hague, Netherlands.
- Eighteen justices elected from Assembly of States Parties adjudicated cases.
- Charges included crimes of aggression, genocide, and war crimes.[1]
- ICC intended as permanent tribunal.

violent protest at the Athens Polytechnic. And in 1974, the military dictatorship invaded the island of Cyprus, launching a bloody coup against its population. In a series of trials held throughout 1975, dealing with the dictatorship in its entirety, more than 150 top officials were tried and punished for crimes including torture, assassinations, and the unlawful suspension of the constitution. Many thousands of others were stripped of governmental and administrative positions—an attempt to 'dejuntify' the country in the aftermath of the coup.

International Justice

Sometimes, however, the national court system is unwilling to carry out these kinds of prosecutions. Furthermore, it may be unable to do so. In these cases, the international community has stepped in to assist with these prosecutions. Such trials began with the post-War **Nuremberg Trials** and Tokyo Tribunal, which were appointed to deal with Nazi war crimes and the crimes of Japanese officials. Thus began the development of the system of international criminal law (see Box 22.3). Previously, any and all laws had existed only at the national/state level (see Chapter 4).

It was several decades, however, until further international criminal legal avenues were pursued. The international community showed little interest in the prosecution of perpetrators of mass atrocities, genocide, and **war crimes**. In the 1990s, several international courts and tribunals were established, in conjunction with the United Nations Security Council. These included the **International Criminal Tribunal for the Former Yugoslavia** (ICTY) and the **International Criminal Tribunal for Rwanda** (ICTR), both established on an ad hoc (single-purpose) basis to try cases pertaining to the genocides, war crimes, and other atrocities that took place in those countries. Most recently, the **International Criminal Court** (ICC), a permanent court with more or less international jurisdiction, was established to try individuals for war crimes, crimes against humanity, and genocide (see Box 22.4).

One other option in the international arena is that various states can step in and conduct trials of people who have committed criminal acts in another country. Such cases are tried under the international legal principle of **universal jurisdiction**, which, until the late 1990s, had rarely been used. Universal jurisdiction is claimed on the grounds that the crime committed is considered to be a crime against all, and therefore any state may claim criminal jurisdiction. The idea, then, is that people

BOX 22.4 CHALLENGING ASSUMPTIONS: THE INTERNATIONAL CRIMINAL COURT

To date, the International Criminal Court has only taken up the prosecution of cases from the continent of Africa—although the Court has carried out preliminary examinations of situations in a number of other states outside Africa, including Afghanistan, Colombia, Georgia, Honduras, Iraq, Ukraine, and Palestine. This has led to charges of bias against the Court, as well as a deep distrust of the Court by a number of African states, who accuse it of being a court for policing Africa.

However, the very reason for the existence of the Court holds an important clue as to the reason for this: the Court is intended for the prosecution of the most serious cases of human rights abuses where the state that has jurisdiction over it is 'unwilling or unable genuinely to carry out the investigation or prosecution' (Rome Statute Art.17.a) of those crimes. In the case of states like Uganda, Democratic Republic of Congo, and Darfur, Sudan, the states themselves have indicated that they are either unwilling or unable to prosecute those who have committed serious crimes.

One other reason must also be considered: courts can only successfully prosecute situations in which clear evidence exists of the crimes that have been committed. Without this evidence, it is much harder to secure convictions. And like any court, the International Criminal Court must have clear evidence. The crimes that have been committed in various African situations, such as in the case of Jean-Pierre Bemba, who was ultimately convicted of enlisting and conscripting children under the age of 15 years and using them to participate actively in hostilities in the context of an armed conflict, reflect the availability of clear evidence that is used in successful prosecutions.

who have committed crimes may be tried in a country other than their own, regardless of nationality, country of residence, or any other relation with the prosecuting country, even though their crimes have been committed outside the boundaries of the prosecuting state.

The case of Rwanda illustrates how retributive justice can be applied by the international community when a state itself is unwilling or unable to prosecute those responsible for criminal violations. Between early April and mid-July 1994, a genocide was carried out in Rwanda in which more than 800,000 mostly Tutsi Rwandan citizens were brutally murdered by mostly Hutu citizens (see Chapter 20). When the genocide came to an end, more than 120,000 Rwandans stood accused of the commission of these crimes. The justice system, as it then existed, was simply unable to deal with such an extreme number of cases. Two separate international mechanisms, along with an intricate national system of *gacaca* courts (pronounced ga-CHA-cha), were established to try those accused. We will describe the international mechanisms in the following sections.

International Trials: Tribunals

The International Criminal Tribunal for Rwanda was established by the United Nations Security Council in 1994, to prosecute those responsible for genocide and other serious breaches of international humanitarian law committed in the territory of Rwanda in 1994. The international community recognized the need to strengthen the rule of law, and to demonstrate that it had held at least the 'big fish' responsible, in an attempt to show other leaders around the world that they could not get away with such crimes. The idea behind the court was that it would try a finite number of cases and then be disbanded, which happened in late 2015. A similar court was appointed for the Former Yugoslavia in 1993.

International Trials: Universal Jurisdiction

The second international mechanism being used in pursuit of retributive justice for crimes committed during the Rwandan genocide is the trial of *génocidaires* by courts of, and located in, other countries, using the principle of universal jurisdiction. Belgium was the first country to try Rwandan *génocidaires* in its civilian courts, based on a law of universal jurisdiction passed in 1993. In 2001, four Rwandans were charged, convicted, and sentenced under the Belgian criminal justice system for crimes that they had committed in Rwanda. Canada, France, and Switzerland have also tried Rwandan genocide cases. Many other states are reluctant to do so.

Restorative Justice

Restorative justice may be a foreign concept to those who have grown up with the idea of retributive justice described above. In this paradigm, justice is about restoring both the victim and perpetrator of crimes back into harmony with the community. Restorative processes always seek to dignify and empower victims. And so, unlike retributive mechanisms such as court cases, which tend to focus only on the perpetrator, victims often play a central role in restorative processes. Ideally, the victim is also empowered through restorative processes. The wider community, too, is often a participant in restorative processes.

Restorative justice can take many forms. A number of these are, and have been, actively used in the West and elsewhere, either instead of, or alongside, retributive mechanisms. In New Zealand, Family Group Conferences, based on traditional Maori principles, including teaching, settlement, and community restoration, are used in conjunction with the court system. In many parts of Canada, aboriginal communities use healing circles instead of the courts to deal with community members who have committed crimes against the community. Ceremonies to 'cool the heart[s]' of former child soldiers on their return to their home communities in Sierra Leone are commonplace.

Truth Commissions

In pursuit of justice in transitional communities, one of the most commonly used restorative mechanisms has been the **truth commission**. Truth commissions are bodies established to look at widespread human rights violations that took place during a specified period of time, on a temporary basis, by the state, often in conjunction with opposition forces and/

KEY POINTS

Retributive justice generally involves the indictment, trial, and punishment of the perpetrators of crimes.

Trials for the perpetrators of crimes may be carried out by national courts.

Retributive justice may also be carried out by international tribunals.

Courts around the world have begun to try the perpetrators of crimes in other countries under the principle of international law known as *universal jurisdiction*.

Critical Thinking Questions:

Who should be held accountable for gross violations of human rights—only the masterminds of the crimes, or also the low-ranking soldiers who carried them out?

Is there moral value in imprisoning people found guilty of these crimes?

or the involvement of the international community. While no two truth commissions ever look or function in exactly the same way, their aim, generally, is to inquire into past events (see Box 22.5). Often, the inquiry includes the collection of details from victims by means of questionnaires, and sometimes by public testimony. For the most part, each truth commission also produces a report that contains detailed or summary accounts of exactly what has taken place. In most cases, these reports are widely publicized. In Argentina, for example, the report published by the National Commission on the Disappeared, entitled *Nunca Más* (*Never Again*), became one of the best-selling books of all time in that country. There have been more than thirty truth commissions established around the world since 1974. The majority of these have been held in Africa and Latin America, although commissions have also been established in Asia and Europe.

The benefits of truth commissions over retributive mechanisms have been hotly debated. First,

truth commissions have a much broader focus than trials. While the scope of a trial is often limited to the actions of one perpetrator, truth commissions focus on widespread abuses perpetrated by any number of individuals and on the suffering endured by hundreds, or more likely thousands, of victims. Second, truth commissions can have an educative effect through the broadcasting of public hearings and testimony or through the publication and dissemination of the final report. Such measures might be the first opportunity that people have to hear about what happened in their own country. Third, truth commissions are not a 'one-size-fits-all' approach. Truth commissions may choose to focus on truth or they may choose to focus on reconciliation, as identified by the people of a particular country. They are also able to tailor their activities to suit the circumstances of the particular country in which they operate. Fourth, truth commissions are often seen as a less costly alternative to retributive approaches. For example, because truth commissions

---

BOX 22.5 WHERE HAVE TRUTH COMMISSIONS BEEN ESTABLISHED?

Uganda	Commission of Inquiry into the Disappearance of People in Uganda since 25 January 1971 (1974)
Argentina	*Comisión Nacional para ka Desaparición de Personas* (1983–4)
	(National Commission on the Disappearance of Persons)
Chile	*Comisión Nacional para la Verdad y Reconciliación* (1990–1)
	(National Commission on Truth and Reconciliation)
South Africa	Truth and Reconciliation Commission (1995–2000)
Guatemala	*Comisión para el Esclarecimiento Histórico* (1997–9)
	(Commission for Historical Clarification)
Sierra Leone	Truth and Reconciliation Commission (2000–4)
Peru	*Comisión de la Verdad y Reconciliación* (2003)
	(Truth and Reconciliation Commission)
Morocco	*Instance Équité et Réconciliation* (2004–5)
	(Fairness and Reconciliation Commission)
Ghana	National Reconciliation Commission (2004–5)
Kenya	Truth, Justice and Reconciliation Commission (2008–13)
Canada	Indian Residential Schools Truth and Reconciliation Commission (2007–)
Tunisia	Truth and Dignity Commission (2014–)

This is not an exhaustive list, but shows selected truth commissions.

require far less in terms of infrastructure, personnel, and other expenses generally associated with a trial, their expenses are considerably lower. The South African Truth and Reconciliation Commission, for instance, had a total budget, for all five years of its operation, of 196 million Rand (approximately US$25 million)—a substantially smaller sum than the ICTR, as we have discussed.

National Implementation

Truth commissions are generally established and run by the *national government*, as happened in Chile. In 1973, the Government of democratically elected President Allende was overthrown by General Augusto Pinochet in a brutal and repressive military coup. More than 3,000 people were killed, and many more were injured. When the subsequent Government came to power in 1990, a truth commission was established. The *Comisión Nacional para la Verdad y Reconciliación* (National Commission on Truth and Reconciliation) worked for a period of nine months. During that time, the Commission received evidence from victims and their families in 3,400 cases, considered this evidence, and finally prepared a report. Testimony was heard, evidence gathered, and decisions made; in the end, all of the evidence was referred to the courts, except for the testimony of those who had been granted a blanket amnesty.

International Involvement

In other cases, however, truth commissions are implemented and/or run by the *international community*. The involvement of the international community may come as a result of one factor or a combination of several factors. First, the national government may be too fragile to carry out such investigations on its own. The involvement of the international community gives legitimacy to the national regime, and the support that the international community can provide often strengthens the process immeasurably. Second, the financial resources of the national government may be too depleted for it to be able to carry out a truth commission on its own. Third, other resources in society, including members of the judicial community, or basic infrastructure needs, may be similarly depleted. The international community can provide for these needs. Fourth, there is enormous expertise in matters concerning truth commissions in the international community that may be lacking at the national level. The inclusion of personnel

from the international community can provide such expertise. Finally, the conditions to bring about the truth commission may have been negotiated between opposing parties under international supervision. The presence of members of the international community can keep disagreements between rival parties that are meant to be working together on the truth commission from flaring up and derailing the process.

The international community was very much integrated in the Haitian truth commission. President Jean-Bertrand Aristide was elected President of Haiti in 1990, but he was forced into exile in 1991 when a coup led by Raoul Cédras erupted. From 1991 to 1994, the military regime waged a campaign of torture against Aristide's supporters. In October 1994, after the US brokered an agreement between Aristide and Cédras, Aristide was returned to power, and appointed the *Commission nationale de vérité et de justice* (National Commission of Truth and Justice) in 1995. The idea for a Haitian truth commission and much of the work towards it was initiated and influenced by the Haitian diaspora community abroad. The Haitian commission was carried out by the Organization of American States (OAS) and the United Nations Permanent Mission to Haiti (*International Civilian Mission in Haiti*). In the end, four of the appointed commissioners were Haitian nationals, all of whom had been living in exile at the time of the violence. The three others were representatives of the international community, from Bahamas, Barbados, and Senegal. The Commission presented its final report in December 1995, as Aristide was again forced out of power—this time because of the terms of the Constitution.

KEY POINTS

Truth commissions are implemented and run by the international community in conjunction with, or in support of, the national government.

Critical Thinking Questions:

If no one is ever punished, can victims really feel like justice has been done?

Is it possible to restore communities back into harmony? How might the mechanisms discussed here help, or hinder, this effort?

Reparative Justice

Reparative justice is a different kind of justice again from either retributive or restorative justice. The reparative paradigm is concerned with making right the things that went wrong. At its root is the idea of repair. The goal, therefore, is to provide a remedy for the suffering and loss that have occurred.

Apology

Reparative justice can take place in one of two ways, or it can contain a mixture of both. The first method of repairing the past is by issuing an *apology*. That is, the perpetrator himself can simply say sorry for what has taken place. Or, if sufficient time has passed that the perpetrator is no longer able to apologize—for instance, if generations have passed since the abuses were carried out and the perpetrator has died—then a representative of the perpetrator may apologize on his behalf. The Government of Canada, for example, apologized in 1992 for the hanging of Métis leader Louis Riel in 1885 for his role in the Northwest Rebellion. None of the elected officials who had been responsible for the decision to hang Riel in 1885 were still alive. Yet the modern-day Government took the initiative, as representatives of that regime, to issue a formal apology for the previous Government's actions.

The benefits of an apology are many. First, the wrong that the victim has suffered is acknowledged by the perpetrator. This kind of acknowledgement—publicly admitting to and accepting a knowledge of the events that have taken place—can allow the victim to move forward, and to begin to 'let go' of the wrong she has suffered. Second, and closely related to the first, is that an apology can lessen the bitterness that the victim feels. This is not to say that she will necessarily become suddenly freed of the loss, or will forget it entirely. Rather, an apology can reduce feelings of anger and hurt. Third, the victim may feel a sense of vindication at being recognized, finally, as being right. Fourth, the trauma of the incident may also be diminished.

Obviously, the hurts that a victim feels will not magically disappear simply because an apology is made. This is particularly the case if the victim feels that the apology is in any way insincere, or if she feels that the apology giver does not have the authority to issue a meaningful apology. An apology is not a panacea. But it does go some way towards repairing the damage that has been inflicted.

For example, the Government of Australia offered an apology for past wrongs to the Aboriginal people who live there. Between 1915 and 1969, thousands of Aboriginal children were forcibly removed from their parents and given to white families or institutions to raise. As a lasting outcome, Aboriginal people in Australia remain the country's poorest and most disadvantaged group. An inquiry into these policies was held in 1997, and a report was released. The following year, a National Sorry Day was instituted, to acknowledge the wrong that had been done. In 2008, the new Prime Minister, Kevin Rudd, issued a formal apology. The apology was issued instead of the billion-dollar nationwide compensation package that Aboriginal campaigners had been calling for.

Restitution

The second method of repair is **restitution**. Restitution can be defined as a token paid in compensation for loss or injury. The idea behind this kind of compensation is similar to the awards offered by civil courts when, for example, a child is killed through an act of negligence. No one can be sure what that child's life might have been worth, yet a sum of money is awarded as payment or repair for the harm that was caused. This is the kind of repair that the Aboriginal community in Australia had been calling for.

To be sure, the idea of compensation is not completely adequate. No amount of money can ever fully compensate someone for loss or damage suffered, and no 'wrong' can be righted with the payment of money. Yet restitution has been utilized by a number of countries in an attempt to right the wrongs that were perpetrated. In Canada, for example, after the attack on Pearl Harbor in 1941, more than 20,000 Canadian citizens of Japanese ancestry, many of whom had lived in Canada for several generations and had Canadian citizenship, were suspected of aiding Japanese authorities in military espionage activities. These Canadian citizens were placed in internment camps, and many of the men were taken to work camps; and homes, fishing boats, and other property were seized by the Government and sold without the permission of their rightful owners. At the end of the war, in 1945, these Canadians of Japanese ancestry were released from the camps, but were banned for the next five years from living near the coast. They were unable to reclaim much of their property. In 1950, the Bird Commission awarded $1.3 million in claims to 1,434 Japanese Canadians, based solely on claims for lost property. More than half a century later, in 1988, the Government awarded CAD$21,000 to each Canadian of Japanese ancestry who had been interned, under the *Japanese Canadian Redress Agreement*.

KEY POINTS

Reparative justice focuses on repairing suffering and loss.

One key method of bringing about reparation is by issuing an apology.

Another way of effecting reparation is by awarding compensation or restitution.

Critical Thinking Questions:

If restitution is purely symbolic, can any amount of money ever be sufficient?

Can an apology serve 'justice' needs?

Putting Transitional Justice into Practice

These three paradigms of transitional justice represent three different visions of how a society can and should be rebuilt in a period of transition. Retributive justice focuses on holding perpetrators of crimes accountable for their actions. Restorative justice focuses on uncovering the truth about past crimes, focusing not only on the perpetrators but also on the victims of criminal activities. Reparative justice focuses on making things right, whether by means of an apology, or by giving a token amount of money, or by replacing what was lost. It is clear that there are both benefits and shortcomings to each of these approaches.

The number of mechanisms employed in the pursuit of transitional justice has grown considerably since the mid-1980s. And with every new attempt, knowledge about how best to carry out such efforts has grown too. Lessons can be learned from past attempts that can inform how new mechanisms will be set up.

In 2004, then-United Nations Secretary General Kofi Annan addressed the subject of transitional justice. One of the things that he stressed the most was the need for these mechanisms to work together:

The international community must see transitional justice in a way that extends well beyond courts and tribunals. The challenges of post-conflict environments necessitate an approach that balances a variety of goals, including the pursuit of accountability, truth and reparation, the preservation of peace and the building of democracy and the rule of law ... Where transitional justice is required, strategies must be holistic, incorporating integrated attention to individual prosecutions, reparations, truth-seeking, institutional reform, vetting and dismissals, or an appropriately conceived combination thereof. The United Nations must consider through advance planning and consultation how different transitional justice mechanisms will interact to ensure that they do not conflict with one another. It is now generally recognized, for example, that truth commissions can positively complement criminal tribunals.

(UN Secretary General, 2004, p. 9)

Indeed, a number of transitional justice mechanisms have been established with just this in mind. One of the biggest needs is for some combination of all the objectives of the three different paradigms (retributive, restorative, reparative) to be fulfilled. In some cases, one mechanism can fulfil more than one of these objectives on its own. The South African Truth and Reconciliation Commission, for example, was established with three distinct objectives, reflected in the three different committees into which it was divided: gross violations of human rights, amnesty, and reparations.

In other cases, more than one mechanism must be employed in order to satisfy the objectives of the three paradigms. For example, in Sierra Leone, the Truth and Reconciliation Commission and the Special Court for Sierra Leone were established, and ran, concurrently. While this caused practical problems, such as the sharing of evidence and sheer amount of resources and capital required to carry out both projects simultaneously, the various needs of the population could be more adequately addressed in this way.

However it works, in the aftermath of violent conflict and human rights abuses, societies in transition have a real need to overcome the social implications of past conflict. Obviously, not every situation will require the same kind of solution. Moreover, not every society will have the same ideas about what must be done. But it is the case that reforms in the justice sector can go a long way towards helping societies to move forwards. And these reforms help, overall, to strengthen a country's chances at a successful

Transitional justice mainly deals with civil and political rights. Claims have emerged that economic, social, and cultural rights should also be considered, whether as a means of providing development or as a means of redress. Scholars like Rama Mani argue that the liberal goals of promoting democracy and legal justice exclude broader 'social injustices and patterns of structural violence that may have been the underlying causes of conflict … [including] practices of discrimination, exclusion and marginalization targeting certain groups or communities' (Mani, 2008, p. 254). The mainstream literature has thus far resisted their inclusion, arguing that courts and other mechanisms are ill-equipped to deal with these types of crimes. Some truth commissions, though, have included some socio-economic crimes in their mandates.

transition towards peace and democracy. (See Box 22.6 for a discussion of claims that economic, social, and cultural rights should also be considered in transitional justice.)

KEY POINTS

The number of mechanisms of transitional justice at work has grown.

Mechanisms can work alone or in tandem.

Where more than one mechanism is in use, they must work together.

Critical Thinking Question:

Is the proliferation of transitional justice mechanisms a sign of progress?

Case Study: Uganda

The country of Uganda has experienced a high level of human rights abuses at the hands of the state since its independence from Britain in 1962. From 1971 onwards, the country experienced a series of coups, which culminated in a concentration of power in the head of state. Under Milton Obote, the country's first post-colonial prime minister, a number of groups carried out riots and armed attacks in protest against his accession to power (Berg-Schlosser and Siegler, 1990, p. 196).

In 1971, Obote was overthrown by his top general, Idi Amin, who carried out a systematic reign of terror, murdering anyone he considered to stand in his way (Wright, 1996, p. 306). The military and paramilitary mechanisms of the state conducted brutal campaigns of torture (Khiddu-Makubuya, 1989, pp. 141–57). It is conservatively estimated that between 300,000 and 500,000 people were killed during this period (Briggs, 1998, p. 23). In 1979, Amin's forces were defeated by forces including those of Obote, of future president Yoweri Museveni, and of neighbouring Tanzania. Amin fled to exile in Libya (Ofcansky, 1996, p. 47). Interim Governments were appointed in 1979 and 1980.

As the result of rigged elections in 1980, Obote returned to power. He remained until 1985, when he was again overthrown by a faction of the Ugandan military. During this period, human rights abuses skyrocketed as the paramilitary forces of the state carried out campaigns of torture, rape, and rampant looting (Khiddu-Makubuya, 1989, p. 153). It is estimated that approximately 300,000 (*Uganda*, 1998, p. 53) to 500,000[2] people were killed, many of them within a small geographic area known as the Luweero Triangle. Obote fled into exile in Zambia (Museveni, 1997, p. 166). A military council ruled for six months, until it, too, was overthrown.

The current President, Yoweri Museveni, and the National Resistance Army (NRA; now National Resistance Movement (NRM)) seized power by means of military force in January 1986. He, too, has ruled with an iron fist. As with his predecessors, Museveni has faced considerable opposition from many of the fifty-six different ethnic groups throughout the country. Between 1986 and 2008, Museveni faced more than twenty-seven armed insurgencies.[3]

One of the most violent was carried out by the Lord's Resistance Army (LRA), a rebel group led by Joseph Kony. The LRA perpetrated thousands of human rights abuses against the population of northern Uganda in its bid to defeat Museveni and take control of the country. Their fighting spilled over to areas including the greater north and east of the country. An estimated 30,000 children were abducted for use as child soldiers and sex slaves. Many thousands of women were raped and gang-raped. And thousands of others were tortured, many with lips, noses, and ears sliced off. Over the years, at least 1.8 million people, representing 80 per cent of the population of northern Uganda, were forced to flee to camps for **internally displaced persons** (IDPs)—and many were in the camps for twenty years or more. The fighting and rebel raids tapered off during periods when peace talks were taking place, and at other times were increasingly violent. One study reported that 79 per cent of community members said they had witnessed torture, 40 per cent had witnessed killing, and 5 per cent had been forced to physically harm another (T. Allen, 2005b, p. 25).

This conflict, although distinct from many of the other conflicts that have taken place, is in many ways representative of the manner in which discord has manifested itself in the country. The scope of abuse, and the devastation of communities, is similar to many of the other conflicts that have seized Uganda. And so Uganda finds itself beleaguered by conflict, with many of the resulting problems untreated and questions unanswered—even though it has attempted, at different times and in different ways, to deal with the perpetrators of such conflicts.

Truth Commission

When Museveni and the NRM came to power in 1986, one of their programmes involved the creation of a truth commission. The role of the 1986 Commission was to inquire into 'the causes and circumstances' surrounding mass murders, arbitrary arrests, the role of law enforcement agents and the state security agencies, and discrimination that occurred between 1962 and January 1986, when Museveni and the NRM assumed power. It was also meant to suggest ways of preventing such abuses from reoccurring (Republic of Uganda, 1994, pp. 3–4). The Commission was expected to determine the role of various state institutions in both perpetrating and hiding gross human rights violations. It collected testimony from thousands of victims and witnesses, and in the end 608 witnesses appeared before the Commissioners at public hearings. Its final report is 720 pages in length.

In actuality, however, the Commission was able to accomplish very little. It faced a considerable number of constraints that ultimately proved its undoing. The Commission was beset by a number of institutional failures. These included a lack of capacity to carry out the kinds of investigations and referrals to prosecution that it was meant to have undertaken. Its mandate, for example, was simply too vast: to investigate *all* human rights abuses committed between 1962 and 1986 would have required many times more than that with which the Commission was invested. And there was a dearth of hard evidence, either because

that evidence was never preserved, or because it went missing (whether innocently or nefariously) in the intervening years. The passing of time also affected the ability of witnesses to testify, as those who might have provided important information had either forgotten crucial details or died before the opportunity arose. Funding, too, was a problem for the Commission, since it was never adequately funded or resourced by the Government. This affected everything from the Commission's ability to pay the commissioners and other staff, to their need for basic items such as file folders, pens, and petrol. In the end, funding came from international non-governmental organizations (NGOs) to enable the Commission to complete its work and publish the final report. Similarly, the Commission suffered from a general lack of political will to galvanize the process. Most citizens were too sceptical of the process to become involved; these people, who had been abused at the hands of their Governments for the better part of forty years, were not in a position to trust that this government-initiated process might be beneficial for them. Likewise, the Government itself backed away from the work of the Commission almost before it started, and its officials, such as the Criminal Investigations Division and the Director of Public Prosecutions, which were supposed to have collected evidence and used it to prepare for prosecutions of perpetrators, failed to fulfil these responsibilities.

In the end, the work of the Commission was negligible. It touched only a marginal segment of the population in any real way. As a testament to the ineffectual performance of the Commission, all of its documents now reside in a locked, bug-infested closet, forgotten by everyone.

Amnesty Act

With the number of armed conflicts and the amount of bush warfare that has paralysed the country since 1962, it is not surprising that there are thousands of former rebel soldiers who could rightly face prosecution. This is especially relevant to the ongoing conflict in northern Uganda, in which thousands of people, including children, have been abducted into the rebel forces and made to commit heinous crimes. The people of Uganda, therefore, 'conceived [of an amnesty] as a tool for ending conflict ... a significant step towards ending the conflict in the north and working towards a process of national reconciliation' (Hovil and Lomo, 2005, p. 6).

After a significant amount of persuasion of Government officials, particularly those in northern Uganda, in November 1999 the Government of Uganda passed an Amnesty Act, which was enacted in January 2000. The Act offers amnesty to anyone who has 'engaged in or is engaging in war or armed rebellion against the government of the Republic of Uganda' (Republic of Uganda, 2000, II.3.i). By 2006, the Amnesty Commission had received more than 20,000 applications for amnesty.

The people of Uganda are deeply divided as to whether those who have committed serious crimes should be punished for them. On the one hand, there is substantial support for the prosecution of those such as Joseph Kony, the leader of the LRA. There is little question among the population, particularly in the north, that Kony should simply go free. On the other hand, however, there is widespread concern that those who have been forced to commit such atrocities might also be held responsible—including those children and adults who were forcibly abducted by the LRA. For these, there is substantially less clarity about the issue of amnesty. Only one point garnered consensus: the conflict must be stopped.

The Government of Uganda has waffled on the issue. Within the Parliament and the Presidential Palace, there is at best 'ambiguous support for the amnesty process: numerous informants questioned whether or not the government was really serious about the Amnesty. Indeed, since its enactment, the government has never presented a consistent position on the Amnesty ... One elderly man in Kitgum articulated a commonly held view: "Parliament said [the Amnesty Act] was OK, but the president himself didn't want it. This is no secret." '

(Hovil and Lomo, 2005, p. 18)

In April 2006, the Government passed the Amnesty Amendment Bill (2003) to enable the Minister of Internal Affairs, with Parliamentary approval, to prevent specific people, most notably the LRA, from being granted amnesty. In January 2012, the Amnesty Amendment Bill was challenged when ex-LRA commander Col. Thomas Kwoyelo was granted amnesty by the International Criminal Division of the High Court.

International Criminal Court

Another piece of the 'justice' puzzle in Uganda has come in the form of the International Criminal Court (ICC). In what has been seen as a further indication of Museveni's dissatisfaction with the Amnesty Act, he formally requested an investigation by the ICC into the actions of the Lord's Resistance Army in northern Uganda in December 2003. This cast a more ominous shadow over the existing amnesty process. The Chief Prosecutor issued warrants for the arrest of Joseph Kony and four other senior members of the LRA, making Uganda the first situation to be examined by the Court. Individually, each of the five warrants details the atrocities attributed to the LRA, and to each of the five men, including more than 2,200 killings and 3,200 abductions in over 820 attacks. Kony, for example, is charged with twelve counts of **crimes against humanity** and twenty-one counts of war crimes.

Yet here, too, opinion is divided. The same justice versus peace debate rages on regarding the role of the ICC. International agencies have, for the most part, been very supportive of the role played by the ICC. On the ground, however, sentiments are mixed. Many Ugandans see the ICC as a troublesome intruder that threatens to take away any chance that they have for peace and a resolution of the conflict through negotiation with the rebels, for Kony and his men are unlikely to surrender in the face of such daunting warrants. Others seem relieved for the international community, finally, to have become involved, when it has been clear that the Government of Uganda had no will to prosecute.

In early 2016, the situation of Uganda at the ICC was still active. None of the warrants had been executed. But in January 2015, one of the five, Dominic Ongwen, surrendered himself to US forces, whereupon he was surrendered to the ICC; at the time of writing, he was awaiting trial.

KEY POINTS

Protracted civil conflict has plagued Uganda since 1962.

Uganda's truth commission (1986–94) failed to acknowledge past events adequately.

The Amnesty Act (2000) has been divisive, as people debate who should be punished, and how.

The warrants issued by the International Criminal Court have been equally divisive.

Critical Thinking Questions:

Many argue that Uganda is still not in transition. Is it too soon for transitional justice?

Can there be too many mechanisms of transitional justice?

Conclusion

The case of Uganda aptly illustrates the difficulty that exists in putting into practice any form of 'justice' through the paradigms of retributive, restorative, and reparative justice, and resolving the social implications of prolonged violent conflict, as we have discussed. What seems, on paper, a reasonable solution to a difficult problem is often no match for the complexity of situations on the ground, or the complicated effects of human rights abuses. Scholars and practitioners of transitional justice are only now beginning to comprehend the manner in which such mechanisms can and should promote greater goals such as peace and democracy, and how these relate to and interact with other concurrent processes of transition, such as economic development, or the demobilization and disarmament of combatants, that are also likely to be under way.

The field of transitional justice is rife with debate about how these different paradigms fit together, and about how we can be sure they have succeeded or failed. Indeed, some have argued that without the rule of law, as demonstrated by a rigorous use of retributive mechanisms, there simply is no justice, and that the restorative and reparative paradigms are neither fully right nor adequate. Others claim that the latter two approaches are merely a second best option, sufficient for use only when all else fails. Yet many contend that each of these approaches is sufficient, in and of itself, to bring about the desired outcome: the rebuilding of a society after human rights violations.

What is clear is that the three paradigms, and the institutions that operate within them, aim towards the same goals. Their methods and rationale, of course, differ greatly. But, in the end, it is entirely possible that the paradigms are themselves concordant pieces of a holistic process of justice. In the years to come, as transitional justice is applied through all three of its paradigms, in different cases and at different times, it will become more apparent whether this is, in fact, the case.

? QUESTIONS

Individual Study Questions

1. What is transitional justice?

2. What good does transitional justice serve?

3. How is universal jurisdiction useful?

4. How does restorative justice differ from retributive justice?

5. What is the value of a truth commission?

Group Discussion Questions

1. Should these three different types of justice always work alone?

2. Is there any benefit to a society as a whole in avoiding retributive punishment?

3. Is there a role for amnesty in encouraging societal participation in restorative processes?

4. What should the responsibility of government be in apology or restitution? Should there be a statute of limitations on this responsibility?

5. What kinds of developments in transitional societies would reflect some measure of 'success' of transitional justice mechanisms?

6. What issues in your own country warrant examination by the kinds of mechanisms outlined in this chapter?

FURTHER READING

Elster, J. (ed.) (2006). *Retribution and Reparation in the Transition to Democracy*. New York: Cambridge University Press.

Elster provides an in-depth treatment of a number of cases from the early stages of retroactive accountability for crimes of war that took place in the twentieth century. Elster also offers overviews of the history of the practice of transitional justice that neatly conceptualize the mechanisms and processes that are used.

Hayner, P. (2001). *Unspeakable Truths*. New York: Routledge.

Hayner deals with the need for and utility of truth commissions as a means of reckoning with past crimes. She provides a number of case studies, and a deep look at restorative justice.

Kritz, N. J. (ed.) (1995). *Transitional Justice: How Emerging Democracies Reckon with Former Regimes*. Washington, DC: United States Institute of Peace Press.

Kritz's three volumes look at the nuts and bolts of transitional justice, from theory (Vol. 1) to country studies (Vol. 2) to legal documentation (Vol. 3).

Mani, R. (2008). Editorial: Dilemmas of Expanding Transitional Justice, or Forging the Nexus between Transitional Justice and Development. *International Journal of Transitional Justice*, **2**/3, 253–65.

Mani provides an alternative viewpoint, exploring the possibility for transitional justice to address socio-economic abuses, rather than just civil and political abuses.

Minow, M. (1998). *Between Vengeance and Forgiveness: Facing History after Genocide and Mass Violence*. Boston, MA: Beacon Press.

Minow unpacks the three paradigms of transitional justice, and presents a thoughtful discussion of the positive and negative impacts of each.

Parliament of Australia (2008). Apology to Australia's Indigenous peoples. *House Hansard*. 13 February. http://australia.gov.au/about-australia/our-country/our-people/apology-to-australias-indigenous-peoples

The full text of MP Kevin Rudd's apology to Australia's Indigenous population can be found here.

Quinn, J. and **Freeman, M.** (2003). Lessons learned: Practical lessons gleaned from inside the truth commissions of Guatemala and South Africa. *Human Rights Quarterly*, **25**/4, 1117-49.

Using primary documents and information obtained by staff from the truth commissions in South Africa and Guatemala, Quinn and Freeman discuss the practical difficulties encountered by truth commissions.

Rotberg, R. I. and **Thompson, D.** (eds) (2000). *Truth v. Justice*. Princeton, NJ: Princeton University Press.

Rotberg and Thompson provide a collection of essays that deal with the essential paradox that paralysed transitional justice in its early years: is truth more important than justice?

Stover, E. and **Weinstein, H. M.** (eds) (2004). *My Neighbour, My Enemy: Justice and Community in the Aftermath of Mass Atrocity*. Cambridge: Cambridge University Press.

The essays provided in this book edited by Stover and Weinstein examine various responses to atrocity in Rwanda and the former Yugoslavia.

WEB LINKS

http://www.icc-cpi.int   The website of the International Criminal Court contains details of each of the cases presently before the Court, as well as documents including the Rome Statute.

http://www.ictj.org   The International Center for Transitional Justice is an NGO that works in countries around the world, helping to develop transitional justice solutions in post-conflict societies.

http://ijtj.oxfordjournals.org/ *The International Journal of Transitional Justice* publishes academic articles dealing with the topic of transitional justice.

http://www.usip.org/ The website of the United States Institute of Peace has a collection of primary documents from a number of truth commissions.

 NOTES

1. The Rome Statute of the International Criminal Court also specifies that the Court will try crimes of aggression. At the time of writing, however, such crimes remain undefined.

2. Confidential interview with Abdul Nadduli, District Commissioner, Luweero District, by the author on 17 November 2004, Luweero Town, Uganda.

3. These include rebellions by Action Restore Peace, Allied Democratic Forces, Apac Rebellion, Citizen Army for Multiparty Politics, Force Obote Back, Former Uganda National Army, Holy Spirit Movement, Lord's Army, Lord's Resistance Army, National Federal Army, National Union for the Liberation of Uganda, Ninth October Movement, People's Redemption Army, Uganda Christian Democratic Army, Uganda Federal Democratic Front, Uganda Freedom Movement, Ugandan National Democratic Army, Uganda National Federal Army, Ugandan National Liberation Front, Ugandan National Rescue Fronts I and II, Ugandan People's Army, Ugandan People's Democratic Army, Uganda Salvation Army, and West Nile Bank Front (Hovil and Lomo, 2004, p. 4; 2005, p. 6).

Visit the Online Resource Centre that accompanies this book for updates and a range of other resources: www.oxfordtextbooks.co.uk/orc/goodhart3e/

23

The Environment

John Barry and Kerri Woods

Chapter Contents

Reader's Guide

The aim of this chapter is to examine the ways in which environmental issues affect human rights and the ways in which human rights are relevant to environmental campaigns, and to consider proposals for extending human rights to cover environmental rights, rights for future generations, and rights for some non-human animals. The structure of the chapter is as follows. We begin by looking at the relationship between human rights and the environment in both academic literature and national and international law and policy, and consider recent defences of claims that all persons have 'environmental human rights'. Thereafter, we consider the impact of the environment on human security and its bearing on human rights issues. Next, we ask two questions: Is the human rights framework an appropriate one in terms of which to address environmental issues? Are there alternative moral/ethical idioms that might better accommodate environmental issues, e.g. the language of justice? Finally, we look at the plausibility and potential advantages and disadvantages of extending the current human rights framework to include environmental concerns. We consider the view that sustainability, understood to encompass environmental, social, and economic concerns, is central to any proposed extension of the human rights framework to encompass environmental concerns. This vision of sustainability is illustrated in our case studies, which look at the impact of climate change and development projects, each of which discloses the central role of the global economy in the human rights impacts of environmental issues. Taken together, this suggests that the appropriate way to think about human rights in this area is to focus on a broader understanding of sustainability rather than environment.

Introduction

In this section our aim is to outline the ways in which the environment and sustainable development or unsustainable development can be understood to be human rights issues.

At the crux of the relationship between the environment and human rights is the inescapable fact that humans are ecologically embedded beings. That is, humans are utterly dependent on, and vulnerable to changes in, their relationships with the non-human world. The United Nations Environment Programme (UNEP) recognizes three respects in which environmental issues relate to human rights:

- the environment as a prerequisite for the enjoyment of human rights (implying that human rights obligations of states should include the duty to ensure the level of environmental protection necessary to allow the full exercise of protected rights);

- certain human rights, especially access to information, participation in decision making, and access to justice in environmental matters, as essential to good environmental decision making (implying that human rights must be implemented in order to ensure environmental protection); and

- the right to a safe, healthy, and ecologically balanced environment as a human right in itself (this is a debated approach). (UNEP, 2009)

In political practice, though, this close interrelationship and its ramifications for our social, political, and economic practices are often neglected. The concept of **sustainable development** can be seen as an attempt to bring to the fore the ecological embeddedness of all human activity (especially economic activities), which entails the need to weigh the ecological consequences of our decisions in developing and refining our social, political, and economic thinking, practices, and structures.

The concept of sustainable development has been embraced by a wide variety of actors, including governments, **non-governmental organizations** (NGOs), environmentalists, Indigenous peoples, trade unionists, women's groups, human rights activists, and also corporations. In developing countries there has been talk of a **right to development**, while in the richer Western countries sustainable development has sometimes been seen as a way of 'greening orthodox economic growth' or translated to mean the 'ecological modernization' of the economy (J. Barry, 2004, 2012, 2014). Sustainable development as a normative concept has been circulating in green political and development theory since at least 1987 (see Box 23.1), when the report of the World Commission on Environment and Development (WCED) called for a strategy integrating environment and development. Development is necessary in the South to achieve social and economic human rights, which in many countries currently are chronically unfulfilled.

BOX 23.1 ALTERNATIVE POINTS OF VIEW—SUSTAINABLE DEVELOPMENT

The dominant view of sustainable development is the one taken from the 1987 Brundtland Commission on Environment and Development. In essence, it suggests that it is possible, with technological, governance, and policy changes, to reconcile economic growth and environmental protection. However, there are at least two criticisms that can be made of this dominant conceptualization.

1. Some have suggested that the entire concept of 'sustainable development' is both an oxymoron (Redclift, 2005) and counterproductive in that it has effectively neutered and marginalized the claim that creating a more sustainable society requires large-scale structural changes to our economy and ways of life. That is, sustainable development allows us the fiction of 'having our cake and eating it',

suggesting a 'painless' and often 'apolitical' transition, rather than requiring redistributive measures in relation to resources, income, and wealth within and between societies and significant economic and political changes to achieve a sustainable development path (Marcuse, 1998; Luke, 2006).

2. Others point out, using the example that it is injustice not justice we should focus on and develop policy and political responses to (Simon, 1994), that much valuable time and effort has been wasted debating and refining and developing 'greenprints' of 'sustainable development'. Rather than working towards some future 'ideal state' of sustainable development, what is needed is a recognition of 'actually existing unsustainability' (Barry, 2012) and a focus on reducing environmental harms.

BOX 23.2 ECOLOGICAL FOOTPRINT

Simply put, the ecological footprint is the total ecological impact of a given thing, be it a consumable product, an individual, a family, a community, or a state. It is a particularly appealing concept in environmental politics because it demonstrates, in a way that market values do not, the full ecological cost of whatever is being measured, and, in sophisticated models, can illustrate the distribution of that cost.

The idea was originally put forward by Matthias Wackernagel and William Rees to measure the 'area of ecologically productive land (and water) … required on a continuous basis to (a) provide all the energy/material resources consumed, and (b) absorb all the wastes discharged … *wherever that land is located*' by a given population (Andersson and Lindroth, 2001, p. 114). The ecological footprint is therefore an accounting tool that enables researchers to identify countries that run an ecological deficit—that is, use up more ecological space than is available within their territory.

Today, humanity's ecological footprint is over 23 per cent larger than what the planet can regenerate (see http://www.footprintnetwork.org/en/index.php/GFN/page/

world_footprint/). Another way of expressing this is 'Earth Overshoot Day'. For example, in 2014, 19 August was Earth Overshoot Day, 'marking the date when humanity has exhausted nature's budget for the year. For the rest of the year, we will maintain our ecological deficit by drawing down local resource stocks and accumulating carbon dioxide in the atmosphere. We will be operating in overshoot' (Global Footprint Network, 2014). As a consequence, environmental resources are being consumed and used unsustainably. Two-thirds of Organisation for Economic Co-operation and Development (OECD) countries run an ecological deficit, including the UK, the USA, the Netherlands, Belgium, and Germany. Among non-OECD countries, the worst offenders are Singapore, Hong Kong, and Israel. The ecological debt of some countries is explicitly recognized in their sustainable development plans—for example, the latest UK sustainable development strategy says 'one planet living' is a core objective.

For further information see the Global Footprint Network's website (http://www.footprintnetwork.org/index.php), where you can also find a number of films on ecological footprint and sustainable development.

The strategy proposed was sustainable development, defined as 'development that meets the needs of the present without compromising the ability of future generations to meet their own needs' (WCED, 1987, p. 24). In short, each generation should ensure that its ecological footprint (see Box 23.2) does not exceed the Earth's carrying capacity. The report of the WCED was the principal inspiration for the United Nations Conference on the Environment and Development (UNCED), popularly known as the Earth Summit, held in Rio in 1992, which produced Agenda 21, a global plan of local action to realize sustainable development. In the years since, climate change (and related concerns about 'peak oil' and energy insecurity) has emerged as a major environmental and political issue (Barry, 2012; Klein, 2014). Responding to both climate change and environmental sustainability more generally, increasing numbers of academics, activists, and policy makers have begun to invoke the notion of 'environmental human rights' as a way of protecting individuals, communities, and future generations from the worst effects of environmental degradation.

An Environmental Human Right?

Various formulations of environmental human rights have been put forward in scholarship and policy forums. In the recent literature we find defences of a human right to a safe environment (Nickel, 1993), to an environment adequate for health and well-being (Hayward, 2005), to ownership of natural resources (Hancock, 2003), against climate change (Caney, 2007), against pollution (Lercher, 2007), access to food (Sage, 2012; IPCC, 2014, p. 18), and 'emergent' environmental human rights to a green future (Hiskes, 2005). No doubt other approaches are possible. What these various arguments share is a conviction that the power of human rights as a political discourse is valuable to the sustainability/sustainable development agenda, and that environmental problems have comparable normative status with other 'standard threats' to human security that require the protection afforded by human rights (Shue, 1980). Sceptics doubt whether the character of the threats that environmental problems pose is consistent with the character of other threats that human rights protect against. Certainly, environmental rights do not track the direct interactional logic of such paradigmatic human rights as the right not to be tortured. Nevertheless, as our understanding of human rights develops and we evaluate the reality of threats to a life consistent with human dignity, we find reasons to take seriously the normative arguments advanced in defence of environmental human rights.

The Environment, Human (In)Security, and Human Rights

Almost every state has formally endorsed the **Universal Declaration of Human Rights** (UDHR). Article 3 of the UDHR asserts that all persons have the right to 'life, liberty and security of person'. Security of person can be threatened by a number of environmental factors. First, environmental degradation and the depletion of resources such as oil and clean water have been a cause of or contributory factor in violent conflict in many parts of the world, from the invasion and occupation of Iraq to the Darfur conflict in Sudan. This is particularly acute in the case of oil as we face the twin threats of 'peak oil' (oil running out and getting more expensive) and climate change (Aleklett, 2012). The dominant economic model of development promoted by the neoliberal 'Washington consensus' is—to put it crudely—addicted to and based on the availability of cheap oil. When oil resources are threatened (as in Iraq under Saddam Hussein) 'resource wars' can follow. A related issue here is both the vulnerability of development based on declining oil sources and how the energy insecurity implications of peak oil (and gas) can render development itself insecure. On the other hand, the environmental, water, and climate change implications of the exploitation of unconventional oil and gas—which presents the dilemma in terms of there being *too much* rather than *too little* oil and gas—still pose enormous socio-ecological dangers. This may be either in terms of creating 'sacrifice zones' as the cost for oil-based development (Alberta's tar sands for example), or in 'frying the planet' by continuing oil-based development and burning more than the scientifically established safe threshold to stay within a stable climate regime.

Second, access to clean air and water is crucial for human life. Access to a sufficient quantity and quality of food is dependent on the environment in important ways and can clearly be regarded as crucial to human security and to the fulfilment of human rights. As Vandana Shiva (1999) argues, the human right to freedom of speech can be undermined by hunger as well as by political repression. Third, human security is threatened when people are removed from their land because of environmental threats, whether these threats are pollution, such as oil spills, other chemical spills, or radioactive contamination, or from flooding and rising sea levels, or landslides and soil erosion. Another relevant consideration here is the removal of people from their lands to make way for development projects, such as mining and dams (see 'Case Studies' section).

There is a vast literature on the ways in which human security has been threatened and compromised in the context of activities associated with globalization and the degradation of the environment. Joan Martinez-Alier's work on 'the environmentalism of the poor' is often cited in this regard. In the face of development strategies to exploit minerals, oil, and timber resources, 'the poor often find themselves fighting for resource conservation and a clean environment even when they do not claim to be environmentalists' (Martinez-Alier, 2003, p. 201). The environmental justice movement emerged largely in response to localized threats to environmental security arising from corporate **externalities**—that is, the ecological costs that are not included in the market price of a given commodity (because the producer does not have to pay for the costs).

The local conflicts that spurred the environmental justice movement disclose a more general conclusion: that humans cannot be said to enjoy security of person when preponderant patterns of production and consumption are ecologically unsustainable. Moreover, there is often a global dimension to localized environmental problems—for example, the oil companies operating in the Niger Delta supply oil to petrol stations in Europe and North America. Globally, current patterns of production and consumption are ecologically unsustainable. The responsibility for addressing this must also be global. If we can be said to have a human right to security of person, it follows that we have a right to certain environmental goods that are crucial to our security: clean water, a sustainable source of food, and the right, perhaps, not to be removed from our land to make way for development or conservation projects.

The basis of the relationship between the environment and human rights is the inescapable fact that humans are ecologically embedded beings.

Environmental scholars propose various formulations of 'environmental human rights'. They typically share the view that environmental problems are comparable with other 'standard threats' that human rights protect against.

Article 3 of the Universal Declaration of Human Rights (UDHR) asserts that all persons have the right to 'life, liberty and security of person'. Environmental degradation and the depletion of resources such as oil and clean water have been a cause of or a contributory factor in violent conflict.

The environmental justice movement emerged largely in response to localized threats to environmental security arising from corporate externalities—that is, the ecological costs that are not included in the market price of a given commodity.

If we can be said to have a right to security, it follows that we have a right to certain environmental goods crucial to that security.

Critical Thinking Question:

What are the main ideas behind and practical implications of 'environmental human rights'?

Problems of Compatibility

In this section we address the assumed compatibility between human rights and the environment. Human rights and environmental sustainability at a first glance look like natural bedfellows—who among those in favour of human rights would say that they do not agree that the environment should be protected? And who among those campaigning on environmental issues would not recognize both the normative status and the strategic value of human rights? Indeed, dominant understandings of sustainable development place a concern with the protection and promotion of human rights as constitutive elements (UNDP, 1998).

Philosophical Underpinnings

Human rights are conventionally understood to be mechanisms for protecting individuals from harm (usually at the hands of the state), and about protecting and extending freedoms: the freedom to say and print what one thinks, and the freedom to live as one chooses subject to the caveat that one does not impede the lives of contemporaries. Human rights are individualistic, liberal (at least in their origins), concern entitlements rather than duties, and, above all, affirm the normative status of humans as special beings deserving of dignity and specific types of appropriate treatment and non-interference. They are in many ways at odds with the most dominant concerns in environmental politics.

Environmental politics is often about the citizen as bearer of duties. It is also sometimes about circumscribing the freedom to behave in ecologically unsustainable ways, rather than protecting and extending freedoms. Some early environmental theorists have sometimes argued that even political and civil freedoms should be restricted for the sake of the environment (Hardin, 1977; Ophuls, 1977), though later green thinkers have comprehensively rejected such eco-authoritarian positions (Barry, 1999; Humphrey, 2007). Environmental citizens are required to live in ways that do not inhibit the same freedoms of future generations as well as those of contemporaries. Yet, most green politics is about asserting the right of individuals and communities to a decent and healthy environment, so there are both duties and rights at the heart of green politics.

Ecocentric theorists have argued that humans do not necessarily have a special moral place in the universe, and, indeed, hold that much of the current and historical damage to the environment has been predicated on the idea that humans are morally more important than other animals and ecosystems. Therefore, ecocentrists hold that we should recognize the environment, as well as humans, as a source of intrinsic value. From this point of view, it is not obvious how environmental human rights can dislodge the deeply rooted human chauvinism that underpins our ecologically unsustainable social and economic practices. Even weak anthropocentrists seek to diminish the extent to which humans are seen as occupying a privileged position in nature, and suggest that what is required is a less 'arrogant' and more reflexive and modest form of 'ecologically enlightened anthropocentrism' that sees humanity as a part of, as well as apart from, the non-human world (Barry, 1999).

Most importantly, environmentalists typically recognize that the persons living today have obligations to future generations to bequeath both a sustainable environment and an adequate resource base as far as that is possible. An environmental ethic without this future orientation would have limited applicability to the most serious environmental problems currently faced, and would yield a very restricted vision of sustainability that could license significant further environmental degradation (K. Woods, 2010). Among the most divisive questions about environmental human rights is whether future generations, either as individuals (Feinberg, 1974) or as collective bearers of group rights (Hiskes, 2005, 2009), can be said to have rights of moral weight comparable to those of persons living now, which would entail claims on persons living now. Defenders of environmental human rights often find it puzzling to think that future persons would not have such rights (Caney, 2007; Read, 2011), while critics find it puzzling to think that they would (Woods, 2010) (see Box 23.3).

Can Human Rights be 'Greened'?

How far, if at all, can the rights framework be 'greened'? Key to this is to recognize the ecological embeddedness of all human freedom. Thus, Klaus Bosselmann proposes an 'ecological limitation' to environmental human rights. Such a limitation 'refers to the fact that individual freedom is determined not only by a social context—the social dimension of human rights—but also by an ecological context' (Bosselmann, 2001, p. 119). But this dimension is easy to neglect when many environmental problems, such as climate change and biodiversity loss, build up slowly and incrementally, and human lifespans are short, relative to the timescales involved. Hence, Richard P. Hiskes defines environmental hazards as 'emergent' risks, and environmental human rights as 'emergent' rights (Hiskes, 2005). Promoting human rights today by, for example, clearing land to grow food for the hungry, may well undermine environmental sustainability over the long term and diminish the environmental resources available to future generations. Such conflicts between the interests and rights of humans now and future generations—as well as the interests and rights of human beings in different parts of the world—are at the heart of sustainable development, which undertakes the almost impossible task of rendering compatible competing claims and rights to the use of the environment for human purposes.

BOX 23.3 ALTERATIVE POINTS OF VIEW: CAN FUTURE GENERATIONS HAVE RIGHTS?

The question of whether future generations can be said to have rights is important in environmental ethics and politics because, if future generations have rights, the present generation may have corresponding duties. Therefore, the present generation would have to ensure that its choices with regard to resource consumption did not threaten to undermine the rights of future generations.

However, philosophically, it is difficult to establish that future generations do have coherent rights. There are a number of reasons for this. First, there is no currently identifiable subject that can be said to be the future generation rights-holder (Macklin, 1981, pp. 151–2; Beckerman, 2001, p. 18). Therefore, there is no subject whose rights can be said to have been violated. In reply to this sort of objection, Joel Feinberg (1974) advances the idea that the rights of future persons are 'contingent' rights, and that the normative force of these rights is contingent on future persons coming into existence. Since we can reasonably expect that future persons will exist, we can be guided now by the claims that will become valid.

An alternative defence of the rights of future persons has turned on analogies such as that of a booby-trapped time capsule, which injures someone eighty years after it was set, first discussed by Robert Elliot (1989). The booby-trapped time capsule, when opened, causes serious injury. Whether the person so injured is born before the time capsule is booby-trapped (and so has rights at the time of the booby-trapping), or afterwards (and so is a future person at the time of the booby-trapping), makes no difference to the judgement that the injury is a violation of the person's rights. The booby-trapper has violated the rights of the injured person, whether she was born at the time of the action or not. By analogy, it is claimed, present persons are violating the rights of future persons by contributing to problems like climate change, which will predictably significantly threaten the lives and well-being of future persons.

Against this sort of argument sceptics often invoke what Derek Parfit (1984) calls 'the non-identity problem', which casts doubt on the feasibility of saying that future persons are harmed by factors that also play a role in determining their having come into existence as the particular individual that they are. So, the life of someone whose family moved to another country because of climate change could not have been 'harmed' by climate change, because they would not have been born as the exact person they are, were it not for the sequence of events (influenced in part by climate change) that led to their birth. While some see very significant problems for intergenerational human rights following from this, others argue that the non-identity problem's relevance to environmental issues is considerably weaker than is sometimes suggested (Tremmel, 2009), and does not offer a strong argument against the ethical claim that future generations place on us now (Read, 2011).

Implementing Environmental Human Rights?

In this section we consider the plausibility of, and prospects for, embedding environmental issues in the human rights framework. We also look at the issue of whether we need to shift our thinking and action from an environmental focus to one in which *sustainability* (understood to contain environmental, social, and economic dimensions and claims) is central.

Environmental Human Rights in Practice?

The major international human rights treaties do not recognize environmental human rights. Nevertheless, there is an emerging body of law and legal practice that points to the tentative recognition of environmental human rights in national, regional, and international human rights bodies. Over ninety states around the world now recognize some form of environmental human right in their national constitutions. In 2012 the United Nations Office of the High Commissioner for Human Rights appointed the first ever Independent Expert on the Environment, Professor John Knox.

Knox's mandate is to review the emerging practice of environmental human rights in regional and international law, and to make recommendations of best practice which can be implemented by states to ensure that their citizens' human rights are not undermined or violated by environmental problems. We are some way yet from a legally binding environmental human right, but there is clear evidence that widely accepted human rights norms are now recognized as having an environmental dimension.

The Green Logic of Human Rights

There are clear reasons to welcome these developments. '[R]ights are a way of marking out a protected area within which the rights-holders are free to pursue their goals' (Merrills, 1996, p. 27). The point of claiming environmental human right(s) is therefore to promote some minimum level of environmental sustainability as being beyond the sphere of political compromise. Thus, debates about whether governments should prioritize the environment over development, or vice versa, are easily settled where further development is not essential to the fulfilment of other human rights. In this context, the advantage of a rights-based approach is that 'it serves to "trump" competing claims for utility maximisation' (Eckersley, 1996, p. 216).

Hayward expands on this line of argument by suggesting that embedding environmental rights in national constitutions serves a broader purpose than simply providing for the protection of the environment by legal action. One effect of environmental human rights would be the mandating of a number of procedural rights, such as rights to be informed of proposed developments in a particular local area, rights to information about environmental impact assessments, rights to freedom of assembly to facilitate protests against unwanted development, and extended rights to self-determination, including rights to participate in decision-making forums. The legal recognition of such rights has a positive impact on the democratic credentials of environmental decision-making procedures, helps facilitate environmental justice, and may foster an ethic of custodianship—all key aspects of a sustainable society. Another positive effect is to introduce environmental ethics to a wider and younger audience wherever citizenship training is part of the national curriculum (Barry, 2012), and to contribute to the environmental education of the general public. Finally, 'Such effects would serve to consolidate the essential aims of environmental protection as being a matter of public interest rather than partisan cause' (Hayward, 2005, p. 126).

Examples of procedural environmental rights include Principle 10 of the 1992 Rio Declaration, which states that:

Environmental issues are best handled with the participation of all concerned citizens, at the relevant level. At the national level, each individual shall have appropriate access to information concerning the environment that is held by public authorities, including information on hazardous materials and activities in their communities, and the opportunity to participate in decision-making processes. States shall facilitate and encourage public awareness and participation by making information widely available. Effective access to judicial and administrative proceedings, including redress and remedy, shall be provided.

(UNEP, 1992)

The 1998 Aarhus Convention on Access to Information, Public Participation in Decision-Making and Access to Justice in Environmental Matters can be seen as an attempt to implement Principle 10, and is often held up as a good example of the positive linking of human rights and environmental concerns. Article 1 of the Aarhus Convention states that:

In order to contribute to the protection of the right of every person of present and future generations to live in an environment adequate to his or her health and well-being, each Party shall guarantee the rights of access to information, public participation in decision-making, and access to justice in environmental matters in accordance with the provisions of this Convention.

(UNECE, 1998, p. 4)

Within European legal jurisdictions, the Aarhus Convention is frequently cited as granting citizens key environmental human rights. Such 'second-order' human rights—rights that facilitate political action and protest—may in practice be more valuable for protecting environmental goods than a distinct right to environmental goods.

Environmental human rights are not only procedural rights. The implications of recognizing a substantive environmental human right (or rights)—such as, say, a right to a healthy environment, or a right not to suffer the adverse effects of anthropogenic climate change—are less clearly understood in current legal practice. Another way to approach the implementation of environmental human rights would be to think of them as group rights held by future generations,

either altogether or as future groups of currently existing states. Hiskes sees in the latter approach an advantage for the political task of garnering support for environmental human rights:

Although they exist only in the abstract and can only be perceived as a group, future citizens will be 'like us', they will share our historical collective identity, will embrace our concepts and culture. Therefore, it is not difficult for citizens to show concern for their own succeeding generation's welfare and environmental rights, even if those rights can only be viewed as group rights.

(Hiskes, 2005, pp. 1356–7)

This approach offers a route to defending environmental human rights claims as readily intelligible to ordinary citizens, against those who find environmental human rights too abstract. (We should also note that the declaratory form of environmental human rights echoes the declaratory form of some traditional rights.) Nevertheless, it also makes evident the extent to which substantive environmental human rights may represent a significant departure from conventional ways of thinking about human rights, so we should also give consideration to potential problems with environmental human rights.

KEY POINTS

Legal recognition of environmental human rights is emerging in a number of jurisdictions at national and regional levels.

Environmental human rights create increasing opportunities for legal action to protect the environment.

The idea of environmental protection and its importance is arguably strengthened, and is authoritatively embedded in the legal and political fabric, if some form of environmental human rights is recognized.

Claiming environmental human rights may create opportunities to reshape the understandings of key elements of our political vocabulary.

Environmental human rights may be thought of as group rights held by future generations.

Critical Thinking Question:

What form should environmental human rights take—procedural rights, substantive rights, or rights held by future generations?

Problems with Environmental Human Rights?

There are a number of reasons for caution with regard to the attractiveness of the idea of environmental human rights. One respect in which the logic of human rights is potentially problematic for environmentalists, already mentioned earlier, is its inherent anthropocentrism. To claim a human right is to say that there is something morally significant about being human. Human rights discourse recognizes that individual humans have a right to what they need, or a right to pursue their own interests, in a way that individual snails, or giant pandas, or (more complicatedly) forest ecosystems do not. This issue raises the question of whether the current human rights framework could or should be extended to include rights for non-human animals, such as great apes (see Box 23.4), for ecosystems, or for future generations (see Box 23.3). The fact that in the present human rights framework individuals of other species are not valued in the same way as individual humans means that, where environmental human rights are accepted and there is a conflict between 'human interests' and 'non-human interests', it seems highly likely that 'the human interest will prevail' (Hayward, 2005, p. 34). Critics describe this priority for humans as 'speciesist' (Singer, 2009).

Indeed, the ecological context that can support human life need not necessarily be as biodiverse as, or be less polluted than, it is today. There is, therefore, reason for concern about the quality of environmental sustainability that a human rights-based approach could offer. If we work to satisfy all humans' rights to adequate food, water, and shelter without regard to increasing population levels, then, over time, we may achieve this at the expense of leaving sufficient ecological resources for many of the non-human animals with whom we share the planet. Environmental human rights protect the habitats of all animals insofar as they protect the Earth, but they protect the Earth for humans first and foremost, an approach that may undermine the already threatened livelihoods of endangered species, especially those that may not be necessary to conserve in order to protect environmental human rights.

Strategic Considerations

Nevertheless, the question is whether, strategically—that is, with the aim of effecting widespread political change in a democratic manner (if not always in a democratic context)—environmental human rights are useful. De-Shalit (2001) advises that the ecocentric approach is often unpersuasive to the public at large, who may be more concerned with immediate economic

---

BOX 23.4 THE GREAT APE PROJECT

There have long been campaigns for the recognition of animal rights. The Great Ape Project (GAP, http://www.greatapeproject.org/), founded by Peter Singer and Paolo Cavalieri, and based in Seattle, USA, argues for humans to extend the 'community of equals' to include humans, chimpanzees, bonobos, gorillas, and orangutans, such that all have a right to life, a right to the protection of individual liberty, and a right to freedom from torture. The GAP calls for a declaration on the rights of great apes in the manner of existing human rights declarations. In 2006, a Spanish Green MP proposed a parliamentary resolution on the rights of great apes, with the effect of ending humans' ownership rights of great apes and instead requiring that great apes be treated as 'legal persons' under Spanish law.

The purpose of extending rights to great apes is neither to frustrate the coherence of human rights, nor to deny that other animals are deserving of rights, but rather to bring coherence to moral standards with regard to the treatment of creatures that are genetically and behaviourally very close to human beings, as Singer (2006) explains:

Recognizing the rights of great apes does not mean that they all must be set free, even those born and bred in zoos, who would be unable to survive in the wild. Nor does it rule out euthanasia if that is in the interest of individual apes whose suffering cannot be relieved. Just as some humans are unable to fend for themselves and need others to act as their guardians, so, too, will great apes living in the midst of human communities. What extending basic rights to great apes does mean is that they will cease to be 'mere things' that can be owned and used for our amusement or entertainment.

An example of this is the legal recognition of an orangutan as a 'non-human person' in Argentina in 2014, where a court ruled that the orangutan, who had spent the last twenty years in a zoo, be granted some legal rights enjoyed by humans. However, this must be contrasted with a US court ruling, in the same year, that a chimpanzee was not entitled to the same rights as people, and did not have to be freed from captivity by its owner.

security than long-term environmental sustainability. Moreover, there has been a shift in green thinking towards a weak or 'reflexive' anthropocentrism that asserts the need for a strong model of environmental sustainability because of the ecological embeddedness of human life (Barry, 1999). In particular, a weak anthropocentrism concerned with protecting the environment for the sake of future generations can yield a robust and coherent model of sustainability, assuming that future generations can be said to have rights.

Environmental human rights are thus tools of use to environmental citizens who take on the role of stewards. For example, if environmental human rights afford me the right to be informed of proposed developments, or rights to access environmental impact assessments, then, as an environmental citizen, I might find these rights crucial in deciding what action I should take for the sake of future generations. Furthermore, such rights would have an impact on some cases within the present generation. Not all environmental problems are gradual and incremental. The decision as to where to site a toxic dump, for instance, can immediately impact negatively on the health and well-being of local people. Similarly, those who have been made environmental refugees by virtue of conservation policies that equated environmental protection with wilderness preservation might well argue that the right to an environment adequate for health and well-being, or the right to ownership of natural resources, would have meant that they ought not to have been removed from their lands. So, although environmental human rights encounter some problems in relation to future generations, this does not render the idea of environmental human rights redundant or incoherent.

Remaining Challenges

What all this suggests is that the idea of environmental human rights is indeed plausible and also has the potential to be useful to environmental citizens. But there are problems with the contemporary international human rights regime that may yet mean that environmental activists should not be too hasty in framing environmental claims in the language of human rights. Human rights are undeniably universalist, and the terms in which human rights are defended by political theorists sometimes do little to assuage the concerns of those who fear that human rights proponents are insufficiently sensitive to cultural difference (Mutua, 2001; Woods, 2014). Non-Western critics of human rights have at times rejected the universalism

they see in the idea of both human rights and sustainable development. Indeed, it is clear from the case of environmental refugees who have lost their homes to conservation projects that there are reasons to be sceptical of externally defined 'universal' standards that are applied without the informed consent, or better, the active participation, of the people affected.

Another concern to be noted is the thought that there are more and less important human rights. We very often encounter a distinction, explicitly or implicitly, between 'basic' and 'non-basic' rights (Cranston, 1967; Rawls, 1999; Williams, 2005). The adoption of the human rights framework enjoins environmentalists to argue for a package, some elements of which are not universally respected. If basic rights are those that are most urgent, given the long-term scale of many environmental threats, it is easily conceivable that environmental sceptics would class environmental human rights as non-basic rights. Nevertheless, over the long term, the importance of environmental goods can hardly be denied; human rights are sometimes thought to best capture the urgency of immediate threats to life and limb. Something like this growing sense of urgency may be emerging with the discourse and political activism on climate change as an 'existential threat' to humanity (Klein, 2014), in spite of the persistence of climate change deniers (see Box 23.5). But an important question for environmental theorists and activists is whether an alternative moral idiom might provide a more hospitable framework in terms of which to present environmental/sustainability claims.

KEY POINTS

Fulfilling humans' rights to adequate food, water, and shelter may be achieved with a less biodiverse world and, therefore, at the expense of non-human animals with whom we share the planet.

Non-human-based arguments for environmental protection, such as ecocentrism, suffer from having little persuasive power in human-centred (anthropocentric) political and legal discourses.

Environmental human rights in terms of intergenerational justice may be said to denote that environmental citizens should take on the role of stewards who have a duty to look after the environment, rather than future people having 'rights' per se.

Critical Thinking Questions:

Talking about environmental concerns in the language of environmental human rights assumes that human beings have the moral right to decide on behalf of other species or of 'nature' about these concerns. Do we have that right? Why or why not?

BOX 23.5 DECONSTRUCTING: CLIMATE CHANGE

Climate change is a complex phenomenon, involving claims of ethics, politics, science, and economics to name but a few (Hulme, 2008). What is meant by climate change is human-caused (or anthropogenic) increases in the global average temperature of the planet caused by human activities such as burning carbon energy (coal, oil, and gas), deforestation, and agricultural practices, which produce climate-changing greenhouse gases (GHGs). The overwhelming majority of the world's climate scientists accept the reality of human-caused climate change, as articulated in peer-reviewed scientific articles and research, as well as the reports of the Intergovernmental Panel on Climate Change (IPCC). While there is scientific agreement on the causes of climate change and the urgent need for a reduction in GHGs, especially carbon dioxide from burning fossil fuels, this has not translated into sustained, credible, or robust international agreement on climate change. While the Kyoto Protocol (agreed in 1997 and implemented from 2008–12) did at least testify to some degree of recognition of the severity of the climate crisis, (a) it only lasted until 2012 and nothing has replaced it despite increasing GHG emissions, and (b) major carbon polluters such as the USA refused to sign it. Our carbon/fossil dependency is the flip side of climate change and may help explain or frame the seeming intractability of the climate problem. Given the power of fossil fuel interests (ranging from large corporations such as Shell or Exxon-Mobil, to those promoting hydraulic fracturing—or 'fracking'—for gas, to major oil-producing states such as Saudi Arabia) it is easy to see how tackling climate change through 'decarbonizing' the world's energy system is a threat. This of course gives them a vested interest to use their enormous economic and political resources to stall, block, and prevent any binding climate agreement, including attempts to produce climate-sceptical 'pseudoscience' and thus 'manufacture doubt' in public discourse around climate change (Nuccitelli, 2015). Thus, with respect to climate change, we are left with an extremely complex, multifaceted, global issue that 'changes everything' to use Naomi Klein's phrase (Klein, 2014). Moreover, the compelling scientific consensus on the reality of climate change being due to human activities, especially burning carbon, sits alongside either public resistance (not all of it manufactured by climate change sceptics) to engage with the topic, or wilful ignorance. 'Cognitive dissonance' is an all too common reaction of people to climate change (Marshall, 2014). A final, and very powerful (and attractive) response is the appeal of the 'myth of techo-optimism', which, while recognizing and accepting anthropogenic climate change, proposes technological solutions to enable the continuation of 'development as usual' (Barry, 2015). All of this means that there are, as yet, no determined moves, especially within developed industrial societies, to seriously consider and implement the large-scale changes to lifestyles and ways of life that tackling climate change requires (Barry, 2012).

Case Studies: Climate Change, Development Projects, and Environmental Refugees

The Impact of Economic Globalization on the Environment and Human Rights

The processes of economic **globalization** make available a greater variety of goods and services, at cheaper prices, to consumers in all corners of the globe, in every season (Stiglitz, 2002). Growth in the worldwide economy is also held by some economists to be more effective than redistribution at alleviating poverty. However, while the economic cost of numerous goods has fallen, the ecological costs are often not counted; rather, they are 'externalized' and not included in the final price or economic calculation. These costs nevertheless accrue, and emerge as environmental hazards such as climate change, biodiversity loss, and toxic pollution, with major impacts on human health and society. The economically driven displacement of environmental costs principally affects the human rights of two constituencies: today's poor, and future generations. It also affects the integrity and well-being of ecosystems and non-human animals.

Ecological footprint analysis (see Box 23.2) suggests that richer communities displace their environmental costs onto poorer ones, both within and between countries, and that past and present generations are displacing costs onto future ones—particularly evident in the case of climate change and biodiversity loss. Environmental damage does not disappear; it simply disappears from the sight of wealthy consumers. This 'out of sight, out of mind' perspective exemplifies, not 'problem solution', but rather 'problem displacement' (Dryzek, 1987)—the rich world effectively shipping the ecological costs of globalization to poorer countries. It is for this reason that many environmentalists view North–South relations in terms of the 'ecological debt': the rich, minority world owes the poorer 'global South' (Simms, 2005). Increasing disparities between rich and poor thus present an ecological problem as well as a social and political one.

One starting place for understanding the environmental impact of economic globalization is the globalizing agenda promoted by the **International Monetary Fund** (IMF) and the **World Trade Organization** (WTO). Former **World Bank** economist Joseph Stiglitz (2002) records that the character and remit of the IMF changed somewhat in the 1980s with the adoption of a **neoliberal** ideological outlook—promoting a global free market, sometimes known as the 'Washington Consensus' (Nitzan and Bichler, 2000)—which also came to dominate the WTO and, to a lesser extent, the World Bank.

Criticism of the IMF centres on the fact that states receiving development loans from the World Bank have, since the 1980s, been required by the IMF to implement **structural adjustment programmes** (SAPs). These typically entail cuts in public spending, which can often undermine environmental protection standards. SAPs also promote pursuit of competitive advantage in agriculture, which pushes farmers away from subsistence crops, increases pesticide use, and increases pressure on irrigation sources. At the same time, dependence on cash crops leaves countries vulnerable to prices falling for such low 'added value' primary products on the world market, as has happened with coffee, fruit, rubber, and other primary resources.

The WTO's record in terms of the outcomes of the environmental dimensions of WTO jurisprudence is better than many of its critics suggest, but the *raison d'être* of the WTO, to promote global trade and continuous economic growth, is itself a problem from an environmental point of view given the inevitable production of externalities and the rapidly increasing scale of the global economy. As Cole points out, 'Nations have traditionally been allowed to do as they please within their own borders, *but in an ecologically interdependent world, where production processes in one country can affect the global environment, such a notion may be outdated*' (Cole, 2000, p. 36; emphasis added). The economic and human rights impacts of climate change presents an enormous challenge both to the global economy in future years and to a 'business as usual' approach in the here and now.

Climate Change and Environmental Refugees

In 2003, Saufatu Sopoanga, Prime Minister of Tuvalu, told the United Nations General Assembly:

We live in constant fear of the adverse impacts of climate change. For a coral atoll nation, sea level rise and more severe weather events loom as a growing threat to our entire population. The threat is real and serious, and is of no difference to a slow and insidious form of terrorism against us.

(http://www.tuvaluislands.com/warming.htm)

Tuvalu is a small island nation in the South Pacific. Its highest point is a few metres above sea level, and it is widely regarded as being under threat from global warming. Rising sea levels cause problems, not only in terms of flooding, but also in terms of increased salt levels, rendering previously fertile land incapable of supporting crops, both of which problems may force people to leave homes on low-lying land. Like other kinds of refugees, environmental refugees typically face a number of problems that can be conceptualized in human rights terms: lack of shelter; lack of livelihood; lack of secure access to food, water, and medical services; and discrimination by host communities that feel threatened by the presence of refugee populations (see Chapter 18). The Intergovernmental Panel on Climate Change predicts that as many as 200 million people will be displaced from their homes by rising sea levels by 2050 (Warner, 2011; IPCC, 2014). The 2014 UN Human Development report, *Sustaining Human Progress: Reducing Vulnerabilities and Building Resilience*, connects climate change and the unequal resilience of people to cope with its negative effects due to already existing development and socio-economic inequalities. It states:

Hundreds of millions of poor, marginalized or otherwise disadvantaged people remain unusually vulnerable to economic shocks, rights violations, natural disasters, disease, conflict and environmental hazards. If not systematically identified and reduced, these chronic vulnerabilities could jeopardize the sustainability of human development progress for decades to come.

(UNDP, 2014, p. 10)

This echoes warnings in previous Human Development reports. For example, the 2008 Human Development report, *Fighting Climate Change: Human Solidarity in a Divided World*, stated:

Climate change is the defining human development challenge of the 21st century. Failure to respond to that challenge will stall and then reverse international efforts to reduce poverty. The poorest countries and most vulnerable citizens will suffer the earliest and most dam-aging setbacks, even though they have contributed least to the problem. Looking to the future, no country—how-ever wealthy or powerful—will be immune to the impact of global warming.

(UNDP, 2008)

The impact of climate change has meant that there are now more environmental refugees in the world than refugees from wars. And this is a trend set to continue throughout the coming decades. This is a major chal-lenge to the international community in coping with millions of people displaced because of climate and environmental change, and it underscores the relation-ship between policies dealing with climate change and environmental sustainability and human and interna-tional security. Creeping environmental deterioration has already displaced up to 10 million people per year and the situation is set to get worse, creating 50 mil-lion environmental refugees by the end of this decade. However, this new category of refugee is not currently recognized in international agreements. Campaigners such as Andrew Simms (Conisbee and Simms, 2003) and the former President of Ireland and former UN High Commissioner for Refugees, Mary Robinson (Robinson, 2015), call for governments and the inter-national legal system to recognize the environmental refugee as a specific status for asylum purposes, to help protect the human rights of 'climate refugees'.

Development Projects and Environmental Refugees

There are many examples of people being displaced from their lands or facing threats to their livelihoods because of development projects, and thus facing threats to their human rights, again in terms of rights to security of person, shelter, secure access to food and water, and so on. There have also been instances of the violation of civil and political rights on the part of governments and private security contractors con-fronted with protests against development projects.

One much publicized example is the judicial kill-ing in 1995 of Ken Saro-Wiwa and eight other activ-ists protesting against Shell Oil exploitation in the Niger Delta. The Movement for the Survival of the Ogoni People has long campaigned against the pol-luting practices of Shell, which have resulted in the contamination of freshwater supplies in the region as well as the destruction of natural habitats (Sachs and

Peterson, 1995). The Movement for the Survival of the Ogoni People has explicitly phrased its campaigns in terms of human rights, arguing for the right to con-trol of its lands and for the local people (and not the Nigerian state) to decide on *what* sort of development takes place in Ogoniland and, equally importantly, *who* decides on development proposals (see http://www.mosop.org/).

Another development project that has been op-posed in explicitly human rights terms is the Narmada Valley Development Plan in India, a substantial dam-construction project that the Asian Human Rights Commission claims has caused 'large-scale abuse of human rights and the displacement of many poor and underprivileged communities' (AHRC, 2003). The In-dian Government's plan is to build 30 large, 135 me-dium, and 3,000 small dams to harness the waters of the Narmada and its tributaries to provide the large amounts of water and electricity that are desperately required for the purposes of development. Opponents of the dam view the forced displacement of Indige-nous peoples as a human rights violation. Indigenous peoples have often been displaced by development projects with little or no consultation, and insufficient compensation (J. O'Neill, 2007) (see Chapter 19).

Opponents have pointed out that 'The controversy over large dams on the River Narmada has come to symbolize the struggle for a just and equitable society in India' (Friends of River Narmada, 2008). Opponents of the dam question the basic assumptions of the gov-ernment and believe that its planning is unjust, and the construction is causing large-scale abuse of human rights and the displacement of many poor and under-privileged communities. At another level, the ques-tions that arise in the Narmada struggle challenge the dominant model of development that holds out the promise of material wealth through modernization but perpetuates an unequal distribution of resources and wreaks social and environmental havoc. In simple terms, the struggle over the river Narmada is a case study in different development futures for India in how development relates to justice, human rights, equal-ity, and democracy. As the novelist and campaigner Arundhati Roy has written about the Narmada dam:

Big Dams are to a Nation's 'Development' what Nuclear Bombs are to its Military Arsenal. They're both weapons of mass destruction. They're both weapons Governments use to control their own people. Both Twentieth Cen-tury emblems that mark a point in time when human intelligence has outstripped its own instinct for survival. They're both malignant indications of civilisation turning upon itself. They represent the severing of the link, not just the link—the understanding—between human beings and the planet they live on. They scramble the intelligence that connects eggs to hens, milk to cows, food to forests, water to rivers, air to life and the earth to human existence. Can we unscramble it? Maybe. Inch by inch. Bomb by bomb. Dam by dam. Maybe by fighting specific wars in specific ways. We could begin in the Narmada Valley.

(Roy, 1999)

KEY POINTS

Environmental issues directly impact on the human rights of those who become refugees because of environmental problems, such as those displaced from lands by the threat of climate change and also by development projects.

The plight of environmental refugees illustrates the complex interlinking of environmental issues with issues of human rights, justice, and democracy in contemporary global politics.

Critical Thinking Question:

What are the main difficulties in establishing international legal rights for 'environmental refugees'?

Human Rights and Environmental Sustainability

The contemporary green movement sees freedom and rights as necessary (not contingent) features of sustainability. Thus greens welcome, though not uncritically, the values of human rights. This represents a move away from a narrow, single-issue 'environmentalism' to a comprehensive 'politics of sustainability', in which concern for the environment is nested within objectives related to such concerns as social and environmental justice, democratic participation, good governance, and human rights (Woods, 2010; Barry, 2014). That being the case, it makes sense for greens

to work to promote human rights, since they are at the heart of an expanded green agenda of sustainability. Equally, this line of argument, which suggests the evolution from a rather narrow 'environmental' focus towards a more expansive politics of sustainability, also offers an answer to the question: what sort of society are we sustaining? To build social and economic 'bottom lines' into green political objectives means that a 'sustainable society' is not simply one that does not undermine ecological conditions, but also one that does not undermine principles of social and environmental justice and democratic values and practices.

Environmental problems are, in the several ways indicated here, human rights issues that require careful thought and concerted, often collective, action. But human rights do not in themselves represent a solution to environmental problems, nor can human rights be uncritically accepted by the environmental movement. Rather, human rights are a resource that environmentalists might make use of, and a set of norms and values that green theorists and activists can work with others to renew and reshape.

KEY POINTS

While some earlier 'eco-authoritarian' green writers were willing to compromise human rights (and democracy and social justice) for sustainability, modern green advocates see human rights as an essential part of their politics and a constitutive feature of a 'sustainability society'.

'Promethean' or 'techno-fix' approaches to the challenge of environmental sustainability advocate a 'business as usual' view in which achieving environmental sustainability does not require major socio-economic or political changes when such transformation is precisely what greens advocate is needed.

Human rights do not in themselves represent a solution to environmental problems, but they are a necessary part of the solution and are now an embedded feature of green politics.

Critical Thinking Question:

What is gained and what is lost in the shift from 'environmentalism' to the 'politics of sustainability'?

Conclusion

This chapter has explored some of the ways in which environmental issues affect human rights, and the complex ways in which human rights are relevant to

environmental campaigns—especially in relation to 'environment versus development' controversies. A key issue in the relationship between human rights and the environment is the economy—its character and how it is structured. This chapter has shown how the neoliberal model of economic globalization has had profoundly negative impacts on the environment and, by extension, on certain human rights. While there are continuing theoretical/philosophical issues concerning the compatibility of human rights and environmental sustainability—particularly in relation to the rights of non-humanity and future people, and ongoing issues of the implementation of environmental human rights—human rights are firmly embedded as constitutive aspects of environmental sustainability in general, and green political theory and practice in particular.

? QUESTIONS

Individual Study Questions

1. How and in what ways are environmental issues related to human rights?

2. What human rights are related to the environment?

3. How does economic globalization impact on the environment? How does this relate to human rights?

4. What are the main areas of tension/incompatibility between green demands for 'sustainable development' and human rights? How can these be reconciled?

5. What are the main features of 'environmental human rights' and how do they differ from other human rights?

6. From a green political perspective, what are the relative advantages and disadvantages of seeking to represent environmental claims in a moral idiom other than human rights?

Group Discussion Questions

1. Does the creation of a sustainable society and one that safeguards human rights require the transcendence of current capitalist forms of economic globalization?

2. Do we need environmental human rights as a 'third generation' of human rights, or can most of the issues raised by greens be dealt with by first- and second-generation human rights?

3. If you were to define and codify environmental rights in a constitution, what would these be (in order of priority), and how might they clash with other rights enshrined in a constitution of a liberal democratic state?

4. Can future persons or non-human animals be said to have environmental human rights?

≋ FURTHER READING

Barry, J. (2007). *Environment and Social Theory* (2nd edn). London: Routledge.

This is an introductory textbook on the relationship between conceptions of nature and environment in Western and non-Western social, political, and economic thinking and explores the complex ways in which thinking about external nature always connects with thinking about internal human nature.

Barry, J. (2012). *The Politics of Actually Existing Unsustainability: Human Flourishing in a Climate-Changed, Carbon-Constrained World*. Oxford: Oxford University Press.

Barry argues that an adequate green politics needs to start from the global reality of 'actually existing unsustainability', and identify the causes of the multiple forms of harm that result from this unsustainability, rather than focusing on abstract and future-oriented concerns of 'sustainable development'.

Boyle, A. E. and **Anderson, M. R.** (eds) (1996). *Human Rights Approaches to Environmental Protection*. Oxford: Clarendon Press.

This is a collection of essays on environmental law from a human rights viewpoint, including conceptual discussions as well as studies of the international law dimension and national case studies.

Hancock, J. (2003). *Environmental Human Rights: Power, Ethics and Law*. London: Ashgate.

Hancock argues for the existence of two environmental human rights: the right to freedom from toxic pollution and the right to ownership of natural resources.

Hayward, T. (2005). *Constitutional Environmental Rights*. Oxford: Oxford University Press.

Hayward explores the implications of embedding environmental rights in national constitutions, and argues that environmental rights ought to be constitutionally guaranteed in any liberal democracy as human rights are now.

Hiskes, R. P. (2009). *The Human Right to a Green Future*. Cambridge: Cambridge University Press.

Hiskes looks here at the question of intergenerational justice in relation to environmental human rights.

Humphreys, S. (2010). *Human Rights and Climate Change*. Cambridge: Cambridge University Press.

A collection of essays addressing several dimensions of the relationship between human rights and climate change, including contributions from Simon Caney, Dinah Shelton, and many other leading scholars.

Nickel, J. (1993). The Human Right to A Safe Environment. *Yale Journal of International Law*, **18**/1, 281–95.

In this article Nickel defends the view that there is a human right to a safe environment.

Woods, K. (2010). *Human Rights and Environmental Sustainability*. Cheltenham: Edward Elgar.

In this book Woods undertakes a detailed analysis of the assumed normative and conceptual harmony between environmental sustainability and human rights. She also offers an extended discussion of the economy and politics of sustainability.

Zarksy, L. (ed.) (2003). *Human Rights and the Environment: Conflicts and Norms in a Globalizing World*. London: Earthscan.

This collection of essays presents discussions of a number of case studies, based on extensive empirical research, of conflicts in which environmental issues and human rights issues come into play.

WEB LINKS

http://www.ehumanrights.org/ Website of Advocates for Environmental Human Rights, with information, resources, and opportunities for online action.

http://environmentandhumanrights.org/inforesources.htm Environment and Human Rights Advisory's website, containing links to further information and resources.

http://www.footprintnetwork.org/index.php The Global Footprint Network website, including an individual footprint calculator as well as national footprint information for most countries.

http://www.unep.org/ The homepage of the UN Environment Programme, with a wealth of data and other information.

http://www.ohchr.org/EN/Issues/Environment/IEEnvironment/Pages/IEenvironmentIndex.aspx Homepage of the UNOHCHR Independent Expert on the Environment

 Visit the Online Resource Centre that accompanies this book for updates and a range of other resources: www.oxfordtextbooks.co.uk/orc/goodhart3e/

Glossary

Abrogation of rights The failure to honour rights.

Accession or accretion The acquisition of territory that has emerged from the action of the forces of nature.

Alien Tort Statute (ATS) An Act of the US Congress passed in 1789 that provides jurisdiction in federal courts over lawsuits by aliens for torts committed in violation either of international law or of treaties to which the United States is a party. It has been used successfully by torture victims and their families to bring civil suits against torturers residing in the United States.

Amnesty Immunity from prosecution, often granted through legislation as part of a peace agreement.

Amnesty International (AI) One of the world's principal human rights organizations. It was founded in 1961 with international headquarters in London. Amnesty International is a non-aligned organization that reports on human rights violations and works for political prisoners in all regions of the world. It is represented at the United Nations and other international bodies.

Androcentrism Being centred on a man. Feminists argue that human rights are androcentric when those rights have features that reflect the biological, political, and social experiences of men.

Asylum seekers Individuals who are seeking international protection. In countries with individualized procedures, an asylum seeker is someone whose claim has not yet been finally decided on by the country in which the claim is submitted.

Autonomy Autonomy refers to self-government, either of states or of individuals.

Behavioural revolution The period of development in political science starting in the late 1930s that sought to provide an objective, quantified approach to explaining and predicting political behaviour. This period of development is associated with the rise of the behavioural sciences, which were modelled after the natural sciences.

Bilateral treaty A treaty concluded between two parties only.

Biopolitical Regulation based on the needs of the population rather than the needs of the ruler or government. The concept derives from the work of Foucault, who counterposes biopolitical regulation based on the public needs of the society to pre-modern rule purely in the personal needs of the Prince (see, for example, Foucault, 2003, 2007).

Bretton Woods institutions The Bretton Woods institutions are the **World Bank** and the **International Monetary Fund** (IMF). They were set up at a meeting of forty-three countries in Bretton Woods, New Hampshire, USA in July 1944. Their aims were to help rebuild the shattered post-War world economy and to promote international economic cooperation. The original Bretton Woods agreement also included plans for an International Trade Organization (ITO), but these lay dormant until the **World Trade Organization** (WTO) was created in the early 1990s. The creation of the World Bank and the IMF came at the end of the Second World War as a central feature of a multilateral framework established to overcome the destabilizing effects of the previous global economic depression and trade battles.

Brown v. Board of Education of Topeka, Kansas The landmark 1954 ruling by the US Supreme Court that overturned previously restrictive laws segregating blacks and whites in public schools. The ruling mandated that separating blacks and subjecting them to systematically poorer learning environments amounted to a denial of equal educational opportunities.

Capacity gap A capacity gap refers to where there is alleged to be an inability on the part of rights-holders to act on their own behalf. An external agent steps in to act in their interest and, in doing so, often claims to enhance their capabilities or to empower them.

Cartagena Declaration of 1984 The Declaration adopted by a colloquium of experts from the Americas in November 1984. The Declaration enlarges the 1951 Convention definition of refugees to include 'persons who have fled their country because their lives, safety or freedom have been threatened by generalized violence, foreign aggression, internal conflicts, massive violation of human rights or other circumstances which have seriously disturbed public order'.

Cession The acquisition of the territory of another state through a treaty.

Child soldiers Children who have been recruited (usually forcibly) by non-state actors for military or forced labour purposes.

Citizenship Citizenship generally refers to the rights and duties of a member of a nation state or city. The work of sociologist T. H. Marshall is seen as a necessary starting point for understanding the modern concept sociologically. He defined citizenship as a status enjoyed by a person who is a full member of a community. It has three components: civil citizenship, which encapsulates individual freedoms; political citizenship, which grants rights to participation in the political process; and social citizenship, which grants rights to enjoy an appropriate standard of living.

Civil Rights Act The seminal law passed by the US Congress in 1964 banning segregation in employment, public schools, and public places.

Civil society Civil society refers to the arena of un-coerced collective action around shared interests, purposes, and values. In theory, its institutional forms are distinct from those of the state, family, and market, though in practice the boundaries are often blurred. Civil societies are populated by a network of social institutions and practices that play an important role in the functioning of democratic societies, comprising groups such as registered charities, community groups, women's organizations, faith-based organizations, professional associations, trade unions, self-help groups, business associations, coalitions, and advocacy groups.

Classical sociology It was not until the nineteenth century, in the aftermath of the industrial revolution, that a concern with 'society' emerged as an object of scholarly inquiry. Cumulatively, the writings of Marx, Durkheim, and Weber during that period are seen as broadly constituting 'classical sociology'.

Coding The practice of assigning a numerical score to a piece of empirical information. In the field of human rights, coding might involve assigning scores to countries for the degree to which they protect different types of human rights or coding treaty ratification and the filing of reservations.

Cold War The period of superpower rivalry between the USA and the USSR from the late 1940s to 1991. The idea of 'cold' war indicates that the two never fought directly, despite a massive arms race and numerous 'hot' proxy wars around the globe. The Cold War reflected traditional great power rivalry, as well as an ideological clash between communism (USSR and allies) and liberal democracy and capitalism (USA and allies). Human rights were one of the key ideological dividing lines in this conflict.

Collective sympathy Bryan Turner uses the concept to partly explain the emergence of human rights norms, the argument being that 'human beings will want their rights to be recognized *because they see in the plight of others their own (possible) misery*'.

Commission on Human Rights A functional body within the United Nations dealing with human rights concerns from 1946 to 2006. It was a subsidiary of the UN Economic and Social Council, though it also worked closely with the Office of the High Commissioner for Human Rights after 1993. Its main functions were to promote human rights, to hear complaints, and to investigate violations. The Commission was widely criticized as ineffective and was replaced in 2006 by the **Human Rights Council**.

Comparative politics The systematic study of domestic politics, or politics within countries. When applied to human rights, comparative politics helps to explain why states practise repression, how societal groups contribute to reforms, and the role of domestic institutions—from democracy to national courts—in changing human rights practices.

Conceptual Dealing with ideas or concepts, or having to do with the structure and coherence of ideas and arguments.

Conquest The acquisition of territory by the victor in a war.

Consequentialism/consequentialist approach to ethics The consequentialist approach to ethics is the notion that we ought to judge the moral worth of an act by its consequences (sometimes expressed simply as 'the ends justify the means'). **Utilitarianism** is one form of consequentialism.

Conservatism/conservatives A political philosophy/ideology emphasizing the organic emergence of society out of historical times. It rejects attempts to radically remould society or human nature, emphasizes continuity and incremental change, and has a generally sceptical outlook towards the claim of either reason or government that the human condition can be morally or substantively improved.

Constructivism A theoretical approach to international relations that emphasizes the role of ideas, rules, norms, discourses, identities, and social relations in the generation of social life. Constructivism conceptualizes actors as being embedded in socially constructed institutional contexts, which are constitutive of actors' identities and interests and can be changed in interaction (see also **social constructionism**).

Contracting states (high contracting parties/state parties) Contracting states are states that have agreed to be bound to a **treaty** through signature, ratification, accession, or succession.

Convention Against Torture and Other Cruel, Inhuman, or Degrading Treatment or Punishment (CAT) The principal international treaty outlawing torture and governing the responsibilities with regard to torture by **states parties**. It entered into force in 1987 and has been ratified by more than 140 countries.

Convention for the Elimination of All Forms of Discrimination Against Women (CEDAW) This was ratified by the UN General Assembly in 1979 and came into force in 1981. It comprises all of the UN's prior initiatives for ensuring the equality of women's human rights and re-emphasizes that all human rights are to be enjoyed equally by men and women. It is distinctive in requiring states to enshrine gender equality in their domestic law and to eliminate customs and practices that perpetuate gender bias or reinforce the idea of women's inferiority to men.

Convention on the Punishment and Prevention of the Crime of Genocide (Genocide Convention) The 1948 international treaty that codifies the crime of **genocide** and obligates state parties to punish and prevent genocide. The treaty came into force in 1951 and is widely accepted around the world today.

Convention Relating to the Status of Refugees This convention established the most widely applicable framework for the protection of refugees. The Convention was adopted in July 1951 and entered into force in April 1954. Article 1 of the Convention limits its scope to 'events occurring before 1 January 1951', but this restriction was removed by the 1967 Protocol relating to the Status of Refugees. The convention has over 150 state signatories.

Corrective rapes Sexual assaults of LGBTQ people, especially lesbians, for the purpose of curing—or 'correcting'—non-normative sexual orientation or gender identity. Corrective rape was first identified as a phenomenon linked to bias against LGBTQ people in South Africa. In 2014, South African government officials held meetings with South African SOGI activists and Western officials to consider implementing hate crimes laws to challenge the impunity of corrective rape perpetrators.

Council of Europe International organization founded in 1949 that seeks to promote democracy and human rights throughout Europe. The main instrument guiding the Council's work is the Convention for the Protection of Human Rights and Fundamental Freedoms (European Convention on Human Rights), which came into force in 1953. The **European Court of Human Rights** is the primary enforcement mechanism of the Convention. The Council presently has forty-seven members. See http://www.coe.int/en/web/about-us/who-we-are.

Crimes against humanity Deliberate widespread or systematic attacks on civilians, including murder, forced deportation, enslavement, imprisonment, torture, rape, or persecution. On the spectrum of humanitarian offences, it is more extreme than a war crime but less extreme than genocide, which requires the intent to destroy a group in whole or in part.

Critique The praise or criticism of an idea, law, institution, policy, practice, etc. Critique can be based on, among others, **conceptual**, **empirical**, or **normative** concerns or perspectives.

Cultural relativism A view that holds that ethics develop within particular social contexts; because social contexts are distinct from one another, there cannot be a moral framework that applies across contexts. Thus all truths are relative (context-specific), so cultures cannot be compared on moral or other normative grounds. In connection with human rights, it is the idea that human rights standards are Western and therefore inapplicable or inappropriate outside the West.

Customary international law State practice binding on states due to a period of uniform practice based on a sense of legal obligation.

Declaration of the Rights of Man and of the Citizen The Declaration of the Rights of Man and of the Citizen (*Declaration des Droits de l'Homme et du Citoyen*) was adopted by the French National Assembly in 1789. Its Article 10 secures freedom of religion subject to rule of law and the maintenance of public order. The Declaration distils French Enlightenment ideas about equality before the law and is an influence on contemporary understandings of universal human rights. See full text: http://avalon.law.yale.edu/18th_century/rightsof.asp.

Declarations Statements made by a state when agreeing to a **treaty**, which may or may not have legal effect. Also refers to an instrument adopted by international organizations that indicates or expresses international opinion but, unless otherwise stated in the organization's constituent instrument, is not legally binding.

Democratic deficit A democratic deficit occurs when decisions, particularly decisions by organizations ostensibly committed to democratic values, are taken without sufficient input from the citizens affected by them. Initially coined to refer to the insufficient impact of European citizens on decisions taken by the European Union, it has come to refer more broadly to the way in which different forms of globalization affect the capacity of citizens to make autonomous decisions in a national or subnational democratic setting.

Deontological approach to ethics The notion that acts are considered intrinsically good or bad without reference to their consequences.

Dependent variable In a quantitative analysis, the dependent variable is the variable whose variation we seek to explain.

Deportation The forcible removal of an immigrant or asylum seeker to another country.

Derogation The suspension of a state's obligation to respect certain human rights during a time of national emergency; it is an emergency power of limited duration.

Detention The practice of holding a person claiming asylum while processing her or his application.

Diaspora The dispersion of a community of people of a particular ethnic, religious, or national group from its original homeland through emigration, persecution, economics, politics, or enslavement. Also refers to the members of the community living outside the original homeland who keep in close contact with their homeland and are frequently politically active.

Disaggregate/disaggregation An effort to break larger analytic units into smaller ones for the purposes of more careful analysis. For instance, one might look at states rather than the federal government in federal polities or at different branches of government rather than government as a whole.

Disappearances The forcible detention or abduction of people by the government (or with its consent), followed by a refusal to disclose their whereabouts.

Doctrine of necessity This refers to the notion that one harmful act may be justifiable to prevent a second, far more harmful act.

Donor In the context of human rights, groups or individuals that donate resources for the purpose of advancing human rights. Donors may be governments (or agencies within governments), non-governmental organizations, corporations, or individuals, and recipients of human rights donations may be organizations or individuals. Donor relationships are often characterized by standards of accountability for the appropriate disbursing of funds on the part of donors and their effective use by aid recipients.

Earmarking Earmarking occurs when a donor state places conditions on the use of aid funds for a specific programme, country, or purpose.

Ecocide The killing of ecosystems, including planet Earth.

Ecological footprint The ecological footprint is a measure of human demand on the Earth's ecosystems and natural resources. Ecological footprint estimates the amount of biologically productive land and sea area needed to regenerate the resources a human population consumes and to absorb and render harmless the corresponding waste, given prevailing technology and current understanding. For example, if everyone in the world was to live the lifestyle of an average American, we would need five planet Earths.

Economic migrants Economic migrants are persons who leave their countries purely for economic reasons or in order to seek material improvements in their livelihood. Economic migrants do not fall within the criteria for refugee status and are therefore not entitled to benefit from international refugee protection.

Empirical Empirical refers to 'what is'. Empirical studies deal with data and information about the real world, gleaned from the real world. Empirical studies seek to describe or observe what is actually going on and to explain what accounts for the patterns and relationships in our observations or predicts what is likely to occur. Contrast this with **normative**.

Empirical ethnographic methodology This refers to the close relationships and sensory experiences utilized in the observation of social groups, in the attempt to describe and explain social phenomena, and in the subsequent production of a written record thereof.

Empowerment rights Empowerment rights are a subset of internationally recognized human rights that includes rights such as workers' rights and the rights to open and free political participation, movement, religion, and a free media, among others.

Encampment The practice of placing refugees in camps in host countries where they are protected and assisted by international organizations or host governments.

Enlightenment The European Enlightenment, also known as the Age of Reason, is usually said to have started between 1660 and 1685, and to have ended with the French Revolution. The Enlightenment philosophers believed in progress through human reason and were critical of superstition and religion, along with monarchical and aristocratic forms of political authority. An elite cultural movement, it laid the intellectual groundwork for political transformation in the eighteenth and nineteenth centuries in Europe and North America.

Entitlement An entitlement is a benefit secured by law or contract; something one is *entitled to*.

Equivalence principle of good governance The principle that stakeholders should have voice equivalent to that of decision makers in matters impacting directly upon their life chances and life choices.

Essentialism/essentialist The attribution of a behaviour or practice to human nature or to natural human tendencies, either generally or specifically in connection with a particular class or group of people. For instance, human rights violations might be attributed to human evil or animosities between social groups, or to specific social or cultural factors. Consequently, this view can be deeply pessimistic about the prospects for human rights reform.

Ethnic cleansing The forced displacement of civilians based on their ethnicity, typically employing threats, fire, rape, or killing. Ethnic cleansing can sometimes constitute **genocide**.

Ethnocide The destruction of the culture and distinct identity of an ethnic group, sometimes described as cultural genocide.

Ethnography/ethnographic Ethnography (Greek εθνος *ethno*: people and γράφειν *graphein*: writing) is a type of research writing that uses fieldwork to generate data and facilitate the study of human societies. Anthropology and sociology, especially the constructivist and relativist paradigms, rely heavily on ethnographic research.

Eugenics An ideology based on a hierarchy of races of people that informed nineteenth- and twentieth-century 'scientific' racism.

European Court of Human Rights (ECHR) The primary enforcement mechanism of the Convention for the Protection of Human Rights and Fundamental Freedoms (European Convention on Human Rights), which came into force in 1953 (see **Council of Europe**). It is widely recognized as being the most evolved supranational mechanism for human rights enforcement. The Court took on its present form through changes implemented with Protocol No. 11 to the Convention, which came into force in 1998. See http://www.coe.int/t/democracy/migration/bodies/echr_en.asp.

Exclusionary ideologies Exclusionary ideologies define the conditions under which it is appropriate to repress certain categories of people. Examples include national security doctrines and broader ideologies of discrimination, targeting people on the basis of political orientation or social identity. Exclusionary ideologies are a fundamental source of state repression.

Executive Committee (UNHCR) The Executive Committee is charged with approving the UNHCR's assistance programmes, advising the High

Commissioner on the exercise of his/her functions, and overseeing the Office's finances and administration. The Executive Committee is composed of representatives of seventy states with a demonstrated interest in refugee issues. Other states may attend, along with intergovernmental organizations and non-governmental organizations, as observers.

Externalities Externalities are the costs or benefits of a decision or policy to third parties—often, although not necessarily, from the use of a public good. A negative externality is one where the producer of a product does not bear all of the costs. Manufacturing that causes air pollution or environmental degradation imposes costs on others when making use of public air that are not borne by the polluter nor reflected in the price of the goods.

Failed and fragile states A failed state is one that has collapsed or is near collapse and cannot provide for its citizens without substantial external support. A fragile state has weak institutions and capacities and is in danger of failing.

Foreign direct investment (FDI) The investment a corporation or business makes outside its home country—either the construction of plants or acquisition of a controlling interest (more than 10 per cent of outstanding stock) in an existing overseas company. FDI is a central part of the **neoliberal** model of economic **globalization**, which encourages governments to lower corporate tax rates and provide other incentives to attract foreign investment capital.

Foundationalism/foundationalist Foundationalism is the view that any theory or principle must be justified by reference to more basic or foundational beliefs, which are held to be self-evident or self-justifying. Thus, a foundationalist position is one that relies on an apparently self-evident claim—e.g. 'Human frailty is a universal experience of human existence' (Turner, 1993, p. 505; Turner and Rojek, 2001, p. 110).

Framing Framing describes the active, dynamic, and evolving process of constructing, adapting, and negotiating frames. Frames refer to 'schemata of interpretation' that enable individuals to make sense of a complex reality by 'locating, perceiving, identifying and labelling' events and occurrences, and thereby function to organize experiences and guide action. Framing implies agency and contention at the level of reality construction.

Freedom Riders Freedom Riders were a group of activists, generally from the northern USA, who travelled to the South in an effort to challenge discriminatory laws mandating segregation in public transportation across state lines.

***Gacaca* courts** Literally translated as 'justice on the grass', the *gacaca* courts were established after the 1994 Rwandan genocide, using a traditional model. Local courts were established to try perpetrators of the Rwandan genocide for crimes that were divided into four categories, based on the seriousness of the offence; judges were elected by the local community to adjudicate these trials.

Gender The power dynamics associated with masculinity and femininity and with expectations about what men and women can do and should do. Gender analysis also focuses on the mechanisms through which these dynamics and expectations become normalized in social, political, and economic arrangements.

Gender Empowerment Measure (GEM) Created and published by the United Nations Development Programme's Human Development Reports, the GEM aims to measure disparity in empowerment by gender. It is a composite index that includes three basic dimensions of empowerment—economic participation and decision making, political participation, and decision making and power over economic resources.

Gender mainstreaming An attempt to institutionalize accountability for design programming and allocating resources in ways that promote human rights for all. An alternative to creating special bureaus, offices, etc. to address women's concerns.

Gender-related Development Index (GDI) Created and published by the United Nations Development Programme's Human Development Reports, GDI is a composite index that measures human development in the same dimensions as the human development index (HDI), while adjusting for gender inequality in those basic dimensions. Its coverage is limited to 136 countries and areas for which the HDI rank was recalculated.

Geneva Conventions and Protocols The Geneva Conventions are four treaties, the first of which was adopted at an international conference in 1864, that set international legal standards regarding humanitarian matters, especially concerning the treatment of non-combatants and prisoners of war during wartime.

The Geneva Conventions are the foundation of modern humanitarian law and have since been expanded (1949, 1977).

Genocide Genocide, as defined by the 1948 UN **Convention on the Punishment and Prevention of the Crime of Genocide**, is a crime under international law comprising acts 'committed with intent to destroy, in whole or in part, a national, ethnical, racial or religious group, as such'.

Genocide Convention See **Convention on the Punishment and Prevention of the Crime of Genocide**.

Global civil society (GCS) The sphere of ideas, institutions, organizations, networks, and individuals operating beyond the confines of national societies, polities, and economies; it is the international analogue of **civil society**. The term also carries **normative** connotations of belonging to a global imagined community, belief in human rights, global social justice, and/or shared responsibility for the environment. However, not all groups operating within the domain of GCS share these normative views.

Globalization Globalization is a historical process that links distant communities and expands the reach of power relations across regions and continents. It involves a shift in social relations and interaction from more local to more global levels. Popularly the term is often used to describe an integrated world economy and society. *Economic* globalization can refer generally to an increase in the worldwide flow of goods, services, labour, and capital or specifically to the implementation of **neoliberal** economic policy reforms.

Global North/South Geopolitical and economic labels that designate countries that were former colonizers/colonies, users/suppliers of natural resources, and places inhabited by people of wealth/in poverty. These terms have begun to replace **Western** and Third World in the literature on development, transnational activism, etc. Global North refers to people and places of political and economic privilege, while global South denotes people and places of political and economic deprivation, either historically or presently.

Governance Governance refers to 'state-like' activity. It is used particularly in reference to the evolving global system of formal and informal political coordination among states and intergovernmental organizations and non-state actors seeking to realize common purposes or resolve collective problems through the making and implementation of global or transnational norms, rules, programmes, and policies.

Guiding principles The United Nations Guiding Principles on Business and Human Rights (also 'Ruggie Principles') are global standards for addressing adverse impacts on human rights linked to business activity. They set out, in three pillars, principles concerning the State duty to protect human rights, the corporate responsibility to respect human rights, and access to remedy for victims of human rights abuse. Although authoritative, the guiding principles are non-binding requirements for companies to respect human rights, and proactively take steps to prevent, mitigate and, where appropriate, remediate, their adverse human rights impacts. The principles were developed by John Ruggie as the UN Special Representative for Business and Human Rights, who presented them to the UN Human Rights Council in June 2011.

Hague Conventions The Hague Conventions are two international **treaties** negotiated in 1899 and 1907 governing the conduct of war itself, the weapons that may and may not be employed under international law, and the definition of war crimes.

Harmonization The process by which domestic laws and rules are aligned with international standards. States are obligated to alter domestic laws, rules, and regulations that conflict with international human rights norms. Harmonization is essential if human rights reforms are to be sustainable.

Helsinki Accords/Agreement Accords signed in 1975 by the United States, Canada, the Soviet Union, and most European states including Turkey. It was the Final Act of the Conference on Security and Cooperation in Europe. The Agreement was seen as a major step in reducing **Cold War** tensions through the recognition of the territorial integrity of Eastern bloc states; its human rights provisions later became the basis for **civil society**-based challenges to Soviet rule.

Helsinki committees Non-governmental organizations formed during the **Cold War** in Eastern European countries to promote human rights. These committees date to the 1975 Helsinki Accords, which inserted human rights issues into East–West relations. Some credit the committees, and the transnational linkages they forged, with ending the Cold War.

Human Development Index (HDI) An aggregate index combining normalized measures of life expectancy, literacy, education, and gross domestic product per capita for countries worldwide. It has become a standard means of measuring human development, a concept that refers to the process of widening the options of individuals, giving them greater opportunities for education, healthcare, income, employment, etc. The HDI is published annually in the United Nations Development Programme's Human Development Reports.

Human development and capability approach (HD/CA) A development approach framed in Amartya Sen's concept of development as capability expansion (Sen, 1989) or freedom (Sen, 1999a). Development is defined by its ends or purpose: expanding capabilities that individuals have to lead lives they value; or alternatively, expanding choices that people have in their lives. As a development approach, HD/CA emphasizes the creation of an enabling environment for pursuing these ends. Economic growth is only one such means.

Human Dimension Mechanism Organization for Security and Co-operation in Europe (OSCE) procedure that allows member states to raise issues of human rights concern with other members. The Moscow Mechanism (established at the last meeting of the Conference on the Human Dimension in Moscow in 1991) provides for the additional possibility for participating states to establish ad hoc missions of independent experts to assist in the resolution of a specific human dimension problem, either on their own territory or in other OSCE participating states.

Human Poverty Index (HPI) Created and published by the United Nations Development Programme's Human Development Reports to measure the level of poverty by focusing on human lives, the HPI is a composite index that complements the human development index. HPI-1 for developing countries includes deprivations in the three basic dimensions captured in the human development index—a long and healthy life, knowledge, and a decent standard of living. HPI-2 for selected high-income Organisation for Economic Co-operation and Development (OECD) countries includes social exclusion, in addition to the three dimensions included in HPI-1. HPI-2 uses indicators and threshold levels more appropriate to high-income OECD societies.

Human rights-based approach to development (HRBA) HRBA is a discourse in the development field. OHCHR (2006) defines it as 'a conceptual framework for the process of human development that is normatively based on international human rights standards and operationally directed at promoting and protecting human rights. It seeks to analyse inequalities that lie at the heart of development problems and redress discriminatory practices and unjust distributions of power that impede development progress'.

Human Rights Council (HRC) The UN human rights body established by General Assembly Resolution 60/251 in 2006. The Council replaced the **Commission on Human Rights**.

Human Rights Watch (HRW) One of the world's principal international human rights organizations, with headquarters in New York City. HRW was founded in 1978 under the name Helsinki Watch to monitor the former Soviet Union's compliance with the **Helsinki Accords**. As the organization grew, it formed other watch committees to cover other regions of the world. In 1988, all of the committees were united under one umbrella to form Human Rights Watch. HRW conducts research and advocacy on a wide range of human rights issues around the world and is represented at the United Nations and other international bodies.

Humanitarian intervention Originally defined as the provision of vital materials (food, water, shelter, and medical care) to at-risk civilians in conflict areas, it now also includes any international action—economic, diplomatic, or military—motivated primarily by the humanitarian desire to protect civilian targets of violence.

Humanitarian law Refers both to laws, such as the **Geneva Conventions and Protocols**, governing the conduct of war (in Latin, *jus in bello*), and laws concerning the circumstances under which war is justified (in Latin, *jus ad bellum*). Sometimes called the 'laws of war'.

Impartiality State of not favouring any side or position. In discussions of humanitarian assistance, impartiality means providing aid solely on the basis of need, without consideration of the political or military allegiance of the recipient or the effect on a conflict's balance of power. Compare with **neutrality**.

Imperialism The subjugation and domination of one group of people by another, usually through violent political and military means; it involves political, economic, and social control over territory and resources.

Comes from the Latin term *imperium*, which means 'to command'.

Impunity Exemption from punishment. Often refers specifically to the status of known human rights violators who are not prosecuted or otherwise brought to justice.

Inclusiveness and subsidiarity principle of good governance The principle that those whose life chances and life choices are most affected by actions and decisions should have the greatest say in deliberations concerning these.

Independent variable In a quantitative analysis, this is a variable used to explain variation in the **dependent variable**. For example, altitude is one independent variable that could be used to explain variations in the time it takes for water to boil (the dependent variable) in different places around the world.

Indivisibility The principle that each and every human right is inherent to the dignity of every human person. Consequently, they all have equal status as rights and cannot be ranked in a hierarchy of importance. This is an important principle in many debates, as some argue that civil and political rights are more significant than economic and social rights, or vice versa.

Interdiction The practice of intercepting refugees and asylum seekers before they cross the border of the country in which they intend to seek asylum.

Intergenerational justice Intergenerational justice is the idea that some form of ethical relationship, framed in terms of justice, can be identified between generations of people separated by time. See also: Lukas Meyer, Intergenerational Justice, *The Stanford Encyclopedia of Philosophy* (Fall 2015 Edition), ed. Edward N. Zalta, http://plato.stanford.edu/archives/fall2015/entries/justice-intergenerational/.

Internally displaced persons (IDPs) Individuals who have been forced or obliged to flee from their home or place of habitual residence as a result of, or in order to seek safety and protection from, the effects of armed conflicts, situations of generalized violence, violations of human rights, or natural or human-made disasters, and who have not crossed an internationally recognized state border.

International Committee of the Red Cross (ICRC) Prototypical humanitarian organization, founded in 1863 at the international conference that also gave rise to the original version of the **Geneva Conventions and Protocols**. The ICRC eschews political criticism of states in order to maintain access to provide humanitarian relief.

International Court of Justice (ICJ or World Court) The principal judicial organ of the United Nations. The only permanent international court with competence to hear inter-state disputes (brought with the consent of both parties).

International Covenant on Civil and Political Rights (ICCPR) One of the 'twin covenants' that forms the backbone of the International Bill of Rights. The ICCPR tabulates in a legally binding form the first half of the rights and freedoms enshrined in the **Universal Declaration of Human Rights**.

International Covenant on Economic, Social and Cultural Rights (ICESCR) One of the 'twin covenants' that forms the backbone of the International Bill of Rights. The ICESCR tabulates in a legally binding form the second half of the rights and freedoms enshrined in the **Universal Declaration of Human Rights**.

International Criminal Court (ICC) Permanent court created by the Rome Treaty (1998) and established in 2002 with jurisdiction to prosecute individuals who have allegedly perpetrated crimes listed in the 1998 Statute of the International Criminal Court. Cases can be referred to the Office of the Prosecutor by the state itself (e.g. Uganda) or by the Security Council (e.g. Sudan).

International Criminal Tribunal for Rwanda (ICTR) The United Nations ad hoc tribunal established to prosecute the major planners of the 1994 genocide in Rwanda. The court is based in Arusha, Tanzania.

International Criminal Tribunal for the former Yugoslavia (ICTY) The United Nations ad hoc tribunal established to prosecute war crimes committed in the former Yugoslavia. The court is based in The Hague, the Netherlands.

International financial institutions (IFIs) IFIs are financial institutions that have been established (or chartered) by more than one country, and hence are subjects of international law. Their owners or shareholders are generally national governments, although other international institutions and other organizations occasionally figure as shareholders. The most prominent IFIs are multilateral institutions.

International Human Rights Day In 1950, 10 December was designated as International Human Rights Day to commemorate the United Nations General Assembly's 1948 adoption of the Universal Declaration of Human Rights (UDHR). International Human Rights Day is celebrated in a variety of ways by member states, including with human rights events, speeches, and the presentation of awards.

International Labour Organization (ILO) International organization established in 1919; now a specialized agency of the United Nations, with primary responsibility for addressing issues of workers' rights and social justice. The ILO adopts many treaties and recommendations on labour and related matters.

International Monetary Fund (IMF) One of the **Bretton Woods institutions** established in 1944 to provide short-term financial help to countries seeking to stabilize exchange rates or improve balance of payments difficulties. Since the 1980s, the IMF has become progressively more involved in the economic decision making of nations through the **structural adjustment programmes** associated with its loans.

Intersectionality The theoretical lens theorists of injustice use to explore the connections across multiple forms of oppression: race, class, gender, sexuality, Indigenous politics, minority politics, cast politics, nationalism, etc. By studying these intersections, feminists identify the ways in which sources of oppression may intersect to render some experiences of injustice invisible.

League of Nations An international organization created after the First World War by the Treaty of Versailles. Its goal was to prevent war from happening again. It had some success in the 1920s, but was ultimately unable to withstand the aggression of the Axis powers in the 1930s. After the Second World War it was replaced by the United Nations.

Legal positivism The view that the law is separate from considerations of morality or justice. On this view the law does not gain its legitimacy from the natural law or other ethical considerations, but from being enacted by an appropriate institutional authority.

Liberalism/liberals A political philosophy/ideology emphasizing humans' rational capacities, the role

of individuals in shaping social life, the harmony of individuals' rights, freedoms, and interests, market economics (in either classical liberal or welfare liberal strands), and democratic government (conceived often as limited government). Freedom or liberty is the primary value that should be instantiated in society and protected by government, in the liberal view; all individuals are equal, and their rights are to be protected equally under the **rule of law**. In international relations theory liberalism is associated with a variety of approaches that emphasize the role of democratic states in generating cooperation internationally as well as the role of international institutions in generating cooperation between states.

Like-minded group A like-minded group is an informal coalition of states who coalesce around a joint position in a particular international forum. In the field of human rights, this has traditionally referred to a group of small Western powers, including Canada, the Netherlands, and the Scandinavian countries, committed to furthering human rights issues in the United Nations. In the negotiations on the **International Criminal Court** the like-minded group grew from this base to encompass a much larger group of states in favour of a strong, independent Court, including most European, African, and Latin American states. But most recently, in the context of the **Human Rights Council**, the term 'like-minded group' has been used conversely to refer to a group of states committed to privileging national sovereignty over human rights.

Limburg Principles on the Implementation of the International Covenant on Economic, Social and Cultural Rights A set of 103 principles drawn up by a group of distinguished experts in international law who convened in the province of Limburg (the Netherlands) in 1986 to elucidate the nature and scope of the obligations of **states parties** to the **International Covenant on Economic, Social and Cultural Rights**. They were supplemented a decade later with the Maastricht Guidelines on Violations of Economic, Social and Cultural Rights.

Magna Carta The Magna Carta ('Great Charter' in Latin) is a document signed by King John in Runnymede, England (1215) following the rebellion of a group of barons. It asserts the idea of the rule of law and places the king beneath the law. Some of its clauses remain part of contemporary British statuary law including the first clause that 'the

English Church shall be free, and shall have its rights undiminished, and its liberties unimpaired'. (See full text: http://www.bl.uk/magna-carta/articles/magna-carta-english-translation.)

Margin of appreciation Margin of appreciation in the broadest sense refers to the degree of freedom accorded to national authorities in fulfilling their obligations under the European Convention on Human Rights. For more details see: Steven Greer, *The Margin of Appreciation: Interpretation and Discretion under the European Convention on Human Rights*, Human rights files No. 17. Council of Europe Publishing.

Millennium Declaration (MD) Declaration made by heads of state convened at the 2000 Millennium Summit committing their nations to 'doing their utmost' for global development. The MD vowed to overcome poverty and achieve peace, human rights, democracy, and environmental sustainability, while respecting the principles of equality and solidarity. It also set out specific goals and targets for development, which were further elaborated in the **Millennium Development Goals**.

Millennium Development Goals (MDGs) A set of eight goals, eighteen associated targets, and forty-eight progress indicators for development, subsequent to the 2000 **Millennium Declaration**. The MDGs address seven key dimensions of poverty: hunger, primary education, gender equality and empowerment of women, maternal mortality, child mortality, HIV/AIDS and other major diseases, and environmental sustainability. The eighth goal calls for stronger global partnerships and cooperation on development.

Moral hazard of humanitarian intervention A perverse dynamic in which the emerging norm of intervention to protect at-risk civilians, or **Responsibility to Protect**, has the unintentional consequence of encouraging rebellion that provokes state retaliation against civilians.

Multilateral treaty Treaty concluded between more than two parties or a treaty concluded by two parties but open to a larger group of states to ratify.

Multinational corporations (MNCs) Corporations that do business and/or have branches in more than one country (sometimes also referred to as a transnational corporations or TNCs).

Naming and shaming Closely related strategies used by human rights activists. Groups document and disseminate evidence of human rights violations with the aim of shaming or embarrassing governments into complying.

National human rights institutions Governmental agencies designed to promote and protect international human rights norms domestically. These institutions have proliferated worldwide since the early 1990s, and they now exist in over a hundred countries. They are commonly tasked with collecting and investigating human rights complaints, issuing recommendations, and engaging in human rights education.

National security doctrines Exclusionary ideologies that legitimate the state's use of coercion to contain social instability and guarantee national security. Influential during the **Cold War**, as well as in today's global 'war on terror', national security doctrines provide a rationale for why it is acceptable and even necessary to respond to societal challenges with repression.

Natural Family In Christian conservative discourse, the model of the family that is ordained by God and consists of a married husband and wife and their biological children. Proponents of this family model consider it to be threatened in contexts in which alternative family forms are recognized by law. They oppose the recognition of alternative family forms such as same-sex families as an issue of fundamental human rights.

Natural law A moral law or code that is supposedly objective because it is built into the cosmos. Natural law has pre-Christian antecedents, but it was the Christian version that provided the theoretical backdrop to the emergence of the **rights of man** and modern human rights.

Natural rights Rights based on the **natural law** and justified in the first age of rights through ideas from Christian theology. As this theology lost favour among philosophers, natural rights were argued to emerge out of our basic humanity, rather than out of God's natural law. But philosophers then disagreed about how such rights should be understood to emerge out of our humanity.

Neoliberal/neoliberalism Neoliberalism is an ideology that defines freedom primarily in terms of the operation of markets with minimal government regulation and the protection of capital from taxation, expropriation, or social responsibilities. Neoliberals hold that the 'free market' leads to the greatest possible degree of freedom and prosperity for everyone. The main tenets of neoliberalism include trade liberalization, deregulation, elimination of or drastic reduction in public spending, and securing of property rights, including the right to make contracts and dispose of assets as one pleases. Policies implementing these aims are said by proponents to increase economic growth by reducing the role of the state in the economy. Critics claim that neoliberalism is a way of reinforcing Western hegemony and note that evidence for the growth claims is scarce.

Neutrality A status of ensuring that one's intervention does not affect the balance of things. In discussions of humanitarian intervention, neutral assistance is assistance that does not alter the balance of power between warring parties. Compare with **impartiality**.

New International Economic Order (NIEO) A set of proposals advanced by developing countries in the 1970s to make the global economic system more fair. These proposals included more trade, tariff reform, increased development assistance, and changes to a system of global economic decision making that was viewed as favouring the rich countries.

No-fly zone Intervention to patrol the skies and shoot down any unauthorized military aircraft, often in support of humanitarian intervention, as in parts of Iraq from 1991–2003 and Bosnia from 1993–5.

Non-governmental organizations (NGOs) Legally constituted, private, not-for-profit organizations that, in the field of human rights, work on advocacy campaigns, develop and set international human rights standards, monitor human rights violations, and provide service delivery primarily in developing countries. Many are active in **global civil society**.

Non-materialist Non-materialist explanations emphasize the role of ideas, norms, and identities (i.e. ideational factors) in human events. They focus less on the calculations and concrete interests that underlie the decision to repress, for example, than on the exclusionary ideologies that render repression appropriate in the first place.

Non-refoulement *Refoulement* is the removal of a person to a territory or frontier of a territory where the person's life or freedom would be threatened on account of the person's race, religion, nationality, membership of a particular social group, or political opinions. The duty of *non-refoulement* or not returning

such individuals at risk is a part of **customary international law** and is therefore binding on all states whether or not they are parties to the **Convention Relating to the Status of Refugees**.

Non-state actors Refers to all actors at the international level who are not states, e.g. terror groups, **multinational corporations**, **non-governmental organizations**, private security contractors, etc.

Normative Normative refers to what ought to be. Normative studies address moral, conceptual, and philosophical questions and are concerned with clarifying and justifying concepts and making moral arguments and **critiques**. Contrast with **empirical**.

Nuremberg Trials/Nuremberg Tribunal (International Military Tribunal (IMT) at Nuremberg) A series of trials held in Nuremberg, Germany by the Allies following the end of the Second World War. These trials prosecuted captured German leaders for crimes against peace, war crimes, and crimes against humanity. (Similar trials were held in Tokyo before the International Military Tribunal for the Far East.) In the most famous trial, nineteen high-ranking German defendants were found guilty in 1946. The court was the first international criminal tribunal of its kind, and is today seen as a precedent for the United Nations ad hoc criminal tribunals and the **International Criminal Court**.

OAU Convention Governing Specific Aspects of Refugee Problems in Africa This regional complement to the 1951 Convention provides for a broader refugee definition. Adopted in 1969, the OAU Convention stipulates that the term 'refugee' also 'applies to those fleeing from external aggression, occupation, foreign domination, or events seriously disturbing public order in either part of or the whole of the country of origin'.

Occupation or discovery The acquisition of territory that is not under the power of another sovereign state.

Offshore processing The practice of processing claims of asylum seekers outside the country that they are bound for.

Palermo Protocol The Protocol to Prevent, Suppress, and Punish Trafficking in Persons, especially Women and Children. The Palermo Protocol supplemented the UN Convention against Transnational Organized

Crime; it was signed in Palermo, Italy in 2000 and provided a contemporary definition of human trafficking that encompassed trafficking for labour and sexual exploitation.

Philosophes A term used to describe those thinkers and authors who were active and influential during the period of the European Enlightenment.

Physical integrity rights/violations A subset of internationally recognized human rights that typically includes the rights to protection from execution, torture, **disappearance**, or political imprisonment. Physical integrity violations, commonly known as state repression or coercion, consist of the use or threatened use of violence by the state and its agents to violate physical integrity rights.

Physical Quality of Life Index (PQLI) Index measuring the quality of life or overall well-being of a country. The index is a single number derived from the basic literacy rate, infant mortality, and life expectancy at age one. It has in many ways been displaced by the use of the **Human Development Index**, but in some studies has been used by political scientists as a measure of 'subsistence' rights.

Polity index This is a data-collection effort pioneered by Ted Gurr that attempts to measure diverse political characteristics of governmental authority on a range of indicators. It focuses on governing institutions rather than discrete and mutually exclusive forms of governance. The index conceives of governmental authority on a spectrum ranging from fully institutionalized autocracy to fully institutionalized democracy using a 21-point scale. The index is used to identify three regime types: autocracies (scores of –10 to –6), 'anocracies' (–5 to +5, plus special values), and democracies (+6 to +10).

Portfolio investment The purchase of stocks and bonds totalling less than 10 per cent of the outstanding stock in foreign firms.

Poverty Reduction Strategy Papers (PRSPs) Policy frameworks for poverty reduction prepared by governments of low-income countries to mobilize donor support. Elaborate documents of several hundred pages, they analyse the causes of poverty and set strategic priorities and define action plans for economic growth and poverty reduction. They are underpinned by a framework of macro-economic policies intended to maintain stability.

Prescription The acquisition of territory based on its effective possession over a period of time.

Proletariat A term used in Marxist theory to refer to those who are wage or salary workers. They are people who do not have ownership of the means of production—that is, who are not part of the ruling capitalist class (the bourgeoisie).

Public/private dichotomy An analytic distinction used to determine what is political and what is left to 'individuals'. Falsely characterizes personal and interpersonal relations, such as family relations, as 'not political' and irrelevant to/inappropriate for politics, economics, and social institutions. This conceptual distinction is also used to reject public intervention in 'private' matters.

Qualitative/qualitative studies Qualitative studies are **empirical** studies that rely on the analysis and interpretation of data in ways that do not involve statistical techniques. These studies often utilize an in-depth case analysis of a particular country, region, or reference group; evidence might include interviews, **ethnography**, historical analysis, etc.

Quantitative/quantitative methods/studies Quantitative studies are **empirical** research studies that rely on statistical techniques for the analysis and interpretation of data (typically, *regression analysis*—a technique for determining the nature and strength of the relationship between a **dependent variable** and one or more **independent variables**). In the human rights field, quantitative methods examine a number of countries together over a period of time in the search for generalizations that can be made from these countries' collective experiences—for instance, to explain state repression or treaty ratification.

Ratification Practice of agreeing to the terms of a **treaty** (in accordance with constitutional national law) to enable it to be enforced.

Realism/realist A school of thought about international relations that emphasizes the nature of the international system as competitive and 'anarchic' (without a world authority able to compel states to act in any given way), and which therefore requires individual states to protect their interests through military means if necessary. For realists, international law and institutions exert almost no constraining effect on the conduct of states. Instead, their behaviour is animated by the unrelenting pursuit of the national interest.

Realpolitik Term used to describe state policies that concern themselves solely with the pursuit of the national interest.

Refugee determination process The process carried out by the UN High Commissioner for Refugees or state governments to determine whether or not a person is a genuine refugee according to international legal refugee instruments.

Regimes Institutions, principles, norms, rules, and decision-making procedures around which actors' expectations converge in international relations. The international human rights regime comprises the UN system, relevant international law, and so on.

Reparations A range of remedies available for a breach of international law; the term is used variously to denote monetary compensation (narrow definition) or to include non-monetary damages (broader definition).

Reparative justice Justice that makes right the things that have gone wrong by provision of a remedy (such as **reparations** or **restitution**) for the suffering and loss that have occurred; comes from the notion of 'repair'.

Reservation A unilateral exemption from specified parts of a **treaty** by a **states party**, usually submitted on ratification.

Resettlement The transfer of refugees from the country in which they have sought asylum to another state that has agreed to admit them.

Responsibility to Protect (R2P) A principle endorsed by the UN in 2005 that recognizes the responsibility of all states to protect their own citizens. When a state is unable or unwilling to provide this protection the responsibility is transferred to the international community, licensing **humanitarian intervention**.

Restitution A token paid in compensation for loss or injury.

Restorative justice A process whereby both the victim and perpetrator of a crime are brought back into harmony with the community.

Retributive justice The dispensing of sanctions (imprisonment, monetary fine) in punishment for a crime committed by an individual.

Returnees Persons who are of concern to the UN High Commissioner for Refugees when outside their country of origin and who remain so for a limited period after returning to their country of origin.

Right to development (RTD) As defined by the Special Rapporteur on the Right to Development, it is a right to a particular kind of development that would set the necessary conditions for the fulfilment of human rights. The rights in the Declaration include: full sovereignty over natural resources; self-determination; popular participation in development; equality of opportunity; and the creation of favourable conditions for the enjoyment of other civil, political, economic, social, and cultural rights.

Rights of man The term used by **Enlightenment** thinkers to refer to the **natural rights** that they wrote into the early rights declarations and associated literature; in its modernized form, it refers to human rights.

Rule of law The principle in which state authorities, including the courts, apply legal standards fairly across cases, rather than arbitrarily or in response to political calculations. State accountability is an essential aspect of any rule-of-law system. Human rights protection, in turn, requires strong rule of law.

Safe areas Enclaves declared off-limits to attacks during war. A tactic of **humanitarian intervention** to protect civilians, but controversial when such areas are misused as rebel bases. In Bosnia, in July 1995, UN peacekeepers failed to prevent Serb forces from capturing the safe area of Srebrenica and slaughtering 8,000 Muslims.

Self-determination The right to choice of one's own acts, free from external compulsion; in connection with human rights, the freedom of the people in a given territory to determine freely their own political arrangements. In the context of Indigenous peoples, it refers to the right to govern according to the wishes of the group, which is seen as a remedial political right of distinct dispossessed 'peoples' and 'nations', in contrast to the individual citizenship rights, or limited rights to land occupation, conferred on them by colonial nation states.

Sexual Orientation and Gender Identity (SOGI) A term that situates minority sexual and gender identities as a significant category for human rights violations; the category also includes minority gender expression and discrimination based on perceived (even if not actual) sexuality and gender. The term and abbreviation are common in human rights groups and communities. A variation is LGBT (for lesbian, gay, bisexual, and transgender), which focuses attention on the groups most likely to be targeted for discrimination on the basis of minority sexual or gender identity.

Social constructionism/constructionist A theoretical approach emphasizing the socially created nature of social life and 'reality'. When the approach is turned to human rights, it views them as social inventions and, invariably, the product of the balance of power between social actors at a particular point in history and in a particular social context.

Social constructivist Alexander Wendt has defined constructivism as seeing 'that the structures of human association are determined primarily by shared ideas rather than material forces, and that the identities and interests of purposive actors are constructed by these shared ideas rather than given by nature' (Alexander Wendt (1999). *Social Theory of International Politics*. Cambridge: Cambridge University Press, p. 1).

Social movements Networks of people in **civil society** who organize efforts to bring or resist change, today often using the language of human rights. Social movements frequently have a significant say in institutionalizing rights.

Social structure This refers to the ordered interrelationships between elements of society, such as the different forms of kinship and legal, religious, economic, political, and other institutions of a society.

Socialism/socialists A political philosophy/ideology that enjoins wholesale change in the structures of society so that the means of production are owned by the workers or **proletariat** rather than by elite capitalist classes, so that the productive power of society is used for the common good, not merely in the interests of a few. Marxists and Communists are socialists who seek radical change to society by altering its economic base, and have historically pursued revolutionary politics to this end.

Soft law Instruments that are not, strictly speaking, legally binding but that nevertheless may influence state behaviour, e.g. a **declaration**.

Sovereign immunity The legal principle that a head of government is immune from prosecution for acts committed in his official role as sovereign (as opposed to acts committed in pursuit of his own private interests). It is generally understood that, while a head of state could be prosecuted for such things as personal corruption or murder of a spouse, he/she could not be prosecuted for the consequences of state policies.

Sovereignty Legal or constitutional independence of a territorial state, entailing the right to govern and control the identified territory and legal and political jurisdiction within that territory without external interference. The concept is conventionally dated to the 1648 Peace of Westphalia, which established a norm of non-interference that was codified in the 1945 UN Charter and is—or was until quite recently—sacrosanct in international law. Sovereignty today is increasingly understood as the shared exercise of public power and authority between national, regional, and global authorities.

Spiral model of human rights change This describes the process by which international norms gradually influence domestic-level human rights changes. The assumption is that states, in responding to human rights pressures, will initially deny abuses, then begin making small concessions, move to more concrete if still sometimes cosmetic reforms, and eventually—in some cases—alter their behaviour so that it is consistent with internationally recognized human rights norms.

Stateless persons Persons who are not considered as nationals by any state under the operation of its law, including persons whose nationality is not established.

States parties See **contracting states**.

Structural adjustment policies/programmes (SAPs) Lending policies of the **International Monetary Fund** and the **World Bank** that are designed to promote economic efficiency and growth in developing countries by minimizing the role of the state in the economy. These policies or programmes take the form of conditions attached to loans and promote a range of **neoliberal** policies.

Sustainable development A form of development in which meeting the needs and rights of the present generation is not achieved at the expense of the needs and rights of future generations. It is often expressed as a form of 'triple bottom line' development that encompasses social, environmental, and economic bottom lines, rather than focusing simply on economic growth. Sustainable development prioritizes social inclusion and social justice, and respect for critical ecological systems.

Sustainable Development Goals (SDGs) A central part of the plan of action for sustainable development—Transforming our World: The 2030 Agenda for Sustainable Development—adopted by the UN General Assembly in September 2015. They include eighteen goals and 169 targets to be achieved by 2030. They succeed the Millennium Development Goals (MDGs) that were set in 2000 to be achieved by 2015.

Terra nullius Latin for 'land of no one'. Colonizing states (especially the British in Australia) conflated the interpretation 'land of no occupying sovereign' with the interpretation 'land without inhabitants with legal personality recognized by civilized nations' to arrive at the meaning 'uninhabited land'.

Tolerance A willingness to accept the beliefs and practices of others when not believing in or being prepared to participate in them oneself. Toleration requires that while we may not agree with another, we do not disagree sufficiently strongly that their beliefs or practices are intolerable to us.

Torture Victim Protection Act (TVPA) A 1991 Act of the US Congress that allows for civil suits to be brought in US courts against individuals acting in an official capacity for a foreign government who are alleged to have committed torture or extrajudicial killings.

Torture warrants Refers to proposed legal orders that could be issued by a judge sanctioning the torture of one or more specified individuals.

Trafficking/traffickers The organized transportation of contraband from one country to another for profit. *Human* trafficking involves the recruitment and transportation of people and/or their exploitation in work and employment. Human trafficking often involves the use of coercion and/or deception throughout, or at some stage in, the process.

Trafficking Victims Protection Act (TVPA) A progressive law defining human trafficking, passed by the United States Congress and signed by President Bill Clinton in 2000. The TVPA established the norms of the '3Ps': prevention of trafficking, protection of victims, and prosecution of traffickers. The TVPA is both a domestic tool to address trafficking and a foreign policy tool to pressure other governments to address trafficking.

Transitional justice A process of helping societies deal with the difficult questions of justice that arise as a society moves from war to peace, or from a repressive or authoritarian regime to democracy. It focuses particularly on social, political, and economic institutions, and on addressing past wrongs and on roles for former combatants. It may be carried out by means of **retributive**, **restorative**, or **reparative justice**, or some combination of these.

Treaty Binding written agreement concluded between states.

Truth commission A mechanism established to uncover the truth about past events, often part of a programme of **transitional justice**.

UN Development Programme (UNDP) The United Nations' global development network, which provides assistance, advice, and resources to developing countries. The UNDP has a presence in 166 countries and has special programmes on democratic governance, poverty reduction, crisis prevention and recovery, environment and energy, and HIV/AIDS.

UN High Commissioner for Refugees (UNHCR) The UNHCR, established on 14 December 1950, is a UN agency mandated to protect and assist refugees at the request of a government or the UN itself. It assists in finding solutions to the plight of refugees, primarily in their return to their home countries or in their resettlement to other countries. The UNHCR is headquartered in Geneva and has offices in over 100 countries worldwide.

UN Peacebuilding Commission Established in 2007 as an intergovernmental advisory body of the UN that supports peace efforts in countries emerging from conflict.

UN Relief and Works Agency for Palestine Refugees in the Near East (UNRWA) Founded in 1948, the UNRWA is the UN agency that provides assistance to millions of Palestinian refugees throughout the Middle East.

Universal Declaration of Human Rights (UDHR) Landmark **declaration** adopted and proclaimed by the General Assembly of the United Nations on 10 December 1948, it marks the dawn of the modern age of human rights. Its thirty articles outline a wide range of civil, cultural, economic, political, and social rights, rights subsequently codified in international law through the **International Covenant on Civil and Political Rights** and the **International Covenant on Economic, Social and Cultural Rights**. The UDHR establishes 'a common standard of achievement for all peoples and all nations, to the end that every individual and every organ of society' shall strive to ensure 'their universal and effective recognition and observance'.

Universal jurisdiction The legal doctrine that certain crimes are so grave that any/all states may prosecute individuals allegedly perpetrating these crimes, irrespective of the existence of any connection to the state seeking to prosecute. Crimes claimed to fall within this jurisdiction include genocide, slavery, and war crimes.

Universality Applicability to everyone everywhere.

Utilitarianism/utilitarians A political philosophy/ideology of the **Enlightenment**, pioneered by Jeremy Bentham. It is a **consequentialist** theory holding (in simplified form) that an act is morally justified if and only if it leads to the greatest good for the greatest number.

Vienna Declaration A human rights **declaration** issued by the **Vienna World Conference on Human Rights** in 1993; it reaffirmed the universality of human rights and their indivisibility and interdependence.

Vienna Process The negotiations leading to the Protocol to Prevent, Suppress, and Punish Trafficking in Persons, especially Women and Children (see **Palermo Protocol**), conducted in Vienna, Austria. The Vienna Process was marked by highly contentious debates between abolitionist feminists, who believe that all forms of prostitution are exploitative and thus forms of trafficking, and human rights feminists, who believe that only forced prostitution should be considered a form of trafficking.

Vienna World Conference on Human Rights (Vienna Conference) A ground-breaking global conference held in 1993. It charted the course of post-Cold War human rights policy. Among other issues, it emphasized the importance of embedding international human rights standards in domestic structures, including legal systems, national human rights institutions, non-governmental organizations, and the media.

Violations approach An approach to measuring human rights that focuses on the violation of particular rights, allowing for an enumeration of violations or a **coding** of country performance on a standardized scale.

Voting Rights Act Landmark 1965 legislation passed by the US Congress outlawing discriminatory electoral practices throughout the United States.

War crimes A violation of the laws or customs of war, including targeting civilians for murder, ill-treatment, or forced deportation. See **Geneva Conventions and Protocols**.

Western Geographic, geopolitical, and cultural label referring to North America and Europe (and sometimes European settler societies, such as Australia and New Zealand), and to the ideas that emerged from the political and economic traditions and practices in these places. Also an ideological reference to the ideas developed during the **Enlightenment**.

White slavery Term used at the turn of the twentieth century to describe the abduction of white girls and women in Western Europe and the United States, who were forced into prostitution in their home countries or trafficked to other countries. Most scholars now believe that the scope of the white slave trade was much smaller than suggested by the hype in the media at the time.

World Bank One of the **Bretton Woods institutions** established in 1944 to provide economic assistance to the reconstruction of Europe after the Second World War. Today it is the leading public development institution in the world, providing long-term loans to governments for development projects.

World Social Forum (WSF) First held in 2001 in the Brazilian city of Porto Alegre as a response by critics of economic globalization to the World Economic Forum, a meeting of political and economic elites held annually in Davos, Switzerland. The WSF defines itself as 'an open meeting place for reflective thinking, democratic debate of ideas, formulation of proposals, free exchange of experiences, and interlinking for effective action, by groups and movements of civil society that are opposed to neo-liberalism and to domination of the world by capital and any form of imperialism, and are committed to building a planetary society directed towards fruitful relationships among Mankind and between it and the Earth'.

World Trade Organization (WTO) Intergovernmental organization that sets the rules governing global trade and provides a mechanism for the settlement of trade-related disputes. The WTO was established in 1994; it grew out of the Uruguay round of negotiations under the framework of the General Agreement on Tariffs and Trade (GATT). The original **Bretton Woods institutions** were to have included an International Trade Organization (ITO), but these plans were never realized. Critics complain about the WTO's **neoliberal** agenda.

References

AAA (American Anthropological Association) (1947). Statement of human rights. *American Anthropologist*, **49**/4, 539–43.

Aaronson, S. and Zimmerman, J. (2006). Fair trade? How Oxfam presented a systemic approach to poverty, development, human rights, and trade. *Human Rights Quarterly*, **28**/4, 998–1030.

Abouharb, M. R. and Cingranelli, D. L. (2006). The human rights effects of World Bank structural adjustment. *International Studies Quarterly*, **50**/2, 233–62.

Abouharb, M. R. and Cingranelli, D. L. (2008). *Human Rights and Structural Adjustment*. New York: Cambridge University Press.

Ackerly, B. and Cruz, J. M. (2010). Hearing the voice of the people: Human rights as if people mattered. *New Political Science*, **33**/1, 1–22.

Adcock, R. and Collier, D. (2001). Measurement validity: A shared standard for qualitative and quantitative research. *American Political Science Review*, **95**/3, 529–46.

Agamben, G. (2005). *State of Exception*. Chicago, IL: University of Chicago Press.

Agamben, G. (2006). *State of Exception*. Chicago, IL: University of Chicago Press.

AHRC (Asian Human Rights Commission) (2003). Electricity for development vs. displacement of people. Available at: http://www.ahrchk.net/ua/mainfile.php/2003/498/. Accessed 12 November 2015.

Akinci, B. (2006). Turkey faces hazelnut crisis as growers protest prices. *Turkish Daily News*, 15 August.

Alderson, A. S. (2004). Explaining the upswing in direct investment: A test of mainstream and heterodox theories of globalization. *Social Forces*, **83**/1, 81–122.

Aleklett, K. (2012). *Peaking at Peak Oil*. Heidleberg: Springer.

Alexander, Michelle (2012). *The New Jim Crow: Mass Incarceration in the Age of Colorblindness*. New York City: The New Press.

Alforte, Andrea, Joseph Angan, Jack Dentith, Karl Domondon, Lou Munden, Sophia Murday, and Leonardo Pradela (2014) *Communities as Counterparties: Preliminary Review of Concessions and Conflict in Emerging and Frontier Market Concessions*. New York: The Munden Project. http://www.rightsandresources.org/wp-content/uploads/Communities-as-Counterparties-FINAL_Oct-211.pdf.

Alfred, T. (2008). *Peace, Power, Righteousness: An Indigenous Manifesto*. Oxford: Oxford University Press.

Alfredsson, G. (2005). Minorities, Indigenous and tribal peoples: Definitions of terms as a matter of international law. *Minorities, Peoples and Self-Determination—Essays in Honour of Patrick Thornberry* (ed. N. Ghanea and A. Xanthaki). Leiden: Martinus Nijhoff.

Alfredsson, G. and Eide, A. (eds) (1999). *The Universal Declaration of Human Rights—A Common Standard of Achievement*. The Hague: Martinus Nijhoff.

Alimi, A. (2015). Why I oppose the United States' special envoy for LGBT human rights. *The Daily Beast*, 10 March. http://www.thedailybeast.com/articles/2015/03/10/why-i-oppose-the-united-states-special-envoy-for-lgbt-human-rights.html (accessed 11 March 11 2015).

Allen, B. (1996). *Rape Warfare: The Hidden Genocide in Bosnia-Herzegovina and Croatia*. Minneapolis, MN: University of Minnesota Press.

Allen, S. and Xanthaki, A. (eds) (2010). *Reflections on the UN Declaration on the Rights of Indigenous Peoples*. Studies in International Law. Oxford: Hart Publishing.

Allen, T. (2005a). *Trial Justice: The International Criminal Court and the Lord's Resistance Army*. London: Zed Books.

Allen, T. (2005b). *War and Justice in Northern Uganda: An Assessment of the International Criminal Court's Intervention*. London: Crisis States Research Centre, Development Studies Institute, London School of Economics.

Alston, P. (1997). Effective functioning of bodies established pursuant to United Nations human rights instruments: Final report on enhancing the long-term effectiveness of the United Nations human rights treaty system. UN Doc. E/CN.4/1997/74.

American Anthropologist (1947). American Anthropological Association: Statement on human rights (Extract). October.

American Anthropologist (2006). In focus: Anthropology and human rights in a new key. **108**/1.

Amin, S. (1976). *Unequal Development*. Hassocks: Harvester.

Amnesty International (2005). *Human Rights for Human Dignity: A Primer on Economic, Social and Cultural Rights*. London: Amnesty International.

Amnesty International (2012). *LGBT Pride 2012: Lesbian, Gay, Bisexual, and Transgender Rights are Human Rights! Activist Resource Packet*. New York: Amnesty International. http://www.amnestyusa.org/pdfs/AIUSA_Pride_Toolkit-2012.pdf (accessed 24 April 2013).

Amnesty International (2014). *Human Rights for Human Dignity: A Primer on Economic, Social and Cultural Rights* (2nd edn). London: Amnesty International. https://www.amnesty.org/en/documents/POL34/001/2014/en/

Amnesty International (2015a). About LGBT human rights. www.amnestyusa.org/our-work/issues/lgbt-rights/about-lgbt-human-rights (accessed 14 April 2015).

Amnesty International (2015b). Nigeria: 'Our job is to shoot, slaughter and kill'. Boko Haram's reign of terror in north east Nigeria. London: Amnesty International. https://www.amnesty.org/en/documents/afr44/1360/2015/en/

Anaya, J. (2010). The right of Indigenous peoples to self-determination in the post-declaration era. *Making the Declaration Work: The United Nations Declaration on the Rights of Indigenous Peoples* (ed. C. Charters and R. Stavenhagen). Copenhagen: IWGIA.

Anaya, J. (2011a). *Report of the Special Rapporteur on the rights of Indigenous peoples. Extractive industries operating within or near indigenous territories*. New York: United Nations. http://unsr.jamesanaya.org/annual-reports/report-to-the-human-rights-council-a-hrc-18-35-11-july-2011.

Anaya, J. (2011b). Report of the Special Rapporteur on the rights of Indigenous peoples *Sami people in the Sápmi region of Norway, Sweden and Finland*. New York: United Nations.

Anaya, J. (2013) Report of the Special Rapporteur on the rights of Indigenous peoples, *Extractive industries and indigenous peoples*. UN Doc. A/HRC/24/4. New York: United Nations. http://unsr.jamesanaya.org/docs/annual/2013-hrc-annual-report-en.pdf

Anaya, S. J. (2004). *Indigenous Peoples in International Law* (2nd edn). Oxford: Oxford University Press.

Anderson, B. and O'Connell Davidson, J. (2002). *Trafficking—A Demand Led Problem?* Washington, DC: Save the Children.

Anderson, C. J., Paskeviciute, A., Sandovici, M. E., and Tverdova, Y. V. (2005). In the eye of the beholder? The foundations of subjective human rights conditions in East-Central Europe. *Comparative Political Studies*, **38**/7 (September), 771–98.

Anderson, K. and Rieff, D. (2000). Global civil society: 'A sceptical view'. *Global Civil Society 2004/5* (ed. H. Anheier, M. Glasius, and M. Kaldor). London: Sage.

Anderson, M. (1999). *Do No Harm: How Aid Can Support Peace—Or War*. Boulder, CO: Lynne Rienner.

Andersson, J. O. and Lindroth, M. (2001). Ecologically unsustainable trade. *Ecological Economics*, **37**/1, 113–22.

Andreassen, B. A. and Marks, S. P. (eds) (2006). *Development as a Human Right: Legal, Political and Economic Dimensions*. Cambridge, MA: Harvard School of Public Health. Distributed by Harvard University Press.

Anheier, H., Glasius, M., and Kaldor, M. (2001). Introducing global civil society. *Global Civil Society* (ed. H. Anheier, M. Glasius, and M. Kaldor). Oxford: Oxford University Press.

An-Na'im, A. A. (1992a). Toward a cross-cultural approach. *Human Rights in Cross-Cultural Perspectives: A Quest for Consensus* (ed. A. A. An-Na'im). Philadelphia, PA: University of Pennsylvania Press.

An-Na'im, A. A. (ed.) (1992b). *Human Rights in Cross-Cultural Perspectives: A Quest for Consensus*. Philadelphia, PA: University of Pennsylvania Press.

An-Na'im, A. (1999). Universality of human rights. *Japan and International Law: Past, Present and Future* (ed. N. Ando). The Hague: Kluwer Law International.

An-Na'im, A. A. (2002). *Cultural Transformation and Human Rights in Africa*. London: Zed Books.

An-Na'im, A. (2011). *Muslims and Global Justice*. Philadelphia, PA: University of Pennsylvania Press.

Annan, K. (2002). Strengthening of the United Nations: An agenda for further change. UN Doc. A/57/387.

Annan, K. (2005). In larger freedom: Towards development, security and human rights for all. UN Doc. A/59/2005.

Antrobus, P. (2005). *The Global Women's Movement*. London: Zed Books.

Apodaca, C. (2001). Global economic patterns and personal integrity rights after the Cold War. *International Studies Quarterly*, 45/4, 587–602.

Apodaca, C. (2002). The globalization of capital in East and Southeast Asia. *Asian Survey*, 42/6, 883–905.

Appiah, K. A. (2005). *The Ethics of Identity*. Princeton, NJ: Princeton University Press.

Arat, Z. (2008). Women's Rights as Human Rights. *UN Chronicle*, 45/2/3, 9–13.

Arbour, L. (2007). Foreword. *Frequently Asked Questions on a Human Rights-Based Approach to Development Cooperation*. Geneva: Office of the United Nations High Commissioner for Human Rights.

Arendt, H. (1959). *The Human Condition*. New York: Doubleday.

Arendt, H. (1972). *Crisis of the Republic*. Harmondsworth: Penguin.

Arendt, H. (1973). *The Origins of Totalitarianism* (new edn). New York: Harvest.

Ariès, P. (1962). *Centuries of Childhood*. London: Cape.

Aristotle. (1962). *Nicomachean Ethics*. Indianapolis, IN: Bobbs-Merrill.

Arnold, D. and Hartman, L. (2006). Workers rights and low wage industrialization: How to avoid sweatshops. *Human Rights Quarterly*, 28/3, 676–700.

Asiedu, E. (2002). On the determinants of foreign direct investment to developing countries: Is Africa different? *World Development*, 30/1, 107–19.

Askin, K. (2006). Prosecuting gender crimes committed in Darfur: Holding leaders accountable for sexual violence. *Genocide in Darfur: Investigating the Atrocities in the Sudan* (ed. S. Totten and E. Markusen). New York: Routledge.

Atkinson, K. (1989). The torturer's tale. *Toronto Life*, March.

Badger, A. (2011). Collective v individual rights in membership governance for Indigenous peoples. *American University International Law Review*, 26/2, 485–514.

Badiou, A. (2001). *Ethics: An Essay on the Understanding of Evil*. London: Verso.

Baehr, Peter R.D (2001). *Human Rights: Universality in Practice*. Houndmills, Basingstoke: Palgrave.

Balakrishnan, R. and Elson, D. (eds) (2011). *Economic Policy and Human Rights: Holding Governments to Account*. London: Zed Books

Bales, K. and Lize, S. (2005). *Trafficking in Persons in the United States*. Washington, DC: National Institute of Justice.

Ball, P. B. (2000). The Guatemalan Commission for Historical Clarification: Generating analytical reports; inter-sample analysis. *Making the Case: Investigating Large Scale Human Rights Violations Using Information Systems and Data Analysis* (ed. P. B. Ball, H. F. Spirer, and L. Spirer). Washington, DC: American Association for the Advancement of Science.

Ball, P. B. and Asher, J. (2002). Statistics and Slobodan: Using data analysis and statistics in the war crimes trial of former president Milošević. *Chance*, 15/4, 17–24.

Ball, P. B., Asher, J., Sulmont, D., and Manrique, D. (2003) *How many Peruvians have died?* Washington, DC: American Association for the Advancement of Science (AAAS). https://hrdag.org/wp-content/uploads/2013/02/aaas_peru_5.pdf.

Ball, P. B., Kobrak, P., and Spirer, H. (1999). *State Violence in Guatemala, 1960–1996: A Quantitative Reflection*. Washington, DC: American Association for the Advancement of Science.

Ball, P. B., Spirer, H. F., and Spirer, L. (eds) (2000). *Making the Case: Investigating Large Scale Human Rights Violations Using Information Systems and Data Analysis*. Washington, DC: American Association for the Advancement of Science.

Ban, K. (2007). Leadership and climate change. UN Secretary General, press article, 23 September. http://www.un.org/sg/articles/articleFull.asp?TID=69&Type=Op-Ed&h=0.

Bandelj, N. (2002). Embedded economies: Social relations as determinants of foreign direct investment in Central and Eastern Europe. *Social Forces*, **81**/2, 411–44.

Barbalet, J. M. (1988). *Citizenship: Rights, Struggle and Class Inequality*. Milton Keynes: Open University Press.

Barnett, H. G. (1948). On science and human rights. *American Anthropologist*, **50**/2, 352–5.

Barnett, M. (2002). *Eyewitness to a Genocide: The United Nations and Rwanda*. Ithaca, NY: Cornell University Press.

Barnsley, Ingrid. (2009). *Reducing Emissions from Deforestation and Forest Degradation in Developing Countries: A Guide for Indigenous Peoples*. Yokohama: UNU-IAS.

Bar-On, A. (1996). Criminalising survival: Images and reality of street children. *Journal of Social Policy*, **26**/1, 63–78.

Barry, J. (1999). *Rethinking Green Politics: Nature, Virtue and Progress*. London: Sage.

Barry, J. (2004). Ecological modernisation. *Debating the Earth* (2nd edn) (ed. J. Dryzek and D. Schlosberg). Oxford: Oxford University Press.

Barry, J. (2007). *Environment and Social Theory* (2nd edn). London: Routledge.

Barry, J. (2012). *The Politics of Actually Existing Unsustainability: Human Flourishing in a Climate-Changed, Carbon-Constrained World*. Oxford: Oxford University Press.

Barry, J. (2014). Green political theory. *Political Ideologies* (4th edn) (ed. V. Geoghegan and R. Wilford). London: Routledge.

Barry, J. (2015). Bio-fuelling the Hummer? Transdisciplinary thoughts on techno-optimism and innovation in the transition from unsustainability. *Transdisciplinary Perspectives on Transitions to Sustainability* (ed. E. Byrne, G. Mulally, and C. Sage). Surrey: Ashgate.

Barry, K. (1979). *Female Sexual Slavery*. New York: New York University Press.

Baxi, U. (2006). *The Future of Human Rights*. Oxford: Oxford University Press.

Bayefsky, A. (1996). The UN human rights treaties: Facing the implementation crisis. Committee on International Human Rights Law and Practice report. International Law Association.

Bayefsky, A. (2001). *The UN Human Rights Treaty System: Universality at the Crossroads*. The Hague: Kluwer.

BBC (2014). Who, what, why: Exactly what does the phrase Boko Haram mean?, 13 May. http://www.bbc.co.uk/news/blogs-magazine-monitor-27390954

BBC (2015a). Attractive jihadists can lure UK girls to extremism, 3 March. http://www.bbc.co.uk/news/uk-31704408

BBC (2015b). Who are Britain's jihadists?, 25 June. http://www.bbc.co.uk/news/uk-32026985

Beckerman, W. (2001). *Justice, Posterity, and the Environment*. Oxford: Oxford University Press.

Bedford, K. and Jakobsen, J. R. (2008). *New Feminist Solutions: Towards a Vision of Sexual and Economic Justice*. New York: Barnard Center for Research on Women.

Bedont, B. and Hall Martinez, K. (1999). Ending impunity for gender crimes under the International Criminal Court. *Brown Journal of World Affairs*, **6**/1, 65–85.

Beetham, D. (1994). *Defining and Measuring Democracy*. Beverly Hills, CA: Sage Publications.

Beetham, D. (2006). The right to development and its corresponding obligations. *Development as a Human Right, Legal, Political and Economic Dimensions* (ed. B. A. Andreassen and S. P. Marks). Boston, MA: Harvard School of Public Health. Distributed by Harvard University Press.

Beitz, C. (2009). *The Idea of Human Rights*. Oxford: Oxford University Press.

Belknap, M. (1987). *Federal Law and Southern Order: Racial Violence and Constitutional Conflict in the Post-Brown South*. Athens, GA: University of Georgia Press.

Bell, D. and Coicaud, J.-M. (eds) (2007). *Ethics in Action: The Ethical Challenges of International Human Rights Nongovernmental Organizations*. New York: Cambridge University Press.

Bell, E. (1910). *Fighting the Traffic in Young Girls or the War on the White Slave Trade*. Chicago, IL: G. S. Ball.

Bellamy, A. J. (2010). *The Responsibility to Protect: The Global Effort to End Mass Atrocities*. Cambridge: Polity.

Bellamy, A. (2014). *Responsibility to Protect: A Defence*. Oxford: Oxford University Press.

Benedict, R. (1961). *Patterns of Culture*. London: Routledge.

Benhabib, S. (2002). *The Claims of Culture, Equality and Diversity in the Global Era*. Princeton, NJ: Princeton University Press.

Benhabib, S. (2004). *The Rights of Others: Aliens, Residents and Citizens*. Cambridge: Cambridge University Press.

Benhabib, S. (2011). *Dignity in Adversity: Human Rights in Troubled Times*. Chichester: John Wiley & Sons.

Bennett, J. (2008). *Where Underpants Come From*. New York: Simon & Schuster.

Bentham, J. (1843). Anarchical fallacies. *The Complete Works of Jeremy Bentham*, Vol. II (ed. J. Bowring). Edinburgh: William Tait.

Berger, P., Berger, B., and Keller, H. (1974). *The Homeless Mind: Modernization and Consciousness*. Harmondsworth: Penguin.

Berg-Schlosser, D. and Siegler, R. (1990). *Political Stability and Development: A Comparative Analysis of Kenya, Tanzania and Uganda*. Boulder, CO: Lynne Rienner.

Berg-Schlosser, D. and Siegler, R., (2000). *Political Stability and Development: A Comparative Analysis of Kenya, Tanzania and Uganda*. Boulder, CO: Lynne Rienner Publishers.

Bernstein, R. (2003). Kidnapping has Germans debating police torture. *The New York Times*, 10 April.

Betts, A. (2009). *Forced Migration and Global Politics*. Oxford: Wiley-Blackwell.

Betts, A. (2013). *Survival Migration: Failed Governance and the Crisis of Displacement*. Ithaca, NY: Cornell University Press.

Betts, A. and Loescher, G. (eds) (2011). *Refugees in International Relations*. Oxford: Oxford University Press.

Betts, A., Loescher, G., and Milner, J. (2012). *UNHCR: the Politics and Practice of Refugee Protection*. (2nd revised edn), Abingdon: Routledge.

Betts, A., Loescher, G., and Milner, J. (2016). *UNHCR: The Politics and Practice of Refugee Protection* (3rd revised edn). Abingdon: Routledge.

Betts, R. (1994). The delusion of impartial intervention. *Foreign Affairs*, **73**/6, 20–33.

Bhagwati, J. (2004). *In Defense of Globalization*. Oxford: Oxford University Press.

Biersteker, T. J. (1978). *Distortion or Development*. Cambridge, MA: MIT Press.

Birchfield, L. and Corsi, J. (2010). The right to life is the right to food: *People's Union for Civil Liberties v. Union of India & Others*. *Human Rights Brief*, **17**/3, 15–18.

Bissio, R. (2003). *Civil Society and the MDGs*. Montevideo: Instituto del Tercer Mundo.

Black, M. (1996). *Children First: The Story of UNICEF*. Oxford: Oxford University Press.

Blackstone, W. (1765-9). *Commentaries on the Laws of England*. Oxford: Clarendon Press. http://avalon. law.yale.edu/subject_menus/blackstone.asp (New Haven, CT: Yale University, Lillian Goldman Law Library, The Avalon Project).

Blanding, M. (2010). *The Coke Machine: The Dirty Truth Behind the World's Favorite Soft Drink*. New York: Avery.

Blasius, M. (2013). Theorizing the politics of (homo) sexualities across cultures. *Global Homophobia: States, Movements, and the Politics of Oppression* (ed. M. L. Weiss and M. J. Bosia). Urbana, IL: University of Illinois Press.

Bloed, A. (1993). Monitoring the CSCE human dimension: In search of its effectiveness. *Monitoring Human Rights in Europe* (ed. A. Bloed, A. L. Leicht, M. Nowak, and A. Rosas). London: Martinus Nijhoff.

Bloxham D. and Moses, A. (2010). *The Oxford Handbook of Genocide Studies*. New York: Oxford University Press.

Bob, C. (2005). *The Marketing of Rebellion: Insurgents, Media and International Activism*. New York: Cambridge University Press.

Bob, C. (2009). *The International Struggle for New Human Rights*. Philadelphia: University of Pennsylvania Press.

Bob, C., Haynes, J., Pickard, V., Keenan, T., and Couldry, N. (2008). Media spaces: Innovation and activism. *Global Civil Society Yearbook 2007/2008* (ed. M. Kaldor, M. Glasius, H. Anheier, and M. Albrow). London: London School of Economics.

Bobbio, N. (1999). *The Age of Rights*. Oxford: Polity.

Boekle, H. (1995). Western states, the UN Commission on Human Rights, and the '1235' procedure: The question of bias revisited. *Netherlands Quarterly of Human Rights*, **13**/4, 367–402.

Bollen, K. A. (1992). Political rights and political liberties in nations: An evaluation of rights measures, 1950 to 1984. *Human Rights and Statistics: Getting the Record Straight* (ed. T. B. Jabine and R. P. Claude). Philadelphia, PA: University of Pennsylvania Press.

Booker, C. (2012). Foreign government may take UK to European court over its 'illegal' child-snatching. *The Telegraph*, 15 September. http://www.telegraph. co.uk/comment/9545361/Foreign-government-may-take-UK-to-European-court-over-its-illegal-child-snatching.html.

Borrows, J. (1999). Sovereignty's Alchemy: An Analysis of *delgamuukw v British Columbia*. *Osgoode Hall Law Journal*, **37**/3, 537–96.

Borrows, J. (2010). *Canada's Indigenous Constitution*. Toronto, Canada: University of Toronto Press.

Bos, A. (1999). The International Criminal Court: Recent developments. *Reflections on the International Criminal Court: Essays in Honour of Adriaan Bos* (ed. H. A. M. von Hebel, J. G. Lammers, and J. Schukking). The Hague: T. M. C. Asser.

Bosia, M. J. and Weiss, M. L. (2013). Political homophobia in comparative perspective. *Global Homophobia* (ed. M. J. Weiss and M. L. Bosia). Urbana, IL: University of Illinois Press.

Bosselmann, K. (2001). Human rights and the environment: Redefining fundamental principles? *Governing for the Environment: Global Problems, Ethics and Democracy* (ed. B. Gleeson and N. Low). Basingstoke: Palgrave.

Bottoni, R. (2013). Legal, political and social obstacles for headscarved women working at state institutions in Turkey. *Religion and Human Rights*, **8**/3, 183–201.

Boudreau, V. (2004). *Resisting Dictatorship: Repression and Protest in Southeast Asia*. New York: Cambridge University Press.

Bowcott, O. (2015). Travel ban for five east London girls over fears they will join Isis in Syria. *The Guardian*, 27 March. http://www.theguardian.com/uk-news/2015/mar/27/five-girls-barred-from-travel-same-school-three-teenagers-syria-bethnal-green-academy.

Bowleg, Lisa. 2008. When black + lesbian + woman ≠ black lesbian woman: The methodological challenges of qualitative and quantitative intersectionality research. *Sex Roles*, **59**/5: 312–25.

Bowring, B. (2008). *The Degradation of the International Legal Order? The Rehabilitation of Law and the Possibility of Politics*. Abingdon and New York: Routledge-Cavendish.

Boyden, J. (1990). Childhood and the policy makers: A comparative perspective on the globalization of childhood. *Constructing and Reconstructing Childhood: Contemporary Issues in the Sociological Study of Childhood* (ed. A. James and A. Prout). London:

Boyden, J. (1994). Children's experience of conflict related emergencies: Some implications for relief policy and practice. *Disasters*, **18**/3, 254–67.

Boyden, J. (1997). Childhood and policy makers: A comparative perspective on the globalization of childhood. *Constructing and Reconstructing Childhood: Contemporary Issues in the Sociological Study of Childhood* (2nd edn) (ed. A. James and A. Prout). London: Falmer.

Boyle, A. E. and Anderson, M. R. (eds) (1996). *Human Rights Approaches to Environmental Protection*. Oxford: Clarendon Press.

Boyle, K. (1995). Stock-taking on human rights: The World Conference on Human Rights, Vienna 1993. *Political Studies*, **43**/Special issue, 79–95.

Boyle, K. (2004). Human rights, religion and democracy: The Refah Party case. *Essex Human Rights Review*, **1**/1, 1–16.

Branch, A. (2007). Uganda's civil war and the politics of ICC intervention. *Ethics and International Affairs*, **21**/2, 179–98.

Brett, R. (1993). The human dimension of the CSCE and the CSCE response to minorities. *The CSCE in the 1990s: Constructing European Security and Cooperation* (ed. M. R. Lucas). Baden-Baden: Nomos Verlagsgesellschaft.

Bricmont, J. (2007). *Humanitarian Imperialism: Using Human Rights to Sell War*. Delhi: Aakar Books.

Briggs, P. (1998). *Uganda*. Old Saybrook, CT: Globe Pequot.

Bristow, E. J. (1977). *Vice and Vigilance: Purity Movements in Britain Since1700*. Dublin: Gill and Macmillan.

Brockett, C. (2005). *Political Movements and Violence in Central America*. Cambridge: Cambridge University Press.

Brookings-Bern Project on Internal Displacement (2007). Disaster risk reduction: A front line defense against climate change and displacement. http://www.brookings.edu/reports/2007/1010_disaster_risk_reduction.aspx.

Brookings-Bern Project on Internal Displacement (2008). Human rights and natural disasters: Operational guidelines and field manual on human rights protection in situations of natural disaster. http://www.brookings.edu/reports/2008/spring_natural_disasters.aspx.

Brown, C. (2001). Cosmopolitanism, world citizenship and global civil society. *Critical Review of International Social and Political Philosophy*, **3**/1 (Summer), 7–27.

Brown, C. (2007). From humanized war to humanitarian intervention: Carl Schmitt's critique of the just war tradition. *The International Political Thought of Carl Schmitt: Terror, Liberal War and the Crisis of Global Order* C (ed. L. Odysseos and F. Petito). London: Routledge.

Brown Thompson, K. (2002). Women's rights are human rights. *Restructuring World Politics* (ed. S. Khagram, J. V. Riker, and K. Sikkink). Minneapolis, MN: University of Minnesota Press.

Bruton, H. (1997). *On the Search for Well-Being.* Ann Arbor, MI: University of Michigan Press.

Brysk, A. and Shafir, G. (eds) (2007). *National Insecurity and Human Rights: Democracies Debate Counterterrorism.* Berkeley, CA: University of California Press.

Bueno de Mesquita, B., Downs, G. W., Smith, A., and Cherif, F. M. (2005). Thinking inside the box: A closer look at democracy and human rights. *International Studies Quarterly*, 49/3, 439–57.

Bunch, C. (1990). Women's rights as human rights: Toward a re-vision of human rights. *Human Rights Quarterly*, 12/2, 486–98.

Bunch, C. and Fried, S. (1996). Beijing '95: Moving women's human rights from margin to center. *Signs*, 22/1, 200–4.

Bunn, I. D. (2000). The right to development: Implications for international economic law. *American University International Law Review*, 15/6, 1425–67.

Bunyan, N. (2015). Senior Muslim lawyer says British teenagers see Isis as 'pop idols'. *The Guardian*, 5 April. http://www.theguardian.com/world/2015/apr/05/senior-muslim-lawyer-says-british-teenagers-see-isis-as-pop-idols

Burg, S. and Shoup, P. (1999). *The War in Bosnia-Herzegovina.* New York: M. E. Sharpe.

Burgers, J. (1992). The road to San Francisco: The revival of the human rights idea in the twentieth century. *Human Rights Quarterly*, 14/4, 447–77.

Burgoon, B. (2001). Globalization and welfare compensation: Disentangling the ties that bind. *International Organization*, 55/3, 509–51.

Burke, E.(1971 [1790]). *Reflections on the Revolution in France.*London: Dent.

Burke, S. (2014). What an era of global protests says about the effectiveness of human rights as a language to achieve social change. *Sur: International Journal on Human Rights*, 11/20, 26–34.

Burkhart, R. E. (2002). The capitalist political economy and human rights: Cross-national evidence. *The Social Science Journal*, 39/2, 155–70.

Burkhart, R. E. and Lewis-Beck, M. (1994). Comparative democracy: The economic development thesis. *American Political Science Review*, 88/4, 903–10.

Burman, E. (1994). Innocents abroad: Western fantasies of childhood and the iconography of emergencies. *Disasters*, 18/3, 238–53.

Burman, E. (1995). Developing differences: Gender, childhood and economic development. *Children and Society*, 9/3, 121–42.

Bybee, J. S. (2005). Standards of conduct for interrogation under 18 U.S.C.—1 August 2002. *The Torture Papers: The Road to Abu Ghraib* (ed. K. J. Greenberg and J. Datel). Cambridge: Cambridge University Press.

Camp Keith, L. (1999). The United Nations International Covenant on Civil and Political Rights: Does it make a difference in human rights behavior? *Journal of Peace Research*, 36/1, 95–118.

Camp Keith, L. (2002). Constitutional provisions for individual human rights (1977–1996): Are they more than mere 'window dressing'? *Political Research Quarterly*, 55/1, 111–43.

Caney, S. (2007). Outcome document of the high level expert meeting on the new future of human rights and environment: An agenda for moving forward. http://www.unep.org/environmentalgovernance/Portals/8/documents/Events/Outcome DocumentHumanRightsEnviroment.pdf Accessed 12 October 2011.

Capotorti, F. (1977). Study on the rights of persons belonging to ethnic, religious and linguistic minorities. UN Doc. E/CN.4/Sub.2/384/Add. 1–7.

Cardenas, S. (2007). *Conflict and Compliance: State Responses to International Human Rights Pressure.* Philadelphia, PA: University of Pennsylvania Press.

Cardenas, S. (2014). *Chains of Justice: The Global Rise of State Institutions for Human Rights.* Philadelphia, PA: University of Pennsylvania Press.

Carey, C. and Poe, S. (eds) (2004). *Understanding Human Rights Violations: New Systematic Studies.* Aldershot: Ashgate.

Carothers, T. (2002). The end of the transition paradigm. *Journal of Democracy*, 13/1, 5–21.

Carr, E. H. (1946). *The Twenty Years Crisis, 1919–1939: An Introduction to the Study of International Relations* (revised edn). London: Macmillan.

Carter, P. (2005). Taxonomy of torture. *Slate*, 26 May. http://slate.com/features/whatistorture/Taxonomy.html.

Cassese, A. (2003). *International Criminal Law*. Oxford: Oxford University Press.

Castellino, J. (2005). Conceptual difficulties and the right to Indigenous self-determination. *Minorities, Peoples and Self-Determination—Essays in Honour of Patrick Thornberry* (ed. N. Ghanea and A. Xanthaki). Leiden: Martinus Nijhoff.

Castro, Daniel. (2007). *Another Face of Empire: Bartolomé De Las Casas, Indigenous Rights, and Ecclesiastical Imperialism*. Durham, NC: Duke University Press.

Chandler, D. (2001). The road to military humanitarianism: How the human rights NGOs shaped a new humanitarian agenda. *Human Rights Quarterly*, 23/3, 678–700.

Chandler, D. (2003). New rights for old? Cosmopolitan citizenship and the critique of state sovereignty. *Political Studies*, 51/2, 339–56.

Chandler, D. (2006). *Empire in Denial: The Politics of State-Building*. London: Pluto.

Chandler, D. (2007a). Hollow hegemony: Theorising the shift from interest-based to value-based international policy-making. *Millennium: Journal of International Studies*, 35/3, 703–23.

Chandler, D. (2007b). The security-development nexus and the rise of 'anti-foreign policy'. *Journal of International Relations and Development*, 10/4, 362–86.

Chandler, D. (2008). The revival of Carl Schmitt in international relations: The last refuge of critical theorists? *Millennium: Journal of International Studies*, 37/1, 27–48.

Chapman, A. (1996). A 'violations approach' for monitoring the International Covenant on Economic, Social, and Cultural Rights. *Human Rights Quarterly*, 18/1, 23–66.

Charlesworth, H. (1995). Human rights as men's rights. *Women's Rights, Human Rights: International Feminist Perspectives* (ed. J. Peters and A. Wolper). London: Routledge.

Charters, C. and Stavenhagen, R. (eds) (2009). *Making the Declaration Work: The United Nations Declaration on the Rights of Indigenous Peoples*. Copenhagen: IWGIA.

Charvet, J. and Kaczynska-Nay, E. (2008). *The Liberal Project and Human Rights: The Theory and Practice of a New World Order*. Cambridge: Cambridge University Press.

Cheng, L. (1999). Globalization and women's paid labour in Asia. *International Social Science Journal*, 52/160, 217–28.

Chong, D. P. L. (2010). *Freedom from Poverty: NGOs and Human Rights Practice*. Philadelphia: University of Pennsylvania Press.

Chowdhry, G. (2004). Postcolonial interrogations of child labor: human rights, carpet trade, and Rugmark in India. *Power, Postcolonialism and International Relations: Reading Race, Gender, and Class* (ed. G. Chowdhry and F. S. Nair). London and New York: Routledge.

Chrétien, J. P. (2003). *The Great Lakes of Africa: Two Thousand Years of History* (trans. S. Straus). New York: Zone Books.

Chuang, J. (2006). The United States as global sheriff: Using unilateral sanctions to combat trafficking. *Michigan Journal of International Law*, 27/2, 437–94.

Cingranelli, D. L. and Richards, D. L. (2007). Measuring government effort to respect economic and social human rights: A peer benchmark. *Economic Rights: Conceptual, Measurement, and Policy Issues* (ed. S. Hertel and L. Minkler). Cambridge: Cambridge University Press.

Cingranelli, D. L. and Richards, D. L. (2008). The Cingranelli-Richards (CIRI) human rights data project. www.humanrightsdata.com.

Cingranelli, D. L. and Richards, D. L. (2010). The Cingranelli and Richards (CIRI) Human Rights Data Project. *Human Rights Quarterly*, 32/2, 401–24.

Clark, A. M. (2001). *Diplomacy of Conscience: Amnesty International and Changing Human Rights Norms*. Princeton, NJ: Princeton University Press.

Clark, P. (2010). *The Gacaca Courts, Post-Genocide Justice and Reconciliation in Rwanda: Justice without Lawyers*. Cambridge: Cambridge University Press.

Claude, R. P. (1976). The classical model of human rights development. *Comparative Human Rights* (ed. R. P. Claude). Baltimore, MD: Johns Hopkins University Press.

Claude, R. P. (1983). The case of Joelito Filartiga and the clinic of hope. *Human Rights Quarterly*, 5/3, 275–95.

Claude, R. P. and Jabine, T. B. (1992). Exploring human rights issues with statistics. *Human Rights and Statistics: Getting the Record Straight* (ed. T. B. Jabine and R. P. Claude). Philadelphia, PA: University of Pennsylvania Press.

Cochabamaba Peoples Conference. (2010). World Peoples Conference on Climate Change and the Rights of Mother Earth. http://pwccc.wordpress.com.

Coetzee, J. M. (1982). *Waiting for the Barbarians*. New York: Penguin.

Cohen, J. (2004). Minimalism about human rights: The most we can hope for? *The Journal of Political Philosophy*, **12**/2, 190–213.

Cohen, R. and Rai, S. (eds) (2000). *Global Social Movements*. London: Athlone.

Cohn, T. (2003). *Global Political Economy* (2nd edn). New York: Addison Wesley and Longman, Inc.

COI (Commission of Inquiry) (2005). Report of the International Commission of Inquiry on Darfur to the United Nations Secretary-General. Geneva, 25 January.

Cole, M. (2000). *Trade Liberalisation, Economic Growth and the Environment*. London: Edward Elgar.

Collings, N. (2010) Environment. *State of the World's IndigenousPeoples*. New York: UN. http://www.un.org/esa/socdev/unpfii/documents/SOWIP/en/SOWIP_chapter3.pdf.

Collins, K. (2007). Thai men sue N. C. contractor. *News and Observer*, 10 March.

Colonomos, A. and Santiso, J. (2005). Viva la France! French multinationals and human rights. *Human Rights Quarterly*, **27**/4, 1307–45.

Comte, A. (1896). *The Positive Philosophy*. London: George Bell. Republished Batoche Books Kitchner (2000) at http://socserv2.socsci.mcmaster.ca/econ/ugcm/3ll3/comte/Philosophy1.pdf.

Conference on Security and Co-operation in Europe, Final Act (1975). Helsinki, 1 August. https://www.osce.org/mc/39501?download=true.

Conisbee, M. and Simms, A. (2003). *Environmental Refugees: The Case for Recognition*. London: new economics foundation. http://www.neweconomics.org/publications/entry/environmental-refugees.

Connelly, M. T. (1980). *The Response to Prostitution in the Progressive Era*. Chapel Hill, NC: University of North Carolina.

Conroy, J. (2000). *Unspeakable Acts, Ordinary People: The Dynamics of Torture—An Examination of the Practice of Torture in Three Democracies*. New York: Knopf.

Copelon, R. (1994). Intimate terror: Understanding domestic violence as torture. *Human Rights of Women: National and International Perspectives* (ed. R. J. Cook). Philadelphia, PA: University of Pennsylvania Press.

Corbin, A. (1990). *Women for Hire: Prostitution and Sexuality in France After 1850* (trans. A. Sheridan). Cambridge, MA: Harvard University Press.

Cornia, G. A., Jolly, R., and Stewart, F. (1987). *Adjustment With a Human Face, Volume 1: Protecting the Vulnerable and Promoting Growth*. Oxford: Oxford University Press.

Corntassel, J. (2008). Toward sustainable self-determination: Rethinking the contemporary Indigenous rights discourse, *Alternatives* **33**/1, 105–32

Corrales, J. and Pecheny, M. (2010). *The Politics of Sexuality in Latin America: A Reader on Lesbian, Gay, Bisexual, and Transgender Rights*. Pittsburgh, PA: University of Pittsburgh Press.

Cossman, B. (2003). Turning the gaze back on itself: Comparative law, feminist legal studies, and the postcolonial project. *Feminist Legal Theory: An Anti-Essentialist Reader* (ed. N. E. Dowd and M. S. Jacobs). New York and London: New York University Press.

Courthoys, A. and Docker, J. (2008). Defining genocide. *The Historiography of Genocide* (ed. D. Stone). London: Palgrave Macmillan.

Cowan, J. K., Dembour, M. B., and Wilson, R. A. (eds) (2001). *Culture and Rights: Anthropological Perspectives*. Cambridge: Cambridge University Press.

Cowell, A. (2000). A call to put social issues on the corporate agenda. *The New York Times*, 6 April.

Cox, R. (1996). *Shaping Childhood: Themes of Uncertainty in the History of Adult-Child Relationships*. London: Routledge.

Cranston, M. (1967). Human rights, real and supposed. *Political Theory and the Rights of Man*. (ed. D. D. Raphael). London: Macmillan.

Crawford, T. and Kuperman, A. (eds) (2006). *Gambling on Humanitarian Intervention: Moral Hazard, Rebellion and Civil War*. New York: Routledge.

Crelinsten, R. (2005). How to make a torturer. *Index on Censorship*, **34**/1, 72–7.

Crenshaw, E. (1991). Foreign investment as a dependent variable: Determinants of foreign investment and capital penetration in developing nations, 1967–1978. *Social Forces*, **69**/4, 1169–82.

Crenshaw, K. (1991). Mapping the margins: Intersectionality, identity politics, and violence against women of color. *Stanford Law Review*, **43**/6, 1241–99.

Cunningham, H. (1995). *Children and Childhood in Western Society Since 1500*. London: Longman.

Czyzewski, K. (2011). Colonialism as a broader social determinant of health. *The International Indigenous Policy Journal*, **2**/1. http://ir.lib.uwo.ca/iipj/vol2/iss1/5.

Daes, E.-I. A. (1993). Some considerations on the Right of Indigenous Peoples to Self-Determination. *Transnational Law& Contemporary Problems*, **3**/ 1, 1–11.

Daes, E. and Eide, A. (2000). Working paper on the relationship and distinction between the rights of persons belonging to minorities and those of Indigenous peoples. UN Doc. E/CN.4/Sub.2/2000/10. http://www.unhchr.ch/huridocda/huridoca.nsf/0/e2bb9e4b569ae37fc12569290050ae93?OpenDocument.

Dahl, R. A. (1966). *Political Opposition in Western Democracies*. New Haven, CT: Yale University Press.

Dahl, R. A. (1971). *Polyarchy: Participation and Opposition*. New Haven, CT: Yale University Press.

Dahlab v. *Switzerland* (2001). European Court of Human Rights, No. 42393/98. 15 February.

Dallaire, R.Beardsley, B. (2003). *Shake Hands with the Devil: The Failure of Humanity in Rwanda*. Toronto: Random House Canada.

Dallin, A. and Breslauer, G. (1970). *Political Terror in Communist Systems*. Stanford, CA: Stanford University Press.

Daly, M. (2007). *Darfur's Sorrow: A History of Destruction and Genocide*. New York: Cambridge University Press.

Danner, M. (2004). *Torture and Truth: America, Abu Ghraib and the War on Terror*. New York: New York Review of Books.

Darrow, M. and Tomas, A. (2005). Power, capture and conflict: A call for human rights accountability in development cooperation. *Human Rights Quarterly*, **27**/2, 471–538.

Dassin, J. (ed.) (1986). *Torture in Brazil: A Report by the Archdiocese of Sao Paulo*. New York: Vintage.

Davenport, C. (1995). Multi-dimensional threat perception and state repression: An inquiry into why states apply negative sanctions. *American Journal of Political Science*, **39**/3, 683–713.

Davenport, C. (1996). 'Constitutional promises' and repressive reality: A cross-national time-series investigation of why political and civil liberties are suppressed. *Journal of Politics*, **58**/3: 627–54.

Davenport, C. (1997). From ballots to bullets: An empirical assessment of how national elections influence state uses of political repression. *Electoral Studies*, **16**/4, 517–40.

Davenport, C. (1999). Human rights and the democratic proposition. *Journal of Conflict Resolution*, **43**/1, 92–116.

Davenport, C. (2004). The promise of democratic pacification: An empirical assessment. *International Studies Quarterly*, **48**/3, 539–60.

Davenport, C. (2007a). *State Repression and the Domestic Democratic Peace*. New York: Cambridge University Press.

Davenport, C. (2007b). State repression and political order. *Annual Review of Political Science*, **10**, 1–23.

Davenport, C. and Armstrong II, D. A. (2004). Democracy and the violation of human rights: A statistical analysis from 1976–96. *American Journal of Political Science*, **48**/3, 538–54.

Davenport, C., Moore, W., and Armstrong II, D. A. (2008). Waterboarding and democracy: Understanding torture and domestic threats. Manuscript.

Davenport, C. and Stam, A. (2003). Mass killing and the oases of humanity: Understanding Rwandan genocide and resistance. National Science Foundation (SES-0321518), Spring.

David, F. (1999). New threats or old stereotypes: The revival of 'trafficking' as a discourse. History of Crime, Policing and Punishment Conference, Australian Institute of Criminology in conjunction with Charles Stuart University, Canberra, 9–10 December. http://www.aic.gov.au/media_library/conferences/hcpp/david.pdf.

Davis, M. (2008). Unforgivable behavior, inadmissible evidence. *The New York Times*, 17 February.

de-Shalit, A. (2001). Ten commandments of how to fail in an environmental campaign. *Political Theory and the Environment: A Reassessment* (ed. M. Humphrey). London: Frank Cass.

de Waal, A. (1998). *Famine Crimes: Politics and the Disaster Relief Industry in Africa*. Bloomington, IN: Indiana University Press.

Deng, F. (1995). *War of Visions: Conflict of Identities in the Sudan*. Washington, DC: Brookings Institution Press.

Deng, F., Kimaro, S., Lyons, T., Rothchild, D., and Zartman, I. W. (1996). *Sovereignty as Responsibility: Conflict Management in Africa*. Washington, DC: Brookings Institution Press.

Dershowitz, A. (2002). *Why Terrorism Works: Understanding the Threat, Responding to the Challenge*. New Haven, CT: Yale University Press.

Dershowitz, A. (2004). Torture warrant: A response to Professor Strauss. *New York Law School Law Review*, **48**/1, 275–94.

Des Forges, A. (1999). *Leave None to Tell the Story: Genocide in Rwanda*. New York: Human Rights Watch.

DESA (UN Department of Social and Economic Affairs) (2009). *The State of the World's Indigenous Peoples* ST/ESA/38. New York: United Nations.

Detrick, S. (ed.) (1992). *The United Nations Convention on the Rights of the Child: A Guide to the 'Travaux Preparatoires'*. Dordrecht: Martinus Nijhoff.

Devetak, R. (2007). Between Kant and Pufendorf: Humanitarian intervention, statist anti-cosmopolitanism and critical international theory. *Review of International Studies*, 33/Special issue, 51–174.

Diamond, L. (2002). Thinking about hybrid regimes. *Journal of Democracy*, 13/2, 21–35.

Diamond, L. (2008). *The Spirit of Democracy: The Struggle to Build Free Societies Throughout the World*. New York: Times Books.

Dicey, Albert Venn (1959 [1889]). *Introduction to the Study of the Law of the Constitution*. London: Macmillan.

Dicke, W. and Holland, F. (eds) (2007). Water: A global contestation. *Global Civil Society 2006/7* (ed. H. Anheier, M. Kaldor, and M. Glasius) London: Sage.

Diebold, J. (1974). Why be scared of them. *Foreign Policy*, 3/1, 79–95.

Doezema, J. (2000). Loose women or lost women? The re-emergence of the myth of white slavery in contemporary discourses of trafficking in women. *Gender Issues*, **18**/1, 23–50.

Doezema, J. (2002). Who gets to choose? Coercion, consent and the UN trafficking protocol. *Gender and Development*, **10**/1, 20–7.

Donnelly, J. (1982). Human Rights and Human Dignity: An Analytic Critique of Non-Western Conceptions of Human Rights. *The American Political Science Review*, **76**/2, 303–16.

Donnelly, J. (1985). *The Concept of Human Rights*. New York: St Martin's Press.

Donnelly, J. (1989). *Universal Human Rights in Theory and Practice*. Ithaca, NY: Cornell University Press.

Donnelly, J. (2003). *Universal Human Rights in Theory and Practice* (2nd edn). Ithaca, NY: Cornell University Press.

Donnelly, J. (2006). *International Human Rights* (3rd edn). Boulder, CO: Westview.

Donner, F. J. (1990). *Protectors of Privilege: Red Squads and Police Repression in Urban America*. Berkeley, CA: University of California Press.

Dooley, K., Griffiths, T., Martone, F., and Ozinga, S. (2011). *Smoke and Mirrors: A Critical Assessment of the Forest Carbon Partnership Facility*. Moreton-in-Marsh: FERN/FPP.

Doran, P., Wanhua, Y., Wagner, L., and Wise, S. (1995). Summary of the Fourth World Conference on Women. *A Daily Report on the Fourth World Conference on Women*, **14**, 12.

Douzinas, C. (2007). *Human Rights and Empire: The Political Philosophy of Cosmopolitanism*. London: Routledge-Cavendish.

Douzinas, C. and Gearty, C. (eds) (2014). *The Meanings of Rights: The Philosophy and Social Theory of Human Rights*. Cambridge: Cambridge University Press.

Drumbl, M. (2012a). Child soldiers and clicktivism: Justice, myths, and prevention. *Journal of Human Rights Practice*, 4/3, 481–5.

Drumbl, M. (2012b). *Reimagining Child Soldiers in International Law and Policy*. Oxford: Oxford University Press.

Dryzek, J. (1987). *Rational Ecology: Environment and Political Economy*. London: Wiley Blackwell.

Du Plessis, M., Maluwa T., and O'Reilly, A. S. (2013), Africa and the International Criminal Court. Chatham House International Law paper 2013/1. http://www.chathamhouse.org/sites/files/chathamhouse/public/Research/International%20Law/0713pp_ic-cafrica.pdf.

DuBois, P. (1991). *Torture and Truth*. London: Routledge.

Duffield, M. (2007). *Development, Security and Unending War: Governing the World of Peoples*. Cambridge: Polity.

Duggan, L. (2002). The new homonormativity: The sexual politics of neoliberalism. *Materializing Democracy* (ed. R. Castronovo, and D. D. Nelson). Durham, NC: Duke University Press.

Dunne, T. and Gifkins, J. (2011). Libya and the state of intervention. *Australian Journal of International Affairs*, **65/5**, 515–29.

Dunne, T. and Wheeler, N. J. (eds) (1999). *Human Rights in Global Politics*. Cambridge: Cambridge University Press.

Duong, K. (2012). What does queer theory teach us about intersectionality? *Politics & Gender*, **8/3**, 370–86.

Durodié, B. (2013). 'War on terror or a search for meaning?' Strategic Multi-layer Assessment Occasional White Paper. US Joint Chiefs of Staff/Department of Defense. http://www.durodie.net/images/uploads/SMA_CT_White_Paper.pdf

Duvall, R. and Stohl, M. (1988). Governance by terror. *The Politics of Terrorism* (ed. M. Stohl). New York: M. Dekker.

Dworkin, R. (1977). *Taking Rights Seriously*. Cambridge, MA: Harvard University Press.

Dyer, A. S. (1880). *The European Slave Trade in English Girls: A Narrative of Facts*. London: Dyer Brothers.

Eastwood, L. E. (2011). Resisting dispossession: Indigenous peoples, the World Bank and the contested terrain of policy. *New Global Studies*, **5/1**. http://www.degruyter.com/view/j/ngs.2011.5.1/ngs.2011.5.1.1114/ngs.2011.5.1.1114.xml.

Eckersley, R. (1996). Greening liberal democracy: The rights discourse revisited. *Democracy and Green Political Thought: Sustainability, Rights and Citizenship* (ed. B. Doherty and M. de Geus). London: Routledge.

Eckholm, E. (2003). Tide of China's migrants: Flowing to boom or bust? *New York Times*, 29 July.

Ecuador (2004). International trade, health, and children's rights. 3D country briefing. September.

Edmundson, W. A. (2004). *An Introduction to Rights*. Cambridge: Cambridge University Press.

Edwards, M. (2003). NGO legitimacy: Voice or vote? *BOND Networker*, February.

Edwards, M. and Gaventa, J. (eds) (2001). *Global Citizen Action*. London: Earthscan.

Edwards, S. (1990). Capital flows, foreign direct investment and debt. NBER working paper no. 3497 Cambridge, MA: NBER.

Egan, S. (2011). *The UN Human Rights Treaty System: Law and Procedure*. Dublin: Bloomsbury Professional.

Eide, A. (1989). Realization of social and economic rights and the minimum threshold approach. *Human Rights Law Journal*, **10/1–2**, 35–51.

Elazar, D. J. (1972). *American Federalism: A View from the States* (2nd edn). New York: Thomas Y. Crowell.

Elliot, R. (1989). The rights of future people. *Journal of Applied Philosophy*, **6/2**, 159–69.

Elson, D. (2006). *Budgeting for Women's Rights: Monitoring Government Budgets for Compliance with CEDAW*. New York: UNIFEM.

Elson, D., Fukuda-Parr, S., and Vizard, P. (eds) (2012). *Capabilities and Rights: An Interdisciplinary Conversation*. London: Routledge. First issued as a special issue of the *Journal of Human Development and Capabilities*, **12/1**.

Elster, J. (ed.) (2006). *Retribution and Reparation in the Transition to Democracy*. New York: Cambridge University Press.

Emmerij, L., Jolly, R., and Weiss, T. (2001). *Ahead of the Curve? UN Ideas and Global Challenges*. Bloomington, IN: Indiana University Press.

Escobar, A. (1995). *Encountering Development: Making and Unmaking of the Third World*. Princeton, NJ: Princeton University Press.

Escobar, A. (1997). The making and unmaking of the Third World. *The Post-Development Reader* (ed. M. Rahnema with V. Bawtree). London: Zed Books.

Etzioni, A. (2006). Sovereignty as responsibility. *Orbis*, **50/1**, 71–85.

Evans, G. (2008). State sovereignty was a licence to kill. Interview with Gareth Evans. *SEF News (Stiftung Entwicklung und Frieden)*, Spring.

Evans, G. (2009). *The Responsibility to Protect: Ending Mass Atrocity Crimes Once and For All*. Washington, DC: Brookings Institution Press.

Evans, G. (2013). R2P down but not out after Libya and Syria, *Open Democracy*. 9 September 2013. https://www.opendemocracy.net/openglobalrights/gareth-evans/r2p-down-but-not-out-after-libya-and-syria.

Evans, M. D. (2011). *Lautisi v. Italy*: An initial appraisal. *Religion and Human Rights*, **6**/3, 237–44.

Evans, T. (1996). *US Hegemony and the Project of Universal Human Rights*. Basingstoke: Macmillan.

Evans, T. (ed.) (1998). *Human Rights Fifty Years On: An Appraisal*. Manchester: Manchester University Press.

Ezzat, H. R. (2004). Beyond methodological modernism: Towards a multicultural paradigm shift in the social sciences. *Global Civil Society 2004/5* (ed. H. Anheier, M. Glasius, and M. Kaldor). London: Sage.

Fagan, A. (2010). *The Atlas of Human Rights: Mapping Violations of Freedom Worldwide*. London and Oxford: Routledge.

Falk, R. (2000). *Human Rights Horizons*. London: Routledge.

Family Law Week (2014) Re E (A Child) [2014] EWHC 6 (Fam). 14 January. http://www.familylawweek.co.uk/site.aspx?i=ed126781.

Fanon, F. (2004). *The Wretched of the Earth*. New York: Grove.

Fariss, C. J. (2014). Respect for human rights has improved over time: Modeling the changing standard of accountability. *American Political Science Review*, **108**/2, 297–318.

Farmer, P. (2005). *Pathologies of Power: Health, Human Rights and the New War on the Poor*. Berkeley, CA: University of California Press.

Farrior, S. (1997). The international law on trafficking in women and children for prostitution: Making it live up to its potential. *Harvard Human Rights Journal*, **10**, 213–55.

Federle, K. (1994). Rights flow downhill. *International Journal of Children's Rights*, **2**/4, 343–76.

Fein, H. (1979). *Accounting for Genocide: National Responses and Jewish Victimization During the Holocaust*. Chicago, IL: University of Chicago Press.

Fein, H. (1995). More murder in the middle: Life-integrity violations and democracy in the world, 1987. *Human Rights Quarterly*, **17**/1, 170–91.

Feinberg, J. (1974). The rights of animals and future generations. *Philosophy and Environmental Crisis* (ed. W. Blackstone). Athens, GA: University of Georgia Press.

Felner, E. (2005). Torture and terrorism: Painful lessons from Israel. *Torture: Does it Make Us Safer? Is it Ever OK?* (ed. K. Roth and M. Worden). New York: New Press/Human Rights Watch.

Fiddian-Qasmiyeh, E., Loescher, G., Long, K., and Sigona, N. (eds) (2014). *The Oxford Handbook of Refugee and Forced Migration Studies*. Oxford: Oxford University Press.

Fields, A. B. (2003). *Rethinking Human Rights for the New Millennium*. New York: Palgrave Macmillan.

Fierce (no date). Police Accountability Work Committee. http://www.fiercenyc.org/news/police-accountability-work-committee (accessed 16 April 2015).

Fisher, T. (1997). *Prostitution and the Victorians*. New York: St Martins.

Flint, J. and de Waal, A. (2008). *Darfur: A New History of a Long War* (revised and updated). London: Zed Books.

Flint, J. and de Waal, A. (2009). Case closed: A prosecutor without borders. *World Affairs*, **171**/4, 23–38.

Florini, A. M. (ed.) (2000). *The Third Force: The Rise of Transnational Civil Society*. Tokyo: Japan Center for International Exchange and Washington, DC: Carnegie Endowment for Peace.

Foot, R. (2000). *Rights Beyond Borders: The Global Community and the Struggle Over Human Rights in China*. Oxford: Oxford University Press.

Forest Peoples Programme (2006). Peoples' rights, extractive industries and transnational and other business enterprises. http://www.business-humanrights.org/Documents/Forest-Peoples-Tebtebba-submission-to-SRSG-re-indigenous-rights-29-Dec-2006.pdf.

Forst, R. (trans. John M. Farrell) (1994). *Contexts of Justice: Political Philosophy beyond Liberalism and Communitarianism*. Berkeley and Los Angeles, CA: University of California Press.

Forsythe, D. P. (ed.) (2000). *Human Rights and Comparative Foreign Policy*. Tokyo: United Nations University Press.

Forsythe, D. P. (2006). *Human Rights in International Relations* (2nd edn). Cambridge: Cambridge University Press.

Forum Social Mundial (World Social Forum) (2005). Programmacao (Programme) 29 30 31.

Foster, H., Raven, H., and Webber, J. (2008). *Let Right be Done: Aboriginal Title, the Calder Case, and the Future of Indigenous Rights*. Vancouver: UBC Press.

Foster, J. (2002). *The Millennium Declaration: Engaging Civil Society Organisations*. New York: World Federation of United Nations Associations.

Foucault, M. (1977). *Discipline and Punish: The Birth of the Prison*. New York: Pantheon.

Foucault, M. (2003). *'Society Must be Defended': Lectures at the Collège de France1975–1976*. London: Allen Lane/Penguin.

Foucault, M. (2007). *Security, Territory, Population: Lectures at the Collège de France1977–1978*. Basingstoke: Palgrave.

Foweraker, J. and Landman, T. (1997). *Citizenship Rights and Social Movements: A Comparative and Statistical Analysis*. Oxford: Oxford University Press.

Fox, F. (2001). New humanitarianism: Does it provide a moral banner for the 21st century? *Disasters*, **25**/4, 275–89.

Francis, R. (2005). *Judge Sewall's Apology: The Salem Witch Trials and the Forming of an American Conscience*. New York: Harper Collins.

Franck, T. M. (1984). Of gnats and camels: Is there a double standard at the United Nations? *American Journal of International Law*, **78**/4, 811–33.

Franck, T. M. (2000). Legitimacy of the democratic entitlement. *Democratic Governance and International Law* (ed. G. H. Fox and B. R. Roth). Cambridge: Cambridge University Press.

Frank, A. G. (1970). *Latin America: Underdevelopment or Revolution: Essays on the Development of Underdevelopment and the Immediate Enemy*. New York: Monthly Review Press.

Frank, A. G. (1971). *Capitalism and Underdevelopment in Latin America: Historical Studies of Chile and Brazil*. Harmondsworth: Penguin.

Frankel, J. and Romer, P. (1999). Does trade cause growth? *American Economic Review*, **89**/3, 379–99.

Franklin, B. (ed.) (1995). *The Handbook of Children's Rights*. London: Routledge.

Franks, D. M., Davis, R., Bebbington, A. J., Saleem, H. A., Kemp, D., and Scurrah, M. (2014). Conflict translates environmental and social risk into business costs. *PNAS*, **11**/21, 7576–81. http://www.pnas.org/content/111/21/7576.short.53.

Freedman, R. (2013). *The United Nations Human Rights Council: A Critique and Early Assessment*. Routledge Research in Human Rights Law. Abingdon and New York: Routledge.

Freeman, M. (1997). *The Moral Status of Children: Essays on the Rights of the Child*. The Hague: Martinus Nijhoff.

Freeman, M. (2001). Is a political science of human rights possible? *The Netherlands Quarterly of Human Rights*, **19**/2, 121–37.

Freeman, M. (2002). *Human Rights: An Interdisciplinary Approach*. Cambridge: Polity.

Frenkel, S. and Kuruvilla, S. (2002). Logics of action, globalization, and changing employment relations in China, India, Malaysia, and the Philippines. *Industrial and Labor Relations Review*, **55**/3, 387–412.

Friedman, E. (1995). Women's human rights: The emergence of a movement. *Women's Rights, Human Rights: International Feminist Perspectives* (ed. J. Peters and A. Wolper). London: Routledge.

Friedman, M. (1962). *Capitalism and Freedom*. Chicago, IL: Chicago University Press.

Friedman, T. L. (2004). *The Lexus and the Olive Tree*. New York: Random House.

Friends of River Narmada (2008). Introduction. http://www.narmada.org/introduction.html.

Fukuda-Parr, S. (2005). Millennium development goals: Why they matter. *Global Governance*, **10**/3, 395–402.

Fukuda-Parr, S. (2006). Millennium Development Goal 8: International human rights obligations? *Human Rights Quarterly*, **28**/4, 966–97.

Fukuda-Parr, S. (2008a). Human rights and development. *Social Welfare, Moral Philosophy and Development: Essays in Honour of Amartya Sen's Seventy Fifth Birthday* (ed. K. Basu and R. Kanbur). Oxford: Oxford University Press.

Fukuda-Parr, S. (2008b). *Are Internationally Agreed Development Goals (IADGs) being Implemented in National Development Strategies and Aid Programmes? A Review of Poverty Reduction Strategy Papers (PRSPs) and Development Cooperation Policy Statements*. Background papers for the 2008 Development Cooperation Forum, Mainstreaming of IADGs. New York: UN Department for Economic and Social Affairs. http://www.isn.ethz.ch/Digital-Library/Publications/Detail/?lang=en&id=92651.

Fukuda-Parr, S. and Yamin, A. (eds) (2015). *Millennium Development Goals, Capabilities and Human Rights: The Power of Numbers to Shape Agendas*. London: Routledge.

Fukuyama, F. (1992). *The End of History and the Last Man*. London: Hamish Hamilton.

Galbraith, J. K. (1964). *Economic Development*. Cambridge, MA: Harvard University Press.

Galbraith, J. K. (1977). *The Nature of Mass Poverty*. Cambridge, MA: Harvard University Press.

Gallagher, A. (2001). Human rights and the new UN protocols on trafficking and migrant smuggling: A preliminary analysis. *Human Rights Quarterly*, 23/4, 975–1004.

Gallie, W. B. (1956). Essentially contested concepts. *Proceedings of the Aristotelian Society*, **56**/1, 167–98.

Garrett, G. (1995). Capital mobility, trade, and the domestic politics of economic policy. *International Organization*, **49**/4, 657–87.

Garrett, G. (1998). *Partisan Politics in the Global Economy*. Cambridge: Cambridge University Press.

Gartner, S. and Regan, P. (1996). Threat and repression: The non-linear relationship between government and opposition violence. *Journal of Peace Research*, **33**/3, 273–87.

Gastanaga, V. and Nugent, J. B. (1998). Host country reforms and FDI inflows: How much difference do they make? *World Development*, **26**/7, 1299–314.

Gastil, R. D. (1978). *Freedom in the World: Political Rights and Civil Liberties, 1978*. Boston, MA: G. K. Hall.

Gastil, R. D. (1980). *Freedom in the World: Political Rights and Civil Liberties*. Westport, CT: Greenwood.

Gastil, R. D. (1988). *Freedom in the World: Political and Civil Liberties, 1986–1987*. New York: Freedom House.

Gastil, R. D. (1990). The comparative survey of freedom: Experiences and suggestions. *Studies in Comparative International Development*, **25**/1, 25–50.

Gatrell, P. (2013). *The Making of the Modern Refugee*. Oxford: Oxford University Press.

Geertz, C. (1983). *Local Knowledge: Further Essays in Interpretive Anthropology*. New York: Basic Books.

Gelleny, R. and McCoy, M. (2001). Globalization and government policy independence: The issue of taxation. *Political Research Quarterly*, **54**/3, 509–30.

Geneva Conventions and Protocols of 1949 and 1977.

Gewirth, A. (1996). *The Community of Rights*. Chicago, IL: University of Chicago Press.

Ghani, A., Lockhart, C., and Carnahan, M. (2005). Closing the sovereignty gap: An approach to state-building. Overseas Development Institute working paper no. 253, September. London: Overseas Development Institute. http://www.odi.org.uk/Publications/working_papers/wp253.pdf.

Gibbons, E. (2006). The Convention on the Rights of the Child and implementation of economic, social and cultural rights in Latin America. *Los Derechos Economicos, Sociales y Culturales en America Latina* (ed. A. Yamin). Ottawa: IDRC and Plaza y Valdes. http://www.idrc.ca/EN/Resources/Publications/openebooks/323-2/index.html.

Gibney, M. and Stohl, M. (1988). Human rights and US refugee policy. *Open Borders? Closed Societies?: The Ethical and Political Issues* (ed. M. Gibney). Westport, CT: Greenwood.

Gibson, M. (1986). *Prostitution and the State in Italy, 1860-1915*. New Brunswick, NJ: Rutgers University Press.

Gilpin, R. (2001). *Global Political Economy*. Princeton, NJ: Princeton University Press.

Glanville, L. (2014). *Sovereignty and the Responsibility to Protect*. Chicago: Chicago University Press.

Glasius, M. (2005). *The International Criminal Court: A GCS Achievement*. London: Routledge.

Glasius, M. (2006). *The International Criminal Court: A Global Civil Society Achievement*. London: Routledge.

Glasius, M. (2012). Economic and social rights and social justice movements: Some courtship, no marriage, no children yet. *Defending Human Rights: Tools for Social Justice* (ed. I. Lintel, A. Buyse, and B. McGonigle Leyh). Cambridge: Intersentia.

Glasius M. (forthcoming). Civil and uncivil society. *Wiley Blackwell Encyclopedia of Sociology* (2nd edn) (ed. George Ritzer). Hoboken, NJ: Wiley Blackwell.

Gleditsch, N. P., Wallensteen, P., Eriksson, M., Sollenberg, M., and Strand, H. (2002). Armed conflict 1946–2001: A new dataset. *Journal of Peace Research*, **39**/5, 615–37. Data available at http://www.prio.no/jpr/datasets.asp.

Glendon, M. A., Gordon, M. W., and Osakwe, C. (1982). *Comparative Legal Traditions in a Nutshell*. St Paul, MN: West Publishing Corporation.

Global Civil Society (GCS) Yearbook Series, 2004 Global Civil Society (GCS) Yearbook Series (2001–) For 2001-3 published by Oxford University Press, Oxford; 2004, onwards by Sage, London.

Global Footprint Network (2014). Earth Overshoot Day. http://www.footprintnetwork.org/en/index.php/GFN/page/earth_overshoot_day/ (accessed 7 March 2015).

Glucksmann, M. (2006). Developing an economic sociology of care and rights. *Rights: Sociological Perspectives* (L. Morris). London: Routledge.

Goldstein, R. J. (1978). *Political Repression in Modern America: From 1870 to the Present*. Cambridge: Schenkman Publishing.

Golston, J. C. (1993). Ritual abuse: Raising hell in psychotherapy: The political, military and multigenerational training of torturers: Violent initiation and the role of traumatic dissociation. *Treating Abuse Today*, 3/6, 12–19.

Gonzalez, J. and Goodman, A. (2014). Naomi Klein: Reject Keystone XL Pipeline, we need radical change to prevent catastrophic warming, *Democracy Now*, 17 November, http://www.democracynow.org/2014/11/17/naomi_klein_reject_keystone_xl_pipeline.

Goodale, M. (2006a). Introduction. *American Anthropologist*, 108/1, 1–8.

Goodale, M. (2006b). Ethical theory as social practice. *American Anthropologist*, 108/1, 25–37.

Goodale, M. (2008). *Human Rights: An Anthropological Reader*. Blackwell Readers in Anthropology. Chichester: Blackwell.

Goodale, M. and Merry, S. E. (2007). *The Practice of Human Rights: Tracking Law Between the Global and the Local*. Cambridge Studies in Law and Society. Cambridge: Cambridge University Press.

Goodhart, M. (2005). *Democracy as Human Rights: Freedom and Equality in the Age of Globalization*. New York: Routledge.

Goodman, A. (2014). Pablo Solón on COP 20 and carbon markets: This is a new mechanism to commodify nature. *Democracy Now*, 9 December. www.democracynow.org/blog/2014/12/9/pablo_solon_on_cop20_and_carbon.

Goodman, A. (2015). Keystone, climate and the cold. truthdig, 15 January. http://www.truthdig.com/report/item/keystone_climate_change_and_the_cold_20141119.

Goodman, L. E. (1998). *Judaism, Human Rights, and Human Values*. New York: Oxford University Press.

Goodwin-Gill, G. and Cohn, I. (1994) *Child Soldiers: The Role of Children in Armed Conflicts*. Oxford: Oxford University Press.

Goodwin-Gill, G. and McAdam, J. (2007). *The Refugee in International Law*. Oxford: Oxford University Press.

Gorbachev, M. (1989). Speech reproduced in *Current Digest of the Soviet Press*, 41/46, 13 December.

Gotkowitz, L. (2008). *A Revolution for Our Rights: Indigenous Struggles for Land and Justice in Bolivia, 1880–1952*. Durham, NC: Duke University Press.

Gould, C. C. (1988). *Rethinking Democracy: Freedom and Social Cooperation in Politics, Economy, and Society*. Cambridge: Cambridge University Press.

Gould, C. C. (2004). *Globalizing Democracy and Human Rights*. Cambridge: Cambridge University Press.

Gover, K. (2010) Comparative tribal constitutionalism: Membership governance in Australia, Canada, New Zealand, and the United States, *Law & Social Inquiry*, 35/3, 689–762.

Gow, J. (1997). *Triumph of the Lack of Will*. New York: Columbia University Press.

Gray, M. M., Kittilson, M. C., and Sandholtz, W. (2006). Women and globalization: A study of 180 nations, 1975–2000. *International Organization*, 60/2, 293–333.

Gready, P. and Ensor, J. (eds) (2005). *Reinventing Development? Translating Rights-Based Approaches from Theory into Practice*. London: Zed Books.

Green, M. (2001). What we talk about when we talk about indicators: Current approaches to human rights measurement. *Human Rights Quarterly*, 23/4, 1062–97.

Greenberg K. J. and Datel, J. (eds) (2005). *The Torture Papers: The Road to Abu Ghraib*. Cambridge: Cambridge University Press.

Greer, D. (1935). *The Incidence of Terror During the French Revolution: A Statistical Interpretation*. Cambridge, MA: Harvard University Press.

Greig, A., Hume, D., and Turner, M. (2007). *Challenging Global Inequality: Development Theory and Practice in the 21st Century*. New York: Palgrave Macmillan.

Griffin, J. (2008). *On Human Rights*. Cambridge: Cambridge University Press.

Grittner, F. K. (1990). *White Slavery: Myth, Ideology and American Law*. New York: Garland.

Gross, O. (2004). The prohibition on torture and the limits of the law. *Torture: A Collection* (ed. S. Levinson). Oxford: Oxford University Press.

Grossfeld, Bernhard (1990). *The Strength and Weakness of Comparative Law*. Oxford: Clarendon Press.

Grotius, Hugo. (1625). *De jure belli et pacis*.

Guibernau, M. (1999). *Nations Without States: Political Communities in a Global Age*. Cambridge: Polity.

Guinier, L. (1994). *The Tyranny of the Majority: Fundamental Fairness in Representative Democracy*. New York: Free Press.

Gunn, T. J. (2003). The complexity of religion and the definition of 'religion' in international law. *Harvard Human Rights Journal*, **16**, 189–215.

Gurr, T. R. (1970). *Why Men Rebel*. Princeton, NJ: Princeton University Press.

Gurr, T. R. (1974). Persistence and change in political systems, 1800–1971. *American Political Science Review*, **68**/4, 1482–504.

Gurr, T. R. (1986). The political origins of state violence and terror: A theoretical analysis. *Government Violence and Repression: An Agenda for Research* (ed. M. Stohl and G. A. Lopez). New York: Greenwood.

Gurr, T. R, Marshall, M., Davenport, C., and Jaggers, K. (2002). Polity IV, 1800–1999: A reply to Munck and Verkuilen. *Comparative Political Studies*, **35**/1, 40–5. Additional source for polity project: http://www.systemicpeace.org/polity/polity4.htm.

Gustafson, B. (2009). Manipulating cartographies: Plurinationalism, autonomy and Indigenous resurgence in Bolivia. *Anthropological Quarterly*, **82**/4, 985–1015.

Guzmán, D., Guberek, T., Hoover, A., and Ball, P. (2007). *Missing People in Casanare*. Palo Alto, CA: The Benetech Initiative. https://hrdag.org/content/colombia/casanare-missing-report.pdf.

Haakonssen, K. (1991). From natural law to the rights of man: A European perspective on American debates. *A Culture of Rights: The Bill of Rights in Philosophy, Politics and Law—1791 and 1991* (ed. M. J. Lacey and K. Haakonssen). Cambridge: Woodrow Wilson International Center for Scholars and Cambridge University Press.

Habermas, J. (1996). *Between Facts and Norms: Contributions to a Discourse Theory of Law and Democracy*. Cambridge, MA: MIT Press.

Habermas, J. (1999). Bestialität and Humanität. *Die Zeit*, 29 April.

Hafner-Burton, E. M. (2005). Right or robust? The sensitive nature of repression to globalization. *Journal of Peace Research*, **42**/6, 679–98.

Hafner-Burton, E. M. (2009). *Forced to Be Good: Why Trade Agreements Boost Human Rights*. Ithaca, NY: Cornell University Press.

Hafner-Burton, E. M. (to appear). *Coercing Human Rights: Why Preferential Trade Agreements Regulate Repression*. Ithaca, NY: Cornell University Press.

Hafner-Burton, E. M. and Ron, J. (2007). Special issue on human rights, *Journal of Peace Research*, **44**/4.

Hafner-Burton, E. M. and Tsutsui, K. (2005). Human rights in a globalizing world: The paradox of empty promises. *American Journal of Sociology*, **110**/5, 1373–411.

Hafner-Burton, E. M. and Tsutsui, K (2007). Justice lost! The failure of international human rights law to matter where needed most. *Journal of Peace Research*, **44**/4, 407–25.

Hagan, J. and Palloni, A. (2006). Death in Darfur. *Science*, **313**/5793, 1578–9.

Hagan, J. and Rymond-Richmond, W. (2009). *Darfur and the Crime of Genocide*. New York: Cambridge University Press.

Hancock, A.-M. (2007). Intersectionality as a normative and empirical paradigm. *Politics & Gender*, **3**/2, 248–54.

Hancock, A.-M. (2011). *Solidarity Politics for Millennials: A Guide to Ending the Oppression Olympics*. New York: Palgrave Macmillan.

Hancock, J. (2003). *Environmental Human Rights: Power, Ethics and Law*. London: Ashgate.

Haney, C., Banks, W. C., and Zimbardo, P. G. (1973). Interpersonal dynamics in a simulated prison. *International Journal of Criminology and Penology*, **1**, 69–97.

Hanson, M. (1994). Democratisation and norm creation in Europe. *Adelphi Paper*, **34**/284, 28–41.

Haq, M. ul (1995). *Reflections on Human Development*. New York: Oxford University Press.

Hardin, G. (1977). *The Limits to Altruism*. Indianapolis, IN: Indiana University Press.

Hardt, M. and Negri, A. (2001). *Empire*. New York: Harvard University Press.

Harff, B. (2003). No lessons learned from the Holocaust? Assessing risks of genocide and political mass murder since 1955. *American Political Science Review*, **97**/1, 57–73.

Haritos-Fatouros, M. (1988). The official torturer: A learning model for obedience to the authority of violence. *Journal of Applied Social Psychology*, **18**/13, 1107–20.

Harrison, A. and Scorse, J. (2003). Globalization's impact on compliance with labor standards. *Brookings Trade Forum*, 45–82.

Harrison, G. (2004). *The World Bank and Africa: The Construction of Governance States*. London: Routledge.

Hart, J. (2006). Saving children: What role for anthropology? *Anthropology Today*, **22**/1, 5–8. http://www.jstor.org/stable/3695095.

Hart, J. (2008). Displaced children's participation in political violence: Towards greater understanding of mobilisation. *Conflict, Security & Development*, **8**/3, 277–93.

Hasselback, D. (2001). Lundins search for the big score. *Financial Post*, 22 June.

Hathaway, O. (2002). Do treaties make a difference? Human rights treaties and the problem of compliance. *Yale Law Journal*, **111**/8, 1932–2042.

Hathaway, O. (2007). Why do countries commit to human rights treaties? *Journal of Conflict Resolution*, **51**/4, 588–621.

Hauser, P. (ed.) (1961). *Urbanization in Latin America*. New York: Columbia University Press.

Havemann, P. (2005). Denial, modernity and exclusion: Indigenous placelessness in Australia. *Macquarie Law Journal*, **57**/5, 57–80.

Havemann, P. (2009). Ignoring the mercury in the climate change barometer: Denying Indigenous peoples' rights. *Australian Indigenous Law Review*, **13**/1, 2–26.

Hayner, P. (2001). *Unspeakable Truths*. New York: Routledge.

Hayner, P. (2002). *Unspeakable Truths: Facing the Challenges of Truth Commissions*. New York: Routledge.

Hayward, T. (2005). *Constitutional Environmental Rights*. Oxford: Oxford University Press.

Hechter, M. (2000). *Containing Nationalism*. Oxford: Oxford University Press.

Held, D. (1995). *Democracy and the Global Order: From the Modern State to Cosmopolitan Governance*. Cambridge: Polity.

Held, D. (1996). *Models of Democracy*. Stanford, CA: Stanford University Press.

Held, D. (2004). *Global Covenant: The Social Democratic Alternative to the Washington Consensus*. Cambridge: Polity.

Held, D. (2005). Democratic accountability and political effectiveness from a cosmopolitan perspective. *Global Governance and Public Accountability* (ed. D. Held and M. Koenig-Archibugi). Oxford: Blackwell Publishing.

Hempel, C. G. H. (1966). *The Philosophy of Natural Science*. Englewood Cliffs, NJ: Prentice Hall.

Henderson, C. W. (1991). Conditions affecting the use of political repression. *Journal of Conflict Resolution*, **35**/1, 120–42.

Henderson, C. W. (1993). Population pressures and political repression. *Social Science Quarterly*, **74**/2, 322–33.

Henkin, L. (1981). International human rights as 'rights'. *Human Rights* (ed. J. R. Pennock and J. W. Chapman). New York: New York University Press.

Hertel, S. (2006). *Unexpected Power: Conflict and Change among Transnational Activists*. Ithaca, NY: Cornell University Press.

Hertel, S. and Minkler, L. (eds) (2007). *Economic Rights: Conceptual, Measurement, and Policy Issues*. Cambridge: Cambridge University Press.

Hibbs, D. A. (1973). *Mass Political Violence: A Cross-National Causal Analysis*. New York: Wiley.

Hill, D. (2015). Is Bolivia going to frack Mother Earth? *The Guardian*, 24 February. http://www.theguardian.com/environment/andes-to-the-amazon/2015/feb/23/bolivia-frack-mother-earth.

Hill, D. and Z. Jones. 2014. 'An Empirical Evaluation of Explanations for State Repression.' *American Political Science Review* 108(3): 661–687.

Hill, K. (1994). *Democracy in the Fifty States*. Lincoln, NE: University of Nebraska Press.

Hirano, K. (2007). Government not persuaded—Ainu hope U.N. move aids Indigenous status quest. *The Japan Times*, 13 October. http://search.japantimes.co.jp/cgi-bin/nn20071013f1.html.

Hiskes, R. P. (2005). The right to a green future: Human rights, environmentalism, and intergenerational justice. *Human Rights Quarterly*, **27**/4, 1346–64.

Hiskes, R. P. (2009). *The Human Right to a Green Future*. Cambridge: Cambridge University Press.

Hitchcock, R. K. and Totten, S. (2010). *Genocide of Indigenous Peoples: Genocide—A Critical Bibliographic Review*. New Brunswick, NJ: Transaction Publishers.

Hitchens, C. (2008). Believe Me, It's Torture, *Vanity Fair*, August.

Hobbes, T. (1968 [1651]). *Leviathan*. New York: Penguin.

Hochschild, A. (1998). *King Leopold's Ghost: A Story of Greed, Terror, and Heroism in Colonial Africa*. New York: Houghton Mifflin.

Holder, C. and Reidy, D. (2013). *Human Rights: The Hard Questions*. Cambridge: Cambridge University Press.

Holmes, S. and Sunstein, C. R. (1999). *The Cost of Rights: Why Liberty Depends on Taxes*. New York: W. W. Norton.

Hopgood, S. (2014) *The Endtimes of Human Rights*. Ithaca, NY: Cornell University Press.

Horowitz, I. (1976). *Genocide: State Power and Mass Murder*. New Brunswick, NJ: Transaction Publishers.

Horowitz, I. (1997). *Taking Lives: Genocide and State Power*. New Brunswick, NJ: Transaction Publishers.

Hovil, L. and Lomo, Z. (2004). Working paper 11: Behind the violence: Causes, consequences and the search for solutions to the war in northern Uganda. Kampala: Refugee Law Project.

Hovil, L. and Lomo, Z. (2005). Working paper 15: Whose justice? Perceptions of Uganda's Amnesty Act 2000: The potential for conflict resolution and long-term reconciliation. Kampala: Refugee Law Project.

Howard, R. (1986). *Human Rights in Commonwealth Africa*. New Jersey: Rowman & Littlefield.

Howard-Hassmann, R. (2005). The second great transformation: Human rights leapfrogging in the era of globalization. *Human Rights Quarterly*, **27**/1, 1–40.

Howell, J. and Pearce, J. (2001). *Civil Society and Development: A Critical Exploration*. Boulder, CO: Lynne Rienner.

HRW (Human Rights Watch) (1999). Human rights trump sovereignty in 1999: Crimes against humanity provoke international action. 9 December. https://www.hrw.org/news/1999/12/09/human-rights-trump-sovereignty-1999.

HRW (Human Rights Watch) (2011). Historic decision at the United Nations (June 17). http://www.hrw.org/news/2011/06/17/historic-decision-united-nations (accessed 5 April 2014).

HRW (Human Rights Watch) (2012). *World Report 2012: Saudi Arabia*. Washington, DC: Human Rights Watch http://www.hrw.org/world-report-2012/world-report-2012-saudi-arabia.

HRW (Human Rights Watch) (2014a). Lesbian, gay, Bbisexual, and transgender rights. http://www.hrw.org/topic/lgbt-rights (accessed 5 April 2014).

HRW (Human Rights Watch) (2014b). 'Maybe We Live and Maybe We Die': Recruitment and Use of Children by Armed Groups in Syria. Washington, DC: Human Rights Watch. http://www.hrw.org/sites/default/files/reports/syria0614_crd_ForUpload.pdf.

Hulme, M. (2009). *Why We Disagree About Climate Change: Understanding Controversy, Inaction and Opportunity*. Cambridge: Cambridge University Press.

Human Rights Committee (1994). General comment 24 on issues relating to reservations made upon ratification or accession to the Covenant or the Optional Protocols thereto, or in relation to declarations under article 41 of the Covenant. New York: United Nations.

Human Rights First (no date a). Our Mission. www.humanrightsfirst.org/about-us/ (accessed 5 July 2013).

Human Rights First (no date b). LGBT Persons http://www.humanrightsfirst.org/our-work/fighting-discrimination/lgbt-persons/; LGBTI Refugees http://www.humanrightsfirst.org/our-work/refugee-protection/lgbti-refugees/ (accessed 5 July 2013).

Human security report (2005). Vancouver: Human Security Centre. http://www.humansecurityreport.info/.

Humphrey, M. (2007). *Ecological Politics and Democratic Theory: The Challenge of the Deliberative Ideal*. London: Routledge.

Humphreys, S. (2010). *Human Rights and Climate Change*. Cambridge: Cambridge University Press.

Hunt, L. (2007). *Inventing Human Rights: A History*. New York: W. W. Norton.

Huntington, S. (1968). *Political Order in Changing Societies*. New Haven, CT: Yale University Press.

Huntington, S. (1991). *The Third Wave: Democratization in the Late Twentieth Century*. Norman, OK: University of Oklahoma Press.

Huseman, J. and Short, D. (2012). 'A slow industrial genocide': Tar sands and the Indigenous peoples of northern Alberta. *The International Journal of Human Rights*, 16/1, 216–37.

Hyland, K. E. (2001). Protecting human victims of trafficking: An American framework. *Berkeley Women's Law Journal*, 16/1, 29–71.

Hynes, P., Lamb, M., Short, D., and Waites, M. (eds) (2011). *Sociology and Human Rights: New Engagements*. London: Routledge.

ICG (International Crisis Group) (2001). International criminal tribunal for Rwanda: Justice delayed. Africa report no. 30.

ICG (International Crisis Group) (2007). Darfur's new security reality. Africa report no. 134. http://www.genocidewatch.org/images/Sudan-26-Nov-07-Darfur_s_New_Security_Reality.pdf.

ICHRP (International Centre for Human Rights Policy) (2009). *Corruption and Human Rights: Making the Connection*. Geneva: ICHRP.

ICISS (International Commission on Intervention and State Sovereignty) (2001). *The Responsibility to Protect*. Ottawa: International Development Research Centre. http://responsibilitytoprotect.org/ICISS%20Report.pdf.

Ignatieff, M. (1998). *The Warrior's Honor: Ethnic War and the Modern Conscience*. New York: Chatto & Windus.

Ignatieff, M. (2001). Human rights as politics and idolatry. *Human Rights as Politics and Idolatry* (ed. Amy Gutmann). Princeton, NJ: Princeton University Press.

Ignatieff, M. (2004). *The Lesser Evil: Political Ethics in an Age of Terror*. Princeton, NJ: Princeton University Press.

Ignatieff, M. and Gutmann, A. (2001). *Human Rights as Politics and Idolatry*. Princeton, NJ: Princeton University Press.

IICK (Independent International Commission on Kosovo) (2000). *The Kosovo Report*. Oxford: Oxford University Press.

Ikenberry, J. (2001). *After Victory: Institutions, Strategic Restraint and the Rebuilding of Order After Major Wars*. Princeton, NJ: Princeton University Press.

Illich, I. (1997). Development as planned poverty. *The Post-Development Reader* (ed. M. Rahnema with V. Bawtree). London: Zed Books.

IMF (International Monetary Fund) (various years). Annual reports on exchange arrangements and exchange controls. Washington, DC: IMF.

Immigration Equality (2015). Immigration Basics: Thorny Issues in LGBT/H Asylum Cases. http://www.immigrationequality.org/get-legal-help/our-legal-resources/immigration-equality-asylum-manual/11-immigration-basics-thorny-issues-in-lgbth-asylum-cases/ (accessed 19 December 2015).

Inglehart, R. (1997). *Modernization and Postmodernization: Cultural, Political and Economic Change in 43 Societies*. Princeton, NJ: Princeton University Press.

Ingram, J. and Freestone, D. (2006). *Human Rights and Development: Development Outreach*. Washington, DC: World Bank Institute.

Institute for the Study of International Migration (ISIM) and Brookings-Bern Project (2008). Global database—guiding principles on internal displacement. http://www.idpguidingprinciples.org/.

International Gay and Lesbian Human Rights Commission (2012) IGLHRC Celebrates Historic UN Panel about Ending Violence and Discrimination Based on Sexuality Orientation and Gender Identity. https://www.outrightinternational.org/content/iglhrc-celebrates-historic-un-panel-about-ending-violence-and-discrimination-based-sexual (accessed 13 November 2013).

International Commission of Jurists and the International Service for Human Rights (no date). The Yogyakarta Principles. http://www.yogyakartaprinciples.org/ (accessed 31 May 2013).

International Gay and Lesbian Human Rights Commission (2013). *In Their Own Words: Documenting Violence and Discrimination against Lesbians, Bisexual Women, and Transgender People in Asia*. New York: IGLHRC.

International Gay and Lesbian Human Rights Commission (2014). http://iglhrc.org/ (accessed 30 June 2014).

International Lesbian, Gay, Bisexual, Transgender, Queer Youth and Student Organisation (2015a). http://www.iglyo.com/about/ (accessed 9 March 2015).

International Lesbian, Gay, Bisexual, Transgender, Queer Youth and Student Organisation (2015b). What we do. http://www.iglyo.com/what-we-do/advocacy/ (accessed 9 March 2015).

International Lesbian, Gay, Bisexual, Transgender, Queer Youth and Student Organisation (2015c).

State-Sponsored Homophobia. http://old.ilga. org/Statehomophobia/ILGA_State_Sponsored_ Homophobia_2015.pdf (accessed 19 December 2015).

International Military Tribunal at Nuremberg (1946). Nuremberg Trial proceedings. Vol. 1. Indictment: Count three—war crimes. http://avalon.law.yale. edu/imt/count3.asp.

International Working Group for Disease Monitoring and Forecasting (1995). Capture-recapture and multiple record systems estimation I: History and theoretical development. *American Journal of Epidemiology*, **142**/10, 1047–58.

IPCC (International Panel on Climate Change) (2014). Fifth Assessment Report—Synthesis for policy makers http://www.ipcc.ch/pdf/assessment-report/ ar5/syr/AR5_SYR_FINAL_SPM.pdf.

Irwin, M. A. (1996). 'White slavery' as metaphor: Anatomy of a moral panic. *Ex Post Facto: The History Journal*, **5**. http://www.walnet.org/csis/papers/ irwin-wslavery.html.

Ishay, M. (ed.) (1997). *The Human Rights Reader: Major Political Writings, Essays, Speeches, and Documents From the Bible to the Present*. New York: Routledge.

Ishay, M. R. (2004). *The History of Human Rights: From Ancient Times to the Globalization Era*. Berkeley, CA: University of California Press.

Jabine, T. B. and Claude, R. P. (eds) (1992). *Human Rights and Statistics: Getting the Record Straight*. Philadelphia, PA: University of Pennsylvania Press.

Jabri, V. (2007). *War and the Transformation of Global Politics*. Basingstoke: Palgrave.

Jackson, R. (1990). *Quasi-States: Sovereignty, International Relations and the Third World*. Cambridge: Cambridge University Press.

Jahic, G. and Finckenauer, J. O. (2005). Representations and misrepresentations of human trafficking. *Trends in Organized Crime*, **8**/3, 24–40.

James, A. and Prout, A. (eds) (1990). *Constructing and Reconstructing Childhood: Contemporary Issues in the Sociological Study of Childhood*. London: Routledge.

James, A. and Prout, A. (eds) (1997). *Constructing and Reconstructing Childhood: Contemporary Issues in the Sociological Study of Childhood* (2nd edn). London: Routledge.

Jay, Alexis (2014). *Independent Inquiry into Child Sexual Exploitation in Rotherham(1997-2013)*. Rotherham:

Rotherham Metropolitan Borough Council. http:// www.rotherham.gov.uk/downloads/file/1407/ independent_inquiry_cse_in_rotherham.

Johansson Dahre, U. (2010). There are no such things as universal human rights—On the predicament of Indigenous peoples, for example. *The International Journal of Human Rights*, **14**/4, 641–57.

Johnstone, D. (2003). *Fools' Crusade: Yugoslavia, NATO, and Western Delusions*. New York: Monthly Review Press.

Jolly, R. (1999). Human development and neoliberalism, paradigms compared. *Readings in Human Development* (ed. S. Fukuda-Parr and A. K. Shiva Kumar). New Delhi: Oxford University Press.

Jolly, R. (2004). Global goals: The United Nations experience. *Journal of Human Development*, **5**/1, 69–95.

Jones, B. (2001). *Peacemaking in Rwanda: The Dynamics of Failure*. Boulder, CO: Lynne Rienner.

Jones, P. (1999a). Group rights and group oppression. *The Journal of Political Philosophy*, **7**/4, 353–77.

Jones, P. (1999b). Human rights, group rights, and people's rights. *Human Rights Quarterly*, **21**/1, 80–107.

Jones, P. (ed.) (2008a). *Group Rights*. Aldershot: Ashgate.

Jones, P. (2008b). Group rights. *The Stanford Encyclopedia of Philosophy* (Winter edn) (ed. E. N. Zalta). http://plato.stanford.edu/entries/rights-group/.

Jordan-Zachery, J. S. (2007). Am I a black woman or a woman who is black? A few thoughts on the meaning of intersectionality. *Politics & Gender*, **3**/2, 254–63.

Junf, A., Knaup, H., Shafy, S., and Zand, B. (2015). The warming world: Is capitalism destroying our planet? *Speigal Online International*, 14 April. http://www. spiegel.de/international/world/climage-change-failed- efforts-to-combat-global-warming-a-1020406.html.

Kaase, M. and Newton, K. (1995). *Beliefs in Government*, Vol. V. Oxford: Oxford University Press.

Kaldor, M. (2003). *Global Civil Society: An Answer to War*. Cambridge: Polity.

Kalyvas, S. (2006). *The Logic of Violence in Civil War*. New York: Cambridge University Press.

Kamenka, E. (1978). The anatomy of an idea. *Human Rights* (ed. E. Kamenka and A. Erh-Soon Tay). Port Melbourne: Edward Arnold.

Kant, I. (1991). Perpetual peace: A philosophical sketch. *Political Writings* (ed. H. Reiss). Cambridge: Cambridge University Press.

Kant, I. (2002). *Groundwork for the Metaphysics of Morals* (trans. A. W. Wood). New Haven, CT: Yale University Press.

Kanyongo, G. Y. (2005). Zimbabwe's public education system reforms: Successes and challenges. *International Education Journal*, **6**/1, 65–74.

Kaoma, K. (2014). Warning: US LGBTQ organizations falling into Uganda's anti-homosexuality trap. *Political Research Associates*, February 20. http://www.politicalresearch.org/2014/02/20/warning-u-s-lgbtq-organizations-falling-into-ugandas-anti-homosexuality-trap/ (accessed 21 February 2014).

Karklins, R. and Petersen, R. (1993). Decision calculus of protesters and regimes: Eastern Europe 1989. *Journal of Politics*, **55**/3, 588–614.

Keal, P. (2003). *European Conquest and the Rights of Indigenous Peoples: The Moral Backwardness of International Society*. Cambridge: Cambridge University Press.

Keating, C. (2013). On the interplay of state homophobia and state homoprotectionism. *Global Homophobia: States, Movements, and the Politics of Oppression* (ed. M. L. Weiss and M. J. Bosia). Urbana, IL: University of Illinois Press.

Keck, M. E. and Sikkink, K. (1998). *Activists Beyond Borders: Advocacy Networks in International Politics*. Ithaca, NY: Cornell University Press.

Keller-Herzog, A. (1996). Globalisation and gender: Development perspectives and interventions. Discussion paper: Women in Development and Gender Equity Division Policy Branch. Canada: Canadian International Development Agency.

Kempadoo, K. (ed.) (2005a). *Trafficking and Prostitution Reconsidered*. Boulder, CO: Paradigm Publishers.

Kempadoo, K. (2005b). From moral panic to global justice: Changing perspectives on trafficking. *Trafficking and Prostitution Reconsidered* (ed. K. Kempadoo). Boulder, CO: Paradigm Publishers.

Kenen, P. B. (1994). *The International Economy* (3rd edn). Cambridge: Cambridge University Press.

Khiddu-Makubuya, E. (1989). Paramilitarism and human rights. *Conflict Resolution in Uganda* (ed. K. Rupesinghe). Oslo: International Peace Research Institute.

Kiernan, B. (2007). *Blood and Soil: A World History of Genocide and Extermination from Sparta to Darfur*. New Haven, CT: Yale University Press.

Kim Dae, J. (1994). Is culture destiny: The myth of Asia's anti-democratic values; a response to Lee Kuan Yew. *Foreign Affairs*, **73**/6, 189+.

King, J. (2000). Exploring the ameliorating effects of democracy on political repression: Cross-national evidence. *Paths to State Repression: Human Rights Violations and Contentious Politics* (ed. C. Davenport). Boulder, CO: Rowman and Littlefield.

King, M. (1997). *A Better World for Children? Explorations in Morality and Authority*. London: Routledge.

Kinley, D. and Joseph, S. (2002). Multinational corporations and human rights. *Alternative Law Journal*, **27**/1, 7–11.

Kirmayer, L. J. and Valaskakis, G. G. (eds) (2009). *Healing Traditions*. Vancouver: PN UBC Press.

Kirsch, P. and Holmes, J. T. (1999). The birth of the International Criminal Court: The 1998 Rome conference. *Canadian Yearbook of International Law*, **36**, 3–39.

Kishlansky, M.C et al. (1995). *Civilizations in the West*. New York: HarperCollins.

Klein, N. (2014). *This Changes Everything: Capitalism vs the Climate*. New York: Simon & Schuster.

Koch, I. E. (2009). *Human Rights as Indivisible Rights: The Protection of Socio-Economic Demands under the European Convention on Human Rights*. Dordrecht: Martinus Nijhoff.

Kollman, K. and Waites, M. (2009). The global politics of lesbian, gay, bisexual and transgender human rights: An introduction. *Contemporary Politics*, **15**/1, 1–17.

Kopecky, P. and Mudde, C. (eds) (2003). *Uncivil Society? Contentious Politics in Post-Communist Europe*. London: Routledge.

Korey, W. (1999). Human rights NGOs: The power of persuasion. *Ethics and International Affairs*, **13**/1, 151–74.

Kramer, P. (2008). The water cure. *The New Yorker*, 25 February.

Kramnick, I. (ed.) (1995). *The Portable Enlightenment Reader*. London: Penguin.

Krasner, S. (1999). *Sovereignty: Organized Hypocrisy*. Princeton, NJ: Princeton University Press.

Kraut, A. (1996). *Records of the Immigration and Naturalization Service. Series A: Subject Correspondence Files. Part 5: Prostitution and 'White Slavery,' 1902–1933*. Bethesda, MD: University Publications of America.

Kritz, N. J. (ed.) (1995). *Transitional Justice: How Emerging Democracies Reckon with Former Regimes*. Washington, DC: United States Institute of Peace Press.

Kucera, D. (2001). The effects of core workers rights on labour costs and foreign direct investment: Evaluating the conventional wisdom. IILS working paper no. 130. International Labour Organization. http://ssrn.com/abstract=313079.

Kuper, A. (1999). *Culture: The Anthropologists' Account*. Cambridge, MA: Harvard University Press.

Kuper, L. (1981). *Genocide: Its Political Use in the Twentieth Century*. New Haven, CT: Yale University Press.

Kuperman, A. (2001). *The Limits of Humanitarian Intervention: Genocide in Rwanda*. Washington, DC: Brookings Institution Press.

Kuperman, A. (2008). The moral hazard of humanitarian intervention: Lessons from the Balkans. *International Studies Quarterly*, **52**/1, 49–80.

Kuperman, A. (2011). False pretense for war in Libya? *Boston Globe*, 14 April, A19. www.boston.com/bostonglobe/editorial_opinion/oped/articles/2011/04/14/false_pretense_for_war_in_libya/.

Kuperman, A. (2013). A model humanitarian intervention? Reassessing NATO's Libya campaign. *International Security*, **38**/1, 105–36.

Kuperman, A. (2015). Obama's Libya debacle: How a well-meaning intervention ended in failure. *Foreign Affairs*, **94**/2, 66–77.

Kurzman, C. (1998). Introduction: Liberal Islam and its Islamic context. *Liberal Islam: A Sourcebook* (ed. C. Kurzman). Oxford: Oxford University Press.

Kurzman, C. (1999). Liberal Islam, prospects and challenges. *Middle East Review of International Affairs*, **3**/3 September, 11-19.

Kymlicka, W. (1995). *Multicultural Citizenship: A Liberal Theory of Minority Rights*. Oxford: Oxford University Press.

Laïdi, Z. (1998). *A World Without Meaning: The Crisis of Meaning in International Relations*. London: Routledge.

Lamony, S. A. (2014). International Justice and the ICC: Neither 'Europe's Court for Africa' nor 'Africa's Court'. *Debating The Endtimes of Human Rights* (ed. D. Lettinga and L. van Troos). Amsterdam: Amnesty International Netherlands.

Landau, D. (2012). The reality of social rights enforcement. *Harvard International Law Journal*, **53**/1, 401–59.

Landau Commission Report (1989). *Israel Law Review*, **23**/2-3.

Landman, T. (2002). Comparative politics and human rights. *Human Rights Quarterly*, **24**/4, 890–923.

Landman, T. (2004). Measuring human rights: Principle, practice, and policy. *Human Rights Quarterly*, **26**/4, 906–31.

Landman, T. (2005a). Review article: The political science of human rights. *British Journal of Political Science*, **35**/3, 549–72.

Landman, T. (2005b). *Protecting Human Rights: A Global Comparative Study*. Washington, DC: Georgetown University Press.

Landman, T. (2006a). Holding the line: Human rights defenders in the age of terror. *British Journal of Politics and International Relations*, **8**/2, 123–47.

Landman, T. (2006b). *Studying Human Rights*. London: Routledge.

Landman, T. (2013). *Human Rights and Democracy: The Precarious Triumph of Ideals*. London: Bloomsbury Academic.

Landman, T. (2015). *Issues and Methods in Comparative Politics: An Introduction*. London and Oxford: Routledge.

Landman, T. and Carvalho, E. (2009). *Measuring Human Rights*. London and Oxford: Routledge.

Landman, T. and Häusermann, J. (2003). Map-making and analysis of the main international initiatives on developing indicators on democracy and good governance. Report for the Statistical Office of the Commission of the European Communities (EUROSTAT). Human Rights Centre, University of Essex.

Landman, T., Kernohan, D., and Gohdes, A. (2012). Relativising human rights. *Journal of Human Rights*, **11**/4, 460–85.

Langbein, J. H. (1977). *Torture and the Law of Proof: Europe and England in the Ancien Régime*. Chicago, IL: University of Chicago Press.

Langlaude, S. (2010). The rights of religious associations to external relations: A comparative study of the OSCE and the Council of Europe. *Human Rights Quarterly*, **32**/3, 502–29.

Langlaude, S. (2011). The rights of religious associations to external relations: A comparative study of the OSCE and the Council of Europe. *Human Rights Quarterly*, **32**/3, 502–29.

Langlois, A. J. (2001). *The Politics of Justice and Human Rights*. Cambridge: Cambridge University Press.

Langlois, A. J. (2004). The elusive ontology of human rights. *Global Society*, **18**/3, 243–61.

Langlois, A. J. (2009). Normative and theoretical foundations of human rights. *Human Rights: Politics and Practice* (1st edn) (ed. M. Goodhart). Oxford: Oxford University Press.

Las Casas, B. de (1992). *The Devastation of the Indies: A Brief Account.* Baltimore, MD: Johns Hopkins University Press.

Lattimer, M. (2010). Peoples under threat 2010 (ed. Preti Taneja). *State of the World's Minorities and Indigenous Peoples.* London: Minority Rights Group. http://minorityrights.org/publications/state-of-the-worlds-minorities-and-indigenous-peoples-2010-july-2010/.

Laughland, J. (2007). *Travesty: The Trial of Slobodan Milošević and the Corruption of International Justice.* London: Pluto.

Lauren, P. G. (1998). *The Evolution of International Human Rights: Visions Seen.* Philadelphia, PA: University of Pennsylvania Press.

Lautsi v. Italy. (2011) (Judgment of 3 November 2009). No. 30814/06 [*Lautisi I*]; GC Judgment of 18 March 2011 [*Lautsi II*].

Layla Şahin v. Turkey. (10 November 2005). European Court of Human Rights. No. 44774/98.

Leader, N. (1998). Proliferating principles; or how to sup with the Devil without getting eaten. *Disasters,* **22**/4, 288–308.

League of Nations (1926). Slavery, servitude, forced labour and similar institutions and practices: Convention of 1926 (Slavery Convention of 1926). 60 L.N.T.S. 253. Entered into force 9 March 1927.

Lechner, F. J. and Boli, J. (eds) (2004). *The Globalization Reader.* Malden, MA: Blackwell.

Lee, E., Bristow, J., Faircloth, C., and Macvarish, J. (eds) (2014). *Parenting Culture Studies.* Basingstoke: Palgrave.

Lemarchand, R. (1970). *Rwanda and Burundi.* London: Pall Mall.

Lemkin, R. (1944). *Axis Rule in Occupied Europe: Laws of Occupation, Analysis of Government, Proposals for Redress.* New York: Columbia.

Lemkin, R. (1947). Genocide as a crime under international law. *American Journal of International Law,* **41**/1, 145–51.

Lercher, A. (2007). Are there any environmental rights? *Environmental Values,* **16**/3, 355–68.

Lerner, D. (1958). *The Passing of Traditional Society: Modernizing the Middle East.* Glencoe, IL: Free Press.

Lerner, D. (1967). Comparative analysis of processes of modernisation. *The City in Modern Africa* (ed. H. Miner). London: Pall Mall.

Lesch, A. (1998). *The Sudan: Contested National Identities.* Bloomington, IN: Indiana University Press.

Levene, M. (2005). *Genocide in the Age of the Nation State.* London: I. B. Tauris.

Levin, M. (1982). The case for torture. *Newsweek,* 7 June.

LeVine, R., Klein, N., and Owen, C. (1967). Father-child relationships and changing life-styles in Ibadan, Nigeria. *The City in Modern Africa* (ed. H. Miner). London: Pall Mall.

Levinson, S. (ed.) (2004). *Torture: A Collection.* Oxford: Oxford University Press.

Levitsky, S. and Way, L. (2002). The rise of competitive authoritarianism. *Journal of Democracy,* **13**/2, 51–65.

Lewis, D. (2002). Civil society in African contexts: Reflections on the usefulness of a concept. *Development and Change,* **33**/4, 569–86.

Lewis, N. (1998). Human rights, law and democracy in an unfree world. *Human Rights Fifty Years On: An Appraisal* (ed. T. Evans). Manchester: Manchester University Press.

Li, Q. and Resnick, A. (2003). Reversal of fortunes: Democratic institutions and foreign direct investment inflows to developing countries. *International Organization,* **57**/1, 1–37.

Lichbach, M. I. (1995). *The Rebel's Dilemma.* Ann Arbor, MI: University of Michigan Press.

Lijnzaad, L. (1995). *Reservations to UN-Human Rights Treaties: Ratify and Ruin?* The Hague: Martinus Nijhoff.

Likosky, M. (2003). Mitigating human rights risks under state-financed and privatized infrastructure projects. *Indiana Journal of Global Legal Studies,* **10**/2, 65–85.

Lim, L. L. (ed.) (1998). *The Sex Sector.* Geneva: International Labour Office.

Lipschutz, R. D. and Rowe, J. K. (2005). *Regulation for the Rest of Us? Globalization, Governmentality, and Global Politics.* London: Routledge

Lipset, S. M. (1959). Some social requisites of democracy: Economic development and political legitimacy. *American Political Science Review,* **53**/1, 69–105.

Locke, J. (1952). *The Second Treatise of Government* (ed. T. P. Peardon). Indianapolis, IN: Bobbs-Merrill.

Locke, J. (1960). *Two Treatises of Government*. Cambridge: Cambridge University Press.

Locke, J. (1988 [1688]). *Two Treatises of Government*. Cambridge: Cambridge University Press.

Loescher, G. (2001). *The UNHCR and World Politics: A Perilous Path*. Oxford: Oxford University Press.

Loescher, G., Milner, J., Newman, E., and Troeller, G. (eds) (2008). *Protracted Refugee Situations: Political, Security and Human Rights Implications*. Tokyo: United Nations University Press.

Loftin, C. M. (2012). *Masked Voices: Gay Men and Lesbians in Cold War America*. New York: SUNY.

Long, L. D. (2004). Anthropological perspectives on the trafficking of women for sexual exploitation. *International Migration*, **42**/1, 5–31.

Lowen, M. (2014). Islamic State crisis: The 13-year-old on 'righteous path'. BBC, 6 November. http://www.bbc.co.uk/news/world-middle-east-29921816.

Luttwak, E. (1999). Give war a chance. *Foreign Affairs*, **78**/4, 36–44.

Lutz-Bachmann, M. and Nascimento, A. (eds) (2014). *Human Rights, Human Dignity, and Cosmopolitan Ideals: Essays on Critical Theory and Human Rights*. Burlington, VT: Ashgate.

Lyman, P. N. and Beecroft, R. M. (2014). *Using Special Envoys in High-Stakes Conflict Diplomacy*. Washington, DC: United States Institute of Peace.

Maastricht Guidelines on Violations of Economic, Social and Cultural Rights (1997). Maastricht, 22–6 January. https://www.escr-net.org/docs/i/425804.

McCall, L. (2005). The complexity of intersectionality. *Signs: Journal of Women in Culture and Society*, **30**/3, 1771–800.

McCamant, J. F. (1981). Social science and human rights. *International Organization*, **35**/3, 531–52.

Macchi, M. with Oviedo, G., Gotheil, S., Cross, K., Boedhihartono, A., Wolfangel, C., and Howell, M. (2008). Indigenous and traditional peoples and climate change—Issues paper, March. Gland: IUCN. http://cmsdata.iucn.org/downloads/indigenous_peoples_climate_change.pdf.

McCorquodale, R. and Fairbrother, R. (1999). Globalization and human rights. *Human Rights Quarterly*, **21**/3, 735–66.

McGillivray, Anne (1994). Why children do have equal rights: In reply to Laura Purdy. *The International Journal of Children's Rights*. **2**/3, 243–58.

MacKenzie, L. (1993). *Peacekeeper: The Road to Sarajevo*. Vancouver: Douglas & McIntyre.

MacKinnon, C. (1987). *Feminism Unmodified: Discourses on Life and Law*. Cambridge, MA: Harvard University Press.

MacKinnon, C. (1993). Crimes of war, crimes of peace. *On Human Rights: The Oxford Amnesty Lectures* (ed. S. Shute and S. L. Hurley). New York: Basic Books.

Macklin, R. (1981). Can future generations correctly be said to have rights? *Responsibilities to Future Generations* (ed. E. Partridge). Buffalo, NY: Prometheus Books.

MacMahon, P. (2007). Parties reject call for legal smacking ban. *Scotsman*, 23 January. Mahoney, J. (2007). *The Challenge of Human Rights*. Oxford: Blackwell Publishing.

Malik, S. and Siddique, H. (2015). 'Britain's youngest suicide bomber' mourned by West Yorkshire family. *The Guardian*, 15 June 2015. www.theguardian.com/world/2015/jun/14/west-yorkshire-teenager-talha-asmal-britain-youngest-suicide-bomber.

Malinowski, B. (1945). *The Dynamics of Culture Change: An Inquiry into Race Relations in Africa* (ed. Phyllis M. Kaberry). New Haven: Yale University Press.

Mamdani, M. (2001). *When Victims Become Killers: Colonialism, Nativism, and the Genocide in Rwanda*. Princeton, NJ: Princeton University Press.

Mani, R. (2008). Editorial: Dilemmas of expanding transitional justice, or forging the nexus between transitional justice and development. *International Journal of Transitional Justice*, **2**/3, 253–65.

Mann, M. (2005). *The Dark Side of Democracy: Explaining Ethnic Cleansing*. New York: Cambridge University Press.

Marcuse, H. (1964). *One Dimensional Man: Studies in the Ideology of Advanced Industrial Society*. London: Routledge.

Maritain, J. (1947). The possibilities for co-operation in a divided world. Inaugural address to the Second International Conference of UNESCO, 6 November.

Maritain, J. (1949). Introduction. *Human Rights: Comments and Interpretations*. New York: Columbia University Press.

Marshall, G. (2014). *Don't Even Think About it: Why Our Brains are Wired to Ignore Climate Change*. New York: Bloomsbury.

Marshall, M. G. and Jaggers, K. (2000). Polity IV Project: Political regime characteristics and transitions, 1800-1999. Data users manual.

Marshall, T. H. (1965). Citizenship and social class. *Sociology at the Crossroads and Other Essays*. London: Heinemann.

Martinez, J. (2008). Antislavery courts and the dawn of international human rights law. *Yale Law Journal*, **117**/4, 550–641.

Martinez-Alier, J. (2003). Mining conflicts, environmental justice, and valuation. *Just Sustainabilities: Development in an Unequal World* (ed. J. Agyeman, R. D. Bullard, and B. Evans). London: Earthscan.

Martinez-Cobo, J. (1986). Study of the problem of discrimination against Indigenous populations. UN Doc. E/CN.4/Sub.2/1986/7 and Add. 1–4, paragraph 379. http://www.un.org/esa/socdev/unpfii/documents/MCS_xvii_en.pdf.

Marx, K. (1987). On 'the Jewish question'. *Nonsense Upon Stilts: Bentham, Burke and Marx on the Rights of Man* (ed. J. Waldron). London: Methuen.

Marx, K. (1990). *Capital: A Critique of Political Economy*, Vol. I. London: Penguin.

Maxfield, S. (1998). Understanding the political implications of financial internationalization in emerging market countries. *World Development*, **26**/7, 1201–19.

May, J. D'Arcy. (2012). A Mounting East-West Tension: Buddhist-Christian Dialogue on Human Rights, Social Justice, and a Global Ethic (Review). *Buddhist-Christian Studies*, 32/1, 167–71.

May, M. (2006). San Francisco is hub for trafficking for sexual exploitation. *San Francisco Chronicle*, 6 November.

Mayer, A. E. (2007). The Islam and human rights nexus: Shifting dimensions. *Muslim World Journal of Human Rights*, 4/1, 1–27.

Mead, M. (ed.) (1953). *Cultural Patterns and Technical Change*. Paris: UNESCO with the World Federation for Mental Health.

Mead, M. and Wolfenstein, M. (1955). *Childhood in Contemporary Cultures*. Chicago, IL: Chicago University Press.

Mears, R. R. (1995). The impact of globalization on women and work in the Americas. Women's Rights Committee Inter-American Bar Association Conference, Quito, Ecuador.

Medcalf, L. (1978). *Law and Identity: Lawyers, Native Americans and Legal Practice*. Beverly Hills, CA: Sage.

Medway Council (2015). Medway Council v A & Ors (Learning Disability; Foster Placement) [2015] EWFC B66 (2 June 2015). http://www.bailii.org/ew/cases/EWFC/OJ/2015/B66.html.

Meijknecht, A. (2001). *Towards International Personality: The Position of Minorities and Indigenous Peoples in International Law*. Antwerp: Intersentia.

Melson, R. (1992). *Revolution and Genocide: On the Origins of the Armenian Genocide and the Holocaust*. Chicago, IL: University of Chicago Press.

Mendus, S. (1995). Human rights in political theory. *Political Studies*, **43**/Special issue, 10–24.

Merrills, J. G. (1996). Environmental protection and human rights: Conceptual aspects. *Human Rights Approaches to Environmental Protection* (ed. A. E. Boyle and M. R. Anderson). Oxford: Clarendon.

Merry, S. E. (2005). *Human Rights and Gender Violence: Translating International Law into Local Justice*. Chicago, IL: University of Chicago Press.

Merry, S. E. (2006). Transnational human rights and local activism: Mapping the middle. *American Anthropologist*, 'In focus: Anthropology and human rights in a new key', **108**/1, 38–51.

Mertus, J. (2009). *The United Nations and Human Rights: A Guide for a New Era*. London: Routledge.

Meyer, W. H. (1996). Human rights and MNCs: Theory versus quantitative analysis. *Human Rights Quarterly*, **18**/2, 368–97.

Meyer, W. H. (1998). *Human Rights and International Political Economy in Third World Nations*. Westport, CT: Praeger.

Midlarsky, M. (2005). *The Killing Trap: Genocide in the Twentieth Century*. New York: Cambridge University Press.

Miéville, C. (2005). *Between Equal Rights: A Marxist Theory of International Law*. Leiden and Boston: Brill.

Milanović, D. (1992). *Postmodern Law and Disorder*. Liverpool: Deborah Charles Publications.

Milgram, S. (1974). *Obedience to Authority: An Experimental View*. New York: Harper Collins.

Mill, J. S. (1972). On liberty. *John Stuart Mill: Utilitarianism, on Liberty, Considerations on Representative Government* (ed. H. B. Acton). London: Everyman.

Mill, J. S. (1985). *On Liberty*. London: Penguin.

Miller, R., Ruru, J., Behrendt, L., and Lindberg, T. (2012). *Discovering Indigenous Lands: The Doctrine of Discovery in the English Colonies*. Oxford: Oxford University Press.

Mills, C. W. (1997). *The Racial Contract*. Ithaca, NY: Cornell University Press.

Milner, W., Poe, S., and Leblang, D. (1999). Security rights, subsistence rights, and liberties: A theoretical survey of the empirical landscape. *Human Rights Quarterly*, **21**/2, 403–44.

Minogue, K. (1979). The history of the idea of human rights. *The Human Rights Reader* (ed. W. Laquer and B. Rubin). New York: New Amsterdam Library.

Minow, M. (1990). *Making All the Difference: Inclusion, Exclusion and American Law*. Ithaca, NY: Cornell University Press.

Minow, M. (1998). *Between Vengeance and Forgiveness*. Boston, MA: Beacon.

Mitchell, C., Stohl, M., Carleton, D., and Lopez, G. (1986). State terrorism: Issues of concept and measurement. *Government Violence and Repression: An Agenda for Research* (ed. M. Stohl and G. Lopez). New York: Greenwood.

Mitchell, N. J. and McCormick, J. M. (1988). Economic and political explanations of human rights violations. *World Politics*, **40**/4, 476–98.

Moghadam, V. M. (1993). *Gender Dynamics of Restructuring in the Semi-Periphery*. WIDER Research for Action Series. New York: United Nations University.

Mokhtari, S. (October 2004). The search for human rights within an Islamic framework in Iran. *The Muslim World*, **94**/4, 469–79.

Monshipouri, M., Welch, C., and Kennedy, E. (2003). Multinational corporations and the ethics of global responsibility: Problems and possibilities. *Human Rights Quarterly*, **25**/4, 965–89.

Montesquieu, Baron de (1949 [1748]).*The Spirit of the Laws*. New York: Hafner Publishing.

Moravscik, A. (2000). The origins of human rights regimes: Democratic delegation in postwar Europe. *International Organization*, **54**/2, 217–52.

Morgan, R. (2004). Advancing Indigenous rights at the United Nations: Strategic framing and its impact on the normative development of international law. *Social and Legal Studies*, **13**/4, 481–500.

Morgenthau, H. (1948). *Politics Among Nations*. New York: Knopf.

Morris, L. (2006). Sociology and rights: An emergent field. *Rights: Sociological Perspectives* (ed. L. Morris). New York: Routledge.

Morsink, J. (1999). Cultural genocide, the universal declaration, and minority rights. *Human Rights Quarterly*, **21**/4, 1009–60.

Morsink, J. (2000). *The Universal Declaration of Human Rights: Origins, Drafting, and Intent*. Philadelphia, PA: University of Pennsylvania Press.

Moyn, S. (2010). *The Last Utopia: Human Rights in History*. Cambridge, MA: Belknap Press of Harvard University.

Moyn, S. (2014). A powerless companion: Human rights in the age of neoliberalism. *Law and Contemporary Problems*, **77**/4, 147–69.

Muehlebach, A. (2003). What self in self-determination? Notes from the frontiers of transnational Indigenous activism. *Identities: Global Studies in Culture and Power*, **10**/2, 241–68.

Muller, E. N. (1985). Income inequality, regime repressiveness, and political violence. *American Sociological Review*, **50**/1, 47–61.

Munck, G. and Verkuilen, J. (2002). Conceptualizing and measuring democracy: Evaluating alternative indices. *Comparative Political Studies*, **35**/1, 5–35.

Murdie, A. and Peksen, D. (2013). The impact of human rights INGO activities on economic sanctions. *Review of International Organizations*, **8**/1, 33–53.

Murdie, A. and Peksen, D. (2014). The impact of human rights INGO shaming on humanitarian interventions. *Journal of Politics*, **76**/1, 215–28.

Murray, A. F. (2008). *From Outrage to Courage: Women Taking Action for Health and Justice*. Monroe, ME: Common Courage Press.

Murray, P. (1951). *State Laws on Race and Color*. Athens, GA: University of Georgia Press.

Museveni, Y. K. (1997). *Sowing the Mustard Seed*. London: Macmillan.

Mutua, M. W. (1996). The ideology of human rights. *Virginia Journal of International Law*, 36, 589–657.

Mutua, M. (2001). Savages, victims and saviours: The metaphor of human rights. *Harvard International Law Journal*, **42**/1, 201–45.

Mutua M. (2013). *Human Rights: A Political and Cultural Critique*. Philadelphia, PA: University of Pennsylvania Press.

Muzaffar, C. (2002). *Rights, Religion, and Reform: Enhancing Human Dignity through Spiritual and Moral Transformation*. London: Routledge.

Nagel, T. (1979). *Mortal Questions*. Cambridge: Cambridge University Press.

Narayan, D. with Patel, R., Schafft, K., Radenmacher, A., and Koch-Schulte, S. (2000). *Voices of the Poor: Can Anyone Hear Us?* Oxford: Oxford University Press.

Narayan, D., Chambers, R., Kaul Shah, M., and Petesch, P. (eds) (2000). *Voices of the Poor: Crying Out for Change*. Oxford: Oxford University Press.

Narayan, U. (1997). *Dislocating Cultures: Identities, Traditions, and Third-World Feminism*. New York: Routledge.

Narayan, U. (1998). Essence of culture and a sense of history: A feminist critique of cultural essentialism. *Hypatia*, **13**/2, 86–106.

Neal, D. and Rick, A. (2014). The prison boom and the lack of black progress after Smith and Welch. NBER Working Paper No. 20283. http://www.nber.org/papers/w20283.pdf.

Neier, A. (2003). *Taking Liberties: Four Decades in the Struggle for Rights*. New York: Public Affairs.

Nell, V. (2006). Cruelty's rewards: The gratifications of perpetrators and spectators. *Behavioral and Brain Sciences*, **29**/3, 211–24.

Nelson, J. (1969). *Migrants, Urban Poverty, and Instability in Developing Nations*. Occasional Papers in International Affairs, 22 Cambridge, MA: Center for International Affairs, Harvard University.

Nelson, J. M. (1987). Political participation. *Understanding Political Development* (ed. M. Weiner and S. Huntington). London: Little, Brown.

Nelson, P. and Dorsey, E. (2003). At the nexus of human rights and development: New methods and strategies of global NGOs. *World Development*, **31**/12, 2013–26.

Neumann, F. (1996). The concept of political freedom. *The Rule of Law under Siege: Selected Essays of Franz L. Neumann and Otto Kirchheimer* (ed. S. William and S. Scheuerman). Berkeley, CA: University of California Press.

Neumayer, E. (2005). Do international human rights treaties improve respect for human rights? *Journal of Conflict Resolution*, **49**/6, 925–53.

new economics foundation (2006). *The UK Interdependence Report: How the World Sustains the Nation's Lifestyles and the Price it Pays*. London: new economics foundation.

Newbury, C. (1988). *The Cohesion of Oppression: Clientship and Ethnicity in Rwanda, 1860-1960*. New York: Columbia.

Nickel, J. W. (1993). The human right to a safe environment. *Yale Journal of International Law*, **18**/1, 281–95.

Nickel, J. W. (2007). *Making Sense of Human Rights* (2nd edn). Oxford: Blackwell Publishing.

Nieuwenhuys, O. (2000). The household economy and the commercial exploitation of children's work: The case of Kerala. *The Exploited Child* (ed. B. Schlemmer). London: Zed Books.

Nieuwenhuys, O. (2001). By the sweat of their brow? Street children, NGOs and children's rights in Addis Ababa. *Africa*, **71**/4, 539–57.

Niezen, R. (2003). *The Origins of Indigenism*. Berkeley, CA: University of California Press.

Nino, C. S. (1991). *The Ethics of Human Rights*. Oxford: Oxford University Press.

Nitzan, J. and Bichler, S. (2000). Capital accumulation: Breaking the dualism of 'economics' and 'politics'. *Global Political Economy: Contemporary Theories* (ed. R. Palan). London: Routledge.

North, D. (1990). *Institution, Institutional Change and Economic Performance*. Cambridge: Cambridge University Press.

Nuccitelli, D. (2015). *Climatology versus Pseudoscience: Exposing the Failed Predictions of Global Warming Skeptics*. Santa Barbara: Praeger.

Nussbaum, M. (1997a). Capabilities and human rights. *Fordham Law Review*, 66. Reprinted in Hayden, P. (ed.) (2001). *The Philosophy of Human Rights*. St Paul, MN: Paragon House.

Nussbaum, M. (1997b). Human rights theory: Capabilities and human rights. *Fordham Law Review*, **66**, 273–300.

Nussbaum, M. (2000a). Aristotle, politics, and human capabilities: A response to Antony, Arneson, Charlesworth, and Mulgan. *Ethics*, **111**/1, 102–40.

Nussbaum, M. (2000b). *Women and Human Development: The Capabilities Approach*. Cambridge: Cambridge University Press.

Nussbaum, M. C. (2010). *Liberty of Conscience: In Defense of America's Tradition of Religious Equality*. New York: Basic Books.

Nussbaum, M. C. (2012). *The New Religious Intolerance: Overcoming the Politics of Fear in an Anxious Age*. Cambridge, MA, and London: The Belknap Press of Harvard University Press.

Nwankwo, E., Phillips, N., and Tracey, P. (2007). Social investment through community enterprise: The case of multinational corporations involvement in the development of Nigerian water resources. *Journal of Business Ethics*, **73**/1, 91–101.

OAU (Organisation of African Unity) (1990). African Charter on the Rights and Welfare of the Child. OAU Doc. CAB/LEG/24.9/49 (1990). Entered into force 29 November, 1999.

OAU (Organisation of African Unity) (2000). Rwanda: The preventable genocide. The report of the International Panel of Eminent Personalities to investigate the 1994 genocide in Rwanda and the surrounding events. Presented by Sir Ketumile Masire. xxii, 318 S. Addis Ababa: Organization of African Unity/IPEP.

Oberleitner, G. (2007). *Global Human Rights Institutions*. Cambridge: Polity.

OECD (Organisation for Economic Co-operation and Development) (1996). *Shaping the 21st Century: The Contribution of Development Co-operation*. Paris: PN OECD.

OECD/DAC (Organisation for Economic Co-operation and Development/Development Assistance Committee) (2007). DAC Action-oriented paper on human rights and development. DCD/DAC (2007) 15. Paris: OECD.

Ofcansky, T. P. (1996). *Uganda: Tarnished Pearl of Africa*. Boulder, CO: Westview.

OHCHR (Office of the High Commissioner for Human Rights) (1993). Fact sheet no. 19, National Institutions for the Promotion and Protection of Human Rights. http://www.ohchr.org/Documents/Publications/FactSheet19en.pdf.

OHCHR (Office of the High Commissioner for Human Rights) (2004). *Human Rights and Poverty Reduction: A Conceptual Framework*. New York: United Nations. http://www.ohchr.org/Documents/Publications/PovertyReductionen.pdf.

OHCHR (Office of the High Commissioner for Human Rights) (2006). *Frequently Asked Questions on a Human Rights-Based Approach to Development Co-operation*. New York: United Nations. http://www.ohchr.org/Documents/Publications/FAQen.pdf.

OHCHR (Office of the High Commissioner for Human Rights) (2007). Mary Robinson, United Nations High Commissioner for Human Rights (1997–2002). http://www.unhchr.ch/html/hchr/unhc.htm.

OHCHR (Office of the High Commissioner for Human Rights) (2008). *Claiming the Millennium Development Goals: A Human Rights Approach*. New York: United Nations.

OHCHR (Office of the High Commissioner for Human Rights) (2012). *Born Free and Equal: Sexual Orientation and Gender Identity in International Human Rights Law*. New York and Geneva: OHCHR. http://www.ohchr.org/Documents/Publications/BornFreeAndEqualLowRes.pdf.

Olson, M. (1993). Dictatorship, democracy and development. *American Political Science Review*, **87**/3, 567–76.

Olympia Monthly Meeting of the Religious Society of Friends (2014). Friends New Underground Railroad. http://www.friendsjournal.org/fnur/ (accessed 15 July 2014).

O'Neill, J. (2007). *Markets, Deliberation and Environmental Value*. London: Routledge.

O'Neill, O. (1992). Children's Rights and Children's Lives. *Children, Rights and the Law* (ed. P. Alston, S. Parker, and J. Seymour). Oxford: Clarendon.

Oosterveld, V. L. (1999). The making of a gender-sensitive international criminal court. *International Law FORUM du droit international*, **1**/1, 38–41.

Ophuls, W. (1977). *Ecology and the Politics of Scarcity*. San Francisco, CA: Freeman.

Orbinski, J. (1999). Nobel lecture by James Orbinski, Médecins Sans Frontières, Oslo, 10 December. http://nobelprize.org/nobel_prizes/peace/laureates/1999/msf-lecture.html.

Orchard, P. (2014). *A Right to Flee: Refugees, States and the Construction of International Cooperation*. Cambridge: Cambridge University Press.

Orchard, P. (2016). *Protecting the Internally Displaced: Rhetoric and Reality*. Abingdon: Routledge.

Orlin, T. S., Rosas, A., and Scheinin, M. (2000). *The Jurisprudence of Human Rights Law: A Comparative Approach*. Abo, Finland: Institute for Human Rights, Abo Akademi University.

Oxfam (2007). Close the gap: Solutions to the Indigenous health crisis facing Australia. A policy briefing paper from the National Aboriginal Community Controlled Health Organisation and Oxfam Australia, April. http://www.ahmrc.org.au/Downloads/CTG.pdf.

Pace, W. R. (1999). The relationship between the International Criminal Court and non-governmental organizations. *Reflections on the International Criminal Court: Essays in Honour of Adriaan Bos* (ed. H. A. M. von Hebel, J. G. Lammers, and J. Schukking). The Hague: TMC Asser.

Pace, W. R. and Thieroff, M. (1999). Participation of non-governmental organizations. *The International Criminal Court: The Making of the Rome Statute; Issues, Negotiations, Results* (ed. R. S. Lee). The Hague: Kluwer Law International.

Parfit, Derek (1984). *Reasons and Persons*. Oxford: Oxford University Press.

Parisi, L. (2002). Feminist praxis and women's human rights. *Journal of Human Rights*, 1/4, 571–85.

Parisi, L. (2010a). Feminist perspectives on human rights. *The International Studies Compendium Project* (ed. R. A. Denemark). Oxford: Blackwell.

Parisi, L. (2010b). Reclaiming spaces of resistance: Women's human rights and global restructuring. *Gender and Global Restructuring: Sightings, Sites and Resistances* (ed. M. H. Marchand and A. S. Runyan). London: Routledge.

Parisi, L. and Corntassel, J. (2007). In pursuit of self-determination: Indigenous women's challenges to 'traditional' diplomatic spaces. *Canadian Foreign Policy*, **13**/3, 81–98.

Parliament of Australia (2008). Apology to Australia's Indigenous peoples. *House Hansard*. 13 February. http://www.australia.gov.au/about-australia/our-country/our-people/apology-to-australias-indigenous-peoples.

Parry, M. L., Canziani, O. F., Palutikof, J. P., van der Linden, P. J., and Hanson, C. E. (eds) (2007). Cross-chapter case study. *Climate Change 2007: Impacts, Adaptation and Vulnerability. Contribution of Working Group II to the Fourth Assessment Report of the Intergovernmental Panel on Climate Change*. Cambridge: Cambridge University Press. http://www.ipcc.ch/pdf/assessment-report/ar4/wg2/ar4-wg2-xccc.pdf.

Parton, N. (1985). *The Politics of Child Abuse*. Basingstoke: Macmillan.

Pashukanis, E. (1978 [1924]). *Law and Marxism: A General Theory* (trans. B. Einhorn). London: Pluto.

Pateman, C. (1988). *The Sexual Contract*. Stanford, CA: Stanford University Press.

Pavlovic, Z. (2007). Are children's rights starting to damage human rights? Unpublished paper. Ljubljana.

Pearson, E. (2005). *The Mekong Challenge: Human Trafficking: Redefining Demand*. Bangkok: International Labour Office.

Pender, J. (2002). Relegitimising intervention: The World Bank and the voices of the poor. *Rethinking Human Rights: Critical Approaches to International Politics* (ed. D. Chandler). Basingstoke: Palgrave.

Pender, J. (2007). Country ownership: The evasion of donor accountability. *Politics Without Sovereignty: A Critique of Contemporary International Relations* (ed. C. Bickerton, P. Cunliffe, and A. Gourevitch). London: Routledge.

Perry, M. J. (1998). *The Idea of Human Rights: Four Inquiries*. New York: Oxford University Press.

Peskin, V. (2008). *International Justice in Rwanda and the Balkans: Virtual Trials and the Struggle for State Cooperation*. New York: Cambridge University Press.

Peters, E. (1996). *Torture*. Philadelphia, PA: University of Pennsylvania Press.

Peters, J. and Wolper, A. (1995). *Women's Rights, Human Rights: International Feminist Perspectives*. New York: Routledge.

Peterson, V. S. and Parisi, L. (1998). Are women human? It's not an academic question. *Human Rights Fifty Years On: A Reappraisal* (ed. T. Evans). Manchester, UK: Manchester University Press.

Pew Research Center (2013). King's dream remains an elusive goal; many Americans see racial disparities, 22 August 2013 http://www.pewsocialtrends.org/2013/08/22/kings-dream-remains-an-elusive-goal-many-americans-see-racial-disparities/.

Pharr, S. (1997). *Homophobia: A Weapon of Sexism*. Berkeley, CA: Women's Project.

Phuong, C. (2005). *The International Protection of Internally Displaced Persons*. Cambridge: Cambridge University Press.

Picq, M. and Thiel, M. (eds) (2015). *Sexual Politics in World Politics*. New York: Routledge.

Pieterse, M. (2004). Possibilities and pitfalls in the domestic enforcement of social rights: Contemplating the South African experience. *Human Rights Quarterly*, **26**/4, 882–905.

Piron, L.-H. (2005). Integrating human rights into development: A synthesis of donor approaches and experiences. London: ODI. Prepared for the OECD/ DAC Network on Governance (GOVNET). http:// www.odi.org.uk.

Platt, A. (1977). *The Child Savers: The Invention of Delinquency*. Chicago, IL: University of Chicago Press.

Plummer, K. (2006). Rights work: Constructing lesbian, gay and sexual rights in late modern times. *Rights: Sociological Perspectives* (ed. L. Morris). New York: Routledge.

Poe, S. and Tate, C. N. (1994). Repression of human rights to personal integrity in the 1980s: A global analysis. *American Political Science Review*, **88**/4, 853–72.

Poe, S., Tate, C. N., and Camp Keith, L. (1999). Repression of the human right to personal integrity revisited: A global cross-national study covering the years 1976-1993. *International Studies Quarterly*, **43**/2, 291–313.

Pogge, T. W. (2002). *World Poverty and Human Rights*. Cambridge: Polity.

Pogge, T. W. (2007). Severe poverty as a human rights violation. *Freedom From Poverty as a Human Right: Who Owes What to the Very Poor?* (ed. T. W. Pogge). Oxford: Oxford University Press.

Pollis, A. and Schwab, P. (eds) (2000). *Human Rights: New Perspectives, New Realities*. Boulder, CO: Lynne Rienner.

Posen, B. (1996). Military responses to refugee disasters. *International Security*, **21**/1, 72–111.

Posen, B. R. (2014). *Restraint: A New Foundation for U.S. Grand Strategy*. Ithaca, NY: Cornell University Press.

Posner, E. (2014). *The Twilight of Human Rights Law*. New York: OUP.

Power, S. (2002). 'A Problem from Hell': America and the Age of Genocide. New York: Basic Books and London: Flamingo.

Prendergast, J. (1996). *Frontline Diplomacy: Humanitarian Aid and Conflict in Africa*. Boulder, CO: Lynne Rienner.

Price, M., Gohdes, A., and Ball, P. (2014). *Updated Statistical Analysis of Documentation of Killings in the Syrian Arab Republic*. Report commissioned by the Office of the UN High Commissioner for Human Rights (OHCHR). San Francisco, CA: HRDAG.

Primeau, T. and Corntassel, J. (1995). Indigenous 'sovereignty' and international law: Revised strategies for pursuing 'self-determination'. *Human Rights Quarterly*, **17**/2, 343–65.

Prunier, G. (1995). *The Rwanda Crisis: History of a Genocide*. New York: Columbia University Press.

Prunier, G. (2005). *Darfur: An Ambiguous Genocide*. Ithaca, NY: Cornell University Press.

Przeworski, A. (2000). *Democracy and Development: Political Institutions and Well-Being in the World, 1950-1990*. Cambridge: Cambridge University Press.

Przeworski, A. and Vreeland, J. R. (2000). The effects of IMF programs on economic growth. *The Journal of Development Economics*, **62**/2, 385–421.

Pupavac, V. (1998). The infantilisation of the South and the UN Convention on the Rights of the Child. *Human Rights Law Review*, **3**/2, 1–6.

Pupavac, V. (2001). Misanthropy without borders: The International Children's Rights Regime. *Disasters*, **25**/2, 95–115.

Pupavac, V. (2002). The International Children's Rights Regime. *Rethinking Human Rights: Critical Approaches to International Politics* (ed. D. Chandler). Basingstoke: Palgrave.

Pupavac, V. (2005). Human security and the rise of global therapeutic governance. *Conflict, Security and Development*, **5**/2, 161–81.

Pupavac, V. (2011). Punishing childhoods: Contradictions in children's rights and global governance. *Journal of Intervention and Statebuilding*, **5**/3, 285–312.

Putnam, R. (1994). *Making Democracy Work: Civic Traditions in Modern Italy*. Princeton, NJ: Princeton University Press.

Quinn, J. and Freeman, M. (2003). Lessons learned: Practical lessons gleaned from inside the truth commissions of Guatemala and South Africa. *Human Rights Quarterly*, **25**/4, 1117–49.

Quinn, S. (2010). *An Activist's Guide to the Yogyakarta Principles*. http://www.ypinaction.org/files/02/85/ Activists_Guide_English_nov_14_2010.pdf (accessed 9 November 2015).

Rahnema, M. with Bawtree, V. (eds) (1997). *The Post-Development Reader*. London: Zed Books.

Ramcharan, B. (2011). *The Human Rights Council*. Abingdon and New York: Routledge.

Rao, Anupama (ed) (2003a). *Gender and Caste*. New Delhi: Kali for Women.

Rao, Anupama (2003b). Indian feminism and the patriarchy of caste. *Himal South Asian*, February.

Rao, Arati (1995). The Politics of Gender and Culture in International Human Rights Discourse. *Women's Rights, Human Rights: International Feminist Perspectives* (ed. J. Peters and A. Wolper). London: Routledge.

Rawls, J. (1971). *A Theory of Justice*. Boston, MA: Harvard University Press and Oxford: Oxford University Press.

Rawls, J. (1973). *A Theory of Justice*. Oxford: Oxford University Press.

Rawls, J. (1993). *Political Liberalism*. New York: Columbia University Press.

Rawls, J. (1999). *The Laws of Peoples with 'The Idea of Public Reason Revisited'*. Cambridge, MA: Harvard University Press.

Raymond, J. G., D'Cunha, J., Ruhaini Dzuhayatin, S., Hynes, H. P., Ramirez Rodriguez, Z., and Santos, A. (2002). *A Comparative Study of Women Trafficked in the Migration Process*. Amherst, MA: Coalition Against Trafficking in Women.

Raz, J. (1986). *The Morality of Freedom*. Oxford: Oxford University Press.

Read, R. (2011). *Guardians of the Future: A Constitutional Case for Representing and Protecting Future People*. London: Greenhouse. http://www.greenhouse-thinktank.org/files/greenhouse/home/guardians_inside_final.pdf (accessed 5 March 2015).

REAL Women of Canada (1998). Canada courts disaster with World Court. *REALity Newsletter*, **16**/10, July/August.

Refah Partisi (The Welfare Party) and others v. Turkey. (31 July 2001). European Court of Human Rights. Nos. 41340/98, 41342/98 and 41344/98.

Refugee Law Project (2015). *Ongwen's Justice Dilemma: Perspectives from Northern Uganda*. Kampala: Makerere University. http://www.refugeelawproject.org/files/briefing_papers/ONGWEN'S_JUSTICE-DILEMMA_-_Perspectives_ from_Northern_Uganda_-_Dialogue_Report.pdf.

Regan, E. (2010). *Theology and the Boundary Discourse of Human Rights*. Washington, DC: Georgetown University Press.

Regan, P. and Henderson, E. (2002). Democracy, threats and political repression in developing countries: Are democracies internally less violent? *Third World Quarterly*, **23**/1, 119–36.

Rehof, L. A. (1993). *Guide to the traveaux préparatoires of the United Nations Convention on the Elimination of All Forms of Discrimination against Women*. International Studies in Human Rights. Dordrecht: Martinus Nijhoff Publishers.

Reid, G. (2012). Two steps forward, one step back. *Global: The International Briefing*. http://www.global-briefing.org/2012/10/two-steps-forward-one-step-back/.

Rejali, D. (2007). *Torture and Democracy*. Princeton, NJ: Princeton University Press.

Republic of Uganda (1994). *The Report of the Commission of Inquiry into Violations of Human Rights*. Kampala: UPPC.

Republic of Uganda (2000). *Amnesty Act*. Kampala: Government of Uganda.

Rettig, M. (2011). The Sovu Trials: The impact of genocide justice on one community. *Remaking Rwanda: State Building and Human Rights after Mass Violence* (ed. S. Straus and L. Waldorf). Madison, WI: University of Wisconsin Press.

Reus-Smit, C. (2001). Human rights and the social construction of sovereignty. *Review of International Studies*, **27**/3, 519–38.

Richards, D. L. (1999a). Perilous proxy: Human rights and the presence of national elections. *Social Science Quarterly*, **80**/4, 648–65.

Richards, D. L. (1999b). Death takes a holiday: National elections, political parties and government respect for human rights. PhD Dissertation. Department of Political Science, State University of New York at Binghamton, NY.

Richards, D. L. (2006). What do citizens mean when they say 'human rights'? A comparative examination of the formation of citizen attitudes about, and understandings of, human rights. 2006 Annual Meeting of the American Political Science Association, 30 August-3 September, Philadelphia, PA.

Richards, D. L. and Carbonetti, B. (2012). Worth what we decide: A defense of the right to leisure. *The International Journal of Human Rights*, **17**/3, 329–49.

Richards, D. L. and Gelleny, R. D. (2002). Is it a small world after all? Economic globalization and government respect for human rights in developing countries. *Coping With Globalization* (ed. S. Chan and J. R. Scarritt). London: Frank Cass.

Richards, D. L. and Gelleny, R. D. (2007). Women's status and economic globalization. *International Studies Quarterly*, **51**/4, 855–76.

Richards, D. L., Gelleny, R. D., and Sacko, D. H. (2001). Money with a mean streak? Foreign economic penetration and government respect for human rights in developing countries. *International Studies Quarterly*, **45**/2, 219–39.

Rights and Resources Initiative (RRI) (2015) *Looking for Leadership: New Inspiration and Momentum amidst Crises*. Washington, DC: Rights and Resources Initiative. http://www.rightsandresources.org/wpcontent/uploads/RRI4087_AR2014r11B3.pdf

Riles, A. (2000). *The Network Inside Out*. Ann Arbor, MI: University of Michigan Press.

Risse, T., Ropp, S. C., and Sikkink, K. (eds) (1999). *The Power of Human Rights: International Norms and Domestic Change*. Cambridge: Cambridge University Press.

Risse, T., Ropp S. C., and Sikkink, K. (eds) (2013). *The Persistent Power of Human Rights: From Commitment to Compliance*. Cambridge Studies in International Relations no. 126 Cambridge: Cambridge University Press.

Risse, T. and Sikkink, K. (1999). The socialization of international human rights norms into domestic practices: Introductions. *The Power of Human Rights: International Norms and Domestic Change* (ed. T. Risse, S. C. Ropp, and K. Sikkink). Cambridge: Cambridge University Press.

Risse-Kappen, T., Ropp, S. C., and Sikkink, K. (eds) (1999). *The Power of Human Rights: International Norms and Domestic Change*, Volume 66. Cambridge: Cambridge University Press.

Robertson, L. G. (2005). *Conquest by Law: How the Discovery of America Dispossessed Indigenous Peoples of their Land*. Oxford: Oxford University Press.

Robinson, M. (2005). What rights can add to good development practice. *Human Rights and Development:*

Towards Mutual Reinforcement (ed. P. Alston and M. Robinson). New York: Oxford University Press.

Robinson, M. (2015). International law is coming up short in its response to climate change. http://www.theguardian.com/sustainable-business/2015/jan/09/mary-robinson-law-coming-up-short-climate-change (accessed 10 March 2015).

Rodriguez, H. (2004). A 'long walk to freedom' and democracy: Human rights, globalization, and social injustice. *Social Forces*, **83**/1, 391–412.

Rodrik, D. (1997). *Has Globalization Gone Too Far?* Washington, DC: Institute for International Economics.

Rorty, R. (1993). Human rights, rationality, and sentimentality. *On Human Rights: The Oxford Amnesty Lectures 1993* (ed. S. Shute and S. Hurley). New York: Basic Books.

Rose, M. (1998). *Fighting for Peace: Bosnia 1994*. London: Harvill.

Rosenau, J. (1997). *Along the Domestic-Foreign Frontier: Exploring Globalisation in a Turbulent World*. Cambridge: Cambridge University Press.

Rosenau, J. (1998). Governance and democracy in a globalizing world. *Re-Imagining Political Community: Studies in Cosmopolitan Democracy* (ed. D. Archibugi, D. Held, and M. Köhler). Stanford, CA: Stanford University Press.

Rotberg, R. I. and Thompson, D. (eds) (2000). *Truth v. Justice*. Princeton, NJ: Princeton University Press.

Roth, K. (2004a). Defending economic, social and cultural rights: Practical issues faced by an international human rights organization. *Human Rights Quarterly*, **26**/1, 63–73.

Roth, K. (2004b). Response to Leonard S. Rubenstein. *Human Rights Quarterly*, **26**/4, 873–8.

Roth, K. and Worden, M. (eds) (2005). *Torture: Does it Make Us Safer? Is it Ever OK?* New York: New Press.

Rothschild, C., Long, S., and Fried, S. T. (eds) (2005). *Written Out: How Sexuality is Used to Attack Women's Organizing*. New York: International Gay and Lesbian Human Rights Commission & The Center for Women's Global Leadership.

Roy, A. (1999). The greater common good. http://www.narmada.org/gcg/gcg.html (accessed 10 March 2015).

Rubenstein, L. S. (2004a). How international human rights organizations can advance economic, social and cultural rights: A response to Kenneth Roth. *Human Rights Quarterly*, **26**/4, 845–65.

Rubenstein, L. S. (2004b). Response by Leonard S. Rubenstein. *Human Rights Quarterly*, **26**/4, 879–81.

Rubin, B. R. and Newberg, P. R. (1980). Statistical analysis for implementing human rights policy. *The Politics of Human Rights* (ed. P. R. Newberg). New York: New York University Press.

Rummel, R. (1994). *Death by Government*. New Brunswick, NJ: Transaction Publishers.

Ruzza, C. (2006). Human rights, anti-racism and EU advocacy coalitions. *Rights: Sociological Perspectives* (ed. L. Morris). New York: Routledge.

Sachedina, A. A. (2009). *Islam and the Challenge of Human Rights*. New York: Oxford University Press.

Sachs, A. and Peterson, J. A. (1995). Eco-justice: Linking human rights and the environment. Worldwatch Paper 127.

Sage, C. (2012). *Environment and Food*. London: Routledge.

Salick, J. and Byg, A. (eds) (2007). *Indigenous Peoples and Climate Change*. Oxford: Tyndall Centre for Climate Change Research, University of Oxford and Missouri Botanical Garden. http://tyndall.ac.uk/sites/default/files/Indigenous%20Peoples%20and%20Climate%20Change_0.pdf.

Samson, C. and Short, D. (2006). Sociology of Indigenous peoples rights. *Rights: Sociological Perspectives* (ed. L. Morris). New York: Routledge.

Sanford, V. (2008). Si hubo genocidio en Guatemala! *The Historiography of Genocide* (ed. D. Stone). London: Palgrave Macmillan.

Sano, H. O. (2000). Development and human rights: The necessary, but partial integration of human rights and development. *Human Rights Quarterly*, **22**/3, 734–52.

Santos, Boaventura de Sousa (1987). Law: A map of misreading: Toward a postmodern conception of law. *Journal of Law and Society*, **14**/3, 279–302.

Santos, Boaventura de Sousa (1995). *Toward a New Common Sense: Law, Science and Politics in the Paradigmatic Transition*. New York: Routledge.

Scarry, E. (1985). *The Body in Pain: The Making and Unmaking of the World*. Oxford: Oxford University Press.

Schabas, W. (2000). *Genocide in International Law: The Crimes of Crimes*. Cambridge: Cambridge University Press.

Scheingold, S. (2004). *The Politics of Rights: Lawyers, Public Policy and Political Change*. Ann Arbor, MI: Michigan University Press.

Scheinin, M. (2005). What are Indigenous peoples? *Minorities, Peoples and Self-Determination—Essays in Honour of Patrick Thornberry* (ed. N. Ghanea and A. Xanthaki). Leiden: Martinus Nijhoff.

Schmitt, C. (1996). *The Concept of the Political*. Chicago, IL: University of Chicago Press.

Schmitt, C. (2003). *The Nomos of the Earth: In the International Law of the Jus Publicum Europaeum*. New York: Telos.

Schock, K. (2005). *Unarmed Insurrections*. Minnesota: University of Minnesota Press.

Schofield, K. (2007). Smacking vital as last resort, insist parents in 'growing up' study. *Scotsman*, 20 January.

Scholte, J. A. (2001). *Civil Society and Democracy in Global Governance*. CSGR working paper no. 65/01. Warwick University: Centre for the Study of Globalisation and Regionalisation.

Schoof, R. (2008). CIA Director: Agency used waterboarding. *The Seattle Times*, 6 February.

Schulman, S. (2011). Israel and 'pinkwashing'. *New York Times*, 22 November. http://www.nytimes.com/2011/11/23/opinion/pinkwashing-and-israels-use-of-gays-as-a-messaging-tool.html?_r=0 (accessed 30 March 2015).

Schulz, W. (2003). *Tainted Legacy: 9/11 and the Ruin of Human Rights*. New York: Thunder's Mouth/Nation Books.

Schulz, W. (ed.) (2007). *The Phenomenon of Torture: Readings and Commentary*. Philadelphia, PA: University of Pennsylvania Press.

Scottish Parliament (2014). Children and young people (Scotland) http://www.legislation.gov.uk/asp/2014/8/contents/enacted.

Seckinelgin, H. (2002). Time to stop and think: HIV/Aids, global civil society and people's politics. *Global Civil Society 2002* (ed. M. Glasius, M. Kaldor, and H. Anheier). Oxford: Oxford University Press.

Seligman, A. (1992). *The Idea of Civil Society*. New York: Free Press.

Sellars, K. (2002). *The Rise and Rise of Human Rights*. Stroud: Sutton.

Sémelin, J. (2007). *Purify and Destroy: The Political Uses of Massacre and Genocide* (trans. C. Schoch). New York: Columbia University Press.

Sen, A. K. (1981). *Poverty and Famines: An Essay on Entitlement and Deprivation*. Oxford: Clarendon.

Sen, A. K. (1988). *The Standard of Living: The Tanner Lectures, Clare Hall, Cambridge, 1985.* Cambridge: Cambridge University Press.

Sen, A. K. (1989). Development as capability expansion. *Journal of Development Planning*, **19**, 41–58. Reprinted in S. Fukuda-Parr and A. K. Shiva Kumar (eds) (2003). *Readings in Human Development*, Dehli: Oxford University Press.

Sen, A. K. (1999a). *Development as Freedom*. New York: Alfred Knopf Publishers.

Sen, A. K. (1999b). Human rights and economic achievements. *The East Asian Challenge for Human Rights* (ed. J. R. Bauer and D. A. Bell). Cambridge: Cambridge University Press.

Sen, A. K. (2004). Elements of a theory of human rights. *Philosophy and Public Affairs*, **32**/4, 315–56.

Sen, A. K. (2005). Human rights and capabilities. *Journal of Human Development*, **6**/2, 151–66.

Sen, A. K. (2006). Human rights and development. *Development as a Human Right: Legal, Political, and Economic Dimensions* (ed. B. A. Andreassen and S. P. Marks). Cambridge, MA: Harvard School of Public Health. Distributed by Harvard University Press.

Senate Intelligence Committee (2014). Committee Study of the Central Intelligence Agency's Detention and Interrogation Program. http://fas.org/irp/congress/2014_rpt/ssci-rdi.pdf.

Sengupta, A. (2006). The human right to development. *Development as a Human Right, Legal, Political and Economic Dimensions* (ed. B. A. Andreassen and S. P. Marks). Boston, MA: Harvard School of Public Health. Distributed by Harvard University Press.

Seybolt, T. B., Aronson, J. D., and Fischoff, B. (eds) (2013). *Counting Civilian Casualties: An Introduction to Recording and Estimating Nonmilitary Deaths in Conflict.* Oxford: Oxford University Press.

Shaw, M. (2000). *Theory of the Global State: Globality as an Unfinished Revolution*. New York: Cambridge University Press.

Shelton, D. (2000). Law, non-lawand the problem of 'soft law'. *Commitment and Compliance: The Role of Non-Binding Norms in the International Legal System* (ed. D. Shelton). New York: Oxford University Press.

Shelton, D. (2006). *Remedies in International Human Rights Law* (2nd edn). Oxford: Oxford University Press.

Shiva, V. (1991). *The Violence of the Green Revolution: Third World Agriculture, Ecology, and Politics*. London: Zed Books.

Shiva, V. (1999). Food rights, free trade, and fascism. *Globalizing Rights: The Oxford Amnesty Lectures 1999* (ed. M. Gibney). Oxford: Oxford University Press.

Shiva, V. (2003). The myths of globalisation exposed: Advancing towards living democracy. *Worlds Apart: Globalization and the Environment* (ed. J. G. Speth). London: Island.

Shiva, V. (2005). *Earth Democracy: Justice, Sustainability, and Peace*. Cambridge, MA: South End Press.

Shor, E. (2008). Conflict, terrorism, and the socialization of human rights norms: The spiral model revisited. *Social Problems*, **55**/1, 117–38.

Short, D. (2007). The social construction of Indigenous 'native title' land rights in Australia. *Current Sociology*, **55**/6, 857–76.

Short, D. (2008). *Reconciliation and Colonial Power: Indigenous Rights in Australia*. Aldershot: Ashgate.

Short, D., Elliot, J., Norder, K., Lloyd-Davies, E., and Morley, J. (2015). Extreme energy, fracking and human rights: A new field for impact assessments? *International Journal of Human Rights*, **19**/6, 697–736. dx.doi.org/10.1080/13642987.2015.1019219.

Shue, H. (1980). *Basic Rights: Subsistence, Affluence, and U.S. Foreign Policy*. Princeton, NJ: Princeton University Press.

Shue, H. (1996). *Basic Rights: Subsistence, Affluence and U.S. Foreign Policy* (2nd edn). Chichester: Princeton University Press.

Sikkink, K. (1993). The power of principled ideas: Human rights policies in the United States and Western Europe. *Ideas and Foreign Policy: Beliefs, Institutions, and Political Change* (ed. J. Goldstein and R. O. Keohane). Ithaca, NY: Cornell University Press.

Sikkink, K. (2004). *Mixed Signals: U.S. Human Rights Policy and Latin America*. Ithaca, NY: Cornell University Press.

Sikkink, K. (2011). *The Justice Cascade: How Human Rights Prosecutions are Changing World Politics*. New York: Norton.

Silverman, A. (2014) *Know Your Rights Related to REDD+: A Guide for Indigenous and Local Community Leaders*. Washington, DC: Tebtebba & Centre for International Environmental Law. http://theredddesk.org/resources/know-your-rights-related-redd-guide-indigenous-and-local-community-leaders.

Simmons, B. A. (2009). *Mobilizing for Human Rights: International Law and Domestic Politics*. Cambridge: Cambridge University Press.

Simms, A. (2005). *Ecological Debt: The Health of the Planet and the Wealth of Nations*. London: new economics foundation.

Simon, M. (1994). Hawks, doves and civil conflict dynamics: A 'strategic' action-reaction model. *International Interactions*, **19**/3, 213–39.

Simpson, G. (2004). *Great Powers and Outlaw States: Unequal Sovereigns in the International Legal Order*. Cambridge: Cambridge University Press.

Singer, P. (2006). The great ape debate. *Project Syndicate*, May. http://www.utilitarian.net/singer/by/200605-.htm.

Singer, P. (2009). *Animal Liberation*. New York: Harper.

Skilling, G. H. (1981). *Charter 77 and Human Rights in Czechoslovakia*. London: George Allen & Unwin.

Skogly, S. (1993). Structural adjustment and development: Human rights. An agenda for change. *Human Rights Quarterly*, **15**/4, 751–78.

Slaughter, A. M. (2004). *A New World Order*. Princeton, NJ: Princeton University Press.

Slovak Ministry of Justice [Ministerstvo spravodlivosti] (2012). Declaration on the Adoption of Slovak children without valid reasons in the UK [Vyhlásenie k prípadom adopcií slovenských detí bez relevantných dôvodov vo Veľkej Británii], 23 August, Bratislava. http://www.justice.gov.sk/Stranky/aktualitadetail.aspx?announcementID=1631.

Slyomovics, S. (2005). *The Performance of Human Rights in Morocco*. Philadelphia, PA: University of Pennsylvania Press.

Smith, J., Bolyard, M., and Ippolito, A. (1999). Human rights and the global economy: A response to Meyer. *Human Rights Quarterly*, **21**/1, 207–19.

Smith, J., Chatfield, C., and Pagnucco, R. (eds) (1997). *Transnational Social Movements and World Politics: Solidarity Beyond the State*. Syracuse, NY: Syracuse University Press.

Smith, R. K. M. (2003). *Textbook on International Human Rights*. New York: Oxford University Press.

Smith, R. (2011). *Textbook on International Human Rights* (5th edn). Oxford: Oxford University Press.

Snow, A. H. (1918). *The Question of Aborigines in the Law and Practice of Nations*. Washington, DC: Government Printing Office.

Snyder, M. (2006). Unlikely Godmother: The United Nations and the Global Women's Movement. *Global Feminism: Transnational Women's Activism, Organizing, and Human Rights* (ed. M. Marx Ferree and A. M. Tripp). New York: New York University Press.

Sobrino Sj, J. (2001). Human rights and oppressed peoples: Historical-theological reflections. *Truth and Memory: The Church and Human Rights in El Salvador and Guatemala* (ed. M. Hayes and D. Tomb). Gloucester: Gracewing.

Solzhenitsyn, A. (1973). *The Gulag Archipelago: 1918–1956: An Experiment in Literary Investigation*. New York: Harper & Row.

Somerson, W. (2010). The intersection of anti-occupation and queer Jewish organizing. *Tikkun Magazine* (July/August). www.tikkun.org/nextgen/the-intersection-of-anti-occupation-and-queer-jewish-organizing (accessed 23 July 2015).

Spade, D. and Willse, C. (2014). Sex, gender, and war in an age of multicultural imperialism. *QED: A Journal in GLBTQ Worldmaking*, **1**/1, 5–29.

Spar, D. (1998). The spotlight and the bottom line: How multinationals export human rights. *Foreign Affairs*, **77**/7, 7–12.

Special Rapporteur on the Rights of Indigenous peoples. (2011). www2.ohchr.org/english/issues/indigenous/rapporteur/.

Speed, S. (2006). At the crossroads of human rights and anthropology: Toward a critically engaged activist research. *American Anthropologist*, 'In focus: Anthropology and human rights in a new key', **108**/1, 66–76.

Speed, S. (2008). *Rights in Rebellion: Indigenous Struggle and Human Rights in Chiapas*. Palo Alto, CA: Stanford University Press.

Spero, J. and Hart, J. (1997). *The Politics of International Relations* (5th edn). New York: St Martins.

Speth, J. G. (2003). Two perspectives on globalization and the environment. *Worlds Apart: Globalization and the Environment* (ed. J. G. Speth). Washington, DC: Island.

Spirit House (no date). The Harm Free Zone. http://www.spirithouse-nc.org/collective-sun-ii (accessed 16 April 2015).

Spivak, G. C. (2005). Use and abuse of human rights. *Boundary2*, **32**/1, 131–89.

Stammers, N. (1999). Social movements and the social construction of human rights. *Human Rights Quarterly*, **21**/4, 980–1008.

Staub, E. (1989). *The Roots of Evil: The Origins of Genocide and Other Group Violence*. Cambridge: Cambridge University Press.

Staub, E. (1990). The psychology and culture of torture and torturers. *Psychology and Torture* (ed. P. Suedfeld). New York: Hemisphere.

Stead, W. T. (1885). The maiden tribute of modern Babylon. *Pall Mall Gazette*.

Steains, C. (1999). Gender issues. *The International Criminal Court: The Making of the Rome Statute; Issues, Negotiations, Results* (ed. R. S. Lee). The Hague: Kluwer Law International.

Steiner, H., Alston, P., and Goodman, R. (2007). *International Human Rights in Context: Law, Politics, Morals* (3rd edn). Oxford: Oxford University Press.

Stern, N. (ed.) (2006). Stern review on the economics of climate change. http://webarchive.nationalarchives.gov.uk/20080910140413/http://www.hm-treasury.gov.uk/independent_reviews/stern_review_economics_climate_change/sternreview_index.cfm.

Steward, J. (1948). Comments on the statement on human rights. *American Anthropologist*, **50**/2, 351–2.

Stiglitz, J. (2002). *Globalization and its Discontents*. London: Allen Lane.

Stone, D. (ed.) (2008). *The Historiography of Genocide*. London: Palgrave Macmillan.

Stover, E. and Weinstein, H. M. (eds) (2004). *My Neighbour, My Enemy: Justice and Community in the Aftermath of Mass Atrocity*. Cambridge: Cambridge University Press.

Straus, S. (2001). Contesting meanings and conflicting imperatives: A conceptual analysis of genocide. *Journal of Genocide Research*, **3**/3, 349–75.

Straus, S. (2005). Darfur and the genocide debate. *Foreign Affairs*, **84**/1, 123–33.

Straus, S. (2006). *The Order of Genocide: Race, Power, and War in Rwanda*. Ithaca, NY: Cornell University Press.

Straus, S. (2007). Second generation comparative research on genocide. *World Politics*, **59**/3, 476–501.

Sudan Divestment Task Force (2007). *Sudan Company Rankings 12/20/2007*. Washington, DC: Sudan Divestment Task Force.

Supreme Court of Israel (1999). Judgment concerning the legality of the General Security Service's interrogation methods. 38 ILM 1471,1488.

Symonides, J. (ed.) (2003). *Human Rights: International Protection, Monitoring, Enforcement*. Aldershot: Ashgate and Burlington, VT: PN UNESCO.

Talbott, W. J. (2005). *Which Rights Should Be Universal?* New York: Oxford University Press.

Tauli-Corpuz, V., de Chavez, R., Baldo-Soriano, E., Magata, H., Golocan, C., Bugtong, M. V., Enkiwe-Abayao, L., and Cariño, J. (2009). *Guide on Climate Change and Indigenous Peoples*. Baguio City, Philippines: Tebtebba Foundation.

Tauli-Corpuz, V. and Lynge, A. (2008). Impact of climate change mitigation measures on Indigenous peoples and on their territories and lands. UNPFII, Seventh Session, New York, 21 April-2 May. UN Doc. E/C.19/2008/10. http://www.un.org/esa/socdev/unpfii/documents/E_C19_2008_10.pdf.

Tauli-Corpuz, V. and Tamang, P. (2007). Oil palm and other commercial tree plantations, mono-cropping: Impacts on Indigenous peoples' land tenure and resource management systems and livelihoods. UNPFII, Sixth Session, New York, 14-25May. UN Doc. E/C.19/2007/CRP.6. http://www.un.org/esa/socdev/unpfii/documents/6session_crp6.doc.

Taylor, C. (1994). *Multiculturalism and the Politics of Recognition*. Princeton, NJ: Princeton University Press.

Taylor, C. (1999). Conditions of an unforced consensus on human rights. *The East Asian Challenge for Human Rights* (ed. J. R. Bauer and D. Bell). Cambridge: Cambridge University Press.

Terry, F. (2002). *Condemned to Repeat: The Paradox of Humanitarian Action*. Ithaca, NY: Cornell University Press.

Thakur, R. (2002). Outlook: Intervention, sovereignty and the responsibility to protect. *Security Dialogue*, 33/3, 323–40.

TheInterim (1998). ICC: Promise of justice or threat of tyranny? *The Interim*, August.

Thomas, D. C. (1999). The Helsinki Accords and political change in Eastern Europe. *The Power of Human Rights: International Norms and Domestic Change* (ed. T. Risse, S. C. Ropp, and K. Sikkink). Cambridge: Cambridge University Press.

Thornberry, P. (1991). *International Law and the Rights of Minorities*. Oxford: Clarendon.

Thornberry, P. (2002). *Indigenous Peoples and International Law*. Manchester: Manchester University Press.

Tickle, L. (2015). Social workers under scrutiny as parents capture sessions on camera. *TheGuardian*, 17June.http://www.theguardian.com/society/2015/jun/17/social-workers-under-scrutiny-parents-camera.

Tilly, C., Tilly, L., and Tilly, R. (1975). *The Rebellious Century 1830-1930*. Cambridge, MA: Harvard University Press.

Tobin, B. (2014). *Indigenous Peoples, Customary Law and Human Rights—Why Living Law Matters*. London: Earthscan/Routledge.

Tomuschat, C. (2003). *Human Rights Between Idealism and Realism*. Oxford: Oxford University Press.

Totten, S. and Markusen, E. (2006). *Genocide in Darfur: Investigating the Atrocities in the Sudan*. New York: Routledge.

Tremmel, J. (2009). *A Theory of Intergenerational Justice*. London: Earthscan.

True, J. and Parisi, L. (2010). Gender Mainstreaming Strategies in International Governance. *Feminist Strategies in International Governance* (ed. G. Caglar, E. Prügl, and S. Zwingel). London: Routledge.

Tsebelis, G. (2002). *Veto Players: How Political Institutions Work*. Princeton, NJ: Princeton University Press.

Tuck, R. (1979). *Natural Rights Theories: Their Origin and Development*. Cambridge: Cambridge University Press.

Tuman, J. P. and Emmert, C. F. (2004). The political economy of U.S. foreign direct investment in Latin America: A reappraisal. *Latin American Research Review*, 39/3, 9–28.

Turner, B. S. (1993). Outline of a theory of human rights. *Sociology*, 27/3, 489–512.

Turner, B. S. (1997). A neo-Hobbesian theory of human rights: A reply to Malcolm Waters. *Sociology*, 31/3, 565–71.

Turner, B. S. (2006). *Vulnerability and Human Rights*. University Park, PA: The Pennsylvania State University Press.

Turner, B. S. and Rojek, C. (2001). *Society and Culture: Principles of Scarcity and Solidarity*. London: Sage.

Uçarer, E. (1999). Trafficking in women: Alternate migration or modern slave trade. *Gender Politics in Global Governance* (ed. M. Meyer and E. Prügl). Lanham, MD: Roman and Littlefield.

Uganda (1998). *Uganda*. Brooklyn, NY: Interlink Books.

UNCHR (United Nations Commission on Human Rights) (2005). Human rights and transnational corporations and other business enterprises: Resolution 2005/69.

UNCTAD (2007). *Doing Business2007*. New York: United Nations Publications.UNDG (2003). The human rights based approach to development cooperation towards a common understanding among UN agencies. http://hrbaportal.org/the-human-rights-based-approach-to-development-cooperation-towards-a-common-understanding-among-un-agencies.

UNDP (United Nations Development Programme) (1990). *Human Development Report*. New York: Oxford University Press.

UNDP (United Nations Development Programme) (1994). *Human Development Report: New Dimensions of Human Security*. New York: United Nations.

UNDP (United Nations Development Programme) (1998). *Human Development Report: Consumption for Human Development*. New York: United Nations.

UNDP (United Nations Development Programme) (1999). *Human Development Report: Globalization with a Human Face*. Oxford: Oxford University Press.

UNDP (United Nations Development Programme) (2000). *Human Development Report: Human Rights and*

Human Development. New York: Oxford University Press.

UNDP (United Nations Development Programme) (2002). *Human Development Report: Deepening Democracy in a Fragmented World*. New York: Oxford University Press.

UNDP (United Nations Development Programme) (2003). *Human Development Report: MDGs: A Compact Among Nations to End Human Poverty*. New York: Oxford University Press.

UNDP (United Nations Development Programme) (2004). *Governance Indicators: A User's Guide*. Oslo: Oslo Governance Centre.

UNDP (United Nations Development Programme) (2006). *Indicators for Rights-Based Approaches to Development Programming: A User's Guide*. Oslo: Oslo Governance Centre.

UNDP (United Nations Development Programme) (2008). *Human Development Report: Fighting Climate Change: Human Solidarity in a Divided World*. New York: Palgrave Macmillan. http://hdr.undp.org/sites/default/files/reports/268/hdr_20072008_en_complete.pdf.

UNDP (United Nations Development Programme) (2014). *Human Development Report: Sustaining Human Progress: Reducing Vulnerabilities and Building Resilience*. New York: United Nations.

UNDP (United Nations Development Programme) (2015). Post-2015 Sustainable Development Agenda. http://www.undp.org/content/undp/en/home/mdgoverview/post-2015-development-agenda/ (accessed 25 June 2015).

UNDP/RIIP (2010). Millennium Development Goals and Indigenous Peoples. Bancock/UNDP/RIPP.

UNDRIP (2007). United Nations Declaration on the Rights of Indigenous People. http://www.un.org/esa/socdev/unpfii/documents/DRIPS_en.pdf

UNECE (United Nations Economic Commission on Europe) (1998). Convention on access to information, public participation in decision-making and access to justice in environmental matters. http://www.unece.org/fileadmin/DAM/env/pp/documents/cep43e.pdf.

UNEP (United Nations Environment Programme) (1992). The Rio declaration on environment and development. http://www.unep.org/Documents.Multilingual/Default.asp?DocumentID=78&ArticleID=1163.

UNEP (United Nations Environment Programme) (2009). Outcome document of the high level expert meeting on the new future of human rights and environment: An agenda for moving forward. http://www.unep.org/environmentalgovernance/Portals/8/documents/Events/OutcomeDocument-HumanRightsEnviroment.pdf (accessed 12 October 2011).

UNESCO (1978). 1978 Study of the procedures that should be followed in the examination of cases and questions that might be submitted to UNESCO concerning the exercise of human rights in the spheres of its competence, in order to make its action more effective. Decision 104, EX/3. 3.

UNFCCC (2010). Information received from the UNFCCC for the 10th Session of the UN PFII. http://www.un.org/esa/socdev/unpfii/documents/session-10-UNFCCC.pdf.

UN High Commissioner for Human Rights (2015). Report of the Office of the United Nations High Commissioner for Human Rights on the human rights situation in Iraq in the light of abuses committed by the so-called Islamic State in Iraq and the Levant and associated groups. A/HRC/28/18. http://www.ohchr.org/EN/NewsEvents/Pages/DisplayNews.aspx?NewsID=15755&LangID=E#.

UNHCR (2006). Colombia: Humanitarian emergency looms for Indigenous communities. UNHCR Briefing Notes, 4 April. http://www.unhcr.org/cgi-bin/texis/vtx/news/opendoc.htm?tbl=NEWS&id=4432474c6.

UNHCR (2015a). *Asylum Trends 2014*. Geneva: UNHCR.

UNHCR (2015b). *Global Trends 2014*. Geneva: UNHCR.

UNHCR (2016). *The State of the World's Refugees*. Oxford: Oxford University Press.

UNICEF (undated). Introduction to the Convention on the Rights of the Child. Definition of key terms. http://www.unicef.org/crc/files/Definitions.pdf.

UNICEF (1963). *The Needs of Children*. New York: The Free Press of Glencoe.

UNICEF (2014). Bring back our childhood. Geneva: UNICEF. http://bringbackourchildhood.tumblr.com/.

Unitarian Universalist Association (2014). Unitarian Universalist United Nations Office. UUA, November 21. http://www.uua.org/international/un/198551.shtml (accessed 22 February 2015).

United Nations (1979). UN Convention on the Elimination of All Forms of Discrimination Against Women (CEDAW).

United Nations (2004). *A More Secure World: Our Shared Responsibility*. Report of the Secretary-General's High-level Panel on Threats, Challenges and Change, 3 December. New York: United Nations. http://www.un.org/en/peacebuilding/pdf/historical/hlp_more_secure_world.pdf.

United Nations (2015). SC/12008, August 17, http://www.un.org/press/en/2015/sc12008.doc.htm.

UNA-USA (2001). The UN Convention on the Elimination of All Forms of Discrimination Against Women (CEDAW) UNA-USA Advocacy Agenda 2001 Fact Sheet, June. New York: United Nations Association of the United States of America. http://www.freerepublic.com/focus/fr/546800/posts?page=2

United Nations General Assembly (1989). UN Convention on the Rights of the Child. General Assembly Resolution 44/25, 20 November.

United Nations General Assembly (1993). Resolution 43/134 endorsing the Paris Principles on National Human Rights Institutions. UN Doc. A/RES/48/134.

United Nations General Assembly (2000). UN Millennium Declaration. UN Doc. A/Res/55/2 http://www.un.org/millennium/declaration/ares552e.htm/.

United Nations General Assembly (2001). *We the Peoples: The Role of the United Nations in the 21st Century*. New York: United Nations. http://www.un.org/en/events/pastevents/pdfs/We_The_Peoples.pdf.

United Nations General Assembly (2005). Resolution adopted by the General Assembly. A/RES/60/1: World Summit Outcome, 24 October. http://www.un.org/womenwatch/ods/A-RES-60-1-E.pdf.

United Nations General Assembly (2006). Human Rights Council. GA Resn 60/251 at 2. UN Doc. A/RES/60/251. http://www2.ohchr.org/english/bodies/hrcouncil/docs/A.RES.60.251_En.pdf.

UN Permanent Forum on Indigenous Issues (UNPFII) (2014). Study of the Impacts of the Doctrine of Discovery on Indigenous Peoples, including mechanisms, processes and Instruments of Redress, UN Doc E/C.19/2014/3. http://www.un.org/esa/socdev/unpfii/documents/2014/3.pdf.

UNPFII (UN Permanent Forum for Indigenous Issues) (2006). Who are Indigenous peoples? http://www.un.org/esa/socdev/unpfii/documents/5session_factsheet1.pdf.

UNPFII (UN Permanent Forum for Indigenous Issues) (2008). Climate change, bio-cultural diversity and livelihoods of Indigenous peoples to be focus of UN forum. Press release, New York, 16 April. http://www.un.org/esa/socdev/unpfii/documents/Opening_%20PR_7th_Sess_PFII.pdf.

UNPFII (UN Permanent Forum on Indigenous Issues) (2010). *State of the World's Indigenous Peoples*. http://undesadspd.org/IndigenousPeoples/LibraryDocuments/StateoftheWorldsIndigenousPeoples.aspx.

UN Secretary General (2001). *We the Children: End-decade Review of the Follow-up to the World Summit for Children*. New York: United Nations. http://www.unicef.org/specialsession/documentation/documents/a-s-27-3e.pdf.

UN Secretary General (2004). Report of the Secretary General: The rule of law and transitional justice in conflict and post-conflict situations. S/2004/616.

UN Secretary General (2006). *Secretary General study on Violence Against Children*. New York: United Nations. https://srsg.violenceagainstchildren.org/sites/default/files/documents/a_61_299_un_study_on_violence_against_children.pdf.

UN Security Council (2011). SC/10180, AFR/2120, Security Council Press Statement on Libya, Department of Public Information, News and Media Division, New York. http://www.un.org/News/Press/docs/2011/sc10180.doc.htm.

UN Task Team on the Post-2015 UN Development Agenda (2012). *Realizing the Future We Want for All*. New York: United Nations Department of Economic and Social Affairs.

United States Code (2000). Code 22, §7101. *Trafficking Victims Protection Act of 2000*.

US Department of Justice (2007). *Attorney General's Annual Report to Congress on U.S. Government Activities to Combat Trafficking in Persons Fiscal Year 2006*. Washington, DC: US Department of Justice.

US Department of State (2006). *Trafficking in Persons Report*. Washington, DC: US Department of Justice. http://www.state.gov/g/tip/rls/tiprpt/2006/.

US Department of State (2008). *Trafficking in Persons Report*. Washington, DC: US Department of Justice. http://www.state.gov/g/tip/rls/tiprpt/2008/.

US Department of State (2011). The Department of State's Accomplishments Promoting the Human Rights of Lesbian, Gay, Bisexual and Transgender People. http://www.state.gov/r/pa/prs/ps/2011/12/178341.htm (accessed 4 May 2013).

US Department of State (2014). *Trafficking in Persons Report*. Washington, DC: US Department of Justice. http://www.state.gov/j/tip/rls/tiprpt/2014/.

US Department of State (no date a). About the Fund. http://www.state.gov/globalequality/about/index.htm (accessed 3 December 2014).

US Department of State (no date b). Bureau of Democracy, Human Rights, and Labor. http://www.state.gov/j/drl/ (accessed 23 February 2015).

Uvin, P. (1998). *Aiding Violence: The Development Enterprise in Rwanda*. West Hartford, CT: Kumarian.

Uvin, P. (2004). *Human Rights and Development*. Bloomfield, CT: Kumarian.

Uvin, P. (2007). From the right to development to the rights-based approach: How human rights entered development. *Development in Practice*, 17/4–5, 598–604.

Valadez, J. (2000). *Deliberative Democracy, Political Legitimacy and Self-Determination in Multi-Cultural Societies*. Boulder, CO: Westview.

Valentino, B. (2004). *Final Solutions: Mass Killing and Genocide in the Twentieth Century*. Ithaca, NY: Cornell University Press.

Valentino, B., Huth, P., and Balch-Lindsay, D. (2004). 'Draining the sea': Mass killing and guerrilla warfare. *International Organization*, 58/2, 375–407.

Van Bueren, G. (1998). *The International Law on the Rights of the Child*. The Hague: Martinus Nijhoff.

Vandenbroeck, M., Roose, R., and De Bie, M. (2011). Governing families in the social investment state. *International Critical Childhood Policy Studies*, 4/1, 69–85.

Verloo, M. (2013). Intersectional and cross-movement politics and policies: Reflections on current practices and debates. *Signs*, 38/4, 893–915.

Verpooten, M. (2005). The death toll of the Rwandan genocide: A detailed analysis for Gikongoro Province. *Population*, 60/4, 331–67.

Vidal, J. (2011). Bolivia enshrines natural world's rights with equal status for Mother Earth. *The Guardian*, 10 April.

Vienna Declaration and Programme of Action (1993). Adopted by the World Conference on Human Rights, Vienna, 14–25 June. UN Doc. A/CONF.157/23. http://www.unhchr.ch/huridocda/huridoca.nsf/(Symbol)/A.CONF.157.23.En.

Village Voice (2001). The case against torture. *Village Voice*, 28 November-4 December.

Vincent, R. J. (1986). *Human Rights in International Relations*. Cambridge: Cambridge University Press.

Vizard, P. S., Fukuda-Parr, S., and Elson, D. (2011). The Capabilities Approach and Human Rights. *Journal of Human Development and Capabilities*, 12/1, 1–22.

Vreeland, J. R. (2003). *The IMF and Economic Development*. Cambridge: Cambridge University Press.

Vreeland, J. R. (2008). Political institutions and human rights: Why dictatorships enter into the United Nations Convention Against Torture. *International Organization*, 62/1, 65–101.

Waldorf, L. (2006). Mass justice for mass atrocity: Rethinking local justice as transitional justice. *Temple Law Review*, 79/1, 1–88.

Waldron, J. (1987). *Nonsense Upon Stilts: Bentham, Burke and Marx on the Rights of Man*. London: Methuen.

Walkowitz, J. R. (1980). *Prostitution and Victorian Society: Women, Class and the State*. Cambridge: Cambridge University Press.

Wallerstein, I. (2006). *World-Systems Analysis*. Durham, NC: Duke University Press.

Walter, E. V. (1969). *Terror and Resistance: A Study of Political Violence, with Case Studies of Some Primitive African Communities*. New York: Oxford University Press.

Walther, T. (1997). *The World Economy*. New York: Wiley.

Waltz, S. (2001). Universalizing human rights: The role of small states in the construction of the Universal Declaration of Human Rights. *Human Rights Quarterly*, 23/1, 44–72.

Waltz, S. (2002). Reclaiming and rebuilding the history of the Universal Declaration of Human Rights. *Third World Quarterly*, 23/3, 437–48.

Warner, K. (2011). *Climate Change Induced Displacement: Adaptation Policy in the Context of the UNFCCC Negotiations*. Geneva: Division of International Protection, United Nations High Commissioner for Human Rights.

Waters, M. (1996). Human rights and the universalisation of interests: Towards a social constructionist approach. *Sociology*, **30**/3, 593–600.

Watson, A. (2006). Children and international relations: A new site of knowledge? *Review of International Studies*, **32**/2, 237–50.

WCED (1987). Our common future, from one earth to one world. http://www.un-documents.net/ocf-ov.htm.

Webber, A. and Shirk, D. (2005). Hidden victims: Evaluating protections for undocumented victims of human trafficking. *Immigration Policy in Focus*, **4**/8.

Webber, J. (2011). *From Rebellion to Reform in Bolivia: Class Struggle, Indigenous Liberation, and the Politics of Evo Morales*. Chicago: Haymarket.

Weber, M. (1954). *Max Weber on Law in Economy and Society*. New York: Simon & Schuster.

Weber, M. (1978). *Economy and Society*. Berkeley, CA: University of California Press.

Weber, M. (2004). Politics as a vocation. *The Vocation Lectures* (ed. D. Owen). Indianapolis, IN: Hackett.

Weiss, M. L. and Bosia, M. J. (eds) (2013). *Global Homophobia: States, Movements, and the Politics of Oppression*. Urbana, IL: University of Illinois Press.

Weiss, T. G. (2012). *Humanitarian Intervention* (2nd edn). Cambridge: Polity Press.

Weitz, E. (2003). *Century of Genocide: Utopias of Race and Nation*. Princeton, NJ: Princeton University Press.

Weldon, S. L. (2008). Intersectionality. *Politics, Gender, and Concepts: Theory and Methodology* (ed. G. Goertz and A. Mazur). Cambridge: Cambridge University Press.

Weller, M. (2009). *Escaping the Self-Determination Trap*. Leiden: Brill.

Wells, H. G. (1940). *The Rights of Man, or, What Are We Fighting For?* New York: Penguin.

Weschler, L. (1990). *A Miracle, a Universe: Settling Accounts with Torturers*. New York: Pantheon.

Wheeler, N. J. (2001). *Saving Strangers: Humanitarian Intervention in International Society*. Oxford: Oxford University Press.

Whitcomb, C. (2002). The shadow war. *Gentlemen's Quarterly*, 22 September.

White, H. and Black, R. (eds) (2002). *Targeting Development: Critical Perspectives on Millennium Development Goals and International Development Targets*. London: Routledge.

Whiteley, P. (1999). The origins of social capital. *Social Capital and European Democracy* (ed. J. Van Deth, M. Maraffi, K. Newton, and P. Whiteley). London: Routledge.

Whiteley, P. (2000). Economic growth and social capital. *Political Studies*, **48**/3, 443–66.

Wilkinson, S. (2004). *Votes and Violence: Electoral Competition and Ethnic Riots in India*. New York: Cambridge University Press.

Williams, B. (2005). *In the Beginning Was the Deed: Realism and Moralism in Political Argument*. Princeton, NJ: Princeton University Press.

Williams, R. (1963). *Culture and Society1789–1950*. Harmondsworth: Penguin.

Williams, R. (2012). *Savage Anxieties: The Invention of Western Civilization*. New York: Palgrave Macmillan.

Williams, R.R. (producer, director) (2013). *God Loves Uganda* (film). New York: Variance Films.

Wilson, R. A. (1997). Human rights culture and context: An introduction. *Human Rights, Culture and Context: Anthropological Perspectives* (ed. R. A. Wilson). London: Pluto.

Wilson, R. A. (2001). *The Politics of Truth and Reconciliation in South Africa: Legitimizing the Post-Apartheid State*. Cambridge: Cambridge University Press.

Wilson, R. A. (2006). Afterword to 'Anthropology and human rights in a new key: The social life of human rights'. *American Anthropologist*, 'In focus: Anthropology and human rights in a new key', **108**/1, 38–51.

Wilson, R. A. and Mitchell, J. P. (eds) (2003). *Human Rights in Global Perspective: Anthropological Studies of Rights, Claims, and Entitlements*. London: Routledge.

Wood, E. J. (2000). *Forging Democracy from Below: Insurgent Transitions in South Africa and El Salvador*. Cambridge: Cambridge University Press.

Woodiwiss, A. (2005). *Human Rights*. New York: Routledge.

Woods, K. (2010). *Human Rights and Environmental Sustainability*. Cheltenham: Edward Elgar.

Woods, N. (2000). The political economy of globalization. *The Political Economy of Globalization* (ed. N. Woods). Basingstoke: Palgrave.

Woods, K. (2014). *Human Rights*. Basingstoke: Palgrave Macmillan.

Woodward, C. V. (1951). *Origins of the New South, 1877–1913*. Baton Rouge, LA: Louisiana State University Press.

Worden, M. (2005). Torture spoken here: Ending global torture. *Torture: A Human Rights Perspective* (ed. K. Roth and M. Worden). New York: New Press/ Human Rights Watch.

World Bank (2005). World Development Indicators on CD-Rom. Washington, DC: World Bank.

World Trade Organization (WTO) (2003). Implementation of paragraph 6 of the Doha Declaration on the TRIPS Agreement and Public Health Decision of the General Council of 30 August 2003. http:// www.wto.org/english/tratop_e/trips_e/implem_ para6_e.htm.

Wright, N. G. (1996). Uganda: History from1971. *Encyclopedia of Africa South of the Sahara* (ed. J. Middleton). New York: Charles Scribner's Sons.

Yasuaki, O. (1999). Toward an Intercivilizational Approach to Human Rights. *The East Asian Challenge for Human Rights* (ed. J. R. Bauer and D. A. Bell). Cambridge: Cambridge University Press.

Yaziji, N. (2013). The sad fate of R2P: From Libya to the lost chance of Syria. *Open Democracy* https:// www.opendemocracy.net/openglobalrights/ nassim-yaziji/sad-fate-of-r2p-from-libya-to-lost-chance-of-syria.

Yergin, D. and Stanislaw, J. (2002). *The Commanding Heights: The Battle for the World Economy*. New York: Touchstone.

Yousafzai, M. (2014). Noble Prize speech dated 10 December. http://www.nobelprize.org/nobel_prizes/ peace/laureates/2014/yousafzai-lecture_en.html.

Zakaria, F. (1994). Culture is destiny: A conversation with Lee Kuan Yew. *Foreign Affairs*, 73/2, 109.

Zakaria, F. (2003). *The Future of Freedom: Illiberal Democracy at Home and Abroad*. New York: W. W. Norton.

Zanger, S. C. (2000). A global analysis of the effect of political regime changes on life integrity violations, 1977–1993. *Journal of Peace Research*, 37/2, 213–33.

Zarksy, L. (ed.) (2003). *Human Rights and the Environment: Conflicts and Norms in a Globalizing World*. London: Earthscan.

Ziegenhagen, E. A. (1986). *The Regulation of Political Conflict*. New York: Praeger.

Zivi, K. (2012). *Making Rights Claims: A Practice of Democratic Citizenship*. New York: Oxford University Press.

Zolo, D. (2002). *Invoking Humanity: War, Law and Global Order*. London: Continuum.

Index